WILSON

AND THE PEACEMAKERS

Combining

WOODROW WILSON AND THE LOST PEACE

and

WOODROW WILSON AND THE GREAT BETRAYAL

THE MACMILLAN COMPANY
NEW YORK · BOSTON · CHICAGO · DALLAS
ATLANTA · SAN FRANCISCO

MACMILLAN AND CO., Limited
LONDON · BOMBAY · CALCUTTA · MADRAS
MELBOURNE

THE MACMILLAN COMPANY
OF CANADA, Limited
TORONTO

WILSON

AND THE PEACEMAKERS

by

THOMAS A. BAILEY

Combining

WOODROW WILSON AND THE LOST PEACE

and

WOODROW WILSON AND THE GREAT BETRAYAL

New York · 1947

THE MACMILLAN COMPANY

PREFACE

MY ORIGINAL PLAN was to publish one large volume entitled *Wilson and the Peace*. But wartime exigencies forced me to modify the plan, and present the story in two smaller volumes entitled *Woodrow Wilson and the Lost Peace* and *Woodrow Wilson and the Great Betrayal*. Now it has proved possible to bring the two books together as one. The timeliness of the subject will not escape those who recognize that we shall be confronted with the problems of peace-making and peace-executing for a good many years to come.

The original titles are being retained, even though they have been subjected to some criticism. The reference to the "Lost Peace" does not mean that Wilson himself was solely or even primarily responsible for the "losing." The reference to the "Great Betrayal" does not mean that Wilson himself did the "betraying." The word "betrayal," as most commonly used, is a strong one, and it was deliberately selected for the purpose of driving home an unpalatable truth. To this day only a sprinkling of Americans will concede that our course in 1919–1920 had anything whatever to do with the chaos of the subsequent years. The lexicographers agree that "betrayal" has several well-recognized connotations, and herein it is legitimately used to mean deserting a responsibility and forsaking a cause regarding which we had raised up great expectations.

THOMAS A. BAILEY

STANFORD UNIVERSITY, CALIF.
June, 1947

WOODROW WILSON

AND

THE LOST PEACE

WOODROW WILSON

AND

THE LOST PEACE

———

by

THOMAS A. BAILEY

New York · 1947

———

THE MACMILLAN COMPANY

SEVERAL YEARS AGO, after I had delivered what was doubtless too pontifical a lecture on the mistakes of Wilson and others at the Paris Peace Conference, one of the girls in the class came up to the lectern to ask a routine question. When she had gone I noticed that she had inadvertently left behind a copy of the university news sheet, on the margin of which she had scrawled, evidently for the edification of her neighbor, "Too bad Bailey couldn't have been there to tell them how to do it."

Lest others react similarly to the account that follows, I must at the outset deny any claim to superior wisdom. If I had been in a position of authority at Paris in 1919, I am sure that I should have made many of the mistakes I criticize, and a good many more besides. I realize that statesmen who are working under the pressure of an avalanche of events, and often under physical disabilities as well, cannot attain the serenity of mind and detachment of judgment that come to the scholar in his cloistered cubicle. I realize perfectly well that the wisdom of hindsight is not difficult to attain, and that twenty-five years after the event anyone can see a great many things that were not currently evident.

But so costly have been our blunders, and so strong is the likelihood that we shall again run through the same tragic cycle of disillusionment and isolationism, that I regard it as a solemn duty to rise above the inhibitions of false modesty and call spades by their right names. I happen to be among those who believe that history has lessons for those who will read, and that the Paris Conference of 1919 presents many striking illustrations of what to avoid. Every generation of apes begins where the previous generation began, because apes can hand down no record of their experience. Man leaves a record; but how much better is he than the apes if he does not study it and heed its warnings?

This is not a one-volume history of the Peace Conference. It is a critical analysis of the part played by the United States in the making of the world settlement of 1919, with particular attention to Wilson and to American public opinion. For this reason I touch but lightly upon purely European considerations. My account is primarily an interpretation—a critical interpretation. For this reason I do not try to tell the story in great detail, but rather to sketch the general outlines and stress what seem at this distance to have been the most costly blunders made by the negotiators. Finally, the book is an attempt to educate American public opinion to its responsibilities in future peace-making and international coöperation. For this reason I have tried to make the account simple, direct, and meaningful.

I must at the outset confess to a great admiration for many of Wilson's qualities, and to complete sympathy for the broad ends that he sought to attain. I should be profoundly distressed were I to think that what I have to say could be interpreted as giving aid and comfort to isolationism. The fact is that Wilson and his colleagues in 1918 were presented with an unexampled opportunity to make a lasting peace. Something went wrong. I am interested in finding out to what extent and in what way the United States was responsible for what happened, to the end that we may not make the same mistakes again.

Some of the things that I say will no doubt prove offensive to those who hold the memory of Woodrow Wilson in reverence. While I regret that this is so, I cannot permit such considerations to turn me aside from my larger purpose. Surely enough time has elapsed, and enough disaster has befallen us, that we can ask both the Wilson-worshipers and the Wilson-haters to shed the scales of prejudice from their eyes. Surely we are privileged to hope that this great nation will not again plunge the world into despair by the spectacle of a President and a Senate unable to agree on the precise means to attain that which they both profess to desire.

This book is concerned with the making of the peace. I plan to follow it with a sequel on the part played by the United States in the breaking of the peace, and in the subsequent collapse of collective security.

My title is adapted from Harold B. Butler's *The Lost Peace.*

The following publishers graciously extended permission to quote brief passages from the books indicated: Harper and Brothers, from George Creel's *The War, the World and Wilson;* Houghton Mifflin Company, from Charles Seymour's *The Intimate Papers of Colonel House,* vol. IV; and Doubleday, Doran and Company, Inc. (and Mr. Ray Stannard Baker), from Ray Stannard Baker, *Woodrow Wilson and World Settlement,* copyright, 1922.

The following persons, all colleagues at Stanford University, graciously read and constructively criticized all or substantial portions of the manuscript: Thomas S. Barclay (who for several months was Henry White's private secretary at Paris), Harold W. Bradley, Harold H. Fisher, Jere King, George H. Knoles, and Alfred Owen Ulph. Without in any way reflecting on the helpfulness of others, I must single out for special mention Dr. Rudolf Holsti, the distinguished Finnish diplomat who is now on the faculty of Stanford University. His intimate knowledge of persons and places in Paris of 1919, as well as his subsequent relationship with the League of Nations, not only saved me from some embarrassing slips but resulted in a number of constructive improvements.

I am indebted to a score or so of other persons for ideas and suggestions of various sorts. Some of these people are colleagues at Stanford University, or temporary colleagues at Harvard University; some were advisers to Wilson at Paris; others had unusual opportunity for observation, either as officials or as private citizens, in postwar Europe. I do not list their names, because my subject matter is controversial, and I do not want to embarrass them by associating them with views which they would not in some cases fully endorse. I am nevertheless deeply grateful to them.

The staffs of the Stanford University Library; of the Hoover Library on War, Revolution, and Peace; and of the Widener Library at Harvard University cheerfully extended the usual courtesies. Miss Ruth S. Watson, of the Nebraska State Historical Society, provided me with a copy of an important manuscript of Senator Gilbert M. Hitchcock. President Charles Seymour and Mr. Russell G. Pruden graciously made available the materials in the Yale House Collection. I am also indebted to Dr. St. George L. Sioussat, Chief of the Division of Manuscripts, Library of Congress; and especially to Miss Katharine E. Brand, Special Custodian, Woodrow Wilson Collection, the Library of Congress.

My wife, Sylvia Dean Bailey, not only helped prepare the index but painstakingly read and constructively criticized both galley and page proofs.

THOMAS A. BAILEY

STANFORD UNIVERSITY, CALIF.

April, 1944

TABLE OF CONTENTS

LIST OF CARTOONS

LIST OF MAPS

WOODROW WILSON

AND

THE LOST PEACE

CHAPTER ONE

THE ROAD TO WAR

"The military masters of Germany denied us the right to be neutral." WOODROW WILSON, *June 14, 1917.*

I

ON JUNE 28, 1914, a fanatical student, in the Bosnian city of Serajevo, stepped toward the royal limousine, and fired two revolver shots, one at the Archduke Francis Ferdinand, heir to the throne of Austria-Hungary, the other at his blonde consort, the Duchess of Hohenberg. Both died within a few minutes.

The flaming pistol of Princip touched off the European powder magazine, and set in motion a series of earth-shaking events that have not yet run their course, and will not soon do so.

Did the American people even faintly foresee that the death of the Austrian Archduke heralded the death of tens of thousands of their sons in France, and within twenty-five or so years the death of tens of thousands more in a dozen or so different theaters of conflict?

The answer is no. The news of the assassination made the headlines and then gave way to local sensations, including the scandal involving Mme. Caillaux in France. A handful of American observers, it is true, suggested that the resulting quarrel between Austria and Servia might widen into a European conflict. But the rank and file of the American people, busied with their everyday affairs, could hardly take seriously the murder of a seemingly obscure archduke, by an obscure assassin, in an obscure town, in an obscure part of the world. The New York *Sun* was not alone when it boldly predicted that the assassinations would make for peace between Austria and Servia.

Europe suddenly regained the headlines when the Balkan maelstrom sucked all the great powers, with the temporary exception of Italy, into its vortex. The American people still could not recognize the significance of the events that were fast unfolding before their eyes. It is true that for more than a decade the teetering balance of power in Europe had inspired constant speculation in the press about the inevitable world conflict. But the cry of "Wolf, wolf" had been heard so often that we could scarcely believe that the whole pack was at last on the loose.

When the clashing armies and the rolling death wagons finally dispelled all lingering illusions, our first reaction was to rejoice that we were not involved in the bloody mess. We gave thanks to Columbus for having discovered America, and to our ancestors for having had the good sense to come here. Like the Pharisees, we were pleased to know that we were not like other people: contentious, greedy, treacherous, blood-thirsty. We felt strong, smug, secure.

The American people, in line with their traditions, were then fundamentally isolationist. They did not want to plunge into the European blood bath; they did not expect to. President Wilson not only issued the routine proclamations of neutrality, but went further and urged the American people to be neutral both "in action" and "in thought."

Neutrality in action was possible; neutrality in thought was impossible. America, the famed "international board-ing house," was "a menagerie of nationalities"; and millions of German-Americans, Irish-Americans, Italian-Americans, British-Americans and others could not be indifferent to the fate of the "old country." Many if not most Americans sym-pathized with one side or the other, and hoped it would win. But this did not mean that they were willing to back up their sympathies with their life blood.

The leading American isolationist—or perhaps one should say noninterventionist—was the President of the United States, Thomas Woodrow Wilson.

This is a fact of enormous significance in the unfolding of our story, and we shall have to come back to it again. Wilson declared at the very outset that we had had absolutely "no part in making" the war. He repeatedly insisted, in both public and private utterance, that this was not our fight; that its causes and objects were "obscure"; that the announced aims of both sides were "virtually the same."

Not all Americans, especially the red-blooded Theodore Roosevelt, agreed with Wilson. But there can be little doubt that the overwhelming majority believed with their President that this war was not our affair. Wilson was a professional teacher of great persuasiveness and power, and we must record that he taught this lesson well—perhaps too well. When events later forced him to change his mind and become the leading internationalist, he expected that his isolationist following would change their minds too, and march right along behind him.

But the great majority of the American people did not. They remained rooted to their traditions. And this is another fundamental fact of immense importance in explaining what happened to the peace.

2

The task of remaining neutral was not nearly so simple as many Americans had anticipated. The British early established a long-range blockade of Germany, which was clearly illegal under the existing rules of international law. The Germans countered with a submarine blockade of the British Isles, which was clearly illegal under the existing rules of international law. Our Department of State protested against both blockades, but took a much stronger tone against the submarine, because it was feared that American ships and American lives might be accidentally destroyed. The British could pay for confiscated cargoes; the Germans could offer no adequate compensation for the lives destroyed by torpedoes. Murderers are worse than thieves.

The whole issue was sensationally spotlighted when, on May 7, 1915, a giant British liner, the *Lusitania*, was torpedoed without warning off the Irish coast by a German U-boat. The stricken Cunarder plunged to the bottom in eighteen minutes, with a loss of 1,198 persons, 128 of whom were American citizens, and a large percentage of whom were women, children, and babes in arms. The corpse of one woman was retrieved from the sea with a twin baby clutched to each breast.

America, in common with the rest of the civilized world, was horrified by this holocaust. Even sober newspapers burst forth with denunciations of "mass murder" and of "savages drunk with blood," while the well-known acrobatic evangelist, "Billy" Sunday, cried, "Damnable! Damnable! Absolutely hellish!"

Many hot-bloods in the East demanded immediate war; but the entire country was not ready for drastic action, and Wilson was determined not to repeat President Madison's tragic mistake of 1812 and lead a disunited people into armed conflict. Instead he lodged a series of forceful protests demanding assurances against the repetition of such a horror. The bellicose Theodore Roosevelt, who thirsted for war and not words, classed Wilson with the "flubdubs," "mollycoddles," and "flapdoodle pacifists" and branded Wilson's last note as "No. 11,765, Series B." Nevertheless Wilson did extort from Berlin a promise not to torpedo unresisting passenger liners.

In March, 1916, a U-boat commander flagrantly violated this pledge when he torpedoed an unarmed French passenger ship, the *Sussex*, without warning and with serious injury to several Americans. Outraged, Wilson took a step fraught with the most fateful consequences. He presented an ultimatum to Berlin, declaring that unless the Germans ended their barbarous methods of making war on passenger and freight-carrying vessels, the United States would have no choice but to sever relations.

This, of course, was a threat of war—an irrevocable threat. For various reasons, the Germans saw fit to avoid a showdown with the United States, and they thenceforth refrained from torpedoing passenger liners without warning—at least for a time. But the *Sussex* ultimatum still stood.

3

On January 30, 1917, two and one-half years after the German hordes had goose-stepped into Belgium, the United States was still neutral. There seemed good reason to hope that we could continue to be. The German submarine—as far as we were concerned—was muzzled; the military situation in Europe seemed to be in a stalemate; Wilson had just appealed to the belligerents to state their war aims so that the groundwork could be laid for a negotiated peace. He had followed this up with a memorable speech before the Senate in which he ringingly declared for "peace without victory."

On January 31, 1917, with the echoes of Wilson's sensational speech still reverberating around the world, the Imperial German government announced that it would launch an unrestricted submarine campaign against all ships, *belligerent* or *neutral*, entering the European war zones. (The previous campaign had been proclaimed against Allied shipping only.) As a special concession, the Americans might send one vessel a week through a specified part of the war zone, provided it arrived at Falmouth, England, on Sunday, carried no contraband, was painted with wide red and white stripes, and flew a checkered flag resembling a kitchen tablecloth. One American newspaper acidly remarked that "freedom of the seas will now be enjoyed by icebergs and fish."

The staggering announcement of unrestricted U-boat warfare was equivalent to a declaration of war on the United

States. The German High Command knew this; they expected us to enter the conflict; and they had counted the cost—or what they confidently believed would be the cost. They not illogically assumed that they could knock the Allies out of the war before we could raise, train, equip, and transport a formidable army.

To Wilson, who was absorbed in his plans for a negotiated peace, the German announcement came as a body blow. During the nine months following the *Sussex* ultimatum, our relations with Germany had been unusually amicable, more so than with the British, who were blacklisting our merchants and searching our mails. Even Wilson, in a moment of anger, burst out that the "poor boobs" in England had "got on his nerves."

Yet there was nothing that Wilson could honorably do but accept the brutal German challenge, for in the *Sussex* ultimatum he had nailed his colors to the mast. The Germans now threatened to sink all ships, including ours, without warning. They had called Wilson's bluff—if it was a bluff. There was no alternative left to notifying the German ambassador that diplomatic relations were formally severed, and this was promptly done.

A few minutes later on that same day, February 3, 1917, the pale professor-President went before Congress to explain in solemn tones where he stood. He sorrowfully confessed that he still could not bring himself to believe that the German government would actually do what it threatened to do. He would not believe it until American ships and lives were destroyed by actual "overt acts" of hostility. If they were, he would call upon Congress for appropriate measures to protect Americans who were exercising their undeniable rights to sail the high seas.

The British were disappointed by Wilson's speech. Prime Minister Lloyd George exclaimed: "And so he is not going to fight after all!" Theodore Roosevelt burst out: "I do not believe Wilson will go to war unless Germany literally kicks him into it."

The next anxious weeks were spent in waiting for the blow to fall—for the first "overt" act.

4

As one leafs through the yellowing newspapers of early 1917, one is struck with a surprising fact. The full significance of the German declaration seems not to have dawned upon the American people. Like Wilson, they still wanted to stay out of war, and hoped to do so. Like Wilson, they recognized that there was nothing to do but sever relations with Germany. And like Wilson, they refused to believe that the Germans would actually do what they said they were going to do. Clearly public opinion was not yet ripe for war, and until it was, the Administration dared not lead the nation into the bloody abyss.

But within a month the American people were jarred out of their fool's paradise. On March 1, 1917, the Zimmermann note was sensationally splashed over the front page of every morning newspaper in the land.

The German Foreign Minister, Dr. Alfred Zimmermann, had most indiscreetly cabled the German minister in Mexico that *in the event of war* with the United States he was to negotiate for a German-Mexican alliance, holding out to the Mexicans the bait of regaining Texas, New Mexico, and Arizona. He was also to ask the President of Mexico to invite Japan to support the scheme.

This fantastic cablegram was intercepted and decoded by the British, and, when published, caused a tremendous revulsion of feeling in America, more so than the vastly more significant announcement of unrestricted submarine warfare. The East had generally been favorable to war following the announcement of the U-boat campaign; but the South and West had been rather apathetic. The Zimmermann note did more than anything else to fuse the disunited United States.

Ships—even American ships—sunk in the Irish Sea were far away. But this was close to home. Mexicans in Texas! Japanese on the Pacific Coast! Americans deluged with inferior peoples! To one Texas newspaper this was Prussian militarism "writhing in the slime of intrigue."

Few stopped to realize that Japan was already an ally of the Allies, or that revolution-riddled Mexico could put no effective force into the field. Few stopped to realize that when nations are at war they seek allies. And Germany, it must be repeated, virtually declared war on the United States the day she announced her unrestricted submarine warfare.

5

Meanwhile American ships had been clinging to port, afraid to venture into the war zone. Mountains of supplies were piling up on Eastern docks, and the transportation system of the country was becoming badly snarled. This is precisely what the Germans wanted, for our supplies were not reaching the Allies.

The country could not long endure economic paralysis. Wilson therefore went before Congress again and asked for authority to arm our merchantmen. Congress and the country were willing, but a handful of antiwar Senators filibustered the ship-arming measure to death. Stung to the quick, Wilson issued a statement to the country on March 4, 1917, in which he lectured the Senate on its inadequate rules, and intemperately declared that a "little group of willful men, representing no opinion but their own, have rendered the great Government of the United States helpless and contemptible." Wilson, to his regret, was to learn more about the "willful men" in the Senate.

Balked by Congress, Wilson discovered authority elsewhere, and sent American merchantmen to sea with mounted guns, and with orders to shoot at hostile submarines in the war zone. The country waited breathlessly for the overdue "overt" act.

It was not long in coming. In mid-March four unarmed American merchantmen flying the Stars-and-Stripes were sunk

Forced into It!

(From the St. Louis *Republic;* courtesy of the
St. Louis *Globe-Democrat*)

by German U-boats on the high seas, with the loss of thirty-six lives. The submarine announcement had been but an announcement; the Zimmermann note had been but a note; but this was an act of war. The German submarines were making war on the United States just as surely as the Japanese bombers were to make war on the United States when they dumped their lethal cargoes on the American fleet at Pearl Harbor.

Again Wilson's hand was forced. He had no honorable alternative to summoning Congress in special session and asking it officially to recognize the hostilities that were being waged on us. It took two weeks for Congress to assemble, but in the meantime the country assumed that we were at war—which we were. The newspapers and the public in general actually united in an unofficial counter declaration of war on Germany before Congress had an opportunity formally to do so.

On April 2, 1917, President Wilson again stood before the packed and hushed audience in the chamber of the House of Representatives. In measured words he stated that the German government was waging war on the United States, and he called upon Congress formally to recognize the state of hostilities that had been "thrust" upon us. He did not then ask Congress to declare war on Austria-Hungary and Bulgaria and Turkey, even though they were allies of Germany, because they were not attacking us. We would fight only those who were fighting us.

Congress responded to Wilson's summons when, on April 4 and 6, 1917, the two houses voted by overwhelming majorities that "the state of war . . . which has thus been *thrust upon the United States* is hereby formally declared."

Why did we go to war with Germany? The answer is that we did not go to war with Germany. She went to war with us. The United States, as a self-respecting, sovereign nation, whose citizens had a perfect legal right to sail the high seas, could not do other than recognize this fact. As Wilson pointedly declared two months later, "The military masters of Germany denied us the right to be neutral."

The submarine was clearly the precipitating cause of our war with Germany, but this does not mean that there were not other and highly important contributory causes. German espionage as betrayed by Dr. Albert's purloined briefcase, German intrigue as nakedly exposed in the Zimmermann note, and German sabotage as high-lighted by such disasters as the Black Tom explosion, mightily aroused the American people against the "Hun."

There was also a widespread and gnawing fear that if the

Kaiser should crush the Allies, he would hardly wait to take a deep breath before coming over here with millions of spiked helmets to make short work of us and our Monroe Doctrine. This view was not too seriously held by those who knew something of Germany's semi-exhaustion, and of the technical difficulties involved in waging a war across the Atlantic. But it made sense to the man in the street, and it was sedulously cultivated by Allied and home-grown propaganda. After all, it was better to fight when one could have strong allies than to wait until one had to fight alone.

These fears and incidents, superimposed upon a strong pro-Ally, anti-German sentiment, caused us to accept Germany's challenge the more willingly when it came. But without the submarine we probably should not have gone to war with Germany, certainly not when we did.

6

In later years, Senator Gerald P. Nye, of North Dakota, achieved great notoriety by alleging, and proving to his satisfaction, that we were dragged into the war by the munitions manufacturers (a German charge of 1917), by the Wall Street bankers, by the war profiteers, and by the Allied propagandists. All such explanations ignore the simple fact that we were not dragged into the war at all. Wilson took an irrevocable stand in his *Sussex* ultimatum; the Germans finally defied him, and then began making war on us. If any "dragging" was done, it was done by the Germans. The decision that we should fight was made in Germany, not in America.

The question naturally arises: Was Wilson wise in issuing his *Sussex* ultimatum? At this distance it now seems that there were only two possible ways of meeting the submarine threat. The first was to forbid our citizens and shipping to enter the war zones, as we later did in the Neutrality Act of 1939. But Wilson, the idealist and moralist, sternly and quite understandably refused to permit such a course. It would, he felt, be dishonorable; and once we began to abdicate certain rights, the whole "fine fabric" of international law would begin to break down.

The second possible course was to build up so powerful an armed force that the Germans would not dare disregard American rights. This Wilson refused to do, for he was a pacifist, or at least an unremitting hater of war. He fought the prepared- ness movement tooth and nail, and not until November, 1915, fifteen months *after* the outbreak of the war and nine months *after* the opening of the German submarine campaign, did he reluctantly and lukewarmly clamber onto the bandwagon. By this time it was too late.

Actually, Wilson adopted neither of the two courses here outlined. He refused to keep American citizens off munitions- laden belligerent passenger ships. He refused to keep Amer- ican ships out of the war zone. He refused, until too late, to build up a strong army and merchant marine. His *Sussex* ulti- matum in these circumstances was hardly less than a colossal bluff.

When the showdown came, we had a strong navy but a con- temptibly small army, ranking in numbers with about that of Spain. Our navy did not worry the Germans, because they con- trolled the underseas, and Britain already controlled the sur- face of the seas. Berlin counted on knocking the British out of the war before we could send an effective army to Europe. When the Germans concluded that they had more to gain than to lose by attacking our ships, they attacked them. And America was forced into the war.

7

In still more recent years another plausible explanation has become fashionable. We went to war in 1917, it is alleged, pri- marily to save the Allies and to redress the balance of power.

The basic difficulty with this explanation is that it is false. The Allies were not visibly collapsing in February and March of 1917. On the contrary, it was generally assumed in the United States that they were winning—or, at the very worst, there was a draw. The capture of Bagdad by the Allies on March 11, 1917, was widely regarded as an offset to the failure of the Dardanelles campaign. The strategic withdrawal of Hindenburg to the famed Hindenburg line, in mid-March, 1917, involved the yielding of 1,300 square miles of French territory on a 100-mile front, and was preceded and succeeded by Allied successes. The Americans not unnaturally regarded this as a great victory, and were pleased to note that the arrogant Germans were developing a "retiring disposition." Submarine sinkings were an old story, and the toll being taken by the new campaign was heavy but not especially alarming.

It is true that the Allies were beginning to scrape the bottoms of their money chests, but this fact was not generally known. The famous telegram of Ambassador Walter Hines Page, describing the alarming financial situation, was not sent from London until March 5, 1917, five weeks *after* the German war lords had announced their intention of forcing the United States into the war.

The naked truth is that the real danger of Allied collapse came *after* we entered the conflict—not before. In the last two weeks of April, 1917, and the first week of May, 1917, the U-boat took a terrifying toll of Allied shipping. Brought face to face with the gaunt specter of starvation, England passed through her darkest hour from Napoleon to Hitler.

Late in 1917, the Italian front crumbled and was reestablished with enormous difficulty. Shortly thereafter Russia withdrew from the war, thus releasing approximately one million German veterans for the Western front, and insuring preponderant man power to Germany for the first time in the war. In March, and again in May, 1918, the gray German flood came within a hairbreadth of breaking through to Paris and knocking France out of the war.

No, America did not enter the conflict primarily to save the Allies, or to reestablish the balance of power. The Allies did not then seem to be in need of saving, and the balance of power was the very last thing in the world that Wilson was willing to fight for. If any one thing stands out clearly in his numerous war addresses it is that he would have none of the old order of armed camps.

America entered the war to vindicate her right to sail the high seas—the historic American principle of freedom of the seas. As Wilson said in his stirring war message, "there are no other means of defending our rights."

If it is true that we were fighting for freedom of the seas, it is no less true that the Allies, notably Britain, were not. Since the imperialistic aims of the Allies were not our aims, why not withdraw from the war the moment Germany agreed to respect our maritime rights?

It is a fact of the highest significance—and one that has been generally overlooked—that during the weeks following the submarine declaration there was widespread expression of this view in the United States. A considerable number of men prominent in public life, as well as a large number of newspapers, gave serious attention to the problem of waging a limited-liability war, and of withdrawing as soon as our rights were acknowledged. There was also serious discussion of the question as to whether we ought openly or officially to join the Allies.

The agitation for a limited-liability war largely died out after the Zimmermann note and the various overt acts, but it was symptomatic of a profoundly important isolationist prejudice. Wilson would have done well to remember this limited-liability sentiment when he outlined his sweeping program for world responsibility.

8

The United States accepted the gage of war in 1917 without overwhelming enthusiasm—certainly not with the enthusiasm that was generated later. The war resolution in Congress actually received the negative vote of fifty-six members. Throughout the country, and especially in the Middle West, influential groups of people were apathetic if not actually hostile to fighting. The conclusion is inescapable that both Wilson and the American public as a whole made their decision to accept the German challenge with the greatest of deliberation and reluctance. It was a dirty job that had been forced upon us, and the only way out was forward.

Wilson realized, just as the American people realized, that the submarine had driven us into this war. But he also realized that the nation, especially the landlocked Middle West, could not be aroused to support a great self-sacrificing crusade with the cry, "Make the world safe against the submarine!" The submarine was the immediate *cause* of the war; but he would have to find some more elevated and inspiring *objective*.

It is highly significant—and also generally overlooked—that in his speeches and letters of the spring of 1917 Wilson was careful to preserve a fine distinction between *causes* and *objectives*. The submarine, of course, was the immediate *cause*, but now that we were in the war we were fighting not only for our rights on the high seas but for our more general rights to go our democratic way in peace. We were fighting to make the world safe for democracy, because our democracy could not be safe—nor could any democracy be safe—in a world in which Prussian militarism was running amuck.

But as the war dragged on, Wilson introduced other objectives which developed logically from his zeal to make the world safe for American democracy. We were fighting also for the "rights of mankind," for the "rights of all peoples," for the "sacred rights of free men everywhere." We were even fighting for "a new international order based . . . on broad principles of right and justice."

When Wilson said that the American people were fighting for the rights of all humanity, he professed to speak for the great mass of his countrymen. But was he faithfully interpreting their views? Had he forgotten the many millions who were reluctant to fight for their own rights, to say nothing of the rights of all peoples everywhere? Had he forgotten the large number who felt that they were fighting for freedom of the seas for the United States, and who were willing to leave the Allies in the lurch once this object was attained? Had he forgotten that the deeply rooted isolationist tradition did not at all square with the ideal that we were our brothers' keeper?

9

It is doubtless true that Wilson was the spokesman for the more liberal elements in the United States. It is doubtless true that his lofty ideals, expressed with glowing conviction in a number of notable war addresses, captivated the imagination of a great many people. But there doubtless is some truth in the charge that Wilson became hypnotized by the eloquence of his own fascinating phrases. Gradually in his thinking the *causes* began to merge with the *objectives*, and before the end of the war he seems to have believed—and he certainly carried a great many with him—that we had actually entered the conflict to save the world from Prussian autocracy, to make the world safe for democracy, and to end all wars.

In view of the blurring that took place in Wilson's mind, is it surprising that present-day students have fallen into the same error? Is it surprising that they have assumed that the *objectives* which we announced *after* we entered the war were the same as the *causes* that brought us into the war?

We must not lose sight of the fact that these exalted objectives did not exist—at least not in clear form—before they were proclaimed by President Wilson. The American people did not accept the war that had been "thrust" upon them with the expectation of embarking upon a great world crusade. They did not even have clearly in mind sending over a large expeditionary force. It was generally assumed at first that, since the Allies were winning, our chief contributions would be financial and naval, while we took steps to raise an army for defense. But the flaming sword of Wilsonian idealism aroused the American people from their apathy and confusion, and united them behind a cause for which men willingly sacrificed their lives.

At this distance it seems as though one of Wilson's gravest mistakes was to lose sight of the distinction between the fundamental *causes* of the war and the possible *objectives* of the peace. He pitched his objectives on too high a plane—objectives which did not command the support of the American people, at least not in their quieter moments. It is true, of course, that his exalted words exercised unprecedented power in arousing men to fight. But unfortunately wars do not end with the shooting, and people often see things differently in the cold, gray dawn of the morning after.

Wilson declared that we were fighting to make the world safe for democracy. Theodore Roosevelt, who was nearer the grass roots, went around the country shouting through clenched teeth that we were not fighting to make the world safe for anything. We were fighting because we had been attacked. We were fighting to beat Germany—not to attain a new international order.

Few forward-looking persons will argue that Wilson should have formulated his war aims in line with the narrowest isolationist sentiment in the country. But a formidable body of such sentiment did exist at that time, and Wilson, as the event was to prove, should either have reckoned with it or have educated it. Nothing was to be gained in the long run by ignoring it. When a President is determined to commit the American people to a self-denying program of world responsibility, he should make sure that he is not out too far ahead of the parade.

CHAPTER TWO

THE PEN IS MIGHTIER

"The phrase [self-determination] is simply loaded with dyna-
mite. It will raise hopes which can never be realized. . . . What
a calamity that the phrase was ever uttered! What misery it will
cause!" ROBERT LANSING, *December 30, 1918.*

———————

1

AN INCREASING number of writers, especially in recent years, are disposed to censure Wilson for what they consider a lamentable oversight. Why, they ask, did he not drive a bargain with the Allies as to the specific terms of the peace at the time we entered the conflict?

The argument is that the Allies were in such critical need of our financial and naval assistance early in 1917 that they could have been forced to make definite pledges in line with our desires for a non-imperialistic peace. If such promises had been extorted—and kept—the tragedy of the peace table might have been avoided.

On the surface, this argument appears plausible. Certainly the time to drive a hard bargain with one's future associates in a war is when they are in desperate need of your help. When the common enemy is crushed, they are much less likely to respect your ideas about the writing of the peace.

Yet there are sound reasons why we should not censure Wilson for having failed to exact his pound of flesh before clasping hands with the Allies. First and foremost, we did not enter the conflict primarily because we desired to, or because we wanted to help the Allies, but because Germany had picked a fight with us. Our quarrel was with the Imperial German government, not with the Allies over the prospective spoils.

We should also note that Wilson did not have his long-range war aims clearly thought out at the time we were pushed into

18

the struggle, and he could hardly have taken the time to work them out and integrate them with those of the Allies before consenting to give immediate assistance. By late April, 1917, the submarine peril had become desperate, and there was no time to be lost in getting our destroyers into action.

Finally, once we had entered the war on the side of the Allies, we were all in the same boat together, and from the military point of view it would have been foolhardy to withhold essential aid from our Associates while haggling over the terms of a peace that lay in the uncertain future. To have done so might well have meant the loss of the war, with Germany on the giving end of the terms.

It is true, of course, that the decision to send a large expeditionary force to France was not taken until some months after our declaration of war, and by that time Wilson could conceivably have discussed peace terms at length with the Allied leaders. Even so, we must not forget that the race to get the A.E.F. to France was a race to meet the impending German spring drive made possible by the collapse of Russia. "A terrible blow is imminent," Georges Clemenceau, the French premier, warned an American newsman early in 1918. "Tell your Americans to come quickly."

We should also remember that by early 1918 the American people had worked up tremendous enthusiasm for "licking the Kaiser," and they would have tolerated no hairsplitting over peace terms at this critical hour. They had also developed a sentimental attachment for their associates, especially France, and they doubtless would have regarded it as dishonorable to take undue advantage of the necessities of their friends. Promises extorted under these conditions certainly could have been repudiated with good conscience in the hour of victory.

Let us suppose, for the sake of the argument, that Wilson had publicly demanded of the Allies a specific renunciation of their territorial and other imperialistic aims before advancing a single dollar or sending a single destroyer to the submarine-infested waters. Let us also suppose that the Allied governments—and very probably this would have happened—had said that they did not dare fly in the face of home opinion by renouncing all such aims. Then where would Wilson have been? He could not withdraw the United States from the war. He could not fight a separate war. In short, it would have been the supremest folly to do other than cooperate wholeheartedly and unreservedly with the Allies—and they knew it.

2

In connection with America's attitude toward the Allies, it appears that Wilson made one avoidable mistake which on the surface seems to have been of a trivial nature. This was his insistence that we be not "allied" with the Allies as "allies," but "associated" with them as "Associates." From this distinction was born that awkward official phrase, "the Allied and Associated Powers."

Wilson was much more than a superficial student of American history and government, as his five-volume *History of the American People* attests. He was keenly aware of the power and persistence of the isolationist tradition, and particularly the antipathy against entangling alliances which had grown out of our military alliance of 1778 with France. He was fully aware that there were few subjects on which the American rabble-rouser could shout with more damaging effect than by misquoting Washington's Farewell Address on the dangers of foreign entanglements.

Wilson therefore insisted that a verbal and psychological barrier be erected between us and our allies in the wordy phrase, "Allied and Associated Powers." In common conversation this circumlocutory mouthful was conveniently discarded, and people referred simply to the Allies as "our Allies"—which was the truth, though the bond was not sealed by a formal alliance. Self-interest and a common enemy were bond enough.

Yet Wilson was constantly on the alert to scotch such evi-

dences of loose thinking as were betrayed by the term "our
Allies." When careless subordinates lapsed into the colloquial
and used this forbidden expression, Wilson rapped their
knuckles with a stern and magisterial rebuke. The frustrated
Theodore Roosevelt, who hated Wilson and all his works,
frothed at this latest exhibition of pedantry. He publicly demanded to know "what the President means by continually
referring to this country merely as the associate instead of the
ally of the nations, with whose troops our own troops are actually brigaded in battle . . ."

Wilson's insistence on this wordy distinction is further proof
that he was well aware of the hereditary American prejudice
against making alliances with "wicked furriners." Yet his later
effort to lead the United States into the League of Nations and
the Security Treaty with France suggests that he forgot the
lesson he had once known so well. The Scripture speaks of men
who strain gnats out of their drink while swallowing camels.
Wilson carefully strained the Allied and Associated Powers
through his thinking, while gulping down the League of Nations and a military alliance with France.

We know that Wilson strongly urged the adoption of a
League of Nations even before the United States entered the
war, notably in his masterly "peace without victory" address
of January 22, 1917. Immediately an outburst of criticism and
denunciation arose from the bitter isolationists in the Senate.
If Wilson was interested in leading us into the League, he
would have done well to insist that we were allied with the
Allies in a common cause, after April, 1917, both in war and
in peace. An entanglement forged in the heat of war, and sanctified by victory, would win acceptance more easily in time of
peace than one newly forged after the fighting had stopped.

The ancient American prejudice against alliances may be
unreasoning, and it may even be childish, but there it was. One
could not overcome it by ignoring it or by paying obeisance
to it. Wilson certainly adopted a curious approach for one who
had already decided to forsake old traditions and embark on

the uncharted sea of international cooperation. His emphatic insistence upon our not becoming allied with the Allies did nothing to break down the hoary isolationist ideal. It did nothing to remove the ingrained suspicion that faithless foreigners on the other side of the Atlantic were people unclean, not fit to be "allied" with, fit only to be "associated" with. By merely "associating" ourselves with the Allies, we could the more easily disassociate ourselves when the fighting ended—and we did.

3

It is one of the prettiest ironies of history that the peace-loving President Wilson, with his pacifist Secretary of War, attained far greater success in making war than in making peace.

As a war leader, Wilson achieved what was probably his greatest triumph in public life. The man and the hour providentially met. Endowed with a fine voice and a splendid platform presence, blessed with a gift for telling phrase, and radiating the sincere spiritual fervor of his Presbyterian forbears, he aroused the American people from their apathy and launched them on a crusade of unprecedented power.

Before we were plunged into the war, Wilson had developed certain ideas about a lasting peace, and from time to time he outlined these in eloquent public addresses. After we entered the war, he clarified and elaborated these same ideas, and added others. Few of these statements attracted much attention: the world was full of announced peace aims, and Wilson's were too vague and too lengthily worded.

By early January, 1918, the situation called for the publication of a peace program with a "punch." The Russian revolutionists were insidiously calling for "peace without annexations or indemnities." They had ripped open the musty archives of the Tsar, and had nakedly exposed Russia's secret and imperialistic treaties with the Allies to the gaze of a shocked world. The Allies, who professedly were fighting for nobler things, suffered a severe moral defeat. Wilson's advisers urged him to frame a specific platform in "snappy" placard paragraphs which could be used for propaganda purposes, and which would serve to offset the propaganda and the damaging revelations of the Bolsheviks.

The Peace Terms

(From the New York *American;* courtesy of the
New York *Journal-American*)

Wilson responded magnificently when, on January 8, 1918, he appeared before Congress with his memorable Fourteen Points. The first five were general in scope: open diplomacy; freedom of the seas; the beating down of economic barriers; the reduction of armament; and the adjustment of colonial claims on a fair basis. Then followed a series of formulas for applying justice to specific countries or areas. The fourteenth and capstone point was a declaration in favor of an Association of Nations to guarantee world peace. (For texts of Wilson's points, see note accompanying this chapter, pp. 333-336.)

In three subsequent addresses, Wilson set forth at least thirteen other points, bringing the total to twenty-seven. Some of the later points were merely a repetition, elaboration, clarification, or contradiction of the earlier ones. When we eliminate the overlapping, the total is about twenty-three.

Among the latter-day points were persuasive declarations in favor of a just and lasting peace; of no bartering of peoples; of the satisfaction of legitimate national aspirations; of honorable international dealing; of the destruction of arbitrary power; and of territorial adjustments in the interests of the peoples concerned. This last point, self-determination, was destined to arouse a vast amount of unrealizable nationalistic sentiment.

Yet did the American people, despite wide editorial acclaim, really understand and approve the Fourteen Points? Was Wilson expressing the aspirations of his countrymen, as he repeatedly claimed, or was he merely setting up a high-sounding goal to which they might aspire, and in which they could acquiesce as long as their enthusiasm was at a high pitch? Colonel House was present at the last of Wilson's great war-aims addresses, that of September 27, 1918, in the Metropolitan Opera House at New York, and he recorded that most of it seemed to be "over the heads of the audience," and that the parts which were least important brought forth the "most vigorous applause." Ominously, the passage which the press reported as most enthusiastically received was that promising stern treatment for Germany. The American people were evidently more interested in dethroning the Kaiser than in enthroning Wilsonian idealism, and it is unfortunate that Wilson did not grasp this crucial fact.

Below the surface, and even above the surface, there were some rumbling criticisms of the Fourteen Points, especially from Republicans who did not like the idea of a Democratic President reordering the world. There were some sneering comments about the "fourteen commandments" of "God Almighty Wilson," and there was considerable disquietude in the ranks of the high-tariff Republicans over Point III, which aimed at the lowering of economic barriers. But it is significant that this muttered opposition did not break out into the open until the fighting had ended, or had nearly ended.

4

Wilson has been frequently criticized for not having worked out a joint statement of war aims with the Allies, rather than stealing the spotlight with a prima-donna performance.

The truth is that Wilson attempted to secure such a joint declaration, and the Allies were unable to agree upon one. It was only after all efforts in this direction had failed that he decided to go it alone.

One must also correct the rather general misconception that the Fourteen Points were original with Wilson. Three days before the President's memorable address, Prime Minister Lloyd George had partially stolen Wilson's thunder by delivering a hardly less spectacular speech in London before the representatives of the trade unions. He mentioned essentially all of Wilson's Fourteen Points, except three: open covenants openly arrived at; a lowering of trade barriers; and freedom of the seas. On the other hand, he strongly stressed reparations for damages caused by the Germans.

It is most interesting to note that the three points not mentioned by Lloyd George appeared in the Bolshevist statement of war aims, published a week earlier. Both the Russian and the British spokesmen had already stressed self-determination for submerged minorities, and Lloyd George out-Wilsoned Wilson when he advocated the extension of this principle to the half-naked natives of Africa. Later, at the Paris peace con-

ference, Lloyd George heatedly told Wilson that self-determination was one of his own points. He might just as well have
claimed authorship of the Bible; self-determination is as old
as nationalism.

While it is clear that we cannot blame Wilson for inventing
the principle of self-determination, he did give it a new emphasis and a new impetus. This, in fact, may be said of most
of his Fourteen Points. What he actually did was to codify the
best of existing war aims, even including some announced by
the Germans and the Bolsheviks, and to add a few of his own.

Some of the Fourteen Points were precise, shockingly precise for old-school diplomacy; others were vague or contradictory. This was especially true of the latter-day points.
Poland, for example, was promised free access to the sea in
Point XIII. But the only possible corridor to the sea ran
through territory inhabited by a considerable body of Germans. If Poland did not get the corridor, one of the points
would be violated; if she did get it (with Danzig) the point relating to self-determination would be at least partially violated.

In short, the Points were idealistic enough and vague enough
to make a splendid platform for waging the war; but they were
too illusory and contradictory to make an adequate platform
upon which to construct the peace. "He [Wilson] could have
preached a sermon on any one of them," writes John Maynard
Keynes, "or have addressed a stately prayer to the Almighty
for their fulfilment; but he could not frame their concrete application to the actual state of Europe." One of the most unfortunate aspects of this whole story is that the Fourteen Points
were finally used for a purpose that was not originally intended.

Admirable though the Wilsonian points were for arousing
the American people to a supreme effort, it now seems that
from the long-range point of view Wilson made a mistake in
pitching them on so high a note. God is on the side of the big
battalions; and the American divisions would probably have
got to France and the Allies probably would have overborne
the enemy about as rapidly if Wilson had held his idealism

somewhat in leash—if he had been more temperate, more precise, more realistic.

One danger inherent in the Fourteen Points was that reaction was inevitable. The ideals that Wilson set forth were, under the best of circumstances, not wholly realizable. Disillusionment—"the slump in idealism"—was bound to come with the cold gray dawn of victory; and unhappily it did come under circumstances that will be described later. The higher the idealism the greater the slump, and if Wilson had fixed his aim on the peace table rather than on the battlefield the reaction might not have been so violent.

5

Wilson not only preached ideals which were clearly unrealizable in this our world, but those who re-preached them grossly "oversold" them.

The dynamic George Creel, who as head of the Committee on Public Information mobilized emotion, took over Wilson and his Points, and advertised him and them all over the world as no one person or program has been advertised before or since. These great "verbiage drives" or "moral offensives" had all the earmarks of a glorified campaign to sell some patent medicine—a development that could hardly have pleased the dignified and sensitive academician in the White House.

More than sixty million leaflets, pamphlets, and booklets—largely featuring "Wilsonisms"—were showered upon Latin America, the Far East, and Europe. They were translated into a veritable babel of tongues. A volume of Wilson's speeches became a "best seller in China"; a leaflet containing one of his addresses was adopted as a textbook in a Madrid school. Always it was the thunderbolts of President Wilson.

Ominously, this great crusade began to arouse Messianic hopes—and President Wilson was the Messiah. In far-away Poland, starry-eyed university students met on the streets, clasped hands, and uttered but one word: "Wilson." Creel, while traveling in a mountainous part of Italy, sought refuge from a storm in a peasant's lonely cabin. Above a shrine on one side of the chimney he observed a wax figure of a local patron saint side by side with a poster picture of Woodrow Wilson. A member of the American Embassy in Rome saw in some barracks an improvised altar, on which burned four candles, above which hung a poster of Wilson, and before which the soldiers were constantly kneeling.

Nor was the enemy neglected, Wilson's Fourteen Points were rained upon the Central Powers from airplanes, balloons, and cannon shell. Among the highly nationalistic Poles, Czechs, and Slavs of Germany and Austria-Hungary the rainbow of self-determination aroused hope, then resistance, and finally rebellion. The winged words of Woodrow Wilson were worth armies.

The people of Germany at first felt that the Fourteen Points were a masterpiece of effrontery, especially in view of the fact that their legions had won most of the battles to date. But Wilson's high-sounding promises insidiously began to bore like termites at the foundations of German morale. German liberals could applaud a great deal in the Points, for Wilson had stolen much of their thunder. German merchants and manufacturers were pleased with the prospect of economic disarmament, for they lived in daily dread of after-the-war reprisals. German imperialists could not quarrel with the promise of a fair adjustment of colonial claims, for this was seemingly a pledge that they might keep some or all of their colonies. Germans everywhere could not refuse to applaud the principle of freedom of the seas, for that would hamstring the hated British navy.

As the great conflict roared into its final stages, and as German morale began to crack, increasing numbers of hungry Germans began to ask themselves: would not a negotiated peace based upon the principles of the Fourteen Points be far better than the continuance of this fruitless struggle?

6

One of the greatest weaknesses of the Fourteen Points as a peace platform was that they lent themselves to sloganizing. "Freedom of the seas," "open covenants openly, arrived at," "self-determination for peoples"—what did all these things mean? The grave danger of slogans is that they shut the door to thinking, while giving people the comfortable feeling that they are thinking. And since people do not ordinarily go to the trouble to find out what slogans mean, and since the Fourteen Points were inadequately explained by their author, it is not surprising that they were made to mean what their readers wanted them to mean. This was splendid—as long as the Points were used to arouse the Allies and seduce the enemy. But a day of reckoning was bound to come.

Obviously, no mortal man this side of the millennium could have hoped to bring about all the things that the world came to expect of Wilson. On the day he sailed from New York for the Paris Conference, a sweatshop worker was heard to remark, "There goes the man who is going to change all this for us." Wilson's own people were bound to feel disillusioned; the peoples of the neutral and the Allied countries were bound to feel deceived; and the peoples of the enemy countries were bound to feel betrayed.

The official authors of war aims should make them clear, reasonable, and as explicit as possible. In the short run, extravagant promises—specific or tacit—may prove effective, but in the long run they cannot but recoil upon the heads of their makers.

7

The Fourteen Points led to another highly unfortunate development. They came to be rather generally regarded as the peace platform of all the Allies, rather than the platform of

Woodrow Wilson, who was merely "associating" with the Allies.

This inference was not wholly Wilson's fault. In his earlier speeches he stated emphatically that he was speaking *only* for the United States. But as time wore on he made this distinction less emphatic, and eventually it was largely lost sight of, certainly in the popular mind. The result probably would have been the same in any event, no matter how many denials he made. The United States was "associated" with the Allies; Wilson was the outstanding figure among the war leaders of the Allied and Associated Powers; therefore Wilson spoke for all the Allied governments. The senior partner is ordinarily presumed to speak for the entire firm.

Perhaps it is unfair to suggest that Wilson should have had the foresight to see that this would happen. But as things turned out it would have been less disastrous if he had been able to work out some common program with the Allies. This would have been difficult, perhaps impossible; it would have taken time; and time was at a premium when the Fourteen Points were issued. But even if no joint Allied statement had been possible, there was no valid reason why Wilson could not have correlated his program with that of the British. We have noted that the original Fourteen Points speech followed that of Lloyd George by only three days; and the program of the British Prime Minister was certainly sweeping enough. The three new points that Wilson added eventually gained little or nothing, and opened a Pandora's box of misunderstanding. From the standpoint of Allied unity it would have been better if Wilson had merely restated Lloyd George's better aims. But this would not have been true from the standpoint of Wilson's prestige or the success of the Allied propaganda campaign.

In truth, the Allied governments did favor the Fourteen Points as a weapon for disarming the enemy, and they viewed with satisfaction how well this weapon was doing its work. But the Allied governments, as distinguished from the more liberal elements in their population, did not favor the Fourteen Points as a platform for the peace they proposed to draw up. They had already made a number of secret treaties among themselves for carving up the enemy's territory; and they had no intention, after long years of bloody sacrifice, of giving up their prospective booty at the behest of the American doctrinaire-President. When the time came for a serious discussion of peace terms Premier Clemenceau of France remarked, perhaps jokingly, that he had never read the Fourteen Points. But, whether joking or in earnest, he betrayed an inauspicious attitude.

So the Allied governments kept quiet, while a large part of the world believed that Wilson was speaking for the entire coalition. What else could the Allied leaders do? Could they rise up and loudly say that they did not believe in what Wilson was saying, and thus arouse the Central Powers for a last-ditch struggle? Could they rise up and proclaim that they had secret aspirations for which they—and indirectly the American people—were fighting?

Wilson himself kept quiet at one critically important time. In October, 1918, when the Imperial German government sued for peace, three supremely important interchanges of notes took place between Washington and Berlin. In the second, that of October 12, the Wilhelmstrasse said: "The German Government believes that the Governments of the powers associated with the United States also accept the position taken by President Wilson in his addresses."

Then was the time for Wilson—for he helped prepare these crucial notes—to make it emphatically clear that he spoke only for the United States. But the American reply completely ignored this whole point. Silence is usually assumed to give consent. In any event, the Germans were not without some grounds for complaint when they discovered to their lasting regret that this presumption was wrong.

8

A final word about war aims in general, and the Fourteen Points in particular.

A vast number of people, especially in America, regarded Wilson's declarations as a hard and fast contract with the public that he would carry out to the strict letter every one of his announced war aims. When he failed to do so—no mortal man could have done so—he was widely and bitterly accused of having broken faith.

The longer and more specific a list of war aims becomes, the more difficult it is to realize it in its entirety. Conditions may so change as the war goes on—and this happened in 1917 and 1918—that what once seemed feasible is no longer feasible, what once seemed desirable is no longer desirable.

A statement of war aims is a statement of what one hopes to attain. In this workaday world one would be both foolish and naïve to assume that there must be no leeway for adjustment in the light of changing circumstances. War aims are to warfare what political platforms are to politics; no one ever expects the latter to be carried out completely. In some cases it would be actually harmful to do so. Why we should expect a different standard in the even more complex field of international relations, it is difficult to say, except perhaps that we have had far more experience with politics than with war.

Wilson, it seems, never promised to carry out to the letter every one of his war aims. He was far more concerned with their spirit than with their letter. "They were articles of faith," writes George Creel, "rather than the hard and fast clauses of a commercial agreement, and if they were to be dealt with in a mean, legalistic spirit, every one of them could be denied without loss of face."

It is difficult enough to carry out literally a long and specific list of war aims when a nation is fighting without allies. It is literally impossible when a nation is fighting with a coalition of nearly thirty other belligerents. The Allied leaders, notably Lloyd George (who wore his promises lightly), had now and again made a passing bow to the Fourteen Points. But Wilson knew perfectly well that our Associates had not formally or even informally subscribed to them in their entirety. To force them to do so, even with reservations, was one of the great diplomatic battles that lay ahead, and he knew it. That struggle won, the next step would be to try to make the Allies live up to as many of their promises as practicable.

If Wilson had made it clear, time and again, that the Fourteen Points were not to be taken too literally, he might have dampened America's war enthusiasm, but he would have cushioned the disillusionment which finally ruined the Treaty of Versailles in America.

CHAPTER THREE

AN ARMISTICE THAT WAS
NOT AN ARMISTICE

*"We have no quarrel with the German people. We have no feel-
ing towards them but one of sympathy and friendship. It was
not upon their impulse that their government acted in entering
upon this war."* WOODROW WILSON, *April 2, 1917.*

1

THERE ARE many who now feel that it was a mistake for
Wilson to insist in his public addresses that we were not really
fighting the German people but their "military masters." This
pleasant fiction led ultimately to tragic consequences.

Governments are the responsible spokesmen—in fact the
only spokesmen—for the peoples they presume to govern. Not
infrequently, to be sure, those governments do not faithfully
represent the wishes of their people. When this happens, it is
assumed that the people will cause the government to change
its policy, or failing that, change the government, either by
ballots or by bullets.

It often happens that peoples, through inertia or ignorance
or fear, tolerate governmental policies of which they do not
approve. It also happens that governments, through control of
the press and other agencies of propaganda, deliberately deceive their own people. But in international relations the only
practicable course is to assume that a government speaks for
the entire nation. To go behind the returns will almost invariably create more problems than will be solved.

The German people bitterly resented and heatedly denied
Wilson's assertions that they were not supporting the Imperial
German government. One has only to turn to the contemporary
German press, from the most liberal journals to the most con-
servative, to find abundant evidence that Germans of all classes,

except for a few pacifists and left-wing Socialists, were loyally
backing their leaders. And we must remember that there was
an extraordinary amount of free speech in the Germany of
1917–1918. Almost to a man it was felt that the Fatherland was
fighting a legitimate war of self-defense, against an encircle-
ment of powerful, unscrupulous, and vengeful enemies. This,
naturally, was the theme of official German propaganda.

Wilson's attempt to drive a wedge between the people and
their leaders, if anything, strengthened the will of the Germans
to resist—as long as they were in a mood to continue fighting.
But there can be little doubt that the distinction which Wilson
made between the German people and their "military masters"
added to the enthusiasm of the American war effort. It also
undoubtedly reconciled the millions of German-Americans to
the thought of killing their own kinsmen.

While the American people undoubtedly generated a great
amount of bitterness against Germans as such, it would have
been difficult if not impossible to arouse a blind and overwhelming hatred against the German people as a whole. We
in America had welcomed millions of them as neighbors, and
we knew them as clean, industrious, and law-abiding citizens.
But the "military masters" of Germany—the arrogant, goose-
stepping, Junkerized, Prussianized aristocracy—could be epit-
omized in the person of the Kaiser, with his sneering, snarling,
upturned mustaches. The cartoonists and orators had a field
day. Against this unfortunate representative of royalty the
American people worked up a paroxysm of hate without parallel in our history.

Nothing could better illustrate the dangers of overpersonal-
izing a great war. When the villain is removed or destroyed, the
victors are at a loss how to deal with the underlying forces that
brought him into being or gave him strength.

2

Then came October, 1918. Bulgaria had collapsed; Austria-Hungary was near collapse; the German defenses in France were crumbling. The Berlin government approached Wilson seeking an armistice and peace negotiations. With stern, uncompromising words the President replied that if the United States had to deal with "the military masters of the monarchical autocrats of Germany," it "must demand, not peace negotiations, but surrender."

This biting reply was undoubtedly Wilson's own idea, for the Allied leaders were completely in the dark as to what his answer would be. Its uncompromising tone was doubtless due in part to the continuance of submarine warfare while the negotiations were in progress, and particularly to the brutal torpedoing of a British passenger ship, the *Leinster*, with a loss of over four hundred men, women, and children.

It is important to note that Wilson did not specifically warn the German people that they must throw the Kaiser overboard, and it is quite possible that he did not intend that they should do so. If this is true, he made a serious error in not specifying more exactly what he wanted. But the inference to be drawn from Wilson's ambiguous injunction was unmistakable, at least to the Germans. If they continued under the yoke of their Kaiser and "military masters," they could expect nothing but unconditional surrender; if they got rid of them and established a republic, there might be negotiation—and lenient terms. There can be no doubt that this general feeling hastened not only the German revolution but also the establishment of a more liberal government and the expulsion of the discredited Kaiser.

Once the German people had lived up to what they thought was their end of the bargain—but which was no bargain at all—they counted on generous peace terms. When the hour of disillusionment came, they vehemently denounced Wilson and the Allies for treachery and betrayal.

The official Allied reply at Versailles in 1919 was a classic of envenomed realism. It pointed out that the German people had supported the war from beginning to end, which was true, and that they could have overthrown their government and its policy at any time they had willed it, which was also true. The German people had kept up the fight as long as there was promise of victory and conquest, and they could not expect to escape responsibility for their misdeeds merely by changing rulers, as one would change clothes, in the hour of defeat.

In the dark days of 1917 and 1918 Wilson had repeatedly proclaimed that we were not fighting the German people but their "military masters." In the glorious days of victory the Allied spokesmen bluntly denied that this was true. They sincerely believed that the German people were guilty as well as their rulers. And even if they had not believed this, they would have found it convenient to do so, for how could they otherwise justify harsh punishments and heavy reparations burdens?

In this case, as in that of the Fourteen Points, Wilson made the mistake of not squaring his program with that of the Allied statesmen, and keeping closely in touch with them. They could not very well tell him to stop talking; and once he had elevated American morale by making the sharp distinction between the German people and their imperial rulers, the Allies could hardly have issued loud protests that this was not so.

It is highly interesting to note that under the impact of the war and the Conference, Wilson shifted ground. Speaking at Columbus, Ohio, on September 4, 1919, during his fatal tour for the League, he said in reference to the Germans that "a people are responsible for the acts of their Government. If their Government purposes things that are wrong, they ought to take measures to see to it that that purpose is not executed."

The German people would have had less justification for charges of betrayal if Wilson had preached this doctrine during the war rather than after.

3

It would have been much better, as we see it now, if the Kaiser had been allowed to stay and face the music. The long-run results probably would have been less disastrous if his government had been forced to sign the peace; and then, if the tide had turned that way, he could have bowed himself out in the face of a genuine democratic uprising.

The Weimar Republic was more or less imposed upon Germany from above; it did not spring from the soil. This partly explains why it lasted no longer than it did. In addition, this unnatural child of war was made to choke down the Treaty of Versailles—"war guilt clause" and all. That would have been a lethal dose for any government, and it was one from which the German Republic never fully recovered. It would perhaps be going too far to say that this discrediting of German liberalism was the primary cause of the rise of Hitler, but no one will deny that he used it as one of his loudest and most effective talking points in his spectacular rise to power.

In the United States, the enforced flight of the Kaiser had far-reaching psychological results. The American people were all keyed up to march on Berlin, assault the proud capital, and put the hemp around the imperial neck. "Hang the Kaiser" was the reiterated promise of song and slogan. Not only did we not get to Berlin, but we did not get the Kaiser. He fled to Holland, and the Dutch government stubbornly refused to deliver him up. Several months later the Brooklyn *Eagle* lamented: "The ex-Kaiser is still at large; unwept, unhonored, and unhung." Not only was he left unhung, but he was never punished, except to remain an exile and saw wood at Doorn and brood for twenty-three years over the glories that were gone—which was perhaps a cruel and inhuman form of punishment.

It would be a mistake to overstress the feeling of frustration that came to America, but it is probably not far from the mark to say that the premature deposition of the "Beast of Berlin" had something to do with the feeling of disillusionment which found vent in the reaction against the League of Nations. We did not hang the Kaiser, but in a very real sense we did hang the League of Nations.

4

We come now to a phase of Wilson's career which involved a decision of momentous consequences, one which could just as well have been made either way. This was his part in the Armistice negotiations of October, 1918.

Late in September, 1918, the German High Command became panicky over the military situation and peremptorily demanded that the Foreign Office make overtures to Wilson for a negotiated peace. They insisted that Wilson be approached because they were sure that the Allies would return a blunt refusal, as they already had done in the case of Austria-Hungary. The High Command was not yet prepared to surrender, but it hoped to lure the presumably naïve and idealistic Wilson into an armistice which would at least enable the German armies to regroup and strengthen their lines.

The first German note to Washington, that of October 6, 1918, unqualifiedly accepted the Fourteen Points as a basis for peace and requested the negotiation of an armistice. It is possible that the Berlin government, knowing that the Allies had not yet agreed on war aims, hoped to create dissension in their ranks by appealing to the Fourteen Points, and thus escape severe punishment.

Wilson had two courses open to him. He could have referred this overture to the Allied Supreme War Council, explaining that he was not in a position to speak for the Allied and Associated Powers, which was true. If he had done this, the Allies almost certainly would have rejected the German proposal, and would then have blasted the German armies into submission on German soil.

The other course was to open independent negotiations with

the Germans, and this Wilson did. The Allied leaders were vastly annoyed and angered at being thus short-circuited, and they broke into a cold sweat of apprehension lest this "dangerous visionary" be inveigled into some kind of trap that would throw away the fruits of victory.

Public opinion in the Allied countries seems generally to have favored fighting the war through. This was particularly true of the United States, which had developed an overwhelming war madness. There was a widespread feeling, largely among Republicans, that a negotiated peace meant a lost war. From the bellicose Theodore Roosevelt came the wild cry, "Let us dictate peace by the hammering guns and not chat about peace to the accompaniment of the clicking of typewriters."

"Our answer to the Hun's twaddle," shouted the Cleveland *Plain Dealer,* "shall be more war." Ominously, from the United States Senate arose loud rumblings of protest against a negotiated peace, including muttered threats of impeaching Wilson. One Democratic Senator, evidently fearing that the President would fall into the German "armistice trap," came to Wilson in great perturbation. The President was not flattered. "I said to the Senator," reported Wilson, " 'Do they think I am a damned fool?' "

There seems little doubt, as Colonel House testified, that Wilson underestimated the war hysteria of the American people. There also seems little doubt, as Wilson's private secretary, Joseph P. Tumulty, pointed out, that the President would have strengthened himself politically if he had flatly rejected the German overture. A march to Berlin—an unconditional surrender without parley—was what the country overwhelmingly wanted. If Wilson took the unpopular course, he would put a rallying cry into the mouths of his Republican opponents—and he did.

There can be little question but that Wilson's setback in the Congressional elections of November, 1918, to which we shall come presently, was in large part due to the fact that he had

entered upon negotiations with the Germans, and that the
war by then was virtually over.

But Wilson sternly closed his ears to the siren song of the
politicians. From a moral point of view he could do no other
than grasp this opportunity to bring the bloody conflict to a
speedy and honorable end. "If I think it is right to accept it,"
he told Tumulty, "I shall do so regardless of consequences.

The Beast That Talks Like a Man:
"I Demand an Honorable Peace—
No Humiliation, etc."
(Courtesy of the Brooklyn *Eagle*)

As for myself, I can go down in a cyclone cellar and write
poetry the rest of my days, if necessary."

5

Wilson pushed ahead with the negotiations, in spite of the
vehement outcry at home and abroad, and skillfully evaded
the traps that the Prussian war lords had laid for him. Once it

was known that the German government had set peace negotiations in motion, the morale of the people began to crack
wide open. The prospect of a peace of justice based on the
Fourteen Points proved irresistible to this war-weary and starving country. As German morale grew weaker, and as the clamor
in Allied countries for a stern peace grew louder, the tone of
Wilson's demands grew correspondingly stronger. A basis for
understanding was finally reached, late in October, and Wilson
passed this on, *without recommendation*, to the Allied Supreme War Council for their approval or disapproval.

This last point is vitally important. Wilson did not draw up
the terms of the armistice. That was left entirely to the Allied
military leaders, who laid down conditions which the Germans, then torn by revolution, were forced to accept. The final
terms were signed on November 11, 1918, in the same railway
car in the same forest of Compiègne that Chancellor Hitler
used for the same purpose in June, 1940.

At eleven o'clock on the eleventh day of the eleventh month
of 1918, an eerie, numbing silence fell upon the Western
Front, and the Great War was over. Or rather, the formal fighting was over.

Wilson's role as an intermediary in the preliminary armistice negotiations undoubtedly shortened the war by a number
of months, and saved tens of thousands of lives. The ultimate
object of the Allies was to disarm the enemy; and if this could
be done by negotiation rather than by prolonged fighting, so
much the better. The Allied military leaders recognized this
fact, and not unwillingly accepted it. Indeed, it would have
been immoral for them to do otherwise. They could hardly
have said: "No, we cannot stop now. There are two hundred
German towns we want to destroy; there are 500,000 more
German soldiers we want to kill."

Wilson's critics condemned him then and later for having
brought the war to an end before full vengeance could be
wreaked upon Germany. They alleged, as we have seen, that
the disappointment and frustration resulting from the failure

to march on Berlin had much to do with the ultimate defeat of his peace program. They insisted that if the Allies had marched into Germany with fire and sword the German people would have really learned what war was at first hand, and that they would have been less willing in later years to worship the false gods of Adolf Hitler.

A Popular Interpretation of Germany's Peace Overtures

(From the New York *Evening World;* reprinted by permission)

There is unquestionably much force in these criticisms. But Wilson's immediate task was to bring the war to a victorious end as quickly and bloodlessly as possible. If the conflict had been prolonged three to five more months, as Marshal Foch had thought possible, Bolshevism might have engulfed Europe, as it almost did anyhow, and the statesmen of the postwar era would have been confronted with a set of different and more disagreeable problems. In this case Wilson's peace program would have encountered even more stormy weather.

As for the frustration of the American people, and the failure of the German people to experience the devastation of war at first hand, these, it seems, were problems that could conceivably have been solved by sane and constructive leadership. Mankind will never get anywhere if it insists on needlessly protracting current evils in order to avoid possible future evils which may be removed by statesmanlike vision.

6

We must return once more to the Fourteen Points before leaving the subject of the Armistice.

The Berlin government, in its first peace feeler of October 6, 1918, announced its unqualified acceptance of the Fourteen Points as a basis for the peace. Wilson, of course, was quite agreeable to this suggestion, but the Allied leaders, who had been preaching the gospel according to Wilson for the purpose of disarming the enemy, were visibly embarrassed, just as the German strategists may have hoped.

The first question of the Allied statesmen was: What do the Fourteen Points mean? There had been little necessity for clear definition earlier in the war: indeed, the more nebulous they were, the easier it was to deceive and disarm the enemy. Colonel House, as Wilson's personal representative in Paris, had Walter Lippmann, the well known journalist, and Frank Cobb, editor of the New York *World*, draw up an elaborate commentary on the Fourteen Points which was cabled to Washington and approved by Wilson on October 30. It was on the table before the Allied leaders during these pre-Armistice negotiations, and was constantly referred to by them as the official interpretation.

The British flatly refused to accept Point II, on the freedom of the seas, because they felt that it would shackle their navy in a future war; and they were determined to continue fighting rather than throw away their most powerful offensive weapon.

Clemenceau had little faith in the Fourteen Points, and he is reported to have sneered: "God gave us the Ten Commandments, and we broke them. Wilson gives us the Fourteen Points. We shall see." He actually issued instructions to draw up a detailed statement of France's objections to the Wilsonian program, but this document was never presented. Italy suspected that the Fourteen Points might stand in the way of realizing her territorial aspirations. Belgium feared that Point III might adversely affect her trade, and Point V her colonies.

But Colonel House, representing the aroused Western giant, held strong cards in his attempts to secure acceptance of the Fourteen Points. The bankrupt Allies, in the hour of victory, were scarcely less in need of American moral and economic support than they had been in the shadow of defeat. House finally threw his ace of trumps on the table when he suggested that the United States might have to withdraw from the war, make a separate peace, and leave the Allies in the lurch. Such a desertion would be disastrous, for the Germans would be enheartened, the Allies would be weakened and demoralized, and the war might result in a stalemate, with the victors unable to gather the fruits of victory. This is so obvious to us now that Colonel House has been bitterly criticized for not having pressed his advantage more relentlessly.

After prolonged debate, the Allied leaders finally accepted the Fourteen Points, with one reservation and one elucidation. The British reserved the right to discuss the issue of freedom of the seas at the Peace Conference. Wilson was most reluctant to make this concession, because next to the League of Nations he seems to have regarded it as his most important point. It was in fact the issue that had plunged the United States into the war. After much hesitation, and after toying with the idea of an appeal to public opinion, Wilson grudgingly acceded to the British reservation.

The one elucidation was presented by the French. Point VIII stipulated, "All French territory should be freed and the invaded portions restored . . ." But this did not specifically say that the Germans would have to make reparation for the devastation they had inflicted. The French insisted upon an elucidation to the effect that the Germans would have to pay "compensation" (reparations) for "all damage done to the civilian population of the Allies and their property . . ." This seemed like a reasonable interpretation to Wilson and the American representatives, and they accepted it without undue difficulty.

The Italians had a reservation regarding their Adriatic territorial aspirations, but they presented it so bunglingly and pressed it so hesitatingly that it was never officially entered on the record. Out of this grew a vast amount of misunderstanding and ill will.

Colonel House was not altogether happy over the result, for he had hoped to secure an unqualified endorsement of the Fourteen Points. Yet it was undoubtedly a triumph for Wilsonian idealism to force an acceptance of all but one. House consoled himself by saying that perhaps it was best to have these reservations after all; they underscored the fact that the Allies had unreservedly accepted all the other points.

The Allied and Associated Powers then presented their reservations on the Fourteen Points to Germany, and this statement forms the basis of what present-day scholars refer to as the pre-Armistice contract. In other words, the victors bound themselves by a solemn legal and moral contract to make peace with Germany on the basis of the Fourteen Points, with one reservation on freedom of the seas, and one elucidation on reparations.

This, it must be emphasized, was not unconditional surrender. There were numerous if vaguely defined conditions in the Fourteen Points which the victors were honor bound to observe. It is incontestable that there was a contract; but what it meant is by no means incontestable.

7

The lawyer will tell us that the basis of any contract is a meeting of minds. There was no meeting of minds in connection with the Fourteen Points. The Germans formally accepted the Fourteen Points of Wilson, points which they read in the light of their own hopes and fears. The Allies formally accepted the Fourteen Points as explained by the Lippmann-Cobb memorandum, but this memorandum was apparently not shown to the Germans. How can there be a contract in good faith when the meaning of its most important clauses is withheld from one set of signatories?

Then there were the mental reservations. As one reads the record of Colonel House's parley with the Allied leaders it becomes perfectly clear that they did not really accept the Fourteen Points. It is perfectly clear, as the Peace Conference was to reveal further, that they and their people all had aspirations regarding security, reparations, colonies, and territory that went far beyond the letter and spirit of the Wilsonian program. To put it baldly, ardent nationalists like Clemenceau, whose people had been bled white by the "Hun," had no intention of carrying through the contract in good faith, at least not in the sense that both Wilson and the Germans interpreted it. Having accepted the points against their will, they were of the same opinion still. Yet they could not stultify themselves before the bar of world opinion, after all the publicity given to the Fourteen Points, by openly announcing that they did not believe in them.

We have already noted that House was later condemned for not using the financial and military resources of the United States to extort a more complete acceptance of the Fourteen Points at the time of the pre-Armistice negotiations. Even if the ethics of using such a club on one's colleagues be granted, it is difficult to see how the final result could have been different. No matter how many or how powerful the clubs, the mental reservations still remained; and they were bound to come out around the peace table. The immediate task was to disarm the enemy; and if the brutal and unscrupulous "Hun" was tricked, that, the American people believed, was what he richly deserved.

The Germans have also been criticized for not having insisted upon a more explicit elaboration of the Fourteen Points before laying down their arms. It appears that they did not want too specific a definition, because it might be phrased to their disadvantage, and because they hoped to interpret the vaguenesses of the Fourteen Points to their advantage at the peace table. As it turned out, they never got to the peace table. But even if there had been a more explicit restatement, the mental reservations of the Allies still existed, and the victors —leaders and people—were in no mood to deal leniently with the Germans. Where the will exists in such cases, "escape clauses" can always be found in the contract, and the Allied statesmen, as we shall later note, were resourceful in finding them.

8

We must touch on one other point before leaving this general subject. Is it true that the Fourteen Points disarmed Germany?

Some writers say that this is completely false. The German armies were being beaten in the field, and the war lords simply sought an armistice so that they could regroup their lines. The Fourteen Points had nothing to do with it.

But this is not the whole story. It is clear that the German High Command sought out Wilson, rather than the Allies, because he, as the idealistic author of the Fourteen Points and moral arbiter of the world, might be easier to handle. And when the news was published that peace negotiations were under way, German morale, already undermined by the Fourteen Points, rapidly deteriorated, and surrender was inevitable.

It seems reasonable to conclude that if the German people had not come to regard Wilson's pronouncements as something more than platitudes, they would not have demanded peace when they did. In this sense, the Fourteen Points disarmed Germany, though forcible disarmament was inevitable within a few months.

As the event proved, it would have been better if Wilson had had fewer points, more clearly defined points, fewer unrealizable points, and more points integrated with the war aims of the Allies and accepted at heart by them. Less delusive and more realistic points might not have lured the Germans into an armistice so soon. But it would have been better to fight the war through to the last barbed-wire entanglement than to make a solemn contract which could not be realized, which the Allies had no intention of fully realizing, and which was not realized.

9

The Armistice of November 11, 1918, with Germany was not a true armistice but a bastard armistice. We must consider this situation briefly because it is fundamental to any understanding of what went on at the Peace Conference. But we need not discuss it at length because Wilson and his advisers had nothing to do with it; in fact, they opposed it.

When the Germans asked for terms, the Allied leaders were anxious to bring about an armistice. Although their armies were moving forward, the current drive was beginning to lose momentum, winter was approaching, and serious problems of man power, morale, and transportation were already at hand. The Allied countries were war-weary, and Bolshevism was sweeping in from the east. Any move in the direction of peace —a victorious peace—could not but be welcomed.

The problem of the Allied leaders was to ask for enough disarmament from Germany to make it impossible for her to renew the war effectively, while not asking for so much that the Germans would be forced to reject the proffered terms. In short, just what the traffic would bear—and no more.

So it was that the German troops were allowed to go home carrying their rifles, and were asked to surrender approximately half of their heavy artillery, machine guns, and other equipment. This meant that, with such military stores as they had captured from their enemies and could manufacture, the Germans were still able to put a veteran army in the field, which would have the advantage of fighting on shortened lines, though without any real prospect of success.

This arrangement was strongly opposed by General Tasker H. Bliss, American member of the Allied Supreme War Council. Bliss favored a formula of complete disarmament and demobilization. General Pershing insisted on unconditional surrender. They both felt that if Germany was beaten she would accept any terms. If she was not beaten, then it was unwise to make terms with her at all.

The American generals were overruled—unwisely many now feel, and certainly to the later regret of at least some of the Allied leaders. After the Armistice was signed, they discovered that revolution-rocked Germany was in much worse shape than they had thought, and that they almost certainly could have imposed far more drastic terms.

This oversight on the part of the Allied generals was partially corrected in the three periodic renewals of the Armistice, in which the French demanded progressively harder conditions. After much protestation and uncertainty, Berlin was forced to yield. The Germans loudly claimed that this was a breach of faith. They had laid down the bulk of their arms on the strength of certain promises, and when they had thus rendered themselves virtually defenseless, they were confronted with new and more onerous terms. President Wilson, Colonel House, and General Bliss were all grieved by what they regarded as "unfair," "unsportsmanlike," and "dishonorable" conduct, not "worthy" of the Allies. The French, on the other hand, advanced plausible reasons for drastic action.

10

A true armistice ordinarily involves the reciprocal granting of concessions and the imposing of restrictions. In this armistice the concessions were made only by the Germans. A true armistice is generally concerned with military matters. In this armistice a number of political considerations were injected, including an important French reservation on reparations; and in the subsequent renewals the so-called Armistice began to take on the aspect of a preliminary peace.

The net result was that the Germans were increasingly exasperated, while being left with enough to put up some kind of resistance. The soldiers in the Allied armies were clamoring to go home, now that the war was seemingly over, and they were unable to understand the necessity of keeping large armies mobilized against a possible resurgence of defeated Germany. Large bodies of men, notably the Belgians, deserted and went home. Tens of thousands of American boys were eager to return to families and sweethearts, and their plaintive cry was, "Lafayette, we are still here."

In this connection one of the great mistakes of the Allies was in the field of public education. They failed to make it sufficiently clear to their people that the war did not end with the fighting, and that it was imperative to keep huge forces under arms if the bitter fruits of victory were to be properly safeguarded.

But the most distressing feature of the seven months of technical warfare following the Armistice was the continuation of the starvation blockade of Germany, against the remonstrances of Wilson and the vehement protests of Herbert Hoover. The Armistice agreement had actually contained a promise—certainly a tacit promise—that the Allies would "provision" the German people "as shall be found necessary."

The fact is that the blockade, though lightened in March, 1919, was made more severe than it had been during the actual fighting, and it was kept in force until July 12, 1919, three days after Germany actually ratified the treaty, and eight months after the signing of the Armistice. During this period uncounted thousands of German men, women, and children died of starvation, or were physically and mentally blighted. This, of course, could be defended on the technical ground of German noncompliance with the Armistice, and also on the ground of military necessity, for at no time before the actual signing of the treaty could the Allies be absolutely sure that Germany would not again take the field. Yet if the disarmament provisions of the Armistice had been made as drastic as they should have been, and could have been, the hunger-blockade could hardly have been defended on any grounds.

At all events, the whole atmosphere of uncertainty and recrimination growing out of this situation contributed immeassurably to the difficulties of the negotiators, and hung like a pall over the Conference. General Jan C. Smuts not unreasonably concluded that the months of the Armistice were "perhaps" as "upsetting, unsettling, and ruinous to Europe as the previous four years of war."

II

Germany, say the Germans (including the Austrian-born Adolf Hitler), was not beaten but betrayed. The truth is that in a very real sense she was beaten and then betrayed. Her armies were reeling when the High Command sought a truce, though they were reeling on foreign soil. But the circumstances surrounding the Fourteen Points, the pre-Armistice contract, and the renewals of the Armistice gave all too valid a basis to the charges of betrayal, which tended to obscure the fact of the beating. With the wisdom of hindsight we can now see that the beating had advanced so far that betrayal was not necessary. The German soldiers marched home with their small arms,

and were greeted under evergreen arches as conquering heroes.
Germany had not been seriously invaded; German arms had
won glorious victories against overwhelming foes. After four
years of fighting the Allies had seemingly recognized that the
war was a stalemate, and they were willing to negotiate a treaty
with the German representatives—a treaty based upon peace
and justice, upon Wilson's Fourteen Points. The chivalrous

The New German War-Song
(Knott in the Dallas *News;* courtesy of the Dallas *News*)

Allied foemen, who had learned to respect German steel, could
be counted upon to recognize the Germans as brothers in arms.

So the Germans thought. It was unfortunate that they
thought so, though circumstances gave some reality to their
illusions. It was also unfortunate that the army, which occupied such a prominent place in German pride and national life,
should not have been portrayed as it was—a beaten army. This
misrepresentation of facts gave strength to Hitler's thesis that
the men at the front had been stabbed in the back by the Jews

and Communists, and helped prepare the public mind for another war in which the "invincible army" would bring home more tangible proofs of success.

Germany failed to learn the one lesson that she most needed to learn: war does not pay.

CHAPTER FOUR

THE MAN WITHOUT A COUNTRY

"He [Wilson] is certainly in splendid humor and in good trim— not worried a bit. And why should he be, for the world is at his feet, eating out of his hand! No Caesar ever had such a triumph!"
SECRETARY OF THE INTERIOR LANE, *November 5, 1918.*

1

THE NEWS of the Armistice caused war-taut America to relapse into a delirium of rejoicing. Streets everywhere were crowded with laughing, weeping, whooping, whistling, tooting, singing, kissing, drinking, dancing, milling masses. The canyons of New York City were filled with flags, confetti, torn paper. The police were powerless to control the crowds bent on window breaking, bonfire building, streetcar wrecking.

Gloating over the downfall of the Kaiser was everywhere unrestrained. He was lampooned in effigy, burned in effigy, tossed from skyscrapers in effigy, trampled underfoot in effigy. One placard announced triumphantly: "There ain't no Kaiser." Another proclaimed: "Let him rule in hell." One imaginative butcher drove about a truck on which he exhibited a stuck pig labeled: "Kaiser."

The Atlanta *Constitution* passed solemn judgment: "And somewhere in Holland an old, old man, the greatest criminal the world has ever known, is shivering before the hosts of accusing shapes who point their ghostly fingers and brand him murderer."

But in Washington, Woodrow Wilson was not shivering. He was responding graciously to one of the greatest spontaneous ovations ever given him.

And why not? He was at the dizziest peak of his incredible career. He had led an unprepared, bewildered, and partially disunited people through the greatest war in history. He had aroused and united them in a gigantic crusade which had proved that a democracy, in spite of its amateurish awkwardness, could make war, and make war with terrible effectiveness. Two million American boys had hurried ashore in France; they had cracked the German lines; they had driven seasoned veterans out of their trenches, hands in air, whimpering "Kamerad!" The Prussian war lords had sued for peace; Wilson had skillfully evaded their traps. He had forced the Germans to accept his proposals and change their government and evict their Kaiser. All that now remained was to make a just and lasting peace.

He did not know—he could not know—that the rest would be an anticlimax. When one is at the summit, the only possible path is down.

Wilson's triumphant position in November of 1918 was not unlike Lincoln's in April of 1865. Both had led their people through the dark days of gloom and disaster; both had united them with inspiring utterances; both had achieved victory.

But here the parallels break down. Lincoln was shot at the climax of his career, and became enshrined as a martyr, while lesser and weaker hands were left to fumble with the problems of reconstruction. Wilson lived on, toppled from his lofty eminence, and was left to wrestle with the problems of peace singlehanded. If Wilson had been shot on the eve of the Armistice, and if Lincoln had lived to complete his term, it is not improbable that Wilson would now rank higher in popular esteem than the Great Emancipator.

Wilson's wartime leadership had been superb. Despite such blemishes as the lagging aircraft program and the shipbuilding muddle, he had succeeded in inspiriting the people, and getting the job done. He had routed his political opponents when they sought to take the power out of his hands and put it into those of a bipartisan war cabinet. He had done his tremendous task with a minimum of fretting and exertion. He had chosen competent men, like Hoover, Baruch, McCormick, Hurley, and Garfield; had handed the reins of power over to them; and had let them run their respective organizations. During the darkest days of the war he played golf and attended the vaudeville with almost clocklike regularity. By delegating authority, by not overstraining, by concentrating his mind and energies on the over-all organization, he had been able to keep his brain clear, his judgment sound. And success had crowned his efforts.

But from October, 1918, to the end of this great tragedy we see a different Wilson. Something happened to becloud his judgment. Perhaps the strong wine of victory went to his head. Perhaps he was borne down by the responsibility of remaking the world. At all events, he fixed his attention upon the immediate problems with the single-track intensity of mind so characteristic of him, and he undoubtedly worked too hard. During the war he had delegated authority; during the peace negotiations he tried to carry the burden himself. It was too important a job to hand over to subordinates.

Whatever the explanation, he launched out upon an independent and stiff-necked course that brought disaster to his program, and physical prostration to himself. This is not to say that in all of these decisions Wilson was wrong. In some he was right; in some, it seems, he was wrong; in others he took courses which to this day are debatable. But from the vantage point of a quarter of a century after the event we can see some things that we could wish he had done differently.

2

Wilson's first great mistake grew out of his unfortunate appeal habit, which was to backfire again and again during the months that lay ahead.

Like Thomas Jefferson, the founder of his own Democratic party, Wilson had unshakable confidence in the teachableness and reasonableness of the masses, once the situation was clearly laid before them. During the war he had repeatedly appealed to the people, and they had not failed him. He assumed that they would never do so. But the pitcher can go to the well once too often.

By October, 1918, Wilson had definitely decided—though he had made no announcement—to attend the Peace Conference in person. The mid-term Congressional elections were about to be held. If the Democrats should suffer a defeat, the President would be seriously embarrassed at the peace table. He might not be able to command the prestige necessary to force through his program of a just peace capped by the League of Nations. At least, so he feared.

These fears were far from groundless. The Democrats had an excellent chance of suffering a severe reverse, now that the enforced unity of the war had disappeared, and they knew it, especially in view of the fact that they controlled the House of Representatives by an extremely narrow margin. A number of Congressmen whose seats were slipping came to Wilson in something of a panic, and urged him to issue an appeal to the country requesting the election of Democrats to the Sixty-sixth Congress.

Wilson had been toying for some time with the idea of publishing such a statement, and he finally yielded to the avalanche of pressure that was brought to bear upon him. The first draft contained bitter references to outstanding Republican opponents of the Administration, like Henry Cabot Lodge, but Wilson was persuaded by his political advisers to leave these out. After much consultation, some misgivings, and considerable redrafting, the appeal was gradually whipped into final form.

Mrs. Wilson relates that one evening in late October she went into the President's study and found him hammering out the finished draft on his portable typewriter. "I would not send it out," she said. "It is not a dignified thing to do." Wilson replied that he had promised to issue the appeal, and that he could not honorably back out now. So he rang the bell and handed the message to the head usher for delivery to the press.

One wonders why Wilson did not adhere to the plan originally proposed, and address his remarks in the form of a letter to some prominent Democrat, who would then publish it. This strategy would have avoided the impropriety and offensiveness of a direct appeal, while serving essentially the same purpose. Wilson evidently preferred less devious methods.

The momentous October appeal asked bluntly for the election of a Democratic majority to both houses of Congress. But Wilson was careful to explain—a point later overlooked—that he did not impugn the patriotism of the Republican party; they had supported the war loyally, although they had tried to embarrass the administration. They were, he said, "pro-war" but "anti-administration." "In ordinary times," Wilson apologized, such an appeal would be out of place. But this was "the most critical period" in the history of the country, and "no scruple of taste" should stand in the way of plain speaking.

Most significantly, the appeal stressed foreign reactions to the outcome of the election. In four different passages, Wilson referred to what people on "the other side of the water" would think. If the Republicans won, he declared, the result would be interpreted abroad "as a repudiation of my leadership." So he asked the American people to vote for Democrats, if "you have approved of my leadership and wish me to continue to be your unembarrassed spokesman in affairs at home and abroad . . ." In short, Wilson was asking for a vote of confidence.

Wilson may be pardoned for perhaps exaggerating the nature of the crisis, but there can be little doubt that this was one of the most important Congressional elections in our history. From the standpoint of foreign affairs, it was up to that time undoubtedly the most important.

3

During the war the catchword had been—in Wilson's own pedantic phrase—"Politics is adjourned." It was unpatriotic to criticize the president.

Upon publication of the October appeal, a Republican roar of anger reverberated from coast to coast. Wilson had wantonly and flagrantly violated the political truce; he had reconvened politics with a vengeance.

Chairman Will Hays of the Republican National Committee (later guardian of movie morality) cried, "Mr. Wilson wants only rubber stamps." Ex-President Taft remarked privately that Wilson had revealed the spirit of the "German autocracy which he claims to be fighting." The envenomed Theodore Roosevelt wrote exultantly to his bosom friend, Henry Cabot Lodge: "I am glad Wilson has come out in the open; I fear Judas most when he can cloak his activities behind a treacherous make-believe of non-partisanship." More urbanely, the Wheeling *Intelligencer* observed: "There is a growing impression that one Woodrow Wilson spilt a large bucket of beans about 3:00 P.M., Friday, October 25, 1918."

As a matter of fact, politics had never been adjourned during the war; politics never are in a democracy, war or no war. They are always present, though at times not trembling so unpleasantly near the surface as others. As early as the spring of 1918 the Republicans had begun a determined and bitter campaign to capture the next Congress. Even the amiable ex-President Taft was writing privately of Wilson's "peanut soul." The less amiable ex-President Theodore Roosevelt had been rampaging around the country against Wilson and his Fourteen Points, and by October was making such unrestrained statements as to suggest that he hoped to goad Wilson into some such blunder as the October appeal proved to be.

Yet until October the partisan activity of the Republicans was not generally known, and they could make a strong point of their nonpartisan record. During the conflict they had backed Wilson's war program, and in certain cases, notably in connection with the Selective Service Act, their aid had saved critically important legislation. The Republicans could now say that they had loyally supported the war, which they had; that they had sent their boys to France, which they had;

that it had been an American war, which it had. But now it was going to be a Democratic peace.

In brief, the Republicans were good enough to help fight the war, but they were not good enough to help make the peace. It was going to be Woodrow Wilson's private peace. At least, this was the charge.

Election day came, and the Republicans won a moderate victory in the House, gaining twenty-five seats and outnumbering the Democrats 237 to 190. The margin in the Senatorial contests was much closer. The Republicans picked up five seats, thus insuring control of the Senate by two votes. Several of the Senatorial elections were very close, and if any one of them had gone for the Democrats, there would have been a tied vote in the Senate, the Democratic vice president would have broken the tie in favor of the Democrats, and the Senate would have been organized along Democratic lines.

The most spectacular Senatorial contest was in Michigan, where the Democratic Henry Ford, the "flivver" magnate and pacifist, was narrowly defeated by the Republican candidate, Truman H. Newberry. The victor enjoyed a majority of fewer than 8,000 votes out of over 430,000 cast. Newberry was later convicted of having spent too much money (or having it spent for him), but was freed on a technicality. In 1922 he was finally forced from the Senate by the pressure of public opinion.

But by that time the Republicans had organized the Senate committees; and, thanks to Newberry's questionable vote, Henry Cabot Lodge, Republican, became chairman of the Senate Committee on Foreign Relations, from which vantage point he could help engineer the defeat of the League of Nations. In many ways, this was the most important single result of the election.

When the returns were all in, the Republicans exultantly announced that Wilson had been repudiated by the country. He had asked in effect that the election be made a vote of confidence. The country had voted for the opposition party; hence

Wilson could no longer be regarded as the spokesman for his country. He had forfeited his leadership—at least so the result was widely interpreted both at home and abroad.

4

The assumption is general that if Wilson had not issued the appeal the Democrats would not have lost Congress in 1918.

This hypothesis is impossible to prove. In fact, it would be just as reasonable to state, and just as impossible to prove, that if Wilson had not issued the appeal the Democrats would have lost the Senate and the House by an even wider margin, perhaps by a landslide. It is highly significant that a considerable number of Democrats whose seats were in doubt warmly thanked Wilson for the assistance that the appeal would presumably give them. When it was all over, a leading Democratic newspaper, the New York *Times,* was of the opinion that the appeal had saved seats.

There were many reasons, entirely apart from Wilson's appeal, why the Democrats should have suffered a serious setback. Even the most superficial student of our political history knows that there is normally a marked reaction against the party in power during the mid-term Congressional elections. He also knows that the party in power has always suffered a sharp reverse when the mid-term Congressional elections have come during a war.

We must also observe that there were extraordinary reasons why the Republicans should have made desperate efforts to recapture control of Congress in 1918. Since 1897, the country had been normally Republican; and Wilson was able to win in 1912 only because the unseemly row between Taft and Roosevelt had split the Republican vote. Four years later foreign affairs were still in a critical state, and even with the cry, "Don't swap horses in the middle of the stream," Wilson had been able to defeat the Republican candidate, Charles E. Hughes, only by the narrowest of margins.

In 1918, Taft and Roosevelt met publicly, shook hands, and buried the hatchet. The discordant factions of the Republican party were drifting back into the fold, and looking forward to the fatted calf when the Democrats should be thrown out. And how the Republican leaders hated Wilson! As the only

German "Repentance"

(Knott in the Dallas *News;* courtesy of the Dallas *News*)

Southerner elected President since Zachary Taylor, and the only Democratic President since the Civil War except Grover Cleveland, he had driven through a sweeping program of social and economic reform which trod heavily upon the toes of Republican big business. Wilson and his works must be defeated at all costs, and the hands of the clock set back to where they had been in the golden days of Republican standpattism.

The collapse of Germany came at a most inopportune hour for Wilson's political fortunes. By the time he had issued his appeal, it was clear that the enemy was beaten, and that the turbulent stream had been crossed. The old slogan about swapping horses now carried little weight.

We should also note that Wilson's dickering with the "Hun" in October for a negotiated peace added immeasurably to his vulnerability. Republican leaders like Roosevelt and Lodge were identifying the party with a drastic peace dictated in Berlin at the point of American bayonets. They much preferred an American victory in the field to a diplomatic victory by a Democratic President. They scoffed at the dreamy idealism of the "Fourteen Commandments"; they deprecated a "soft peace." "Unconditional Surrender Clubs" were formed throughout the country by Republicans: Germany must be made to pay for her misdeeds. There can be no doubt that this was the popular mood.

The Republicans insisted that a vote for Republican Congressmen was a vote in support of the President at the peace table. They were not only behind him; they were way ahead of him—in their insistence on Carthaginian terms. When it was all over, they claimed that they had won because they were the "unconditional surrender" party.

5

One important reason why Congressmen lost seats—this point is generally overlooked—is that the country as a whole regarded the incumbent Congress as an unusually poor one. It had been dilatory and inept in dealing with critically important war legislation. Its important committees had been headed by long-lived "Dixie" Democrats, "parochial politicians," and "political nondescripts." The chairman of the all-important House Committee on Ways and Means, Claude Kitchin of North Carolina, had been accused of "a fierce joy" in devising schemes for "soaking the rich"—the Northern Republican rich. The Southern Democrats had embittered the

Northern wheat-growing sections by voting to put a ceiling on the price of wheat, while refusing to put a similar ceiling on cotton. Northern resentment against Southern sectionalism unquestionably contributed to the November debacle.

Finally, the country was in an angry mood, tired of the necessary wartime dictatorship and "the patriotism of the lean garbage can." It was wearied of heatless, wheatless, meatless days, and determined to "take it out on someone." The party in power happened to be a convenient if illogical target.

Yet when all these things are said the fact remains that the contest was basically fought out over local issues. While there was some talk about letting the Germans off too easy, about the possibility of free trade under the Fourteen Points, and about the ineptitudes of the Administration, the average voter was not concerned with remaking the world but with electing a man that would look after the local interests of, say, the Nineteenth Illinois district. There is no evidence that the electorate believed that a vote of confidence for Wilson was the real issue, or even a primary issue, though the Democratic leaders tried to make it so.

Whatever interpretation one may wish to place upon this election, it seems reasonably clear that Wilson was stronger than his party. The vote was more pro-Republican and anti-Democratic than it was anti-Wilson. It is entirely probable that if a parliamentary form of government had existed in America, and the issue had been a vote of confidence, the President would have polled a comfortable majority.

Wilson asked in effect for a vote of confidence, and he got neither a vote of confidence nor a vote of lack of confidence. Under our presidential form there can be no true vote of confidence. In Congressional elections the issue is normally the vindication of incumbent Congressmen, not the vindication of a President. The rank and file of the electorate did not have the remotest idea that their vote would have any bearing upon the subsequent defeat of the Treaty of Versailles.

6

Some critics have charged that Wilson made a mistake in putting his appeal on so narrow a basis. Why did he not adopt the strategy later used by President Franklin D. Roosevelt and ask for the election of men, whether Democrats or Republicans, who would loyally uphold his hands in the making of the peace? This is what Colonel House and some of his other advisers urged, because it would have avoided making an issue of Republican patriotism.

We may well doubt whether a nonpartisan appeal of this sort would have worked out successfully. Wilson was a deep-dyed partisan, and he had a profound distrust of Republicans. His Democratic followers needed his support; and what would their feelings have been if Wilson had proclaimed that it was quite all right to elect Republicans, as long as they favored his peace aims as announced in the Fourteen Points? It is altogether probable that Wilson would have lost more through Democratic anger than he would have gained through Republican support.

Nor do those who point to the superior political finesse of President Franklin D. Roosevelt choose too happy a comparison. Roosevelt was conspicuously unsuccessful when he intervened in the state elections of 1938 for the purpose of securing Congressmen and Senators to his liking. In general, our people regard the election of members of Congress as their own local business, and they resent interference by the President or any other outsider.

The blunt truth is that the Republican leaders hated Wilson, and they were out to "get" him at all costs. They probably would have been just as determined if he had issued the appeal on a broad, nonpartisan basis. Indeed, they probably would have voted Republican just the same and just as hard, even if there had been no appeal of any kind. From their point of view the ides of November witnessed the fall of two great autocracies: that of the Kaiser and that of Wilson.

It now seems evident that Wilson committed a serious error when he issued the October appeal in the form that it took. All fair-minded persons will recognize, of course, that the decision was a difficult one to make. If he had kept quiet, his followers would not have had the benefit of his support; and, whether they won or lost, he would have earned their lasting resentment. There was in fact considerable grumbling already among the leaders of his own party.

At best, the appeal was a gamble. But from the point of view of foreign affairs Wilson could not have lost at all, or could not have lost much, if he had kept quiet. If he had issued no appeal, and the result had been the same, he could have waved aside the result as the normal, mid-term reaction against the party in power, in this case accentuated by wartime restrictions and local issues. As it was, he burned all his bridges behind him.

If he had kept quiet and won, as is conceivable, then he would have been in an extraordinarily strong position. He could have triumphantly announced that the result was a vote of confidence in his administration, and a mandate from the people to go ahead and make the kind of peace he had been preaching—a peace based on the Fourteen Points. This, of course, would not have been true, for, as previously noted, a Congressional election is primarily an election of Congressmen. But it is the privilege of the victor in politics to place his own interpretation on the result, whether sound or not. And when this interpretation is proclaimed loudly enough in the moment of victory, and repeated frequently enough under the sanction of victory, it is more often than not accepted as the gospel truth.

7

Next to making the appeal itself, Wilson's most costly error was in declaring so pointedly that a loss for the Democrats would be regarded as a repudiation of his leadership. Wilson

was one of the greatest living authorities on American government. He knew that we did not have a parliamentary system;
he knew that a Congressional election could not be a vote of
confidence. Then why did he lend the weight of his own
authority, even by indirection, to this false interpretation?

We know that he admired the parliamentary system of England, and felt that a government could not function smoothly
unless the executive and legislative branches were of the same
party. He planned to attend the Peace Conference in person;
and if he sat down with the prime ministers and premiers of
Britain, France, and Italy after a defeat in the November elections, he would be embarrassed by knowing that he was the
only one there not entitled to his place under a parliamentary
arrangement.

Immediately after the election, and several weeks before
Wilson reached Paris, his critics on both sides of the water
were clamorously claiming that he had no business to go
abroad as a delegate, because he had been repudiated by the
electorate. He himself had implied that he would be if the
Democrats were defeated; and these critics, both domestic and
foreign, could hardly be blamed for taking his own words at
their face value. It is an ironical fact that this great authority
on American government, by giving a misleading interpretation to our electoral system, thrust a lethal weapon into the
hands of those who wished to attack him. They undoubtedly
would have seized upon it even if he had issued no appeal, but
his unfortunate emphasis undoubtedly gave it greater potency.

In mid-December, 1918, following an appeal to the country
by Prime Minister Lloyd George, the British held a rousing
general election, and vindicated the administration by a landslide. Late in December, Premier Clemenceau asked for a vote
of confidence in the Chamber of Deputies, and was supported
by a thumping majority of 380 to 134.

The essential difference between the appeals of Lloyd
George and Clemenceau on the one hand and Wilson on the
other was that the British and French leaders were trium-

phantly successful, whereas Wilson was apparently repudiated. There can be no doubt whatsoever that the outcome of
the November election, and particularly Wilson's implied insistence on a vote of confidence, was extremely damaging to
his prestige. Premier Hughes of Australia said that Wilson
"had no claim to speak even for his own country," and certainly not for the whole world.

He Got There!
(Courtesy of the St. Louis *Post-Dispatch*)

Wilson's own seat was secure until March, 1921, but for
whom did he speak? The taunt was thrown in his face that in
no other great nation in the world would he even be in office,
much less at the peace table. His threats at the Paris Conference to appeal to American and world opinion over the
heads of the Allied leaders were greeted with cynical and
incredulous smiles.

Foreign criticisms to the effect that Wilson was a repudiated leader were largely ill informed or for political effect, designed to humiliate and embarrass the President. Discerning Europeans knew perfectly well that Wilson was still a power to be reckoned with; they knew perfectly well that we did not have the parliamentary form of government; they knew perfectly well that Wilson had not been legally repudiated.

Those who think otherwise will have to explain how it was that the French and the British accepted commitments from Wilson of the most vital importance to themselves merely on his verbal assurance that he could persuade the American people to endorse them. A repudiated leader cannot be relied on to make such deliveries.

Ominously, the apparent rebuke at the polls merely made Wilson more obstinate. He wrote with the utmost cheerfulness that he was not at all "dismayed or disheartened" by the results, and he boasted that "you may be sure that the stubborn Scotch-Irish in me will be rendered no less stubborn and aggressive . . ." This, unfortunately, was all too true.

CHAPTER FIVE

JOVE STEPS DOWN FROM OLYMPUS

"When he [Wilson] stepped from his lofty pedestal and wrangled with the representatives of other states upon equal terms, he became as common clay." COLONEL HOUSE, *June 29, 1919.*

1

THE OCTOBER appeal was sensational; the November election no less so. But the sensations did not end here. On November 18, 1918, less than two weeks after Wilson's presumed repudiation at the polls, the White House made the startling announcement that the President was going to attend the Peace Conference in person.

A heated debate immediately started as to the wisdom of this move, and it continues in an academic way down to the present time. But one thing is certain. The critics of Wilson are virtually unanimous in agreeing that the trip abroad was one of his most serious blunders—perhaps the most serious in a long sequence of blunders. If he had not gone, they say, the peace would have been a more lasting one, and it undoubtedly would have been accepted by the United States Senate.

At precisely what time Wilson made this momentous decision it is difficult to say. But we do know that from an early date he thought of himself as an important influence at the peace table. His futile attempts to mediate between the Allies and the Central Powers late in 1916 showed him how difficult it was to exert effective pressure while the United States was a mere spectator of the great events which were then unfolding. Reluctant as he was to accept the arbitrament of war, he found some consolation in the thought that as an active belligerent, and as a leader of the strongest of the victor nations, he would have a far better opportunity to remake the world along the lines of a just and permanent peace. As he told Jane

Addams, the voice of the United States would be more compelling at the peace table than calling through the crack of
the door.

When Germany began to sue for peace terms in October,
1918, this question of attendance was thrust prominently to
the fore of Wilson's mind. He discussed it with a number of
advisers, and even sought the counsel of several Democrats
in the Senate, though there apparently is no record of his having discussed the problem with Republicans. Whatever else
may be said about this hotly disputed question, the fact is clear
that Wilson was amply forewarned of the probable consequences of his going. A number of his closest advisers begged
him to stay at home.

The announcement of Wilson's plans evoked an immediate
outburst of condemnation, chiefly from partisan Republicans.
There was also a good deal of quieter dissatisfaction among
Democrats in the Senate and elsewhere, for they felt that the
President should stay at home and rally the shattered and
dispirited ranks of the party. One Democratic newspaper let
the cat out of the bag when it remarked that it was "fright-
fully afraid that while we are making Europe safe for democracy the party will lose every post-office in the United States."

The thing that most infuriated leading Republicans was
that Wilson should presume to go to Europe and speak for
the United States after his recent rebuke at the polls. Ex-
President Theodore Roosevelt, who next to Wilson was the
most influential American abroad, cried across the Atlantic
to the European statesmen in stentorian tones:

Our allies and our enemies and Mr. Wilson himself should all
understand that Mr. Wilson has no authority whatever to speak
for the American people at this time. His leadership has just been
emphatically repudiated by them. . . . Mr. Wilson and his Fourteen Points and his four supplementary points and his five complementary points and all his utterances every whichway have
ceased to have any shadow of right to be accepted as expressive of
the will of the American people.

Such extreme statements were not only reprinted in the European press; they were played up to the exclusion of news items more flattering to Wilson. All this did nothing to strengthen the President's prestige when he finally sat down at the peace table.

2

Some of the criticisms of Wilson's pilgrimage to Paris were sound, some unsound; some trivial, some weighty; some contemporary, some latter-day. Let us briefly examine some of the principal criticisms, with attention to the domestic scene first:

Wilson's going was unconstitutional.

The argument was that Wilson could not properly discharge the constitutional duties of the President in Paris, and for this reason he should either stay at home or resign in favor of Vice President Thomas R. Marshall. Senator Sherman of Illinois, a violent Republican critic of Wilson, actually introduced a resolution designed to declare the Presidential office vacant. Marshall was urged to assume the Presidency, but he was too good a Democrat to create this kind of schism in the party's ranks.

Wilson's European trip was unprecedented.

Up to this time no other President had ever set foot on European soil during his term of office. Previous Presidents had in fact made extraordinary efforts to avoid leaving the country at all during their administrations. Theodore Roosevelt, with characteristic Rooseveltian love for shattering traditions, had gone down to Panama in 1906 on a battleship to "see the dirt fly." But this was in the Western Hemisphere, the Canal Zone was a leasehold of the United States, and the Republic of Panama (which he also visited) was a creature and virtual protectorate of the United States. Even so, Roosevelt's bold act was criticized, chiefly by Democrats, who then happened to be the party of the "outs."

Wilson was needed at home.

The greatest industrial machine thus far in history had just been stopped at full speed, and overpowering problems of domestic reconstruction—finance, railroads, industrial and human demobilization—were clamoring for immediate solution. The country was eager to get back to a normal footing after the orgy of war. Wilson should stay in Washington, provide Congress with the necessary leadership, and devote the major portion of his energies to the pressingly important domestic difficulties. Of course, the Republicans did not care for the kind of attention that Wilson would give these problems, either at home or abroad, but they felt that they could keep a closer watch on him if he stayed in the United States.

Wilson was needed to guide public opinion in the problems of peacemaking.

No treaty could be ratified that was not supported by popular sentiment and approved by the Senate. Wilson would do well to keep closely in touch with both these important coadjutors, provide the necessary information as to the progress of the negotiations, and carefully educate both the Senate and the public to the new responsibilities which he was asking the country to assume. As we shall see, both public opinion and the Senate were kept largely in the dark, and herein lies one of Wilson's greatest failures.

Wilson's venture abroad was merely an unseemly display of swell-headedness.

The President's moral leadership of the world, it was alleged, had inflated his vanity and had given birth to a Messiah complex. The wine of world domination had affected his head. His junket abroad was additional evidence of a desire "to hog the whole show"—to use the earthy phrase of William Howard Taft.

3

We come now to certain objections which bear more directly upon the actual negotiation of the peace.

The Old Girl Who Wasn't Invited to the Show
Turns Up Her Nose at the Program
(Courtesy of the St. Louis *Post-Dispatch*)

Wilson was a poor negotiator.

Although he had visited England and Scotland a half-dozen times, he knew little of Europe at first hand, having made only one hurried summer trip to the Continent sixteen years ago. No American, it was currently said, could ever understand Europe, yet this egoist-idealist was going to reorder not only

the mother continent but the whole world. He could understand or speak no European language, and his Ph.D. "reading
knowledge" of French and German had grown rusty since his
graduate years at the Johns Hopkins University. He was a rank
amateur as a diplomatist. He was an idealist and a chaser after
moonbeams. He was a poor horse trader, inept in the give
and take of the conference table. The "slick" European diplomats would wrap this honest greenhorn at the poker table
around their little fingers, and "trade him out to his eyeteeth."

Wilson would make a "soft peace."

A great many Americans, preponderantly Republicans, felt
that Wilson had robbed them of a satisfying victory, and they
were afraid that this "mushy" sentimentalist would now rob
them of a victor's peace. He would be too lenient with the
Germans, who admittedly were rejoicing at the coming of their
American savior. The Allied diplomats would, of course, favor
stern terms, but the strong-willed and imperious Wilson
would use the enormous influence of the United States to "put
over" a "soft peace." (This, it will be noted, rather contradicts
the charge that he would be putty in the hands of the wily
European diplomats.)

Wilson would jeopardize his overshadowing moral ascendancy.

Sitting quietly in the White House, at one end of the wire
and aloof from the hurly-burly of the conference, he would
still be the arbiter of the world. His voice would resound across
the Atlantic with the authority of Jove. He could appeal to
the peoples of Europe, to his own people, to the people of the
world—and they would listen. But to go down from Mount
Olympus to Paris, to sit at the same table with tricky and unscrupulous diplomats, to haggle over the sordid details of the
loot, to rub elbows with treacherous and dishonest wirepullers
—all this would sully his raiment and undermine his authority.
What would the European masses think of their new Messiah

if he had intimate converse with this discredited breed of publicans and sinners?

If things did not go well, and Wilson bolted the Conference and appealed to the people, he would be jeered at as an egoist who was piqued because he could not have his own way all the time. If he stayed at the Conference, he would be outvoted; at best he could expect only a shabby compromise. If he stayed at home and played the game his own way, he could not lose; if he went abroad and played the game their way, he could not win. And all the disappointed peoples in the world would condemn him for not winning.

Wilson could work more efficiently at home.

Securely ensconced in his ivory tower at the White House, receiving cabled reports daily from his representatives, issuing instructions over the same wire, and keeping closely in touch with public opinion, he could preserve detachment and sound judgment. This is what McKinley had done in 1898 during the negotiations with Spain in Paris, and the results had been satisfactory.

At Paris, Wilson would come to know the other negotiators personally. He would have to say "No" to them so often that he would become seriously embarrassed; the pressure to say "Yes" would finally become so great that he would have to yield occasionally against his better judgment. It is much easier in such circumstances to say "No" by cable.

The Paris Conference was bound to be a madhouse of confusion, with hundreds of people desperately seeking something, and with little or no opportunity for Wilson to get off and view the whole scene with sanity before making an earth-shaking decision. He could not ask his colleagues to wait while he appealed to Washington for instructions. He was the source of instructions; there was "no appeal from himself."

In Washington, at the other end of the wire, he could make his decisions impersonally, without the "pneumatic hammer of daily personal contacts." His representatives could bring about a wholesome delay by cabling to him for instructions. And he could drive off into the arboreal quietness of Rock Creek Park and have a chance to think.

4

A final argument against Wilson's going—though not generally known at the time—was that the leading European statesmen, as distinguished from their people, did not want him to come.

This feeling is quite understandable. Wilson overshadowed Clemenceau of France, Lloyd George of England, and Orlando of Italy like a veritable colossus. This stiff-necked schoolmaster would doubtless lecture heathen Europe on its congenital wickedness and hold out for a "soft peace"; he might even arouse the people against their leaders by stirring appeals; he would almost certainly throw all kinds of monkey wrenches into the plans of the Allies for partitioning the spoils of war. And who was this eleventh-hour laborer in the vineyard to come to them, after they had sacrificed millions of their sons on the altar of Mars, and tell them what they might or might not keep?

The idealist-professor was all well enough in framing and preaching the Fourteen Points, which had proved terribly effective in disrupting and disarming the enemy. But when it came to the cold, hard, realistic business of peacemaking he had better stay at home and let Europeans settle the affairs of Europe. They were old hands at the game; they knew best.

When Wilson announced that he expected to attend the Conference, Clemenceau and Lloyd George could not very well make their real objections known. So they resorted to a quibble. Wilson, they said, would be the only "head of a state" present, and the head of a state could properly negotiate only through accredited agents. If he insisted on coming, then it might be necessary to invite the King of England, the President of France, the King of Italy, and others. Premier Clemenceau was insistent that his implacable political foe, President Poincaré, be given no opportunity to attend the Conference in an official capacity.

Wilson was clearly much annoyed by this transparent attempt to sidetrack him. He was determined to go; he expected to preside; he planned to take an active part in the deliberation; and he had no intention, so he said, of hanging around the Conference as "the centre of a sort of sublimated lobby." The sharp cablegram he sent to Colonel House in Paris on this point suggests that the enormous power which he was then wielding had to some extent affected his ego.

The quibble about being the head of a state was especially annoying to Wilson. The United States had the presidential system of government, and the head of the government, unlike the prime ministers of Europe, happened also to be the head of the state. Wilson, as we have seen, admired the parliamentary system, and liked to think of himself as a prime minister. If the other prime ministers and premiers were entitled to go, he felt that he should enjoy the same privilege, not as the head of the state, but as the head of the government—and also as the herald of a new age. He had no intention of being kept at home by this hollow subterfuge, which his opponents knew very well was a subterfuge. If anything, this attempt to "pocket" him— to use his own word—aroused his Scotch-Irish stubbornness, and made him all the more determined to go.

Clemenceau's opposition to the coming of the inconvenient idealist waned with the passage of time. Wilson tactfully yielded the presidency of the Conference to the doughty French premier, an honor which could not be denied France once Paris was made the seat of the Conference. Clemenceau also perceived that "the theocrat of the White House" would prove more manageable than he had been led to suppose. What more could he ask than that Wilson should forsake the lofty advantages of Mount Olympus and go to the mat with him—a mat which Clemenceau would dominate as both wrestler and referee? If Wilson opposed French demands, he could be (and was) branded a pro-German. And, as President Poincaré shrewdly observed, if he did not come, all the failures of the Conference "would be attributed to his absence."

5

Many, if not most, of the arguments advanced by Wilson's critics could be strongly challenged.

It is a debatable point whether his going was unconstitutional; and Wilson secured competent legal advice on this question before departing. The Constitution does not forbid the President to leave the country; and Wilson's being physically absent probably did not amount to disability within the meaning of the Constitution, because he could arrange to keep in contact with Washington by wire and sign bills on his return trips. Besides, the Constitution does not vest in any person or body the authority to declare the office of President vacant.

It is true that Wilson's trip to Paris was unprecedented, but what of it? Times had changed. America, as Wilson now recognized with increasing clearness, was no longer isolated but was part and parcel of the rest of the world. The making of the peace concerned our future welfare as well as that of Europe and the other continents. It has often been said that the United States wanted nothing and asked for nothing at Paris, and had no direct stake in the terms of the settlement. Nothing could be farther from the truth. We had invested billions of dollars and tens of thousands of lives in a war to end wars, and we had a direct and vital interest in the task of making sure that it would not all happen again.

Nothing could be more silly, Wilson's defenders say, than to argue that America should not play the role that was rightfully hers simply because of a horse-and-buggy precedent. President Coolidge went to Cuba in 1928, while Franklin D. Roosevelt ranged by boat and by plane from Buenos Aires in

South America to Casablanca and Cairo in North Africa, and to Teheran in Asia. If there should be a great peace conference today in Paris, no one would think it strange that a President of Franklin D. Roosevelt's stature should go. On the contrary, he would be expected to go. Every trail-blazer, every precedent-breaker, is criticized for what his successors are frequently praised, and Wilson was no exception.

No one could deny that the problems of reconstruction were pressing, but they could be worked on by Wilson's able administrative assistants, who would keep closely in touch with their chief in Paris. Domestic reconstruction could wait; world reconstruction could not. As Wilson told Congress on the eve of his departure, he could think of no other "business or interest" that should take precedence. Foreign affairs, for one of the few times in our history, seemed to be of more pressing importance than domestic affairs. It was eloquent testimony of the changed position of the United States in the world theater that this should be so. Those who thought that wars end when the fighting ends were living in a fool's paradise. From the long-range point of view, it was of paramount importance that a just and enduring peace be made. Otherwise, as Wilson himself told Congress, we should break faith with those boys who had joyfully sacrificed their lives for such a noble end.

It is self-evident that Wilson could theoretically have remained in closer contact with public opinion, and could have guided it more surely, if he had stayed in the United States. Whether he would have done so had he remained behind, one cannot say. As we shall repeatedly observe, one of his gravest mistakes was to fasten his eyes so steadfastly on the distant vistas of a new world order as to ignore the mundane problem of keeping up his fences at home. Star-gazing is just as easy on either side of the Atlantic. Even while in Paris, Wilson was kept constantly informed as to the state of public opinion by Joseph P. Tumulty and others, though he evidently did not pay much attention to what they reported. At all events, he could not be in two places at once; and for reasons that were undeniably weighty he thought it best to be on the other side.

It seems reasonable to suppose that Wilson's new earth-shaking role had to some extent gone to his head. But what mortal man, for that matter, would have been completely immune? Lloyd George chucklingly and perhaps inaccurately recalls that at Paris the President once startled Clemenceau by telling how he was going to avoid the mistakes that Jesus had made.

Wilson was undoubtedly aware of the charges that he was going to the Conference merely to gratify his Messiah complex. But why should he turn aside from the noble deeds that only he could do because of the cavilings of mean spirits? He was moral arbiter of the world, and why should he not go and don his mantle? The common people of all lands were counting on him to do so, and he could betray neither the living nor the dead. A stern sense of duty, rather than selfish motives, probably more than anything else sent Wilson to Paris.

6

No one will dispute the fact that Wilson knew little at first hand of the machinations of European chancelleries. But he was no babe in the woods when it came to either politics or foreign affairs. His public career had been relatively brief but spectacular and concentrated. Two years as governor of New Jersey followed by six years of the Presidency of the United States had been an incomparably rigorous training school, and had left him with few illusions about men and their motives. As a politician and political leader Wilson had up to this time established a record which still ranks among the most sensationally successful in American history.

It is true that Wilson was not a professionally trained diplomat, and that he was not at his best in the give and take of a free-for-all discussion. It is also true that he did not speak foreign languages; but interpreters could be used and were used. Although he did not know a great deal about Europe at first hand, he had an unusually wide theoretical knowledge, and when he reached Paris he gave the more important problems intense study. It was not unusual to find him on all fours over a geographical or ethnological map. He had a keen, perceptive mind, which kept on the main track; he was a comprehending listener; and he spoke with precision, intelligence, and force. This is the well-nigh unanimous testimony of the American experts who were intimately associated with him at Paris.

In all fairness to Wilson, one must point out that the problems harassing the world were so complex and far-ranging that no mortal mind could master them. Lloyd George made the incredible confession at the Peace Conference that he had never heard of the notorious Twenty-one demands presented by Japan to China in 1915. On the floor of Parliament he also made the no less incredible admission that before going to Paris he had never heard of the industrially important area of Teschen, the bone of contention between Poland and Czechoslovakia. Lloyd George may not have known some things, but he knew enough to keep up his fences at home, which Wilson did not.

English writers like John Maynard Keynes and Harold Nicolson have done the cause of truth no service by stereotyping Wilson as an ignorant fumbler who was "bamboozled" by the European frock coats. He made his errors, as they all did, but his average of constructive achievement was high. And he was far from being dull-witted. His mind did not scintillate as sparklingly as that of Lloyd George, who darted from point to point with kingfisher rapidity, and who reversed himself with the greatest of ease when he found his information incorrect. Wilson preferred to get the facts first, and then move more slowly in one direction.

It is clear that Wilson was an idealist, but idealism may be—and much of Wilson's was—long-range realism. The pothouse politician, who sees only one move at a time, brands anyone an idealist who spurns the short-run advantage in favor of the larger, less immediate gain. Wilson was dealing in long-range realities, and he failed largely because the great mass of humanity is unable to see more than one jump ahead. From a practical point of view he should have recognized this fact, and trimmed his sails accordingly.

Wilson, his critics to the contrary, did not favor a "soft peace." He favored a just peace—just retribution for Germany's misdeeds—and this meant a stern peace. We shall have occasion to refer to this later.

It is perfectly true that Wilson risked his political standing at home and his moral ascendancy abroad when he went to Europe. He knew that the popular thing to do would be to stay in America. He knew that he would be throwing his enormous prestige on the gaming table if he went to Paris. But the problems to be solved were so tremendous, and the chances of establishing a new world order were so unprecedented, that he decided to take the risk. This was no time to be selfishly thinking of one's popularity. This was no time to stay at home mending political fences when the entire world needed mending. There was no one else whom he could entrust with such a colossal responsibility. To shirk this tremendous task would, to him, have been nothing short of immoral.

7

On the positive side, there were weighty reasons why Wilson should go.

He had been the leading spokesman of the Allied and Associated Powers, and his peace aims had commanded general popular acceptance. The Germans had laid down their arms on the basis of the Fourteen Points, and it was perfectly natural that Wilson should go to Paris as the author of the Points, explain them more fully, and see that they were written into the peace. This was all the more true since he knew that they had been accepted with mental reservations by the Allied leaders.

Wilson was the moral arbiter of the world, and the masses everywhere, not just in the United States, expected him to go to Paris and give them a lasting peace. They did not trust the Old Diplomacy, but they had a childlike faith in his ability to usher in the new era. How could he disappoint this tremendous and expectant following? Like Jesus, Wilson found that a prophet is more honored abroad; and it is an ironical fact that the Europeans, who knew Wilson least, trusted him more than did his own countrymen.

Could Wilson have worked better through subordinates, as McKinley had done? At the outset we must note that the problem in 1898 was of kindergarten simplicity when compared with the Augean tasks confronting Wilson. In 1919 there were multipartite negotiations, involving not two powers but some thirty; the reshaping of the world, not the crumbs of Spain's once proud empire. With so many hundreds of threads in the tangled skein; with so many different and clashing interests; with so many reasons for moving with the utmost speed, it seemed desirable to Wilson that he be on the ground. There were too many problems that could not be settled, at least not expeditiously, without oral discussion. Terse cablegrams, laboriously coded and decoded, were slow, misleading, and often inaccurate.

The question of working through subordinates may be answered in part by fact and not speculation. In February, 1919, after getting off to a seemingly splendid start, Wilson left Paris for a flying trip to the United States, leaving Colonel House and Secretary Lansing in charge. Though he kept closely in touch with House by wire and wireless, he found upon his return after a scant month that his subordinates, in his judgment, had given ground alarmingly, and he had to struggle desperately to regain what they had lost, or what he thought they had lost. We shall return to this episode later.

Present-day scholars like Dr. Paul Birdsall—and their evidence is convincing—conclude that Wilson, by being present

and exercising his great personal prestige, was able to force
more of his program into the peace than would have been possible through subordinates. This does not necessarily mean
that the peace was better because he did so; perhaps it would
have been more workable and more lasting if he had stayed at
home and let the Europeans write the kind of treaty they
wanted. But for the moment we are concerned with his efforts
to incorporate his own ideas in the peace; and, as we shall note
in the last chapter, he achieved a very considerable degree of
success.

8

When Wilson announced, on November 18, 1918, that he
was leaving for Paris, he was at pains to say that he was not going as a delegate, and he was careful to suggest that he might
find it possible to take part in only preliminary meetings.

This was hardly candid, for Wilson had every intention of
attending as a delegate, and of staying for the main work of the
Conference. But knowing that his move was unpopular he took
the precaution, at Colonel House's suggestion, of breaking
the news gently. It was not until eleven days later that the five
American delegates to the Conference were publicly named,
and Wilson headed the list.

During this eleven-day period criticism of Wilson was not so
severe as it otherwise would have been, and much of that which
was expressed quickly waned. There were many who felt that
it would be a good thing for him to go to Europe, get the "feel"
of the situation, meet the leading statesmen, engage in preliminary discussions with them, and then leave for home to
direct the concluding negotiations by wire. If he should do
this, his influence would remain unimpaired: in fact, it might
be enhanced.

The Cleveland *Press* struck a not uncommon note when it
remarked that those who were criticizing Wilson for "going
across" should wait to see whether he "puts it across."

CHAPTER SIX

WILSON AND HIS
"ERRAND BOYS"

"[The Commission] is a cheap lot of skates. I could swear if it would do any good." WILLIAM HOWARD TAFT, *December 23, 1918.*

1

THE COUNTRY was shocked by the October appeal, and by the announcement that Wilson was going to Paris. It received another rude shock on November 29, 1918, when the personnel of the Peace Commission was announced.

Wilson, of course, headed the list. The other four commissioners were Robert Lansing, Secretary of State; Colonel Edward M. House, confidential adviser to the President; Henry White, an experienced diplomat; and General Tasker H. Bliss, a member of the Supreme War Council in Paris and the expert on military affairs.

The outburst of condemnation that greeted the announcement of these names was loud, prolonged, and insistent.

The first criticism was that the group contained no really big men comparable in stature with Wilson. The Republicans in particular cried that the new Messiah was so determined to remake the world himself in his own way that he did not want the counsel and interference of really competent advisers. He wanted only "rubber stamps"—soft-spoken and self-effacing "yes men" like Colonel House. The Republicans distrusted Wilson's exalted idealism, and they wanted able and hard-headed realists around him to apply the brakes when necessary.

It is true that, politically speaking, there was no really "big" man on the Peace Commission. Robert Lansing had to be chosen *ex officio,* because the other foreign ministers were being sent to Paris, and it would have been an intolerable insult to ignore him. As it turned out, he was taken to Paris and there ignored—at least according to his own embittered book.

Lansing—handsome, prematurely white, fussily precise— was an able international lawyer who had been serving as Counselor for the Department of State when Secretary Bryan resigned in 1915 over the *Lusitania* crisis. Wilson was pre- occupied, and rather than comb the entire country for an out- standing successor, he followed the path of least resistance by merely moving Lansing up, though all the time he had grave doubts as to his fitness for the job. In all important matters, Wilson served as his own Secretary of State, and for this reason he probably thought that he needed nothing better than a com- petent and experienced administrative assistant.

At all events, Lansing was an able rather than an outstanding man. Although he spent much of his time in conference at Paris absent-mindedly penciling sketches and grotesque figures on a pad, he nevertheless gave serious thought to the problems at hand, spoke cogently when the occasion demanded, and grew steadily in the esteem of his colleagues. Being an inter- national lawyer, he was thoroughly out of sympathy with Wilson's flights into the future, and a rift rapidly widened be- tween the two men over the League of Nations and other issues. He probably would have resigned, but was restrained in part by the conviction that this would weaken the hands of the President by advertising dissension within the Commission. Wilson seriously considered asking him to resign, but refrained from doing so, probably for the same reason. In any case, Lansing was a stern realist, with his feet on the ground, and Wilson would have done well to heed some of his advice at Paris.

2

Colonel House was not a big man, though he was far from being a stupid one. The keen but erratic British critic, Harold Nicolson, who was at the Conference in a minor capacity, char- acterizes him "as the best diplomatic brain that America has

,yet produced." While there are many who will quarrel with this sweeping judgment, it is true that House had behind him an unusual amount of experience. As Wilson's personal representative and *alter ego,* he had made several extensive trips abroad, and he not only had come to know many of Europe's problems at first hand, but had made the acquaintance of many of the leading European statesmen. They respected him and had confidence in him. The American people, on the other

Wilson's Peace Delegation
(Malicious satire from *Harvey's Weekly*)

From left to right: Wilson, House, Lansing, White, Bliss,
Baruch, Hoover, Creel

hand, regarded him as something of a sphinx-like man of mystery.

Small of stature, gentle, soft-spoken, and retiring to the point of shyness, the quiet Texan Colonel—a geographical not a military colonel—had never run for public office, and had never been elected or appointed to one, much preferring the role of the power behind the throne. His portfolio as peace commissioner was the only quasi-official public appointment of any kind he had ever held. He was the only one of the four commissioners whom Wilson took into his confidence; indeed, on important matters the other three were virtually ignored.

It may not have been a mistake to take Colonel House to

Paris, but it probably was unwise to appoint him as one of the five official commissioners. If he had not gone in this capacity, Wilson could have made room on the commission for someone else whose political standing would have reassured the country. House had faithfully served Wilson as an invaluable personal and confidential adviser, and there is no good reason why he could not have continued in the same role at Paris. Despite recent criticism, he was generally levelheaded, well informed, and experienced in European statecraft. He has been sneered at as a compromiser; but in complicated human relationships, such as the making of a peace treaty by twenty-seven victorious powers, there can be no agreement without compromise, and no achievement without agreement. But even granting all this, Colonel House's advice would have been just as sound, perhaps more sound, if he had not gone in an official capacity.

3

A word about the remaining two commissioners, General Bliss and Henry White.

General Bliss was a gruff, honest soldier, of medium height, thick-set, and slightly stooping. "Nature," says Ray Stannard Baker, "intended him to be a hairy man, gave him thick eyebrows and bristling moustache and then changed its mind and made him bald—an extreme shiny baldness, except for a bristling fringe of hair at the back and sides of the head." Surprisingly enough, he was a classical scholar, and interlarded his correspondence with erudite Latin expressions. *Harvey's Weekly,* a bitterly critical sheet, remarked that "his presence at an international peace conference is about as fitting as that of an army mule would be in a church choir."

General Bliss was not a big man politically, but he proved to be a lucky "find." He not only had a firm grasp of the military questions involved, but had a broad comprehension of the general economic and political problems that were then vexing

Europe. He was that rare combination: statesman, humanitarian, scholar, and soldier. His advice was sound and far-sighted, startlingly so for one who was presumed to be a narrow military man. He was in fact one of the few figures who came out of the Conference with enhanced stature. To this day there are some who believe that he was the ablest man on the American commission.

There is no reason to suppose that it was a mistake to have General Bliss in Paris, but in some ways it was unfortunate that he should have had an official place on the Peace Commission. As a technical military adviser he could have been kept close at hand, like Colonel House, while his place on the Commission could have been taken by a more impressive political figure.

The fact is often overlooked that there were scores of American legal, economic, and other technical advisers at Paris, many of whom overshadowed—at least in the public mind—the four commissioners whom Wilson appointed. The names Herbert Hoover, Bernard M. Baruch, Norman H. Davis, and Vance C. McCormick at once come to mind. There is no valid reason why Wilson could not have added indefinitely to this list, and why he could not have reserved room on the official Peace Commission for men of outstanding stature.

4

Handsome, affable Henry White was not a big figure politically, though he was physically. A man of independent wealth, he had been able to afford the luxury of a lifetime in the diplomatic service, and was unquestionably the outstanding "career" diplomat of his generation. But he had not held a post for about ten years, and there was a tendency to sneer at him as a "has-been."

White was an open-minded and broad-gauged man, with sound judgment, polish, tact, and great conciliatory powers.

He knew Europe, European statesmen, and European problems. Having lived in England and France for many years, and
having a daughter married to a German nobleman and suffering from the Allied blockade, he could to an unusual degree
sympathize with the conflicting points of view. He had played
the leading role for the United States in the critical Algeciras
conference of 1906, which is credited with having postponed
the World War. In fact, he was the only man in the entire
country who had behind him responsible, first-hand experience
with the interplay of international forces at a great conference.
He was the only American on the commission of five who knew
French well enough to carry on an official conversation.

From every possible viewpoint except the political—which
we shall come to shortly—Henry White was an excellent choice.
His services should have been utilized in some way, either
officially or unofficially.

5

The Republicans were not so much disturbed by the small
caliber of the men on the Commission as by the fact that there
was only one Republican on it, Henry White, and he was not
at all prominent in party councils. He was a registered Republican, and when living in the United States, which had
been intermittently, he had voted the Republican ticket. Ex-
President Taft, an unfriendly critic, thought he was "more of
an Englishman than he is an American." He was not a bitter
partisan; if he had been, Wilson would have passed him by.
The Republicans consequently insisted that they did not have
a single representative on the Commission of five. Henry
White was a pleasant man, but as a political figure he simply
did not count. No one was more surprised at the appointment
than White himself.

Harvey's Weekly satirized the whole Commission, and
Wilson's domination over it, with diabolical cleverness:

Name	Occupation	Representing
Woodrow Wilson	President	Himself
Robert Lansing	Secretary of State	The Executive
Henry White	None	Nobody
Edward M. House	Scout *	The Executive
Tasker H. Bliss	Soldier	The Commander-in-Chief

Senator Henry Cabot Lodge sneered that Wilson had appointed himself four times—and Henry White.

The charge that the Republicans had been deliberately slighted was, unfortunately, all too true, and it was one of the mistakes which had most to do with the disaster that finally befell Wilson.

The Republicans undeniably had a strong and well founded grievance. They had supported the war enthusiastically and loyally, more so in certain respects than Wilson's party. They now represented, at least on the basis of their recently won Congressional majority, more than 50 per cent of the voters of the country. Yet they were to have only 20 per cent of the numerical representation on the Commission, and not even 5 per cent when one considered the fact that Henry White was not a strong and vengeful Republican. No wonder they cried that the President had been glad enough to have the Republicans fight the war, but he did not want them hanging around when it came to making the peace. The cowboy humorist, Will Rogers, had Wilson say to the Republicans, "I tell you what, we will split 50–50—I will go and you fellows can stay."

The disconcerting truth is that there was only one prominent partisan of either party on the Commission, and that was Woodrow Wilson.

Why, demanded the Republicans, was there not at least one distinguished Republican who could give to the majority party in the country the feeling that their views, as well as those of Wilson, would be written into the peace? Why not take men

* A reference to House's several secretive trips to Europe as representative of Wilson.

like Charles Evans Hughes, Republican presidential standard-bearer in 1916; or ex-President Taft, an outstanding advocate of the League of Nations; or Elihu Root, a former Secretary of State, a friend of international collaboration, and the distinguished elder statesman of the party?

6

It seems reasonably clear that Wilson made a mistake in not appointing one or more of these three men. But in fairness to him we must note that from his point of view there were strong objections to all of them.

They were all distinguished lawyers; and Wilson, who had begun life unsuccessfully as a lawyer, had a deeply ingrained dislike for the narrow mental processes of the legal profession. He wanted to work for a broad, sweeping program, and did not care to be constantly annoyed by the realistic and legalistic objections of the precedent-bound "library lawyers." He bluntly told Robert Lansing, himself a lawyer, that he did not intend to have lawyers drafting the treaty of peace. Lansing was hurt.

The three "big-gun" Republicans most commonly mentioned—Taft, Hughes, and Root—were all strong partisans, though perhaps not narrow and bitter partisans. Theodore Roosevelt was narrow, bitter, and unbridled, and he had been ranting around the country making "skin-'em-alive" speeches against Wilson. But no one seriously proposed taking him along.

Wilson himself was a strong partisan and a good hater. Born a Democrat—a Southern Democrat—in the state of Thomas Jefferson, and dedicated to the principles of Thomas Jefferson, he believed that Republicans were tolerable people, but not to be trusted too far in high places. He believed in the two-party system: one party governing, the other watching—with the Republicans doing the watching.

During the summer and fall of 1918, Root, Hughes, and Taft had all made speeches attacking the Administration. Hughes and Taft had both assailed the October appeal in public, and Taft had gone so far as to criticize Wilson's Fourteen Points and his thirst for power. As a presidential rival, Taft had thrown some heavy verbal punches at Wilson in 1912, and Hughes had done the same thing in 1916 when courting the German-American vote. And Wilson, despite his policy of hitting such people "with a chunk of silence," took these things to heart.

Root, Taft, and Hughes were all big men, comparable in stature with Wilson. But Wilson did not like to have big men around him giving advice, and therein lay one of his gravest weaknesses. He naturally sought the counsel and enjoyed the company of inferior if not mediocre minds. Colonel House, his most intimate adviser, was not a big man. Most of the time the self-effacing House agreed with Wilson; but when he did disagree he was careful to phrase his objections in the most inoffensive manner. Much of the time he indicated dissent by a period of silence. Wilson, contrary to the popular misconception of the know-it-all professor, was fully able to listen to counsel, and there is abundant evidence that he did so intelligently and appreciatively. But he apparently did not want advice crammed down his throat by men of his own level of ability. He had great confidence in his own undeniably superior mental equipment, and he preferred associates whose minds "went along with his"—to use one of his favorite phrases.

From one point of view Wilson was perfectly right in not asking outstanding Republicans of a strong partisan bent to serve with him. He was responsible to the American people for the kind of peace that was to be made, and he doubtless felt that harmony would be better in the long run than outstanding but contentious ability. He may have remembered that the United States had suffered from such embarrassments in making peace with England at Ghent in 1814. As it was, the Commission of 1919 developed enough disharmony. Taft had been President; and although he was amiable and had an infectious laugh which bubbled up from his abundant abdomen, he distrusted Wilson and had ideas of his own. And men who have been President are not accustomed to taking orders. Root and Hughes also had ideas of their own, and Hughes had come within a hairsbreadth of attaining the Presidency in 1916.

There were additional reasons for not taking along these outstanding Republicans. Taft was a strong and faithful supporter of the idea of the League of Nations, which was coming under increasing attack in the Senate. Would it be wise to weaken the home front, where Taft was doing such effective work, by taking him abroad to serve in a purely advisory capacity?

Several members of Wilson's official family strongly urged that he take Root. But Wilson peremptorily dismissed him as a "hopeless . . . reactionary," whose "appointment would discourage every liberal element in the world."

No one will deny that Root was conservative—perhaps reactionary. But Wilson undoubtedly exaggerated the importance of this objection. Even granting that liberals and labor would have been seriously antagonized, which is debatable, the selection of Root would have done a great deal to mollify the Republicans. The objections to Taft and Hughes were much less applicable to Root; and temperamentally he should have been able to work harmoniously with Wilson. Having recently served a term in the United States Senate, he also would have represented the point of view of that body, and could have used his great influence to get the treaty approved.

In fairness to Wilson it must be repeated that he had reasons —strong reasons in his own mind—for ignoring the outstanding Republicans. It was most unfortunate that he could not bring himself to invite at least one of them, preferably Root. The tragedy is that he was temperamentally incapable either of inviting them or of serving wholeheartedly with them.

7

Two other questions naturally arise. If Wilson could not bring himself to appoint "big" Republicans, why did he not take along several smaller ones? And in particular why did he not invite a Republican or two, perhaps a Democrat also, from the Senate?

One difficulty was that the number of five commissioners was decided upon in consultation with the Principal Allied Powers. The possibilities ranged from three to seven, and the figure finally agreed upon was five. After Wilson had taken care of himself, as well as Lansing and House, there were only two places left, and one of these was earmarked for a Democratic military adviser.

So far as the records show, the idea never occurred to Wilson that he could have appointed House and Bliss as unofficial advisers. He could in fact have taken along any number of Republicans in an unofficial capacity. When he reached Paris he largely ignored both his official and unofficial advisers, and it is just as easy to ignore a large delegation as a small one— perhaps more so. But one danger is that some of them will come back and write bitter books.

If Wilson had put House and Bliss in the unofficial group, this would have left room on the Commission for three Republicans, besides himself and Lansing. The appointment of three Republicans, who could have been ignored if they had proved unmanageable, would have been a master stroke from the standpoint of meeting the charge that the Commission was "packed" with Democrats. On the other hand, the Democrats would have been acutely unhappy over the "packing" of the Commission with Republicans, and Wilson could not afford to antagonize both his own and the opposition party.

Then what about the Senate? Republican President McKinley had appointed three Senators, one of whom was a Democrat; and would not Wilson have flattered that body by the selection of two or three of its members? Would not Senatorial advisers in Paris have been able to tell him at every stage of the negotiations what the Senate would or would not be likely to approve? Would they not have warned him against omitting a reservation regarding the Monroe Doctrine from the first draft of the League of Nations Covenant, and would they not have told him that the Security Treaty with France did not have even a fighting chance in the Senate? Would they not have been able to inform their Senatorial colleagues at home what was going on, and thus forestall the damaging criticism that Wilson was purposely keeping the Senate uninformed?

If Wilson had chosen three Senators, would he not have had three votes assured for the treaty before it was even signed? The influence and votes of McKinley's three Senatorial commissioners had saved the treaty of 1898 with Spain, and certainly Wilson's appointees could not have stultified themselves by throwing out their own handiwork. If Wilson had chosen prominent Senators, would they not have been able to carry their friends with them? And during the debates in the Senate would they not have been able to provide information at every stage as to what certain provisions actually meant and what had really happened at Paris?

8

All things considered, it would have been perfectly feasible to take one Democratic Senator and one or even two Republican Senators. The press rather generally spoke of Senator Walsh, of Montana, a Democrat of high ability, and Senator Knox, of Pennsylvania, a distinguished lawyer who had served under Taft as Secretary of State and who, as a consequence, had a broader grasp of foreign affairs than the great majority of his colleagues. He was passed over, and developed into one of the most unrelenting critics of Wilson's handiwork.

Whether he would have done differently if he had served on the Commission, one cannot say.

Another alternative was to take the Democratic chairman of the all-important Senate Committee on Foreign Relations, Senator Hitchcock of Nebraska, an excellent choice. If this had been done, propriety would have suggested that Wilson also choose the ranking Republican member of the same committee, who would be the chairman when the next Congress assembled. This happened to be Henry Cabot Lodge of Massachusetts.

Aye, here was the rub. Lodge and Wilson were on conspicuously unfriendly terms. The Senator from Massachusetts was a Boston Brahmin of the Charles Sumner tradition, educated at Harvard, and profiting from the social and cultural advantages of inherited wealth. Chauncey M. Depew once remarked that his mind was like the soil of New England, "naturally barren, but highly cultivated."

Lodge had enjoyed the distinction of being "the scholar in politics" until Wilson came along, and then the Senator's scholarly and political attainments were overshadowed by the greater scholarly and political attainments of Wilson. Lodge had openly and enthusiastically supported the idea of the League of Nations before Wilson took it up, and when Wilson came out in favor of it, Lodge somersaulted over into the opposition camp. During the heated presidential campaign of 1916, Lodge had made a not altogether groundless charge as to Wilson's handling of the *Lusitania* affair, and Wilson had politely given Lodge the lie. From then on the two men were at daggers drawn.

There is no evidence that Wilson ever seriously considered the appointment of a Senator. If he had chosen a Democrat, he presumably would also have had to take a Republican. The natural Republican choice was Henry Cabot Lodge—and this may have caused Wilson to shy away from the Senate altogether. If Lodge had been invited, he could have been expected to cause much embarrassment at a time when there was enough embarrassment over larger matters. He might also have been disloyal, for he tried to persuade his delegate-friend, Henry White, surreptitiously to circulate a memorandum at Paris among the Allied statesmen to the effect that Wilson did not really represent the American people. Perhaps, on the other hand, Lodge would have been loyal if he had been invited into the family and stroked the right way; he might have caused less trouble in Wilson's "bosom than on his back."

It probably would have been unwise to appoint Henry Cabot Lodge, but some other leading Republican Senator, such as Knox, could well have been invited. This would have caused some raising of the eyebrows; but the feud between Wilson and Lodge was no secret, and the country would have understood. Of course, Lodge would have been mortally offended, but he was mortally offended anyhow, and out to get his knife into Wilson's back.

The reason that Wilson actually gave to his Attorney General for passing by the Senate was a constitutional one. He remarked that "the Senate was an independent body and that it did not seem fair to him to influence its free judgment of diplomatic negotiations by appointing Senators who would take part in the negotiations and then act upon them as judges."

At the time of the approaching negotiations with Spain in 1898, certain prominent Senators had protested vigorously that it was unconstitutional to have the same men serve as both negotiators and ratifiers. This would break down the fine system of checks and balances in our federal system.

Even granting this point of propriety, there was in 1918 ample precedent for appointing Senators, as there has been since then. And if one may credit the reports of the Washington press correspondents, the Senate would not have been displeased by such a compliment. Some of the Senators expected to have representation on the Commission, and they were deeply disturbed when they were completely ignored.

The stakes at Paris were stupendous. With the future peace

and stability of the world involved, it is strange that Wilson should have been squeamish about an obscure point which was sanctified by precedent. He did not scruple to throw overboard a century of isolationist tradition, yet he was a stickler for a constitutional point which at the most was unconstitutional only in spirit. One is again reminded of men who strain at gnats and swallow camels.

One suspects—though proof is lacking—that Wilson would have found this constitutional argument less satisfying if it had not provided such a convenient excuse for leaving Lodge and other Republican encumbrances at home.

9

It is possible to understand why Wilson should not have appointed Senators, but it is difficult to explain why he snubbed that all-important body in almost every other way. He seems to have made little or no effort to defer to it either on the question of selecting the Commission or on that of shaping the peace.

General Ulysses S. Grant, upon being thrust into the Presidency, thought that Congress and not the Senate approved treaties; but gradually he learned something about the Constitution at the taxpayers' expense. Yet Wilson, the internationally known authority on government, could certainly not plead ignorance.

The simple facts are these. Wilson knew, or should have known, that the Senate is a powerful body, sleeplessly jealous of its prerogatives; that it had defeated treaties before and might do so again; and that only one-third of its membership (plus one) could undo any pact brought before it. He knew, or should have known, that the Senate Republicans were in an ugly mood following his October appeal, and that the Senate was eager to regain the power and prestige it had enjoyed before Wilson had assumed his wartime dictatorship under the Constitution. He knew, or should have known, that the next

Senate would be controlled by the Republicans, with the chairman of the Senate Committee on Foreign Relations none other than the implacable Henry Cabot Lodge. He knew that he was going to try to force a League of Nations into the treaty of peace, and he also knew, or should have remembered, that when he had earlier broached this idea he had stirred up a hornets' nest among isolationist Republicans in the Senate.

As recently as 1908, Wilson had written in one of his better

"Seein' Things"
(Courtesy of the Brooklyn *Eagle*)

known books that there was nothing to prevent the President from making the Senate a useful partner rather than a jealous rival. He received a forceful reminder of his own dictum when, early in November, 1918, ex-President Taft appealed to him publicly to defer to the foreign relations committees of both the House and the Senate.

It is true that previous Presidents had not ordinarily followed the practice of consulting the Senate in advance of negotiating a treaty; but a few had done so, and there was nothing to prevent Wilson's doing so. This, it must be repeated, was to be no ordinary treaty; the destiny of the world hung upon it; money and blood had been poured out like water to achieve it. Then why should the President stand on punctilio?

Wilson, it must be confessed, did not entertain great respect for the Senate, and he viewed it with irritated aloofness. It must also be confessed that he was not discreet in his private references to the "pigmy-minded" gentlemen in that body. He tactlessly insisted in a public speech, after his return from Paris, that he owed nothing to the Senate. Both he and the Senators were elected and paid by the American people to do their respective jobs. His job was to draw up treaties; theirs was to pass upon them. If any accounting was to be made, he would make it to the people who had hired him. The Senate could do likewise.

There can be no doubt, either, that Wilson did not like the two-thirds rule. But the fact remains that the Senate was just as much a part of the treaty-making power as he was, and there was nothing that could be done about it short of amending the Constitution, which, if possible, would have taken too long. As Wilson was condemned to live with the Senate, he would have done well to invite its cooperation rather than excite its antagonism.

10

The members of Congress, and in particular the members of the Senate, were vitally interested in making the peace, as was true of all thoughtful Americans. On December 2, 1918, Senator Cummins introduced a resolution in the Senate designed to send a bipartisan Senatorial committee to Paris for the purposes of watching the negotiations and keeping Congress posted. Administration forces, after sarcastically proposing that all ninety-six Senators go to Paris, were able to sidetrack this unwelcome move.

The members of the Senate would doubtless have been flattered, and made to feel that they were partners in the enterprise, if their advice had been sought in advance of Wilson's
going. They would have been able to give some excellent advice as to what to put into the treaty and what to leave out, in
order to insure prompt approval. Even assuming that the
Senate had not responded graciously to Wilson's gesture, there
was nothing to be lost and everything to be gained by making
it.

Why, then, did Wilson ignore the Senate?

Perhaps it was because he had not got his fingers badly
burned in any previous treaty fight, though he had encountered annoying difficulties over the Colombia indemnity treaty,
over the canal-tolls repeal, and over the armed-ship filibuster.
Perhaps it was because he felt that the Senate did not matter as
long as public opinion was on his side. Perhaps it was because
he did not believe that the Senate would dare incur the oppro-
brium of ruining his plans for world reorganization. This
thought cropped out later in one of his public speeches.

Possibly the true explanation is that Wilson, as he himself
admitted, had a "one-track" mind, and that he tackled this
problem with "single-track" intensity. While he was concentrating on the colossal task of making a new world order, the
Senate did not seem important. As has been well said, "he
was like the man who knocked the ball into the left-field
bleachers, but forgot to touch the home plate."

In any event, either Wilson overlooked what he already
knew about the Senate, or he thought it unimportant.

But the Senate was not unimportant—and it was to be heard
from again.

11

The uproar over the appointments had not died down
when, on December 2, 1918, Wilson appeared before Congress
to deliver his annual message. He was to sail for Paris two days

later, and it was generally anticipated that he would take the country into his confidence and outline in general terms the kind of peace he expected to bring back.

But the address was largely the conventional and prosaic presidential discourse on the state of the nation. At the very end, Wilson appealed to the people to support him in what he was going to do, but he did not make it at all clear what he was going to do.

The Democrats who were present generally applauded his remarks. The Republicans, and a considerable sprinkling of Senate Democrats, sat in sullen silence. The press voiced keen disappointment at Wilson's secretiveness, and partisan journals remarked that Wilson treated the American people like a class in political economy at Princeton. There can be no doubt that Wilson completely muffed a splendid opportunity to win popular support and acquaint the American people with their new responsibilities.

Two days later he sailed from New York. Ominously, he left behind him an ill-tempered, resentful, and suspicious Republican opposition, and a confused, preoccupied, and drifting Democratic following.

CHAPTER SEVEN

THE COMING
OF THE MESSIAH

"If he [Wilson] has any sense he will get back to America as soon as he can." SIR HENRY WILSON, *December 22, 1918.*

1

ON THE morning of December 4, 1918, the good ship *George Washington* (a former German luxury liner) nosed slowly out of New York harbor, bearing Woodrow Wilson to Europe on one of the greatest adventures of all time. No argosy—not even that of Columbus—ever ventured out into the unknown more heavily freighted with the hopes of humanity.

Airplanes droned overhead, tugboats shrieked hoarsely, and the black masses of humanity on shore shouted enthusiastically, as President Wilson, standing beside Mrs. Wilson on the topmost deck of the *George Washington,* waved his dark felt hat in response, and flashed his famous smile. Gradually the up-pointing Statue of Liberty hazed into the background, and the great adventure had begun.

On the way out of the harbor, the *George Washington* met the transport *Minnehaha* bringing home a cargo of khaki-clad American boys from Europe. They waved and cheered as if to remind him that he must not break faith with their buddies who would never come back; as if to remind him that if he succeeded in making the right kind of peace they would not have to go back and do the bloody job again.

But Wilson needed no reminders. He knew full well the ghastly cost of the recent war. He knew full well that it lay within the power of the victorious nations to dictate the terms of settlement and to erect the structure of an enduring peace. This was an opportunity such as had never before come to mortal man—an opportunity that might never come again. If

the peacemakers succeeded, their names would be blessed; if
they failed, their names would be cursed by generations yet
unborn.

No one was more completely convinced than Wilson that
there could be no enduring peace without the participation of
the United States in his League of Nations. He was therefore
determined that the American people should underwrite the
military, political, territorial, and financial terms of the yet
unnegotiated peace. But would they? He assumed that the
American people had changed their minds, much as he had
changed his mind, on the subject of close cooperation with the
rest of the world. But had they?

We have already referred to Wilson's capacity for changing
his mind in recognition of changing realities, and to his assumption that others could change their minds also. We have
also considered the "one-track" intensity with which he pursued large objectives, while losing sight of smaller ones. In
making up the personnel of the Peace Commission, he lost
sight of the Senate. In making plans for the new and enduring
peace, he lost sight of the American people.

For some unaccountable reason, Wilson did not properly
appreciate the magnitude of the sacrifice he was calling upon
his countrymen to make. From the days of George Washington
onward, with the single exception of the brief interlude of
Theodore Roosevelt, the United States had generally pursued
a policy of isolation—a policy of having as little political connection with Europe as possible.

Yet here was Wilson—singlehanded—about to change the
main current of American foreign policy, a policy sanctified by
time and hallowed by association with the names of the Founding Fathers. To Wilson's penetrating mind the reversal seemed
simple, and altogether necessary in the light of changed conditions. To the less penetrating minds of millions of his countrymen, this was a momentous step, not to be taken lightly,
certainly not without the greatest of deliberation.

Not the least among the ironies of this great tragedy is the fact that Wilson was sailing to Europe on the *George Washington*—a ship named after the very President whose policy he was seeking to reverse. If this was a gentle warning from the great Disposer of Events, Wilson seems to have paid little or no attention to it.

2

Wilson was by no means without assistance in his plans for remodeling the world. Accompanying him on the *George Washington* were scores of specialists in history, geography, ethnography, economics, finance—a veritable "brain trust," to which Wilson referred as his "brains."

The principal Allied and Associated Powers, including the United States, had been at work for many months on the problems of the peace. Some months after America entered the war, a group of experts, predominantly college professors, was brought together in New York City under the direction of Colonel House. For many months this earnest group, named The Inquiry, had been giving meticulous study to the numerous problems that were bound to vex the makers of the new map of Europe.

There can be no doubt that the American experts amassed a great deal of sound, factual information. The *George Washington* groaned under the cartloads of books, maps, reports, and other data which had been so carefully assembled—"peace conference munitions." But American opinion, suspicious of academicians, was not too favorably impressed. One New York journal irreverently described the whole organization as "Colonel House's troupe of performing professors." William Allen White, another journalist, wrote:

"Down the gangplank walked this Yankee knight errant followed by a desperate crew of college professors in horn-rimmed glasses carrying textbooks, encyclopaedias, maps, charts, graphs, statistics, and all sorts of literary crowbars with which to pry up the boundaries of Europe and move them around in the interests of justice, as seen through the Fourteen Points."

This lurid picture is not only unfriendly but unfair. The nationally known experts who went to Europe were not carrying textbooks; they had advanced far beyond the textbook stage. Harold Nicolson, a minor member of the British delegation, cheerfully concedes that the American delegation was the best informed at Paris. Dr. Charles Seymour, who was one of the specialists in question, relates that at a meeting of a commission in Paris, an American expert proposed that a decision be altered in the light of new facts, and offered to present the evidence. A foreign delegate thereupon suggested "that we accept the amendment without asking for the evidence. Hitherto the facts presented by the Americans have been irrefutable; it would be a waste of time to consider them."

3

Three days before the *George Washington* reached France, Wilson assembled the American experts for a discussion of some of the problems that loomed menacingly on the horizon. The conference took place behind closed doors, and we are much indebted to Dr. Isaiah Bowman, who had the foresight to take careful notes, from which he shortly thereafter reconstructed the President's entire speech.

We need not analyze this revealing address at length, but we should carefully weigh two remarks which throw a flood of light upon Wilson's thinking, and which in some measure explain his conduct at Paris.

At the very beginning Wilson declared that the Americans would be the "only disinterested people at the Peace Conference, and that the men whom we were about to deal with *did not represent their own people* . . ."

This is an astonishing statement. What Wilson evidently had in mind was that the greedy and grasping premiers and prime ministers of Great Britain, France, and Italy did not represent the finer aspirations of their people, to whom Wilson had appealed in his Fourteen Points. The actual experience at the Conference revealed that the people not only were behind their representatives but were to some extent ahead of them in clamoring for the spoils of war.

But whether well founded or not, this attitude on the part of Wilson did not augur well for harmonious cooperation with his associates at the peace table. He seems to have felt all along that in case of a deadlock all he had to do was to appeal over their selfish heads to the nobler impulses of their people. He seems to have felt that he represented, not merely an American, but a world constituency. In a very real sense he represented neither.

The second point of Wilson's address that needs emphasis appeared in his peroration. After urging his experts to keep constantly in touch with him and to bring to his attention any matters of critical importance, he pleaded: "Tell me what's right and I'll fight for it; give me a guaranteed position."

Here we see the workings of the careful academic mind. Trained as a specialist, Wilson respected specialists—academic specialists. They were "his kind"; they spoke the language he understood. He also respected facts. He did not want opinions from his specialists; he wanted only the facts. On the basis of the facts, he would form the opinions. And when he was assured that the position which he took was based on facts, he would fight for that position, "agreeably if we can, disagreeably if necessary."

We shall presently see how this pledge worked out.

4

The *George Washington* sighted Brest, France, on Friday the 13th, a date which bore no terrors for Wilson, for he had long regarded thirteen as his lucky number.

As the ship steamed slowly into the harbor, he was greeted with the strains of "The Star-Spangled Banner," with thunderous presidential salutes from the near-by warships, and with the huzzas of the populace. With high silk hat in his left hand, he bowed and smiled while acknowledging the plaudits of the people.

He did not tarry long at Brest. Through lines of cheering soldiers, flower-bearing children, and peasants in their picturesque Breton costumes, he pushed on to the train, and with waving hand began his triumphal trip to Paris. Lincoln Steffens records that here and there peasant families knelt beside the track in the dark to pray for him and his mission.

The capital gave Wilson an ovation that would have warmed the heart of a Caesar or a Napoleon. Proudly he rode down the beflagged Champs-Elysées with President Poincaré, while two million people, held back by tens of thousands of cheering soldiers, shouted "Vive l'Amérique!" "Vive le Président!" Countless bouquets of roses and violets were rained upon the open carriage. Wilson gracefully acknowledged the cheers, gray head bared, while the procession passed under a great banner bearing the words, "Honour to Wilson the Just."

This tremendous tribute was partly personal, partly an expression of gratitude to America for having helped rescue France from the heel of the Boche. It was also partly the manifestation of a belief that Wilson would carry through his ideals and bring a lasting and just peace—which meant, of course, that Germany would be ground down so far into the dust that she could never clench her mailed fist again.

After nearly two weeks in France, Wilson journeyed to England, where he was greeted by cheering throngs, reverberating salutes, and all the pomp and pageantry of a millennium of royalty. He dined at Buckingham Palace, and ate from golo services of plate valued at fifteen million dollars. At Carlisle he visited the church in which his grandfather had served as pastor, and delivered a few beautifully chosen extemporaneous words. His several formal addresses were all brief, dignified, and not especially revealing.

The six-day reception in England was noticeably cooler than that in France. Perhaps it was Gallic excitability; perhaps it was that England had already poured out her soul to Foch and Clemenceau only a few weeks before.

There is one other explanation. The British remembered how reluctant Wilson had been to bring his people into the fray on their side. Blood was not thicker than water; he had been "too proud to fight"; he had favored "peace without victory." In none of his speeches in England did he pay a graceful and eloquent tribute to the tremendous sacrifices of England in the war that had just ended, sacrifices far greater than those of late-coming America. British leaders, notably Lloyd George, were hurt and angry. But Wilson was probably thinking of the bright vistas of the future rather than the bloody sacrifices of the past.

One portentous development occurred while Wilson was in England. On December 29, 1918, Clemenceau appeared before the Chamber of Deputies, and with a sneering reference to Wilson's *noble candeur* ("noble simplicity") came out four-square for the old balance of power—with France the dominant end of the balance. He was resoundingly supported by a vote of confidence, 380 to 134, the greatest of his tempestuous career. Tactfully, the compositors of the official record of the debates changed *noble candeur* to *noble grandeur*.

The next day, speaking at Manchester, England, Wilson stated sharply that the United States was not in the slightest degree interested in supporting the old balance of power. We would join only a combination which was a combination of all.

The British press interpreted Wilson's statement as a rejoinder to Clemenceau, as doubtless it was, and printed the two speeches side by side. Clearly there was going to be a head-on collision between the leading spokesman for the Old Order, and the leading spokesman for the New.

5

Returning to rain-soaked Paris, Wilson made hasty preparations for a four-day journey to Italy. As his train snaked along under cloudless skies, thousands of peasants poured down from the hills to wave an enthusiastic Godspeed. At Rome, the hysterical masses, held back by the soldiery with great difficulty, cheered wildly, "Viva Wilson, god of peace," and poured a cascade of purple violets and golden mimosa upon him. At Milan, he stood on the balcony, led the band, and with both hands threw kisses to the delighted populace.

The Italian reception was nothing short of delirious. In Milan, wounded soldiers had attempted to kiss his clothes. Europe had seen nothing like it since the days of Peter the Hermit. Streets and public squares were renamed in Wilson's honor. Men thought of the millennium, of the second coming of Christ. A story—undoubtedly apocryphal—told of an Italian laborer who hoped that the Pope would not die, because "Voovro Veelson," as he was affectionately called, might appoint a Protestant.

One ugly incident marred the triumphal Italian tour. As George Creel tells the story—and he was there—some 50,000 people packed the Piazza Venezia in Rome, waiting for Wilson to speak to them as scheduled. They waited five hours, and then the Presidential procession swept by without stopping. A great groan rose up from the expectant multitude, and with Latin emotionalism women wept and men threw their hats upon the ground and tore wildly at their hair.

The explanation is that while Wilson wanted to meet the people, and expected to do so, the Italian leaders did not want him to. They were afraid that he would make such a moving appeal as to spoil the plans that they were secretly laying for imperialistic loot. So they took him in hand and saw to it that he was not permitted to make such an appeal, while officially announcing in the press that the President had never had any intention of speaking at the Piazza Venezia.

Mrs. Wilson vividly recalls in her memoirs the anger which both she and the President felt over these transparent attempts to keep him at arm's length from the masses. The common people would have heard him "gladly"—only they were not allowed to.

Returning to Paris after making a half-dozen fatiguing speeches, and after sightseeing in the Coliseum and elsewhere, Wilson on the whole had reason to be happy. He apparently believed that all the cheering meant that the peoples of Europe were enthusiastically in favor of the proposed League of Nations. But were they? Was it not relief from war; joy over the approaching peace; gratitude to the United States; appreciation of Wilson's leadership? Time would tell.

6

One cannot help feeling that these pre-Conference junkets were unfortunate, though it is difficult to see how they could have been avoided. But as long as Wilson decided to take them, it was well that he went before the Conference, rather than after. Had he gone later, he would have been the recipient of things less pleasant than flowers, especially in Italy.

There can be little doubt that the pressure to make these tours was great. The Conference would not meet for several weeks, and what valid excuse could be offered for disappointing all these worshipful people? We should also note that Wilson would have been less than human if he had failed in some measure to enjoy such unprecedented outpourings of devotion and good will. Besides, he did not believe that the statesmen represented their people, and here, he assumed, was a splendid opportunity to bring his message directly to the masses.

If Wilson had been looking for an excuse not to go on these presidential pilgrimages, he could have found an excellent one. All of his time and energy were needed in Paris for working out the preliminaries of the Conference. The trips consumed precious time, and sapped his slender store of energy. It is probable that at this early date he did not fully realize how valuable time was, and how much there was to be done. But if he could have applied the many days that were frittered away on trips to the tasks that came rushing to a head in April, the final story might have been different.

7

Wilson, in fact, did say "No" to one invitation—perhaps the one invitation he should have accepted.

The French and Belgians had made extensive preparations for taking him on a trip to the devastated areas and the graveyards, where the President could see with his own eyes the incredible damage inflicted by the Hun, and the countless acres of white crosses—mute testimony of the terrible sacrifices of France.

Wilson stubbornly declined these repeated invitations, and possibly was irked by them. He had come from America to make a peace of justice, and he did not want his mind beclouded with long rows of white crosses when he considered the fate of Germany. "The French want me to see red," he remarked. "I could not despise the Germans more than I do already." Wilson, the scholar, was going to make a determined effort to retain some of his scholarly objectivity. Wilson, the Southern boy brought up in devastated Georgia, already knew that war was what General Sherman actually made it and reputedly called it. He was too busy with more important things.

But from the political point of view Wilson made a serious error. France was eager to show the wounds of her still-bleeding body to him who would have much to do with binding them up. If the good physician had looked at them, he would have offended no one, and he would have given the patient a strong psychological "lift." Lloyd George went out to visit the devastated regions at the first possible moment, and made a speech about them at the first possible opportunity. But Lloyd George was a politician who overlooked few tricks.

"Pay for That!"
(From the New York *Evening World;* reprinted by permission)

The most curious thing about this entire episode is that Wilson finally did go out to the battlefields—when it was too late fully to appease the French. On January 26, 1919, he and Mrs. Wilson made a hurried, one-day excursion to Rheims. Lloyd George stresses the bad impression that was made when Wilson allegedly remarked that the damage to the priceless cathedral was not so great as he had been led to expect. One cannot be sure that Wilson said this, but in any case the trip was another instance of too little and too late. The Conference had already been in session for some two weeks, and the area visited was but a small sector, and not the most badly damaged one at that. It was not until late in March that Wilson made a hurried, one day trip to the more seriously devastated areas.

8

We have already observed that the trips to England and Italy were a waste of precious time. There are additional reasons why they were most unfortunate.

Wilson by his very presence exaggerated the hopes and aspirations of the masses of the people, and these hopes and aspirations, some of them territorial, were already sufficiently exaggerated. When the hour of disillusionment came, as it was bound to come, Wilson could not escape the wrath born of disappointment.

More important, perhaps, Wilson came away from these tumultuous ovations with mistaken ideas of his personal influence with foreign peoples. In all the hysterical cheering he saw convincing proof of his smug assertion on the *George Washington* that the masses favored the unselfish ideals that he stood for rather than the selfish principles that their rulers stood for. Possibly this would have been true—though one may doubt it—if the rulers had permitted him to present those ideals to the masses directly.

At the peace table the "dumb eyes of the people" continued to haunt Wilson. He knew that they were counting on him to give them a better world; he felt that they were so enthusiastically behind him that if it came to a showdown he could appeal directly to them over the heads of their rulers. Even the ordinarily levelheaded Colonel House believed that Wilson might "possibly" overthrow the governments of England, France, and Italy by exerting his influence among the liberals and laboring classes.

It is not surprising that Wilson should later have made one disastrous attempt to appeal over the heads of the rulers to their people. Perhaps he would not have done so if their uproarious vivas had not been still ringing in his ears.

CHAPTER EIGHT

BLUNDERING BEGINNINGS

"Bolshevism is gaining ground everywhere. Hungary has just
succumbed. We are sitting upon an open powder magazine and
some day a spark may ignite it . . ." COLONEL HOUSE,
March 22, 1919.

———

1

THE PARIS Peace Conference did not begin its formal deliberations until January 12, 1919, almost exactly one month
after Wilson landed at Brest. The first plenary session was not
held until January 18.

This delay is incomprehensible, particularly when we remember that the crying need of the hour was haste. The red
bacillus of Bolshevism was gradually spreading westward from
Russia, and anarchy was smoothing its path. Europe was bankrupt, starving, and sick, both mentally and physically. "The
wolf," said Herbert Hoover, "is at the door of the world."
Unless peace was made, and made quickly, Germany might
yield to Bolshevism, clasp hands with Russia, and reopen the
war. Or there might be no responsible government in Germany
to accept the peace when once it was drawn up.

The race was a breath-taking one between the makers of
peace and the makers of anarchy. Yet the makers of peace
dawdled away two months after the Armistice before putting
their feet together under the table. All the while their armies
melted away, their strength ebbed, and with it went the power
to enforce their decisions and garner the fruits of victory. In
what way was Wilson responsible for this perilous delay?

The answer is: he had little or nothing to do with it. This
judgment becomes all the more significant when we realize that
he was later criticized with great bitterness for delaying the
peace by forcing the League of Nations into the treaty. We

shall consider this point later, but for the moment we may observe that the time, if any, lost in making the League Covenant
was as nothing when compared with the early weeks of thumb-
twiddling, while Europe slowly crumbled to pieces.

Wilson could have settled down to serious work shortly after
arriving in mid-December, and expected to do so on or about
December 17. He had postponed his departure so that he could
deliver his annual message to Congress in person, but if it had
been imperatively necessary he could have sailed shortly after
the Armistice, three weeks earlier. The President is not required by the Constitution to make personal appearances before Congress; in fact, Wilson was the first one in over a century
to do so.

The common criticism that the Conference had to wait for
Wilson may be met in still other ways. Far-away Japan, China,
Siam, India, Australia, New Zealand, and South Africa were
all entitled to send representatives, and under the best of circumstances they could hardly have been brought to Paris
earlier than December 14, when Wilson arrived. And if, as
alleged, the Conference was waiting breathlessly for him, why
was there a delay of another month before it actually began its
deliberations?

The true explanation of the delay must be sought in a
number of different quarters. The victory had to be celebrated
with processions and state visits. The fiery general election in
England, which Lloyd George had called for December 14, the
day of Wilson's arrival in Paris, had to be cleared out of the
way. The Christmas holiday letdown had to be surmounted. It
was also necessary to take stock of the situation; to let war-
fevered emotions die down; to erect peace machinery on the
foundations of war machinery. It was necessary to allow the
revolutions in Russia and Germany to shake down, so that the
Allied statesmen could see more clearly whom and what they
had to deal with. It was necessary to give Wilson an opportunity
to get the "feel" of the European situation; to visit the devastated regions; to absorb the Allied point of view. There is

finally a not unfounded suspicion that the Allied leaders purposely delayed meeting earlier because they knew that delay would cool the enthusiasm of the populace for Wilson and his idealism. They would also have time to take the measure of their idealistic adversary, and find the weak joints in his armor. There is, in fact, some evidence that they deliberately set out to do so in advance of his coming.

Whatever the explanation, the results were highly unfortunate.

The nationalistic aspirations of France and especially of Italy were given time to develop in an overblown fashion. If the territorial terms could have been written earlier, they probably would have been more reasonable than they were later.

Public opinion began to lose faith in the negotiators—the "dawdlers of Paris." Everywhere there was a mounting impatience to get the thing over with and "bring the boys home," in spite of the fact that the war would not technically be over until the peace was signed.

During the weeks of delay, Wilson, having nothing pressing to do, consented to make his triumphal appearances in England and Italy, with the unfortunate results already described.

Finally, the frittering away of the costly weeks in December and January meant that the work of the Conference had to be rushed forward with frantic speed in April, when a number of hasty and regrettable decisions were made.

2

The selection of Paris as the site of the Conference was one of the cardinal misfortunes of the negotiation. The atmosphere of this shell-shocked city—"gashed to her very soul"—was the complete reverse of that serenity which should surround the making of great and lasting decisions.

Paris in the winter of 1918–1919 was underfed and under-heated. It swarmed with penniless refugees, soulless profiteers, and profligate women. Countless German cannon were piled up in the squares. Women in black walked the leafless boulevards, and mutilated veterans stumped through the streets, grim reminders of the Hun. The ruins left by the long-range Big Bertha were there for all to see. Excitable and gesticulating mobs sprang from the pavements, voicing their sentiments with Gallic intemperance.

One of the worst things about Paris was the clatter of the corrupt and corruptible French press. A dozen or so sheets responded to the commands of the government with servile precision. When Wilson opposed French claims in private conferences, denunciations of the pro-German President would immediately pour from the Parisian press, just as though Clemenceau had turned on a giant faucet. Some of this criticism was diabolically clever, and beyond a doubt vastly annoying to Wilson. At one time he declared that if the clamor kept up he would have to suggest moving the whole Conference to some quieter place.

Another reason why Paris was an unfortunate choice was that it gave to the nerve-racked French a disproportionate control of the program and machinery of the Conference. The able but domineering Clemenceau became chairman—a courtesy that could not be denied the host nation. This meant that the French had a disproportionate voice in the vastly important decision of what should be taken up, and when it should be taken up.

From the very outset the French favored Paris as the meeting place; the Belgians, Brussels. Colonel House cabled Wilson from France late in October that the only objection to Paris was that if sharp differences should arise between the French and their Allies, "it might be embarrassing." This was advice worth remembering.

Wilson promptly replied that he regarded a "neutral place of meeting" as "much wiser," and expressed a preference for the quiet of Lausanne, Switzerland, where pro-Ally influences were strong.

A few days later the representatives of the four powers in Paris came to a tentative decision to take Switzerland. Even Clemenceau voiced no objection at the time, though he clearly did not want Geneva.

But Wilson suddenly changed his mind and cabled House on November 7: "On second thought it occurs to me that Versailles may be the best place for the peace conference where friendly influences and authorities are in control rather than Switzerland which is saturated with every poisonous element and open to every hostile influence in Europe."

The "poisonous elements" to which Wilson referred were probably the Bolshevist and pro-German agents and the pro-German press, which were offset to a considerable degree by pro-Ally influences. In any event, it is doubtful if these "poisonous elements" would have proved as harmful as those of Paris.

The decision to shift from Switzerland to France seems clearly to have been made by Wilson. Although the hotel accommodations of Lausanne or Geneva were inadequate for the host that finally descended upon Paris, it is probable that the tentative decision to take Switzerland could have been made to stand if Wilson had thrown all of his enormous influence behind it. Lloyd George says that he favored Geneva, but had to give up the battle when Wilson shifted ground.

3

Wilson presumably changed to Versailles because he regarded it as much quieter than Paris and entirely without the pro-German influences of Switzerland. There can be no doubt that Versailles would have been better than Paris if it had been used, but it was not used except to present the draft treaty to the Germans, and later to provide the setting for the signing ceremony.

The explanation seems to be almost entirely a practical one. Versailles is virtually a suburb of Paris, and lacking in the spacious hotel accommodations of the metropolis. The delegates would have to live in Paris anyhow, and it would have been an indefensible waste of time, when time was at a premium, to commute to Versailles for the daily deliberations. So the Conference met in the sad and sick city of Paris.

There were other compelling reasons, both practical and sentimental, why the capital of France should have been honored. The hotels, as already noted, were large and numerous, but not too large or too numerous to accommodate without some strain the scores of delegates and their thousands of assistants. The city was centrally located, and the communications were excellent. The Allied leaders had met there for their principal war conferences, and it was logical that they should do so for the peace.

Finally, there was the honor due France. London, in many ways, would have been a more satisfactory meeting place; but if there was going to be a belligerent capital, that capital had to be Paris. France had sustained on her pulverized soil the bulk of the fighting; and she had given up more of her sons than any of her Allies. Arthur J. Balfour remarked to Clemenceau that one good reason for choosing Paris was the communications. Clemenceau, evidently thinking of France's ghastly sacrifices, sourly replied that he could think of other and better grounds.

One may suspect that the true explanation of Wilson's action is that in November, 1918, the question of locale seemed to be relatively trivial. The responsibility of creating a new world order was so overpowering, and the necessity for haste was so apparent, that the natural impulse was to choose a convenient place and get on with the task.

Yet, as it turned out, Paris was just about the last place that should have been chosen. Perhaps it is unfair to blame Wilson for not having recognized this in advance. There certainly was enormous pressure on the Allies to grant what seemed to be so modest and harmless a request. The French had fought the longest and had suffered the most. And who were the Americans—laggard converts to the Allied cause—to deny them this slight consolation?

Little courtesies may be fraught with big results. The green baize table cannot be dumped anywhere, and the negotiators told to go to work.

Even granting all this, one cannot be sure that the Treaty of Versailles would have been a substantially better peace if the Conference had met in Switzerland. Possibly it would have been somewhat better, but the fact remains that if the negotiators had met at the North Pole they would have carried with them the war hatred aroused by propaganda and passion. This is something that can be remedied only by time—not by place.

4

Ray Stannard Baker, who was director of the American Press Bureau at the Conference and who should have known, concludes that "the great failure" of the Americans was a "failure in constructive publicity."

This goes back to the first of the Fourteen Points, and to Wilson's disinclination to explain more precisely and more persistently what he had in mind.

Point I of the Fourteen was "Open covenants of peace, openly arrived at . . ." This easily slipped into the slogan, "Open covenants openly arrived at." Nothing could better illustrate the dangers of imprecision resulting from the oversimplification of a complex situation, and nothing could better illustrate the dangers of hastily phrasing statements that lend themselves to sloganizing.

Countless thousands of Americans mouthed this catchword, confidently believing that henceforth there would be no more hole-in-the-corner diplomacy, and that henceforth the whole world could gaze at every move at the peace table, much as masked doctors look down from the observation gallery upon a delicate operation.

This was not what Wilson meant at all. During the war the news had leaked out that various secret treaties had been made, treaties by which the signatories bound whole nations to dangerous courses. In all these cases the peoples concerned had not been told of their commitment, and in some cases large numbers of them would have opposed it if they had been. Wilson quite logically concluded that this was the very negation of the democratic process.

Wilson, of course, was not so naïve as to propose that there should be no confidential interchanges in the shaping of treaties. He knew perfectly well that the soul of negotiation is the principle of give and take: of asking for more than one expects, and then accepting less. If a negotiator took an extreme position, and then retreated from it, and the news came out in the press the next day, he would be driven from office with cries of: "Britain is betrayed!" "France is betrayed!" If all stages of negotiation proceeded under the full floodlight of publicity, the negotiators would have to move so slowly, if at all, that the whole procedure would be paralyzed. It would be either a farce or a free-for-all.

Wilson did not believe that the "birth pangs" of the peace should be exposed to the public gaze, or that newspaper readers all over the world should enjoy the spectacle of statesmen washing their soiled linen in public. What he meant was that, once a treaty was negotiated, the people concerned should know of its existence and be given a chance to discuss it. (One of the genuine contributions of the Covenant of the League of Nations was to make provision for the registering of treaties at Geneva.)

If this is what Wilson meant, why did he not say so in unambiguous terms—not once, but many times?

The answer seems to be that Wilson, unlike many college professors, hated to repeat himself; and he hated to have people repeat things to him. At the Conference, Ray Stannard Baker once urged him to explain something to the correspondents, but Wilson refused by saying, "But I've already said it." Yes, he had; *in a speech.*

The October appeal, we remember, had been savagely criticized and misrepresented. Yet Wilson issued no qualifying statement—no rebuttal. He had already said it, clearly, precisely, and finally. And that was that.

Wilson had stated his position with rigorous economy of words in the first of the Fourteen Points, and as it was clear to him, he thought it must be clear to everybody else. The good academic lecturer—and Wilson was an outstanding expositor—assumes that the students are all there, that they are awake, that they are interested, that they get the point, and that they will retain it. In a distressing number of cases none of these assumptions is valid.

The blunt truth is that the brilliant Princeton professor failed as a teacher. His classroom was the American public, and he overestimated their capacity to read his mind. Ray Stannard Baker, his understanding biographer, well says that many a "humbler politician could have told him" that an idea "had to be repeated a thousand times, published in every newspaper, put in the movies, set to music!"

The point to bear in mind is that the American people confidently expected to see an abolition of all secret conferences, and a perfect example of housetop diplomacy. They had been led to believe that there was no essential difference between delicate diplomatic discussions and dickering for a horse.

5

About five hundred of the world's ablest newsmen, expecting to capitalize on the new "open diplomacy," poured into Paris. American newspapers and news associations, at great expense, had sent some one hundred and fifty of their crack reporters. The Conference was one of the big news stories of all time, and these "ambassadors of public opinion" were there to see that nothing went unreported.

In mid-January the deliberations formally began. The delegates filed into the high-ceilinged halls of the French Foreign Office on the Quai d'Orsay, and the double doors were slammed in the faces of the expectant news hawks, and then carefully guarded. At the end of the day a secretary slipped out and read a juiceless, five-line summary of what had happened.

The disillusioned correspondents laid aside their freshly sharpened pencils and emitted an outcry of exasperation, disgust, and wrath. There was loud and angry talk about "gag rule," "diplomacy in the dark," and "the Congress of Vienna over again." So these were "open covenants openly arrived at"!

Wilson was strongly in favor of letting the reporters in. He hated censorship of any kind, for he believed that publicity was the lifeblood of public education in a democracy. The United States was the only great power that had no secret treaties, no territorial aspirations. Wilson had nothing to conceal, nothing to be afraid of. No matter what came out of the Conference, he would be President of the United States until March 4, 1921—barring death, resignation, or impeachment.

But, as we must constantly bear in mind, Wilson was the representative of but one of the five great powers, and he could not always have his own way. His position was secure for two more years; but Lloyd George and Clemenceau could be thrown out of office overnight if they made the wrong move, and the news leaked out. A disappointed public, backed by an unscrupulous press, would not hesitate to cry, "Off with his head!" Orlando, the Italian premier, was in fact politically decapitated before he even had an opportunity to sign the Treaty of Versailles.

We must also remember that the war had not ended; the armistice was technically a truce. The secrecy that had governed military councils during the war had also to govern

diplomatic councils during the nominal peace. News of disagreement would encourage—and in fact did encourage—the
enemy to resist the prospective terms.

The jostling nations of Central Europe, which had sprung
from the ashes of revolution and defeat, were quarrelsome,
suspicious, and greedy. Premature news as to the thwarting of
their aspirations would evoke a tremendous outcry, and a consequent increase of pressure at Paris. There was enough clamor
at the Conference as it was without encouraging any more from
this source.

Altogether, complete publicity would have added immeasurably to the confusion and delay—and delay was deadly.

6

Wilson's determined fight for greater publicity was only
partially successful. It was finally agreed that the correspondents might be admitted to the "staged shows" that were called
the plenary sessions, but not to smaller private councils. The
net result was that there were only six plenary conferences, and
little of any consequence was ever done at these window-dress-
ing affairs—dubbed "washouts" by the journalists—except to
ratify decisions made in private. The necessity for even more
secret discussions became evident as the Conference went on,
and this is one of the main reasons why the Council of Four
later established itself as the real power. When it became clear
that little genuine news was to be given out while the Conference was in progress, a considerable number of the journalists disgustedly left for home, with little love in their hearts
for Wilson.

It is interesting to note that certain of the French journals,
which should have known better, blamed the American President for the lack of publicity. One of them satirized both
Wilson and the "daily dope" of the official releases when it had
the American President say: ". . . I have discovered that

Spring always follows Winter. That is the secret of my policy. I can also tell you another of my profound views, namely, that the weather will improve more quickly than will Europe. But this is a diplomatic confidence. Don't repeat it."

The correspondents were finally forced to fall back on the

When Truth Is Kept Within Doors
Lies Come Out at the Window
(Courtesy of the Brooklyn *Eagle*)

official, timetable communiqués, supplemented by "calculated indiscretions," "grapevine" rumors, and other "drippings" from the Conference, many of which were designed to conceal rather than reveal. Much of this "publicity by leak" came through the officially inspired French press, and this accounts for the French bias given a great deal of the news.

The more resourceful newspapermen were able to cultivate "leaks" and establish contacts with "inside" sources of information. On the whole they were able to penetrate the steel curtain of secrecy and send home a fairly satisfactory running account of what had happened. Lloyd George to this day insists that nothing was withheld which the public was entitled to know at the time. Certainly a vast amount of wordage was put on the wires; but unfortunately much of it was speculation of the most harmful kind.

7

This whole controversy over closed-door diplomacy got the Conference off to a bad start. To countless thousands of Americans it seemed as though the very first of the Fourteen Points had been flagrantly disregarded on the very first day of the Conference. Such disillusionment inspired no confidence as to what would happen to the remaining Points. It is small wonder that Wilson's private secretary, Joseph P. Tumulty, cabled in alarm from Washington that the country was up in arms; and that it would be better for the President to bolt the Conference than to submit to a "gag rule."

The rumor and speculation which were given wings at Paris by "calculated leakages" inspired a vast amount of suspicion and distrust. Hopes for a New Order began to take flight as the diplomats fell back upon the secrecy of the Old.

One cannot help feeling that much of this was avoidable.

First, Wilson should have publicly iterated and reiterated his views on open diplomacy until it was reasonably clear that American public opinion knew what he had in mind.

Second, the American press associations should have been emphatically warned about what to expect. If this had been done, they probably would not have sent over so many restless newsmen. This unfortunate situation was made infinitely worse by the month of delay in starting the Conference. There was little news to report, and where news does not exist the resourceful newspaperman makes it, whether through speculation or through imagination. Unfortunately also, many of the American correspondents had won their spurs in reporting domestic politics, and they knew little about the deep, underlying forces that were agitating Europe. The result was that their eyes were caught by the superficial, and their prognostications, often of the wildest sort, aroused unwarranted suspicions and expectations in America. The newsmen made up for the inadequacy of their information by the prodigality of their criticism.

Third, Wilson failed to tell the correspondents that he had put up a vigorous battle for them. As it was, they were resentful for the small favors they did receive, not knowing how energetically he had espoused their interests. Ray Stannard Baker urged Wilson to tell them everything, but Wilson more or less brushed the matter aside, evidently not thinking it important. The story finally did leak out in the press several months later, but at a time when it would do little good.

Wilson not only failed to cultivate the correspondents in this connection, but William Allen White, who was one of them, testifies that he was the only one of the Big Four who refused to meet the news representatives of his own country regularly and personally. He did so once in February; but someone betrayed a confidence, and he never appeared again. Perhaps he wanted to conserve his strength; probably he thought there were more important things to do. This was all most unfortunate. If he had kept up his fences with the correspondents, if he had told them of his battle for publicity, they would have been behind him foursquare. He did not, and they were not. The upshot was that he did not have the "good press" in America which he might have had, and which he so desperately needed when the real fight began.

Finally, this blundering beginning gave ammunition to Wilson's opponents in the Senate when they charged that he had gone to the Conference in order to "put something over on them." The Senate "irreconcilables" gave loud voice to their disappointment, and to the very end never ceased to complain that they did not know what was going on—and yet they were a part of the treaty-making power. Of course, Senators like Borah and Johnson and Brandegee would have found other grounds for complaint, but the inept rationing of news gave additional point and vigor to their denunciations

CHAPTER NINE

THE PERILS OF IMPRECISION

*"I am disquieted to see how hazy and vague our ideas are. We are
going to be up against the wiliest politicians in Europe. There
will be nothing hazy or vague about their ideas."*
GENERAL TASKER H. BLISS, *December 18, 1918.*

1

I T I S difficult to find an eyewitness who was not impressed by
the indescribable confusion and disorganization at Paris.
Wickham Steed, the eminent British journalist, says that a
true history óf the Conference will never be written because
mere words cannot re-create the atmosphere of Paris in 1919.
Harold Nicolson speaks of "that sense of riot in a parrot
house."

The explanation is not far to seek. There were twenty-
seven Allied and Associated Powers, plus the five British
Dominions, and each of the thirty-two was entitled to send
delegates. The American contingent alone, counting various
kinds of subordinates, totaled about 1,300. The British delegation occupied five hotels. And yet England, a century before,
had sent only fourteen men to the great Congress of Vienna.

In addition to the official representatives, Paris swarmed
with unofficial representatives of minority and other groups
which had something to seek. Strange-looking men in strange-
smelling garments walked the streets of Paris demanding recognition of some long-sought nationalistic aspiration.

There were Kirghizes, Circassians, Mingrelians, and Bury-
ats, to say nothing of better known Koreans, Hindus, and
Malays, from such far-away places as Tartary, Kurdistan,
Samarkand and Bokhara—men with patriarchal beards and
scimitar-shaped noses, clad in turbans and flowing mantles.

One of them, Emir Feisal from Arabia, bore a striking physical resemblance to the accepted likenesses of Jesus. But there the resemblance rather sharply ended.

Wilson gave ear to many of these people gladly, though he could in no case understand their language, and though he later confessed from the platform that he had not previously known of the existence of some of the places they represented. How he managed to work such suppliants into his already full day will remain one of the many minor mysteries of Paris.

The Conference set up more than sixty different commissions to deal with territorial, economic, and other problems. These groups, which held over 1,600 meetings, worked more or less in the dark, and often at cross purposes with other groups, whose functioning they were only dimly aware of. The reparations section labored long and hard on the question of exacting payments from Germany; the economic section labored long and hard to effect arrangements that would, as it turned out, make impossible the payment of expected reparations. The right hand seldom knew what the left hand was doing; sometimes the right hand did not even know what the right hand was doing.

Dr. James T. Shotwell, who was at Paris, remembers that the American experts were supposed to work on their respective specialties more or less in a vacuum. It was regarded as poor form to inquire what their colleagues in other fields were doing; only an exchange of gossip at luncheons or other casual meetings enabled them to glimpse faintly and imperfectly what was going on. The British, on the other hand, worked out a fairly satisfactory system of circularizing information among themselves as to the progress of the Conference.

Several years ago the present writer asked a distinguished American expert—one who had had a large hand in the drafting of the League Covenant—for some information about the Conference. "I do not know anything about it," he smiled. "I was only there." To the same question another distinguished American expert replied, "I do not know because I was there." "I would go further," he added, "and suggest that those who were there could not know."

What these men were saying, of course, was that while they knew something about what had happened in connection with their own narrow specialties, they did not have and could not have the over-all view of the Conference that was necessary for a well rounded picture. They were like soldiers in a campaign who know only their part of the trench on the battlefield; they are unable to glimpse the general plan of battle.

It would be unfair to suggest that the delegates at Paris did not work hard. Most of them did—perhaps too hard. At the Congress of Vienna, a hundred years before, they took nine months to dance their way to peace. Everyone seemingly danced except the club-footed Talleyrand: he had to content himself with playing whist. At Paris, in 1919, time was too short for much frivolity, at least among the leaders. Possibly the results would have been more lasting if there had been more relaxation.

The confusion was worse confounded by the complexity of the problem. The Allied statesmen were immediately concerned with making peace with the fallen enemy. They were also concerned with reordering the world in the interests of international stability. And finally, they found it necessary to keep their home governments functioning smoothly in their absence.

This last is very important. Every one of the heads of government at Paris had to spend a considerable part of his time looking after the home front. Wilson had to peck out his long message to Congress on his portable typewriter at odd moments before and after the regular meetings of the Council of Four. The sheer fatigue resulting from such numerous and oppressive duties undoubtedly contributed to some of the unfortunate decisions at Paris. This, it will be noted, is another argument for having the work done by representatives, rather than by a head of government.

2

The machinery of the Conference was gradually perfected by trial-and-error methods. A great body of several hundred delegates was too unwieldy, too dilatory, too loquacious, and too leaky for the efficient dispatch of business. So the plenary sessions became rubber stamps for the smaller groups.

The Supreme Council, or the Council of Ten, which evolved from the Allied Supreme War Council, at first did the most important work. It consisted of the two ranking delegates from each of the five great powers: Great Britain, France, Italy, Japan, and the United States. President Wilson and Secretary Lansing represented the United States.

The Council of Ten in turn proved to be too cumbersome and too leaky, but it was not until March, 1919, when the Conference came squarely to grips with the problem of Germany, that it gave way to the Council of Four—the Big Four—which more or less usurped authority. We shall consider the personnel of this remarkable body later, but for the moment we may note that it consisted of Wilson for the United States, Lloyd George for Great Britain, Clemenceau for France, and Orlando for Italy. Some of the time it was the Council of Three, for Orlando was not infrequently absent. At the early meetings there were neither secretaries nor written records. Three lone men in a room deciding the destiny of the world! An ironically undemocratic ending indeed for a war that had been proclaimed as a crusade to make the world safe for democracy.

After the Council of Ten resolved itself into the Big Four, the Foreign Secretaries met separately as the Council of Five (Council of Foreign Ministers). Although their work was not of the first importance, they nevertheless served a useful function.

Once the machinery of the Conference was set up, the next question was: what should be the plan of procedure? What subjects should be taken up, and in what order?

This was a question of supreme importance. All experienced negotiators recognize that the man who has written down a well thought-out plan has an advantage over those who have none. He can seize the initiative and propose positive measures; they can only criticize, object, or amend. The man with a plan will seldom secure the adoption of all his proposals, but he will almost invariably retain a considerable residuum of them.

Much better than having one man come to a conference with a plan is the procedure by which the conference agrees in advance what the plan shall be.

Harold Nicolson attributes many of the woes of the Paris Conference to the "marsh of imprecision"—and properly so. If ever a conference needed a carefully worked-out program, as well as a precise definition of terms, this one did. Let it not be forgotten that the basis of the pre-Armistice contract was the Fourteen Points, which were only vaguely defined and hesitatingly accepted. The isolationist Washington *Post* not inaptly remarked that "the trouble is not so much with the fourteen points as it is with the fourteen interpretations."

Yet the amazing fact is that the ever-logical French, alone among the great powers, had a carefully outlined plan for the agenda. The British had none. The United States not only had none, but Wilson had quashed all attempts to frame one or to agree upon one. It may well be argued that his great error was not in going to Paris but in going without a plan.

This almost unbelievable blindness to the elementary facts of negotiation by conference requires some explanation.

3

While it is true that the Americans went to Paris without a detailed plan of procedure, it is not true that they went without information. There were cartloads of information; the great problem was to coordinate it and give it meaning.

One basic explanation of the lack of coordination is that the war came to an end unexpectedly soon. The military men had been looking forward to administering the finishing blow in 1919, and the unexpected crumbling of German resistance caught both the warmakers and the peacemakers off balance and unprepared. In the summer of 1918, when the Allied

The Race
(Courtesy of the St. Louis *Post-Dispatch*)

drives were progressing favorably, Winston S. Churchill, then First Lord of the Admiralty, remarked that if these victories continued peace might "come upon us like a thief in the night." It did. Churchill later wrote that, for the British, the transition to peace "was more violent than the entry into war . . ." It is worth repeating that in time of war one must prepare for peace.

Yet we cannot be sure that the result, as far as Wilson was concerned, would have been different if the conflict had lasted another six months. He was strongly opposed to any carefully worked-out plan, though he was firmly wedded to a few basic principles. It was easy enough, says Ray Stannard Baker, for the representatives of the Old Order (the Powers of Darkness) to draw up a precise program based upon the procedure of the Congress of Vienna. But Wilson represented the New Order (the Powers of Light), and he had no precedents to work on. When one is venturing out into an unknown sea, it is both useless and dangerous to make charts in advance. One must feel one's way slowly, inch by inch, and chart the rocks and shoals as one finds them. One's only compass must be sound general principles.

So Wilson, the amateur diplomat, would go to Paris and work out his program on a day-to-day, catch-as-catch-can basis. Lloyd George would do likewise; but the tough, resourceful, and opportunistic Welshman loved rough-and-tumble grappling, with no holds barred, and Wilson did not. This, of course, would make for informality and flexibility; but flexibility gave a distinct advantage to the hand that held the lever which moved the machinery of the Conference. That hand was the gray-gloved hand of "The Tiger"—Georges Clemenceau.

Ray Stannard Baker rather indignantly rejects the charge that the Americans had no program. He says that Wilson's program was first the principles of justice as laid down in his public utterances, and secondly the application of these principles by his experts. This, one must confess, is not a program but a nebulous statement of general principles.

After reaching Paris, Wilson presented to the Council of Ten five general topics that he wanted to have discussed. This, one must concede, was not a program but a skeleton list of subjects.

Before leaving Washington, Secretary Lansing took it upon himself to inform Wilson that the experts in the Department of State had already worked out a tentative draft of a skeleton treaty. According to Lansing, Wilson resented this usurpation of authority, and rebuked him stingingly with the remark that "he did not propose to have lawyers drafting the Treaty."

The French evolved several detailed programs, and one of them, dated November 29, 1918, was presented by the French Ambassador in Washington, and put into Wilson's hands on December 2, two days before his departure for Paris. He took it along with him, but there is no evidence that he ever bothered to reply to it, much less indicate acceptance. He may have discussed it orally upon reaching Paris, but it is clear that he made no determined effort to secure its adoption.

Wilson's failure to seize upon this program and use his enormous prestige to push it through, with modifications, is regarded by certain critics as a blunder of the first magnitude.

4

We need not analyze the French program in detail, but merely consider certain features that have an important bearing on the failures of the Conference—failures which will be discussed later at length.

First, preliminary terms were to be imposed upon the Germans without discussion. (The Conference began as a preliminary conference, got into a hurry, and hastily made the preliminary terms the final ones.)

Second, provision was made for the representation of both enemy and neutral states at the Conference. (Neither was permitted to take part in the final oral discussions.)

Third, reparations were to be levied only for direct damage resulting from German aggression. (The Conference most unfortunately added pensions and other charges.)

Fourth, all secret treaties were to be suspended. (We shall presently consider the disastrous effect of these agreements.)

Fifth, a detailed schedule was set forth under which the most important problems would be considered first, and the less important ones postponed for subsequent discussion. (The less pressing problems were actually considered first, and the fundamental task of making peace with Germany was postponed for about two months.)

This French program, one must grant, was far from perfect, but it was reasonably comprehensive and precise, and it embodied several supremely important features that were conspicuously lacking in the final terms. It also gave a prominent place to the League of Nations, and it referred repeatedly to specific Fourteen Points. Some writers have said that Wilson was offended because the French proposal tactlessly mentioned the vagueness of the Points, but this probably had no important effect on his thinking. More important, one may suspect, were the references to the peace congresses of the past. Wilson simply did not want to be shackled by the precisions of the Old Order.

If Wilson had adopted with enthusiasm the better parts of this program, if he had thrown the weight of his then enormous prestige behind it, could he have secured its adoption at the outset?

Any answer would be pure speculation. It may well be doubted whether he could have forced Japan, Italy, and Great Britain to "suspend" the secret treaties under which they were to receive the spoils of war. But there seems to be no good reason why Wilson could not have secured substantially all of the other more desirable parts of the French program, and this would have been an immense gain for precision and sanity.

As it was, the discussions began with no agreed-upon agenda. The Conference drifted along from day to day like a rudderless ship, with the powers combating one another's proposals, and forming combinations against one another. Then, when it became clear that the race between chaos and peace would be perilously close, the Conference buckled down and in a spasm of work gave birth to a treaty that was as ill coordinated as its parent. Heredity will tell.

It is all well enough to have new ideas and to propose New Orders. But one cannot cut loose completely from the lessons of the past. Even the Old Order can tell the New Order some valuable things learned in the rough school of experience.

5

We must come back once more to the secret treaties, for our indifference to and ignorance of them must take rank as one of the inexcusable blunders of American diplomacy.

During the course of the war the various Allied powers had made a dozen or so secret bargains with one another for parceling out the skin of the yet unskinned bear. We need single out only two, the two that caused Wilson the most sleepless nights.

In 1915, Italy was for sale to the higher bidder, prepared to enter the war on the side that could make her the more attractive offer. The territory that she most wanted belonged to the Central Powers, so the Allies were able to outbid their enemy. Put brutally, Italy's assistance was bought with liberal promises of territory in the secret Treaty of London of 1915.

In 1917, enemy submarines were taking an alarming toll of British shipping in the Mediterranean, and the British and French were desperately anxious to induce the Japanese to provide destroyer escort. The Japanese drove a hard bargain when they extorted a secret pledge from Great Britain (and later from France) that Japan should have German rights in Shantung (China), and all of Germany's Pacific islands north of the equator. The British on their part were to obtain all of Germany's islands south of the equator.

Some of these secret deals were being made after the Allies had proclaimed unselfish war aims, after they had accepted the Fourteen Points, and after the Conference had actually convened. No one could tell behind whose back some kind of trade was being cooked up. Certain promises, for example, were made to the Rumanians which conflicted with the aspirations of the Serbs, who were fighting on the side of the Allies, and on the whole more valiantly. The slimy trail of the serpent of secret diplomacy led into strange places.

Such Machiavellian machinations were shocking to moralists and non-professional diplomatists like Wilson, and the tendency was to dismiss all these agreements as evidence of the incurable wickedness of the Old Diplomacy.

This is entirely too narrow a view. Diplomacy had been carried on this way for untold centuries, and the leopard was not going to change his spots overnight. Secret treaties were not immoral until Wilson made them so.

Nor can we ignore the fact that the Allies probably would have lost the war if they had not made these clandestine bargains. We should not forget that Germany and her allies were bargaining also, and that if the proposals of the enemy had proved more seductive, Italy would doubtless have gone over into the other camp, with disastrous results to the Allied cause. The more liberal British diplomats held their noses as they negotiated these malodorous pacts; but military necessity condones many acts that would not pass muster in the days of peacetime morality. The enemy was using such methods, and it was necessary to fight the devil with fire.

6

During the course of the war, rumors had leaked out from time to time as to the existence of the secret treaties. But the real exposure came with the Bolshevist revolution of late 1917. Rummaging through the archives of the Russian Foreign Office, the Bolsheviks found these dynamite-charged pacts, and seeking to discredit the imperialism of the Tsarist regime, forthwith published them.

The surprising thing is that these sensational revelations, which came to light in November, 1917, made scarcely a ripple in the United States. Only a few newspapers gave them any notice whatsoever; only one seems to have published them all; and only six of some two thousand journals published them in part.

One would think that the American people should have been profoundly concerned about the secret and selfish aims of their Allies, with whom they were associated. Why were they not?

One answer—and one that disposed of much unpleasant truth during the war—was that this was pure enemy propaganda, and as such beneath notice. Besides, the publication of the treaties coincided with the collapse of the Italian front, and this served to focus attention on the fact that we were in a desperate war, and that we had better concern ourselves with really important things. It would be folly at this critical period to weaken Allied morale and prestige by deigning to notice such wicked deals.

There was also the feeling—and this probably accounts in part for Wilson's indifference—that even if these commitments existed, they did not bind the United States. It must be re-emphasized that we were not allies of the Allies, merely Associates—a thing apart; and their unsavory bargains seemingly were of no direct concern of ours. Upon reaching Paris and learning of the Sykes-Picot secret treaty for the partitioning of Turkey, Wilson remarked disgustedly that it sounded like the name of a tea.

Finally, the secret treaties were complicated, and they involved the disposition of strange-sounding places about which we knew nothing, cared less, and had no desire to learn anything. A real comprehension of the foreign affairs of Europe involves a background which the average American did not have then, does not have now, and is unwilling to go to the effort to obtain. This means hard intellectual labor, and the American voter is not distinguished for a capacity to inform himself on domestic problems which are on his very doorstep, let alone three thousand miles away on the other side of a very wide ocean. So the tendency was to skip the finely printed texts of these complicated treaties, when they were printed, and get on to the more important world of sports heroes or comic-supplement villains. Everything would work out all right once we had "licked the Kaiser."

We can find some excuse for the indifference of the average American, whose business is not primarily foreign affairs, but how about the Department of State, whose business is foreign affairs? Incredible though it may seem, Secretary Lansing told the Senate Foreign Relations Committee in the summer of 1919 that before going to Paris he had learned something of the Treaty of London with Italy, but as for the others, he did not even know that they existed. He registered considerable surprise when he was told that they had been published in the New York press.

This does not mean that there were not officials in the State Department who were taking cognizance of these treaties. But Lansing's attitude is dumbfounding. He was Secretary of State; he was the prospective head of the American peace delegation; he could not approach the Conference problems intelligently without a fairly exact knowledge of such secret agreements as had been published. Unlike Wilson, he was a stern realist; he had little faith in the League of Nations; he was well aware of the implications of balance-of-power politics. He could not have been so simple-minded as to believe that the acceptance of Point I of the Fourteen Points—that regarding open covenants—would invalidate all preexisting secret treaties.

Of course, Lansing might have dismissed the published treaties as German propaganda, just as the man in the street did. But, unlike the man in the street, it was his business to look into these revelations, and he had at his command the long tentacles of the State Department. If we may take his word at its face value, he evidently did not regard these things as important.

It seems reasonably clear—if it is not clear already—that we should exercise more care in selecting our Secretaries of State. If they will not concern themselves with important aspects of our foreign affairs, then who will?

7

One approaches the subject of Wilson and the secret pacts with considerable hesitancy, because it involves the odious question: "Was he a liar?"

After returning from Paris with the completed treaty, Wilson allowed himself to be catechized by the members of the Senate Committee on Foreign Relations, and he apparently answered all the questions fired at him with the greatest of candor.

Senator Borah asked him if, before arriving in Europe, he had known about the secret deal with Japan regarding Shantung. Wilson replied in the negative, and went on to say that upon reaching Paris "the *whole series*" of secret treaties was revealed to him for the first time. This is doubtless true, because the "*whole series*" was extremely complicated, and to some extent was being reshaped after the Conference assembled.

If the questioning had ended here, Wilson would appear to better advantage. But after other subjects had been reviewed, Senator Johnson, with the zeal of a prosecuting attorney, came back to the embarrassing question of the secret treaties. The Senator categorically listed the various pacts, including the Treaty of London. Wilson flatly asserted that none of these had been brought to his attention before reaching Paris, and he denied having had any previous knowledge of any of them.

This, we know, was not the truth. Numerous references in Wilson's private papers, large excerpts from which have been published recently by his biographer, relate to the provisions of some of the secret pacts. We know also that the original Fourteen Points, especially the first point about open covenants, were deliberately designed in part to offset the disastrous effect on world opinion caused by the Bolshevist revelation of the secret treaties.

Why Wilson told a different story to the Senators is still a major mystery. He could hardly have been guilty of a mere slip of the tongue, as sometimes alleged, because two different Senators at two different points approached the same question from different angles and repeatedly got the same reply. The true explanation may be confusion of dates or mental fatigue, as sometimes stated. But this excuse is open to the objection that during the course of the questioning Wilson freely and accurately gave intimate details of no less important subjects.

It is not altogether improbable that Wilson was in the position of a doctor who finds that he must tell the patient something that is not true. We must not forget that the whole Treaty of Versailles was under heavy fire at this time, and the arrangement giving German rights in Shantung to Japan under a secret treaty was being bitterly condemned. Wilson must have realized by this time that the fight might be close, and it is altogether likely that he did not want to introduce any new and confusing elements into the struggle. Certainly it would have been embarrassing to explain why, knowing in advance about the secret treaties, he did not do more at Paris to head them off.

8

But the question of Wilson's truthfulness is relatively minor. It seems clear that while he knew the general terms of these secret bargains, he did not know enough. It also seems clear that he did not recognize their importance, for if he had, he would have made it a point to find out more about them. At Paris he flatly refused to be bound by secret treaties, except in so far as their provisions were just, and this determination may explain why he declined to give them more careful study. But the mere refusal to recognize disagreeable realities does not dispose of those realities.

One other explanation may account for Wilson's indifference. In the summer of 1917 he wrote Colonel House that the peace aims of the Allies were not the same as those of the United States, but he was confident that by wielding the enormous economic power of the United States he could force our associates to his way of thinking. So why become concerned too much about the specific terms of secret pacts?

The proverb tells us that he who is forewarned is twice armed. If Wilson had known as much about the secret treaties as he should have known, and as he subsequently learned, he could hardly have refrained from showing more interest when the French, in the program which he spurned, suggested that they be scrapped.

In this connection some critics reasonably argue that Wilson made another costly mistake. If, early in the Conference, when his prestige and influence were still overshadowing, he had insisted that all of the secret treaties be officially disavowed, he might well have carried the day. Instead, he took the purely negative and defeatist attitude of refusing to recognize them at all.

Later, when his influence had waned, they were brought out of their secret pigeonholes, and then they could not be waved aside. Their beneficiaries even argued that one reason why the Allies had fought was to make Germany recognize "scraps of paper," and the victors would merely be aping the Hun if they refused to recognize their own treaties.

Even if Wilson had been unwilling to sweep all these pacts from the table with one bold gesture, he should have studied them. If he had known of their full import, he could have made plans in advance for coping with them, and these plans could have been made quietly, after mature reflection, and with adequate counsel. As it was, new and totally unforeseen situations were sprung upon him at Paris, while he was worn down with overwork and while the Conference was moving into its final hectic stages. With his head in a daze, and his feet tangled in the web of secret treaties, he battled his adversaries at a serious disadvantage.

CHAPTER TEN

THE OLYMPIANS

"It is going to be a rough-and-tumble affair, this Peace Conference." ARTHUR J. BALFOUR, *November 28, 1918.*

1

WE MUST now consider briefly each of the great protagonists in the Council of Four—"The Olympians"—before turning to the actual work of the Conference.

Woodrow Wilson was both the best known and the most influential, for he represented the bursting energy of the wealthiest and most powerful of the nations. At heart a Scotch-Presbyterian clergyman but trained as an academician, he was, up to this time, the darling of the gods. Within the two short years from 1911 to 1913, and by a series of incredible political accidents, he had been catapulted from the President's house in Princeton to the White House in Washington.

Though gracious in a rather stiff manner, he was innately shy and sensitive; and unlike Clemenceau his skin had not been toughened by prolonged years of exposure in the rough and tumble of the political arena. An idealist, a philosopher, a moralist, a religionist, he was born, as someone has well said, halfway between the Bible and the dictionary, and he never lost his faith in the power of words. There have been philosophers who were more profound, there have been politicians who were more powerful, but the world had never before seen a philosopher-politician who combined with his ideals such tremendous physical power to carry them into effect.

At the Conference table Wilson made an excellent impression, and he certainly belied Roosevelt's barb that he "looked like an apothecary's clerk." Immaculately if soberly dressed, he was alert, dignified, modest, soft-spoken, patient, conciliatory, and pleasantly stubborn, with Scotch stubbornness. Thirsting for and respecting facts, he largely ignored his fellow commissioners, except Colonel House, but sought information from his experts, who frequently sat on a cushion behind him and whispered promptings into his ear. Professor Douglas W. Johnson, an American expert on the Adriatic, remembers that on one occasion, late at night, the telephone rang in his bedroom, and Wilson asked for some papers which Johnson had promised but which had not arrived with sufficient promptness.

Wilson at the Conference was by no means the inflexible, know-it-all professor of popular fancy. When the Commission on the League of Nations assembled, he expressed the hope that no minutes would be kept. He wanted to feel free to change his mind, and he felt that a written record would handicap him in doing so. Changing his mind was one of Wilson's most distinguishing characteristics.

Clemenceau knew more about French interests than Wilson, but Wilson probably saw the over-all picture better than any of the other members of the Big Four. He was one of the hardest-working men at the Conference, unwilling to delegate important responsibilities, and laboring late at night over much paper work that should have been left to subordinates. Lord Riddell relates that Wilson once asked for his typewriter (a word then used for "stenographer"). Riddell conjured up a picture of a beautiful blonde secretary, but the messenger brought in a portable typewriter, on which the President proceeded to tap out a long memorandum.

Wilson's fine brain rapidly grasped a great deal in the few weeks at Paris, but no one man could have mastered in a lifetime all of the subjects that were dumped onto the sagging peace table. Sir Henry Wilson recalls that the American President deliberately absented himself from one session, to the anger of some of those present, because he had not had time to study thoroughly the question under debate.

Wilson tried hard—too hard—to do the impossible. Being an academician, he was reluctant to make important decisions until he had all the facts and all the points of view; but the world would not stand still while he carried on his researches. He would squat down over a gigantic map, listen to his experts, pencil the boundary where he thought it ought to go—in Asia Minor or some other place he had never seen—while all the others were made to squat around him. Mrs. Wilson once came upon them thus, and perhaps thinking of the parlor pastime of hunt the thimble, remarked that they looked as though they were playing a game. "Alas," replied Wilson, "it is the most serious game ever undertaken"—a game involving the lives and happiness of millions living and millions yet unborn.

The European statesmen resented Wilson's attempt to master their problems in a few short weeks, and to choke a ready-made solution down their throats. Europe had been the battle-ground; Europe had sacrificed millions of her sons. And now this closet-philosopher, who had held off to the last moment before entering what he now admitted had been America's fight—whose holding off had prolonged the war—was here to tell France what she might or might not do. As Lord Riddell put it: "What sort of peace would the Americans have imposed if a German army had been encamped for four years within fifty miles of New York?"

We have already seen that Wilson was not led around by the nose by his colleagues of the Big Four. At one stage, Dr. Isaiah Bowman, Chief Territorial Specialist of the American Commission, suggested to some of the British experts, following a debate between Lloyd George and the President, that they should keep tabs on their respective chiefs to see which one scored the more points. The British replied, "Up to now, at least, your chief has won them all!"

2

Clemenceau was in many ways the dominating figure of the Conference, though less well known and less influential than Wilson in the world theater. As head of the French government, he controlled the press; as head of the Conference, he controlled the agenda; as presiding officer, he controlled debate.

The stormy petrel of French politics, Clemenceau was then seventy-seven years of age—"the grand young man of France," as Lloyd George graciously described him. He was nicknamed "The Tiger," obviously because of the unrelenting ferocity and savage energy with which he had attacked his enemies over a long and checkered career. Known as a destroyer rather than a builder, he had sunk his fangs into the jugular veins of more than a dozen ministries, and had brought about their downfall. He feared nobody and nothing.

In personal appearance, Clemenceau suggested the gorilla rather than the tiger. Short, squat, and stooped, but powerfully built, he presented a striking figure with his black skullcap protecting a white-fringed bald spot on a massive head; drooping white mustaches that curved downward as if to shield a powerful jaw that needed no shielding; bushy, interrogatory, and skeptical eyebrows; glittering brown eyes, half masked in repose by ivory eyelids; and the eternal gray suède gloves, which covered eczema-cursed hands and which gave him the formal air of an undertaker.

The Tiger had one great love—France; and one great hate—Germany. As a young man of twenty-nine he had seen Paris under the heel of the Hun invader, and the smoke billowing up from the brutal burning of the palace at St. Cloud. As an old man of seventy-two, he had seen the gray German hosts pour into his beloved France. He was determined that it should not happen again. Motivated though he was by this great hate, he was not so vindictive as Marshal Foch or President Poincaré.

Clemenceau had a commanding presence, and he was one of the great orators of his day, with fine voice, logical mind, and forceful delivery, though sparing of Gallic gesticulation. As presiding officer of the Council of Ten he was on the whole patient and deferential, and most of the time he slumped back in his chair, apparently half asleep, with an expression of bored tolerance. But as presiding officer of the plenary sessions he drove a steam roller through the opposition. *"Y a-t-il des objections? Non? . . . Adopté,"* he would rattle off with machine-gun rapidity, and despotically rush on to rubber-stamp something else before a voice could be raised in protest.

Trained as a doctor, Clemenceau had early forsaken the scalpel for journalism and politics. He visited America for several years shortly after the Civil War, and wrote a number of stories for a French newspaper. This American sojourn had helped him perfect his English, which he spoke fluently, though he had experienced early difficulties. He used to amuse his hearers by telling how he had once ordered "smashed potatoes" in an American restaurant.

In November, 1917, during one of the darkest hours of the war, he was called to the premiership of France. Grim, dogged, and courageous, Dr. Clemenceau did not shrink from prescribing heroic medicines. Infusing new spirit into the drooping nation, by sheer power of will he snatched victory from the furnace of defeat. It was not for nothing that he was called "le Père la Victoire" (Father Victory).

3

Clemenceau was deeply puzzled by his Calvinist colleague, the American President. He had lived a long time, and he had seen the seamy side of mankind. Realistic, cynical, logical, he had no faith in the League of Nations. France had been saved by bayonets, not ideals. If she were invaded again, America would perhaps come rushing to her assistance—after three long years—with two million words. Words were all right; but first there must be bayonets.

The Tiger was the incarnation of the Old Order—of Europe as it had been. Wilson was the incarnation of the New Order—of Europe as he hoped it would be. Clemenceau could not understand all this. He believed that mankind should be taken as it is, and not as it was unlikely to be. He called Wilson "Jupiter," sneered at his "elevated simplicity," and made cutting remarks about the "Fourteen Commandments." He told Colonel House: "I can get on with you. You are practical. I understand you, but talking to Wilson is something like talking to Jesus Christ!"

Occasionally, but only occasionally, there were sharp words

"Great Expectations"

(Courtesy of the Louisville *Times;* the cartoonist, Paul A. Plaschke, is now editorial cartoonist on the Chicago *Herald-American*)

between Clemenceau and Wilson. Once the Tiger hotly accused Wilson of being a pro-German, and bolted from the room, eyes flashing, voice vibrating. From long experience in debate he knew the trick of simulating passion, and perhaps he was doing so at this time. When the Conference was over, Clemenceau was reported to have said of Wilson: "He is a nice man and means well." Later, in 1925, the Tiger wrote: "Wilson was a noble figure, but he did not appreciate the facts or the significance of European history."

There were few who did not fear Clemenceau's withering tongue. His *bons mots* were the talk of France, and there are few enduring epigrams from the Conference that are not attributed to him, whether correctly or not. He loved the racy phrase, the biting epigram, the sarcastic sally, and when one came to him, whether at the expense of friend or foe, he seemed powerless to hold it back. His voice was penetrating, and his terrible audibility frequently brought blushes to the cheeks of all his hearers. At one session of the Council of Four, a Japanese delegate made some remark. Clemenceau understood English, but not Japanese-English, so he turned and said in a loud stage whisper, "*Qu'est-ce qu'il dit, le petit?*" (What's the little fellow saying?)—as if a small child had spoken out of turn at the dinner table.

Dogged, domineering, honest, courageous, realistic, and narrow—this was the Tiger. Wilson respected him because one could tell where he stood—back in 1871. There was no deceit or equivocation about the man: he had the courage to meet his problems head on. If he seemed to be dozing at some of the sessions, there could be no doubt as to his vigilance when the interests of France were concerned. And here, as the record reveals, he yielded remarkably little.

4

David Lloyd George, the British Prime Minister, was short and stocky, like Clemenceau, and he had a white mustache, like Clemenceau, and he had had a checkered political career, like Clemenceau. But here the comparisons, physical and political, end. Unlike the bald Clemenceau, Lloyd George had a bristling shock of white hair, which he brushed straight back. Unlike the grim and stolid Tiger, the "Welsh wizard" was amiable and charming, with a genial smile and twinkling eyes;

at times jovial and cheery with bluff heartiness. Bursting with personal magnetism and sleepless energy, he was vivacious and impulsive, given to sudden enthusiasms and panics, and always a torrential talker. He brought with him to Paris the habits of a British lifetime. He insisted on having his afternoon tea, and got it—much to the consternation of French formalism. He also had the British passion for fresh air. Ray Stannard Baker once saw him burst out of the stuffy French foreign office, exclaiming, "I don't believe the air in that room has been changed since the time of Louis Philippe!"

One always knew where the dour Tiger stood; one never could be sure where Lloyd George stood. He was the master opportunist of his time; expediency was his guiding principle. He had a sixth sense for the changes in the pulse of public opinion, and like the chameleon he changed with them. If they wanted vengeance, he promised vengeance; if they wanted leniency, he worked for leniency. Whatever his catapultic public wanted was right. Though gifted with vision and ideals, he could never completely rise above the arts of the demagogue. His opportunism bordered on shiftiness.

The magnetic Welshman had a scintillating mind, the quickest of the Big Four, and like many another man with a scintillating mind, he used it as a substitute for hard work. One of the greatest debaters of his generation, he relied on intuition, imagination, nimble wit, and a ready tongue to confound and discomfit his adversaries.

His ignorance of some things was astounding. As already noted, he had never heard of Teschen before the Conference; he confused Silesia with Cilicia—places that were more than a thousand miles apart. But his skin was tough. When he stubbed his toe, he would brush himself off with a laugh and plunge off in some other direction. When he found that he had taken a position that was untenable because his facts were incorrect, he would blithely or blusteringly shift to the other side and carry on with equal brilliance. To him consistency was the mark of a small mind, and strict truth an insuperable handicap to political preferment. He once quoted to Lord Riddell the cynical adage: "If you want to succeed in politics, you must keep your conscience well under control."

Lloyd George was as reliable as quicksilver, as direct as a zigzag, as unwavering as a weathercock. One day he was immovably for a certain position, the next he was as immovably for another. Sometimes he changed his mind overnight; at others the electorate changed, so he changed with it. Yet with all his wobbliness, shiftiness, and superficiality, such was the man's personality that one could hardly help liking him.

Wilson was for the New Order; Clemenceau was for the Old Order. Lloyd George was for whatever order would promote the best interests of Great Britain and endear him to the electorate. His general strategy was to whittle down Clemenceau's extreme demands on Germany, and for this reason he seemed more moderate at times than Wilson. But there was a reason for Lloyd George's leniency. Clemenceau must not be allowed to create any new Alsace-Lorraines, for that would mean a new world war, and Britain would inevitably be dragged into it. Clemenceau must not be allowed to prostrate Germany, for that would mean no reparations for England, and above all the loss of a valuable customer, one essential for postwar economic recovery. Lloyd George was willing to leave Germany with enough strength to trade and to pay reparations, but not enough to fight with. And France must not be allowed to dominate Europe too completely; that was contrary to traditional British policy.

Wilson and not Lloyd George was Clemenceau's principal antagonist. The Welsh weathercock generally stood on the side lines and threw his weight on the side of moderation, except where Britain's reparations and colonial spoils were concerned, while Wilson carried the burden and heat of the day. On a few occasions Lloyd George aroused the Tiger, and Wickham Steed relates that after Clemenceau had once repeatedly charged inaccuracy of statement, Lloyd George seized him by the collar, and there was mumbled talk about challenges to a duel. But the storm quickly blew over. "Lloyd George," the Tiger growled, "believes himself to be Napoleon, but President Wilson believes himself to be Jesus Christ."

5

Vittorio Emanuele Orlando, the Italian premier, was the least influential of the Big Four. Italy was the weakest of the four powers, and Orlando was the weakest of the four representatives, both in personal and in political force. He had relatively little to say during the discussions, because Italy was concerned primarily with the fate of Austria-Hungary, rather than Germany, and the other three men were primarily concerned with Germany. And when the showdown came over Italian claims, Orlando bolted the Conference, under circumstances which will be described later.

The Italian premier was short and rotund, with a thick white pompadour, white mustache, and full lips. When he smiled, which was often, he revealed dimpled cheeks. Amiable and attractive, he was a learned and cultured gentleman of the south Italian school. Though florid in manner, he was eloquent in speech—a skilled debater and a really gifted orator. Lansing, a fellow lawyer, admired his fine legal mind, and regretted that there were not more lawyers on the Big Four. Generally genial, Orlando would occasionally reveal a volatile temper and burst into tumultuous speech. At other times he would give way to the emotionalism of the Latin, and shed copious tears.

Orlando labored under a serious linguistic handicap. He was the only one of the Big Four who could not speak English, and everything he said had to be resaid by an interpreter. David Hunter Miller relates that Orlando was once asked at the Conference if he knew any English. "Nothing," Orlando replied, "except these words, 'eleven o'clock, I don't agree, good-bye.'"

Apparently these were useful and easily learned words in the Paris of 1919.

Of his three colleagues, Orlando had the most in common with Wilson. Both had studied law, though Orlando had become a distinguished barrister, and both had been professors, Orlando of law, Wilson of government. Both had progressive ideas, and Orlando gave Wilson loyal and unwavering support in the framing of the League of Nations. The Italian premier no doubt expected Wilson to return the favor when Italian claims came up for consideration.

In some respects Orlando was overshadowed by Baron Sidney Sonnino, his foreign minister. The son of an Italian Jew and an English mother, the Baron revealed the native shrewdness in bargaining characteristic of his father's race. With white mustaches, florid complexion, eagle features, powerful nose, and viselike jaw, he was cold, intractable, taciturn, and scheming.

Sonnino, unlike Orlando, had no weakness for the New Order. With cold logic he favored the Old Order, the balance of power, naked imperialism, and all Italy could grab—and then some. Wilson did not get on well with this son of Machiavelli, who had arranged to keep him away from the people in Rome; and Wickham Steed relates how Wilson, when mentioning his name, once clenched his fist and used unparliamentary language.

Orlando, though somewhat slippery, was progressive; Sonnino, reactionary. Each tended to cancel the efforts of the other. Orlando's political position was precarious, and he could not go far with the ball and chain of his foreign minister on his leg. At times the two men were not even on speaking terms. Near the end of the Conference, Wilson told his experts: "I can get along with Orlando, and could quickly arrange matters with him, if he was not scared to death of Sonnino."

6

Each one of the Big Four, save Wilson, had come into his high office during a war crisis—Lloyd George late in 1916, and Clemenceau and Orlando in 1917. Clemenceau and Lloyd George in particular had distinguished themselves for the unrelenting zeal with which they brought hostilities to a victorious conclusion. Each was naturally continued on in office for the making of the peace, yet neither had ever given careful, first-hand attention to the direction of foreign affairs. Not the least among the handicaps of the Conference was that the war-makers became the peacemakers, as was inevitable; but unfortunately the two tasks require different talents and temperaments.

Each one of the Big Four without exception was in some measure, and with varying success, a politician. Yet the arts of the politician are on the whole the very arts that are not wanted in the negotiator. Lloyd George was a brilliant politician, but his gifts handicapped him at the peace table. He could overwhelm his enemies with invective; but there is no place for invective in peacemaking. He could rout his enemies with brilliant sallies; but the peace table needs the judge and not the prosecuting attorney. The situation called for statesmen, not politicians.

Each one of the Big Four without exception had to spend a distressing amount of time in keeping up his political fences at home. Lloyd George had to absent himself from the Conference for protracted periods; Wilson had to make a return trip to America to explain the Covenant of the League; Clemenceau did not have far to go, but he had Foch, Poincaré, and others constantly yipping at his heels. If Wilson had his Senate, Clemenceau had his Chambers, and Lloyd George his House.

Each one of the Big Four had to get out beyond his depth in passing upon the problems that pressed for settlement. Lloyd George lightheartedly confessed his ignorance; but Wilson made a supreme effort to grasp too much. Only the individual experts were competent to rule upon their specialties, and even they often disagreed among themselves. When they agreed, they could not in a number of cases grasp the larger political implications of the recommendations they were making.

The decisions had to be made by the Big Four, because they alone could assume political responsibility for what they were doing. The result was that these four lone men, who were experts in nothing, had to be experts in everything. Giants in the political sphere at home, they were cut down to the size of mortal men in the international theater.

As one reads how the Big Four, out of the depths of their ignorance, divided portions of the world as if they had been parts of a gigantic cake, one can but regret that man has so ordered his affairs that the peacemaking of 1919 had almost inevitably to be a kind of blindman's buff

CHAPTER ELEVEN

THE WHITE MAN'S BURDEN

"The German colonies were to be disposed of. They had not been governed; they had been exploited merely, without thought of the interest or even the ordinary human rights of their inhabitants." WOODROW WILSON, *July 10, 1919.*

1

WILSON ATTENDED the formal sessions of the Conference for about five weeks before returning to America for a brief interlude. During this period he fought two great and successful battles: one for the mandate principle, the other for riveting the League of Nations into the treaty of peace. If his reputation as a negotiator rested on these two achievements, it would be much higher than it was at the end of the Conference. Henry White believed that Wilson's mistake was not in going to Paris but in returning after he had won these two initial engagements. This may be doubted, but even if true Wilson was not one to put his personal reputation above the responsibility of making an enduring peace.

We have already observed that peacemaking was essentially a desperate race against the rising tide of anarchy and Bolshevism sweeping in from the east. Yet it is significant that the negotiators became involved at once and for many weeks to come over two problems that had only indirect relevance to the immediate task of restoring peace to Central Europe.

The natural tendency, of course, is to do the easy and pleasant things first, especially when overwhelming problems loom in the offing. The pleasantest job of all, and the one which seemed to present no great problem, was dividing the booty. The expectant delegates were there with whetted knives and whetted appetites, and the first cry was, "When do we eat?"

Upon one thing they all agreed, and this was very important, for agreement was at a premium. They all agreed—even Wilson—that the former German colonies, with their approximately 15,000,000 helpless natives, should not be returned to

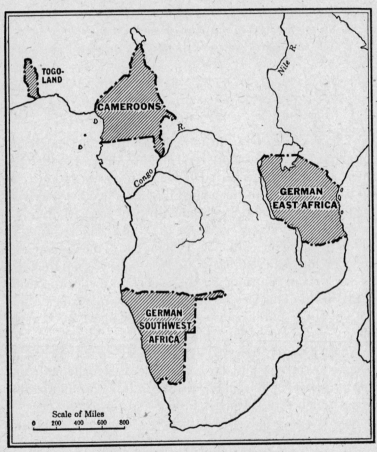

Germany's Prewar African Colonies

Germany. But here agreement ended. The apple of discord proved to be the first fruit of victory.

The British of South Africa had fought desperately, and with heroic sacrifices, to conquer German Southwest Africa, and they had no intention whatever of allowing the Germans to come back and reestablish military and naval bases from which to threaten them in the future. The British of New Zealand and Australia had captured Samoa, New Guinea, and other South Pacific islands, and they had no intention of allowing the Germans to return and jeopardize their security.

These reasons were sound enough, but they did not apply so forcibly to regions like German East Africa and particularly the Cameroons and Togoland, which were so far distant from large areas of British and French population as hardly to constitute a menace. It is true that they could have been used as bases from which to threaten British shipping lines, and this was pointed out by the submarine-conscious Allies in their written interchanges with the Germans. As things turned out, such bases would have been pinched off rather quickly in 1939 by the British and French; but in 1919 the threat seemed very real. So to cover all possible contingencies, and to reinforce the strategic argument, the allegation was made and generally accepted by the Allies that the Germans were not fit to be entrusted with the guardianship of cannibals and other backward peoples.

This convenient article of faith was not difficult to accept in view of the exaggerated but far from groundless atrocity stories which had come out of Belgium. The Hun was a brute, and there the argument ended. It was unfortunately true that while German colonial administration had many bright chapters, which were conveniently overlooked, it also had some dark chapters. These had been repeatedly aired in Germany by opponents of imperialism, who charged that the soil of the colonies had been "manured by the blood of natives"; and the words of these critics were now put into the mouths of the enemies of the Fatherland. Not only did the Allies overlook the bright chapters of German colonialism, but they kept tightly closeted some of the horrible skeletons of their own, including those from the Belgian Congo.

Wilson completely and sincerely agreed with the Allies that the Huns were not fit to be entrusted with the White Man's burden, and he further agreed that they should not have so much as one coral atoll of their former vast colonial empire.

We cannot fairly criticize Wilson for not having been wiser than all of his contemporaries, for suffering from the shell-shocked psychosis of the Allied statesmen, and for not having seen at this early stage the meteoric rise of the paper-hanging corporal who had recently fought in the German army. But the fact is that two far-reaching mistakes were made, and Wilson seems to have made no attempt to head off either.

2

With the wisdom of hindsight, we can see that it was probably an error to take away every single one of Germany's colonies. We can understand why New Zealand and Australia and the Union of South Africa were adamant on the principle of security; but, as we have seen, places like the Cameroons and German East Africa were in a somewhat different category. Neither was a real strategic threat; neither was a vitally important economic asset; and both covered large and satisfactorily delusive areas on the map.

The complete loss of all the colonies was a bitter enough pill in itself, but the bitterness was increased by the fact that Germany expected to retain most of them, or at least a share in some of them. Point V of the Fourteen promised "a free, open-minded, and absolutely impartial adjustment of all colonial claims," with due regard for "the interests of the populations concerned . . ." The Germans felt that they had done a good job of colonial administration, at least comparatively, and there was nothing in this Point to indicate that they would not get their overseas possessions back. It is true that the publicly expressed war aims of the Allies gave no basis for such a hope; but the Fourteen Points (the heart of the pre-Armistice contract) did. One may again point to the perils of imprecision.

We all know that one of Hitler's most telling arguments in

his rise to power, and one with which he lashed huge audiences to near frenzy, was his condemnation of the robbing of Germany. There can be no doubt that, if the Germans had been allowed to retain some of their least profitable and harmless colonies, the Führer would have found other grounds for complaint; but certainly the wind would have been partially taken out of his sails.

To take all the colonies was a harsh enough blow; but partially to justify the taking on the pretext that the Germans were brutes was to turn the knife in the wound. As a student of history, Wilson should have remembered that all colonial powers have their black chapters, and that not even the United States, with its "water cure" scandals in the Philippines, was in a position to cast stones. If all the colonies had to be taken, it would have been much more candid to write them off as reparations, and credit them to the total bill. The distinguished German liberal, Matthias Erzberger, estimated that they were worth nine billion dollars. Granted that this is an exaggerated figure, it is clear that any reasonable allowance would have helped to reduce reparations payments to manageable proportions, and would have been a powerful contribution toward a lasting settlement. It would also have spared Germany the additional humiliation of losing all her overseas possessions, under the hypocritical guise of humanitarian motives, much as we dispossess a feeble-minded person of his property.

Perhaps one should be more careful in using the word "hypocritical." To us in a different age and in a different atmosphere, this may seem like hypocrisy. To men of that age—men who had seen the devastation of France and Belgium, who knew of Big Berthas and Zeppelin raids—there was no room for argument as to Hunnish barbarity. Among a few men there may have been some conscious dissimulation. If so, it was hypocrisy; if not, it was not.

But whatever the motive, the net result was the same. The Treaty of Versailles, with its long train of humiliations, created a vast inferiority complex in the German people which ultimately found expression in the insane leadership of Adolf Hitler. Some of these humiliations were inevitable, no matter how wise the treaty, for defeat in itself was a bitter enough draught for this proud and military-minded people. But we who live in a later generation can but wonder that the colonial question was handled so shortsightedly.

The great problem before the Peace Conference was to work out some order under which Germany would be peaceable and reasonably contented. If the negotiators had sat up nights devising ways and means of rekindling German nationalism and developing a spirit of revenge preparatory to a new war, they could hardly have done better than in their handling of the colonies.

The victors finally saw their mistake in the 1930's, when it was too late. By then they could not make restitution because that would merely be throwing scraps of fresh meat into the mouth of a hungry lion.

Wilson's errors, as we have seen, were negative rather than positive. When he might have protested, he was silent; when he might have been drawing parallels from history, he was apparently thinking of something else. This something else was the mandate system.

3

The mandate idea, though not entirely original with Wilson, apparently came to him independently. Its chief feature was that the German colonies should not be ceded outright to any one power, but should be handed over to certain nations for administration under the general supervision of the League of Nations. Wilson's original plan was for certain of the neutrals, such as Holland and the Scandinavian countries, to act as mandatories.

The scheme was unquestionably ingenious. On paper, it would please Germany, because the League and not her enemies would get the colonies. In the course of time, she would presumably be admitted to the League and have a voice in the control of her former possessions. The mandate scheme would please liberals everywhere, because it would fulfill Wilson's "no annexations" pledge; it would redeem Point V regarding the colonies; and it would hold out to subject peoples the hope of self-determination. It would also please the imperialistic powers, because they could make off with the substance while leaving the League with the shadow.

The mandate idea was also thoroughly in keeping with the American tradition of trusteeship or temporary tutelage, under which our territories had become states. In places like Cuba and the Philippines, we had pursued or were pursuing a policy of temporarily shouldering the White Man's burden, and then, when the natives were strong enough to carry it themselves, or when we were tired of carrying it ourselves, handing it over to them.

Wilson was further attracted to the mandate idea because it would give the League of Nations something specific and important to do from the very start. Perhaps he remembered that the American Union had been held together from 1781 to 1789 in part because the weak government under the Articles of Confederation was charged with the trusteeship of a vast area of public lands. Similarly, the mandate system might insure the success of the League.

The interested British Dominions battled bitterly for the outright annexation of the German colonies, and the intractable and cynical Premier Hughes of Australia led the fight. "And you mean, Mr. Hughes," queried Wilson, "that in certain circumstances Australia would place herself in opposition to the opinion of the whole civilized world?" Hughes, who was deaf but heard all that he wanted to hear through a machine-gun-like contraption, replied bluntly, "That's about it, Mr. President."

But Wilson kept up the fight. The Conference was already under fire, and he felt that it would be doomed if the powers began with a snarling division of the booty contrary to the

Fourteen Points but in keeping with the imperialism of the Old Order.

The French press began a vitriolic attack upon the "impracticable ideals" of the American doctrinaire, evidently securing their information secretly through French official channels. Wilson protested strongly against this misrepresentation, and even went so far as to threaten to publish his own side of the controversy. The direct attacks of the French press immediately ceased.

With the support of Lloyd George, Wilson finally won a partial victory when he secured the mandate system in modified form. But not until he had threatened to break up the Conference and go home.

4

The mandate system as finally worked out was a compromise with Wilson's original ideas—a compromise between lofty idealism and naked imperialism.

No neutral nation was given a mandate over any former German territory, although Wilson had originally planned to invite these small countries to participate.

The great powers, except Italy, all got substantially the areas that they had claimed. These, to be sure, were mandates, and they were hedged about with certain rather illusory restrictions. But possession is nine points of the law.

The mandates for Constantinople and Armenia were left up in the air. The tribulations sure to arise in these two areas were certain to exceed the profits to be taken from them— there were no rich oil fields there—so it was assumed that rich Uncle Sam would play the role of the Good Samaritan. On one occasion, when Constantinople was under discussion, Clemenceau turned to Wilson and said jokingly: "When you cease to be President we will make you Grand Turk." The gibe was not appreciated.

Wilson, though at first expressing some misgivings, gave unaccountably strong encouragement to the belief that the United States would assume a mandate over at least Armenia. That he should have done so, even to the extent of later recommending an Armenian mandate to Congress, is further evidence of his blindness to realities. American public opinion was virtually unanimous on one thing: it would have no mandates, especially outside this hemisphere. The trusteeship over Armenia would involve an estimated 50,000 troops and millions of dollars. The American people sympathized abstractly with the sufferings of the Armenians at the hands of the "terrible Turk," but they had no intention of going over there and suffering along with them.

Various critics, like Nicolson and Keynes, have condemned the "appalling hypocrisy" and "Jesuitical exegesis" of the Treaty of Versailles. Certainly the division of Germany's colonies seems to give them some support.

We have seen that the fifth of the Fourteen Points provided for "a free, open-minded, and absolutely impartial adjustment of all colonial claims" based on the principal that the "interests of the populations concerned must have equal weight with the equitable claims of the government whose title is to be determined."

When the Germans formally protested at Versailles against the unfairness of the mandate system, the Allies replied that they had "placed *before every other consideration* the interests of the native populations . . ." Perhaps, in that poisoned atmosphere, they sincerely thought so. Yet it later developed that France was privileged to conscript the natives of the former German colonies into her army, where they could be used, if need be, to fight a defensive war against Germany.

In 1919 it was embarrassing to explain how it came about that the parceling out of the mandates bore so close a relation to the secret treaties negotiated during the war. The great powers made off with oil fields and other incalculably rich resources, while looking after the "interests of the native population," though, thanks to Wilson, they did not secure as complete control as they desired.

In February, 1919, a week after Wilson's departure from Paris for a hurried trip to the United States, Lloyd George privately remarked to Lord Riddell that while America had obtained a bundle of dubious paper money in the form of the League of Nations, he had "returned with a pocket full of sovereigns in the shape of German Colonies, Mesopotamia, etc. Everyone to his taste."

Ideally, perhaps, the mandates should have been under the complete control of the League of Nations. But the powers would have none of this. They had fought a grueling and exhausting war of self-defense for over four years, and they had to have something to show on the credit side of the ledger. They had not entered the conflict to seize German colonies, but they could hardly be blamed for wanting to salvage something from the economic ruin that Germany had seemingly forced upon them. The alternative to outright annexation was the modified form of Wilson's mandate plan that was finally adopted.

From the larger point of view, the system as finally worked out was preferable to undisguised imperialism. It provided for a species of control, and it gave promise of getting the League off to a good start. Certainly the mandate system proved to be one of the more successful and creditable enterprises of the League of Nations. It was, as someone has said, "an angel conceived in sin."

On the debit side of the ledger, we must weigh the effect of this whole arrangement on the German mind. It was disillusioning to be deprived of all colonies; it was humiliating to be informed that Germans were unfit to govern natives; and it was insulting to be told that all this was being done largely in the interests of backward peoples. To the great body of Germans—and to many liberals elsewhere—the mandate scheme seemed like a clumsy camouflage for outright annexation. Even the Socialist press in France damned the arrangement as "a bastard compromise between Wilsonian idealism and imperialism." There were many liberals who were still convinced that the White Man's Burden was nothing but the loot sack.

5

One of the most persistent latter-day criticisms of Wilson is that he stupidly permitted the German islands of the North Pacific to fall into Japanese hands. The assumption is general that if he had been gifted with any foresight at all, he would have wrested them away from Japan, and that in 1941 we should have held them as fortified outposts.

Yet what else could Wilson have done? Neither he nor his countrymen had any more than the dimmest conception of the value of these islands in the waging of naval and aerial warfare in the Western Pacific. And why become alarmed about Japan? She was one of our Associates; and while we had some suspicions of her motives, we were certainly not at that time seriously contemplating war with her even in the remote future. There were many other problems at the Conference of really pressing importance. Why worry about global flyspecks when one is busy reshaping the world?

Even before Pearl Harbor, some Americans began to see a new light; and certainly after Pearl Harbor an increasing number of our citizenry came to appreciate the value of these numerous stationary and unsinkable aircraft carriers in the hands of a resourceful and tenacious foe. Here we have a striking example of after-the-event wisdom, for it has not been until relatively recent times that the American people have come to see what they assume Wilson should have seen at Paris.

If we are going to blame anyone for not having been able to part the veil of the future, why not pick on President McKinley? Presumably he could have gathered in the Carolines and the other islands from vanquished Spain without the slightest difficulty if he had only had the wit to do so.

As a matter of fact, there is much excuse for McKinley. Germany had begun negotiations to purchase these islands in the 1880's, and in 1898–1899 she exerted very strong pressure

Disposition of Germany's Pacific Colonies

both at Paris and at Washington to induce us to keep our hands off. Our relations with Germany were then rather embittered, and when it was discovered that our missionary and cable interests were adequately safeguarded we stepped aside and let the Germans buy the islands from Spain.

It seems hardly fair to blame McKinley for this oversight, if it was an oversight. He had no way of knowing that Japan would one day get the islands and attack Pearl Harbor. He had no way of foreseeing the coming of aerial warfare. If he had been a soothsayer, he perhaps would have done differently. But we cannot expect our statesmen to be crystal gazers; the best we can expect them to do is to weigh possibilities and probabilities, and make their decisions accordingly. In an age which knew neither the airplane nor the long-range submarine, it did not seem reasonable to suppose that these islands could ever be used effectively against us.

If our statesmen adopt the policy of acquiring everything that can be purchased or seized, from the Antarctic to the Arctic, for fear that at some distant day and in some unforeseen manner it may be used to our disadvantage, then we shall surely embark upon a sea fraught with more than ordinary peril.

6

The American naval experts in 1919 thought that it would be desirable to have the German islands, but they recognized that the best they could hope for was some form of international control. Wilson later recalled before the Senate committee that there had been one memorandum presented in behalf of "some base" in the German group, but he did not seem to think the matter of any vital importance. His only real concern seems to have been for American cable rights on the island of Yap, and he vaguely entered a reservation which later returned to plague our relations with Japan. Incidentally, this was the only request even remotely resembling a territorial claim that the United States presented at Paris.

On technical grounds, the American negotiators in 1919 had much less excuse than McKinley's negotiators in 1898. The submarine had been recently used with devastating effect, and the aircraft had clearly foreshadowed enormous destructiveness. While it is true that our relations with Japan were superficially amicable, there were many points of friction, and there had been occasional war scares on both sides since 1906. It would be difficult enough to defend the Philippine Islands and Guam, in the event of war with Japan, without having our communications flanked by innumerable Japanese bases.

The inescapable fact is that even if Wilson had fully recognized the value of these tiny islands, which he did not, he could not have pried them away from Japan, no matter how desperately he tried. He had a difficult enough time as it was with our cable rights on Yap, and this controversy was not settled until after he had left the Presidency.

When the Conference met at Paris in 1919, the Japanese had already occupied the islands for over four years. They had been guaranteed permanent possession of them by the secret agreement with London and Paris early in 1917, under which Britain was to get the German islands south of the Equator, and Japan was to provide antisubmarine reinforcements for Mediterranean waters. The Japanese had faithfully carried out their end of the bargain, and the British and French were in honor bound to carry out theirs. More than honor was indeed involved, for if the British had repudiated their agreement at this late date, they could hardly have claimed the German islands south of the equator which New Zealand and Australia were demanding.

Early in the Conference, Wilson flatly announced that he would not recognize the secret understanding with Japan. But he eventually had to, in connection both with the Pacific islands and with Shantung. We must not forget that he was only one of the Big Four; and that the United States was only one of the Big Five Powers at Paris. He was quite willing to tear up this secret agreement, but how about the Japanese, the British, and the French?

As a result of the war the British Empire was to pick up over

950,000 square miles of former German territory as mandates; the Japanese were asking for only 830 square miles of North Pacific islands—an area less than that of Yosemite National Park. This was all the territory they were claiming as a reward for their participation in the war, and they would lose face intolerably if they did not get it. They were in possession of the islands; they were determined to stay; the only way they could have been thrown off was by force of arms. And since the United States, which was the only nation interested in dislodging them, was not willing to go to war for this purpose, the Japanese were there to stay.

Thus Wilson was able to win a partial victory when, on the advice of his own experts, he secured the adoption of the mandate system. We did not get the islands; neither did Japan—in fee simple. She was made a mandatory of the League, and pledged herself never to fortify the places entrusted to her care. If she could be depended upon to keep her word, these tiny atolls would seemingly present no menace to our Pacific communications.

7

It now seems clear that the alternatives were not: would the Japanese or the Americans get these islands? We went to Paris not wanting or asking for a square foot of territory, and we could hardly have reversed our position at this late hour. The alternatives were: would Japan get these outposts in fee simple, or as mandatories of the League? If Japan had got them in fee simple, she would have been free to fortify them. If she got them as a League mandate, as she did, she *might not* fortify them. So, granting honor on the part of Nippon, we should gain by this arrangement. If she should prove false to her promises, the United States would be no farther behind than it would have been in the first instance.

When Japan left the League in 1933 she did not return the islands. Whether she fortified them before Pearl Harbor or not is a disputed question; the important point is that she certainly did after Pearl Harbor.

Those who blame Wilson for not having brought these islands back from Paris assume that, if he had, we should have had them in 1941. No assumption could be farther from reality. Following Pearl Harbor we lost everything west of the Hawaiian group, including Wake, Guam, and the Philippines. We had pursued a policy of not fortifying these outposts for fear of annoying Japan. There is not the slightest reason to believe that we would not have followed the same policy regarding the Japanese mandated islands, if we had then held them. In fact, with these potential bases in hand, our false sense of security probably would have been increased, and we probably should have been even less disposed to take vigorous defensive measures.

It seems reasonably clear that Wilson made the best of a bad bargain, and that the picture would not be appreciably different if he had done the impossible and got the islands. The basic blunder was not in letting Japan have these places, or in setting up the mandate system, even in modified form, but in handling the problem of Germany's colonies so shortsightedly as to provide combustibles for future Adolf Hitlers.

CHAPTER TWELVE

A LIVING THING IS BORN

"It is the spirit back of the Covenant that counts more than the text." COLONEL HOUSE, *February 7, 1919.*

———————

1

A GREAT many people still think of the Covenant of the League of Nations and the Treaty of Versailles as two separate instruments. This, of course, is incorrect. The League of Nations Covenant was incorporated in the Treaty of Versailles as Section I. Not only was it placed at the very first, but considerable portions of the rest of the pact were so interwoven with it that the United States Senate could not cut out the Covenant without unraveling the whole fabric.

This is of vast importance, for it is clear that the League of Nations, with its vulnerable Article X, was what defeated the Treaty of Versailles in the United States. To put it another way, if the Covenant had been a separate instrument the treaty would almost certainly have been approved by the Senate.

We have already seen that Wilson won two great diplomatic victories during his first month in Paris. The first was wringing from the Conference an acceptance of the mandate principle. The second was forcing the detailed Covenant of the League of Nations into the text of the treaty. This represented a triumph over those who wanted to postpone consideration of the League to the indefinite future, notably the French, and those who wanted merely to outline the general principles of a League in the Treaty. This latter view initially commanded much support from the British.

Wilson regarded the League as the "key to the whole settlement," and from the start he favored the bodily incorporation of the Covenant in the Treaty. He encountered some opposition, chiefly from the French, but in the end he was able to have his way. It was a great personal triumph for him when, on January 22, 1919, the Council of Ten went on record as favoring his plan, and three days later the plenary session formally and unanimously gave its approval to the integral idea in the very first resolution of the Conference.

This unanimity does not mean that there was tremendous enthusiasm for the League. Wilson had made it clear, notably in his Manchester reply to Clemenceau's balance-of-power

Two Votes for the League of Nations
(Knott in the Dallas *News;* courtesy of the Dallas *News*)

speech, that acceptance of the League was the price that Europe would have to pay for America's coöperation in the peace settlement. The price seemed small indeed for the benefits that the wealthy United States could confer on a sick and impoverished Europe. One usually humors a rich uncle.

The efforts of Wilson to secure an acceptance of the League as an integral part of the treaty have erroneously been pictured as a last-ditch struggle against the wicked powers of the Old

Order. While it is clear that Clemenceau had little desire to put the League first, it is true that Wilson received considerable support from the British, who actually drafted the resolution adopted by the Council of Ten and strongly supported it in the plenary session. But it is significant that the original resolution read that the League should be a "part of the peace." Wilson objected. This might mean that his pet project would in some vague manner be associated at a later time with the entire peace settlement, and this in turn might mean that the League would be sidetracked. He promptly proposed an amendment to read that the League should be "an *integral* part of the general treaty of peace." The amendment carried without difficulty.

One need not overdramatize Wilson's part in this episode to conclude that he must bear the major part of the responsibility for forcing the Covenant bodily into the Treaty of Versailles.

2

We must note at the outset that there were powerful arguments for Wilson's position. The League was the Fourteenth Point—the capstone point—and he could conceive of neither a satisfactory treaty nor a lasting peace without the Covenant's being the heart of the whole arrangement. He believed that liberal opinion throughout the world, which had rallied to his stirring war aims, would be profoundly disappointed if he should bring home from Paris the corpse of a treaty which did not include the League—a League that would smooth out the inevitable imperfections of the entire pact.

Not only would the League be the keystone of the edifice but, if adopted in principle at the outset, it would strike the keynote of the Conference—a clarion call for the new order. It would also facilitate the making of the rest of the treaty, for— to take only one example—if a puissant League existed to maintain order, there would be less need of haggling over such problems as strategic frontiers.

A great many of the European leaders, especially those of lesser rank, rather mildly favored the League of Nations; but they generally regarded it as of secondary importance when compared with the urgent necessity of making peace with Germany. Once this was done, and the spoils were divided, and the enemy was enchained, it would be in order to draw up a League in a leisurely fashion—a powerful League which would make sure that the Allies could keep what they had taken away from their fallen foe. The problem was merely one of first things first. "Why," it was currently asked, "should the roof be put on before the foundations are solidly laid?"

This argument was unanswerable—if Wilson could take it for granted that when the loot was parceled out, and the treaty signed, the weary delegates would not pigeonhole the League and go home. Yet this was precisely what he could not take for granted. He knew that neither Lloyd George nor Clemenceau really believed in the League. Clemenceau not only had sneered at it quite openly, but had, as we have noted, come out unabashedly for the old balance of power. The French delegation at the Conference had the League last on their agenda.

It is true that the security-obsessed French would have been enthusiastic about the League if they could have had the kind of arrangements they wanted: a League of Allies rather than a League of Nations. From first to last they fought for an international army under League jurisdiction, preferably with a French general in command, or at least an international general staff, which could take vigorous action against Germany at the slightest sign of assertiveness. In other words, a powerful military machine for freezing the status quo, and keeping the heel of the victor permanently on the neck of the vanquished.

From first to last, Wilson fought this proposal. There were various objections to it, but one need only point to the fact that the Constitution of the United States puts the war-declaring power in the hands of Congress, not in that of an international body in Geneva. Wilson was amply warned by his advisers—and this must have been evident to him without such advice—that a treaty providing for an international police force would not have a ghost of a chance in the Senate. To paraphrase William Allen White, a superstate with a superarmy and a superstaff might even be tempted to knock the superdaylights out of the United States.

In short, the French conceived of the League as an instrument for perpetuating the military alliance of the victors, and they were quite willing to call it a League of Nations or a Society of Nations or any other name that would please Wilson. When Clemenceau found that the League might be forged into such an instrument, he ceased to sneer at it. But when it turned out to be a milk-and-water League, he had no enthusiasm for it. He felt that it was not totally useless, because it might add something to French defenses when taken in connection with other guarantees; but he placed no reliance on it, and would not accept it as a substitute for real security. One Gallic wit reflected a common view when he said that the League was "impossible" but "indispensable."

It is clear from all this that Wilson had unassailable grounds for believing that if the Covenant was not forced into the Treaty, it might easily be sidetracked for all time

3

On the whole it seems as though Wilson's instincts and strategy were sound, though, as will become evident, the same cannot be said for his tactics. Like a great gambler, he was staking everything on a new world order and a new era of perpetual peace. If such a new world order were to be established, there would have to be a League; and the only way to be sure of a League, Wilson felt, was to have it in the treaty.

Public opinion throughout the world seemed ripe for such an innovation. The time to strike was when the iron was hot.

When the iron cooled off, and public opinion began to lose sight of the horrors of war and become absorbed in domestic reconstruction, enthusiasm for the League would undoubtedly wane, if not evaporate. The world in 1919 was hot and malleable; the time to reshape it was before it grew cold and hard.

We do not know what would have happened—we can only guess—if Wilson had been willing to postpone the League to a subsequent pact. We do know that he waged a determined fight to force it into the Treaty of Versailles, and that the whole Treaty was defeated by a narrow margin in the United States, largely if not primarily because it contained the League. But so many other factors contributed to this narrow defeat—a number of them much more foreseeable than this particular one—that it is hardly just to censure Wilson for it. One must repeat: Wilson was gambling for enormous stakes; the odds seemed to be not altogether unfavorable. If he won, he might win enormous benefits; if he lost, the world could hardly be worse off than it had been under the bankrupt old system of power politics.

But it does not seem to have entered Wilson's head at this stage of the game—and perhaps never—that he could lose. He simply took it for granted that the Senate would approve what he brought home, and he ill advisedly assured his British and French colleagues at the Conference that this was so. He was confident that the American people would rise up in righteous wrath and not permit their representatives to defeat his treaty. He did not believe that the Senate would dare incur the odium of committing so dastardly a crime against humanity.

His strategy was obvious to the Senators, and they were infuriated by it. Before he reached Paris, some of them had served public notice on him not to put the League into the treaty. But he had gone right ahead and done so. The only way the Senators could kill his League was to kill the whole treaty: throw out the baby with the bath. Would they dare incur this terrible responsibility? Time alone would tell.

4

The Senators fought desperately to head off the frightening dilemma which Wilson was preparing to present them, and one of their strongest arguments was that the making of the League at that time would delay the making of the peace. The urgent task, they said, was to stop the war, halt Bolshevism, and "bring the boys back." The time that Wilson wasted on the League might be the very margin by which anarchy would triumph over stability. There would be plenty of time to frame and discuss a League when the dangers of the moment were surmounted.

This was a potent argument, and Wilson recognized its force. He finally went so far as to issue a public statement, explaining that work on the drafting of the League was invariably carried on during odd hours, after regular sessions of the Council of Ten. This was true, for the Commission on the League of Nations, of which Wilson was made chairman, met after the day's tasks were done, in Colonel House's spacious headquarters, Room 315 of the Hotel Crillon. Some of these sessions ran to midnight, and at least one until after one o'clock. It is therefore utterly fantastic to allege, as Lansing did, that the framing of the League prolonged the Conference by a matter of weeks.

Even granted that the League delayed the Conference by a few days, had not the Allies already held up the sessions for a month after Wilson's arrival? And was not the Senate of the United States to dally with the treaty for more than eight months, three months longer than the Conference took to frame it?

It may even be argued that the League Covenant actually expedited the drafting of the treaty. Article XIX was the great expediter. It provided that the Assembly might advise from time to time the "consideration of international conditions whose continuance might endanger the peace of the world."

After the delegates had wrangled fruitlessly over a problem without prospect of agreement, an unsatisfactory solution was not infrequently adopted in the hope that Article XIX would ultimately take care of it. Harold Nicolson speaks of the many errors and obstructions that were passed over "under the aegis of that blessed Article XIX."

If one were asked to guess, it probably would be safe to say that the existence of the League Covenant with its "blessed" Article XIX saved much more time than was lost by the actual drafting of the Covenant. This catch-all article proved to be a convenient kind of attic into which the Conference could thrust all unfinished furniture. We need not discuss at this point the question whether time saved in this way was time profitably saved. It will suffice to observe that some of the problems which the Conference could not solve and which it left to the League, notably disarmament, the League could not solve either. And the failure to do so contributed directly to the League's final collapse, and to that of the whole postwar settlement.

5

While we may argue that the drafting of the Covenant did not seriously delay the making of the Treaty, it is clear that Wilson's preoccupation with his brain child led to serious, not to say disastrous, consequences. Time is not necessarily important in itself; the important thing is what is done with it.

During the month before the Conference met, Wilson was much wrapped up in the League. As it turned out, some of the attention that he then devoted to this subject might better have been given to other problems of more pressing importance.

Specifically, there was the vexatious question of the secret treaties. We have already suggested that if Wilson, at the opening of the Conference, had taken a bold stand against these pacts, he might have been able to sweep them from the green baize board. Instead, he spent his initial momentum in behalf of the League, and when he had to grapple with the secret treaties he was forced to fight on much less advantageous ground.

The Commission on the League of Nations was a distinguished body, which at times eclipsed the Council of Ten, and which for the entire Conference was exceeded in importance only by the Council of Ten and the Council of Four. The prolonged after-hour sessions on the League, superimposed upon an exacting day's labor with the Council of Ten, doubtless preoccupied Wilson's mind, possibly dulled it, and certainly lessened his efficiency for the important sessions of the next morning, when he had to contend with the fresh Lloyd George and Clemenceau, neither of whom was carrying such an overtime burden.

These midnight meetings were undoubtedly a severe drain on Wilson's meager stock of nervous and physical energy, and this would certainly have been true of a younger or more robust man. He had no time for his customary golf or other systematic recreation, and it is altogether probable that this onerous double duty had a real bearing upon his final tragic collapse.

6

But the question of delay and preoccupation seems to be less important in some ways than that of the hasty and imperfect drafting of the Covenant.

The Constitutional Convention, meeting in Philadelphia in 1787, took twelve weeks of exacting labor to complete a constitution for thirteen thinly populated provincial states.

The Commission on the League of Nations, working at night and after a grueling day's work, took only ten meetings, totaling about thirty hours, to strike off a constitution for the entire world. Laboring under such pressure, and confronted with such an enormous responsibility, it could hardly have brought forth a perfect instrument. And it did not. The Covenant bristled with imperfections, many of which, it now seems, were avoidable.

This picture, of course, is oversimplified, and it is necessary to correct a series of common misconceptions.

Many people still believe that Wilson thought up the idea of the League of Nations all by himself, that the British and the European peoples were not much interested in it, that he rammed the general principles of a League down their throats, and that as Chairman of the League of Nations Commission he sat down and dashed off the Covenant in a few days.

The League idea was not original with Wilson; it may be traced at least as far back as Dante. Many Americans had been much more forward and enthusiastic than he in accepting it, and this group includes Senator Henry Cabot Lodge. Wilson in truth was a belated if zealous convert.

In England, a distinguished group of liberals had been actively at work for many months on the League principle, and the famous Phillimore Report was in a very real sense the backbone of the final Covenant. Ray Stannard Baker is free to admit that there were many men at Paris as well prepared for the task of covenant-making as Wilson. The League could hardly have been brought into being without the cordial teamwork of Frenchmen like Léon Bourgeois, and Britons like General Jan C. Smuts and notably Lord Robert Cecil.

No, Wilson did not force the idea of the League upon the powers at Paris against their vigorous opposition. There was more apathy and indifference than actual hostility; more of a feeling that the League should come last rather than first. In brief, the question was not: Shall there be a League? It was: Shall the League be a part of the Treaty or a separate instrument?

Several months before reaching Paris, Wilson had worked out with House a rather careful draft of the proposed League. This explains why the Covenant could be struck off so rapidly. The problem was basically an editorial one of comparing and composing the differences in the several drafts that already existed. If Wilson had sat down to the task with empty hands, he simply could not have brought out of the committee an instrument so nearly complete as this one.

7

Reference to Wilson's early draft of the League Covenant leads us to what may be regarded as one of his most costly errors in the handling of public opinion.

If, as we have seen, he had rather carefully worked out the specific outlines of the League of Nations several months before leaving America, why did he not make his general principles public? He could then have studied the comments of the press, the criticisms of the opposition, and above all the reactions of the Senate. If he had done this, he would have been able to anticipate and meet many of the objections that were finally raised against the draft which was so hurriedly pasted together in Paris.

Wilson was at pains to keep his draft secret, and he also desired that the British withhold theirs from the press. The explanation is obvious. He did not want to arouse premature controversy.

We cannot deny that there was much force in Wilson's objections. But the same objections would not have been so weighty if he had been willing to publish the general outlines of his scheme, rather than specific details. And even if he had balked at publishing general outlines, he could have let them come out anonymously as trial balloons, and then have watched the reaction. Certainly he could have taken the leading Senators into his confidence, Democrats if not Republicans, and got their criticisms. But one finds no record that he did so. Here, as elsewhere, he simply failed to keep up his fences. He was evidently supremely confident that the Senate would not dare reject his handiwork.

The net result was that serious imperfections cropped out in the first draft of the League, imperfections which Wilson could have ironed out much more easily during the drafting than later. As it turned out, he had to go back to Paris, hat in hand, and beg the powers to insert certain amendments that would appease the angry Senate. This weakened his position, and opened the door for embarrassing counter favors, which were advanced either sincerely or as bargaining levers. We shall have to come back to this later, but for the moment we may note that the whole process of securing amendments increased the strain on Wilson, added to the general confusion at Paris, and introduced a not inconsiderable amount of genuine delay.

8

The decision to force the Covenant into the Treaty led to a train of tragic consequences. It necessitated a hasty and imperfect drafting; it introduced an element of distraction and confusion which diverted energy from the primary business of making peace with Germany. It tarred the Covenant with the black brush of Versailles, and caused neutrals to feel uncomfortable about going into a League which was embedded in a punitive treaty of peace. And finally, as already noted, the Covenant brought about the complete defeat of the Treaty in the United States, and in this way contributed powerfully to the collapse of the whole postwar settlement. All this, it seems, might have been avoided if Wilson had not stubbornly refused to accept a compromise between his point of view and that of his critics.

Certain leaders at Paris, including Secretary Lansing, Lord Robert Cecil, Colonel House, Arthur J. Balfour, and others, believed that the ideal solution was neither to postpone consideration of the League until after the Conference, nor to insert the Covenant bodily into the Treaty. Rather, there should be a general statement in the Treaty committing the signatories to the broad principles of a League, and making specific provision for the formation of a commission to erect the machinery in a saner and less hurried atmosphere.

Once the Senate had approved the Treaty, with the general outlines of the Covenant in it, and had sanctioned the creation of a commission to draw up the final instrument, the resulting League Covenant possibly could have been adopted by a simple executive agreement. In this case the Senate would have been by-passed, and Senators Lodge and Borah and Brandegee would not have had a chance to attach a long list of qualifying reservations.

In other words, the negotiators at Paris might have planted an acorn in the Treaty, with the expectation that it would grow into a lusty young oak in the sunshine of experience. As it was, they planted an oak and finally got only a sickly acorn.

The acorn-planting method undoubtedly had much to commend it. It would have prevented that sidetracking of the League which Wilson very properly feared. It would have avoided any serious delay, because the drafting of a few general principles would have taken little time and would have commanded general assent. It would have enabled neutral representatives to take part in the subsequent discussions. It would have given time for passions to cool, and would have made possible the deliberate working out of the specific problems in a more wholesome atmosphere.

Above all, a general statement of principles in the Treaty would have choked off hostile criticism in America. It would have given ample opportunity to the opponents and proponents of such a plan to advance their ideas—as co-authors if you will—for the guidance of those who were later to be charged with the task of drafting the League Covenant.

This is vastly important. General principles, as a rule, do not offer much for critics to attack. Everyone—or almost everyone—favors peace and good will toward men, and some measure of international collaboration toward that end. But when anyone advances specific and detailed plans for achieving those ends, the critic has something definite to sink his teeth into. He will raise questions and doubts; and questions and doubts tend to multiply in the minds of the public. Details were what ruined the League in America.

This does not mean that the Covenant was an unnecessarily wordy instrument. It was an admirably succinct and simple statement, in the tradition of the United States Constitution. Wilson was opposed to elaborate machinery, and insisted that it was the spirit of the thing that counted. Yet, even so, the Covenant was too detailed for its enemies. Some found it too strong, some too weak; some too vague, some too specific. A determined and jaundiced critic could find lurking in it all the hobgoblins he was looking for.

Why Wilson did not listen to Lansing and the others when they advanced the acorn-planting idea, one cannot say. He was a stubborn man, and did not compromise readily. He had made up his mind that the Covenant—a detailed Covenant—should go into the Treaty. And it did.

9

On a snowing and raining St. Valentine's day, February 14, 1919, Wilson stood before the plenary conference, cool and self-possessed, to present the still-warm draft of the League Covenant. It was a day of great personal triumph for him—perhaps his last great day of triumph—for he had forced his will upon those who were bent on postponement. The document which he held in his hand bore the unanimous approval of the fourteen nations represented on the drafting committee.

Without heroics or histrionics, but in quiet and measured tones, he began reading this charter for a new world order. The occasion in itself was so impressive, and the atmosphere was so heavy with big events, that Wilson's almost studied casualness was extraordinarily effective.

Upon completing the reading, he added a few explanatory

words. Quietly yet exultantly he announced: "A living thing is born . . ." Mrs. Wilson smiled proudly. There was not even a flutter of applause; one does not applaud after a prayer.

Others spoke. Significantly a French delegate said that France reserved the right to present further suggestions, and a Japanese delegate announced that Japan would later offer a proposition, presumably on the racial equality question. These remarks merely underscored the fact that the Conference had not yet approved the League; only the drafting committee had. A number of rough edges remained to be filed off.

Wilson was far too optimistic when he proclaimed that a living thing was born. The living thing was stillborn. The Senate, which Wilson did not think would dare take such liberties, was yet to have its say. It had in fact been doing some preliminary saying before and during the birth of the Covenant—enough to alarm a less preoccupied and confident man.

Following the presentation of the Covenant, the President and Mrs. Wilson left hurriedly in a torrential downpour to take the train for Brest, whence they would sail for a brief visit to America. An epoch in their lives and in the life of the League had ended, and another had begun.

CHAPTER THIRTEEN

A PROPHET IS NOT
WITHOUT HONOR

"No matter what I do, they will continue the attack."
WOODROW WILSON, *March, 1919.*

1

O N A wintry February 15, 1919, the *George Washington*
glided out of Brest harbor, bearing the weary Wilson home-
ward for a brief sojourn. The guns from the forts boomed a
noisy farewell, while lines of French marines stood rigidly at
salute along the walls.

Wilson had every reason to feel jubilant. He had won his
first two battles: the first, against a brazen division of the spoils;
the second, for the incorporation of the League in the Treaty.
More than that, he had in his pocket the draft of a Covenant
which he had driven through a committee of fourteen nations,
and which he had triumphantly read to the assembled Conference.

Then why go home? Why not stay on, and without loss of
momentum push on to other victories? Why delay the Conference further by a junket back to the United States?

Mrs. Wilson relates that her husband had hoped to have the
Treaty far enough toward completion by mid-February so
that he could leave Paris and not have to return. But the delays
of December and January, combined with difficulties both
expected and unexpected, had retarded progress to such an
extent that this was a vain hope. The treaty with Germany had
not yet even begun to take shape.

Wilson had now been absent from America for two and
one-half months. The Sixty-fifth Congress was about to adjourn, and it seemed imperatively necessary that he return,
sign the essential bills, and take care of other important ad-

ministrative matters. Above all, he must explain in detail the
nature and purposes of the newly born Covenant, for it was
already being grossly misrepresented.

It is difficult to see how this return trip, or a similar return
trip, could have been avoided. Without it, Wilson would have
been absent from the United States for more than seven
months; and we may well doubt whether the pressure of
domestic business or the temper of public opinion would have
permitted such a prolonged absence.

Nor is it at all clear that this return trip appreciably delayed
the work of the Conference. During Wilson's absence, the various committees were assiduously at work, and they made remarkable progress in the direction of the real task at hand—
peace with Germany. Lloyd George had to be absent in England looking after his political fences; while Clemenceau was
convalescing from an assassin's bullet in the lung. "My enemies
never could shoot straight," he was reported to have muttered
as he pitched forward.

2

Probably, as already remarked, the most important reason
in Wilson's mind for returning home was to explain and defend his League before the American public. Even before the
publication of the draft there had been growing criticism of
his yet unborn child; now that the child, crooked limbs and
all, was exposed to the public gaze, the Senatorial and other
flaw pickers could get down to cases.

Before sailing from France, Wilson had cabled an invitation
to the members of the House and Senate committees that deal
with foreign affairs, asking them to dine with him shortly after
his arrival in Washington for the purpose of discussing the
Covenant. He also requested that in the meantime they refrain
from debating the subject in Congress.

This was a gracious gesture, and on the face of it indicates that Wilson was recognizing the importance, even though belatedly, of enlisting Senatorial support.

The fact is that Wilson did not favor this move at all. When Colonel House first suggested it to him, he insisted that the most he would do would be to make an address to Congress. Upon House's pointing out that Congress would resent being

Anxious Moments—Will He Give Me His Boot or His Blessing?

(Courtesy of the Spokane *Spokesman-Review*)

called together and lectured to as the professor lectures his class before handing them an assignment, Wilson reluctantly gave in.

This is a classic example of locking the barn door after the theft. The time to have deferred to the Senate was when Wilson was making up the personnel of the Commission, and considering what his program would be. When he finally got around to making conciliatory gestures, the Senate was in an angry mood, and too many bitter things had already been said, both publicly and privately.

On the day of the sailing from Brest, it was announced that Wilson would land at Boston and there deliver a speech. The Senators thereupon declared that it was unfair of Wilson to ask them to keep silent while he was making public addresses, so they paid no attention to his request for postponing a discussion of the League. Perhaps they would have spoken anyhow, but this was a plausible pretext. While the *George Washington* was steaming swiftly toward Senator Lodge's bailiwick, Senators Poindexter, Borah, and Reed were thundering against the League. Senator Reed's scorching attack received an unprecedented five-minute ovation, in which the Senators and the gallery joined, while the presiding officer made no effort to check the demonstration. The Newark *News* acidly observed that "in the Senate it's the League of Fulminations."

3

The *George Washington* almost ran ashore, on the mid-afternoon of February 23, 1919, while trying to make Boston harbor in a dense fog. "I don't care if it is the beach," exclaimed one returning soldier. "It's the good old U.S.A., whatever it is, and I say hurray for it!" Nothing could better epitomize the growing isolationist sentiment.

The next morning an estimated 200,000 Bostonians cheered the conquering hero en route from the pier to his hotel, while business houses and schools declared a holiday.

That afternoon some 7,000 persons elbowed their way into Mechanics' Hall to hear Wilson speak, while thousands more milled around outside. The first part of his address was pitched on a plane of high and nebulous idealism—the customary "prose poem." Wilson's supporters gazed glumly at their abstruse gladiator. But toward the end he aroused tremendous

cheers when he came down to earth and revealed a determination to strike back at his Senatorial critics. "I have fighting
blood in me," he boasted, "and it is sometimes a delight to let
it have scope . . ."

Was the speech in Boston a mistake? Was it tactically wise
to stop off in the largest city of Senator Lodge's state and make
a provocative address? Would not the Senator resent this apparent insult, and sharpen his knife to razor edge?

There is little reason to suppose that the Boston speech made
any difference one way or another. Lodge was out to "knife"
Wilson anyhow, and it is difficult to see how this incident had
any relation to his subsequent course. As for the other hostile
Senators, they had already thrown down the gauntlet while
Wilson was on the Atlantic, if not before.

On the evening of February 26, 1919, two days after landing in Boston, Wilson kept his dinner rendezvous at the White
House with the Senate and House foreign relations committees. The atmosphere was tense. The attacks on the League
had been continuing in the Senate. Senator Borah refused to
attend on the ground that he would be honor bound not to
reveal confidential information, and he wanted to reveal all
the information he could. Senator Fall, of later Teapot Dome
infamy, also stayed away.

Wilson discussed the League with the Congressional representatives until nearly midnight. He explained various provisions at length, and expressed the hope that the Covenant
would be accepted without fundamental change.

The President's friends testified that he appeared to very
good advantage, answering questions with completeness and
candor. His critics came away with a different story. Senator
Brandegee of Connecticut, an intense man who later committed suicide, subjected the President to the cross-examina-
tion of a prosecuting attorney. Lodge wrote in his diary that
Wilson's performance was "anything but good." The next
day Senator Brandegee was quoted as saying: "I feel as if I

had been wandering with Alice in Wonderland and had tea with the Mad Hatter."

The conference was clearly a failure. Certainly no new converts had been made. Those who were hostile to the League had evidently come for the purpose of finding confirmation of their suspicions.

Wilson was much irritated by the whole affair, and when he returned to Paris he told Colonel House that "*your* dinner" was a "failure as far as getting together was concerned." Senators Lodge and Knox, he said, had sat in sullen silence, refusing to enter into the spirit of the discussion. Colonel House replied that Wilson had done something to mollify public opinion, for he had refuted the charge that he was so dictatorial that he could not consult Senators. Wilson supposed that this was so, but he still felt that little or nothing had been gained with the Senate.

Apparently nothing had. One cannot recapture one's horse by locking the door after it is stolen.

4

Many people still labor under the delusion that criticisms of the hastily drafted League Covenant were voiced only or primarily by Senators. As a matter of fact men in public and private life, both at home and abroad, as well as newspapers throughout the country, were all airing their opinions. The Covenant was not yet in final form, and the possibility of amendment doubtless encouraged many persons to express their views.

It is not fair to suggest, either, that all those who criticized the Covenant were motivated by partisan or malicious motives. Earnest friends of the League of Nations are prone to give the impression that the Covenant was attacked only by those who were stupid, depraved, or ill intentioned.

This is far from the mark. Many of the suggestions that were made, notably those by men like Taft and Root, were designed to be helpful, and genuinely to improve the Covenant. Many other persons sincerely believed that this was too sharp a break with the past to be taken all at one leap. They argued that the policy of Washington—nonentanglement in the purely political affairs of Europe—had served the Republic well, and that it would be folly to throw it into the ash can, and then dash madly after Wilson's will-o'-the-wisp. Although this point of view did not take properly into account the nature of our shrinking world, the names of the Founding Fathers could be used with great effect to give it support.

But it is undoubtedly true that partisan and other less worthy motives were also present. It is a noteworthy fact that the great bulk of support for the League of Nations came from the Democratic press of the country, while the great bulk of the opposition was voiced by the Republican and Hearst press. Relatively few Democratic newspapers of importance opposed the League; though a considerable number of Republican journals were to be found in the same camp with the Covenant.

This is a curious situation. The League was designed to benefit all the nations, including ourselves; and if peace came to the world as a result of the League, the benefits would accrue not only to Democrats but to the entire country as well. Surely if any issue in foreign policy should have been completely divested of partisanship, it was this one.

But American politics move in a mysterious way. We have a two-party system, and it is the business of the party out of power to criticize the proposals of the party in power. Wilson happened to be President. He happened also to be a Democrat. If he drove through his tremendous program and brought lasting peace to the world, he would add new and greener laurels to his already laurel-wreathed brow. He might, on the strength of his great diplomatic victory, consent to run for a third term, and if he did, he might well win. There was in fact considerable third-term agitation already.

Yet even if Wilson did not choose to run again, his success

with the League would shed a brilliant luster on his party. The Democratic platform would point with pride to his transcendent achievement; Democratic spellbinders would gloat from a thousand stumps. Their great cry would be that only the Democratic party, on the basis of its accomplishments, could be entrusted with the national administration, and particularly with the launching of the League which Wilson had fathered.

The Democrats, of course, insisted that the League was not a partisan issue, but an organization for the good of the entire country. Yet if it had been finally accepted, they would have made partisan capital out of it. On these narrow grounds, at least, the Republicans were justified in anticipating such partisan praise by interposing partisan obstruction. Such are the vagaries of politics. Such are the difficulties when delicate problems involving foreign affairs are thrown into the dusty arena of partisanship.

So it was that political motives became intermixed with sincere ones. The true partisan will put the good of his party above the good of his country. If he is also conscientious and resourceful, he will not find it difficult to discover reasons for believing that the good of the party is also the good of the country.

The supreme goal of a political party is to attain power, and then to stay in power. If, in so doing, it is necessary to throw overboard all plans for a new international order, those plans will be thrown overboard—or at least the attempt will be made.

5

Some of the criticisms of the League Covenant were of a general nature. It was a war-breeding, entangling alliance—an unjustifiable and dangerous departure from the precepts of Washington. It involved yielding a substantial part of our sovereign rights. It was a superstate which would jeopardize and overbear its constituent members. It was a manifestation of Wilson's "Messiah complex"—of his desire to become the "drum-major of civilization."

Most of these arguments were advanced with greater vehemence at a later date, when the Covenant was put into final form and the real fight began. But in February and March of

It's So Sudden—We'd Like a Little
Time to Think It Over
(Courtesy of the Columbus *Dispatch*)

1919, when the Covenant was still in a formative state, certain specific objections were raised so insistently and persistently that something obviously had to be done about them.

First, public opinion demanded a reservation regarding our sacred Monroe Doctrine, which few Americans understood but which most of them would defend unto death. Suppose that the members of this new superstate should come over and threaten us or interfere with us, just as the Holy Alliance had seemed about to do in 1823?

Second, the Covenant contained no provision for with-drawal from the League. After we had stuck our heads into the lion's mouth, and did not like the prospects, there we should have to stay.

Third, there was no provision for exempting purely domestic disputes from the purview of the League. Suppose that this superbody should lay unhallowed hands on the sacred ark of our tariff? Suppose that the Japanese, or the Chinese, or the Hindus should try to flood our fair land, and the League prevented us from excluding them?

Fourth, the Covenant did not specifically permit a nation to refuse an unwelcome mandate. Suppose that the League should assign us Armenia, or some other place that would involve a large army of American boys and vexatious entanglements in the Old World?

Wilson did not believe that any of these four proposed changes was either necessary or desirable. Most of the things to which the American people were objecting had been fully discussed in the League Commission, and finally rejected for what seemed to be good reason.

But so evident was the determination of the public not to accept the Covenant without these four changes that Wilson was finally convinced of the necessity of going back to Paris and reopening the whole issue. Of his success, more will be said later.

6

The various objections to the Covenant have here been discussed at such length as perhaps to give the erroneous impression that public opinion was generally in opposition. On the contrary, the indications are that in March, 1919, the American people were on the whole strongly if not overwhelmingly favorable to the League.

At best, public opinion is a phantom thing, difficult to measure. This was before the age of the various public opinion "sampling" polls, which on the whole have proved surprisingly accurate. Fortunately the *Literary Digest* had already begun to pioneer in the field by polling newspaper editors throughout the country, and its only general poll on the League, published on April 5, 1919, is highly significant.

The *Literary Digest* had sent an inquiry to all daily newspapers in the United States, asking: "Do you favor the proposed League of Nations?" The replies were tabulated as follows: Yes, 718; No, 181; Conditional, 478. From the standpoint of circulation, the figures were: Yes, 9,886,449; No, 4,326,882 (2,488,976 represented the circulation of Hearst newspapers); Conditional, 6,792,461.

On the basis of these statistics, those who had definite opinions on the League were favorable to it by a margin of two to one. The Democratic press, especially in the solid South, was almost unanimous for the League, while the great body of conditional votes was Republican. The most formidable opposition came from Hearst, who was bitterly anti-British, and who resented any League of Nations in which the British Empire would have six votes. His position was vociferously applauded by Irish-Americans.

At this point one highly important fact must be particularly emphasized. If, as seems clear, a strong majority of those who had made up their minds were for the League, their support must have been very strong indeed, because they were asked to pass judgment on the unrevised draft. If, without the proposed amendments, the League could command this much popular support, it would presumably enlist even more if and when the suggested changes were written into the Covenant.

The figures compiled by the *Literary Digest* are not satisfactory, but they are all we have. The newspaper editors were asked to give not merely their own views but those of the section in which they lived, and their replies square with such other fragmentary evidence as we have. Even Senator Lodge was then conceding in private that a majority of the American people favored the League.

Wilson boasted publicly and said privately that an "over-whelming" sentiment supported the Covenant. He doubtless saw the *Literary Digest* figures, and they may have given him a false confidence in his dealings with the Senate. A majority of the country may have favored the League, but a two-thirds majority was necessary in the Senate. It was in fact theoretically possible for Senators representing about 10 per cent of the nation's population to kill the Treaty.

One other point. Doubts are often slow in germinating. Given a little time, and assiduous cultivating and watering, the minority might blossom forth into a majority.

7

Early in March, 1919, shortly before Wilson's return to Paris, the opposition in the Senate bared its teeth in an ugly fashion.

The Republican minority deliberately filibustered vital appropriation bills to death before the short session ended on March 4, 1919. Ordinarily, Congress would not meet again until December, 1919, some nine months later, at which time the Republican majority would take control of the Senate. But with the appropriation bills killed, Wilson would have to summon Congress in extraordinary session if the government was to carry on. This meant that the Republicans could organize the Senate some six months in advance of the normal time, and keep a more careful watch on the President. More important, they could use the floor of Congress as a sounding board for echoing criticisms against the League, and thus weaken his position in Paris.

The stratagem worked perfectly. Wilson was forced to call Congress in special session for May 19, 1919, and it stayed in session until November 19, 1919, the day the Treaty was first laid to rest.

Much more spectacular was a bold move by the opponents of

the League. At two minutes after midnight on the morning of March 4th, Senator Lodge presented to the Senate an extraordinary document that has come to be known as the Round Robin. This was a pronunciamento, drawn up by the Republican leaders at the instance of Senator Brandegee, which announced to the world that the signatories did not find the Covenant of the League acceptable "in the form now proposed." The Round Robin further urged that the Conference address itself to the urgent task of making peace with Germany, while deferring such proposals as the League for later "careful consideration." The document was signed, or soon signed, by thirty-nine Republican Senators or Senators elect. Only thirty-three votes were needed to defeat a treaty.

The New York *Sun* loudly rejoiced: "Woodrow Wilson's League of Nations died in the Senate to-night." George Harvey, a vitriolic editor and a venomous foe of Wilson, who had been castigating "the President's League of Nations Claptrap" and "the League of Denationalized Nations," cried "Honor and Praise" to Lodge and the others who had fathered the Round Robin.

The Round Robin was promptly put on the wires and published in the European press, as the authors intended it to be. Clemenceau, Lloyd George, and the other statesmen in Paris took due notice, as the authors intended they should. When Wilson returned, his voice would ring with much less authority.

Yet the Round Robin, as Senator Hitchcock wrote the President, was not necessarily a sure guarantee of failure. The saving clause regarding the League was "in the form now proposed." This meant that Wilson would have to go back and secure amendments to his Covenant; and this meant that the other powers would seek to extort corresponding concessions before giving in. His position was definitely weaker than it had been when he sailed from Brest.

It is possible that the Round Robin, among other things, was designed to sting the President into some rash declaration or act which could be used against him. If so, it was strikingly successful. Wilson had come home extending the olive branch, belatedly, to the Senate. For his pains he had got a sullen reception at the White House dinner; then a vicious Senate filibuster; then an unprecedented Round Robin. Wilson's vaunted fighting blood was now boiling; henceforth it was war to the death with the Senate.

8

Wilson was scheduled to deliver a farewell speech at the Metropolitan Opera House, in New York City, on the evening of the day the Round Robin was presented, and the day before his sailing for France. From the Pennsylvania Station, in the nation's metropolis, all the way to the meeting place, he received a prolonged ovation, comparable only with the demonstrations on Armistice Day.

Five thousand people jammed the Opera House. Enrico Caruso, immortal tenor, sang "The Star-Spangled Banner." Wilson and ex-President Taft walked onto the platform arm in arm, together with Governor Alfred E. Smith, who introduced them. Taft, who had been engaging in a strenuous barnstorming campaign for the League, and whose portly frame was so fatigued that he came against the advice of physicians, spoke forcefully and effectively.

When Taft sat down amid warm applause, the band played George M. Cohan's stirring "Over There." Wilson rose and, after waiting for a mass handkerchief salute to subside, announced that he accepted the implications of the stirring song. "I will not come back," he pledged, "till it's over, over there." Then he launched into a fighting speech, during the course of which he said:

". . . When that treaty comes back gentlemen on this side will find the Covenant not only in it, but so many threads of the treaty tied to the covenant that you cannot dissect the cove-

nant from the treaty without destroying the whole vital structure. The structure of peace will not be vital without the
League of Nations, and no man is going to bring back a cadaver
with him."

This revealed a fighting but indiscreet Wilson. Granted that
his strategy was sound, it was poor tactics to boast about it.
The "irreconcilables" in the Senate were out to unhorse him
anyhow, but this ill-tempered outburst publicly revealed an
angered, self-centered, headstrong Wilson, who was determined to have his own way at any cost, and who was apparently
unwilling to listen to the sweet reasonableness of compromise.

Many persons in our democracy react unfavorably to such a
leader, and there can be no doubt that this flare-up gained
Wilson little or nothing. The Indianapolis *Star* found that
"it is hard to escape the impression that President Wilson is
riding for a fall."

That evening the *George Washington* drew slowly away
from the pier at Hoboken on the return trip to France. There
was no pomp or display comparable to that of the first departure, though a few hundred of the faithful were there to cheer
their President. To the newspaper reporters Wilson remarked
that the people were with him, even if the politicians were not.

The auguries were not nearly so bright as they had been
when the hope-freighted *George Washington* had sailed in
December. The Senate was up in arms. The country was beginning to mutter about the stubborn President. And the real
fight at Paris for a treaty with Germany had not yet begun.

CHAPTER FOURTEEN

THE BATTLE BEGINS

"The difficulties here would have been incredible to me before I got here." WOODROW WILSON, *April 25, 1919.*

I

IN THE early evening of March 13, 1919, the good ship *George Washington* again steamed into the harbor of Brest. Although a few banners were hastily hung out proclaiming "Welcome to Wilson," and although the shouted greetings were spontaneous and cordial, this reception naturally lacked the magnitude and exuberance of the first one. Messiahs tend to arouse less enthusiasm the more they show themselves: the role requires aloofness and the spell of mystery. And the French people were beginning to have grave doubts as to the ability of this particular Messiah from the West to deliver the Promised Land of Perpetual Peace.

Wilson was anxious to discover precisely what had happened in his absence, for no general can leave the battlefield for a month and find things just as he had left them. Colonel House met Wilson at the dock, and hastened to tell him in detail how the battle had gone. The two men were closeted together for several hours, and when Wilson emerged from the conference his wife was shocked by his appearance. Seemingly he had "aged ten years." He smiled bitterly and said: "House has given away everything I had won before we left Paris. He has compromised on every side, and so I have to start all over again . . ." In this incident Mrs. Wilson sees the beginning of her husband's tragic collapse.

The testimony of a loving spouse must always be accepted with caution, and in this case it is clear that Mrs. Wilson entertained a strong distrust of the quiet Colonel. But it is also clear that Wilson, with good reason or not, was displeased with what he heard, and his growing coolness toward House seemingly dates from this time.

Briefly, the story is this. Before the Conference assembled it was generally though hazily taken for granted that there would be two treaties, a preliminary and a final one. The preliminary peace would impose military, naval, and aerial terms on Germany. Then the Conference could move on in a leisurely fashion to the larger problem of making the final economic, territorial, and other terms; and in these discussions the German delegates could take part.

The plan for two treaties had a great deal to commend it. The immediate military situation would be taken care of, and then there would be no need for frantic haste in the making of the definitive peace. Perspective would sharpen; passions would cool off; and sanity would return. The Allies would also have an opportunity to discuss terms among themselves, and then present a solid front to the enemy. This would prevent the Germans from playing one Ally against another, much as Talleyrand had done at the Congress of Vienna in 1814–1815.

Wilson was quite favorable at first to the idea of a preliminary military peace. Upon sailing for America, he left Colonel House to work for it, and even to discuss the inclusion of territorial and economic adjustments, but these were to be withheld from final decision pending his return.

During Wilson's absence the Conference for the first time rolled up its sleeves and came squarely to grips with the problem of making a treaty with Germany. The French did not want the preliminary peace to contain military and naval terms only, as Wilson had originally planned and as was generally intended. If this were done, the Allied armies would feel free to demobilize, and the victors might be unable to club the Germans into an acceptance of the final treaty. Steps were therefore taken to include in the preliminary peace certain territorial and other terms that had not been originally contemplated. The League would be postponed until the final treaty, because much work remained to be done on it, and because it seemed imperative to rush through the preliminary pact at once.

When Wilson returned to Paris he found the Conference pushing through a preliminary treaty which would dispose of the most pressing military, economic, and other problems, while leaving the League for later consideration. This might mean that in the last-minute scramble the Conference would forget all about Wilson's pet scheme. Everywhere people were saying, "The League is dead."

Alarmed by this prospect, Wilson hastened to issue an emphatic statement to the press on March 15, 1919, the day after his return to Paris. He announced that the Conference had formally voted to make the Covenant an integral part of the Treaty, and that he would stand on that decision. This verbal bombshell caused a sensation, and aroused strong resentment among the anti-League newspapers of England, France, and particularly of the United States.

2

Certain writers of the more dramatic school, notably Ray Stannard Baker, have seen in this episode a gigantic and sinister conspiracy on the part of the British and the French, aided and abetted by Colonel House, to "sidetrack" the League of Nations.

There apparently was no such conspiracy. Colonel House kept closely in touch with Wilson by wire, and faithfully informed him of all important developments. It does not appear that in any important particular House deviated from the parting instructions of his chief, although he was by nature a compromiser, and he may have misunderstood the President's views. Nor is there evidence that the British and French officials had any intention of backing down on their agreement to include the League in the final treaty.

But Wilson evidently feared that this might happen; otherwise it is difficult to explain why he should have issued his proclamation out of a clear sky. It is possible, of course, that he had no deep-seated suspicions, but was merely trying to make assurance doubly sure. In any event, he must have suspected, whether rightly or not, that something was afoot.

This reverberating declaration was the epitaph of the preliminary peace. Wilson had gone home favoring such a scheme; he returned opposing it. There is some direct evidence, and a great deal of circumstantial evidence, that he was thinking of the Senate, about which he had forgotten, but which he had now seen at first hand. And he did not like the looks of what he had seen.

If there were to be two treaties, one preliminary and one final, they would both have to be approved by the Senate. If the preliminary peace covered only military and naval terms, but not a League, as originally planned, the Senate almost certainly would consent to it. But if the final peace contained the League, as contemplated, the perverse Senators, having approved the preliminary peace, might balk. If there was only one treaty, with the League firmly riveted in, then the Senate would have to accept it, and the League would come into being.

So it was that all plans for framing a preliminary peace were thrown out the window, and, incredible though it may seem, the Conference realized for the first time that what had started out in January to be a preliminary peace was now to be the definitive peace. By inserting the League, by adding here and patching there, the final draft could be thrown together.

3

Wilson's torpedoing of the preliminary-peace plan led to far-reaching and momentous consequences.

The ultimate result—and the supreme irony—was that the Peace Conference never really met. The official title of the gathering was, and remained, the Preliminary Conference of the Allied and Associated Powers. The original plan, as already noted, was for the Preliminary Conference to draw up the preliminary peace, decide on the final terms to be presented to the Germans, and then discuss those terms orally with the German representatives. Now, with the preliminary conference telescoped into a final conference, and the preliminary

"Look Out, or I Won't Consider Myself Defeated."

(From the New York *World*; reprinted by permission)

peace into a final peace, there was no place for face-to-face conferences with the enemy. This, as we shall see, was a development of the greatest importance in arousing German bitterness against the Treaty of Versailles.

We should also observe that when the negotiators in Paris began drafting what they supposed was a preliminary treaty, they included a number of "maximum demands." They naturally expected that when the German delegates arrived, and the bargaining began, the "maximum demands" would be whittled down by the usual compromises.

When the decision was made to rush the preliminary peace through as a final peace, many of these "maximum demands" remained as final terms. This, as Harold Nicolson says, accounts in considerable measure for the severity of the Treaty of Versailles.

It is not fair to suggest that all this was Wilson's fault. He was only partially responsible—and largely in a negative way—for the disorganization and planlessness at Paris. One may indeed say in his defense that there would have been ample time to draw up a preliminary treaty if the Conference had met in mid-December, when he had expected it to meet.

In the final analysis, two important factors apparently killed the preliminary peace. One was French fear of a general demobilization before Germany was brought to heel. The other was Wilson's determination that the League of Nations—which he put ahead of everything else—should run no unnecessary risks, either at the hands of the Conference or at those of the Senate.

4

Wilson was now in an extremely embarrassing position, for the Covenant of the League—that "living thing" which had been "born" at the last plenary session—was in need of surgery.

Not only the Senate, but American public opinion as well, was demanding amendments. Sincere friends of the League in the United States, men like William Howard Taft and A. Lawrence Lowell, were telling Wilson bluntly that without these amendments the Senate probably would reject the treaty; with them, it could not avoid approving the treaty.

Wilson's own impulse was to stand pat, for he still did not think that the Senate would dare to incur the odium of putting

the axe to the whole treaty in order to chop out the League.
To him the proposed amendments were irrelevant or repetitious. Why, for example, insert any special mention of the
Monroe Doctrine when the Covenant of the League merely extended the security principle of the Monroe Doctrine to the
entire world?

Colonel House exerted strong pressure to budge the stubborn Wilson from his position, and in this he had the loyal
support of Lord Robert Cecil, the most distinguished British
advocate of the Covenant. Cecil was anxious that the League
should not fail, and he recognized the necessity of meeting
Senatorial opposition. This is an ironical situation indeed: a
British statesman more keenly aware of the necessity of placat-
ing the Senate than the American President himself! Significantly and ominously, Cecil found that Wilson was receptive
to amendments on their own merits, but when any suggestion
was made of appeasing the Senate, he was "up in arms in a
moment."

But Wilson's reluctance to propose amendments was by no
means pure stubbornness. For one thing he would have to re
convene the League of Nations Commission. If he brought in
new amendments, then the other powers would be privileged
to bring in theirs. The European premiers, hardly less than
Wilson, had Senates of their own to appease. Old amendments
which had been voted down would be dusted off and brought
back; new and even more offensive ones would doubtless be
presented. Some of these would be introduced in good faith;
others, for their bargaining power in securing additional concessions from the United States.

Wilson was finally convinced that there was no other way
out, and the League of Nations Commission was again convened. Colonel House records a revealing incident which
further disposes of the charge that the President was a dull-
witted professor. On March 26, Wilson announced to the
League Commission that he intended to appoint the "old drafting committee." At this point House slipped him a memoran-

dum containing the names of a new drafting committee, so Wilson, without a halt, continued, "but I think it would be an imposition to ask them to serve again, therefore I name the following."

To gain time, the League of Nations Commission met in the evening, as before; and it debated the various amendments in five exhausting sessions, two of which lasted until after midnight.

5

Two of the amendments that American public opinion was demanding went through the League Commission without undue difficulty. These were the right to refuse a mandate, and the exemption of domestic questions such as immigration and tariffs from League jurisdiction.

But two other American demands—the right to withdraw from the League and a reservation safeguarding the Monroe Doctrine—encountered stormy weather. Even Lloyd George tried to bludgeon the United States into abandoning its current naval program in return for British support of the Monroe Doctrine. He seems to have succeeded to the extent of securing from Wilson an informal pledge to suspend the second three year building program then before Congress.

The strongest opposition, as might be expected, came from the French, who vehemently argued that the two American amendments would further weaken a League which was already well-nigh toothless. If the Americans could walk out whenever they wanted to, what would become of French security? If the great powers should recognize the Monroe Doctrine, did this not mean that the United States would not have to intervene in the Old World to honor its commitments? Then where again was French security?

The French were shrewd bargainers, and they played their cards for all they were worth. They knew that they had the Americans at a serious disadvantage, because newspapers on both sides of the Atlantic contained emphatic statements from United States Senators and other leading Americans to the effect that no League could be approved without these amendments.

Privately, the French admitted that they did not attach much importance to the Monroe Doctrine, and that they were making all this outcry for bargaining purposes. But their obstruction, whether serious or not, was a great trial to those who sincerely wanted to make progress. At one session the quiet but exasperated Colonel House growled that the French "could go to Hell seven thousand miles deep."

Wilson put up a brilliant fight for a reservation on the Monroe Doctrine, and one of his extemporaneous speeches before the League Commission was of such "witching eloquence" that even the hardened secretaries forgot to take notes. In the end the French yielded, but the circumstantial evidence indicates that they utilized their "nuisance value" by forcing Wilson to accord them a limited military occupation of the Rhine. Whatever the price, the Monroe Doctrine was specifically safeguarded, which in itself was a signal victory, for Europe until then had persistently refused to give formal recognition to the American dogma.

But the victory was Pyrrhic. American demands encouraged the French, the Italians, and the Japanese to press for concessions, including the bothersome "racial equality" amendment of Japan. France's confidence in the League, already at a low point, was further undermined, and this partly explains the French acceptance of the Security Treaty, which, as we shall see, opened a new Pandora's box of woe.

It seems reasonable to conclude that Wilson could have secured all these amendments with less effort and at less cost if he had written them into the first draft of the League. He probably would have done so if he had paid more attention to what the American people were saying, and especially if he had given them an opportunity to criticize his general ideas before the League Commission began its work.

Wilson nevertheless had reason to be pleased when the plenary session of the Conference, on April 28, 1919, unanimously approved the final draft of the Covenant with its twenty-six articles. Although one of the French delegates put in the usual word for security, Clemenceau peremptorily cut him short, and presumably in accord with the Rhineland-Monroe Doctrine deal, gavelled the pact through.

The stillborn infant, after a good deal of surgery at the hands of the doctors, had been given a patched-up and not too satisfactory birth certificate—yet it was a birth certificate, and it was unanimously approved.

6

The last week of March and the first three weeks of April were the crisis of the Conference—what Ray Stannard Baker calls "the Dark Period." To expedite business and plug up leaks (Lloyd George was angry over newspaper attacks), the Big Four began meeting together officially for the first time as the Council of Four, thus superseding the Council of Ten. The convalescing Clemenceau, not fully recovered from the assassin's bullet, was much less alert than before; and the walls re-echoed his violent paroxysms of coughing.

The world weighed heavily on Wilson's shoulders, as events tumbled over one another with breath-taking rapidity. Hungary and Bavaria were going Bolshevik; the "succession states" of Jugoslavia, Czechoslovakia, and Poland were keeping up a constant clamor for their claims. At night, Wilson spent his energies fighting for amendments with the League of Nations Commission; during the day he wrestled with reparations, the Saar Basin, a Rhineland buffer state, French occupation of the Rhine; security for France, Fiume for Italy, Shantung for Japan. The past, the present, and the future were locked in death grapple.

All these problems ran concurrently with one another, and a decision on one frequently had a good deal to do with helping to solve another. The Saar Basin was one of the key logs in the jam—if not the key log itself—and we shall turn to it first.

This area adjoined Lorraine on the north and east, and derived its importance from immensely rich deposits of coal, which, taken in conjunction with the iron ore of Lorraine, furnished the key to an industrial empire. In prewar days, the Saar Basin had annually produced some 17,000,000 tons of coal, or about 8 per cent of the entire output of the German Empire. The reserves of the Saar alone were estimated to exceed those

Germany's Territorial Losses

of all France, which was a country relatively poor in coal.

The French wanted the Saar at all costs. They realized that war with Germany was probable in the future, and whatever they took away from their hereditary foe would weaken him by that much, and make aggression less likely. Whatever they subtracted would add to their own industrial potential; and they were well aware that modern wars are fought as much with smokestacks as with guns. They also knew that the German Reich had been built not so much by blood and iron as by coal and iron. Finally, the Saar Basin was in itself an important strategic link in France's proposed eastern defenses.

The French claimed the Saar coal on two grounds. First, restitution. From 1793 to 1815 roughly one-half of the area had been in the possession of France, and as the historical argument was being used in Poland and Alsace-Lorraine, why should it be overlooked here? Second, reparation. The retreating German armies had deliberately and diabolically wrecked the French coal mines, both as an act of presumed military necessity and as a means of hamstringing French industrial competition after the war. France could therefore claim as compensation—and reasonably so—her historical half of the Saar, plus ownership of the mines in the German half. Hence the issue became entangled with both reparation and security.

There was only one catch—and a very serious one. The population of the Saar was overwhelmingly German, and Wilson regarded it as an intolerable flouting of self-determination, already badly flouted, to hand over several hundred thousand Germans to the tender mercies of French rule. This would also do violence to his "no annexations" pledge of February, 1918. The crux of the problem was how to get the coal without the people.

7

On the *George Washington*, Wilson had urged his experts to tell him what was right and he would fight for it. But in this case "right" was not a simple matter of black and white. The Point on self-determination cried out against French annexation; yet Point VIII promised France restoration and reparation. What was to be done when the Points clashed with one another?

The American experts, it is important to note, were im-

pressed by the historical and economic arguments. Some of the
ruined French mines would not come into production for an
estimated five years, and it seemed only fair that France should
have the coal of the Saar. This certainly was in keeping with
both the spirit and the letter of the Fourteen Points.

But Wilson was more moved by self-determination, and completely unmoved by the argument that France had held a part
of the territory for a brief period under Napoleon more than
a century ago. He rightly contended that much injustice could
be perpetuated by citing previous acts of injustice. Besides, as
he told Clemenceau, "That was a hundred years ago—a hundred years is a very long time." "Yes," replied the Tiger cut-
tingly, "a very long time in the history of the United States."

The atmosphere between Clemenceau and Wilson became
more and more tense. The Tiger made the utterly preposterous statement that there were 150,000 Frenchmen in the
Saar; Wilson branded this as a deliberate misstatement. Clemenceau hotly accused Wilson of being a pro-German. Wilson
thereupon asked whether he should go home to America if
France did not get what she wanted. "I do not wish you to go
home," said Clemenceau, "but I intend to do so myself." With
that, he flung himself out of the room.

Interested intermediaries smoothed the Tiger's fur, and
asked him to have a talk with Wilson. "Talk with Wilson!" he
snorted. "How can I talk to a fellow who thinks himself the
first man in two thousand years to know anything about peace
on earth?"

8

At the very height of the crisis over the Saar and other pressing problems, Wilson's health gave way, and it may be doubted
whether he ever fully recovered. Herbert Hoover found that
during the period of convalescence Wilson had lost his former
alertness and flexibility of mind, and had to be pushed into
decisions.

Wilson had never been robust. Nervous, high-strung, and suffering from indigestion and neuritis, he had entered the White House in 1913 with a stomach pump and a generous supply of headache pills. The distinguished Dr. S. Weir Mitchell, of Philadelphia, had predicted that he would not finish out his first term without a physical collapse. The first years of Wilson's administration had been unusually turbulent on the domestic front; then came the outbreak of the European war, the death of the dearly beloved wife of his youth, the vexations of neutrality, the gigantic task of mobilizing an unready America for war; and then piled on top of all that, the inferno of a peace conference abroad and venomous political opposition at home. We can believe Mrs. Wilson when she says that her husband grew thin and visibly grayer during the hectic weeks at Paris.

Why Wilson did not collapse sooner will always remain something of a mystery. The explanation is perhaps to be found in his indomitable spirit, his iron self-discipline, the four restful trips across the Atlantic on the *George Washington*, and the unrelenting vigilance of his personal physician, Dr. Cary T. Grayson.

At Paris, Wilson worked too hard, and delegated too little authority. Only occasionally would he go for a hurried automobile ride or a brief walk. Between conferences he would step quickly to the window, and hastily inhale a few breaths of fresh air, as if to seek a few additional ounces of energy to revive the sputtering machine.

Much of the time he was running on sheer nerve. Ray Stannard Baker would go up to his room at night after the meetings of the Big Four, and find him "utterly beaten, worn out, his face quite haggard and one side of it and the eye twitching painfully . . ." But the next morning he seemed refreshed and eager to get on with the fight.

On April 3, 1919, Wilson took to his bed, with what the press said was a "cold." The befuddled newsmen had no real inkling either of the seriousness of the crisis over the Saar or the seriousness of Wilson's condition. The attack was very sudden; he was seized with violent coughing; and his fever shot up to 103 degrees. Dr. Grayson was deeply worried, fearing at first that poison had been placed in Wilson's food, but he quickly diagnosed the malady as an attack of the deadly influenza then sweeping the Continent.

But the show had to go on. In the book-lined outer room, beyond Wilson's bedroom, Lloyd George, Clemenceau, and Orlando continued to sit, with the faithful Colonel House representing the ailing President. From time to time House would bring into the bedroom some new French proposal, or a revamped old one. To every demand for surrender the feverish Wilson sent back a firm "No."

By April 7, Wilson's patience was at an end. On that day he dispatched a dramatic cablegram to Washington inquiring how soon the *George Washington* could be put in readiness for the return trip to France. To those on the "inside," the implication was plain that Wilson was going home if he could not have his way. Either that, or he was bluffing.

This sensational telegram was headline news in America. It was interpreted as meaning one of two things: either the Conference was hopelessly deadlocked, or the work was so nearly completed that Wilson could plan to go home. Nothing could better illustrate the fog in which the newsmen had to grope.

The precise effect of this bluff—if it was a bluff—is a matter of dispute. From Washington, Joseph P. Tumulty cabled in alarm that American opinion was reacting unfavorably to what seemed an act of petulance: it looked as though Wilson would not play with the other boys unless they played his way. The French press took up the refrain and jeered that he was going home to mother. The Tiger muttered privately, "I am disgusted . . . Wilson acts like a cook who keeps her trunk ready in the hallway. Every day he threatens to leave."

The Tiger could go home when things went badly; he had only to step around the corner. But Wilson could not run away without creating an international sensation.

The French knew that Wilson could not afford to leave the Conference in the lurch. If he did so, it would probably collapse, Europe would go Bolshevik, there would be no treaty, above all there would be no all-important League of Nations, and Wilson's prestige would hit bottom. His departure would be a public and spectacular confession of failure.

Yet the French realized that they could not afford to take too many chances: Wilson was a stubborn man, and he might just possibly bolt the Conference. If this blind Samson should pull down the temple, they, as dwellers within the temple, would suffer the most. And by now they were beginning to count on a strong defensive military alliance with both Great Britain and the United States.

9

Whether as a result of the *George Washington* incident, or in spite of it, the French at this time began to reveal a less obdurate spirit. This was due partly if not primarily to Wilson's willingness to meet them at least halfway, and during the period of the President's convalescence a compromise was worked out.

The French would not get the Saar in fee simple, but they would secure ownership of the coal mines for a period of fifteen years, during which time the entire area would be governed by a Commission representing the League of Nations. This aspect of the solution undoubtedly appealed to Wilson, for it would further dignify his League by giving it something important to do.

At the end of fifteen years, there would be a plebiscite to determine whether Germany or France should retain the coveted basin. This meant that unless the French in the meantime could convert the German population to French allegiance, the Saar would go permanently to the Reich.

The compromise solution on the Saar had much to commend it. Self-determination would be respected—after fifteen years; and full reparation would be exacted, because the French coal mines certainly could be repaired within that period. Thus the principal claim of both Wilson and the French could be met. As for the historical argument, if the French lost the Saar, they would merely lose what they had lost a hundred years before. And a hundred years is a long time, even in the history of France.

Wilson's bold stand for self-determination in the Saar was not without far-reaching aftereffects. The French press sneered at the settlement as "neither fish, flesh, fowl, nor good red herring." Deprived of this additional economic and military security, France sought compensation elsewhere, and this in part accounts for her insistence upon the Rhineland and for her acceptance of the Security Treaty, to which we shall turn shortly.

The temporary solution of the Saar problem set the stage for a tremendous boost to German nationalism, and a public humiliation of France. With so much depending on the vote of each inhabitant of the basin, a protracted electioneering campaign began, which came to a climax in 1935, when Adolf Hitler was in the saddle. Over 90 per cent of those who marched to the polls voted a vigorous "Ja" for Hitler and the Reich. It was a bloodless yet impressive triumph for the paranoiac paperhanger.

On the other hand, if the Saar had been ceded outright to France, it would have become another Alsace-Lorraine. As much as Danzig or the Sudetenland it would have figured in Hitler's program of reconquest.

On the basis of abstract justice, as seen through the lenses of the Fourteen Points, Wilson was probably right in opposing the French claims. On the basis of history, economics, and reparation, France had a strong case—a case that appealed to the American experts. On the basis of security, the French had perhaps an even stronger case; the partial loss of the Saar, later a complete loss, removed an important cornerstone from the edifice of security which they planned to erect. We shall see later what the French feeling of insecurity had to do with the wrecking of the peace settlement.

A cynic, especially a French cynic, would say that Wilson should have listened to his experts and kept quiet. If he had done so, France almost certainly would have won the Saar. This would have meant an act of injustice, but there were already injustices in the Treaty. And since there were already enough to infuriate an enchained Germany, why not let the French have the Saar, so that they could fight more effectively when the giant burst his chains? If this was done, the inevitable war might not come so soon, and Germany would wage it with less prospect of success.

But Wilson was gambling for greater stakes. If there were injustices in the Treaty—the full number could not yet be counted—the League would iron them out. And there surely would be enough without deliberately putting them in

CHAPTER FIFTEEN

THE PHANTOM OF
FRENCH SECURITY

"I quite admit that the French cannot see beyond their noses; but after all they are their noses: and, my word, what they do see, they see damned clearly." HAROLD NICOLSON, *May 1, 1919.*

1

SCRATCH THE surface of any problem at the Conference, a recent critic has written, and you get French security. The League, German colonies, the Saar, the Rhineland, Poland, Upper Silesia, reparations, and other questions were all tied in with security, and with one another.

The British were not especially concerned about security. Their principal worry, the German naval arm, had been neatly amputated, and it would take many years to grow another.

But with the French it was different. They were an exhausted nation of 40,000,000, with a declining birth rate, wedged against a neighbor of 60,000,000, with a prolific birth rate and a warlike tradition. And that neighbor did not take kindly to defeat.

France, quite understandably, was suffering from national shell-shock. The mark of the German beast was on her northern departments; upon every empty chair in a widowed or orphaned cottage. After a war which had seared both her soil and her soul, and which had turned on a hair, France was now on top, and she was determined to stay there. Men still living, including Clemenceau, had seen the hated invader twice pour over the French frontier. "My house was in the hands of the Germans in 1814, again in 1870, and again in 1914," sadly remarked Abbé Dimnet. "I pray God that He will make it impossible that it shall ever be in their hands again."

The memory of German incursions deeply colored the attitude of the French. "Each of us lives encased in his own past," observed Clemenceau. "Auguste Comte said that we live dead men's lives and it is true." Everywhere and at all times the constant refrain of the French press was, "Guarantees, guarantees, guarantees." The hated invader must not be permitted to come again.

The crux of the French security problem was the strategic

In Memory of Wilhelm II
(Courtesy of the Chicago *Tribune*)

Rhineland. If the Germans should retain a foothold on the west or French side of the Rhine River, they would have a dangerous springboard for future invasion. But if they were kept on the east side of the Rhine, the French would have the springboard.

The most important French demands in this connection were two. First, the German area west of the Rhine (excluding

Alsace, Lorraine, and the Saar) must be erected into a buffer state, which would be demilitarized and put under the tutelage of France. While it is true that there was a rather vocal pro-annexationist group in France, the Paris government did not demand outright ownership of this region. Clemenceau was content to keep the area a satellite state, though satellite states have a way of gravitating permanently into the embrace of the controlling body. But whether annexed outright or not, the loss of the Rhineland to Germany would mean the loss of some ten thousand square miles of territory, containing vitally important industries, and some five million German people. If this area were shorn away, Germany would be correspondingly weakened, and France correspondingly strengthened. (See map on p. 219.)

The second French demand in connection with the Rhine-land was that Allied troops must occupy bridgeheads on the east bank of the Rhine for thirty years. From these strategic springboards, it would be possible to point a pistol at the heart of a disarmed Germany, and demand the full pound of flesh under the Treaty of Versailles.

2

Both Lloyd George and Woodrow Wilson emphatically opposed tearing the west bank of the Rhine from the side of the Reich. Lloyd George's stock argument was that there must be no new Alsace-Lorraines to agitate Germany for the next generation and threaten Britain with a new world war. Wilson, in addition, objected to the scheme on the ground of self-determination. It would be immoral to detach some five million loyal Germans from the Fatherland in which they had been born, and to which they ardently desired to belong.

After many prolonged sessions in the Council of Four, Clemenceau finally and reluctantly consented to a compromise in which he made two important concessions. First, Germany was to keep her territory *west* of the Rhine. But she was never to fortify it, nor an area fifty kilometers *east* of the Rhine. Second, Allied troops were to occupy strategic bridgeheads on the *east* bank of the Rhine for a maximum of fifteen years, as compared with the thirty that the French had been demanding.

The unreliable Lloyd George sadly relates in his *Memoirs* that one part of the "deal" by which Wilson consented to a limited French occupancy of the Rhine was that Clemenceau would call off his journalistic dogs, which were then yawping at the American President with indecent ferocity. It is possible, however, that Lloyd George was misled by some rather interesting circumstantial evidence. We do know that at this very time Colonel House went to Clemenceau and expressed the hope that the violent attacks on Wilson would cease. The Tiger summoned his secretary and told him emphatically that all these intemperate criticisms must be stopped. The next day the Parisian papers broke out in enthusiastic praise of the President.

While this part of the story is probably correct, we may doubt if it was part of a "deal" with Wilson on the Rhine issue. Wilson was not one to yield great principles for purely personal reasons. When he compromised on principle, it was to yield a lesser principle to save a greater one. The evidence is not conclusive, but it seems that one of the reasons why he gave way on the Rhine occupancy was to save his League of Nations by inducing France to accept a reservation on the Monroe Doctrine.

In any event, the French did consent to give up the Rhineland buffer state, and they did consent to an occupancy of the Rhine for fifteen rather than thirty years. These were apparenly great concessions, and they were naturally opposed with extreme bitterness by President Poincaré, Marshal Foch, and the other French generals. What did Clemenceau receive in return for his seeming surrender?

The answer is: a hard and fast military alliance with Great Britain and the United States, under the terms of which both nations would come to the aid of France in the event of another German invasion.

3

The extraordinary proposal of a security treaty seems to have originated in the fertile brain of Lloyd George. Two days before Wilson's return to Paris in March, 1919, the British Prime Minister told Colonel House that Great Britain was willing to come immediately to the assistance of France should the Germans launch another attack.

Lloyd George discussed the scheme with Wilson upon the latter's arrival in Paris, and out of these discussions came the proposal of the new Triple Alliance. Both Great Britain and the United States would sign separate treaties with France, pledging themselves to come to the aid of their ally in the event of an "unprovoked movement of aggression . . ." But there was one highly significant "escape clause." If either Great Britain or the United States failed to ratify the alliance, then the other signatory power would be released from its commitments.

Clemenceau was bitterly criticized in France for his alleged surrender, but it is highly significant that the Security Treaty was approved by both the Chamber and the Senate without a dissenting vote.

The British House of Commons, which had never before thus pledged its military support in advance to another nation, promptly approved the Security Treaty without a single negative vote and without serious debate. The House of Lords did likewise. It was self-evident in both London and Paris that if the two great Anglo-Saxon powers were to pool their might in support of France, a resurgent Germany would never dare risk war against such an overpowering combination. There could be no surer guarantee of peace in Europe.

What happened in America? The Security Treaty died of inanition in a pigeonhole of the Senate Committee on Foreign

Relations. It was not even accorded the honor of a formal and loquacious rejection by the Senate. There was so little sentiment in favor of it, and so much against it, that it was not even reported out of the committee.

When the United States failed to live up to its part of the bargain—or rather the bargain that Wilson had made for it—the whole structure of the Security Treaty crashed to the ground.

4

Wilson's acceptance of the Security Treaty turned out to be one of his most far-reaching blunders, and one of the least excusable, because he should have been able to foresee the result. He knew—or at times did know—that one of the most pervasive and potent American prejudices was that against military alliances. Ironically, this tradition had grown out of an earlier entanglement with the very same nation with which Wilson was now proposing to entangle us again. Already, as Wilson knew—or did he forget?—the Senatorial big guns were thundering against the weak, permissive entanglement in Article X of the League of Nations. What would they do to a hard and fast military alliance?

Not only did such an entanglement run counter to American tradition but it also ran counter to Wilson's own pronouncements. One of the most telling of his supplementary Fourteen Points had struck hard at military alliances. Not only would he contradict himself but he would seemingly undermine the whole structure of the League if he opened the door for separate military engagements. He would merely be confessing to the world that he had no faith in the new order which he was bringing into being.

All these objections and others were forcefully raised by Wilson's advisers, notably Bliss, Lansing, and White. Such criticisms were promptly seized upon and reechoed by the opposition press at home, just as soon as the rumor leaked out that such a pact was in prospect.

The argument about undermining the League seemed plausible, but on this point at least Wilson could defend himself with vigor. It is true that the Security Treaty was a military alliance, but it was a purely defensive alliance (not contrary to the spirit of the Covenant), and it was to last only during the interim when the League was being established on such strong foundations that it could guarantee French security. Surely if the Senate would swallow the League, it should have no difficulty in swallowing this preliminary and tentative military pact. Wilson seems to have completely rejected the ugly thought that the Senators might refuse to swallow both.

But Wilson did recognize the necessity for compromise and concession. The French would not yield the Rhineland without a Security Treaty—at least, so it seemed—and the deadlock could not continue forever. If he gave them the Rhineland, he would merely be sowing the seeds of a war that would undo all he was doing. The Security Treaty seemed to be much the more desirable alternative.

But was this the only alternative? Lloyd George had suggested a Franco-British treaty of assurance; and it is possible that the French would have accepted this instead of the tripartite treaty, particularly in view of the uncertainties of American ratification. A strong Anglo-French alliance would have been infinitely better than an Anglo-American-French alliance which never came into being, and which had scant prospects of ever coming into being.

Whether Lloyd George would have gone ahead with a purely bilateral treaty, and whether the French would have accepted it, we cannot say. But it seems clear that Wilson's willingness to share the responsibility ended whatever chance there may have been for a dual pact. If he had told Lloyd George and Clemenceau the brutal truth—namely, that a military alliance of any kind was completely out of the question—they probably would have made other arrangements or perhaps no military arrangements whatever. As it turned out—and this eventuality Wilson should have foreseen—the treaty which was drawn up was vastly worse than no treaty at all.

5

We come now to an interesting problem in ethics. What shall we say in defense of statesmen who put their names to treaties which they have good reason to believe will not be approved by the Senate?

If Wilson did not have such doubts, his mental condition must have been deplorable indeed. Even if he had been blind to what was then going on in the Senate, he could hardly have been deaf to the warnings of his own advisers. Colonel House was fearful of the Senate; Henry White dismissed the treaty as simply impossible; Lansing thought it preposterous.

Wilson may have been guilty of self-deception, but one may doubt that he deliberately tried to deceive Clemenceau. Wilson knew—as the worldly-wise Clemenceau knew—that no executive can guarantee in advance what a legislative body will do. Wilson was aware, certainly in his less preoccupied moments, that every treaty which enters the Senate arena runs some risk—often serious risk—of mutilation or death.

It seems fair to assume that Wilson, misreading both history and the signs of the times, entered into this pact in good faith. He doubtless knew that there would be opposition, as there almost always is, but he probably concluded that there was a better than even chance to secure senatorial approval, particularly after he had explained that the treaty merely supplemented and implemented the League, which he took for granted would be approved.

Above all, Wilson had supreme confidence in his expository powers, and especially in his ability to build a fire of public opinion under the recalcitrant Senate. Clemenceau records that when he expressed doubts Wilson "invariably replied with an imperturbable confidence." "America," he said in another connection, "has taken much from me. She will take this also."

But if Wilson was naïve, what shall we say about Clemenceau? The wily old Tiger was giving up French claims to a Rhineland buffer state, and reducing Allied occupation of the Rhine from thirty to fifteen years, in return for a guarantee that rested on the whims of a fickle and already hostile United States Senate. Had the assassin's bullet affected his head as well as his lung?

The answer is that Clemenceau knew all about the uncertainties of Wilson's position—possibly better than Wilson did himself—and made what seemed to be ample provision to meet them.

By the specific terms of the Treaty of Versailles (Article 429), the Allied (including French) troops were not required to leave the Rhineland at the end of fifteen years *if France deemed that her position was not secure*—that is, if the Security Treaty had not been ratified. Provision was also made for the Allies to stay if the reparations clauses were not fully lived up to (Article 430). It is clear that a resourceful French government could have so read the treaty as to keep the Rhineland for generations.

So all that France really gave up was the buffer state, which would be of little military value to Germany, because this area would be demilitarized and French troops would be keeping the watch on the Rhine. France would have preferred the Rhineland, for it would have given her definite economic and military advantages; but before surrendering it she made doubly sure of her eastern frontier. As early as April, 1919, she was also busy forging the network of alliances with the nations of the Little Entente on Germany's eastern flank. France believed in forming all the leagues and pacts she could, while keeping her powder dry.

In return for the Rhineland concession, Clemenceau had a fair chance—so it seemed—of effecting a military alliance of transcendent importance to French security. If he won his gamble, he would win a tremendous advantage. If he lost, French soldiers could camp on the Rhine indefinitely. So what could France lose?

6

What else should Clemenceau have done? What else could he have done?

As we have seen, his critics in France assailed him mercilessly for letting the Rhineland go, and for turning up with nothing better than the Security Treaty. But they voted for it.

This was a colossal opportunity. Never before had the British been willing to commit themselves in advance to a guarantee of France's eastern border. Never before had the United States been willing to commit itself in advance to protect the borders of any European nation. The two overseas giants, taken together, could form a combination that would frighten Germany into perpetual submission. This would in effect be a continuation of the core of the alliance of the victors. What more could France ask for?

Clemenceau did not solicit the alliance. It was freely offered by Lloyd George and Wilson. Should The Tiger have spurned it? Could he have said that a tiny Rhineland buffer state was worth more than an alliance with the irresistible Anglo-Saxon combination?

All things considered, Wilson is more to be censured for having offered the alliance than Clemenceau for having accepted it. Where the stakes are enormous, a gamble is often worth while, or at least excusable. But this was not even a gamble. The treaty simply did not have as much as a fighting chance in the Senate of the United States, and Wilson should have recognized this. If he had taken Senators to Paris, they doubtless would have told him. Whether he would have listened, after disregarding the advice of House, White, and Lansing, one cannot say.

Even where the odds are a thousand to one, a gamble may be justified if one does not sacrifice too much when the dice fall wrong. On paper, France did not stand to lose a great deal if the Security Treaty did fall through. On paper, she had taken ample steps to protect herself. But there were certain disastrous psychological results that were neither foreseen nor entirely foreseeable.

After the signing of the Treaty of Guarantee, the people of France naturally began to paint roseate pictures of the thousands of ships and millions of men that would come to their aid. When the bottom fell out of the pact, the French were actually not appreciably worse off than they would have been without any treaty. But their expectations had been so great, and their disillusionment was so keen, that they felt betrayed and deserted. They had given up the Rhineland state for false promises of security; now security was denied them; they would have to seek it themselves. "There is nothing in the long run," said the French, "to stand between us and invasion, but the bayonets and breasts of our soldiers."

Bitterness rapidly developed among the erstwhile Allies. The security-obsessed French felt that they had to take stringent, lone-hand measures to guarantee their security, measures for which they now felt they had complete moral if not legal justification. And some of these measures recoiled disastrously upon their authors and played an important part in the undoing of France in 1940.

CHAPTER SIXTEEN

MAKING THE PIPS SQUEAK

"We have been attacked; we want security. We have been despoiled; we demand restitution. We have been devastated; we want reparation." STEPHEN PICHON, *French Minister for Foreign Affairs, December 30, 1918.*

1

WE MUST continue to bear in mind that the problems of the Rhineland occupation, the Rhineland buffer state, and the Treaty of Guarantee, as well as the Saar, were all related to security and to one another, and that they were all solved more or less concurrently. Precisely the same thing may be said of reparations.

The first great battle over reparations was waged by the American delegation in connection with the Allied demand that Germany should pay the entire cost of the war. This, of course, was directly contrary to the pre-Armistice contract, which stipulated that Germany should pay only for civilian damages.

But as the Allies viewed their staggering bills, and observed that the enemy was now completely at their mercy, they began to repent of their bargain. Why should they pay the cost of Germany's aggression, and especially why should France pay—France, whose only crime, in the words of Clemenceau, "is to have taken up arms against the invader!"

Under the pre-Armistice agreement, a French peasant should obviously be compensated for the loss of his ruined farm. But, demanded Prime Minister Hughes of Australia, how about the Australian shepherd who had lost his farm through a mortgage foreclosure resulting from the war? When the American experts objected to this line of reasoning, Hughes accused them of being pro-German, and shouted, shaking his finger in their faces: "Some people in this war have not been so near the fire as we British have, and, therefore, being unburned, they have a cold, detached view of the situation."

The cold Americans stood their ground, and the Allies gave up the fight for total war costs (except for Belgium) in March, 1919. The American delegation received strong support from Wilson, who was then returning to Paris on the *George Washington,* and who wirelessed that he would have to dissent, publicly if necessary, because total war costs were "clearly inconsistent with what we deliberately led the enemy to expect and cannot now honorably alter simply because we have the power."

In the whole struggle over reparations the Americans could preserve a high degree of detachment, in large part because they were asking nothing for themselves. Perhaps they should have asked for something. Ex-President Herbert Hoover thinks that Wilson might well have demanded a share of both territorial spoils and reparations, and then have yielded them in return for concessions to his views. But Wilson was neither a good horse trader nor a poker player. Advancing insincere proposals for bargaining purposes was foreign to his nature and rasping to his Calvinist conscience. Under the new order of things, one laid one's cards on the table as completely as possible.

2

The second great battle over reparations raged about the Allied demand that Allied pension bills should be added to civilian damages. After unaccountably weak resistance, Wilson hoisted the white flag, and in doing so committed what was perhaps his most disastrous and far-reaching blunder at the Conference. This was all the more regrettable because he could almost certainly have held his ground if he had shown the stubbornness on this issue that he did on others.

The economic results of Wilson's capitulation may be

quickly described. The reparations bill, as finally presented to Germany in 1921, totaled approximately $33,000,000,000, of which roughly one-third represented damage to Allied property, and one-half to two-thirds, pensions and similar allowances. In short, Wilson's decision doubled and perhaps tripled the bill. It spelled the difference between a sum that Germany could reasonably be expected to pay—say $10,000,000,000— and one that she could not or would not pay.

But what was wrong with the decision morally? If we accept the proposition that Germany had deliberately and wantonly forced the war on the Allies—and this was an article of faith in the Allied camp—then why should she not be forced to pay for the support of maimed Allied soldiers, and of the widows and orphans whose breadwinners had fallen on the Somme and a dozen other fronts?

There are several answers. First, Wilson had announced in one of his supplementary Fourteen Points speeches, on February 11, 1918, that there should be "no annexations, no contributions, no punitive damages." The inclusion of pensions with actual damages would swell reparations to a point where they probably would be punitive. The word "reparation" itself suggests the repairing of damage done. To multiply this sum by two or three would cause the reparations payments to take on the character of indemnities.

Germany had accepted the Fourteen Points, and they were solemnly written into the pre-Armistice contract. According to both the letter and the spirit of that contract, it would be illegal and immoral to ask for anything beyond actual reparations for civilian damages, the more so since the Germans were now partially disarmed and virtually at the mercy of the Allies.

3

How can we account for Wilson's flagrant flouting of his own principles?

England, unlike France, had no great devastated area, though her merchant marine had suffered heavily. If the British were to receive a substantial share of German reparations, they would have to establish the validity of pension charges. Lloyd George recognized this, and, consummate politician that he was, evolved an argument which appealed to the heart. If France was to be compensated for the loss of a peasant's hut, then why not for the crippled soldier who had once occupied that hut? Was not life more precious than property?

Shortly after Wilson's return to Paris in March, the British financial experts drew up a lengthy memorandum in support of pensions. Wilson, still disliking lawyers, especially verbose lawyers, rather contemptuously threw it out as "very legalistic."

Then Lloyd George had General Smuts, the great South African liberal, try his hand at virtually the same argument, which in this case was concisely and beautifully written. Wilson greatly admired Smuts, and was undoubtedly grateful to him for unwavering support on the League of Nations Commission. So where the legalists had failed, Smuts succeeded. Wilson was persuaded that pensions might be included with reparations.

This unfortunate decision, though supported by some of the American financial experts, was contrary to the unanimous opinion of the American legal experts, whom Wilson had previously asked to tell him what was right. It was contrary to the Fourteen Points. It was contrary to the spirit, if not the letter, of the pre-Armistice contract. It was contrary to every tenet of good faith and honorable dealing.

But Wilson was a stubborn man. He had given his word, and a man of honor must keep his word. The legal experts—these lawyers were most annoying—objected that the decision was illogical. "Logic! Logic!" Wilson burst out somewhat petulantly. "I don't give a damn for logic. I am going to include pensions!"

Wilson had also given his word of honor—and the word of honor of the Allies—to the entire German nation. Then why should a statesman who set such great store by honorable international dealing have wavered at this critical time? Should not a pledge given to some 60,000,000 people take precedence over one later given to a single individual?

The most plausible explanation comes from Wilson's official biographer, Ray Stannard Baker. At this time the American financial experts were contending for a reasonable lump-sum payment, based upon Germany's capacity to pay over a specified number of years. This figure would presumably not cover more than actual damages, and if the Allies, in apportioning the money among themselves, chose to set aside a certain amount for pensions, rather than for reconstruction, this would obviously have no effect upon Germany.

The tragedy is, as we shall presently see, that the total sum was not fixed in the treaty, and it was not based upon a reasonable estimate of Germany's capacity to pay. Why Wilson or his economic experts should have been so confident at this time that they could carry their point is another unsolved mystery. It seems clear that Wilson did not understand the full implications of what he was doing. Certainly, as he said on his first trip to France, he was "not much interested in the economic subjects" which were to be debated at Paris. This was most unfortunate, for about half the treaty was devoted to economic arrangements.

There is one other aspect of the problem. The French wanted pensions included in reparations, if for no better reason than that they would add to Germany's burden. The heavier the reparations, the more difficult it would be for Germany to struggle to her feet again and be a threat to France. The French are a traditionally thrifty people, but so great was their passion for security that if they had been forced to choose between a

powerful Germany able to pay and a prostrate Germany unable to pay, they would almost certainly have chosen the latter.

At the time of the pensions decision, Wilson was opposing
French demands on the Saar, the Rhineland, and other matters.
This constant opposition to France on issues of seemingly vital
importance may have had something to do with his willingness
to yield on an issue which seemed to be of no real importance.

But it *was* important—terribly so. It bloated the bill to a
point where there was grave doubt as to Germany's capacity to
pay. And it gave the Germans additional moral justification
for evading payment.

4

The third and final battle was waged by the Americans in
behalf of a reasonable, specific lump sum to be named in the
treaty and paid over a definite period of years. The Americans
lost this too.

The final treaty did not stipulate the maximum Germany
would have to pay, or at what time her obligations, when fixed,
would end. That was left to the future—in effect a demoralizing
blank check on Germany's resources. Nothing is so disheartening to a debtor as not to know how much he owes. If the figure
is fixed within his reasonable capacity to pay, he has some incentive to roll up his sleeves and rid himself of the burden. But
if it is beyond his capacity to pay, and if he must keep on paying indefinitely through generation after generation, there is
no will to pay. There is instead every incentive to evade.

Winston Churchill has well described the Paris Conference
as "a turbulent collision of embarrassed demagogues." Nowhere is this better illustrated than in the handling of the
reparations problem.

The Allied leaders, Lloyd George in particular, had led
their people to believe that Germany could be forced to pay the
entire cost of the war which, so it seemed, had so wantonly been
forced upon them. In the general election of 1918 the welkin

had rung with cries of "Hang the Kaiser"; "Make Germany pay to the last pfennig"; and "Search their pockets." Sir Eric Geddes had cried: "We will get out of her all you can squeeze out of a lemon and a bit more. I will squeeze her until you can hear the pips squeak." George Creel relates that Lloyd George came to Paris grinning, as if it were all a huge joke, "Heaven only knows what I would have had to promise them if the campaign had lasted a week longer."

We may say in defense of Lloyd George—and this is admittedly a lame defense—that he started the campaign on a more moderate note; but when he sensed that this was unpopular he instinctively raised the pitch. We may also say in his defense—and this too is a lame defense—that it was Geddes, and not he, who promised to squeeze Germany until the pips squeaked. A politician cannot be held accountable for every wild outcry of his followers. The canny Welshman had said in effect: "They shall pay to the utmost farthing—*if they can do so without delaying the economic revival of the world.*" "They shall pay the maximum possible—*but what is the maximum possible must be ascertained by financial experts.*"

These were supremely important qualifications, and they provided Lloyd George with a perfect "out." But the masses either do not hear such qualifications, or rapidly forget them. They hear and remember only what they want to hear and remember. Lloyd George was an experienced enough politician to know this, and therein lay the enormity of his crime. Like a pyromaniac scattering firebrands around England, he deliberately whipped up passions at a time when peacemaking demanded a subsidence of passion; he deliberately aroused a feeling of greed when he probably knew in his heart that it could not be completely satisfied. In so doing he did perhaps more than any other one man to make impossible the insertion of a reasonable reparations figure in the treaty. And in a very real sense reparations were the heart of the entire settlement.

Lloyd George came to the Conference distinctly disheveled by his electoral gymnastics, and with the blatant and provocative posters of the recent campaign pinned to his coattails. He was displeased when the austere Woodrow Wilson declined to congratulate him on the success of his demagoguery. Wilson was too honest a Presbyterian to conceal his disgust.

The essential point is that Lloyd George had whipped up unrealizable expectations. He could not collect what he had led his people to believe he could collect; but if he failed to collect they would have his head. The magnetic Welshman would have to employ his unusual talents for tightrope walking to the utmost if he was to get out of this corner.

In April, 1919, over 200 members of the Coalition in the British House of Commons, fearing that the Prime Minister was weakening on his election promises, telegraphed him a famous ultimatum, and extorted from him a renewed pledge of delivery. It is an ironical fact that in the actual making of the peace Lloyd George was more embarrassed by his victory than Wilson was by his defeat in the November elections.

5

French estimates of Germany's capacity to pay ran as high as the utterly fantastic figure of $200,000,000,000. Some calculators even included the repayment of France's indemnity to Germany, of 1871, at 5 per cent interest, plus the capital value of all French lives lost in the recent war. Additional moral justification for such colossal sums was provided by the recollection that the Germans, in their hours of triumph, had boasted of the indemnities—$500,000,000,000 was mentioned by some irresponsible persons—that they would exact from their foe. In certain German quarters satisfaction even had been expressed over America's entry into the war: rich Uncle Sam could be gouged for a pretty penny.

Two leading British experts, appropriately called the "heavenly twins," went to work on German reparations and produced the astronomical sum of $120,000,000,000. American

advisers estimated that Germany could not pay more than $30,-
000,000,000 at the outside. The figure as finally established by
the Reparations Commission in 1921 was approximately $33,-
000,000,000, but this was ultimately whittled down to about
$8,000,000,000 in the Young Plan of 1929. If this sum had been
settled upon in 1919, the Germans might have accepted it with
good grace, and the whole story might well have been different. But the men of 1919 were looking at their problem
through the colored glasses of 1919, not of 1929.

Thus it was that the estimates made so lightly in the enthusiasm of victory remained to embarrass the demagogues at the
Conference. Their sober second thought recognized that Germany could not pay anywhere near these maximum figures,
and that to put them into the treaty would completely remove
all incentive to payment. Perhaps the Germans would refuse to
sign the treaty at all, and Europe would lapse into anarchy.
If they did sign and tried to pay such monstrous amounts, they
might be plunged into economic chaos and not be able to pay
anything. Or, worse yet, they might pull the victors down into
the economic morass with them.

Yet the demagogues could not go back to their people on
bended knees and say that they had made a mistake. They
could not confess that Germany was unable to pay more than
one-tenth of the amount expected. If they did this, they would
be replaced immediately by new demagogues. And this would
mean further delay in making the treaty.

There was one possible way by which the negotiators could
save face, and in some measure justify a manageable sum. If
the Americans would renounce all claims to the approximately
$10,000,000,000 which the Allies had borrowed from them,
then the Allies could reduce by that much the amount that
Germany could reasonably be expected to pay.

This proposal was made repeatedly at the Conference, and
repeatedly after the Conference. Wilson opposed it, his economic advisers opposed it, the United States Treasury opposed
it, the United States Congress opposed it, and the American

taxpayers opposed it. Our perfectly understandable attitude on the debt problem had a great deal to do with the reparations muddle.

6

The demagogues had no alternative but to postpone the fixing of the final figure. Speed was still at a premium; the Bolsheviks were on the march; pressing problems of boundaries had to be settled. There was no time to make a careful and scientific estimate of Germany's capacity to pay. A lump sum, worked out by rule-of-thumb methods, might conceivably prove too small, and leave the goose with a few unplucked feathers. Clemenceau argued that, no matter how much he got, French public opinion would demand twice as much, and call him a traitor.

The Americans, as we have seen, fought for a lump sum, based on Germany's capacity to pay, set at a reasonable figure, and paid over a thirty-year period. Norman H. Davis, one of the American experts, pleaded that "the enslavement of one generation was enough." The Allies fought for an indefinite figure, to be paid over an indefinite period, and based not upon capacity but upon Allied claims.

The Americans lost every one of these points. The crucial decisions were made when Wilson was ill with influenza, and when House was representing him on the Council of Four. On some of these matters House consulted Wilson; on others he acted on his own responsibility, thus committing Wilson to a position which he later reluctantly endorsed.

From the American point of view there was one saving feature: the all-important Reparations Commission. This body, which grew out of the proposal of an American expert, would be clothed with enormous powers to fix and collect reparations. The United States would be represented on it; and under moderate American influence, and in a sane, peacetime atmosphere, the reparations problem would be dispassionately

studied, and the final figure set at a reasonable sum. The demagogues would save face; Germany would be fairly dealt with.
And the Americans in the end would win the battles they had
lost on pensions, on a fixed sum, and on a definite time for payment.

The supreme irony is that the United States never ratified
the treaty, and never took a seat on the Reparations Commis-

Soaked!

(Courtesy of the Columbus *Dispatch*)

sion. Control fell into other and less moderate hands, and the
purposes of the Americans were defeated by other Americans.
But this is another story.

The net result was a house-that-Jack-built debacle. Wilson
surrendered on pensions, presumably because he assumed that
the reparations figure would be fixed and reasonable. It was
neither. Colonel House and Wilson surrendered on a fixed and

reasonable figure, to be paid over a limited period, partly because they assumed that the Reparations Commission would
be moderate. It was not.

We have observed that the Americans won the first of the
three battles on reparations: that against saddling the entire
cost of the war on Germany. In the end they lost this battle too,
because the final figure was put so high as to amount in effect
to the same thing.

7

The budget of blunders does not end here. A word must be
said about Article 231 of the Treaty of Versailles—the famous
"war guilt clause," which was the preamble to the reparations
section. It reads: "The Allied and Associated governments
affirm and Germany accepts the responsibility of Germany and
her allies for causing all the loss and damage to which the
Allied and Associated governments and their nationals have
been subjected as a consequence of the war imposed upon them
by the aggression of Germany and her allies." This did not say,
as the Germans attempted to make it say, that Germany was
solely responsible for starting the war. It merely said that Germany accepted for herself *and her allies,* which included Austria-Hungary, the responsibility for causing all the losses
growing out of the war—a war brought on by the aggression of
Germany and her allies. Whatever the causes, immediate or
remote, it is clear that the fighting started when Austrian
troops invaded Serbia.

But, whether true or not, this war-guilt statement is a classic
example of how political chickens can come home to roost and
embroil international relations.

From the German point of view there were two figures:
what Germany could pay, and what she would pay. There
was a wide gap between the two sums. From the point of view
of the Allies there were two figures: what they had led their
people to think they could collect, and what they could actually

collect. There was a tremendous gap between the two sums.

By this time it was clear that nothing like the entire cost of the war could be extorted from exhausted Germany. But from a political point of view it did not seem wise to let the Hun off without some statement of liability. He should be made to confess that he was responsible for the cost of the conflict, even though he was not going to pay for it all. This, presumably, would do something to cushion the disappointment of the Allied electorates. It would also provide a moral and legal basis for collecting reasonable reparations.

The irony of this whole wretched controversy is that it was thoroughly unnecessary, because the "war guilt" clause was unnecessary, except perhaps as a weak sop to home opinion. The Armistice contract, which Germany had signed, had provided a perfect legal basis for collecting reparations for civilian damages, without dragging in the inflammatory issue of moral turpitude and punitive exactions.

The Germans did not then believe, have never believed, and will never believe that they and their allies were solely responsible for all the damage caused by the war. They even cited Wilson's pre-1917 pronouncements to the effect that no one nation had brought on this terrible catastrophe. They had the effrontery not only to deny their own guilt but to believe that the Allies were guilty instead. They cried out bitterly against having to sign such a lie as was embedded in Article 231, and when forced to sign under duress they mentally and orally repudiated what they were signing.

8

The moral indignation of the German people was kept warm by the fuel of a more practical consideration. The Allies, it was felt, were assessing reparations because Germany and her allies had been solely responsible for the war. If the Germans could prove that this was not true, why could they not reasonably demand that the burden be lightened or removed?

This seemingly innocent "war guilt" clause, which was flagrantly misrepresented by German propaganda, erupted into a veritable volcano of passion. It caused liberal sentiment throughout the world to sympathize with the Germans and encourage them. It caused German opinion to keep up a constant clatter against this clause and the entire treaty of which it was a part. And no German demagogue appealed more successfully to this anti-war-guilt prejudice than Adolf Hitler.

One finds no evidence that either Wilson or his advisers put up a fight against the "war guilt clause." Why did Wilson fail to do so? If he had statesmanlike vision at all, should he not have foreseen, even faintly, some of the evil consequences lurking in this seemingly innocent statement?

There are several possible explanations. Perhaps he was not interested in this preamble to the dull reparations section, and read it hurriedly or not at all. Perhaps he was worn down by trying to head off what were seemingly more disastrous things. It was both embarrassing and nerve-racking to have to say "No, no, no."

The true explanation probably lies elsewhere. Wilson and his advisers and practically everyone else of any consequence at the Conference believed that this simple statement of Germany's guilt was true. Whatever doubts Wilson may have had before 1917 quickly melted away when he entered the fiery furnace with the Allies. And since the war guilt clause was true—indeed self-evident—what was wrong with it?

Wilson breathed the same war-charged air as his contemporaries; he viewed problems through the same heavy fog of passion and prejudice. We cannot condemn him for not having seen what no one else could see. We can only regret that the peace had to be made in such an atmosphere.

CHAPTER SEVENTEEN

OPEN DISAGREEMENTS
OPENLY ARRIVED AT

"The whole world is speculating as to whether the Italians are 'bluffing' or whether they really intend going home and not signing the Peace unless they have Fiume. It is not unlike a game of poker." COLONEL HOUSE, *April 22, 1919.*

1

EVEN THE most ardent admirers of Woodrow Wilson find it difficult to explain, much less to justify, his extraordinarily inept handling of the Italian question.

Shortly after reaching Paris, and before the Conference formally convened, Wilson made his first costly blunder. He promised the Italians that their northern frontier might be drawn along the line of the Brenner Pass—which meant that more than 200,000 Austrian-Germans would be handed over to alien rule.

This was a flagrant violation of two of the Fourteen Points. Wilson had proclaimed that the frontiers of Italy should be readjusted along "clearly recognizable lines of nationality." This readjustment completely overshot the mark. He had proclaimed the sacred principle of self-determination. The Germans of the Austrian South Tyrol wanted no part of Italian overlordship.

Liberal observers were profoundly shocked and disillusioned. The area involved was not large, but the principle was. At the very outset of the Conference anxious inquirers began to ask themselves and one another: "Can Wilson be trusted?" Harold Nicolson, who was there, later wrote of the current feeling that, "if Wilson could swallow the Brenner, he would swallow anything."

No one will deny that the peace settlements contained a

number of glaring violations of self-determination. But these generally came about after long discussion and final compromise: a discussion often involving historical, geographical, economic, linguistic, religious, strategic, political, cultural, nationalistic, and racial considerations. The new boundary lines, thousands of miles in length, had to be run somewhere, and it is scarcely ever possible to draw a line without doing violence to at least one of these many factors. In some instances the negotiators decided—and properly so—that economic, strategic, and other advantages were of more importance to the inhabitants than self-determination.

But in the case of the South Tyrol, there was no long debate and no compromise. Wilson apparently asked for nothing in return. He just promised the Italians the 200,000 Germans.

Various explanations have been offered, none of them completely satisfying. Perhaps Wilson felt that this concession was necessary to enlist Italian support for the League. Perhaps he believed that he could moderate even more objectionable Italian demands in the Adriatic—much as one would moderate the appetite of a ravenous animal by throwing it a choice morsel of raw meat. Almost certainly he was impressed by the plea of the Italians that they needed the line of the Brenner as a strategic frontier against future invasion. (The Italians were careful not to point out that a defensible line excluding the great bulk of the Germans could have been drawn farther south.)

The most reasonable and least flattering explanation is that Wilson was ignorant of what he was promising. After the Conference was over he admitted to one of the experts that the decision was due to "insufficient study." The general feeling among the American delegation was that he had made the promise hastily, that he afterwards regretted it, but that he felt bound by his word.

The clarion call, "Tell me what's right and I'll fight for it," was still ringing in the ears of the American advisers. In many instances Wilson fought for what the experts recommended; in some instances he ran counter to their recommendations; in this instance he apparently did not even consult them. Wilson did not very often make similar promises out of

Proposed Italian Gains Under Treaty of London

the depths of his ignorance, but this one went far beyond the personal fortunes of the Tyrolese, who, as the result of a "deal" between Hitler and Mussolini, were brutally uprooted in 1939 and driven back onto German soil.

2

Italy, in pursuance of her policy of *sacro egoismo* ("sacred selfishness" or "consecrated selfishness"), had entered the war in response to inducements held out in the secret Treaty of London. This pact, among other things, promised Italy the Brenner frontier.

We have already noted that Wilson might have brought about a repudiation of all the secret treaties at the very outset of the Conference by a resounding declaration against them. His prompt and premature surrender on the South Tyrol indicated to the Italians that he was not only prepared to recognize but even support the unsavory Treaty of London. Italian "selfishness" became even more "consecrated," and the appetite for other forbidden fruit began to grow.

The choicest of the forbidden plums was the Austro-Hungarian port of Fiume. If Wilson would lightly yield the South Tyrol, with its 200,000 pure Germans, why would he not also yield Fiume, which contained a considerable colony of pure Italians?

The South Tyrol surrender was more than a violation of two of the Fourteen Points; it was a violation of the ABC's of diplomacy. When Wilson offhandedly promised Italy the Tyrol, he asked for nothing in return. Perhaps he expected something in return; but in diplomacy, as in other fields of human endeavor, it is usually unwise to pay in advance.

In any game—and diplomacy is no exception—a player does not discard his ace of trumps on the very first round. This is precisely what Wilson did. When the Italians later demanded Fiume, which was not promised them by the Treaty of London, Wilson had nothing to offer them in return for giving up their demands.

Technically speaking—and this Wilson conceded—the Italians were not bound by the Fourteen Points in their claims for the South Tyrol and other parts of the defunct Austro-

Hungarian Empire. The pre-Armistice contract with Germany included the Fourteen Points, but this did not concern the Italians because Germany had nothing they particularly wanted. Besides, Italy had entered a mumbled reservation during the pre-Armistice negotiations in Paris regarding her territorial aspirations. As for Austria-Hungary, which had what the Italians wanted, there was no pre-Armistice contract based on the Fourteen Points. The Austrians were so far gone when they surrendered that they were in no position to claim such a safeguard. When Clemenceau read the terms offered them he remarked: "We have left the breeches of the Emperor, and nothing else."

Yet there was a strong moral obligation which Wilson failed to exploit to its full advantage. Italy, we remember, had officially accepted the Fourteen Points with regard to Germany, though with unclear reservations. If Wilson, at the outset of the Conference, when his prestige was still paramount, had emphatically announced that there could be no double standard, and that Italy was also bound to observe the Fourteen Points with regard to Austria, he might conceivably have carried the day. Having won this redoubt, he might then have moved on to an assault against the Treaty of London.

Wilson took no strong stand at the outset, and during the later negotiations rather weakly argued that it was immoral to have two standards. Above all, he surrendered on the South Tyrol, which seemed to indicate that the Fourteen Points did not apply to Austria, and that the Treaty of London had the full sanction of the United States.

Apologists for Wilson speak of the Tyrol decision as a "slip." It was more than a slip: it was a blunder. And a blunder, as the proverb has it, may be worse than a crime.

3

If the Tyrol was a "slip," what shall we say of Fiume?

The bothersome Treaty of London promised Italy certain Italian-inhabited areas along the eastern shore of the Adriatic Sea, but, contrary to the principle of self-determination, about 500,000 unwilling Slavs would have to go along with the Italians. The vital port of Fiume was not awarded to Italy: it was specifically reserved to the yet unborn Jugoslavia. Significantly, Italian opinion was not then counting on Fiume: the great battle cries were "Trento" and "Trieste."

If the Conference had moved rapidly, it is possible that Italy would have pressed no serious claims for Fiume. But as time dragged on, Italian appetite (*sacro egoismo*) increased, especially when it was noted that Italy, for all her sacrifices, was not going to get much out of the war, while France and Great Britain were making off with vast colonial empires. Verily, complained the Italian press, the scriptural dictum was being fulfilled: "For whosoever hath, to him shall be given . . ."

So the Italians entered their claim to Fiume, buttressed it by an armed occupation which angered Wilson, and pressed it with noisy insistence during the height of the crisis over the Saar, the Rhineland, reparations, and other problems. Even this early in the game it was rumored that the Italian delegation was threatening to bolt the Conference if its demands were not granted. Wilson was not unnaturally annoyed by this technique of bargain, bluff, bluster, and grab.

On the face of it, the Italians had a fairly good case. Fiume would strategically strengthen their northeastern frontier. It would enable them to dominate the Adriatic both militarily and commercially. It would stifle the military and commercial rivalry of the powerful and much-hated new Serb state. Finally, it would vindicate the principle of self-determination, for a majority of the dwellers within Fiume proper were Italians.

4

Actually, the case against Italy was very strong. She was evidently trying to play both ends against the middle: standing on the Treaty of London for the other parts of Austria-Hungary, and brushing aside the Treaty of London because it gave Fiume to Jugoslavia. She was denying self-determination to the Germans of the Tyrol, while insisting on self-determination for the Italians of Fiume.

The fine Italian hand even went so far as to produce faked photographs. Pictures were shown of a great crowd in Fiume, with uplifted hands, allegedly voting in an informal plebiscite for annexation to Italy. Upon investigation it was discovered that Italian officials had gone to this hunger-ridden city with supplies, and had asked all those who wanted bread to raise their hands.

As a matter of fact, while the heart of Fiume was Italian, the suburbs and the surrounding area were Slav. Italy had to annex thousands of Slavs in order to reclaim 30,000 countrymen: an islet of Italians in a great Slavonian sea. It was ridiculous, as Wilson pointed out, to claim little islands of nationals wherever they might be: the map of Europe would have spots all over it. The Italians might on the same basis as logically claim the hundreds of thousands of their compatriots in New York City.

The Italians disclaimed self-determination in the Tyrol; claimed it in Fiume; and then got angry when it was pointed out that Fiume was not Italian. What of it, they said? The Allied leaders had already violated self-determination in handing over Germans to the Poles in the Danzig corridor. Then why get so self-righteous, especially at Italy's expense? Baron Sonnino, who went so far as to threaten suicide, charged that Wilson, having lost his virginity in dealing with Germany, was now seeking to regain it at the expense of Italy.

The already tangled situation was further snarled by the

emergence of the new Serb-Croat state. When Italy was promised the Dalmatian coast and other parts of the Adriatic area,
those places had belonged to the common enemy, Austria-
Hungary. Now a new nation had arisen which not only was
friendly to the Allies but had rendered them substantial help
in the closing stages of the war. After all, one has to deal more
generously with an ally than with an enemy.

Jugoslavia needed Fiume, because this was her only feasible
outlet to the sea, and it would be inviting trouble—Balkan
trouble—to bring a vigorous new nation into the world and
then try to smother it economically. President Wilson had
recognized this explosive situation when in Point XI he had
promised the new Serb state a "free and secure access to the
sea." The logical "access" was Fiume, to which Jugoslavia was
also entitled by a later point, self-determination. The Treaty
of London also promised Fiume to Jugoslavia, and Italy took
her stand on this treaty—where it was to her advantage to do so.

Clemenceau and Lloyd George, having already disposed of
the German problem, did not view the squabble with Italy as
of transcendent importance. They did not like the Treaty of
London; it was a disagreeable bargain. But England and
France had given their word, Italy had entered the war, and
there was nothing to do but honor the bond—which excluded
Fiume. Italy might have Fiume or she might have the Treaty
of London, but she could not have both.

The Italians had one sentimental argument that they
harped on constantly: their terrible sacrifices in the war. They
also insisted that they had saved the Allies five times, once in
1914 when they had declined to stab France in the back. But
Clemenceau and Lloyd George were not much moved. They
remembered that the Italians had hardly pulled their own
weight in the boat. They had moved with painful slowness,
except at Caporetto, when the roof fell in; and then they had
moved very rapidly—to the rear. The situation had been saved
only by the prompt diversion of French and British forces to
this sagging front.

The white-bearded Serbian Premier, Nikola Pashitch, weary of listening to tales of Italian sacrifices, remarked quietly: "In battle many more men are killed in running away than in fighting."

5

Wilson's Tyrol blunder was probably the result of too little study; his Fiume blunder was perhaps the result of too much study. He worked on this problem as on no other, assimilating lengthy reports from the experts, and getting down on his hands and knees and poring over a large and specially prepared relief map of the Dalmatian coast. He finally concluded that Italy had no legal or moral right to Fiume, and there he took his stand.

At one time Wilson seriously considered making Fiume a free city, not unlike Danzig. But on this issue his best qualified experts were against him. Some of the experts, like Professor Douglas W. Johnson, were experts on this particular region, and some of them, like David Hunter Miller (the "House group") were experts on other matters. The expert experts were for denying Fiume completely to Italy; the non-expert experts were for a compromise which would save the face of the Italians by giving them actual though not nominal control.

The real experts claimed that the establishment of a free port at Fiume would be an injustice to Jugoslavia, and unworkable. Wilson was not convinced. Then they drew up an eloquent and moving appeal, reminding him of his splendid ideals, and of his pledge on the *George Washington*: "Tell me what's right and I'll fight for it." This turned the tide. They told him, and he fought to the last ditch.

This quarrel among the experts bore evil fruit. Colonel House took his stand for compromise with the non-experts, and pursued so ambiguous a course as to raise the suspicion that he was deliberately trying to deceive Wilson as to the anti-

Italian position of the real experts. The Colonel was also so indiscreet as to meet with Clemenceau and Lloyd George in his room (the "Little White House") for a secret conclave. Wilson found them there with their heads together, and in a stern voice said: "Hello, what is this about?" Colonel House's well-meaning but somewhat devious handling of this whole situation aroused Wilson's growing suspicions, and paved the way for the final break.

Ill-feeling between House and Wilson was paralleled by ill-feeling among the experts. The real experts resented the intrusion of the non-experts, and the non-experts felt that the experts were so blinded by a close study of geographical, ethnographical, and strategic maps that they could not grasp the larger and more statesmanlike view—that is, compromise. The Italians got wind of this quarrel in the American delegation, and were emboldened to stand more adamantly for their claims.

Wilson personally disliked having to oppose the Italian demands. Orlando was a delightful person, and he had supported Wilson foursquare on the League of Nations Commission. After a particularly unhappy conference with Orlando, Wilson remarked that only once before had he experienced such a distressing time. When he was President of Princeton, a woman who was about to have a serious operation came to him and pleaded for an hour and a half against the expulsion of her son, alleging that the double shock would kill her. Wilson denied her request on the ground that his responsibility to the university was greater than his responsibility for her health. The son was expelled; the mother had the operation—and recovered. Principle triumphed.

6

Wilson always had—or thought he had—one ace in the hole. He could always, as a last resort, appeal to the people—to his own people, or to the people of the world. During the war his own people had responded gratifyingly (except for the October appeal); and the people of the rest of the world had rallied magnificently to his Fourteen Points. At various times during the Conference he had toyed with the idea of making public statements to gain his point, but now was the time to cut the Gordian knot.

He would draw up a friendly appeal setting forth the unvarnished facts of the Fiume controversy, so that the people of Italy would know the exact situation, as well as the attitude of the United States. There might, he felt, be a temporary uproar; but with the passage of time his manifesto would correct the false picture presented by the poisoned Italian press.

The appeal was discussed in the Council of Four, and hence could not have been a surprise to Orlando. It was studied and approved by Wilson's advisers. It was a well written, temperate, and logical statement; and if presented through the regular channels as a diplomatic note it would have been unobjectionable. One wonders why Wilson did not address his statement first to Orlando, and then publish it in the press. In this way he could have made known his views to the world, as well as to Italy, without intolerably affronting the Italian government.

But the appeal was not sent through the ordinary diplomatic channels. It was given directly to the press, on April 23, 1919, and promptly emblazoned on the front page of every important newspaper. It was in effect an unprecedented appeal to the Italian people over the heads of their regularly constituted representatives. Lord Riddell, remembering the secrecy which had enshrouded the Conference up to this time, sneered: "Which of the Fourteen Points does that come under?"

This was open diplomacy with a vengeance, and the results were sensational. Orlando and Sonnino quit the Conference, ostensibly in high dudgeon, but not in high enough dudgeon to forget to keep their experts on the job looking after Italy's "sacred" interests. Actually Orlando left in sorrow rather than in anger, and allegedly to seek new instructions from Parliament, now that his authority had been called into question.

Upon returning to Rome, Orlando was greeted by cheering throngs like a conquering Caesar. When he shouted to an enormous crowd, "Have I properly interpreted the will of the Italian people?" he was greeted with a tremendous "Yes." From the turbulent throng came cries: "Down with Wilson! Long live America!" The Italian press and public in effect made a counterappeal to the American people over the head of Wilson to support them in their "sacred selfishness." Orlando received a tremendous vote of confidence, which was unanimous in the Senate, and 382 to 40 in the Chamber.

Wilson was a fallen idol in Italy. Lips that had blessed him now cursed him; tablets that had honored him were draped in cloth; streets that had been named after him were rechristened —Fiume or D'Annunzio. A story, probably apocryphal, drifted back to Paris of a perfervid Italian orator who was discoursing on the glory that had once been Italy's. He mentioned Tasso (loud cheers), Dante (loud cheers), Galileo (loud cheers), and finally Cristoforo Colombo (dead silence broken by a few hisses).

7

Why did Wilson make this reverberating blunder? Did he not realize that all people resent having an outsider appeal to them over the heads of their own authorities? Did he not remember enough of the five-volume American history that he had written to know that when Citizen Genêt, the French envoy in 1793, threatened to appeal over the head of Washington to the admiring masses, he too became a fallen idol?

The answer is difficult to find, the more so since Wilson's fellow commissioners knew in advance about the projected appeal, and apparently favored it. Even Clemenceau and Lloyd George impliedly approved, at least by silence.

We have already referred to Wilson's appeal habit, which no

doubt had something to do with his decision. It is also probable that his head had been turned to some degree by the
overwhelming adulation of the Italian masses in January. Only
a scant few weeks earlier, hundreds of thousands of Italians
had shouted for Wilson and a peace of justice. Did he not have
reason to feel that they would put him above Orlando; justice
above greed? If so, Wilson misread not only history but human
nature.

In one other respect Wilson revealed an almost unbelievable naïveté. It is true that the appeal was published in Italy;
but not until Orlando had prepared a misleading reply, and
had followed it up with others that utterly obscured or mis-
interpreted the facts which Wilson was trying to lay before the
Italian people. Knowing that Italy was inflamed by war passions, and that she had lost hundreds of thousands of her
sturdiest sons, and that she was greedy for territory, and that
she was getting little out of the war, and that her press was
controllable, and that her leaders were unscrupulous, how
could Wilson have hoped to present the facts to the Italians,
or to have swayed them with the facts if presented fairly?

8

In a very real sense the repercussions of this unfortunate
appeal have not to this day subsided.

The Italian withdrawal precipitated a crisis of which the
Japanese took full advantage to press their claims to Shantung.
We shall have more to say about this distressing business in
the next chapter.

The Germans, enheartened by the rift in the ranks of the
Allies, were encouraged not to sign the Treaty of Versailles,
and this added greatly to the tension of May and June.

Lloyd George took advantage of the absence of the Italians
to induce Wilson and Clemenceau to consent to a Greek landing at Smyrna, on the Turkish coast of Anatolia, an operation

which was supported by British, French, and *American* warships. This area had been provisionally promised to Italy, but
Lloyd George was anxious to rush through other arrangements before the Italian delegates should come back to Paris.
Why Wilson consented to have a hand in this secret deal is
difficult to explain; Ray Stannard Baker shamefacedly dis-

"Are We Downhearted? Nein!"
(Courtesy of the Brooklyn *Eagle*)

misses it as the most "disreputable intrigue of the Conference."
He thinks that Wilson was moved by the eloquence of Eleu-
therios Venizelos, the Greek premier, and by the fact that
Smyrna was a Greek city. (Self-determination could be used to
cover many sins.) In any event, the landing of the hated Greeks
aroused prostrate and dispirited Turkey, and ultimately

led to the undoing of the whole Near Eastern settlement.

This is not the least of the ironies at Paris. While laboring for a League to end wars, Wilson consented to unleash the Greeks against the Turks, and thus start a war which lasted for three years, and cost tens of thousands of lives.

While Orlando and Sonnino sulked, the British and French arranged to divide up Germany's African colonies, leaving the Italians completely out in the cold. Italy later accepted these arrangements with the understanding that she would receive compensations elsewhere, but these were never satisfactorily forthcoming. Here we find one basis for Italy's enduring bitterness over the final settlement, for the rape of Ethiopia in 1935, and for Mussolini's "stab in the back" of 1940.

Fiume was to the Italians but a third-rate port, and one for which they had but recently developed a synthetic appetite. History can offer few comparable instances where so small a matter set in train such momentous consequences.

American public opinion on the whole applauded Wilson's sensational excursion into the field of open covenants. This was shirt-sleeve diplomacy in the American tradition, and it was perhaps his one act at Paris that was most heartily praised. Wilson was right, or so it seemed; and those who thought that he had been wobbling badly on the Fourteen Points were delighted by this startling exhibition of backbone. Joseph P. Tumulty cabled from the White House that he had never been so proud of Wilson. A number of congratulatory telegrams poured in on the President from Serb and Croat groups in America.

But the Italian-American element did not applaud: the "old country" was not being properly treated. Henry Cabot Lodge of Massachusetts did not applaud; hundreds of thousands of indignant Italian-Americans lived in his constituency. This learned "scholar in politics" publicly informed the Italians of Massachusetts that Fiume was as essential to Italy as the mouth of the Mississippi had been to the United States in the nineteenth century. Henry White patiently wrote Lodge

from Paris that this was true of Jugoslavia but not Italy. Yet
the learned Senator refused to see the error of his ways. Could
it be that this was because there were more Italian than Jugo-
slav voters in his state?

9

Yet what else could Wilson have done?

We can hardly blame him for opposing Italy's claim to an
unconditional cession of Fiume, for he had the right on his
side, and he was pledged to redeem his Fourteen Points. But
one can hardly escape the conclusion that the appeal was a
tremendous blunder, the more so since its immediate results
were both avoidable and predictable.

One of the most unfortunate aspects of this whole affair is
that Wilson received the blame for having robbed Italy of
Fiume. The fact is that both Lloyd George and Clemenceau
privately stood squarely with Wilson on this issue, and submitted their views to Orlando in a powerful *unpublished*
memorandum, just as the latter was about to entrain for Rome.

Wilson was evidently led to believe, according to Ray Stannard Baker, that Lloyd George and Clemenceau would follow
up the public appeal with supporting statements of their own.
When they failed to do so, and when the storm broke in all
its fury, Wilson, according to his wife, grew "white with
anger." Mrs. Wilson says that, when an explanation was asked
for, the answer was that Wilson's statement was so comprehensive that there was no point in adding anything to it.

There is no further evidence, not even in Ray Stannard
Baker, that this story is correct in the sharp outlines that Mrs.
Wilson gives. If it is true, then Wilson erred in not coming
to a more definite understanding with Lloyd George and
Clemenceau, in not arranging for the simultaneous publication of statements, and in not guarding against the unfortunate trap into which his wife claims he fell.

But one thing stands out clearly. Lloyd George and Clemen-

ceau, though privately supporting Wilson, were quite content
to let him subject his idealistic head to the delirium of indignation that burst upon it. They quite naturally had no desire to
run from cover and become co-sharers of the storm. Wilson's
seeming isolation enabled Orlando to give the false impression
that Wilson stood alone, and this made the Italian people even
more determined in their demands.

If Wilson had avoided a public scandal, the three great
Allied leaders would have continued to present their views
to Orlando privately, either individually or collectively, and
Orlando would have been put in an intolerable position. If he
had then bolted the Conference, he would not have returned
to Rome as a conquering hero but as one who was publicly confessing failure. He would have been written down as a touchy,
huffy person, who had bungled the game.

Things could hardly have worked out better for Orlando if
he had planned them that way. Wilson played right into his
hands; and Orlando became the hero, while Wilson became
the "goat." The London *Morning Post* referred caustically
to "Wild-west diplomacy," and added: "Mr. Wilson's name
among the Allies is like that of the rich uncle, and they have
accepted his manners out of respect for his means." The
London *Daily Express* said that this was "open diplomacy gone
mad," and urged that Wilson follow Orlando's excellent example and go home.

10

The Fiume affair has often been represented as a victory
for Wilson—which it was not, except perhaps morally.

The Italians came back to the Conference just before the
treaty was formally presented to the Germans. Negotiations
over Fiume went tiresomely on. Lloyd George tried a new
tack. He offered to buy the Italians out of Fiume with Turkish territory, to which he had no right, and when the Italians
began to nibble at the bait, he sought to buy them out of

Turkish territory with Fiume, to which he had no right. The Italians were confused, as was everyone else, including Lloyd George. Wilson had to sit through these sordid discussions, and they must have been a trial to his sensitive soul. Certainly by taking part in these negotiations he sullied his raiment, and compromised the high idealism of his Fiume manifesto.

The American experts went to work on a compromise plan, under which there would be a plebiscite at Fiume. If the Jugoslavs lost, a new port would be constructed for them. Wilson finally vetoed the proposal when it became evident that only the United States had money for building seaports, and that the American people would probably balk at such extravagances. It was enough of a burden to feed Europe without going to the expense of creating fancy ports.

In 1920 a treaty between Italy and Jugoslavia recognized Fiume as a free state in perpetuity. This proving unsatisfactory, a new treaty was negotiated in 1924 giving Italy Fiume, while awarding Jugoslavia the harbor of Porta Baros and a fifty-year lease of a part of the harbor of Fiume. So Italy got Fiume, in spite of Wilson's dramatic effort.

In retrospect it seems as though Wilson's most fundamental mistake in this matter was not to press for the free-city solution. Here he was confused by the two groups of experts, each of which was right from its point of view. On the narrow grounds of race, geography, and economics Jugoslavia should have had Fiume. The non-expert experts like Colonel House did not know much about these technicalities, but they did recognize the explosiveness of the political situation and the necessity of not driving the Italians into a corner. A peace settlement of this nature cannot be made in a geological laboratory.

The basic explanation of Wilson's stubbornness on the Fiume issue is no doubt partly psychological. He had slipped badly on the Tyrol, and there was a natural impulse to retrieve his moral position, at least partially. He had been forced to yield so much to the French and the British, and had been criticized so savagely for doing so, that when the time came to stand up against Italy he did so, especially since he had an iron-clad case and also the silent backing of both Lloyd George and Clemenceau. So he stood up, and the heavens descended.

One tragedy of the Peace Conference was that men compromised when they should have stood up, and they stood up when they should have compromised. But they were mortal men, and it was not given them to see the future.

CHAPTER EIGHTEEN

THE YELLOW PERIL

"They [the Japanese] are not bluffers, and they will go home unless we give them what they should not have." WOODROW WILSON, *April, 1919.*

1

THE ATTITUDE of the Japanese delegates at Paris was something of a mystery. They were primarily concerned with the Far East; and the Conference was essentially a European affair. They did not claim membership on the Council of Four, but they faithfully attended the various other councils, commissions, and committees on which they were assigned seats. They always seemed interested and awake, which could not be said of their Occidental associates; but what they were thinking lay behind an impenetrable Oriental mask. They intently examined the various charts and maps which were presented, but whether they studied them right side up or bottom side up one could not always tell. They were the "silent partners of the peace."

On one occasion, in a minor commission, there was a tied vote, and the chairman turned to the Japanese delegate for the deciding voice. "Do you vote," he asked, "with the French and the Americans, or with the British and the Italians?" The inscrutable little yellow man sucked in his breath and responded simply, "Yes."

If the Japanese sat like brown Buddhas when non-Asiatic interests were involved, they left no doubt as to where they stood when their own interests were affected. Having kept quiet on matters that did not concern them directly, they spoke with all the more authority when they finally broke their silence. And they did so with directness, clarity, and pertinacity.

The Japanese came to Paris with three demands: first, a formal recognition of the principle of race equality; second, title to the German islands of the North Pacific; third, acquisition of Germany's economic and other rights in the Chinese province of Shantung.

We have already considered the disposal of the German islands in the North Pacific, which Japan finally received under a League mandate. Let us now turn to the Japanese fight for a formal and explicit recognition of the principle of racial equality.

Some writers insist that Japan was not really sincere in pushing this proposal, but that she was merely advancing it as a bargaining lever. If, as she had reason to fear, she was rebuffed, she would be able to advance other and more tangible claims with greater force.

There can be little doubt that the racial equality issue was used as a bargaining lever, and to some extent was intended as such. But the evidence indicates strongly that the Japanese were sincere in making this proposal, and that they regarded it as of the greatest importance. One has only to follow the Japanese press during the Conference to recognize that racial equality was bracketed on a more or less equal basis with the North Pacific islands and German rights in Shantung.

2

The Japanese are a proud and sensitive people. Judged by Western standards, they are too proud and sensitive, and they ought to mend their ways. But some day we may discover that our disapproval will not cause people to change their national characteristics. The very first principle of diplomatic intercourse is that we must take people as we find them, and make due allowance for their distinctive traits.

The basic facts are that the Japanese are small in stature, and that they were then small in territory. Until 1904 they were looked down upon with a certain degree of amused tolerance by outside peoples. But this feeling quickly changed to respect when, in the Russo-Japanese War of 1904–1905, Nippon administered a sound beating to the largest and most populous of the white nations.

As a result of this bloody conflict, the Japanese began to display a certain cockiness. Not only that, but large numbers of energetic coolies began to emigrate to the sun-bathed slopes of our Pacific Coast. The white laborers, fearing for their standard of living, demanded and secured barriers against this influx, and even established restrictions against the owning of land by Nipponese.

Similar bars were erected by the Canadians and by the people of Australasia. The Australians, facing as they did the teeming hives of the Orient, and thinly peopling a vast land, lived in almost daily dread of a yellow tidal wave.

Basically, the objection to the Japanese coolie was economic. He could allegedly live on a handful of rice and beat down the living standard of the white man. The gravest part of the yellow peril was that a Japanese could apparently get rich on what a white man threw into his garbage can. But economic undesirability shades imperceptibly into social and racial undesirability, and there was undoubtedly a strong race prejudice against the Japanese in the threatened areas.

The plain truth is that Japan was suffering from an inferiority complex, for she felt that she had "arrived." She bitterly resented the interference of the European powers in 1895, when, at the close of the Sino-Japanese War, they had intervened to deprive her of some of her richest spoils. She resented the intrusion of the European powers in the Far East, and especially their blocking out of spheres of interest in China— an area which Japan looked upon as her legitimate field of exploitation. She resented knowing that her nationals were not wanted in the white man's country; that the Japanese, with their centuries-old civilization, were not good enough to associate with whites, or own land, or become citizens.

The Japanese state of mind was further colored by a consciousness that Japan had emerged from the World War as the
dominant power in the Far East. Russia had been bled white,
and was in the throes of revolution. Germany was completely
eliminated. Great Britain and France were war-weary and tax-
burdened. The United States could not even defend its own
Philippines.

Encouraged by all these factors, the Japanese were determined to make a strong bid for racial equality.

3

The big fight came in the commission which drafted the
Covenant of the League of Nations. The Japanese wanted a
specific recognition of the principle of racial equality, but they
were finally willing to compromise on a seemingly innocuous
clause in the preamble. It endorsed the "principle of the
equality of Nations and the just treatment of their nationals."
The dynamite-charged word "race" did not even appear.

Wilson was personally sympathetic with the basic principle
of this innocent-looking clause, for he favored any general
move toward international understanding. But he recognized
that it was a rock upon which his whole program might be
wrecked. Prime Minister Hughes of Australia put up an impassioned fight against racial equality, for "White Australia"
would not tolerate even the faintest suggestion of a wedge that
might be used to pry open her anti-Oriental barriers. Other
British statesmen, with their hundreds of millions of uneasy
colored subjects, preferred to sidestep the whole dangerous
issue.

The question was finally forced to a vote in the League of
Nations Commission, on April 11, 1919. Lord Robert Cecil,
the liberal-minded British statesman, acting under instructions from his government, rather shamefacedly registered an
objection. Wilson, as chairman, then called for the affirmative

vote, and the proposal received eleven votes from the seventeen members present. Wilson did not ask for the negative vote, but in line with previous decisions ruled that the motion had lost because it failed to command unanimous support. The objection of Cecil alone was sufficient to defeat the proposal.

This ruling was technically correct, and Wilson doubtless would have acted as he did even if there had not been tremendous pressure to sidetrack the explosive issue. Hughes of Australia loudly threatened, if the racial equality clause was adopted by the Commission, to tear the Conference wide apart by dragging the whole question out into the open of a plenary session. This, as Wilson well knew, would arouse colored people the world over, and inflame the Japanese-conscious Pacific Coast. Senator Hiram W. Johnson of California and others could be counted on to build up a strong backfire of opposition to the entire League.

The Japanese persisted in their demand for racial equality; but since they perceived that the fight was hopeless, and since they had apparently received assurances from the British on the Shantung deal, they declined to press it. This was the end of the troublesome issue as far as the Conference was concerned, but it was not the end as far as the Japanese were concerned.

The much-misunderstood vote on racial equality came after Wilson's return from the United States, and after he was forced to reassemble the League of Nations Commission for the purpose of considering amendments demanded by the American people. If, as we have already observed, Wilson had taken the necessary steps to anticipate some of these amendments when preparing the original draft, this embarrassment might not have arisen. The Japanese almost certainly would have pressed the racial equality issue to a bitter conclusion in the plenary session, but in this case Wilson would not have been the presiding officer, and he would not have had to make the unfortunate but necessary ruling.

One of the most distressing aspects of this entire episode is that Wilson—and indirectly the United States—was savagely condemned by the Japanese for having seemingly thwarted their desires. The Osaka *Mainichi* went so far as to charge that the President had a "female demon within him."

Premier Hughes of Australia, whom the benign Lord Robert Cecil referred to as "that shrimp Hughes," did nothing to set the record straight. He informed the Japanese delegates and the Japanese press that the Americans had strongly opposed racial equality, and had been primarily responsible for its defeat.

This was not true. It was the irascible Hughes more than any other one man who had led the fight. But whether true or false, the impression was made, and the Japanese have never forgiven Wilson—or the United States.

4

By mid-April the Japanese could point to one partial diplomatic victory, a mandate over the North Pacific islands; and one complete defeat, racial equality. They had one demand left: German economic rights in Shantung; and to Japan this was by all odds the most important, at least economically.

Tactically, the position of the Japanese delegates was strong. They had just suffered a stinging defeat on the race issue, and the natural tendency of the Allies was to appease them with something else they wanted.

The Japanese withheld their heavy fire with Oriental patience until late in April, when the desperate situation was all in their favor. Italy had just left the Conference, and might never return. Belgium, bitter over the apportionment of reparations, was seriously threatening to bolt too. If the Japanese, denied Shantung, had gone home, the Conference almost certainly would have collapsed, and with it Wilson's precious League of Nations.

The false impression has gone abroad that the Japanese demanded in fee simple the entire province of Shantung—the home of Confucius, the Holy Land of China—with its 56,000 square miles of territory and its population of some 30,000,-000 Chinese. The false impression has also gone abroad that Wilson surrendered to these demands, and handed over to the

Reaching Out

(Courtesy of the San Francisco *Chronicle*)

tender mercies of the Japanese these 30,000,000 souls—a gross violation of self-determination.

The simple truth is that the Japanese did not ask for, and did not expect to get, sovereign rights over the province of Shantung. They were merely asking for the German economic rights and holdings, which were principally railroad and mining properties. They were also asking for the German leasehold at Kiaochow, but in accordance with a previous agreement with Peking, they were willing to hand it back to China if their claims to German economic holdings were recognized. This leasehold the Japanese had wrested from Germany early in the war at the cost of their own blood—not a great deal of blood to be sure, but nevertheless Japanese blood.

One of the most striking of the many ironies at the Conference is that two of the biggest disputes were stirred up over

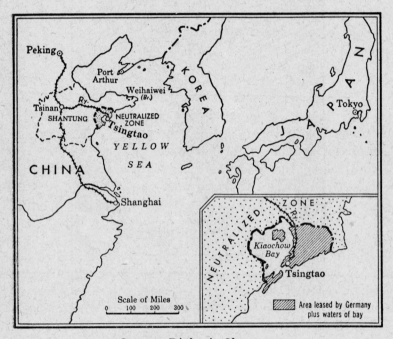

German Rights in Shantung

two of the smallest issues. Fiume, as we have seen, was from the point of view of Italy but a third-rate port. The German leasehold in Shantung, that at the bay of Kiaochow, embraced only 117 square miles. There is some little difference, as Senator Hiram Johnson and others were unwilling to recognize, between taking over 117 square miles temporarily, and 56,000 square miles in perpetuity.

It is clear that self-determination had little to do directly with the Shantung issue, except in so far as economic privileges and railroad supervision may restrict the sovereignty of a nation. And these, it will be readily recognized, may be used as powerful instruments of oppression.

The only Wilsonian principle that seemed directly involved was the second of the Supplementary Points of July 4, 1918, to the effect that "every question" "of economic arrangement" should be based upon "the free acceptance of that settlement by the people immediately concerned . . ."

5

The Japanese, at least as far as German rights in Shantung were concerned, had an almost ironclad legal case. They had been promised those rights by the secret arrangement of 1917 with Britain and France. They had also been promised those rights by the Chinese in the treaties of 1915 and 1918, one of which had been signed by one of the Chinese delegates at Paris. Finally, they had captured the German holdings, and they were apparently there to stay.

Space does not permit a discussion of the merits of the treaties with China, which on various grounds the Chinese now declared invalid. But the agreement of 1917 with Britain and France was certainly binding, the more so since under it the British were making off with Germany's South Pacific Islands. And why apply self-determination to Japan when the British and the French still clung to their Chinese holdings, including the British leasehold at Weihaiwei, which was also in Shantung province? The Japanese expressed a willingness to yield their demands if the British and French would show similar solicitude for China. While there was no danger that this offer would be accepted, it was proffered, and it did bolster Japan's moral position.

The Japanese made it unmistakably clear that if they did not get what they were after, they would bolt the Conference and not sign the treaty. Various compromise proposals were advanced, among them one to the effect that German rights be handed over to the Allied and Associated Powers, who in turn would deal fairly with Japanese interests. This Japan flatly rejected. She wanted to establish once and for all the principle that she was the dominant power in the Far East, and that she was privileged to settle her differences with China without the unwelcome interference of the Western Powers. She would hand Kiaochow back to China, but she would do the handing herself. In short—and this is vastly important—it was largely a matter of "face."

The Japanese delegates, with an aroused public opinion at home, dared not lose face by yielding on Shantung; the Chinese delegates, with an aroused nationalistic feeling at home, dared not lose face by failing to get the German holdings in Shantung; and Wilson, with a strong anti-Japanese element at home, dared not lose face by yielding to the Japanese demands. If he saved face by resisting those demands, he would lose even more face if and when the Japanese withdrew from the Conference and ruined his League of Nations.

6

Critics of Wilson have charged that the Japanese were merely bluffing, and that he weakly bent the knee when he did not have to. Japan, they claim, had much too vital a stake in the League to run out on the Conference. Two of Wilson's Far Eastern experts insisted that Japan was bluffing. Lansing thought so too, but we must bear in mind that he was strongly pro-Chinese, and that he subsequently served for a number of years as legal adviser to the Chinese Embassy in Washington.

Wilson did not agree with Lansing. "They are not bluffers," he said, "and they will go home unless we give them what they should not have." Colonel House agreed with Wilson.

It seems reasonable to conclude that Wilson was right; or to put it another way, he was right in not taking a chance. The Japanese are not notorious bluffers. It was generally thought that they were bluffing before they made war on China in 1894, and on Russia in 1904; when they left the League in 1933; and before they attacked Pearl Harbor in 1941. But they were not.

The Japanese had already lost completely on racial equality, and partially on the mandated islands: the Tokyo government simply could not sustain another defeat. If Japan left the Conference, what could she lose? She still had the North Pacific islands; she was entrenched in Shantung; and who was going to evict her? From the short-run point of view all that she could lose was racial equality, and she had already lost that.

If the Japanese walked out on the Conference they would have potentially formidable and dangerous company. Russia and Germany were outside the pale, and prospective partners in an alliance—an alliance which, in the case of Germany and Japan, finally took shape in 1940. If the old and discredited system of alliances and balances of power was brought into being, this would be the undoing of the League. Ray Stannard Baker believes that the possibility of Japan's joining hands with the other outcasts was one of the most decisive factors in the President's thinking.

Wilson was profoundly worried about the Shantung tangle, and at the height of the crisis he told Baker that he had not slept the previous night. If he made the wrong move, the Conference might well break up, and Europe lapse into anarchy. But if he made the right move, Japan would stay on the reservation, and the League would be saved. As for China, she would have a better chance of securing ultimate justice if Japan were in the League with her rather than outside and against her. If all else failed, the League could be used to right the Shantung wrong.

On this one issue Wilson showed a sensitiveness to home opinion that was conspicuously lacking in his dealing with certain other problems. America was as suspicious of the rising power of the Japanese as she was sympathetic with the position of the underdog Chinese. To hand German rights over to Japan instead of back to China seemed unpleasantly like awarding the loot to the policeman who recovers the stolen goods. Above all, any surrender on Shantung was bound to be attacked in the Senate, and particularly by Senators from the immigration-conscious Western states.

7

The Japanese finally won a substantial victory. They were to receive Germany's economic rights and holdings in Shantung, which was precisely what they had been contending for from the first. In a separate unsigned declaration, entirely apart from the Treaty of Versailles, they promised ultimately to withdraw their troops and restore Shantung in full sovereignty to China, retaining only the German economic holdings and the right to establish a settlement under the usual conditions at Tsingtao. They also gave certain assurances as to Chinese control of the vital railroad.

The Chinese were acutely unhappy. Coming to Paris with the hope of recovering Germany's holdings in Shantung Province, they succeeded in recovering the astronomical instruments which the German troops had baldly removed from Peking during the Boxer disorders of 1900–1901. The Chinese delegates indignantly refused to put their signatures to the Treaty of Versailles. (It was reported that their heads would be cut off if they did.) In China, schools and business houses closed their doors in protest; mass meetings were held; a boycott was begun against Japanese goods; and a few fanatical Chinese committed suicide.

In America, as Wilson feared, there was a wild outburst of condemnation. Numerous newspapers referred to "Japan, the Possessor of Stolen Goods," "The Crime of Shantung," "The Far-Eastern Alsace-Lorraine," "inexcusable injustice," "conspiracy to rob," "a damnable enterprise," "the rape of Shan-tung." Hearst's headlines blared: "SOLD—40,000,000 PEOPLE."

The demagogic Senator Hiram W. Johnson, who knew bet-ter but who also knew the prejudices of his California con-stituency, branded this as "the blackest page in all our history":

To the Japanese Empire, with only 60,000,000 of people, we turned over shamefully and cruelly 40,000,000 of Chinese. To the autocracy of the Orient we delivered 40,000,000 republicans of China. We made the Orient "safe for democracy" by dismember-ing its only democracy and handing the parts to the strongest autocracy on earth.

It would be difficult to compress more errors into fewer words; but one essential fact looms up: the Japanese kept their promise. In 1922 they made final arrangements to turn Shan-tung back to the Chinese government in full sovereignty, though they came back some fifteen years later under different circumstances. This discharge of a solemn obligation received little attention in the press, especially from those newspapers and persons who were proved false prophets.

The alleged Shantung surrender seemingly gave point to Clemenceau's biting remark that Wilson "talked like Jesus Christ but acted like Lloyd George." Writers like Harold Nicolson, forgetting that statesmen must all too often choose between the bad and the less bad, and that the greatest good is sometimes the smallest evil, condemn the Shantung settlement as "the worst surrender of all." On the contrary, it may be regarded as perhaps the most defensible of Wilson's many surrenders.

Unlike the Italians in Fiume, the Japanese had a powerful legal case, buttressed by actual possession. The final arrange-ment was one which involved the honor of Japan, and she kept her promise. The alternative was probable disruption of the entire Conference, with all that it entailed. From many points of view Wilson would have been unjustified in taking such a perilous chance.

8

Perhaps the most unfortunate thing about the so-called
Shantung surrender is that it lent itself to malicious misrepresentation. Face-saving for Japan rather than self-determination

In the Neck!
China's Nine Requests Denied

(From the Bakersfield [Calif.] *Echo;* courtesy of the
Bakersfield *Californian*)

for China was the basic issue. Yet many of the same people
who vociferously condemned Wilson for not giving the Slavs
of Fiume to Italy held up their hands in holy horror when

Shantung—or the economic holdings of Germany in Shantung —went to Japan.

Shantung, as much as any other clause except Article X of the Covenant, defeated the Treaty in the United States. But other things, which were quite avoidable, and which if avoided could have saved the pact, contributed to this end. The Shantung deal could hardly have been avoided, certainly not without running a risk which no responsible statesman should have assumed.

Wilson was acutely unhappy over the result, as he candidly confessed, but he consoled himself as best he could by saying that it was about as clean a settlement as could be made out of a "dirty past." Certainly, it was no dirtier, in fact not so dirty, as some of the things that the European powers were scheming for or actually doing at Paris. Besides, the League was specifically designed to correct such injustices.

There was one final consolation for Wilson. He had faith that when he returned home and explained the situation to the American people they would see that he had no other way out.

But other tutors, less scrupulous about facts, canceled out his efforts.

CHAPTER NINETEEN

THE DAY OF RECKONING

"The Germans don't like the peace terms, but they ought to remember that if they did nobody else would." PHILADELPHIA NORTH AMERICAN, *May, 1919.*

1

ON APRIL 14, 1919, when it seemed as though a settlement were in sight, the German delegates were summoned to Versailles to receive the Treaty. Upon arriving late in the month, they were assigned as virtual prisoners to a hotel, about which a fence was hurriedly erected to shield them from the stares of the curious and from the possible violence of the mob. This precaution was far from foolish, for several weeks later the delegates were assailed by a crowd of angry Frenchmen, and two of the Germans were injured by stones. Nothing could better illustrate the poisonous atmosphere surrounding the Conference.

The German delegates had arrived, but still there was no treaty. The explanation is that during the closing days of April the Fiume and Shantung crises came to a head, and for a while it seemed as though there would be nothing to present to the Germans. Agreement was finally reached, and the various parts of the Treaty on which the numerous committees had been working were thrown together and sent to the printer. The first printed copies were not available until the early morning of May 7, 1919—the day of the presentation of the pact to the German delegates. It is an almost incredible fact that probably no single one of the Allied statesmen had read the Treaty as a whole until the day it was handed to the Germans.

Herbert Hoover remembers that a messenger brought a copy to him on the morning of May 7, and he was so disturbed by what he found that he went for a walk in the early morning air.

He met General Smuts, who was similarly agitated, and who was also walking to cool off. The two men despondently compared notes and expressed fear for the future.

We have already noted that the various parts of the Treaty were fashioned more or less in a vacuum, and then assembled without proper editorial coordination. Lloyd George remarked in the Council of Four that he expected to find in-

Not Fourteen—Only Two—Points Left
(Courtesy of the Cincinnati *Post*)

consistencies, as one always did in a complicated bill in Parliament. He was right: there were serious inconsistencies.

As one examined the individual clauses of the Treaty by themselves the various provisions did not seem altogether unreasonable. But when they were all put together, and when it was observed that certain exactions made it difficult or impossible to carry out other exactions, the whole effect was stunning. Dr. James T. Shotwell has pointedly said that "when all the sacrifices were added together, the whole was greater than the sum of the parts."

2

The Treaty of Versailles was formally presented to the German representatives on May 7, 1919, by coincidence the fourth anniversary of the sinking of the *Lusitania*.

The scene was the Trianon Palace at Versailles. The day was one of surpassing loveliness, and brilliant spring sunlight flooded the room. Dr. Walter Simons, Commissioner-General of the German delegation, noted that "outside of the big window at my right there was a wonderful cherry tree in bloom, and it seemed to me the only reality when compared with the performance in the hall. This cherry tree and its kind will still be blooming when the states whose representatives gathered here exist no longer."

The crowd was small, for the room was small—merely the delegates of both sides, with their assistants, and a few carefully selected press representatives. The grim-visaged Clemenceau sat at the center of the main table: Wilson at his right, Lloyd George at his left.

The air was surcharged with electricity: German and Allied diplomats had not met face to face since the fateful summer of 1914. Would the Germans do something to offend the proprieties?

When all were seated, the doors swung open. At the cry, *"Messieurs les plénipotentiaires allemands!"* the whole assembly rose and stood in silence while the German delegates filed in before their conquerors and sat at a table facing Clemenceau.

The Tiger rose to his feet, and, his voice vibrant with the venom of 1871, almost spat out his speech with staccato precision: "It is neither the time nor the place for superfluous words . . . The time has come when we must settle our accounts. You have asked for peace. We are ready to give you peace."

Already a secretary had quietly walked over to the table at which the Germans sat, and laid before them the thick, two-hundred-odd-page treaty—"the book."

With Clemenceau still standing, the pale, black-clad Count Brockdorff-Rantzau, head of the German delegation, began reading his reply—*seated*.

An almost perceptible gasp swept the room, for the failure of the German to rise was taken as a studied discourtesy. Some felt that he was too nervous and shaken to stand. Others felt that he wanted to snub his "conquerors." The truth is that he planned to sit, not wishing to stand like a culprit before a judge to receive sentence.

Nothing could better reflect the spirit of the Germans. They felt that the war had been more or less a stalemate; they had laid down their arms expecting to negotiate with a chivalrous foe. As equals, why should they rise like criminals before the Allied bar?

3

If Brockdorff-Rantzau's posture was unfortunate, his words and the intonation of his words were doubly so.

The Germans had not yet read the Treaty, but they had every reason to believe that it would be severe. They had not been allowed to participate in its negotiation; they would not be allowed to discuss its provisions *orally* with their conquerors. Brockdorff-Rantzau decided to make the most of this his only opportunity to meet his adversaries face to face and comment on the unread Treaty. Both his manner and his words were sullen, arrogant, unrepentant.

Speaking with great deliberation and without the usual courteous salutation to the presiding officer, he began by saying that the Germans were under "no illusions" as to the extent of their defeat and the degree of their "powerlessness."

This was not true, for both he and his people were under great illusions.

Then he referred defiantly but inaccurately to the demand that the Germans acknowledge that "we alone are guilty of having caused the war. Such a confession in my mouth would be a lie." And the word "lie" fairly hissed from between his teeth.

Bitterly he mentioned the "hundreds of thousands" of German noncombatants who had perished since Armistice Day as a result of Allied insistence on continuing the blockade during the peace negotiations. This shaft struck home, especially to the heart of Lloyd George.

When the echo of Brockdorff-Rantzau's last tactless word had died away, Clemenceau spoke. His face had gone red during the harangue, but he had held himself in check with remarkable self-restraint. Harshly and peremptorily he steamrolled the proceedings to an end: "Has anybody any more observations to offer? Does no one wish to speak? If not, the meeting is closed."

The German delegates marched out, facing a battery of clicking moving picture cameras. Brockdorff-Rantzau lighted a cigarette with trembling fingers.

Lloyd George, who had snapped an ivory paper knife in his hands, remarked angrily: "It is hard to have won the war and to have to listen to that."

Thus, within a half-hour, was compressed one of the greatest dramas of all time.

4

Brockdorff-Rantzau's ill-timed tirade was followed with intense concentration by President Wilson. Dr. Simons noted that the German argument "obviously made its impression upon him, although not a favorable one."

This was absolutely correct. Wilson might have been deeply moved by a clear, dispassionate reference to concrete cases, but this blanket condemnation left him indignant and stubborn. To Lloyd George he turned and said, "Isn't it just like them!"

The German delegate undoubtedly made a grave error in judgment. A short, tactful speech would have kept the door open to compromise; his long, defiant diatribe forced the victors to defend what they had done. Colonel House wrote that if he had been in Brockdorff-Rantzau's position he should have said: "Mr. President, and Gentlemen of the Congress: War is a great gamble; we have lost and are willing to submit to any reasonable terms." But Colonel House might not have been able to say this if he had been the representative of a starved, defeated, and embittered nation.

The Germans were allowed fifteen days—later extended—to file written objections to the provisional terms. It will be remembered that the original plan was to allow enemy delegates to share actively in the final negotiation, but when the preliminary conference merged with the final conference, there was no place for German or other enemy representatives. Besides, it was feared that they might engage in intrigue of the Talleyrand variety, and provoke further dissension at a time when there was already enough dissension. The most serious trouble at the Conference was caused by differences within Allied ranks rather than by differences with the enemy. "To the victors," remarked the Boston *Herald,* "belong the broils."

So it was that the Germans were handed the Treaty on the point of a bayonet and told to file protests. This represented a compromise between giving them an oral share in the discussions and giving them no part at all. The Paris Conference was a conference only in so far as the victors conferred among themselves.

This was most unfortunate, for there was no one during the negotiation of the treaty to present the German point of view to the inevitably hate-ridden victors. The very fact that the Germans, in the short time at their disposal, and with only written protests, were able to secure some concessions and im-

plant more doubts is proof in itself that with tactful negotiators and oral discussions the vanquished might have secured
a more moderate and workable treaty.

The reaction of German opinion to the published terms
was bitter in the extreme. President Ebert called the Treaty a
"monstrous document," and the government instituted a week
of mourning. General Ludendorff cryptically remarked: "If
these are the peace terms, then America can go to hell."

5

The days that followed were anxious and uncertain. The
Germans were studying the Treaty and preparing their replies. The Allied delegates also had to study the Treaty to find
out what was in it, for, as previously noted, few if any of them
had read it as a whole.

During this tense period of waiting for the German reply,
a strong feeling began to develop among liberal elements that
the Treaty had been made too severe, and that it ought to be
softened. This "remorse complex" was especially marked in
Great Britain and among certain members of the British delegation, and Lloyd George, the Welsh weathercock, began to
veer with it. If the Germans should refuse to sign the Treaty
on the ground that it was too drastic, the fiery Welshman
would doubtless be unhorsed. Wilson noted that he had got
into a "perfect funk"; and he insisted on ameliorating the
Treaty, notably at the expense of France rather than of Great
Britain.

Clemenceau brought Lloyd George sharply to book. Great
Britain, he said, had come off very well: German colonies,
reparations, ships, cables, the destruction of Germany's naval
power. If Lloyd George wanted to appease Germany, let him
hand back some colonies and ships, and not weaken French
security by withdrawing the Allied army of occupation, by

returning Upper Silesia to Germany, and by reducing claims for reparations.

Lloyd George's antics, if anything, confirmed Wilson in his stubbornness. During the negotiations the capricious Briton had demanded severe conditions on reparations and other matters, against the better judgment of Wilson, and now that the Germans were threatening not to sign the Treaty, he was insisting on backing down. Wilson remarked disgustedly that such people made him "tired" and "very sick." The terms of the Treaty were either just or unjust; but the time to have decided that was when the Treaty was being drafted.

There is undoubtedly much to be said for Wilson's refusal to countenance a last-moment rewriting of the pact. The race between peace and anarchy was going to be terribly close, and the peacemakers had already been at their task for more than five months. If Lloyd George was permitted to reverse himself, others would be entitled to reverse themselves. Concessions to the Germans would beget demands for further concessions, and the process would go on interminably.

On the other hand, it is possible—though we shall never know—that the importance of haste was exaggerated, and that it would have been better in the long run to take several more weeks or even months, and, if possible, thresh out a more workable treaty.

In any event, the German delegates labored frantically to prepare adequate replies in the inadequately short time allowed them. They were encouraged by learning that all was not well in the Allied camp, and they were spurred on by knowing of the terribly unsettled conditions in revolution-ridden Germany.

The waters were so troubled that a German diplomat of the caliber of Talleyrand undoubtedly could have fished to advantage. If the Germans, instead of vehemently attacking every objectionable feature of the treaty, whether minor or major, had tactfully concentrated their fire on a few essential points, they might conceivably have won substantial concessions. But they had no Talleyrand. They tactlessly and angrily filed voluminous objections to everything objectionable, and in this way forced the Allies into a blanket defense of their admittedly unsatisfactory handiwork.

The German replies, the most important of which was some 50,000 words long, protested violently against the complete loss of all colonies, against the amputation of approximately

Diplomacy!

(From the New York *Evening World;* reprinted by permission)

one-eighth of Germany's territory and one-tenth of her population, against the refusal of the victors to disarm, against Germany's ostracism from the League of Nations, and against the "financial thralldom" established by the reparations and other economic clauses, many of which were impossible of fulfillment. "Those who will sign this Treaty," wrote Brockdorff-Rantzau, "will sign the death sentence of many millions of German men, women and children."

Above all, the Germans insisted that they had laid down their arms after having been solemnly promised a peace based on the Fourteen Points, a peace of right and justice—a peace, as Wilson had said, of "no annexations, no contributions, no punitive damages." Now, they alleged, the points had been cast aside one by one, in the interest of keeping Germany economically and politically prostrate.

6

The 35,000-word Allied reply to the German counterproposals began with an unchallengeable statement: "The protest of the German Delegation shows that they utterly fail to understand the position in which Germany stands today."

Sharply rebutting the German contentions, the Allied statement asserted that the peace proposed "is fundamentally a peace of justice." The Allied conception of justice was further elaborated:

Justice is what the German Delegation ask for and say that Germany had been promised. Justice is what Germany shall have. But it must be justice for all. There must be justice for the dead and wounded and for those who have been orphaned and bereaved that Europe might be freed from Prussian despotism. There must be justice for the peoples who now stagger under war debts which exceed £30,000,000,000 that liberty might be saved. There must be justice for those millions whose homes and land, ships and property German savagery has spoliated and destroyed.

When the Germans laid down their arms on the basis of Wilson's promises of a peace of "right" and "impartial justice," they were clearly laboring under a very serious misapprehension. They were evidently thinking of "mercy" and "leniency" when they thought of "right," "fairness," and "justice." They evidently did not realize that these three words mean different things to different men and at different times. They evidently failed to observe that "justice" meant one thing to them, a different thing to the Allies, and a still different thing to the neutrals. They evidently failed to understand that what is "justice" in a war-charged atmosphere may be something different from "justice" in a peaceful atmosphere. Anyone who talked about genuine "justice" was regarded as pro-German.

Such relative and flexible terms need definition and application by impartial judges. And the Germans failed to realize that the Allies, in determining what justice should be, would be the sole determinants. Wilson, who was one of the chief judges, thought of himself as impartial and disinterested. He had in fact told his experts on the *George Washington* that they would be the "only disinterested people" at the Conference. The truth is that Wilson was not impartial or disinterested: no man could be who had passed through the recent bath of propaganda, war hatred, and atrocity stories.

"Justice" is a word that has several definitions, but a primary meaning is "merited reward or punishment."

There can be no doubt that the great body of Allied negotiators, including Wilson, felt that the severities of the Treaty were a "merited punishment"—in fact, less than a "merited punishment"—for having wantonly forced this horrible calamity upon humanity. Wilson was a stern rather than a merciful man, and his idea of justice was the Calvinist concept of an angry God meting out just deserts to depraved sinners. In his later public defense of the Treaty, he declared time and again that the pact was severe but just.

Lloyd George privately said—and the humane Herbert Hoover wrote essentially the same thing—that if "right" and "justice" were granted to the "Boches" they would be crushed out of existence. Public opinion in the Allied countries felt the same way. The press of the United States abounded in such statements as "Her offenses considered, Germany gets off lightly, indeed"; the terms were "essentially just in view of the colossal calamity which Germany brought upon the world"; "It is a harsh treaty, but it could not have been otherwise and be just."

We may not unreasonably conclude that since "justice" admits of several definitions, and since in 1919 the Allies were doing the defining, the Germans would have to seek other grounds for a legal protest.

7

On the question of the Fourteen Points the Berlin government was treading—or seemed to be treading—on firmer ground.

The Germans in their protests against the Treaty asserted that they had made a solemn pre-Armistice contract with their enemy, in which they were promised a peace based on the Fourteen Points, with one reservation and one elucidation. They now alleged that many of those Points had been broken, and as a consequence the contract had been violated.

The Allies in their reply candidly admitted that they had entered into such a contract, but they unequivocally denied that they had broken the Fourteen Points. Their defense was devastating.

It will be remembered that Berlin had sued for a peace based on the original Fourteen Points and *all the subsequent points and principles relating to peace which Wilson had set forth in his public utterances*. Unluckily for the Germans, some of these supplementary Points contradicted and wiped out all the others. The Allies made powerful use of these forgotten Points in rebutting the German claims.

At Mount Vernon, on July 4, 1918, Wilson had asserted that every "arbitrary power" which might "disturb the peace of the world" must be "destroyed," or at least reduced to "virtual impotence." The Germans solemnly signed this appalling blank check when they accepted *all* of Wilson's Points.

Assuming, as the Allies all did, that Germany was a disturber of world peace, then any measures would be justified that would reduce her to "virtual impotence," including the loss of colonies and German-inhabited areas like Danzig and Upper Silesia.

On February 11, 1918, Wilson had told Congress that each part of the coming settlement should be based not only upon "essential justice" but upon *"such adjustments as are most likely to bring a peace that will be permanent."* In short, any "adjustment" of any kind which *in Allied eyes* would make for a "permanent" peace would override any or all of the other Fourteen Points.

By using these "escape clauses," and the contradictions in the Fourteen Points, the Allies could invoke those principles that operated to Germany's disadvantage, and discard those that did not. Let it not be forgotten that in the application of the Fourteen Points the Allies were both prosecutor and judge; and from their technically defensible point of view there were no violations of the Fourteen Points at all.

8

The shyster lawyer will deliberately introduce "escape clauses" into the contract; but it is hard to believe that Wilson, with his high sense of honor, realized fully what he was doing when he made his numerous speeches. If a man in public life talks enough he will almost inevitably contradict himself.

We do not know whether the Allied leaders immediately detected these "escape clauses" and made careful note of them. The Germans probably did not, for their natural tendency was to seize upon those statements that held out promise of leniency, while overlooking the rest. It is possible, of course, that they did notice them, and rather than press for a more careful definition, preferred to take their chances with oral discussion in the negotiation of the peace—an oral discussion which never came.

But why did Wilson, the man of honor, keep quiet on this issue at Paris? Why did he not, as the author of the Fourteen

Points, issue a peremptory protest against the palpable mis-use of his sacred principles? As a matter of fact, he sat through the meetings of the Council of Four while the Allied reply was being discussed, yet, according to the records now available, he merely said that the document "conveyed a slight feeling of inadequacy," and that "it would not prove satisfactory to the future historian."

The explanation is not easy to find. Perhaps Wilson resented the attacks on his Fourteen Points, and the effrontery of the Germans in quoting Wilson to refute Wilson. Perhaps his con-science hurt him so keenly over the infractions of his principles that he was willing to take refuge in technical escapes. Cer-tainly he was angered by Brockdorff-Rantzau's defiant ha-rangue. Certainly he saw the folly of reopening the whole issue again and further delaying the Treaty. And certainly he was counting on the League of Nations to iron out the in-equities that had inevitably crept into the Treaty.

Enlightened opinion in the Allied countries knew perfectly well in a general way what the Fourteen Points meant. This was the meaning that the Germans had accepted, or thought they had accepted. But the practical application of the Four-teen Points involved, perhaps inescapably, a moral, though not a strictly legal, breach of contract.

A later generation might be tempted to call this dishonest. But the negotiators were too close to their problem and too close to their unrepentant foe not to take full advantage of these loopholes.

9

Clemenceau stood foursquare with Wilson in refusing to alter the Treaty in any fundamental way. The French press changed its tune overnight and began to praise the splendid American President. After all these voluminous interchanges with the Germans, the Allies made only a few minor conces-sions, and only one of any real consequence. They relented on turning over Upper Silesia, with its considerable German population and highly important industries, to the tender mercies of the Poles. Instead, provision was made for a plebiscite. (See map on p. 219.)

We need not discuss this interesting problem at length, because Lloyd George was primarily responsible for it, as he had been in making the German port of Danzig a free city rather than an outright Polish possession. In both cases Wilson, after considerable indecision, and contrary to the wishes of his pro-Pole experts, gave in. Upon mature reflection Upper Silesia seemed to him so clear-cut a case of self-determination as to require the vote of the inhabitants.

It is hardly fair to criticize Wilson because the plebiscite did not work out happily, and because the Germans were exceedingly ungrateful for the substantial part of Upper Silesia which they finally received. This was a situation of terrible explosiveness, and it seems probable that Germany would have been even more bitter if the entire area had been awarded outright to the Poles.

During the hectic weeks when these concessions were being debated, the question on every lip was: Will Germany sign? Opinion varied in every quarter, and from day to day. The Germans showed their defiance by burning certain French battle flags which they were supposed to return, and by spectacularly scuttling their battle fleet in the British harbor of Scapa Flow, rather than have it fall into Allied hands. This was a flagrant violation of the Armistice terms, and aroused the French to new bitterness. "Germany," remarked *L'Action Française* (Paris), "may one day, if we are not careful, scuttle the League of Nations as she scuttled the fleet."

At the last moment, the German government reluctantly offered to sign, subject to an abrogation of the "war guilt" clause, to a renunciation of the article providing for the surrender of German war "criminals" for trial, and to a solemn protest against shearing away all of Germany's colonial possessions.

The Allies flatly rejected these overtures. They were in no mood to dicker, and in no position to have to. Instead, they instructed Marshal Foch, on June 20th, to march into Germany if the Treaty was not approved by 7:00 P.M. on June 23rd.

There was nothing the Germans could now do but sign. Marshal Foch's armies were poised to strike, and both he and

The Fifteenth Point!

(From the New York *Herald*; courtesy of the New York *Sun*)

many of his men would have enjoyed a jaunt through Germany. The American boys of the A.E.F. were delighted with the prospect of a long-deferred march down Unter den Linden.

Germany was bankrupt, revolution-torn, starving. Thousands of Berliners were surging through the streets bearing banners that clamored for immediate signing: "We have had enough; peace, for God's sake." "We want bread not bullets."

On June 23, 1919, a few scant hours before the dead line, the terrible suspense was ended. The new German government

—the old one had resigned in protest on June 20th—announced
that it approved the Treaty, unconditionally.

10

The signing ceremony was staged in the great Hall of
Mirrors in Louis XIV's Palace of Versailles. This was the place
where the Germans had humiliated the defeated French in
1871 by proclaiming William I the Emperor of united Germany, and obviously for the purpose of a counter humiliation
it was chosen for the scene. The Hall of Mirrors was at once
the cradle and the grave of the German Empire.

The date was June 28, 1919, by coincidence the fifth anniversary of the murder of the Archduke Francis Ferdinand at
Sarajevo. The precise time was midafternoon. The occasion
lacked the dignity and suspense of the presentation ceremony
in the small room of the Trianon Palace. Everyone knew that
the Germans would sign; and the event was too elaborately
staged in too large a place. There were about a thousand people
in the audience, many of them ladies, and the air buzzed with
conversation.

The two German delegates were marched in—Brockdorff-
Rantzau had resigned with his government—and after a brief
speech by Clemenceau, they signed the Treaty. The Allied
plenipotentiaries added their signatures. Outside the hall
cannon boomed, the great fountains gushed forth for the first
time since the war began, and the assembly broke up in confusion, with autograph hunters ferreting out the delegates.

A young German was heard to say: "All passes. It will seem
so different in ten, in twenty years . . ."

Colonel House was sad. "I had," he wrote, "a feeling of
sympathy for the Germans who sat there quite stoically. It was
not unlike what was done in olden times, when the conqueror
dragged the conquered at his chariot wheels."

Two incidents marred the ceremony. General Smuts, the

South African liberal, signed under protest. "I feel," he said, "that in the Treaty we have not yet achieved the real peace to which our peoples were looking."

The Chinese refused to sign at all. They could not forget Shantung.

The Germans signed because they had to. They presented no more formal reservations; their reservations were mental. Those that they had offered so vehemently, only a few days before, they would not soon forget. They morally repudiated the Treaty while they signed it.

In Berlin, some of the newspapers announced the signing with black borders, and with captions: "Germany's Fate Sealed." The Berlin *Vorwärts*, which was regarded as a mouthpiece of the government, cried: "We must never forget it is only a scrap of paper. Treaties based on violence can keep their validity only so long as force exists. Do not lose hope. The resurrection day comes."

11

It is highly significant that much of Germany's bitterness against the Treaty turned against America, and particularly against Wilson. His name is still cursed in German.

The fall, rise, and again the fall of Wilson in German esteem was most spectacular. In 1914 he was regarded with considerable respect; from 1915 to 1917 he was branded as a sniveling hypocrite, sympathetic with the Allies and thwarting German victory; from 1917 to 1918 he was a remorseless enemy; from the Armistice to the presentation of the Treaty he was seized upon as Germany's last hope—her sole chance of being delivered from the vengeance of her enemies.

With the publication of peace terms, Wilson again became a treacherous deceiver. All Germany cried with Philipp Scheidemann, head of the German ministry, "President Wilson is a hypocrite and the Versailles Treaty is the vilest crime in history."

It would be amusing, if it were not so tragic, to note how German devotion to the pristine Fourteen Points increased in proportion as the Allies forsook them. "The further President Wilson gets away from the Fourteen Points," chortled the Washington *Post,* "the closer the Germans nudge up to them." By June, 1919, the Germans were far more enthusiastic about the original Wilsonian program than anyone else.

American public opinion was not impressed by German "bleating" about the Fourteen Points. Journals like the New York *World* insisted that Wilson's principles had been generally carried out, which was not difficult to establish, depending on one's premises. Other newspapers bluntly reminded the Germans that they would have fared much less well if it had not been for Wilson and his Points, which was undoubtedly true. Others insisted that Germany had not been disarmed by the Fourteen Points at all but by several million Allied bayonet points, including those of American doughboys.

Other explanations or justifications were more cynical. The Philadelphia *Public Ledger* reminded its readers that the purpose of the Fourteen Points was to "impale German militarism," and this they were doing, and doing well. A good many Republican newspapers shrugged aside the Points by saying that they were Wilson's Points, and they did not represent the wishes of the American people—which was probably more true than Wilson wanted to believe. The *Wall Street Journal* went a step further in perverting history. It declared that the American people had "repudiated the Fourteen Points at the Congressional election in November," when a Republican majority was elected "on the straightforward slogan of 'unconditional surrender.'"

While there was some doubt in America as to the status of the Fourteen Points, there was none as to Germany's general attitude. She had clearly signed under great protest, and she regarded this treaty as another "scrap of paper." She was, in the judgment of the St. Louis *Star,* "a disarmed trickster rather than a reformed conspirator." The Kansas City *Journal* agreed: "It took force to make Germany sign. And it will take force to make her honor the signature." This situation was regarded in certain quarters as all the more reason why the United States should protect itself by joining the League of Nations.

12

The American people wasted little sympathy on the Hun. The press abounded with references to his "yellow streak" in surrendering before taking his beating, to his cowardly and treacherous sinking of his fleet, and to his constant "yawping" for food. There was little appreciation of the terrible straits to which the German population had been reduced by the Allied hunger blockade, which was kept on in some fashion for eight full months after the Armistice. When Congress, in February, 1919, finally appropriated $100,000,000 to provide food for devastated Europe, Germany and her allies were specifically denied a single crumb of bread or a single drop of soup. The Philadelphia *Evening Ledger* caught the spirit of the hour when it declared: "If Germany can be made safe only by hunger and torment and relative poverty, then it is better for the rest of the world that she be made to endure hunger and torment and poverty."

It is a fact of the greatest significance, particularly in view of the later unpopularity of the Treaty in the United States, that there was no serious objection to its severity, except among a numerically small group of liberals. Everywhere there was satisfaction that this was a "hard" peace, and not a "soft" one, such as the Republicans had feared that the dreamy Wilson would make. "The wild beast that sprang at the throat of civilization has been muzzled," rejoiced the New York *Tribune*. Most of our newspapers regarded the terms as just, even merciful, when judged in relation to Germany's offense against civilization. The Atlanta *Constitution* felt that the Germans, "instead of bewailing the fact that they must consign themselves to the mercies of God, should be thanking God that they got off so lightly." "It's a hard bed, Heinie, but who made it?" gibed the Cleveland *Press;* while the Chicago *Daily News* sneered: "What did Germania think—that the nations were going to make her Queen of the May?"

An occasional jarring note was introduced by the liberals, the pro-Germans, the Socialists, and others.

The liberal *New Republic* published a telling indictment of the Allied breach of faith, and concluded that the Treaty "gives the Germans too many reasons for feeling themselves thoroughly abused." The Springfield *Republican,* a liberal newspaper, declared: "The Treaty was dictated in a paroxysm of hate."

The German-language New York *Staats-Zeitung* discreetly refrained from comment on its editorial page and merely published the Fourteen Points.

The Socialist New York *Call,* branding this a "peace that passeth all understanding," cried with savage irony: "Accept it, children, with faith and resignation—and prepare for the next Armageddon."

CHAPTER TWENTY

BLESSED ARE THE PEACEMAKERS

"How splendid it would have been had we blazed a new and better trail!" COLONEL HOUSE, *June 29, 1919.*

———————

1

SHORTLY AFTER the signing ceremony, Wilson left Paris for Brest, where he was to board the *George Washington* for home. A large and enthusiastic crowd, many of them notables, saw him off at the Paris railway station. For the last time the red carpet was rolled out, and he and Mrs. Wilson walked between potted palms to their train.

Just before leaving, Wilson gave a mass interview to some two hundred newspaper correspondents. To the query of Lincoln Steffens he replied: "I think that we have made a better peace than I should have expected when I came here to Paris." His opinion was probably colored, as he privately wrote, by "the consciousness that the results are so much better than at one time I feared . . ."

Nevertheless Wilson was so deeply disturbed by France's blocking of his plans that he had seriously considered declining an invitation to a farewell dinner given by President Poincaré. Fortunately for international amity, Wilson was dissuaded by Henry White and others from administering such a resounding rebuke. But it is evident that he was in a fighting mood.

House had a final word with the departing President. He pointed out that if Wilson were as conciliatory in dealing with the Senate as he had been with his foreign colleagues in Paris, all would be well. Ominously, Wilson rejected this counsel of compromise and concession, and said: "House, I have found

one can never get anything in his life that is worth while without fighting for it."

House replied that "Anglo-Saxon civilization was built up
on compromise . . ." Into these few words were compressed
the divergent viewpoints of the two men.

They never saw each other again.

2

What manner of treaty was Wilson carrying home for the
hostile scrutiny of the United States Senate?

It has been fashionable in recent years to condemn the
Treaty of Versailles as thoroughly bad. The truth is that it
contained much that was good and much that was bad. We
need not try to determine whether the good outweighed the
bad; but, all things considered, it is remarkable that the de-
fects were not more numerous, more pervasive, and more glaring. One could even go so far as to say that the most surprising
thing about the Treaty is not that it was unsatisfactory but
that any kind of treaty came out of the madhouse at Paris.
Certainly no other conference was ever confronted with such
a complex of problems, and certainly none has ever dealt with
a comparable task more scientifically and expeditiously. As
compared with other great conferences of the past, this one
moved at a dizzy pace.

We have considered the blunders—at least some of the
blunders—that the statesmen made. But in all fairness it must
be pointed out that there were certain conditions over which
the negotiators had no control whatsoever, and these conditions would have left their imprint on any peace at that time.

The vision of the delegates and of their people was clouded
by the passions of a war that was still too close. The Peace of
Versailles was almost literally negotiated on the ruins of a
smoking battlefield. As Lloyd George told the House of Commons: "I am doubtful whether any body of men with a diffi-

cult task have worked under greater difficulties—stones crackling on the roof and crashing through the windows, and sometimes wild men screaming through the keyholes." The tragedy is that in order to win the war the Allies had been forced to whip up such passions at home as to make difficult if not impossible the winning of the peace. "Once lead this people into war," Wilson had said in 1917, "and they'll forget there ever was such a thing as tolerance."

The Bolshevik menace, rising like an ominous flood, cried aloud for haste. Its red rivulet licked into Hungary, into Bavaria. There was every temptation to build hastily and quickly, rather than permanently and well. "Better a bad treaty today," was the saying, "than a good treaty four months hence."

The situation in Central Europe was nothing short of chaotic. Succession states were rising like phoenixes from the ruins of the ramshackle Austro-Hungarian empire. They could not wait for the quiet dictates of the Conference; they moved in and took what they wanted, thus presenting the negotiators with accomplished facts. In many cases the oppressed became the oppressors, and all the more savage because of their soul-searing experience.

Men cried, "Peace! Peace!" but there was no peace. While the peacemakers were busy in Paris, the warmakers were busy in Russia and Central Europe. It would in fact be difficult to name a single year following the Armistice when a serious armed disturbance was not agitating some part of the world. Bonar Law told the House of Commons, a few days before the Germans signed the treaty, that twenty-three different wars were raging in various parts of the world. It was as if some giant monster, threshing about in death agony, had broken into twenty-three convulsive parts. No wonder men spoke cynically of "the terrors of peace."

Peace is not in itself a condition: it reflects a condition. We should never forget that one of the insuperable obstacles at Paris was that the frock-coated negotiators were expected to produce a settlement in lands where there was no settlement, in lands where their authority did not extend.

3

There were several other conditions over which the negotiators could have no control.

Behind everything and permeating everything were politics. Clemenceau, Lloyd George, and Orlando—yes, even Wilson—were but the servants and mouthpieces of their people. If they yielded too much, if they did not bring back the spoils of victory, they would be thrown out and replaced by men of sterner stuff. Clemenceau and Lloyd George generally tried to give the public what it wanted. They survived. Orlando failed to give the people what they wanted. He was unhorsed. Wilson tried to give the people what *he* wanted. He was broken.

Where there were so many clashing interests, there had to be compromise or there would be no settlement. The representatives of great nations will not voluntarily consent to sit down at a table and be outvoted by an unfriendly majority. Compromise between two groups is often difficult and always unsatisfactory; but at Paris there had to be compromise among four or five of the great powers, and this increased the difficulty and dissatisfaction vastly more than four- or five-fold. It was simply impossible for Wilson to have his own way all—or perhaps most—of the time, even though he had powerful economic weapons in his arsenal. The marvel is that he got as much of his program written into the Treaty as he did. The explanation probably is that the European nations, despite the muttering in the American press and the sniping in the Senate, did not realize the extent to which he was losing his hold on public opinion.

Not a single one of the great powers was satisfied with the Treaty. This was because it had to be a compromise, and no

compromise, as we have observed, is ever completely satisfactory to all the parties concerned. Each power felt that it had
yielded too much and received too little. In France, Clemenceau was condemned as the dupe of Wilson and Lloyd George;
in England, Lloyd George as the dupe of Wilson and Clemenceau; in America, Wilson as the dupe of Clemenceau and
Lloyd George.

Another unavoidable difficulty at Paris was that the peace
was a coalition peace, just as the war had been a coalition war;
and a coalition can seldom move with complete singleness of
purpose.

Napoleon once remarked that his brilliant victories had been
easy because he was fighting a coalition of enemies. The Allies
of 1914–1918 had prosecuted the war in a disorganized fashion,
until the spring of 1918, and they framed the peace in a disorganized fashion, under the additional handicap of having
disposed of the enemy who had forced them to unite. When we
consider that it is on the whole a more delicate and complicated
task to make an enduring peace than to prosecute a successful
war, it is all the more surprising that the results were not less
satisfactory.

4

Finally—and ominously—Russia, the blind Cyclops of the
East, had no part in the Conference.

It is not altogether clear that this was an avoidable blunder.
Russia was in the throes of one of the bloodiest civil wars in
history, and it was impossible to tell which group of officials
represented the nation. Wilson and others backed an attempt
to bring the discordant elements together on the isle of Prin-
kipo in the Sea of Marmora; but this failed, partly because of
Russian recalcitrance, and partly because of French opposition. It is probably true that the problem was an insoluble one,
but the fact is that France ruined whatever scant prospects
there were for success. She would have no traffic, in the colorful

phrase of Winston Churchill, with the "foul baboonery of Bolshevism."

Repeated reference has been made in these pages to the Big Four. It was really the Big Five. Lenin was the fifth member—an invisible member occupying an invisible chair. He was more important than Orlando. He held the Conference to its labors, and applied the whip and spur. Russia was more important at Paris than Prussia; Prussia had no voice, Russia had a loud though ghostlike voice.

Thus the peace settlements of 1919 embraced only Western and Central Europe and Turkey, with due attention to Germany's overseas empire. The powers could delineate Poland's western borders; but they could not delineate her eastern borders. These could be settled only between her and Russia.

It seems self-evident that there can be no European settlement without Russia, for Russia is about one-half of Europe. It seems self-evident that there can be no world settlement without Russia, for Russia is about one-seventh of the world.

So it came about that peace—an uneasy peace—was made with only one side of Europe. The other side was still in chaos. The wonder is that the settlements lasted as long as they did.

5

Wilson at Paris conceived of the problem before him as a dual one. He tried to make peace with Germany, which was the immediate task, and at the same time reorder international relations, which was the long-run task. The two became hopelessly entangled, and neither was satisfactorily handled.

One of the results—and a fatal result—was that the Treaty of Versailles fell between two stools. It was neither a thoroughgoing victor's peace nor a peace of accommodation.

There are two ways of dealing with a fallen foe. The one is to make a peace so generous that he may forgive and forget. Whether Germany would have responded favorably to such treatment is still a matter of speculation, but there was a possibility that it might have worked. The second method is to impose a victor's peace, with the purpose of keeping the con-

"Chust See If I Don'd Get Oudt of It Yet!"
(Courtesy of the Baltimore *American*)

queror's heel on the enemy's neck as long as physically possible. This method is certain to breed another war.

The Treaty of Versailles contained some of the most severe terms that one civilized nation has ever imposed on another, while elsewhere it soared heavenward in the lofty idealism of the Covenant of the League of Nations. It was harsh enough to humiliate and anger the Germans but not drastic enough permanently to enchain them—assuming that this could ever be done. It was idealistic enough to create the illusion of workable peace machinery, but selfish enough to make that machinery unworkable in a real crisis.

The seeds of war were planted by the statesmen at Paris in many of the articles of the Treaty, but in that impassioned atmosphere they knew not what they were doing. Before 1914, France was the aggrieved power, nursing memories of Alsace-Lorraine and vanished *gloire,* while preparing for a war of revenge; after 1919, Germany was the aggrieved power, nursing memories of Danzig and lost colonies and frustrated plans of European domination, while preparing for a war of revenge. The "guilt clause" was a verbal Alsace-Lorraine.

Wilson recognized that there were inequities in the Treaty, but he confidently counted on the League to iron them out at a later date and in a saner atmosphere. This was a splendid ideal, but utterly unworkable, because Article V of the Covenant called for a unanimous vote in the Assembly and Council on all questions of substance. France, Poland, and others could always be counted on to veto any proposition that would show leniency toward Germany or her vanquished satellites. This was one of the prices that Wilson had to pay for France's adherence to the League of Nations.

Wilson also had to yield to French insistence that Germany be kept out of the League, which she was until 1926. The opposition of France was natural, but it had the most unfortunate result of causing the League to appear like a new Anglo-French alliance—a kind of exclusive international club from which Germany was excluded because of her moral blemish. This weakened the League in the eyes of both Germany and the other non-member nations, and subjected it to an incessant barrage of criticism and denunciation.

In the final analysis the League of Nations turned out to be an organization designed to freeze the status quo and keep the victorious Allies permanently in the saddle. The League was in essence an alliance of the victors, without the binding force of a true alliance. It evolved into an organization designed not to create a new balance of power but to preserve the existing imbalance of power.

This, of course, was not what Wilson wanted. "You cannot go forward," he said, "with one foot in the Old Order and the other in the New." But this was the best he could bring back from Paris, and he hoped that it would work out better than it did. Ironically, the very concessions that he was forced to make in order to give life to the League were the very concessions that ultimately gave it death.

The New Order, far from being established, merely "fouled the Old"—to use the phrase of Harold Nicolson. In the view of many Europeans the idealistic bungler from America should have stayed at home and allowed the Europeans to make a good old-fashioned victor's peace. War probably would have followed, but perhaps it would have been delayed for two generations instead of one. Possibly that is the best humanity can hope for. But Wilson was unable to resign himself to such defeatism.

6

A strong point should be made of the fact that a large part of Wilson's achievement at Paris was purely negative. It can even be argued that his most important contribution was not what he did but what he prevented others from doing, notably in connection with the Saar, saddling Germany with the entire cost of the war, and dividing Germany's colonies on a purely imperialistic basis, illusory though all of these solutions may have been.

It is true that many things went through which he did not approve. But there were so many iniquitous heads popping up at Paris that he could not tilt a lance at every one he saw. He concentrated his efforts on what he regarded—in some cases mistakenly—as the most iniquitous. It is worth repeating that the punitive parts of the Treaty undoubtedly would have been more harsh had he not been at Paris.

The critics of Wilson almost unanimously charge that his most conspicuous failure at Paris had to do with self-determination. Instead of Poles being forced to live under German domination, Germans were forced to live under Polish domination; instead of Italians being forced to live under Slavs, Slavs were forced to live under Italians. New if smaller minorities were seemingly exchanged for old.

Most conspicuous of all, the nearly seven million Germans of Austria were forbidden to join hands with their compatriots in Germany. The French, with their decimated man power and declining birth rate, found it unthinkable that Germany should emerge from this bloody war with a larger population of Germans than in 1914. Austria was to be made so independent that she could not exercise the right voluntarily to yield her independence. She was left an economic shell: a tremendous capital without a hinterland; a heart without a body. In all this Wilson reluctantly acquiesced.

The most glaring violations of the principle of nationality were in some instances avoidable, in others unavoidable. But on the whole the Paris settlement was a victory for self-determination. This principle was far more often honored in the observance than in the breach. Many more millions of minority groups were released from alien domination than were consigned to alien domination. The result was the closest approximation that modern Europe has ever had to an ethnographic map coinciding with a political map.

This raises the question whether an ethnographic map was what Europe needed: whether it would not have been better to have fewer states rather than more, whether it would not have been better to have more economic self-sufficiency and less self-determination, less abstract justice and more economic viability. Man does not live by bread alone, but he cannot live without bread.

7

The critics of Wilson say that at Paris he sacrificed his Four-teen Points one by one in order to save the League, just as a mother would throw her younger children to the pursuing wolves in order to save her first-born. Harold Nicolson, at least by indirection, accuses Wilson of having abandoned nineteen of his twenty-three points and principles.

This statement is pure nonsense, but it should be examined to determine how intelligent men can arrive at so erroneous a conclusion.

Critics like Nicolson assume that because a point, like self-determination, was not fully achieved, it was completely be-trayed: 90 per cent success is total failure. This, in all honesty, is unfair. Winston Churchill estimated that fewer than 3 per cent of the people of Europe were condemned to live under governments whose nationality they repudiated. On the whole, the territorial readjustments in Europe were the most reason-able part of the settlement, and they generally benefited the small states rather than the great powers.

Nicolson takes it for granted that because a point was not achieved at Paris, it was completely betrayed. This also is un-fair. Wilson assumed, for example, that the League of Nations would take care of freedom of the seas, and he had confidence that the machinery specially set up by the League would deal satisfactorily with disarmament. It did not do so, but that was not because he betrayed his principles, but because others be-trayed the League.

Certain other points could not be carried out at Paris, no-tably those having to do with Russia and Turkey, because the confusion in those places had not sufficiently subsided.

When we rule out Russia and Turkey, and consider what the League was supposed to do, and include those points that were in large part carried out either in letter or in spirit, we have a far different picture. This is why men like Secretary

Lansing could honestly testify, after the Treaty of Versailles was signed, that in so far as circumstances then permitted, the Fourteen Points were "substantially" carried out. This could not have been said a few years later, but by that time a situation had developed over which Wilson could have no control.

Even so, the fact cannot be blinked that when the Germans laid down their arms they were tendered a solemn contract promising, with specified exceptions, the Fourteen Points. The contract did not say that the points would be "substantially" carried out, or carried out in so far as circumstances would permit. The contract was terribly binding; and from the German point of view no excuses were valid.

In any case, the word "betrayal" is far too strong when applied to Wilson and his Fourteen Points. There are errors of commission and errors of omission. Most of the criticism of Wilson is directed not at what he did but at what he failed to do. Most of his critics assume that he should have forced his Points fully and completely upon colleagues who did not want them, and who under no circumstances would accept them. Not even Wilson could do the impossible. The original error was to permit his name to be used in giving currency to the belief that he could.

Wilson was never willing to confess—and probably never believed—that he had betrayed his Points. He told the newspaper men before leaving Paris that he had secured more than he had expected when the Conference began, and he insisted that the general spirit of the Fourteen Points had permeated the discussions. As for betraying Germany, he declared to the very end that the Treaty was severe but just.

Allied apologists not only agreed with him on this last point, they also made much of the fact that the Treaty of Versailles was not so bad as that of Brest-Litovsk, which the Germans had imposed upon a vanquished Russia early in 1918.

This is all beside the point. It is true that Brest-Litovsk was a bad peace, so bad in fact as to provide unanswerable justification for the charge that the Germans would have dictated a

Carthaginian treaty had they been the victors. But two wrongs still do not make a right. The task before the negotiators at Paris was not to pay off old scores, or to make a treaty as bad as Brest-Litovsk, or as bad as the Germans might have made had they won, but to construct a workable and lasting peace which both the victors and the rest of the world so desperately needed.

8

The Treaty of Versailles in general and Wilson in particular have been savagely blamed for many sins that they did not commit.

Much of the Treaty was concerned with righting century-old wrongs. A wrong that old sometimes ceases to look like a wrong. The aggressions of Prussia, for example, had netted her territory, notably in Poland, which on the basis of self-determination had to be taken away. Yet the eggs had long been scrambled, and the unscrambling process created newer but perhaps lesser wrongs. It was no easy problem to thrust back into Central Europe a populous nation which had passed out of existence during the Presidency of George Washington in America. The ghosts of those who had partitioned Poland in the eighteenth century stalked through the halls of Versailles.

The men of Paris were blamed for creating the quarrelsome "succession states" of Czechoslovakia, Jugoslavia, and Poland, all of which were destined to sow dragon's teeth of trouble in Central Europe. But the Conference did not create these states. They sprang into being before the negotiators could meet. The task at Paris was to delineate their boundaries and erect safeguards to insure that they would live in peace with their minorities and their neighbors.

The Treaty of Versailles has been blamed for all the ills that befell Europe from 1919 to 1939. The truth is that there had been a grueling, demoralizing conflict of more than four years' duration before the Conference met. It has been competently estimated that the war alone cost Germany $100,000,000,000. If the negotiators at Paris had been angels from heaven they could not have drawn up a treaty which would have prevented many of the calamities of exhaustion and reconstruction. Europe was sick, desperately sick; and Harold Nicolson is correct when he says that those who write about Versailles are not describing a conference but a serious illness.

Lloyd George insists that most of the sins of the Treaty must be laid at the doors of the men who carried it out—or who failed to carry it out. With all due allowance for exaggeration, we must concede that the former prime minister has put his finger on a fundamental truth. Commissions were to be set up, plebiscites were to be held, reparations were to be determined and collected. The treaty in itself was no magic formula; no man-made document can be. Everything depended on the energy, intelligence, loyalty, broad-mindedness, and singleness of purpose of those who were charged with administering it. In many respects the executors of the Treaty are unquestionably far more censurable than its makers.

There is one final observation. The Treaty of Versailles—the treaty with Germany—was but one part of the European settlement. The treaties with Austria, Hungary, Bulgaria, and Turkey were intimately connected with it, just as Wilson had planned and later boasted. The very first section of every one of these treaties was the Covenant of the League of Nations. Not only was the Covenant the first section of the Treaty of Versailles, but other provisions of the same treaty were interlocked with it, and all the treaties were interlocked with one another. The Reparations Commission established by Versailles, for example, was charged with supervising the collection of reparations under the treaty with Austria.

The essential point is that the interlocking postwar settlements were a complicated and topheavy structure which could only endure if its most important foundation stone was put into place. The whole edifice was erected on the assumption, and with Wilson's assurances, that the United States would bear its share of the responsibility for guaranteeing the new world order. The Europeans did not like the architecture of the new building, but they accepted it as a cheap price for the cooperation of a powerful America.

Milestones

(From the St. Louis *Republic;* courtesy of the
St. Louis *Globe-Democrat*)

The most important foundation stone, as we all know, was never put into place. The precarious structure teetered along for more than a decade, and then crashed in ruins.

If the Europeans had been told at the outset that they could not count on our support, they would have built a different structure. Whether it would have been better, one cannot say;

but it would have been different, and perhaps it would have lasted longer.

9

We have already considered the blunders of the Paris negotiation at such length that their applicability to a future conference should be self-evident. But for purposes of re-emphasis and summary, it seems desirable to stress certain basic principles which the American people should keep in mind in connection with a general peace at the end of a great world conflict.

War aims should be unambiguous, practicable, acceptable to American public opinion, and closely correlated with the pronouncements of our allies.

The people should be so led during the conflict that their emotionalism will be held in leash. The greater the passions aroused by the fighting, the greater the difficulties in making a lasting settlement. One may win the war but lose the peace, as we did last time. The objective should be to pace one's self so as to win both.

American public opinion should be educated *in advance* to its responsibilities in world affairs, and more particularly to its responsibilities in executing the peace treaty. This campaign should be undertaken as early in the war as possible, for when the fighting ends the time is always too short for adequate instruction. Wilson made an heroic attempt to educate the country *after* the treaty was completed, but by that time the Senate had gained too big a head start.

Unconditional surrender on the part of the enemy is imperative, unless the conditions are defined with unmistakable clarity, unless they are capable of fulfillment, and unless the victors intend in good faith to fulfill them. Even so, unconditional surrender is no sure guarantee of an enduring peace.

The American peace commission should be bipartisan, with

adequate representation accorded the two great political parties, as well as the Senate of the United States.

The President should enter into the closest and most cordial possible relations with the leaders of both parties in the Senate —*before*, *during* and *after* the negotiations.

A preliminary peace should precede the final treaty, and it should speedily outline the military and other terms most pressingly in need of solution. This will enable the world to adjust itself to a peacetime footing, while giving passions time to cool off. At a later date the negotiators can approach the general settlement with greater deliberation and clearer vision.

The defeated powers should be privileged to discuss, both orally and in writing, the terms of the definitive treaty *while they are being drawn up*. This is the only practicable way in which the reasons for the unworkability of certain provisions may be adequately set forth.

The detailed covenant for a new world organization, if any, should not be written into the treaty of peace. General provision may be made in the pact for creating some such system at a subsequent time and under different auspices. Making peace with the enemy should not be confused with making a constitution for a new order.

No treaty can last unless it provides *workable* machinery for peaceful change in the light of changing conditions.

The victor can have vengeance, or he may have peace, but he cannot have both. In 1919 the Allies got neither, for vengeance was incomplete and short-lived. No great nation can be kept in bondage forever. The vengeance of 1919 enlisted neutral sympathy, created a "remorse complex" in the minds of liberals in the victor nations, and revived German nationalism. Germany needed to be persuaded that war was bad; instead she was convinced that the peace was bad. All these factors contributed to the final undoing of the Treaty of Versailles.

The Constitution should be amended so as to reduce the great obstructive power of the one-third minority in the Senate. Opponents of any treaty are armed with two votes; the proponents with only one. This is illogical, undemocratic, and in 1919 it was probably disastrous. The same thing could easily happen again. The sooner the Constitution is changed the better, because amendment takes time, and procrastination is easy. When treaty-making is not in prospect, the two-thirds rule seems unimportant; when it is in prospect, time is too short for amendment. If we wait for Congress to take steps to reduce its own power, we shall doubtless have to wait a long time. But the Constitution provides adequate machinery for the states to initiate and ratify amendments without the voluntary action of Congress.

The President of the United States should never again make promises which the Senate cannot reasonably be counted on to honor or public opinion to support. It will be a long time before the world recovers from the disillusionment of 1919.

The temple of peace must be built on the foundations of what people are likely to accept and what they will accept, not on what they should ideally accept.

Wilson had a noble vision but he made the tragic mistake of thinking that mankind, without the proper preparation and education, could attain a kind of international millennium at a single bound. As he told his associates on the *George Washington*, "If it won't work, it must be made to work." He assumed that human nature—with its suspicion, fear, selfishness, and greed—could be substantially changed overnight, especially American human nature. He took it for granted that our people would respond gladly to his gospel of unselfishness, speedily assume responsibilities commensurate with their new power, and willingly shoulder burdens from which they could expect no direct gains. Unto America much had been given; she should repay her debt to the rest of the world. It was to be a new era of joy through service.

Instead, we got Harding and "normalcy."

Statesmen must ever remember that mankind is shortsighted and perverse, and that he who would make haste too fast will almost inevitably fail. We shall not see the millennium in our day, or in our children's day; the best we can hope for is a substantial step forward on the tortuous path of international understanding and cooperation. If we can but learn the lessons from our last experience which are there for all to see, the price paid for them, though far too high, will not have been spent altogether in vain.

BIBLIOGRAPHICAL NOTES

INTRODUCTION

THIS BOOK is primarily a synthesis, not a research project on a monographic scale. It is largely, though by no means solely, a re-interpretation of facts that have for some little while been generally available, and for this reason, among others, it has not seemed desirable to present elaborate footnote documentation. Biblio-graphical comments are confined to moot questions, or to problems which need further amplification.

The bibliographies here listed are not exhaustive, but in a general way they indicate the most important sources of information, as well as the materials from which the basic facts have been drawn. This is primarily a study of the peace from the American point of view, and more particularly from that of Wilson, and consequently no effort has been made to present extensive references bearing upon purely European problems, though there exists a vast body of literature on this phase of the subject. Where translations exist, the English version is cited. Interest in the Treaty of Versailles has been so great that fortunately for the general reader most of the important French and German secondary accounts have been translated.

This study is particularly concerned with the reactions of American public opinion, and extensive use has been made of the newspaper press, notably the New York *Times,* and of the periodical press, notably the *Literary Digest.* Use has also been made of the important documentary collections in print, as well as other published materials, official or otherwise. It has been necessary to borrow heavily from the researches of others, and it can only be hoped that they have been given adequate recognition. In most cases it would have been a profitless expenditure of time to go behind their findings.

The archives of the Department of State are not currently available to investigators, though the publication by the Department of the first four volumes of its monumental peace collection has done much to fill this gap. The Woodrow Wilson papers in the Library of Congress were returned from their evacuation center in time to be consulted during two hurried vacation trips; and while the limitations of time did not permit so careful an examination as this great collection deserves, it was possible to consult, among other things, all of Wilson's "out" letters and cablegrams during the Conference period, and in addition a file of the secret minutes of the Council of Four. Fortunately, the task was simplified by Ray Stannard Baker's earlier researches with these papers. The manuscript minutes of the Council of Ten were originally examined in the Hoover Library, Stanford University, though they were subsequently published in the Department of State series referred to above.

The writer was also privileged to examine the House Papers, at Yale University; and certain other manuscript collections in the Library of Congress, notably those of Robert Lansing, Henry White, Ray Stannard Baker, and Senator Gilbert M. Hitchcock. Most of these collections have to some extent been worked over, and, with certain exceptions, they contributed shading to the picture rather than striking new lines. The most significant new revelations bear upon the fight for the ratification of the treaty, which will be dealt with in a sequel volume.

In the bibliographies and notes that follow, the full citation is given the first time only; thereafter the shortened form.

THE ROAD TO WAR

FOR EXTENDED bibliographies relating to this chapter, consult Samuel Flagg Bemis and Grace Gardner Griffin, *Guide to the Diplomatic History of the United States, 1775–1921* (Washington, 1935), pp. 655–672, and the bibliographies and footnotes of my *A Diplomatic History of the American People* (2nd ed., New York, 1942), chaps. XXXVII–XXXVIII. Among the better secondary accounts, one must single out for special mention C. C. Tansill, *America Goes to War* (Boston, 1938); Charles Seymour, *American Diplomacy During the World War* (Baltimore, 1934); Harley Notter, *The Origins of the Foreign Policy of Woodrow Wilson* (Baltimore, 1937); Edwin M. Borchard and W. P. Lage, *Neutrality for the United States* (New Haven, 1937); and Charles Seymour, *American Neutrality, 1914–1917* (New Haven, 1935). These are all substantial works by recognized scholars.

THE QUESTION OF PUBLIC OPINION. The role of American public opinion in connection with our entrance into the war in 1917 has been largely neglected by scholars, probably because the subject is not only enormous but nebulous. Yet it is of the greatest importance, because one indisputable fact is that Wilson would never have asked Congress to declare war unless certain that public opinion was ripe for it. Two unpublished studies have been of value: Emlyn David Jones, "Pacific Coast Press Opinion and the Break with Germany, 1917" (MS. master's thesis, Stanford University, 1942), and Albert Russell Buchanan, "European Propaganda and American Public Opinion, 1914–1917" (MS. doctoral dissertation, Stanford University, 1935). Dr. Buchanan has revised this study in the light of an extensive examination of newspaper and manuscript materials in the Library of Congress, and the present writer has been privileged to consult it in unpublished form. Dr. Buchanan has also published a valuable analysis of the editorial opinion of sixty-eight newspapers, from forty-eight states, for the month immediately following our entrance into the war, "American Editors Examine American War Aims and Plans in April, 1917," *Pacific Historical Review*, IX (1940), 253–265. Granted that newspaper opinion is not a thoroughly satisfactory index to public opinion, the fact is that this is the only study of its kind that has yet been published, and scholars would do well to examine it. Significantly, the newspaper editors overwhelmingly agreed on one thing: the United States had been forced into the war (p. 254).

WAR CAUSES AND WAR AIMS. The present chapter is concerned largely with pre-1917 attitudes and war aims, because any real understanding of the defeat of the Treaty of Versailles in the United States must go back to them. As George Creel well says: "The peace tangle will not unravel unless related to war aims, and war aims stand unsupported and somewhat overstrained unless related to the various emotional stages that marked the period of our neutrality" (*The War, the World and Wilson* [New York, 1920], p. 39).

WERE THE ALLIES LOSING EARLY IN 1917? During February and March, there was relatively little military news on the front page of the New York *Times*, and it was uniformly favorable to the Allies. Many reports were printed regarding starvation in Germany, and these stories were confirmed by the returning Ambassador Gerard (*ibid.*, March 12, 23, 1917). Shipping losses made the first page, but they were not spectacularly more serious than those of the months before the unrestricted submarine campaign was begun. By mid-March, it was recorded that the sinkings were slackening off (*ibid.*, March 15), though the toll became terrific late in April, *after* we entered the war. See J. A. Salter, *Allied Shipping Control* (Oxford, 1921), pp. 357-358. It is true that the Russian Revolution occurred in mid-March, but this was not generally regarded as an ominous portent: it was in fact widely believed that the Russians would fight harder now that they were becoming democratized. Further evidence of Allied strength and German weakness is to be seen in the Austrian peace overtures, begun in February, 1917; the confident paper partition of Germany by France and Russia in February, 1917; the Allied offensive under Nivelle in April and May, 1917; and the Reichstag resolution of July, 1917, favoring a liberal peace.

FEAR OF GERMANY IN THE UNITED STATES. It is undoubtedly true that there was much unreasoning fear of a German victory in the United States, but that this has been overemphasized is indicated by the delay with which the American people accepted the German

submarine challenge. More than two months elapsed between the
submarine announcement and the actual declaration of war, and
during this time there were a number of incidents that could be
regarded as "overt acts." At the Cabinet meeting of Feb. 2, 1917,
two days *after* the German announcement, Wilson said, in response
to a question as to which side he "wished to see win," that "he
didn't wish to see either side win . . ." (A. W. Lane and L. H.
Wall, eds., *The Letters of Franklin K. Lane* [Boston, 1922], p. 234).
About one o'clock of the very same morning on which he presented
his war message to Congress, Wilson exclaimed to Frank Cobb, "If
there is any alternative, for God's sake, let's take it" (John L.
Heaton, comp., *Cobb of "The World"* [New York, 1924], p. 270) .
The story of this interview was told by Cobb to one of his associates,
who later recorded it. For this reason the exact words may be
doubted, but the statement is in character. Both what Wilson said
in Cabinet meeting and what he told Cobb indicate that he was
not impressed with the German menace. On Jan. 4, 1919, Colonel
House, Wilson's closest adviser, scoffed at the fear-of-Germany
argument (Charles Seymour, *The Intimate Papers of Colonel
House* [Boston, 1926], IV, 268). There is some reason to believe that
the chief concern of Wilson and others was what would happen to
American institutions if they had to be revamped so as to stand
guard against aggressions on the part of German militarism. If the
American people had felt themselves to be in immediate danger
from Germany, it is difficult to understand why they were so leisurely in their war preparations, and why they delayed so many
months before undertaking to send a large A.E.F.

WILSON'S CONFUSION OF CAUSES AND OBJECTIVES. This analysis is
based on a reading of all of Wilson's published writings and addresses relevant to the problem. See Woodrow Wilson, *War and
Peace: Presidential Messages, Addresses, and Other Papers (1917–
1924)*, eds. Ray Stannard Baker and William E. Dodd (2 vols.,
New York, 1927), I, 22, 50, 158, 169, 170, 179, 198, 206, 259, 380,
397, 527, 538, 549, 637; II, 117, 118, 162, 211, 258, 366. Wilson's
letter to Heflin (May 22, 1917) shows that at this time he still had
the distinction between causes and objectives clearly in mind. On
Aug. 19, 1919, testifying before the Senate Foreign Relations Committee, Wilson made the often quoted statement that we would
have gone to war with Germany anyhow without the submarine

attacks. (*Sen. Docs.*, 66 Cong., 1 sess., no. 76, p. 40). Whether this was another instance of Wilson's memory being warped by current war hatreds, or a projection of a "wish-phantasy" into the past, one cannot say. It should be noted that in this same testimony he said that he knew nothing of certain of the secret treaties before reaching Paris, which was not true. On Nov. 8, 1918, George Creel wrote Wilson that, while Wilson's leadership had made it a war to "make the world safe for democracy," it "was not that sort of war when we entered it" (*The War, the World and Wilson*, p. 145). Yet Wilson told the Council of Four, on April 20, 1919, that when he wrote his war aims he was writing the point of view of the American people, and on these principles the United States had entered the war (Woodrow Wilson Papers, IX–C).

LIMITED-LIABILITY WAR. This is a highly significant point which has never been adequately stressed. Two revealing symposia on the subject appear in the *Literary Digest* (March 3, 1917, pp. 538–539; April 7, 1917, pp. 965–967—the leading article).

THE BALANCE OF POWER IDEA. It is difficult to understand why latter-day writers, like Nicholas John Spykman, in *America's Strategy in World Politics* (New York, 1942), and Walter Lippmann, in *U.S. Foreign Policy* (Boston, 1943), assert that we entered the war primarily to insure our own safety and preserve the balance of power, except that this theory so closely fits the situation in 1941. Lesser minds than these have fallen into the error of reading the present back into the past. Such a theory presupposes that the Allies were visibly collapsing, and that we were in mortal fear of Germany, neither of which was the case. It would doubtless have been better, from the standpoint of America's acceptance of her share of world responsibility, if this had been true; and the fact that we ran out so lightly on our obligations in 1919–1920 is further evidence that it was not. For Wilson's abhorrence of the balance of power, see Woodrow Wilson, *War and Peace*, I, 257, 353, 410, 411.

CHAPTER TWO

THE PEN IS MIGHTIER

THE BEST source for Wilson's war-aims addresses is Woodrow Wilson, *War and Peace*, vol. I. Valuable background material appears in Ray Stannard Baker, *Woodrow Wilson: Life and Letters* (New York, 1939), vols. VII and VIII; and more generally in F. L. Paxson, *America at War, 1917–1918* (Boston, 1939). The publicity given to the Fourteen Points is described by its director, George Creel, in *How We Advertised America* (New York, 1920), and more briefly in the same author's *The War, the World and Wilson*. A revealing account of more recent date is James R. Mock and Cedric Larson, *Words That Won the War* (Princeton, 1939). For the effect of Allied propaganda on the German collapse, see George G. Bruntz, *Allied Propaganda and the Collapse of the German Empire in 1918* (Stanford University, 1938). David Lloyd George's *Memoirs of the Peace Conference* (2 vols., New Haven, 1939), vol. I, has a useful introductory chapter on Allied war aims. Lloyd George takes credit to the Allies for having anticipated Wilson in the formulation of war aims, and he believes that they were substantially carried out in the Treaty of Versailles. A useful study of this important subject is Ebba Dahlin, *French and German Public Opinion on Declared War Aims, 1914–1918* (Stanford University, 1933). An indispensable compilation is James B. Scott, ed., *Official Statements of War Aims and Peace Proposals, December 1916 to November 1918* (Washington, 1921).

WILSON AND SELF-DETERMINATION. While the idea of self-determination was not original with Wilson, he was doubtless attracted to it because it was so closely in harmony with American tradition as embodied in the Virginia Bill of Rights and the Declaration of Independence. It is also worth noting that Wilson was a Southerner, reared in war-ravaged Georgia; and the war fought by the South was one of the most perfect examples of self-determination in modern history. Wilson's expression of faith in self-determination preceded America's entry into the war. A clear statement appeared in his address of May 27, 1916 (Woodrow Wilson, *The New Democracy: Presidential Messages, Addresses, and Other Papers* [1913–1917], eds. R. S. Baker and W. E. Dodd [2 vols., New York, 1926], II, 187). For Wilson's assertion that the Fourteen Points were not his but an expression of the will of the American people, see Woodrow Wilson, *War and Peace*, II, 410.

Wilson's Fourteen and Supplementary Points

ADDRESS TO CONGRESS, JANUARY 8, 1918

1. Open covenants of peace, openly arrived at, after which there shall be no private international understandings of any kind but diplomacy shall proceed always frankly and in the public view.

2. Absolute freedom of navigation upon the seas, outside territorial waters, alike in peace and in war, except as the seas may be closed in whole or in part by international action for the enforcement of international covenants.

3. The removal, so far as possible, of all economic barriers and the establishment of an equality of trade conditions among all the nations consenting to the peace and associating themselves for its maintenance.

4. Adequate guarantees given and taken that national armaments will be reduced to the lowest point consistent with domestic safety.

5. A free, open-minded, and absolutely impartial adjustment of all colonial claims, based upon a strict observance of the principle that in determining all such questions of sovereignty the interests of the populations concerned must have equal weight with the equitable claims of the government whose title is to be determined.

6. The evacuation of all Russian territory and such a settlement of all questions affecting Russia as will secure the best and freest cooperation of the other nations of the world in obtaining for her an unhampered and unembarrassed opportunity for the independent determination of her own political development and national policy and assure her of a sincere welcome into the society of free nations under institutions of her own choosing; and, more than a

welcome, assistance also of every kind that she may need and may herself desire. The treatment accorded Russia by her sister nations in the months to come will be the acid test of their good will, of their comprehension of her needs as distinguished from their own interests, and of their intelligent and unselfish sympathy.

7. Belgium, the whole world will agree, must be evacuated and restored, without any attempt to limit the sovereignty which she enjoys in common with all other free nations. No other single act will serve as this will serve to restore confidence among the nations in the laws which they have themselves set and determined for the government of their relations with one another. Without this healing act the whole structure and validity of international law is forever impaired.

8. All French territory should be freed and the invaded portions restored, and the wrong done to France by Prussia in 1871 in the matter of Alsace-Lorraine, which has unsettled the peace of the world for nearly fifty years, should be righted, in order that peace may once more be made secure in the interest of all.

9. A readjustment of the frontiers of Italy should be effected along clearly recognizable lines of nationality.

10. The peoples of Austria-Hungary, whose place among the nations we wish to see safeguarded and assured, should be accorded the freest opportunity of autonomous development.

11. Rumania, Serbia, and Montenegro should be evacuated; occupied territories restored; Serbia accorded free and secure access to the sea; and the relations of the several Balkan states to one another determined by friendly counsel along historically established lines of allegiance and nationality; and international guarantees of the political and economic independence and territorial integrity of the several Balkan states should be entered into.

12. The Turkish portions of the present Ottoman Empire should be assured a secure sovereignty, but the other nationalities which are now under Turkish rule should be assured an undoubted security of life and an absolutely unmolested opportunity of autonomous development, and the Dardanelles should be permanently opened as a free passage to the ships and commerce of all nations under international guarantees.

13. An independent Polish state should be erected which should include the territories inhabited by indisputably Polish populations, which should be assured a free and secure access to the sea, and whose political and economic independence and territorial integrity should be guaranteed by international covenant.

14. A general association of nations must be formed under specific covenants for the purpose of affording mutual guarantees of political independence and territorial integrity to great and small states alike.

ADDRESS TO CONGRESS, FEBRUARY 11, 1918

15. That each part of the final settlement must be based upon
the essential justice of that particular case and upon such adjustments as are most likely to bring a peace that will be permanent;

16. That peoples and provinces are not to be bartered about
from sovereignty to sovereignty as if they were mere chattels and
pawns in a game, even the great game, now forever discredited, of
the balance of power; but that

17. Every territorial settlement involved in this war must be
made in the interest and for the benefit of the populations concerned, and not as a part of any mere adjustment or compromise of
claims amongst rival states; and

18. That all well-defined national aspirations shall be accorded
the utmost satisfaction that can be accorded them without introducing new or perpetuating old elements of discord and antagonism that would be likely in time to break the peace of Europe and
consequently of the world.

ADDRESS AT MOUNT VERNON, JULY 4, 1918

19. The destruction of every arbitrary power anywhere that can
separately, secretly, and of its single choice disturb the peace of
the world; or, if it cannot be presently destroyed, at the least its
reduction to virtual impotence.

(17) (Compare with No. 17 above.) The settlement of every
question, whether of territory, of sovereignty, of economic arrangement, or of political relationship, upon the basis of the free acceptance of that settlement by the people immediately concerned,
and not upon the basis of the material interest or advantage of any
other nation or people which may desire a different settlement for
the sake of its own exterior influence or mastery.

20. The consent of all nations to be governed in their conduct
towards each other by the same principles of honor and of respect
for the common law of civilized society that govern the individual
citizens of all modern states in their relations with one another; to
the end that all promises and covenants may be sacredly observed,
no private plots or conspiracies hatched, no selfish injuries wrought
with impunity, and a mutual trust established upon the handsome
foundation of a mutual respect for right.

(14) (Compare with No. 14 above.) The establishment of an organization of peace which shall make it certain that the combined
power of free nations will check every invasion of right and serve

to make peace and justice the more secure by affording a definite
tribunal of opinion to which all must submit and by which every
international readjustment that cannot be amicably agreed upon
by the peoples directly concerned shall be sanctioned.

ADDRESS IN NEW YORK CITY, SEPTEMBER 27, 1918

(15) (Compare with No. 15 above.) The impartial justice
meted out must involve no discrimination between those to whom
we wish to be just and those to whom we do not wish to be just. It
must be a justice that plays no favorites and knows no standard
but the equal rights of the several peoples concerned;

21. No special or separate interest of any single nation or any
group of nations can be made the basis of any part of the settlement
which is not consistent with the common interest of all;

22. There can be no leagues or alliances or special covenants and
understandings within the general and common family of the
League of Nations.

23. And more specifically, there can be no special, selfish economic combinations within the League and no employment of any
form of economic boycott or exclusion except as the power of
economic penalty by exclusion from the markets of the world may
be vested in the League of Nations itself as a means of discipline
and control.

24. All international agreements and treaties of every kind
must be made known in their entirety to the rest of the world.

CHAPTER THREE

AN ARMISTICE
THAT WAS NOT AN ARMISTICE

THE BEST account in some detail is Charles Seymour, *American
Diplomacy During the World War*. The same author has made
available many of the invaluable papers of Colonel House in *The
Intimate Papers of Colonel House,* vol. IV. House was Wilson's
representative in the Paris negotiations. David F. Houston, *Eight

Years with Wilson's Cabinet, 1913 to 1920 (2 vols., Garden City, N.Y., 1926), vol. I, contains records of Cabinet discussions of the German peace overtures. Valuable background material appears in R. S. Baker, *Wilson*, vol. VIII, and Joseph P. Tumulty, *Woodrow Wilson As I Know Him* (Garden City, N.Y., 1921). Tumulty was Wilson's private secretary. The standard life of General Bliss, based on his private papers, is Frederick Palmer, *Bliss, Peacemaker* (New York, 1934); see also Tasker H. Bliss, "The Armistices," in *American Journal of International Law*, XVI (1922), 509–522. Bliss, an American, was on the Supreme War Council, and his observations are of great value. C. E. Callwell, *Field-Marshal Sir Henry Wilson* (2 vols., New York, 1927), vol. II, reflects British bitterness at Wilson's lone-hand conduct of the pre-Armistice negotiations. An able defense of the Armistice is J. J. H. Mordacq, *La guerre mondiale, pages vécues: la vérité sur l'armistice* (Paris, 1929) ; and a penetrating discussion of the series of armistices has recently been published by the distinguished military writer, Sir Frederick Maurice, *The Armistices of 1918* (London, 1943). See also George B. Noble, *Policies and Opinions at Paris, 1919* (New York, 1935), chap. II; and Harold Nicolson, *Peacemaking, 1919* (New York, 1939), chap. I. Important documents bearing upon the negotiation of the Armistice may be found in *Foreign Relations of the United States, 1918*, Supp. 1 (Washington, 1933), vol. I; and James B. Scott, ed., *Preliminary History of the Armistice: Official Documents Published by the German National Chancellery by Order of the Ministry of State*, transl. by the Carnegie Endowment for International Peace, Division of International Law (New York, 1924). See also Gabriel Terrail, *Les négociations secrètes et les quatre armistices* (Paris, 1921).

WILSON AND THE ARMISTICE NEGOTIATIONS. Wilson's willingness to enter into negotiations may be explained in part by his statement to Colonel House that he did not want the stain of invading and ravaging Germany to tarnish Allied arms. Charles Seymour, *House Papers*, IV, 83. Wilson's pressure on the German people to get rid of the Kaiser seems to have been a latter-day development. It may have been in part a throwback to his earlier policy of trying to force undesirable rulers out of the Latin American countries, notably Huerta in Mexico.

CHAPTER FOUR

THE MAN WITHOUT A COUNTRY

AN EXHAUSTIVE study of the campaign of 1918 needs to be done, with attention to trends in preceding and succeeding elections. The most careful investigations to date are Selig Adler, "The Congressional Election of 1918," *South Atlantic Quarterly,* XXXVI (1937), 447–465; and Denna Frank Fleming, *The United States and the League of Nations, 1918–1920* (New York, 1932), chap. II. These should be supplemented by Charles P. Howland, ed., *Survey of American Foreign Relations, 1928* (New Haven, 1928), which pays some attention to an analysis of the contests in the various states. Valuable background material appears in R. S. Baker, *Wilson,* vol. VIII; George Creel, *The War, the World and Wilson;* D. F. Houston, *Eight Years with Wilson's Cabinet,* vol. I; J. P. Tumulty, *Woodrow Wilson As I Know Him;* H. C. Lodge, ed., *Selections from the Correspondence of Theodore Roosevelt and Henry Cabot Lodge, 1884–1918* (2 vols., New York, 1925), vol. II. See also A. D. H. Smith, *Mr. House of Texas* (New York, 1940), pp. 272–276. The text of the October appeal may be conveniently found in Woodrow Wilson, *War and Peace,* I, 286–288.

REPUBLICAN INCONSISTENCY. It is an ironical fact that there was ample Republican precedent for the Democratic appeal, notably in 1898, when President McKinley asked for support on the eve of the negotiations with Spain. Young Theodore Roosevelt and Henry Cabot Lodge, who were later to criticize Wilson for doing essentially the same thing, vigorously applauded their President. It should be noted, however, that earlier appeals were less spectacular or less bald than that of Wilson. This subject is well treated in Fleming, *op. cit.,* pp. 47–51.

WILSON AND THE PURGE IDEA. During the summer of 1918 Wilson had interfered with some success in the Democratic primaries to secure the election of loyal Democrats. This, of course, was not the same as urging the defeat of Republicans; but it may have given Wilson false notions. See *Literary Digest,* Aug. 24, 1918, pp. 10–11.

DEMOCRATIC DISORGANIZATION. The Democratic national organization had suffered because the able national chairman, Vance C. McCormick, had been devoting his energies to the War Trade Board, while the Republican Committee, under Will Hays, was very active. Wilson's influence with the party was not so strong as it might have been, in part because he was certain to go out of office in 1921. The current influenza epidemic prevented public meetings, which the Democrats would have found useful in combating the last-minute Republican misrepresentations inspired by Wilson's appeal. Ray Stannard Baker interviewed Mr. McCormick, July 15, 1928, on the subject of the October appeal, and an interesting memorandum of this interview appears in the Baker papers, Library of Congress.

THE FORD-NEWBERRY ELECTION. Spencer Ervin, in *Henry Ford vs. Truman H. Newberry: The Famous Senate Election Contest* (New York, 1935), presents a strong brief in support of the proposition that Newberry was more sinned against than sinning. Whatever the technicalities of the case, the election was very close, and may have been decided by too liberal a use of money by the Republicans.

F. D. ROOSEVELT AND THE 1942 CONGRESSIONAL ELECTION. Wilson lost 5 seats in the Senate and 25 in the House. In 1942, also in the midst of war, Roosevelt lost 9 in the Senate and 46 in the House. (See *The American Year Book,* 1942, p. 66.) Roosevelt's defeat, though numerically more severe than Wilson's, did not result in a loss of control of either body. The Republicans in 1942 actually polled more than 50 per cent of the popular vote. Roosevelt issued no appeal, and was criticized by many Democrats for not having provided the necessary leadership. Perhaps he was deterred by Wilson's unfortunate experience, and his own rather unhappy attempts at "purging." In any event, this shows that in time of war Congressional reverses may be suffered, with or without a Presidential appeal. In 1942 few informed persons seriously claimed that Roosevelt was a repudiated President.

CHAPTER FIVE

JOVE STEPS DOWN FROM OLYMPUS

THE MOST important new material appears in *Papers Relating to the Foreign Relations of the United States, 1919: The Paris Peace Conference* (Washington, 1942), vol. I. (Hereafter cited as *U.S. Peace Documents*.) This is the monumental series of documents currently being published by the Department of State. Considerable light is thrown on the problem of Wilson's going by R. S. Baker, *Wilson*, vol. VIII, and Charles Seymour, *House Papers*, vol. IV. Observations by those close to Wilson appear in D. F. Houston, *Eight Years with Wilson's Cabinet*, vol. I; J. P. Tumulty, *Woodrow Wilson As I Know Him;* Robert Lansing, *The Peace Negotiations: A Personal Narrative* (Boston, 1921); and George Creel, *The War, the World and Wilson*. See also Allan Nevins, *Henry White: Thirty Years of American Diplomacy* (New York, 1930).

WAS WILSON PERSUADED TO STAY IN PARIS? Robert Lansing, in his *The Big Four and Others of the Peace Conference* (Boston, 1921), pp. 13–14, says that, for two or three weeks after Wilson reached Paris, Clemenceau and his colleagues exerted all of their powers of persuasion to induce Wilson to stay as a delegate. David Lloyd George, in his *Memoirs of the Peace Conference*, I, 89, publishes what purports to be evidence along the same lines. While it is doubtless true that Clemenceau relaxed his opposition to Wilson's presence after the latter reached Paris, it is clear that from the very beginning Wilson had every intention of acting as a guiding force, and he needed no persuasion to do so. As early as Nov. 13, 1918, he cabled House that he expected to preside. (*U.S. Peace Documents*, I, 129. See also Charles Seymour, *House Papers*, IV, 209.)

CHAPTER SIX

WILSON AND HIS "ERRAND BOYS"

THE MOST important new light appears in *U.S. Peace Documents*, I. See also R. S. Baker, *Wilson*, vol. VIII; Charles Seymour, *House Papers*, vol. IV; J. P. Tumulty, *Woodrow Wilson As I Know Him*. A good brief discussion is in D. F. Fleming, *The United States and the League of Nations*. For Lansing, see Robert Lansing, *The Peace Negotiations*. For House, consult Charles Seymour, *House Papers*, vol. IV, and A. D. H. Smith, *Mr. House of Texas*, the only full-length biography of House, and undocumented. Also the unreliable but suggestive George Sylvester Viereck, *The Strangest Friendship in History* (New York, 1932). For White, see Allan Nevins, *Henry White*, one of the most revealing biographies of the period. For Bliss, consult Frederick Palmer, *Bliss*, which is based on Bliss's private papers. On Root and Taft, see Philip C. Jessup, *Elihu Root* (2 vols., New York, 1938) , vol. II, and Henry F. Pringle, *The Life and Times of William Howard Taft* (2 vols., New York, 1939), vol. II, both of which are outstanding biographies.

COMMISSION POSSIBILITIES. There was considerable pressure from labor groups to put Samuel Gompers on the Commission, and there was also some talk about having a woman and' a representative from the West. Wilson sternly resisted all efforts to secure group representation (see *U.S. Peace Documents*, I, 173). Secretary of the Treasury McAdoo and ex-President Charles W. Eliot of Harvard were prominently mentioned, but apparently were not seriously considered by Wilson. There was also some support for Bryan, but Wilson dismissed him for obvious reasons. Wilson planned to take his Secretary of War, Newton D. Baker, as a representative on military matters; but when it was learned that Secretary McAdoo was going to resign, it seemed unwise to weaken the Cabinet further and thus disquiet the country. General Bliss was then chosen. Most of the above facts are taken from *U.S. Peace Documents*, I, 155–192.

REPUBLICAN ALTERNATIVES. So far as the records reveal, Wilson never planned to take more than one Republican out of five. He

seriously considered asking the pro-Wilson Governor McCall of
Massachusetts, who would have been most distasteful to his fellow
Republicans. He actually did invite Republican Justice Day of the
Supreme Court, a veteran of the 1898 negotiations with Spain; but
the aged jurist declined (*ibid.*, p. 159), presumably for reasons of
health, but possibly also because it seemed unwise to involve the
Court in peacemaking. Wilson then turned to Henry White.

THE ROLE OF ROOT. Root had served as head of an American mission to Russia in 1917, and apparently some friction developed between him and Wilson as a result of it. Root was doubtful whether
he would have accepted a place on the Commission after Wilson
announced he was going as a delegate (P. C. Jessup, *Root*, II, 380).
Shortly before Wilson left for Paris, House enthusiastically sec-
onded a suggestion that Root be invited to come as general adviser
with the title of Counsel to the American Plenipotentiaries. Wilson declined on the ground that to appoint Root at that time
would suggest a lack of confidence in the delegation as formally
constituted (*ibid.*). Whether this was the real reason or a good one,
the fact is that Wilson did not want Root along. In connection with
Taft, Hughes, and Root, it is to be noted that Lloyd George was
also criticized for not appointing his political rival, Herbert Henry
Asquith. Clemenceau likewise ignored commanding political figures. See Geoffrey Bruun, *Clemenceau* (Cambridge, Mass., 1943),
p. 187.

CHAPTER SEVEN

THE COMING OF THE MESSIAH

FOR THE work of the Inquiry, see James T. Shotwell, *At the Paris
Peace Conference* (New York, 1937), an important work by one
of the members. Consult also the account by Dr. Sidney E. Mezes
(the Director) in Edward M. House and Charles Seymour, eds.,
What Really Happened at Paris (New York, 1921), chap. I; also
Ingram Bander, "Sidney Edward Mezes and 'The Inquiry,'" in
Journal of Modern History, XI (1939), 199–202. Wilson's remarks

to the experts on the *George Washington* are conveniently found in Charles Seymour, *House Papers,* IV, 280–283; Wilson's speeches on his European tour, in Woodrow Wilson, *War and Peace,* vol. I. Revealing comments on Wilson's ovations appear in David Lloyd George, *Memoirs of the Peace Conference,* vol. I; Norval Richardson, *My Diplomatic Education* (New York, 1923), an account by an American diplomat in Italy; Irwin Hood Hoover, *Forty-two Years in the White House* (Boston, 1934), which is a rather superficial description by the White House usher; George Creel, *The War, the World and Wilson,* by the Chairman of the Committee on Public Information; and especially Edith Bolling Wilson (Mrs. Woodrow Wilson), *My Memoir* (Indianapolis, 1939), which is intimate and stresses the feminine viewpoint. The biographies of Wilson by David Lawrence and William Allen White contain some color and anecdote. The reactions of the French press are well presented in George B. Noble, *Policies and Opinions at Paris,* chap. III, and in R.C. Binkley, "Reactions of European Public Opinion to Woodrow Wilson's Statesmanship from the Armistice to the Peace at Versailles" (MS. doctoral dissertation, Stanford University, 1927). See also H. H. Merriman, "The French and Woodrow Wilson, 1912–1918: A Study in Public Opinion" (MS. doctoral dissertation, Harvard University, 1937).

ATTEMPTS TO KEEP WILSON FROM THE MASSES. The incident in Italy is taken from Creel, *op. cit.,* pp. 168–171, and is corroborated by Mrs. Wilson's *My Memoir,* p. 217. Mrs. Wilson also tells how a group of French soldiers were deliberately kept in quarters while Wilson was visiting the devastated regions, but were set at liberty as soon as the Presidential party had passed (p. 235).

CHAPTER EIGHT

BLUNDERING BEGINNINGS

FOR GENERAL bibliographies on the Peace Conference, consult S. F. Bemis and G. G. Griffin, *Guide to the Diplomatic History of the United States,* pp. 673–684; Nina Almond and Ralph H. Lutz,

An Introduction to a Bibliography of the Paris Peace Conference (Stanford University, 1935); and two outstanding bibliographical articles, R. C. Binkley, "Ten Years of Peace Conference History," *Journal of Modern History,* I (1929), 607–629; and Paul Birdsall, "The Second Decade of Peace Conference History," *ibid.,* XI (1939), 362–378. The same author has the most scholarly single-volume analysis of the whole problem in *Versailles Twenty Years After* (New York, 1941).

On the whole, the most valuable work on the Conference from the point of view of Wilson and the United States is still Ray Stannard Baker's *Woodrow Wilson and World Settlement* (3 vols., Garden City, N.Y., 1923). It supersedes Mr. Baker's sketchy *What Wilson Did at Paris* (Garden City, N.Y., 1919). Though the larger work is marred by too sympathetic an attitude toward Wilson, it reproduces many documents from the Wilson collection, notably from the secret minutes of the Council of Four, which to this day have not been published. No less useful in many ways is Charles Seymour's *House Papers,* vol. IV, which corrects Baker's *World Settlement* on a number of points. An extremely valuable narrative and diary by one of the American experts is J. T. Shotwell, *At the Paris Peace Conference.* A series of lectures by experts who were at the Conference was published in E. M. House and Charles Seymour, eds., *What Really Happened at Paris.* Charles Seymour has a brief but sound general account, *Woodrow Wilson and the World War* (New Haven, 1921). Two leading experts, Charles H. Haskins and Robert H. Lord, collaborated in writing *Some Problems of the Peace Conference* (Cambridge, Mass., 1920). H. J. Coolidge and R. H. Lord, in *Archibald Cary Coolidge: Life and Letters* (Boston, 1932), present some interesting data on an American expert who was primarily concerned with the Central European settlement. Herbert Hoover has some brief observations from the isolationist point of view, chiefly on the economic questions, in his *America's First Crusade* (New York, 1942).

H. W. V. Temperley, ed., *A History of the Peace Conference of Paris* (6 vols., London, 1920–1924), is a cooperative work in the nature of a semiofficial British history. The British point of view is further set forth in David Lloyd George's *Memoirs of the Peace Conference;* in Winston S. Churchill, *The World Crisis, 1918–1928, The Aftermath* (New York, 1929); and in Harold Nicolson, *Peace-*

making 1919, which, though out of focus in its characterization of Wilson and other persons, is a brilliantly penetrating account of the Conference. The present writer is indebted to this work for a considerable number of his ideas. Valuable glimpses also appear in *Lord Riddell's Intimate Diary of the Peace Conference and After, 1918–1923* (New York, 1934); in C. E. Callwell, *Field-Marshal Sir Henry Wilson,* vol. II; and in Henry Borden, ed., *Robert Laird Borden: His Memoirs* (2 vols., New York, 1938). See also R. H. Beadon, *Some Memories of the Peace Conference* (London, 1933). The French point of view is most ably set forth by André Tardieu, one of the French Commissioners, in *The Truth About the Treaty* (Indianapolis, 1921). Consult also Geneviève Tabouis, *The Life of Jules Cambon* (London, 1938, trans. by C. F. Atkinson). G. B. Noble, *Policies and Opinions at Paris, 1919,* discusses French policy and opinion against the general background of the Conference.

Among the numerous books by British journalists, one must single out H. Wilson Harris, *The Peace in the Making* (New York, 1920), which is remarkably fair and accurate for the time; Sisley Huddleston, *Peace-Making at Paris* (London, 1919), which is less satisfactory; the same author's *In My Time* (New York, 1938); Henry Wickham Steed, *Through Thirty Years, 1892–1922* (2 vols., Garden City, N.Y., 1924), whose author was close to some of the leading statesmen; and E. J. Dillon, *The Inside Story of the Peace Conference* (New York, 1920), which is not trustworthy.

Material of some value by American journalists may be found in O. G. Villard, *Fighting Years;* C. T. Thompson, *The Peace Conference Day by Day* (New York, 1920), which is in the nature of a newspaper diary; Harry Hansen, *The Adventures of the Fourteen Points* (New York, 1919); Lincoln Steffens, *The Autobiography of Lincoln Steffens* (2 vols., New York, 1931); and Ella Winter and Granville Hicks, eds., *The Letters of Lincoln Steffens* (2 vols., New York, 1938). See also M. P. Briggs, *George D. Herron and the European Settlement* (Stanford University, 1932).

The most important single documentary collection that has appeared in full to date is David Hunter Miller's monumental *My Diary at the Conference of Paris* (21 vols., New York, 1924–1926), though it is being superseded in part by *U.S. Peace Documents.*

Other titles have already been cited, or will be cited in successive Bibliographical Notes.

On the general subject matter of Chapter VIII, R. S. Baker, *World Settlement,* vol. I, and Charles Seymour, *House Papers,* vol. IV, are especially valuable. Baker's chapter on publicity is revealing; he was in a position to know as much about the problem as anyone else. On the question of the locale of the Conference, *U.S. Peace Documents,* I, 119–127, provides important new information. See also David Lloyd George, *Memoirs of the Peace Conference,* vol. I. On the problem of publicity see J. P. Tumulty, *Woodrow Wilson As I Know Him,* and J. T. Shotwell, *At the Paris Peace Conference.* Shotwell was in Paris with the American delegation, while Tumulty watched the home front. The viewpoint of the journalists is effectively set forth by the well-known American liberal, O. G. Villard, *Fighting Years,* and by the British liberal, H. W. Harris, *The Peace in the Making,* and by the internationally known correspondent, Sisley Huddleston, *Peace-Making at Paris.* The French point of view on these problems is well described in G. B. Noble, *Policies and Opinions at Paris.*

WILSON AND OPEN COVENANTS. While Wilson did not publicly explain his precise views on the subject of open covenants, he did make several feeble gestures in the interest of clarification. On March 12, 1918, he wrote a letter to Secretary Lansing, setting forth exactly what he had in mind. This was transmitted to Congress, and finally embalmed in the *Congressional Record* on June 12, 1918 (*Cong. Record,* 65 Cong., 2 sess., p. 7653). Wilson also approved the explanation of open covenants prepared by Messrs. Lippmann and Cobb in their glossary on the Fourteen Points. But this was not made public until long after the Conference. At Paris, Wilson set forth his views at a secret session of the Council of Ten (Jan. 13, 1919), but this statement was not published until much later. See *U.S. Peace Documents,* III, 536. Speaking at Tacoma, Washington, on September 13, 1919, while touring the country on behalf of the Treaty, Wilson still failed to make it clear that there must be secret discussions preliminary to open covenants. See Woodrow Wilson, *War and Peace,* II, 178.

CHAPTER NINE

THE PERILS OF IMPRECISION

ON THE organization of the Conference see R. S. Baker, *World Settlement*, vols. I, II; Charles Seymour, *House Papers*, vol. IV; Robert C. Binkley, "New Light on the Paris Peace Conference," in *Political Science Quarterly*, XLVI (1931), 335–361; 509–547; C. H. Haskins and R. H. Lord, *Some Problems of the Peace Conference;* Robert Lansing, *The Peace Negotiations* and *The Big Four;* and Harold Nicolson, *Peacemaking 1919,* chaps. IV–VI. The text of the French proposal of Nov. 29, 1918, may be found in R. S. Baker, *World Settlement,* III, 55–63. On the secret treaties, see R. S. Baker, *Wilson,* vols. VII, VIII; Charles Seymour, *House Papers,* III, chap. II; *Senate Docs.,* 66 Cong., 1 sess., no. 76 (Wilson before Senate Foreign Relations Committee); and *ibid.,* no. 106 (Hearings on the Treaty of Versailles); also *Papers Relating to the Foreign Relations of the United States: The Lansing Papers, 1914–1920* (Washington, 1939–1940), II, 23–25.

PUBLICATION OF THE SECRET TREATIES. The material in the text on the republication by American newspapers is taken largely from R. S. Baker, *World Settlement,* I, 32 n. The figures given by Oswald G. Villard, editor of the New York *Evening Post,* which first published the treaties in the United States, are somewhat different. He says that the treaties were syndicated in nine other daily newspapers, and then reprinted in pamphlet form and sold on the news stands of New York, Boston, Philadelphia, Chicago, Washington, and other cities. Two copies were also mailed to the White House. Colonel House apparently received two of them. See Villard, *Fighting Years,* pp. 470–472.

WILSON'S UNTRUTHFULNESS. Only the naïve will be shocked at Wilson's misstatements before the Senate Committee. Few men have gone far in politics without having occasionally "to chip the cube of truth to make it roll." A careful analysis of the writings and addresses of politicians, especially if they make many speeches, will almost invariably reveal inconsistencies and contradictions. There are a number in Wilson's speeches. Two days before he sailed to Europe, for example, he told Congress that the Allied governments "desire my personal counsel," which does not square with his anger over their opposition to his coming. See Woodrow Wilson, *War and Peace*, I, 322. Although, as pointed out in the text, Wilson was clear on many details of the Conference while before the Senate Committee, he did not remember that he had invited China to sever relations with the Central Powers in 1917, which he had and which was an important step (*Senate* Docs., 66 Cong., 1 sess., no. 76, p. 30).

CHAPTER TEN

THE OLYMPIANS

THE BEST general characterization of the Big Four as a group is Robert Lansing's *The Big Four*, which is penetrating. There are few books bearing upon the Conference which do not contain some reference to the Big Four, but one must single out for special mention R. S. Baker's *World Settlement;* Charles Seymour's *House Papers,* vol. IV; Harold Nicolson's *Peacemaking 1919;* and Gabriel Terrail, *Le combat des trois* (Paris, 1922), which contains excerpts from the yet unpublished and confidential minutes of the Council of Four. Nicolson, though brilliant, must be used with caution, for in his unfriendly characterization of Wilson he is as far from the mark as J. M. Keynes in his *The Economic Consequences of the Peace* (New York, 1920). Lloyd George stands self-revealed (and partially self-concealed) in his *Memoirs of the Peace Conference.* Glimpses of Lloyd George appear in Winston S. Churchill's brilliant if somewhat lurid *The World Crisis;* in Lord Riddell's *Intimate Diary of the Peace Conference and After;* in C. E. Callwell's *Field-Marshal Sir Henry Wilson,* vol. II (Wilson is bitterly outspoken); and in H. W. Steed's *Through Thirty Years,* vol. II, which is by a high-grade journalist who had intimate contacts with the leading statesmen. Georges Clemenceau's *Grandeur and Misery of Victory* (trans. by F. M. Atkinson, New York, 1930), is an embittered defense of his making of the peace; while the most recent and most useful biography of the Tiger is Geoffrey Bruun, *Clemenceau*. Colonel Stephen Bonsal, an American interpreter, saw a good deal of Clemenceau during the latter's convalescence, and sets forth some amusing anecdotes in *Unfinished Business* (Garden City, N.Y., 1944), Pt. III. An excellent bibliography on Wilson is published by Charles Seymour in the *Dictionary of American Biography*, XX, 367–368. Intimate glimpses appear in Edith Bolling Wilson, *My Memoir*, and I. H. Hoover, *Forty-two Years in the White House*. Of the various biographies of Wilson, that by William E. Dodd suffers from an excess of sympathy; that by William A. White from a lack of sympathy. David Lawrence, *The True Story of Woodrow Wilson* (New York, 1924), is worth consulting. Two outstanding character sketches of Wilson are in Gamaliel Bradford's *The Quick and the Dead* (Boston, 1929), chap. II; and D. F. Houston, *Eight Years with Wilson's Cabinet*, II, 155–254.

CHAPTER ELEVEN

THE WHITE MAN'S BURDEN

AMONG THE numerous works touching upon the adoption of the mandate system, one must particularly mention David Lloyd George's *Memoirs of the Peace Conference*, I, chap. X; R. S. Baker's *World Settlement*, I, chap. XV; Charles Seymour's *House Papers*, vol. IV; David Hunter Miller, *The Drafting of the Covenant* (2 vols., New York, 1928), chap. IX; and G. L. Beer, *African Questions at the Paris Peace Conference* (New York, 1923). Beer was one of the American experts on colonies. The views expressed by the Germans at Paris are conveniently compiled in Alma Luckau, *The German Delegation at the Paris Peace Conference* (New York, 1941). For an excellent brief discussion see Paul Birdsall, *Versailles Twenty Years After*, chap. III.

ORIGINS OF THE MANDATE IDEA. Wilson apparently conceived of the idea independently of General Jan C. Smuts, of South Africa, who is sometimes given credit for it. Smuts would have applied the scheme only to territories formerly belonging to Russia, Austria-Hungary, and Turkey, and not to the former German colonies (Charles Seymour, *House Papers*, IV, 284–285).

THE IDEA OF AN AMERICAN MANDATE. Late in Oct., 1918, Colonel House reported to Wilson that Lloyd George had suggested that the United States take over the trusteeship of German East Africa. House was under the impression that the British wanted the United States to secure something so that the British could with better grace take what they desired (*U.S. Peace Documents*, I, 407). This was undoubtedly one of the motives behind the later request that the United States assume a mandate for Armenia and Constantinople.

THE ARMENIAN MANDATE. Professor William L. Westermann, one of the American experts at Paris, is strongly critical of America's failure to assume its responsibilities toward Armenia. See his chapter in E. M. House and Charles Seymour, *What Really Happened at Paris*, chap. VIII. Herbert Hoover recalls that he was approached by Colonel House on the subject of being named governor of the Armenian mandate (Herbert Hoover, *America's First Crusade*, p. 48). On May 21, 1919, Wilson told his colleagues on the Council of Four that while in his judgment the American people would oppose taking a mandate over any part of Asia Minor where they had no material interests, he was nevertheless hopeful that he could secure acceptance of a mandate over Armenia and Constantinople, where the United States had missionary and other interests (Woodrow Wilson Papers, IX–C).

JAPANESE MANDATED ISLANDS. The conclusions here expressed regarding the 1898–1899 negotiations between Germany and Spain for the Pacific islands are based primarily on the manuscript records of the Department of State for that period, now in the National Archives. There is also considerable material in *Die Grosse Politik der Europäischen Kabinette*, Band XV, Kapitel XCVIII. It is possible that Wilson attached little importance to the islands, partly because he expected that America would leave the Philippines, in line with Democratic policy, and in that event we should not need bases for strategic support of our possessions in the Far East. A number of years later, Admiral A. T. Mahan, the world-famous naval authority, recalled: "When the Caroline and Ladrone Islands were about to be ceded to Germany by Spain in 1898, I received more than one letter urging me to use any influence I could exert to induce our government to resist the step. My reply was that, besides having no influence, I saw no sufficient reason for our opposition." (*Armaments and Arbitration* [New York, 1912], p. 80.) It is hardly fair to blame McKinley for not seeing what Admiral Mahan could not see.

Under date of Dec. 14, 1918, Third Assistant Secretary of State Breckinridge Long prepared for the United States peace delegation a memorandum of extraordinary interest. His plan was that at the Conference the United States should work for the return of the islands to Germany, and then, when the Conference had adjourned, take them over on an indemnity or some other basis. There is no evidence that this proposal was looked upon favorably; certainly not by such a stern advocate of morality in international dealings as Wilson. It is interesting that Long did not make any mention of the islands as potential air bases. (*U.S. Peace Documents*, II, 512–515.)

On Feb. 13, 1919, the Intelligence Section of the American experts at Paris submitted a lengthy report ("Black Book") on the German North Pacific islands. It recommended that they be turned over to Japan as a mandate, with proper safeguards regarding fortification. The American experts concluded that the islands had "slight importance," except "possibly" from the standpoint of military strategy. The possible strategic value of the islands seemed even more negligible to the experts in view of the prospective establishment of the League of Nations and the possible abolition of the submarine. The report concluded that the United States had no legitimate claim to the islands, and that to demand them would not only offend Japan but undermine America's strong moral position at the Conference. (Woodrow Wilson Papers, IX–A.)

CHAPTER TWELVE

A LIVING THING IS BORN

THE MOST important single work is D. H. Miller, *The Drafting of the Covenant*. The author was an American expert and one of the chief architects of the finished Covenant. Consult also his monumental *My Diary*, and his brief account in E. M. House and Charles Seymour, *What Really Happened at Paris*, chap. XVII. Colonel Stephen Bonsal, who was the interpreter for Wilson and House on the League of Nations Commission, has just published his contemporary notes under the title *Unfinished Business*. While they add little to Miller and Seymour on the formation of the Covenant, they reproduce a good deal of useful color and corroborative data. The difficulties of transacting business through the medium of an interpreter are effectively portrayed. See also Charles Seymour, *House Papers*, vol. IV, and Robert Lansing, *The Peace Negotiations*. Lord Robert Cecil tells his part in the story in *A Great Experiment* (London, 1941). There is also some important light on the place of the Covenant on the agenda in André Tardieu, *The Truth About the Treaty*. R. S. Baker's *World Settlement*, vol. II, contains an important account, which tends to overstress European opposition to the League idea. Lloyd George, in his *Memoirs of the Peace Conference*, vol. I, chap. XIV, swings the pendulum violently the other way. On the question of origins, consult Theodore Marburg, *Development of the League of Nations Idea* (2 vols., New York, 1932); Florence Wilson, *The Origins of the League Covenant* (London, 1928); and Charles Howard-Ellis, *The Origin, Structure, and Working of the League of Nations* (Boston, 1928). Useful secondary accounts are G. B. Noble, *Policies and Opinions at Paris*, chap. IV; and Paul Birdsall, *Versailles Twenty Years After*, chap. V.

THE INTEGRAL PRINCIPLE. David Hunter Miller is of the opinion that the incorporation of the Covenant in the treaty was "itself of the substance of the pre-armistice agreement," and something which was owing to Germany under it. See E. M. House and Charles

Seymour, *What Really Happened at Paris,* p. 399. Wilson believed that the Covenant should be in the treaty, for in this way Germany could be made to approve the League and would not later be in a legal position to challenge the arrangements under it. If she signed the treaty and not the Covenant, there would be no way of compelling her to do so at a later date. At least, this was Wilson's argument before the Senate Foreign Relations Committee (*Sen. Docs.,* 66 Cong., 1 sess., no. 76, p. 16). Yet in the Treaty of Versailles, Germany was compelled to approve, sight unseen, the yet unmade treaties of the Allied and Associated Powers with her former allies. If this could be done, it seems evident that she could have been forced to approve the yet unborn League Covenant.

The incorporation of the Covenant in the Treaty was a source of great embarrassment to the neutrals who wanted to join the League, but who did not want to be associated with the Treaty. As late as 1937 the Assembly of the League of Nations was still debating the question of separating the Covenant from the Treaty. See J. T. Shotwell, *At the Paris Peace Conference,* p. v.

The workability of the plan for putting the general outlines of the League into the Treaty is borne out by the Covenant itself. Article XIV embodies the idea of the Permanent Court of International Justice, which was later worked out by a Committee of Jurists. Article XXIII of the Covenant and Part XIII of the Treaty made rather detailed provision for the International Labor Organization, which was later brought into being. In both of these creations the neutrals played an important role.

CHAPTER THIRTEEN

A PROPHET IS NOT WITHOUT HONOR

THE BEST brief secondary account is D. F. Fleming, *The United States and the League of Nations.* Henry Cabot Lodge's own embittered account of the Round Robin is given in his *The Senate and the League of Nations* (New York, 1925). See also J. P. Tumulty, *Woodrow Wilson As I Know Him;* George Creel, *The War, the World and Wilson;* Allan Nevins, *Henry White.*

THE LITERARY DIGEST POLL. A breakdown of the figures by party is most revealing (*ibid.,* April 5, 1919, p. 14):

DEMOCRATIC NEWSPAPERS

Yes	4,327,052
No	121,912
Conditional	508,384
Total	4,957,348

REPUBLICAN NEWSPAPERS

Yes	1,911,256
No	1,249,264
Conditional	3,836,417
Total	6,996,937

INDEPENDENT NEWSPAPERS

Yes	3,648,141
No	2,955,706*
Conditional	2,447,660
Total	9,051,507

WILSON'S INDISCREET SPEECH. On Feb. 28, 1919, Wilson spoke to the Democratic National Committee at the White House, and while some of his remarks were reported in the press the text was not published until 1921, when it appeared in J. P. Tumulty's *Woodrow Wilson As I Know Him,* pp. 367–379. Wilson referred to the opponents of the League (clearly meaning among them the Senators) as "of all the blind and little, provincial people, they are the littlest and most contemptible. It is not their character so much that I have a contempt for, though that contempt is thoroughgoing, but their minds. They have not got even good working imitations of minds." There was much more in the same vein. Here Wilson betrayed his characteristic contempt for people with "bungalow minds"; and though his speech was presumably not meant for public consumption, he should have known that his remarks would leak out and do nothing to smooth the already ruffled feathers of the Republicans in the Senate.

* Including the 2,488,976 circulation of the Hearst papers.

WILSON AND LEAGUE AMENDMENTS. While it is true that Wilson expected to amend the Covenant to some extent upon his return to Paris, it seems clear that he was hoping for nothing more serious than minor verbal changes in the interests of clarification. See Wilson to Senator Thomas J. Walsh, Feb. 26, 1919, Woodrow Wilson Papers, IX–A. It is interesting also that when Colonel House cabled from Paris advising that the League be put into operation at once, Wilson declined to do so, except possibly on a very provisional basis. He feared that the Senate would resent an attempt to railroad the Covenant through. This indicates that Wilson, then in America, was becoming increasingly aware of the temper of the Senate, while Colonel House experienced an extraordinary lapse from his usual political acuteness. (Wilson to House [cablegram], March 3, 1919, Woodrow Wilson Papers, IX–A.)

CHAPTER FOURTEEN

THE BATTLE BEGINS

ON THE dropping of the preliminary conference see Charles Seymour, *House Papers*, vol. IV; R. S. Baker, *World Settlement*, vols. I, II; and Harold Nicolson, *Peacemaking 1919*, chap. IV. On the amending of the League Covenant, consult David Hunter Miller, *The Drafting of the Covenant*; Stephen Bonsal, *Unfinished Business*; Seymour, *op. cit.*; Baker, *op. cit.*; and D. F. Fleming, *The United States and the League of Nations*. Harold and Margaret Sprout, *Toward a New Order of Sea Power* (Princeton, 1940), have an excellent analysis of the naval problem at Paris. On the Saar, there is an exceptionally able discussion by Professor Haskins in C. H. Haskins and R. H. Lord, *Some Problems of the Peace Conference*. Haskins was one of the American experts and was generally regarded as the prospective head of the Saar Commission. See also Paul Birdsall, *Versailles Twenty Years After*, chap. IX. The French point of view is ably set forth in André Tardieu, *The Truth About the Treaty*; also in G. B. Noble, *Policies and Opinions at Paris*, chaps. VI, IX. See also Seymour, *op. cit.*; Baker, *op. cit.*; and

David Lloyd George, *Memoirs of the Peace Conference,* vol. I, chap. VIII. The standard work on the subject is Sarah Wambaugh, *The Saar Plebiscite* (Cambridge, 1940).

THE "SIDETRACK PLOT." The alleged plot in its most dramatic form is set forth in R. S. Baker, *World Settlement,* vol. I, chap. XVII. Many of the details are sharply challenged by Charles Seymour, *House Papers,* IV, 363–376. Winston S. Churchill enters the lists against Baker most vigorously in *The World Crisis,* pp. 187–191. Robert C. Binkley ably analyzes the whole controversy in "Ten Years of Peace Conference History," *Journal of Modern History,* I (1929), 612–621, and acquits Baker of dishonesty in handling the evidence. The truth seems to be that while there was no real plot, Wilson evidently thought that Colonel House had compromised too far, and that there was real danger to the League.

SUMMONING THE GEORGE WASHINGTON. There is also a controversy over the effectiveness of the summoning of the *George Washington.* R. S. Baker, in his *World Settlement,* II, 57–62, stresses its influence. Charles Seymour, in his *House Papers,* IV, 403–404, belittles it. It is certainly true, as Seymour says, that this incident marks no sharp turning point in the Conference, for in the subsequent days the President himself yielded ground, as well as the French, in effecting compromises over vital issues. On the other hand, Henry White wrote repeatedly in his letters that the possibility of an American withdrawal filled the French and others with consternation. (Allan Nevins, *Henry White,* p. 438 n.) Dr. Grayson, Wilson's personal physician, who presumably knew more about medicine than politics, cabled Tumulty that the *George Washington* incident had had a "castor oil effect" on the slow-moving French (April 10, 1919, Woodrow Wilson Papers, IX–A). Certainly the incident was headlined luridly in the press. Perhaps the fairest conclusion is that the affair has been overplayed, but that it was probably not without some effect. It is to be noted that the original cablegram of April 7, 1919, from Admiral Benson to the Navy Department, did not order the *George Washington* to sail, but asked how soon she could sail. (The text is in Charles Seymour, *House Papers,* IV, 403.) For alleged irregularities attending the sending of this cablegram from London, and for the sailing of the ship on the afternoon of April 11 from New York, see New York *Times,* April 11, 12, 1919.

CHAPTER FIFTEEN

THE PHANTOM OF FRENCH SECURITY

A SPIRITED and able defense of the French position on the Security Treaty appears in André Tardieu, *The Truth About the Treaty,* chap. VI. Tardieu was one of the French commissioners, and the right-hand man of Clemenceau. The Tiger defends himself with less fact and more emotion in *Grandeur and Misery of Victory.* Robert Lansing has an informative statement of the problem in his *The Peace Negotiations,* chap. XV. There is also useful material in David Lloyd George's *Memoirs of the Peace Conference;* in R. S. Baker's *World Settlement,* vols. II, III; and Charles Seymour, *House Papers,* vol. IV. An excellent analysis of French policy, chiefly as reflected in the press, is G. B. Noble, *Policies and Opinions at Paris,* chap. VII. See also C. H. Haskins and R. H. Lord, *Some Problems of the Peace Conference,* chap. IV. There are a number of books on French backgrounds of Rhine policy, but they add little or nothing to the above references with regard to Wilson and the policy of the United States. A summary account appears in Paul Birdsall, *Versailles Twenty Years After,* chap. VIII.

THE RHINELAND DEAL. It is commonly but erroneously supposed that France gave up her demands for the annexation of the Rhineland in return for the Security Treaty. There was never any official demand at the Conference for outright annexation. It is also sometimes thought that the French gave up occupation of the Rhine in return for the treaty. The facts are as stated in the text: France got limited occupation *in addition* to the treaty. It is also a common error to say that France foolishly gave up real security for the fancied security of the treaty. As pointed out in the text, she had ample technical safeguards in addition to the treaty.

THE SECURITY TREATY. Some critics are disposed to blame Britain for exercising her indisputable right to withdraw from the agreement when the United States declined to ratify. They feel that the history of postwar Europe would have been different if Britain had been willing to accept a dual alliance. It is interesting to note that there was considerable support for the Security Treaty in the press of the United States, and it seems probable that public opinion was considerably ahead of the Senate on this issue. See *Literary Digest,* May 3, 1919, p. 20; July 19, 1919, p. 12; and Dec. 31, 1921, pp. 5–9. This last article was based on a newspaper poll on the idea of aiding France. On the other hand, there was strong opposition in the American isolationist press to the proposed Security Treaty, even while it was only in the rumor stage. See Tumulty to Wilson (cablegram), April 22, 1919, Woodrow Wilson Papers, IX–A.

CHAPTER SIXTEEN

MAKING THE PIPS SQUEAK

THE MOST exhaustive study of the subject from the American point of view, and a model of its kind, is Philip Mason Burnett, *Reparation at the Paris Peace Conference from the Standpoint of the American Delegation* (2 vols., New York, 1940). The present study has drawn heavily on this work for some of its conclusions. The most important volume to come down to us from one of the American experts is Bernard M. Baruch, *The Making of the Reparation and Economic Sections of the Treaty* (New York, 1920). A brief chapter by another expert, Thomas W. Lamont, is published in E. M. House and Charles Seymour, *What Really Happened at Paris,* chap. XI. The French viewpoint is set forth in André Tardieu, *The Truth About the Treaty;* the British, in David Lloyd George, *Memoirs of the Peace Conference,* vol. I, chap. IX. John Maynard Keynes, a British economic expert who resigned from the British delegation in protest, wrote a daring and on the whole farsighted analysis in his *The Economic Consequences of the Peace,* which he supplemented with *A Revision of the Treaty* (New York, 1922). Additional material appears in Charles Seymour, *House Papers,* vol. IV; and R. S. Baker, *World Settlement,* vol. II. Brief secondary accounts appear in Paul Birdsall, *Versailles Twenty*

Years After, chap. X; and G. B. Noble, *Policies and Opinions at Paris,* chap. VI.

THE FRENCH RESERVATION ON REPARATIONS. The French, during the Armistice negotiations, succeeded in inserting into paragraph 19 of the final agreement a clause "that any future claims and demands of the Allies and the United States of America remain unaffected . . ." (*For. Rels., 1918, Supp. 1,* I, p. 466). The French later used this seemingly innocent safeguard to support their demands for war costs and pensions. The circumstantial evidence is overwhelming that no such construction was then accepted or could properly be made. John Maynard Keynes concludes that the clause was "merely the usual phrase of the draftsman, who, about to rehearse a list of certain claims, wishes to guard himself from the implication that such list is exhaustive." *Economic Consequences of the Peace,* p. 114. The whole controversy is ably discussed in Burnett, *op. cit.,* I, 7–8.

THE PENSIONS DECISION. The American experts reconciled themselves to this decision on the ground that even if the swollen figure was finally accepted, it would be too big for Germany to pay anyhow, and hence the burden on her would be substantially the same in the long run (Burnett, *op. cit.,* I, 64–65).

THE REPARATIONS COMMISSION. The British apparently did not want American representation; the French, for various reasons, did. Wilson finally threw his weight in favor of American participation. He later told the Senate Committee on Foreign Relations that the United States did not want membership, but that he yielded to the importunities of those nations who "wanted our advice and counsel" (*Senate Docs.,* 66 Cong., 1 sess., no. 76, p. 55). He contemporaneously (April 15, 1919) wrote to Herbert Hoover, who had protested against American participation, that "that commission will undoubtedly need an umpire, and I am afraid we must take the necessary risks in that matter" (Herbert Hoover, *America's First Crusade,* p. 48).

WAR GUILT CLAUSE. A great controversy has raged over the question whether the "war guilt clause" implied moral turpitude on the part of the Germans. It is clear that this clause was originally designed primarily as a political safeguard and not as a moral indictment. A careful reading of the text of the Treaty gives strong support to those who claim that no sense of wrongdoing was implied. But if the instrument is taken in connection with the German replies and the Allied rejoinders, as it must be to determine the intent of the framers, the opposite is true. The Germans took the ground that the clause did involve moral guilt, and that they were blameless. The Allies, whether they wanted to or not, were placed in a position where they had to deny German claims of innocence. The whole controversy is academic, however, because the Germans *thought* that theirs was the correct interpretation, and what they thought in this case was supremely important. Burnett, *op. cit.*, vol. I, chap. XVII, has a penetrating and well balanced discussion of this mooted question.

CHAPTER SEVENTEEN

OPEN DISAGREEMENTS OPENLY ARRIVED AT

THE FULLEST account, based largely on yet unpublished documents, is R. S. Baker, *World Settlement,* vol. II. David Lloyd George's *Memoirs of the Peace Conference,* vol. II, also reproduces significant documents, but is less reliable. There are important materials in Charles Seymour, *House Papers,* vol. IV, and also in J. T. Shotwell, *At the Paris Peace Conference.* Dr. Shotwell was intimately concerned with the quarrel among the American experts over Fiume. Allan Nevins, *Henry White,* pp. 430–433, is revealing on Senator Lodge's attitude regarding Fiume. Professor Douglas W. Johnson, a geographical expert on the Dalmatian area who was on the whole sympathetic toward Jugoslavia, has a compact chapter, which avoids controversial political issues, in E. M. House and Charles Seymour, *What Really Happened at Paris,* chap. VI. Johnson is the authority (p. 117) for the statement herein made regarding a defensible frontier south of the Brenner. Edith Bolling Wilson, *My Memoir,* gives intimate feminine glimpses of Wilson during this dispute. See also George Creel, *The War, the World and Wilson,* chap. XIX. Of the purely secondary accounts, that by René Albrecht-Carrié, *Italy at the Paris Peace Conference* (New York, 1938), is outstanding, and embodies the fruits of the most recent scholarship. The same author also has published "New Light on Italian Problems in 1919," *Journal of Modern History*, XIII (1941), 493–516; "Italy and Her Allies, June 1919," *American Historical Review*, XLVI (1941), 837–843; and "Italian Colonial Problems in 1919," *Political Science Quarterly*, LVIII (1943), 562–580. For brief analyses see Harold Nicolson, *Peacemaking 1919*, chap. VII; and Paul Birdsall, *Versailles Twenty Years After*, chap. XI.

WILSON'S APPEAL HABIT. It will be remembered that Wilson twice toyed with the idea of a public appeal at the time of the Armistice negotiations (Charles Seymour, *House Papers*, IV, 168, 183), in connection with the mandates question *ibid.*, (298 n.), and in connection with the Allied demand for war costs (*ibid.*, 343 n.). His summoning of the *George Washington* was in the nature of a public appeal, and in the case of Fiume he actually went through with it. Wilson should have been a keen enough student of human nature to know that it is one thing to appeal to one's own people; another to appeal to strangers over the heads of their own government. The time was not especially well chosen, because only a few months before, in the October appeal, he had apparently not been able to induce his own people to respond favorably. This experience with the Italians apparently did not change Wilson's views as to the efficacy of direct methods. On May 11, 1919, he told the Council of Four (Orlando absent) that he was so deeply angered by Italian machinations in Asia Minor that he could not much longer refrain from exposing Italy's course to the entire world, and thus visiting upon her the reprobation of mankind (Woodrow Wilson Papers, IX–C).

THE WILSON–HOUSE "BREAK." It is a curious fact that Colonel House often said he never knew precisely when the break actually occurred or what caused it. (See G. S. Viereck, *The Strangest Friendship in History*, chap. XXXV.) A. D. H. Smith, in his *Mr. House of Texas*, pp. 270–272, quotes the Colonel as later seeing the beginnings of coolness when, in the spring of 1918, Smith published a series of laudatory articles under the title, "The Real Colonel House." Mrs. Wilson seems to date the rift from Wilson's first return to Paris, at the time of the alleged "sidetrack plot"

(*My Memoir,* pp. 245–246). J. T. Shotwell, in his *At the Paris Peace Conference,* p. 200, stresses the Fiume affair. The incident regarding Wilson's having been annoyed by House's conclave with Lloyd George and Clemenceau appears in Lloyd George's *Memoirs of the Peace Conference,* I, 159. Shortly after House's death, a statement which the Colonel is said to have given to newspapermen was published by the press. In it he recounts two instances when Wilson was annoyed because Clemenceau and Lloyd George were seeking him out rather than Wilson. From the second of these incidents House is reported to have said that he dated the end of his friendship with the President. See North Adams (Mass.) *Transcript,* May 3, 1938, as quoted in Paul Birdsall, *Journal of Modern History,* XI, 372. This account is subject to some suspicion because House apparently on no other occasion was prepared to date the break so definitely. See also Viereck, *op. cit.,* pp. 247, 262. There can be no doubt that busybodies were at work during the Conference turning Wilson against House, and that the events of the Fiume controversy did nothing to restore the President's peace of mind. It is also clear that there was a "drifting apart" rather than an outright "break." See Seymour, *op. cit.,* IV, 506–517.

ORLANDO AND THE COUNCIL OF FOUR. Contrary to a common misconception, Orlando did not immediately bolt the Conference after Wilson's appeal, and he did not leave in anger. He and Sonnino met with the Council of Four the next day (April 24, 1919), and Orlando said that his esteem for Wilson was unshaken; that he believed Wilson's attitude to be that of a friend; that he had no intention of bolting the Conference (his authority had been called into question, and he must return home to seek new instructions); and that he owed his thanks to Wilson for the latter's "noble declaration." This was in response to the President's explanation that he had never thought of his appeal as going over the head of Orlando to the Italian people; that if this were the effect he personally regretted it; and that he had felt it necessary to issue the appeal because the French and Italian press was not setting forth the true facts. Near the end of the discussion, Orlando said that he had to leave to catch his train, whereupon Sir Maurice Hankey, on behalf of Lloyd George and Clemenceau, handed him the joint letter of April 23, 1919, signed by the British and French premiers. (Minutes of the Council of Four, Woodrow Wilson

Papers, IX–C.) The untrustworthy Lloyd George (*Memoirs of the Peace Conference,* p. 546) leaves the false impression that this letter was handed to Orlando *the day it was dated,* which was the day of Wilson's appeal. Actually it was presented the next day.

ORLANDO AND THE MANDATES. It is not true, as alleged by several writers, that the mandates were finally parceled out while Orlando was absent. The semifinal steps for their allocation were taken while the Italian premier was in Italy, but he was present at the afternoon meeting of May 7, 1919, when the final division was made. He rather mildly protested against Italy's being excluded from African mandates, but did not press the point, presumably because he expected compensations elsewhere. (Minutes of the Council of Four, May 7, 1919, Woodrow Wilson Papers, IX–C.) Some of the confusion probably arises from the fact that there were three meetings of the Council of Four on May 7. Orlando, who had just arrived, came late to the one which met at 11:00 A.M.; was not present at the one which met at noon (here the Smyrna decision was taken); and was present at the one which met at 4:15 P.M. House relates that Sonnino told him on May 8 that both he and Orlando greatly regretted the intemperate things that had been printed and said in Italy, and had tried to curb them. (House to Wilson, May 8, 1919, Yale House Collection.)

CHAPTER EIGHTEEN

THE YELLOW PERIL

ON THE Japanese problem at Paris, see David Hunter Miller, *The Drafting of the Covenant.* The account in R. S. Baker, *World Settlement,* vol. II, is useful, as is that in Charles Seymour, *House Papers,* vol. IV. Robert Lansing, *The Peace Negotiations,* chap. XVIII, is highly critical of Wilson. See also Frederick Palmer's *Bliss,* chap. XXXVI, for an account of Bliss' vigorous protest against the Shantung deal. Wilson's own thinking on this matter is best revealed in his testimony before the Senate Foreign Relations Committee, Aug. 19, 1919 (*Sen. Docs.*, 66 Cong., 1 sess., no. 76), and in his speeches in behalf of the Treaty which are published in Woodrow Wilson, *War and Peace*, vol. II. See also Lansing's testimony before the Senate Committee in *Sen. Docs.*, 66 Cong., 1 sess., no. 106. An excellent monographic account of the problem, with emphasis on Shantung, is T. E. La Fargue, *China and the World War* (Stanford University, 1937). George Creel has a spirited and on the whole able defense of Wilson in *The War, the World and Wilson*, chap. XVIII.

WAS RACIAL EQUALITY A BLUFF? An examination of the *Japan Times and Mail* (Weekly Edition), which reproduced translations of leading editorials in the Japanese press and which also maintained an excellent news service, reveals that Japanese opinion was much concerned over this issue (*ibid.*, XL, 153, 254, 333, 380, 391, 417, 457, 515, 524–525, 568, 571). See particularly the statement of Viscount Uchida, Minister of Foreign Affairs, before the Diet, in which he said that the issue was one of great importance (*ibid.*, p. 420). It is interesting to note that while opinion in the United States felt that Japan got too much at Paris, opinion in Japan was critical of the Japanese negotiators. There was a widespread feeling that Japan, as in 1895 and 1905, had been outmaneuvered by the great powers. But this feeling was not uncommon in the press of all the participating nations.

THE RACE EQUALITY VOTE. Various secondary accounts state that the vote was 11 to 6. This perfectly natural error probably stems in part from the statement in Charles Seymour, *House Papers*, IV, 428 n., which was written without benefit of David Hunter Miller's revelations. While it is true that eleven members did vote in the affirmative, six did not vote in the negative because no negative vote was called for. Thus the votes of the United States (Wilson and House) and Great Britain (Cecil, with Smuts absent) and Portugal, Poland, and Rumania were not recorded. It is not safe to assume that they all would have been negative if asked for; possibly some would have refrained from voting. Wilson, previous to the vote, spoke against the amendment, not because he opposed it in principle, but because he thought that it should not go into the Covenant. (He doubtless was thinking of the opposition which such a clause might arouse among the anti-Japanese elements in the United States.) For this episode see D. H. Miller, *The Drafting of the Covenant*, I, 461–466; also Miller, *My Diary*, VIII, 259.

Wilson's ruling that the motion had lost because it failed to secure unanimous support was objected to by one of the French delegates. Wilson stood his ground, declaring that the practice had been to insist upon unanimity unless those in the opposition were willing to let the motion pass with a reservation. The one apparent exception involved the selection of Geneva rather than Brussels as the seat of the League; but in this case the Belgians did not insist on their point, and any other procedure would have made a decision impossible. See Miller, *op. cit.*, I, 442; II, 392.

CHAPTER NINETEEN

THE DAY OF RECKONING

THE PROTESTS presented by the Germans at Versailles, together with the Allied replies, are all conveniently printed in Alma Luckau, *The German Delegation at the Paris Peace Conference*. The relevant pages in R. S. Baker, *World Settlement*, vol. II, and Charles Seymour, *House Papers*, vol. IV, are revealing, as are those in C. E. Callwell, *Field-Marshal Sir Henry Wilson*, vol. II, and Herbert Hoover, *America's First Crusade*. There are materials on the "funk period" in David Lloyd George's *Memoirs of the Peace Conference*, vol. I, chap. XVI. See also G. B. Noble, *Policies and Opinions at Paris*, chap. X. The German point of view is ably presented in Karl F. Nowak, *Versailles* (trans. by Norman Thomas and E. W. Dickes, London, 1928); Victor Schiff, *The Germans at Versailles, 1919* (trans. by Geoffrey Dunlop, London, 1930), an expert on the German delegation; and Alfred von Wegerer, *A Refutation of the Versailles War Guilt Thesis* (trans. by Edwin H. Zeydel, New York, 1930) . For purposes of comparing Versailles with the Treaty of Brest-Litovsk, consult John W. Wheeler-Bennett, *The Forgotten Peace: Brest-Litovsk* (New York, 1939).

BROCKDORFF-RANTZAU'S FAILURE TO RISE. The stock explanation is that the German delegate was so nervous that he found it difficult or physically impossible to stand. There can be no doubt that he betrayed signs of extreme nervousness, but the evidence as presented in Dr. Simon's diary is conclusive on the point that he had decided in advance not to rise like a criminal before the bar of justice. See Luckau, *The German Delegation at the Paris Peace Conference*, p. 119.

WILSON'S CONCEPT OF JUSTICE. Wilson seems not to have doubted for one moment that the treaty was just, for he believed with his associates that Germany's sins were far greater than she could atone for. She must be punished severely lest she sin again. On his "swing around the circle" in behalf of the Treaty, Wilson told an audience at Columbus, Ohio, on Sept. 4, 1919: "She [Germany] attempted an intolerable thing, and she must be made to pay for the attempt. The terms of the treaty are severe, but they are not unjust." (Woodrow Wilson, *War and Peace*, I, 590–591. For similar expressions on the same tour see *ibid.*, pp. 591, 592, 644; II, 34, 104, 266, 400.)

CHAPTER TWENTY

BLESSED ARE THE PEACEMAKERS

MANY OF the works already cited are relevant to this concluding chapter. General commentaries appear in Paul Birdsall, *Versailles Twenty Years After*, chap. XII; Harold Nicolson, *Peacemaking 1919*, chap. VIII; René Albrecht-Carrié, "Versailles Twenty Years After," *Political Science Quarterly*, LV (1940), 1–24; W. C. Langsam, "Maladjustments of the Peace Settlement," *Annals of the American Academy of Political and Social Science*, CLXXV (1934), 1–10. Sketchy generalizations, some by British experts, are published in Lord Riddell, *et al.*, *The Treaty of Versailles and After* (London, 1935). See also T. E. Jessop, *The Treaty of Versailles: Was It Just?* (London, 1942), an able but biased brief for the treaty. For a French indictment see Alcide Ebray, *A Frenchman Looks at the Peace* (trans. by E. W. Dickes, New York, 1927); for a British, with emphasis on reparations, J. M. Keynes, *A Revision of the Treaty;* for a German, Wilhelm Ziegler, *Versailles: die Geschichte eines missglückten Friedens* (Hamburg, 1933); for an American, Frank H. Simonds, *How Europe Made Peace Without America* (Garden City, N.Y., 1927). See also Hermann Stegemann, *The Mirage of Versailles* (New York, 1928, trans. by R. T. Clark), another unfavorable discussion from the German point of view; and W. H. Dawson, *Germany Under the Treaty* (London, 1933), which is critical of the treaty. The minorities problem is discussed in William O. Molony, *Nationality and the Peace Treaties* (London, 1934); and L. P. Mair, *The Protection of Minorities* (London, 1928), which is an account of the minorities treaties under the League of Nations. W. E. Stephens, *Revisions of the Treaty of Versailles* (New York, 1939), though useful, contains little that is directly relevant to the United States. J. T. Shotwell, *What Germany Forgot* (New York, 1940), shows that the war and not the Treaty was responsible for many of Germany's ills. Critics of Versailles in America and elsewhere also forgot this.

VIOLATIONS OF THE FOURTEEN POINTS. In this connection, see the discussion of the contradictions and the "escape clauses" in Chapter XIX, above. If there was bad faith, it was not on the part of Wilson, who on the whole sincerely tried to honor his bond.

For the text of the Fourteen Points and their supplements see pp. 333–336 above. Point I (open covenants) was fulfilled in the sense that Wilson intended, though certainly neither he nor anyone else could have put an end to secret understandings. Henceforth treaties were to be registered with the League (Article XVIII of the Covenant). Point II (freedom of the seas) was not discussed at Paris. The British were hostile to it, and Wilson assumed that under the League there would be no neutrals, and consequently no issue involving maritime rights. (See R. S. Baker, *World Settlement,* I, 383.) It has often been remarked that the Treaty of Ghent, which ended our conflict with England in 1814, made no mention of freedom of the seas, one of the primary causes for our declaring war. Exactly the same thing may be said of Versailles.

Point III (removal of economic barriers *"so far as possible"*) was carried out literally "so far as possible," which meant that the principal immediate reductions were at the expense of Germany. The rest was left to Article XXIII of the Covenant. Point IV (arms reduction) was left to Article VIII of the Covenant. Point V (impartial adjustment of colonial claims) was presumably though only partially fulfilled in the mandate system. Point VI (Russia) could not be carried out at Paris, owing to current disorders; but Germany was forced to renounce the Treaty of Brest-Litovsk, and Wilson refused to support with American troops any schemes for crushing the Bolsheviks.

Point VII (restoration of Belgium) was completely discharged, as was Point VIII (restoration of France). Point IX (Italian frontier on lines of nationality) was more than carried out, though a number of aliens were thrown in for good measure, contrary to self-determination. Point X (autonomous development for the peoples of Austria-Hungary) was eventually worked out in the "succession states." Point XI (Balkan restoration) was generally fulfilled. Point XII regarding Turkey could not then be carried out because a settlement had not been effected. Point XIII (an independent Poland) was substantially discharged, as was Point XIV (a League of Nations).

The supplementary points were more nebulous in character, and on them some of the most serious of the German charges were based. Point 15 (essential justice of each case) was carried out only in part. Point 16 (non-bartering of peoples) was certainly more honored than not. The same thing may be said of Point 17 (territorial and other settlements in the interests of the people), at least in regard to Europe. In some cases it was discovered that where economic or other ties would be severed, or general interests would not be served, the people were better off without self-determination. A number of these decisions were made on the urgent recommendation of the American experts, and if blame must be apportioned it would be fairer to attack them than Wilson. Point 18 (recognition of national aspirations) was generally observed. Point 19 (destruction of arbitrary power) was certainly carried out, temporarily, in the case of Germany and her allies. Point 20 was the expression of a noble ideal which could hardly be realized as long as national states are what they are. Point 21 (no special interests) was only partially carried out. Point 22 (no alliances within the League) was apparently violated by Wilson in the Security Treaty with France; but this was an interim arrangement. Besides, the League, when founded, did not regard defensive alliances as reprehensible provided they contained no secret clauses. Point 23 (no economic combinations within the League) was carried out at least in part. Point 24 (registration of treaties) was achieved by the League.

It is impossible to tell an accurate story in these few brief words; the whole subject with all its ramifications would fill a book. For unfavorable judgments on the carrying out of the Fourteen Points, consult Harold Nicolson, *Peacemaking 1919*, pp. 43–44, 202–205; and Herbert Hoover, *America's First Crusade*, pp. 66–72. Both writers stress the nonobservances, rather than the important observances. Nicolson blames Wilson for his sins of omission; Hoover blames the wicked Europeans. He says (p. 71): "America has been accused of running out on Europe after the treaty. As a matter of fact, Europe ran out on America in twenty of the Twenty-five Points." Hoover further confuses the picture by turning up with another set of supplementary points than Nicolson has, or than is conventionally accepted. For evidence that every one of the original Fourteen Points was faithfully observed in Paris, in so far as conditions would permit, see Lansing's testimony before the Senate Committee (*Sen. Docs.*, 66 Cong., 1 sess., no. 106, p. 169); also George Creel, *The War, the World and Wilson*, chap. XX. David Lloyd George is unable to "discover a single particular" in which the Allies departed from their war aims (*Memoirs of the Peace Conference*, I, 88).

THE OTHER TREATIES. The Treaty of Versailles was the first to be signed (June 28, 1919), but the main lines of the others were blocked out before the Big Four went home. The final details were left to the members of the delegations who remained behind. The Treaty of St. Germain, with Austria, was signed on Sept. 10, 1919. Undersecretary of State Frank L. Polk, Henry White, and General Tasker H. Bliss acted for the United States. The Treaty of Neuilly, with Bulgaria, was signed on Nov. 27, 1919, with the same three men affixing their signatures. The Treaty of Trianon, with Hungary, was signed on June 4, 1920, with Hugh Campbell Wallace representing the United States. The Treaty of Sèvres, with Turkey, signed on Aug. 10, 1920, was not subscribed to by the United States, for we had not declared war on Turkey. All these treaties were modeled to a considerable extent on the Treaty of Versailles, and the Covenant of the League of Nations was Part I of each of them. A convenient compilation is *The Treaties of Peace, 1919–1923* (2 vols., New York, 1924), published by the Carnegie Endowment for International Peace. A highly useful abstract is Arthur P. Scott, *An Introduction to the Peace Treaties* (Chicago, 1920).

INDEX

WOODROW WILSON

AND

THE GREAT BETRAYAL

WOODROW WILSON

AND

THE GREAT BETRAYAL

by

THOMAS A. BAILEY

New York · 1947

THE MACMILLAN COMPANY

THIS IS an account of one of the supreme tragedies of human history—the Great Betrayal which occurred when the United States turned its back on Wilson's pledges and failed to ratify the Treaty of Versailles and join the League of Nations.

The narrative presented herewith is a sequel to *Woodrow Wilson and the Lost Peace,* although each of the two volumes is an entity in itself and is designed to stand on its own feet. The first deals with peacemaking; the second deals with peacebreaking, with special emphasis on the role of the United States. My original plan was to tell the whole story in one book, but the exigencies of time and space, to say nothing of other considerations, suggested the desirability of two separate volumes.

My purposes are essentially those set forth in the preface of the preceding account. History never repeats itself, but statesmen and their people repeat the same mistakes. I am presenting this narrative, from the American point of view and *with emphasis on what went wrong,* in the hope that we may better recognize certain disastrous pitfalls, and not stumble into them again.

If the American people are handicapped by ignorance of what happened in connection with the making of the peace, they are no less handicapped by wrong notions as to what happened in connection with the breaking of the peace. The tendency is to resort to the absurd oversimplification of saying that Senator Henry Cabot Lodge alone kept us out of the League of Nations. People are lazy, and they like mental short cuts; people are sentimental, and they like real villains in their dramas—villains with long whiskers. Hence Senator Lodge occupies a conspicuous place in American demonology.

My object is neither to kick the corpse of Lodge nor to whiten the tomb of Wilson. Neither the whitewash brush nor the tar brush is going to help us much if we seek a real appreciation of the many forces that entered into this vast tragedy, some of which forces exist today in latent or active form. I fear for the future if the American people are still so simple-minded as to think that one wicked man was to blame for everything that happened.

I must again confess that I am in complete sympathy with Wilson's broad program and with his vision for the future. He spoke with unchallengeable realism when he said that isolationism had been repealed by the forces of history; he spoke with prophetic vision when he said that if we did not set up an agency to prevent war, another and more terrible holocaust would engulf the next generation.

I agree with Wilson that it would have been desirable for the United States to ratify the Treaty of Versailles without any reservations whatever. But, since that proved impracticable, I feel that an agreement on reservations should have been worked out, *in keeping with the American way of resolving deadlock by compromise.* The United States had a world to gain and virtually nothing to lose by joining the League of Nations.

As this narrative unfolds, it will become increasingly clear that Wilson's tactlessness and stubbornness had much to do with our colossal failure. I realize that it is ungracious to criticize an eminent man with a noble vision who did unreasonable things—especially a sick and crippled man. But the historian is not a Hollywood script writer; and he serves neither the cause of an exacting truth nor the cause of a fumbling humanity if he glosses over pertinent but unpalatable facts.

Wilson presumably had the highest motives for what he did, and he doubtless had valid reasons in his own mind for the unyielding course he took. His experiences with compromising had not been altogether happy, and he distrusted some of the men with whom he had to compromise. Although it is possible to argue that he was right in demanding all or nothing, the present account is written with the conviction that in complicated matters of this nature mankind, if it moves forward at all, must proceed "leg over leg" and demand not what is ideally desirable but what is practically attainable.

Every generation has to make its own blunders, and no doubt ours will. An old English proverb says, "Wise men learn by other men's mistakes, fools by their own." On the one hand, there is grave danger in ignorance of the past; on the other, there is grave danger in misapplied knowledge of the past. We must not attempt to scrap the entire machine—as certain earnest souls urge—simply because some parts of it failed to work. What we did right, we should do again; what we did wrong, we should avoid doing again.

These two books on Wilson may serve, I hope, as a rough guidepost to the future. The labor of preparing them will not have been altogether in vain if they do something to show the public that peacemaking is immensely difficult and complicated, that peoples should be tolerant of a failure to achieve the impossible, that to wait for perfection is to wait forever. Peace ratifying and peace execution require a high degree of intelligence, patience, persistence, and vigilance, as well as a courageous assumption of responsibility, and a clearheaded pursuit of long-range rather than short-range interests.

A number of individuals have graciously provided information, among them the Honorable Bainbridge Colby, the late Senator William E. Borah, and Mr. Robert V. Shirley, Clerk of the Senate Committee on Foreign Relations. Dr. Thomas S. Barclay, professor of political science at Stanford, helpfully criticized several chapters relating to political developments. The distinguished Finnish diplomat, Dr. Rudolf Holsti, now a member of the faculty at Stanford, was kind enough to check my observations on the Lodge reservations against his extraordinary background of thirteen years of official participation in the work of the League. Dr. Victor E. Hall, professor of physiology at Stanford, read the manuscript with particular attention to medical problems, and saved me from several embarrassing errors. My present chief, fifteen-year colleague, and former teacher, Dr. Edgar E. Robinson, Margaret Byrne professor of history at Stanford, read the manuscript with meticulous care and prepared a masterly critique, most of the suggestions in which I was able and happy to accept. He also placed at my disposal certain personal data, including copies of letters from James M. Cox, Josephus Daniels, Homer S. Cummings, and others. I am also indebted to Dr. Robinson for his maps on the elections of 1916 and 1920, which appear in his *The Presidential Vote, 1896-1932* (Stanford University, 1934), and which are herewith produced in slightly modified form with the blessing of Mr. Will A. Friend, manager of the Stanford University Press.

I am indebted, as before, to the staffs of the Stanford University Library, especially to Miss Ruth Scibird; of the Hoover Library on War, Revolution, and Peace (Stanford University); of the Widener Library at Harvard University; of the Boston Public Library; and of the Periodicals Division, Library of Congress. Miss Ruth S. Watson, of the Nebraska State Historical Society, cooperated by providing me with an important Hitchcock manuscript. President Charles Seymour and Mr. Russell G. Pruden graciously extended courtesies in connection with the Yale House Collection. For assistance in examining manuscript materials in the Library of Congress, my thanks are due to Dr. St. George L. Sioussat, Chief of the Division of Manuscripts, and to Miss Katharine E. Brand, Special Custodian, Woodrow Wilson Collection. I am particularly grateful to Mrs. Woodrow Wilson for permission to use this valuable collection.

My wife, Sylvia Dean Bailey, typed notes, helped edit the manuscript, read and constructively criticized both galley and page proofs, assisted in the preparation of the index, and tolerated my irascibility. *Nihil est superius benigna conjuge.*

THOMAS A. BAILEY

STANFORD UNIVERSITY, CALIF.
          March, 1945

TABLE OF CONTENTS

LIST OF CARTOONS

LIST OF MAPS

WOODROW WILSON

AND

THE GREAT BETRAYAL

THE RETURN OF THE MESSIAH

"Dare we reject it [the League] and break the heart of the world?" WOODROW WILSON, *July 10, 1919.*

1

ON JUNE 29, 1919, the presidential liner, *George Washington,* steamed out of Brest harbor, France, filled with singing boys in baggy khaki. But their eminent fellow passenger, Woodrow Wilson, was not singing. To him home meant not quiet and repose but the beginning of yet another battle to secure ratification of the Treaty of Versailles, a copy of which he was bringing back with him.

Wilson was not altogether happy over the pact which he had helped frame, even though it did contain the League of Nations. He had done his very best in the face of superhuman obstacles, but no one in far-away America could possibly appreciate the web of difficulties in which he had become entangled. He was painfully aware that he had been forced to mortgage some of his ideals in order to salvage others. But he confidently hoped that the inevitable contradictions and injustices of the treaty would eventually be smoothed away by a powerful League of Nations, of which the United States would be both a charter member and a guiding force.

The ten-day trip through smooth July seas was relatively uneventful, despite rumors of loose mines in the path of the ship. The *George Washington* was met outside New York harbor on the morning of July 8 by a flotilla of superdreadnoughts, headed by the *Pennsylvania,* carrying members of the Cabinet and of Congress. The presidential liner was escorted to the pier at Hoboken, New Jersey, by battleships, destroyers, subchasers, airplanes, and dirigibles. Even smoky

Hoboken looked beautiful to Wilson, for it was home; and he was glad to be there, although bitter struggles lay ahead.

The much-traveled President was taken by automobile from the Twenty-third Street ferry to Carnegie Hall, where he was to make his first public speech. Along the way full-throated cheers rose from the jostling mass of humanity, demonstrations which brought him to his feet, hat in hand. School children waved, and white-haired women leaned from windows to throw him a tearful "God bless you!"

The climax came at Carnegie Hall, where four thousand throats were supplemented by shrilling police whistles. When the din died down, Wilson spoke briefly and "from the heart" —a "homesick" heart. He described the peace as a just one which, if it could be preserved, would "save the world from unnecessary bloodshed." But he made no specific reference to the much-debated League of Nations.

The speech was a disappointment to those who had expected a concrete explanation of what Wilson had done "over there," and why he had done it. Instead, he spoke in characteristically exalted tones of "unselfishness," "distant horizons," and "new tasks."

Leaving Carnegie Hall, Wilson entrained for Washington, and late that same night reached the Union Station in the nation's capital. Some ten thousand people, defying the late hour, were there to give a warm welcome to their most distinguished fellow townsman. A few hundred of the curious were also waiting at the White House grounds. Among them was Mrs. Alice Roosevelt Longworth, who nourished all the bitterness of her Rough Riding father for the professor-president. As the presidential party passed, she made the sign of the evil eye, and muttered, "A murrain on him, a murrain on him, a murrain on him!"

The weary warrior was now home to stay, after an unprecedented six months abroad. There was much point to the current quip that Wilson was visiting rather than returning to the United States. "Just think," exclaimed the Macon *Telegraph,* "we will have a President all by ourselves from now on!"

2

Wilson's next important step in peacemaking was to submit his official copy of the treaty to the Senate, even though that body had secured an unofficial copy about a month earlier. Thereby hangs a curious tale.

When preliminary terms were presented to Germany in May, 1919, Wilson and his colleagues had agreed to keep the exact provisions secret until they were final. This was to prevent the inevitable outcry that would go up in Allied countries if the original draft was softened in response to German complaints.

Yet the Germans were not bound by the non-publication agreement, and within a short time copies of the treaty were being sold all over Europe for a trifle. When this became evident, Wilson could well have asked to be released from his promise so that he might do the Senate the honor of submitting an unofficial draft to it.

But the President was a proud and stubborn Southern gentleman. He had given his word; and besides it seemed ridiculous to communicate a draft treaty to the Senate, and then a month or two later present another draft with the request that the Senate forget all about the first one. Wilson often found it difficult to perceive that a man may be technically right but politically wrong.

The premature publication of the treaty further rasped senatorial sensibilities. Wilson had told the senators before he left for Europe that they would know all that he was doing. Yet they had been kept pretty much in the dark. They were a coordinate part of the treaty-making power. Yet others had received a copy of the pact before they had. The senators had approved the very first of Wilson's Fourteen Points: "Open covenants of peace, openly arrived at . . ." Yet Wilson could now be represented—though unfairly—as a champion of secret covenants.

Various unofficial versions of the treaty speedily reached the United States. The Chicago *Tribune,* a violently anti-League newspaper, secured and published a copy. Senator Henry Cabot Lodge was shown one which had been procured through Thomas W. Lamont, one of the American financial experts at Paris and a member of the House of Morgan. This revelation aroused a great uproar in senatorial circles about the sinister hand of Wall Street. Things had come to a pretty pass indeed when the Senate could not have a copy of the treaty, whereas Wall Street could. The unthinking masses found in this incident strong confirmation of their suspicion that Wall Street was really running the government.

Senator William E. Borah of Idaho, a bitter opponent of the treaty, secured a newspaper copy and on June 9 had it read into the *Congressional Record.* This was highly unconventional, for the Senate is supposed to consider only treaties formally laid before it by the President, not garbled documents in the draft stage. But Borah was highly unconventional, unalterably determined to undo the pact, and completely impervious to caustic remarks about "sagebrush diplomacy."

This whole pother over publication irregularities, trivial though it may now seem, was most unfortunate. It rubbed salt in old sores, confused an issue that was already confused enough, and diverted attention from the main business at hand. It further ensured that the official treaty, when presented, would have a chilling reception.

3

On the afternoon of July 10, 1919, President Wilson, immaculately dressed, arrived at the Senate chamber carrying a bulky copy of the treaty under his arm. A burst of applause greeted him, principally from the galleries and from the Democratic side of the aisle. The Republican senators for the most part sat in stern silence.

The presentation speech was not one of Wilson's best, either in content or in delivery. Perhaps he sensed that a large part of his audience was unsympathetic, for now and then he stumbled over a word. At times it seemed as though he were speaking to the people in the gallery and beyond the gallery, rather than to the senators themselves.

Wilson dealt throughout, as was his wont, in generalities. He explained that time did not permit a detailed account of what had happened at Paris. But he issued a significant invitation when he made it clear that he was at the disposal of the Senate and of the all-important Senate Committee on Foreign Relations, "either informally or in session, as you may prefer . . ." The League Covenant, he said, not only was the most important part of the treaty but was inseparable from the treaty. "Shall we or any other free people hesitate to accept this great duty? Dare we reject it and break the heart of the world?"

At the very end Wilson laid aside his manuscript, and in a superbly eloquent passage pleaded with his audience to "follow the vision" of leadership which we had "dreamed at our birth." His moving words were greeted by an ovation from the galleries and from the Democratic senators, with an occasional "rebel yell" rising above the hand clapping. Yet, ominously, only a scattering of the Republican members were seen to applaud.

Comments on the speech among senators ran the whole gamut of partisanship. The Democrats regarded it as clear, effective, informative, convincing. Senator Williams of Mississippi described it as "the greatest thing ever uttered by any President of the United States since Lincoln died."

The Republicans, as usual, found Wilson's apocalyptic prose too vague, too idealistic, too full of "glittering generalities." Senator Medill McCormick of Illinois declared that it was "soothing, mellifluous, and uninformative"; Senator Brandegee dismissed it as "soap bubbles of oratory and soufflé of phrases"; while Senator Harding (Wilson's successor) criticized this appeal of the "internationalists" as "utterly lacking in ringing Americanism."

Clearly Wilson, in his first appearance before Congress in

It Doesn't Happen to Be a Parrot

(Courtesy of Chicago *Tribune*; cartoonist Orr)

seven months, had not made the most of an unusual opportunity. Foes of the treaty were spreading broadcast the seeds of doubt and misinformation; and the presentation of the pact provided an enviable chance for the President to meet his enemies head on and regain much ground that had been lost during his absence. This was what Secretary of Agriculture Houston urged him to do; but Wilson, for reasons that no doubt seemed valid, ignored such advice. Instead, he appeared aloof, noncontroversial, and confident, refusing to take the people into his confidence by telling them what had happened, and thus giving further support to the charge that he was arrogant and uncompromising.

4

The irregular publication of the pact and Wilson's rather inept manner of presenting it were not the only incidents that confused the picture in July, 1919. There was also the French Security Treaty, and thereby hangs another curious tale.

At Paris, Wilson had finally persuaded the French to give up their claims to the German Rhineland in return (among other things) for a treaty of guarantee. This unprecedented pact pledged both the United States and Great Britain to spring to the aid of France should she again be wantonly attacked by Germany.

Surprisingly enough, considerable approval was expressed in the United States for the French treaty. It was only a temporary arrangement, pending the effective establishment of the League of Nations. It merely put on paper what most Americans felt: that having gone across to save France (and their own skins) in 1917, they would do so again (as they did). The memory of our debt to the land of Lafayette was still fresh.

But many Americans voiced serious objections to the French Security Treaty. It was an alliance; and George Washington had solemnly warned against alliances. It seemed to take the war-declaring power out of the hands of Congress. Finally, it complemented the League of Nations; and the League of Nations was a red flag to many ardent nationalists and isolationists both in and out of the Senate.

Yet it is a significant fact that many of those who were unfriendly to the Treaty of Versailles, such as Senator Henry Cabot Lodge and the journalist, George B. M. Harvey, were not unfriendly to the idea of a French pact of guarantee, *pro-*

vided it could be divorced from the League and specifically limited to five or so years.

But the Security Treaty had been signed, and according to the explicit terms of the fourth article, it was to be submitted to the Senate simultaneously with the Treaty of Versailles. This Wilson signally failed to do. In a statement for the newspapermen he said that he had not had time to prepare a message, and he wanted to take up the issue separately because it was "complicated."

The senatorial foes of Wilson roundly condemned him for not carrying out the plain dictates of the Security Treaty. They made much of the fact that he (and not Germany) was the first to violate the terms of the Paris settlement. The clamor finally became so loud that Wilson on July 29, 1919, *nineteen days late,* submitted the pact with an appropriate message.

Having insisted on speed in submission, the Senate displayed lethargy in taking action. The Security Treaty, to which France pinned extravagant hopes, was not even reported out of the Foreign Relations Committee. It lay for many months silently yellowing in a senatorial pigeonhole. There was obviously no point in taking action on this pact until it was clear that we were going to ratify the Treaty of Versailles. When we failed to do so, the Security Treaty was forgotten in America, but not in France, where Wilson and the United States were bitterly charged with betrayal.

Wilson clearly should have submitted the French pact on the day stipulated; and in neglecting to do so he laid himself open to legitimate criticism at home and abroad. But the people in America who condemned him had already been condemning him on other grounds, and it is difficult to prove that his action (or inaction) had any appreciable bearing on the final tragic failure of the Treaty of Versailles.

5

If the Senate was irked by Wilson's handling of both the French Security Treaty and the Treaty of Versailles, Wilson was no less irked by what had been going on in the Senate. On the same day that he presented the main pact, he gave a most revealing interview to the newspapermen. Obviously annoyed by the efforts of the Senate Republicans to sever the League Covenant from the treaty, and disturbed by their preparations to load the pact down with vexatious qualifications, he struck sharply at the proposed reservations.

One of the correspondents spoke up and asked whether the treaty could be ratified if the Senate were to adopt reservations. Wilson replied bluntly: "I do not think hypothetical questions are concerned. *The Senate is going to ratify the treaty.*"

Such statements as these, taken in connection with Wilson's general aloofness, reveal a spirit of confidence, not untinged with arrogance, which subsequent events were to prove but poorly grounded. What is the explanation?

Wilson's faith in the sound judgment of the masses, once the facts were laid before them, was still unshaken. He shared Thomas Jefferson's conviction that in the long run, if not in the short run, the people could be counted upon to decide correctly on a great moral issue, such as the League of Nations. The truth was mighty and would prevail.

This perhaps is sound doctrine, where the issues are clearly drawn, and where truth and righteousness stand openly arrayed in shining armor against ignorance and deceit. But what will happen when the issues are blurred or falsified by master confusionists like Senators Lodge and Borah and Johnson?

Wilson also had unbounded confidence in his power to appeal to the people and lead them into the paths of right thinking. He had suffered a severe setback in November, 1918, when he had pleaded for a Democratic Congress and had got a Republican majority. But that was a different matter. Even though Congress was Republican, he certainly could marshal enough nonpartisan support to carry the day. Surely, if the enthusiastic outpourings in New York and Washington meant anything, the great mass of the voters was behind him on this issue.

Wilson had not yet learned—perhaps he never learned—that not all those who come to stare and mayhap to cheer will follow the object of their acclaim through fire and water. H. H. Kohlsaat, the well-known Chicago newspaperman, was of the opinion that the people were behind Wilson—but some little distance behind him.

The supreme self-confidence of the President was fortified by a consciousness of his powerful strategic position. Every kind of agency for revealing public opinion—polls, resolutions of legislative bodies and mass meetings, speeches, editorials, letters to the press—showed that the masses were demanding some kind of League to prevent a repetition of the horrors which were still fresh in mind. Even Senator Lodge admitted that all "the vocal classes" were friendly to the League.

While at Paris, Wilson had remarked in the presence of Colonel Stephen Bonsal that the "Senators do not know what the people are thinking. They are as far from the people, the great mass of our people, as I am from Mars." This almost certainly was not true; but, even if true, it bespoke a dangerous attitude of mind.

6

Wilson had other sound reasons, aside from the support of public opinion, for his feeling of confidence.

The Senate had never before rejected a peace treaty, though the one with Spain in 1899 had squeezed through by the narrow margin of two votes.

The Senate could not separate the Covenant of the League of Nations from the treaty, and kill the one while approving the other. Wilson had foreseen the possibility of such a move,

and had cleverly forestalled it. He had interwoven the Covenant with the treaty and with the other peace settlements so
intimately that the League could not be cut out without unraveling the whole arrangement. Wilson not only had planned
it this way, but had unfortunately boasted of his strategy in
public. Some of the senators were angered because the President had deliberately confronted them with a horrible dilemma. Apparently they had to kill all or accept all; and they
wanted to do neither.

The Senate could not even seek the hollow solace of delay.
The people were clamoring to get the war officially over and
to bring the rest of the boys home. Bankers and merchants
and manufacturers and shippers were demanding that peace
be concluded at once so that the Allies would not get a head
start in the race for enemy markets.

And what valid reason could be offered for delay? The Republican senators, in their resounding Round Robin of
March, 1919, had announced that they could not vote for the
League in "the form now proposed." But it was no longer in
"the form now proposed." Reluctantly, and at the behest of
senatorial and other critics, Wilson had gone back to Paris
in March, 1919, and had secured safeguarding amendments.
He had not done it gracefully, but he had done it. "I am
yielding to the judgment of men," he groaned, "who have
little knowledge or appreciation of the world situation, but
who, alas! control votes."

Finally and unanswerably, the Senate could not escape its
moral obligation. The League could not be torn from the
treaty; so the only choice was to approve the treaty, or to reject
the treaty and make such terms as we could with Germany.

A separate peace during the war had been regarded as treasonable; it still seemed treasonable. We could not honorably
forsake our recent comrades in arms and leave them still bleeding on the common field of battle. We could not turn back
when the task was only half done, for we should break faith
with the dead, and the mothers of the dead, whom Wilson

had promised to make this a "war to end wars." We could not refuse to honor the commitments which Wilson as President had made in the name of the American people. We could not betray the high hopes of the lesser nations of Europe who were counting on us to finish the job. We could not cravenly reject the world leadership which the logic of events had forced upon us.

In a speech several months earlier Wilson had spoken of the poor people of Europe who had trustingly thrust flowers upon him. "It is inconceivable that we should disappoint them," he declared, "and *we shall not.*"

7

With all the high cards seemingly in his hand, Wilson may perhaps be pardoned for having developed considerable complacency in his attitude toward the Senate. The Democrats could be counted on to support him. If they did not, he would flourish the patronage bludgeon, and appeal to their constituents not to reelect them. The Republicans could in the end be counted on to support him. If they did not, he would brandish the bludgeon of public opinion. He could not lose.

At Paris the situation had been different, and Wilson had been different. He had been considerate, acquiescent, open to compromise. He had stooped to conquer. He had walked into the French Foreign Office to visit Foreign Minister Pichon, instead of waiting, as custom dictated, for Pichon to visit him.

Wilson might approach the diplomats of Europe on a friendly and conciliatory basis, because he knew them not. But the Senate he had had "on his hands" for six long years. With his characteristic intolerance of inattentive students and sluggish brains, he entertained little respect for the senatorial representatives of the sovereign people. "Bungalow minds" and "pygmy minds" were favorite expressions of his when referring to certain members of Congress. There were in fact many important senators, especially among the Republicans, with whom he had already had some kind of brush. Finally, he had never before faced a Republican majority in either house of Congress; *now hostile majorities controlled both the Senate and the House of Representatives.*

Colonel House had urged Wilson in Paris to treat the senators with more deference, and even to extend the olive branch to Hoke Smith, Democratic senator from Georgia, with whom the President had been "feuding" for many years. Smith and Wilson had both hung out their law shingles in Atlanta in the same month of the same year. Smith was a "hustler," and he had prospered; Wilson was a gentleman, very much on his dignity, and he had failed. "That man is an ambulance-chaser," exclaimed Wilson to House with blazing eyes. "I scorn to have any relations with him whatsoever."

House remonstrated that even if the man had chased ambulances thirty years ago, his vote was now necessary to save civilization. But Wilson was imperturbably confident. He did not think Smith's vote important; certainly not decisive. He would "receive him, of course, as the senator from Georgia, if he calls, but, House, no nosegays, no olive branches in that direction."

Wilson's attitude toward the Senate had, understandably enough, gradually taken on a degree of belligerence. He had with good reason been angered by the Republican Round Robin during the previous March, and had flashed back defiance in his speech of March 4, 1919, at the Metropolitan Opera House. Senator Martin of Virginia, then the Democratic Senate leader, had expressed doubts as to whether a two-thirds vote for the treaty could be mustered. "Martin!" snapped Wilson. "Anyone who opposes me in that, I'll crush!"

In the late spring of 1919 Wilson had been further aroused by the attempts of the Republican senators to amputate the League Covenant from the treaty, and particularly by efforts to propose reservations to the all-important Article X, which undertook to guarantee peace by pledging all members of the

League to protect one another against external aggression (see page 385 for text). On May 24, the President cabled Secretary Lansing that the Senate would have to accept this vital Article X or reject the entire treaty and abide the consequences. He hoped that the friends of the treaty in America would take a most militant and aggressive course, *such as he meant to take the minute he got back.*

Herbert Hoover, then in France, undertook to criticize certain aspects of the treaty, and Wilson, regarding this as a personal affront, flashed back angrily and thenceforth excluded Hoover from his private councils. Colonel House's parting words at Paris, the last he ever spoke to his chief, were an admonition to deal with the Senate in a conciliatory manner. But Wilson sternly rejected such timid advice.

8

It is clear that Wilson returned home in a mood that did not augur well for an amicable adjustment of differences with the Senate. He held the highest office; he held the highest trumps. It was unthinkable that the Senate would dare reject the treaty; we simply could not go back to our fallen foe and beg for new terms. Then why should he accept compromise of any kind, especially reservations and amendments, when he was sure to have his way anyhow? He had the Senate in a bad corner, and he would press his advantage mercilessly.

Dr. Nicholas Murray Butler records in his reminiscences that, in June, 1919, he worked out certain tentative reservations to the treaty which proved satisfactory to an important group of Republican senators. Jules Jusserand, French Ambassador in Washington, cabled the draft to Paris and subsequently was informed that it was acceptable to both the French and the British foreign office. Jusserand then went directly to the White House and said that if Wilson would consent to these reservations the treaty would certainly be ratified. To

Jusserand's horror, the President replied in a stern voice: "Mr. Ambassador, I shall consent to nothing. *The Senate must take its medicine.*"

As we see it now, Wilson would have been well advised not to press the Senate so remorselessly. A stitch in time saves nine; a minor compromise or two in July probably would have saved a half-dozen major ones in October. In July, when the tide was running strongly for the League, the Republicans probably would have accepted trivial concessions which would have enabled them to save face. In October, the advantage was more definitely with them, and it was they who pressed their advantage relentlessly.

It is easy to criticize Wilson for not having seen what is now plainly evident. Most statesmen cannot see their errors as they make them. In fairness to Wilson we must note that almost everyone in July took it for granted that the treaty would be approved substantially as it was signed at Versailles, with perhaps a few face-saving reservations. Even the bitterest foes of the League in the Senate were nursing no more than a forlorn hope. The ill concealed despair of this little group of "irreconcilables" is convincing proof that Wilson was not altogether unjustified in his confidence and optimism.

CHAPTER TWO

THE PARADE OF PREJUDICE

*"We of all peoples in the world . . . ought to be able to under-
derstand the questions of this treaty . . . for we are made up
out of all the peoples in the world."* WOODROW WILSON, *at Columbus, Ohio, September 4, 1919.*

1

THE UNWARY observer is apt to conclude that during the
summer and autumn of 1919 the one consuming interest of
the American people was the treaty with its League of Nations. This is not true. If it had been, the story might well
have been different.

Only a sprinkling of Americans had more than the foggiest
notions as to what the treaty was all about. The pact itself, of
which the League was the very first section, filled a bulky book
of 268 large quarto pages. If a copy had been placed in the
hands of each voter, it still would not have been read. It was
too long, and the language was so technical as to be largely incomprehensible to the lay mind. "This is a strange world,"
lamented the Peoria *Transcript.* "Nobody is competent to
discuss the Versailles Treaty until he has read it, and nobody
who would take the time to read it would be competent to
discuss it."

The League of Nations Covenant was of course much less
technical. It was written in simple language and could be read
in about twenty minutes. Hundreds of thousands of copies
were scattered broadcast by newspapers and interested pressure groups, but we have no way of knowing how many people
read them. One observer took an informal poll of the voters
of a middle western city and found that only one in twenty-
five had done so. This seems like a high percentage, certainly
if we stipulate a comprehending reading.

The disconcerting conclusion is that what little the "average American" knew about the treaty came to him second-, third-, or fourth-hand. Others read the pact and interpreted it for him. Or others read the interpretations of others and then did some additional interpreting of their own. The small-town newspaper editor, the lurid magazine writer, the ill informed local forum, or the loud-mouthed tub-thumper were primary sources of information or misinformation. It must ever be thus when immeasurably complex issues are thrown into the turmoil of public debate.

The American people certainly wanted no more of wars, and they hoped that their leaders would work out some kind of inexpensive and self-operating organization to prevent future conflicts. But the man in the street was too inert or too unintelligent or too preoccupied to give these delicate issues sustained thought. Overpowering problems on his very doorstep clamored for immediate attention. While Wilson was still in Paris, twenty-six Democratic members of the Massachusetts legislature actually cabled that the American people wanted him to come home and reduce the high cost of living, "which we consider *far more important than the League of Nations.*"

The world will never stand still while men debate the issues of peace and war. As the statesmen in their frock coats moved the pawns back and forth on the diplomatic chessboard, the men in blue denim worked and sweated and played and married, as they ever will. Foreign affairs cannot be conducted, much less discussed, in a vacuum. In all our history there have been few times when outside dangers seemed more fearful than domestic dangers; and the post-Armistice period appears not to have been one of them. The power of autocratic, Prussianized Germany had been broken, apparently forever. With the setting of each sun the recent war seemed less real, and the prospects of a future war so remote as to cause little concern.

Delay was the great enemy of the peacemakers in America.

For delay was the culture bed for all the prolific forces of prejudice, partisanship, confusion, and doubt.

2

A mere catalogue of some of the distractions and worries of
the American people during these hectic months will shed a
flood of light on the problem of the peace-ratifiers.

Seldom have times been more out of joint for great masses
of Americans. A restless army of some four million men had
to be demobilized, and each discharged soldier had to find a
peaceful niche in civilian life. Some were maimed, some were
shell-shocked, and most of them were in need of more or less
emotional and mental reconditioning. And the one gnawing
question above all others in their minds was: "Will the old
job be there, or a new one in its place?"

Industrial demobilization was a colossal undertaking. To
the capitalist, financial losses were inevitable; to the laborer,
transitional unemployment was inevitable. To the businessman who faced general insecurity and possible bankruptcy,
the League of Nations did not seem an unmixed blessing.
Would it be, as alleged, a superstate which would beat down
our tariff barriers, flood the nation with the sweated handiwork of foreign labor, and force the American producer to
the wall?

Labor was restive. The cost of living had shot up like a
whale spout; wages, as usual, had lagged behind. Profiteering
and the high cost of living were burning issues well into the
1920's. The labor market was in danger of being glutted by
destitute hordes from Europe.

It had been unpatriotic to lay down one's tools during the
war; now the lid was off. Serious strikes broke out among the
steel workers of Gary, Indiana, and among the begrimed host
of John L. Lewis' coal miners. The very foundations of government trembled when in September of 1919 the police of
Boston struck and left the city at the mercy of hoodlums, who

smashed windows and defiantly rolled dice on the Boston Common—near the "cradle of American liberty."

Some of the labor disorders shaded off toward radicalism. The Socialists were unusually active; the I.W.W.'s were on the loose. The fear was widespread that Russian Bolshevism would sweep the United States. In the spring of 1919 a total of more than thirty bombs, addressed to prominent personages, was found in the mails. Several bombs were thrown, including one which, on June 2, 1919, wrecked the home of Attorney General A. Mitchell Palmer. Palmer, with understandable zeal, redoubled his efforts to herd "reds" behind bars or harry them out of the land. Conservatives were turning witch-hunters, and talking of rope and lampposts and "100 per cent Americanism."

3

The railroads were in a muddle. Taken over as a war measure for war purposes, they had been administered by Wilson's son-in-law, Secretary of the Treasury William G. McAdoo. They had been "McAdoodled," said conservative critics like George Harvey, who did not want government in business except when it helped business.

The Negro problem had been made more explosive. Colored men had gone North, or to France, and they had enjoyed undreamed-of privileges. When they came home it was more difficult to "keep them in their place." Terrifying race riots broke out in Washington, Chicago, Omaha, and elsewhere. Scarcely more than a week after Wilson returned from championing the rights of suppressed minorities, a frightening outburst occurred between blacks and whites almost under the White House windows.

Vexatious legislative issues were still unsettled. The fight for a woman suffrage amendment to the Constitution was going into its final rounds. The Eighteenth Amendment was riveted to the Constitution, but the "wets" and the "drys" were still doing battle over enforcement legislation. The boys in khaki were muttering that while they had been abroad fighting for human liberty, the "bluenoses" had taken advantage of their absence to "put over" this infringement on their personal liberty.

Even when Americans looked up from the harrowing domestic scene, their eyes did not necessarily seek Europe. American boys were still fighting Wilson's undeclared war against the Bolsheviks in the vastnesses of Siberia, and there was a growing demand that they be brought home. Relations with Mexico were normal—that is, teetering on the precipice of war.

The current crop of headline diversions was more than ordinarily thrilling. The air was dark with transatlantic airplanes or dirigibles, guided by men seeking either a watery grave or immortality. The British dirigible *R-34* made the crossing while Wilson was en route, thus crowding him from the front page.

New sports idols were springing into prominence. On July 4, while the President was in mid-ocean, Jack Dempsey battered the huge Jess Willard into a bleeding pulp, and thus became one of the most potent and unpopular of heavyweight champions. The baseball season was now on, with "Babe" Ruth thumping the ball over right-field walls with unprecedented frequency, and with the Chicago White Sox (soon to become the "Black Sox") about to treat the public to the most reverberating scandal in the history of the game.

One South Carolina newspaper half jokingly concluded that the people were getting more interested in the National League than in the League of Nations, and another journal discovered that some Americans actually thought that the new League of Nations was a baseball league.

4

Ignorance, apathy, inertia, and preoccupation were only negative obstacles in the path of the treaty. More dangerous in many ways were the active ingredients of the opposition, for they were able to bend large bodies of public opinion to their way of thinking.

Noisy rather than numerous, yet withal exceedingly influential, were the liberals. In view of later condemnations of the Treaty of Versailles it is highly significant that they alone of the purely American groups thought it too severe; most Americans thought that it erred, if at all, on the side of leniency.

The liberals had pinned their faith to Wilson and his Fourteen Points. Yet he had sat down in secret conclave with international "brigands," he had seemingly bartered away his ideals, and he had brought back a "hell's brew" that would merely beget World War II. The American liberals, joined by many of their brethren abroad, pronounced a solemn curse on Wilson and his handiwork.

The most important liberal journals to turn their guns against the treaty were the *New Republic* and the *Nation*. The *New Republic*, which was widely regarded as a mouthpiece for Wilson on progressive issues, broke with him and fought ratification, lock, stock, and barrel. This decision cost the magazine much of its support among the more reasonable liberals, and undoubtedly weakened its prestige.

The *New Republic* published serially a part of John Maynard Keynes' devastating indictment of the treaty. Keynes was one of the British experts who had resigned in protest; his book, *The Economic Consequences of the Peace*, became a non-fiction best seller, and undoubtedly had a powerful effect in stirring up opposition both within and without the halls of Congress.

The venerable New York *Nation* was then under the militant editorship of Oswald Garrison Villard (grandson of the fanatical abolitionist William Lloyd Garrison), a professional pacifist with a high degree of sympathy for the German point of view. He fought the entire treaty with all the slashing weapons at his command. He was somewhat embarrassed to find himself in the company of such bitter reactionaries as

"Boss" Boies Penrose and Henry Cabot Lodge, but politics makes strange bedfellows.

Not all liberal sheets, notably the Springfield *Republican,* broke with Wilson. But in general, as is usually true of liberals, they tended to seek perfectionism. Only dimly aware of the practical problems that had confronted Wilson at Paris, and of the necessity for give and take, they insisted on the whole loaf or none. When they saw that the loaf was not whole, they fought for none—and got it.

Former Progressives—those who in 1912 had fought to purge the Republican party and many of whom had sung "Onward, Christian Soldiers"—may be roughly classed with the liberals. Prominent among them were Senators Johnson of California, Borah of Idaho, Norris of Nebraska, La Follette of Wisconsin (who represented a constituency where many Germans lived), and ex-Senator Beveridge of Indiana.

Strangely enough, progressives in domestic affairs became reactionaries in foreign affairs. Those who had been crusaders for internal reform became crusaders against international reform. Possibly some of them felt that adventures abroad would interfere with housecleaning at home. But hatred of Wilson, pro-Germanism, and pure partisanship were curiously commingled with the most exalted liberal ideals.

5

Even louder and more bitter than the liberals were the immigrant groups in America, commonly referred to as "hyphenates"—German-Americans, Irish-Americans, Italian-Americans, and the others—all of whom were tied to the mother country by an umbilical hyphen three thousand miles long. Millions had been born in the "Old Country"; other millions —wives, husbands, children—fell under the same influence.

Ironically enough, Wilson expected that the United States would be the most eager of all powers to accept the League of Nations, for we were a league of nations in miniature. Millions of people from all races and climes had been dumped into the giant melting pot, and they had fabricated the New America. The United States seemed to be living proof of the workability of the League of Nations.

But the comparison proved to be misleading. People can live side by side in peace, but nations find it more difficult to live side by side in peace. The ties of nationalism are long and enduring, tenaciously resistant to the heat of any melting pot. This was why the British ambassador could sneer, after the outbreak of war in 1914, that we were "no nation, just a collection of people who neutralize one another."

The Irish-Americans were probably the most important politically of the hyphenate groups arrayed against the League; but they fall into a special category and will be treated later.

The German-Americans were a force of tremendous power, especially in the Middle West. Those of German birth and those with at least one German-born parent numbered about 7,000,000, or approximately 7 per cent of the population. A great body of them had patriotically supported the recent war effort; others had been bulldozed into silence and browbeaten into buying Liberty Bonds. It was now safe for them to come out of their holes, give vent to their pent-up emotions, and work for the Fatherland.

These people hated Wilson for having asked Congress to declare war, and for having prosecuted the war. They hated him for having visited a punitive peace on Germany, with its reparations, territorial excisions, and various humiliations— all seemingly in violation of the Fourteen Points. They were completely impervious to the argument that if it had not been for Wilson the peace would undoubtedly have been more severe than it actually was.

The German-Americans held rousing mass meetings, and undertook to organize their several million voters for the anti-League presidential candidate in 1920. At the forefront of these propagandists was George Sylvester Viereck, who castigated the Covenant as the "League of Damnations," and who was later, during World War II, to serve a prison term as an alien agent.

The Republican foes of the League assiduously wooed the German-Americans, though this group needed little wooing. To preserve America it seemed necessary to appeal to the prejudices of non-American groups in our midst.

Nor did the anti-League agitators overlook the hundreds of thousands of Italian-American voters, who were especially numerous in New York and Massachusetts, and who bitterly resented Wilson's persistent efforts to force the Yugoslav port of Fiume from the grasp of Italy. On Columbus Day, 1919, one Dr. Joseph Santosuosso, speaking to a crowd of Italian-Americans in Boston, vigorously attacked Wilson's Fiume policy, and evoked hisses for the name of Mrs. Wilson when he condemned her for having accompanied her husband to Europe. Fiorello H. La Guardia, then president of the New York City Board of Aldermen and future mayor of the metropolis, was active in organizing Italian-American strength against Wilson.

Other hyphenate groups blamed Wilson because their national aspirations had been denied, or grudgingly granted. Among them were the Poles, the Czechs, the Jews, the Chinese, and the Japanese. Some of these carried no real political weight, but they all added up to a loud, snarling, embittered opposition which controlled millions of votes. There was much point in the remark of a Boston journal that "the United States is a country of quiet majorities and vociferous minorities."

6

A final hyphenate group of great importance was the Irish-Americans. These colorful people had been closely associated during the war with German-Americans and pro-Germanism, not because they particularly loved Germany but because they violently hated Britain.

The mercurial sons of the shamrock were more important politically than the Germans, though outnumbered by them nearly two to one. First of all, the German-Americans were normally Republicans anyhow, and could be counted on to oppose the Democratic Wilson. Secondly, the Irish were generally Democratic and were vital elements in the great urban machines which controlled pivotal states like New York and Massachusetts. Every Irishman whom the Republicans could turn against Wilson represented a gain of more than one vote: one taken away from the Democrats and one added to the Republicans.

The Irish in America, it has often been said, are more Irish than the Irish of Ireland. Certainly those who came to the United States kept their memory of England's sins, real and fancied, as verdant as the landscape of their Emerald Isle. American politicians had long since learned that it was politically profitable to twist the British lion's tail periodically, and receive the acclaim, often in a rich brogue, of hate-ridden Irish voters. It is significant that Senator David I. Walsh of Massachusetts, himself of Irish lineage, was one of the few Democratic senators who refused to support Wilson four-square on the League. He could not overlook the Boston Irish or the Massachusetts Italians, nor for that matter could his senior colleague, Henry Cabot Lodge.

In the late spring of 1919, the British ambassador in Washington told Henry White that he had been approached by two "prominent Republicans" (possibly senators), who confessed that their party would have to attack England on the Irish question but they wanted it known privately that they felt no real animosity toward the Mother Country.

The Irish problem in America would have been less troublesome if during 1919 and 1920 conditions in the ever vexed and ever turbulent isle had not verged on civil war. Rioting, burning, and murdering were daily occurrences. Irish prisoners of the British went on "hunger strikes," notable among them Terence MacSwiney, Lord Mayor of Cork, who died on October 25, 1920, after a voluntary fast lasting seventy-four days.

"President" Eamon de Valera, of the so-called Irish "Republic," toured the United States in the spring and summer of 1919, stirring up fresh hate. The champions of Irish independence held overflow mass meetings, at which the League of Nations was viciously assailed, and the name of Wilson was repeatedly booed and hissed.

"No European Entanglements"

(From New York *Tribune*; courtesy of *Herald-Tribune*;
cartoonist Darling)

German-Americans and Irish-Americans made it a point to attend public meetings en masse, and by their vocal and manual approval of attacks on the treaty they gave the false impression that public sentiment was overwhelmingly opposed to the League. The Brooklyn *Eagle* was not far from the mark when it complained, "Too many people in this country are enjoying the right of free screech."

7

One of the chief grievances of the Irish-Americans against Wilson was that he had failed to secure self-determination for Ireland. At Paris he had courteously but informally talked with an Irish delegation from the United States, though privately confessing that his first impulse was to tell them "to go to hell." Yet he refused to accede to their wishes and press for Irish self-determination, primarily because the problem of Ireland was not relevant to the task in hand.

The United States had fought Germany, not Britain (though some Irish-Americans would have preferred to fight Englishmen); and self-determination was generally applied only to former enemy territory. Wilson had enough insoluble and vexatious problems worrying him at Paris without taking up the questions of self-determination for India, Afghanistan, Egypt, and Ireland. Yet the Irish-Americans never forgave him for not doing the impolitic and the impossible.

The Irish were also infuriated by Article X of the League Covenant, which obligated each member of the League to assist its fellow members against "external aggression." In the voluble mouths of pro-Irish agitators this meant that American boys of Irish ancestry might be sent abroad to help England crush out an Irish revolt. How then could Ireland ever win her independence?

This of course was malicious misrepresentation. By no stretch of either imagination or phraseology could an internal revolt in Ireland be interpreted as "external aggression" against the British Empire.

No less damaging in the mouth of the demagogue was the article of the Covenant which gave the British Empire six votes in the Assembly of the League, while assigning only one to the United States. Wilson, it was hotly charged, had been taken into camp by the wily British diplomats. Henceforth Great Britain would dominate the world, and the Land of the

Free would play second fiddle to King George V of England.

This, too, was malicious misrepresentation or inexcusable ignorance. We shall later consider the problem in some detail, but for the moment we may note that while the British Dominions had six votes in the Assembly, they had only one, like the United States, in the all-important Council. *And our one vote could block any decision on any question except where we were parties to a dispute.*

After viewing the intemperate Irish outbursts, and considering our proposed mandate over Armenia, the Philadelphia *Press* concluded that the League should not ask "Uncle Sam to be mandatory for nations abroad until after he has successfully mandated a few things right here at home."

8

Closely allied with the professional Irishmen were the professional British-haters. They were the men who had not outgrown the influence of their fife-and-drum textbooks, and who were still shooting Redcoats at Bunker Hill and New Orleans. They hated the British, and, like the Irish, feared that something was being "put over" on the United States. Specifically, they pointed to the undeniable fact that the League in its preliminary stages had been largely drafted by such eminent Britons as Smuts, Cecil, and Phillimore. England under George III had failed to enslave America in 1776 by force of arms; now she was seeking to do it under George V by trickery —the trickery of Article X and six votes to one. The United States would have none of a Smuts-sired League.

The high priest of the Anglophobes in the Senate was James A. Reed of Missouri. Neither pro-German nor pro-Irish as such, he castigated the British-controlled League, and satirically nominated for its presidency "that great British statesman" "Sir Herbert Hoover," whom he scorned for having lived many years under the British flag.

Most influential of all the British-haters was William

Randolph Hearst, who marshaled his newspaper empire, with its 3,000,000 or so henchmen, against Britain and the "British-spawned League." His syndicated blasts of hostility were unrelenting, and he directed his fire indiscriminately against both the white peril of British imperialism and the yellow peril of Japanese expansionism.

George Bernard Shaw is reported to have said that the two great English-speaking peoples are separated—not united—by a common language. The British could read what we said about them, and we could read what they said about us. Expressions of sympathy in America for Ireland, whether passed by Congress or by other bodies, were resented in England—and we resented their resentment. Soon influential British writers like Horatio Bottomley in *John Bull* were muddying the waters by crying that America came into the war "not to save her honor but to save her skin," and that Uncle Sam "filled his pockets years before he filled his cartridge belt."

Ere long this transatlantic bickering broadened into an utterly senseless debate as to who had won the war. Before the Armistice there had been some dispute among the American forces as to whether the marines or the infantry deserved the real credit. Now responsible British commanders like Field-Marshal Sir Douglas Haig were saying to English audiences (for home consumption) that Britain had won the war. This seemed like an intolerable insult to the American dead.

During the war America had accelerated her gigantic naval construction program in the face of the German threat. Now the war had stopped, but the riveters had not. Against whom could we be building, unless England? At the rate we were going we should soon be able to wrest Neptune's trident from her grasp.

This general atmosphere of acrimony drove the two nations farther apart at a critical time in world history. Working together, the two great Anglo-Saxon powers could preserve the peace; pulling in opposite directions, they would surely bring about the downfall of the League.

9

Fundamentally more important than any other group was the great mass of isolationists in the United States—those who wanted to keep out of the broils of Europe, and who thought they could do so by merely trying to mind their own business.

The myth still persists that a few wicked men, like Senators Lodge and Borah and Johnson, converted the American people to an isolationist course, and thus engineered the ruin of the League.

This is paying far too high a tribute to the persuasive powers of these master obstructionists. The truth is that the American people had always been basically isolationist in their aspirations, that they had been forced into the war by German U-boat attacks, and that they had temporarily lost sight of their ancient policy under the enthusiasm of war and the lofty exhortations of Wilson.

When the shooting stopped, and the menace to our security was (temporarily) enchained, the natural tendency of the American people was to slip back into the old groove. The New York *Sun* confidently and accurately predicted that "a lot of people will pick up their 1913-14 thoughts right where they laid them down." The foes of the League recognized that this would happen, and their great fear was that action might be pressed on the treaty before the nation had cooled off. Time must be purchased at any price.

France had fought in 1914 because she was attacked; Britain had fought because her age-old policy had been to keep any strong power from occupying the Lowlands and pointing a pistol at her heart; America had fought because she was attacked by Germany. When the war was over, France went back to her ancient policy—older than Louis XIV—of seeking to dominate the continent. Britain went back to her ancient policy—older than Queen Elizabeth—of trying to prevent any one power from becoming too dominant on the continent.

America went back to her ancient policy—older than George Washington—of attempting to keep out of the political broils and wars of the mother continent.

"Nationalism" would be a better description than "isolationism" for the postwar mood of the United States. Wilson had been belatedly converted to a policy of internationalism, and hence his quarrel was with nationalism wherever he found it. He fondly believed that he represented a world constituency rather than an American constituency. He opposed Italian nationalism, and was frustrated by Orlando and others; he opposed French nationalism, and was thwarted by Clemenceau and others; he opposed British nationalism, and was blocked by Lloyd George and others.

When Wilson came home his struggle was still with nationalism. Instead of Orlando and Clemenceau and Lloyd George, he encountered Borah and Lodge and Johnson. And the subsequent battles were more bitter, and the results even less successful, than the battles had been in Europe. Borah was a more obdurate "irreconcilable" than Clemenceau, because he wielded power without commensurate responsibility. The Senate foes of the League, who at first glance may have seemed like less redoubtable antagonists than the European diplomats, were even more formidable because they could be sure of a definite term in office, and be reasonably sure of reelection.

10

Wilson could do battle with live men, and he did. But he could not do battle with dead men. Some of his most formidable antagonists were in the spirit world: George Washington, Thomas Jefferson, James Monroe, and even Theodore Roosevelt. Skeleton hands as well as muscular hands pulled the United States back from the threshold of the League of Nations.

The sacred policy of George Washington—of keeping out

of the broils of Europe—was sanctified not only by time but, said the isolationists, by common sense. Washington would stir uneasily in his tomb at Mount Vernon if he should learn that we were going to underwrite a League of Nations and keep an army of American boys ready to fight strange peoples in strange lands—all at the behest of some superbody. Senator Philander C. Knox of Pennsylvania cried out in the Senate that accept-

Not Room for Both

(Courtesy of San Francisco *Chronicle*; cartoonist Bronstrup)

ance of the League would mean "centuries of blood-letting."

Why surrender our sovereignty to some foreign superstate? In isolationist eyes the League was a species of self-emasculation, a fundamental change in our government, a subversion of our great Constitution. Ex-Senator Beveridge insisted that America was being inveigled into a partnership "where Europe furnishes the liabilities and the United States supplies the assets." It was a sinister conspiracy that would, in the judgment of the New York *Sun*, mark the "sunset of our independence." A League for the Preservation of American Independence was actually organized.

Critics of the League beat the tomtoms of nationalism, and cried out against denationalization. "If I were an Englishman, a Frenchman, or an Italian," cried George Harvey, "I should want this League. But I am an American." His vitriolic *Harvey's Weekly* condemned the "Denationalists," the "League of Denationalization," and the "Covenant of Denationalization." It published "The International Hymn," a part of which ran:

> Our foreign countries, thee,
> Lands of the chimpanzee,
> Thy names we love . . .

As a political issue denationalization had tremendous possibilities, especially in the hands of the unscrupulous rabble rouser. Senator Reed of Missouri made the most of the potent new issue—of a hybrid flag flapping above the glorious Stars and Stripes. "I decline," he shouted, "to set up any government greater than the government of the United States of America!"

Inconsistency was a bugbear that did not trouble the isolationists and nationalists. We must keep free from the broils of the Old World; yet we must rush into the broils of Ireland. The League was such a powerful "superstate" that it would submerge our independence; yet the League was such a weak "sewing circle" that it would be a waste of time to join it. The League was a vicious entanglement; yet the League was "as entangling as any other rainbow."

But the enemies of the League had no scruples about being all things to all men. Such a horrible calamity awaited America that the end would justify the means. And the great mass of the people would not note these inconsistencies. There would be a doubt for everyone, and the gullible could seize upon the doubt which most alarmed them. "Senator Borah," said the Des Moines *Register,* "is not an unthinking man. But he voices the sentiments of the unthinking."

A great many of the isolationists were no doubt as sincere as they were shortsighted. It made sense to them that we should follow the time-honored precepts of Washington, steer clear of foreign broils, and keep our necks out of the noose of internationalism. Aloof from the century-old quarrels of Europe, disinterested, detached, and powerful, the United States as a free agent could best throw its weight on the side of peace. We could dole out loaves to the hungry, proffer do-good advice to the quarrelsome, and preen ourselves on our righteousness. Or, as one journal put it, we could serve most usefully by being a sister to the world rather than by marrying it.

11

Hardly less important than isolationism in the tragedy which befell Wilson and the world was what is known as "the slump in idealism."

Until the Armistice, Wilson had been able to sustain the idealism of the people at a high pitch, high enough in fact to bring the self-denial of prohibition. Even if he had been able to do at Paris all that was expected of him, the slump doubtless would have come sooner or later, as in fact it did in Europe. Human nature is able to sustain an emotional orgy for only a relatively short time.

The barometer of idealism was visibly falling even before Wilson brought the treaty back from Paris. In the heat of combat one does not usually feel so keenly the pain of wounds. But we now had time to take stock of the situation: to scan our incoming casualty lists, and our outpouring disbursements to the Allies. There was the chill that comes with the doctor's bill. We were weary of well-doing. We were tired of war and wartime restrictions and wartime taxes; we recoiled from the very thought of troublesome and expensive international police work.

Many unselfish souls in America had been shocked by the scrambling for spoils at the peace table, and they were disillusioned because their ideals had gone sour. Others felt that they had been victimized by Allied propaganda. Men like Senator Johnson of California had entered the war with the highest motives; they had listened respectfully to the eloquent preachments of Allied spokesmen—spokesmen whose pockets all the while bulged with secret treaties. When the veil was ripped aside at Paris, these senators branded the whole lot as a gang of double-crossing crooks, and vowed to wash their hands of the whole business.

If the Allies had proved faithless, our newly found friends of the succession states were little better. Nations like Poland had received much, but they were greedily reaching out for more. The Balkans were still a caldron of hate and warfare. Peace had not come to earth. "The trouble with the new nations," remarked the Greenville (S.C.) *Piedmont,* "is that they have the old quarrels." Everywhere men were sneering, "Where is Wilson's millennium?"

The President had gone to Paris, seeking nothing for the United States but peace. We not only had lost the friendship of Italy, China, and Japan, but had gained nothing from the whole mess except a questionable League of Nations, while the imperialistic powers had apparently made off with valuable oil reserves and other properties. Observers like the Socialist Victor L. Berger could say with more than a grain of truth that all America got out of the war was the flu and prohibition. Others would add high prices, heavy taxes, and bad debts.

This general picture of course was not fair to the Allies, but it was the picture that a large number of Americans retained.

12

Nor was this all. The "ingrate" nations of Europe, while cursing us for our sins of commission and omission, were stretching bony arms across the Atlantic and begging for more food, more money. Would the appalling cost of this thing ever stop? The Brooklyn *Eagle* struck a popular note when it said, "We don't mind feeding the small nations, but we should like them to stop fighting between meals."

Every returning passenger ship dumped into American ports a fresh cargo of homesick and disillusioned soldiers. They had gone abroad to save the world, believing from their storybooks that war was something romantic and glamorous. They had received a deflating dose of trenches, poison gas, mud, hardtack, and lice. Mark Sullivan tells of the returning Negro soldier who gazed rapturously at the Statue of Liberty from a transport, and solemnly vowed, "Lady, once I gets behind you, I promise I never will look at yo' face again."

All had not been harmonious on the other side. Our boys had engaged in fisticuffs with their British cousins. They had been overcharged by French shopkeepers. The baseless rumor had spread that our government had actually had to pay rent for the trenches our doughboys occupied. The starry-eyed lads in khaki had reached France believing that Frenchmen wore wings and Germans horns. Now that many of our warriors had seen the clean German cities and the clean German people, they were not so sure as they had once been that they had fought on the right side. Anyhow, they were home, and home to stay, and they were not going to be summoned from their plows by any superstate blowing a blast on the trumpet of Article X.

Saddened and disgusted though they were, the "Yanks" at least had the satisfaction of knowing they had won the war. Yet now Field-Marshal Haig was openly proclaiming that the British had turned the trick!

The titanic conflict which had been fought to "make the world safe for democracy" and to "end wars" had turned to dust and ashes. A score or so of minor wars now grew where only one had grown before. Our military leaders were talking openly of peacetime conscription; the War Department was asking Congress for a standing army about five times the normal complement. There was a growing feeling that, as one journal put it, "until the League proves itself, we had better beat our swords into convertible plowshares."

Wilson had won the war by arousing the American people to the fervor of a great moral crusade. He could win an acceptance of the peace, and above all a carrying out of our responsibilities under the peace, only by arousing them to a new idealistic crusade. But would he be able to do so in the face of the obstacles confronting him? A sober review of the forces in opposition reveals little to justify his optimism.

CHAPTER THREE

THE PALL OF PARTISANSHIP

"No party has a right to appropriate this issue [the treaty] and no party will in the long run dare oppose it." WOODROW WILSON, *March 4, 1919.*

———

1

BLIND PARTISANSHIP, as much as any other single factor, ruined the League of Nations in the United States. This is not to condemn any one individual or group of individuals; it is merely to state a fact which, in the circumstances, was as inescapable as the law of gravitation.

The treaty was too much bound up with Wilson, and especially with Wilson's League of Nations, to leave any room for hope that the issue could escape the reefs of partisanship. One competent writer has estimated that four-fifths of the opposition to the League was nothing more than unreasoning hatred of Wilson. This is probably an exaggeration, but there can be no doubt that the Republican leaders, and many of the Republican rank and file, hated the President with a consuming bitterness, and were prepared to stop at nothing to bring about his downfall and at the same time (so they claimed) save the Republic.

The Republicans could not forgive Wilson for having beaten them in 1912, especially since his victory was their own fault. They could not accustom themselves to the role of a minority party: this was contrary to the natural order of things since 1861. They could not forgive Wilson for having won again in 1916, by the narrowest of margins and with the slogan, "He kept us out of war." It was in fact the first time an incumbent Democrat had been elected since the redoubtable Andrew Jackson, in 1832.

The Republicans distrusted Wilson because he was a Southerner, with Southerners in his Cabinet, and with long-lived Southern Democrats in control of the Congressional committees. He was believed to be conspiring to impoverish the North to the advantage of the South through the income tax and other devices. The New York *Tribune* charged that Wilson's internationalism was developed as a screen to cover his Southernism. William E. Dodd alleges that certain "eminent" Republicans announced in his presence that it would have been better if the South had won the Civil War, for "then we should have escaped Wilson."

Wilson believed that a President should lead, and he had stood over Congress with a dictatorial rod. Worse than that, he had liberal ideas about the tariff and trusts and income taxes, all of which notions were anathema to Republican big business. Republican journals referred angrily to the "crimes of Wilson"; and the oil magnate, Edward L. Doheny, later to be besmeared with the Teapot Dome scandal, growled that the President was a "college professor gone Bolshevik."

Bitterly though the Republicans reacted against Wilson's peacetime leadership, their resentment increased when war came and Wilson ("Kaiser" Wilson) assumed the dictatorial powers that were lawfully his under the Constitution. The Republicans could not reconcile themselves to the fact, nor forgive themselves for it, that a Democrat was running the biggest of our wars up to that time. They cried out against huge expenditures of money, as if penny-pinching were in order when the fate of America was at stake; and their bitterness mounted to fury when, search though they did, they could find no real taint of scandal.

2

Wilson not only had run the war, but had kept prominent Republicans from winning glory and making political capital out of it. General Leonard Wood, a potential Republican President and a close friend of ex-President Theodore Roosevelt, was suddenly ordered away from the embarkation port and condemned to stay at home while the troops which he had trained went overseas. Colonel Theodore Roosevelt, who was regarded as the logical Republican nominee in 1920, almost got down on his knees before the hated Wilson, pleading for a chance to take a division of volunteers to France and inspirit the flagging Allied cause. Wilson austerely rebuffed him, thus visiting upon the graying Rough Rider the greatest disappointment of his life.

Wilson of course had good or at least plausible reasons for snubbing both Wood and Roosevelt; but the important point is that the Republicans neither forgot nor forgave. Roosevelt had once shown some friendliness to the idea of a league of nations, notably in his address accepting the Nobel Peace Prize. But when Wilson espoused the League, Roosevelt attacked it with all his unbridled vehemence. He literally plotted on his deathbed to defeat the yet unborn League of Nations.

The venom engendered by the Roosevelt-Wilson feud persisted, and gave strength to the foes of the League during those dark hours when it seemed as though theirs was a losing cause. Looking back through the mists of thirteen years, Mrs. Alice Roosevelt Longworth, the doughty Rough Rider's doughty daughter, could write, "How we did cherish and nourish our hatreds in those days!"

During the war, politics had been nominally "adjourned." Both partisanship and pro-Germanism took cover, but they were still very much alive. Now that the shooting had stopped, partisanship could flare forth with all the greater explosiveness for having been repressed.

Wilson, it must be conceded, played directly into the hands of the Republican partisans. Before going to Paris, he bluntly called upon the country for a Democratic Congress to uphold his policies; then, when the voters returned Republicans, he snubbed the Senate by refusing to consult with its leaders and by taking abroad a peace commission of five which contained no senators and only one Republican, a minor figure at that. Wilson was going to make a Wilsonian peace, a Democratic peace, with the glory unipartisan but with the responsibility bipartisan. All right, said the Republicans, that was a game that two could play.

Partisanship in some degree could not have been kept out of

The Stars and Stripes First
(From New York *World*; cartoonist Kirby; reprinted by permission)

the death struggle over the treaty. Yet if Wilson had been more deferential to the Republicans, if he had honored them with prominent places in his councils, if he had accepted more of their ideas, he would no doubt have removed some of the sting. Certainly he would have given the Republicans less excuse for going before the country in a blaze of indignation crying that the President was playing politics with the treaty.

In short, the Republicans were forced to oppose the League, at least in unamended form, if for no other reason than that it was a Wilson League. As the Greenville (S.C.) *Piedmont* baldly put it, "The Senate's chief objection to the League idea is that Wilson is a Democrat." A few prominent Republicans, notably ex-President William Howard Taft, could rise above their dislike of Wilson and support the League with unflagging devotion. But such men were the exception. The Columbus *Ohio State Journal* whimsically remarked, "The attitude of most of us thoughtful Republicans seems to be that we're unalterably opposed to Article X, whether we know what's in it or not."

3

The high officials of both parties naturally considered their position on the League issue in the light of their political fortunes. The chairman of the Republican National Committee, Will H. Hays, was in constant touch with the party leaders, senatorial and otherwise, as to what attitude the Republicans should take. Should they accept the Wilson League? Should they strive to amend it slightly, or fundamentally? Or should they scrap the whole thing, as Senators Borah and Brandegee and Johnson were demanding? Would not the ringing cry of "Americanism versus internationalism" win the most votes in the end? The Republicans, in brief, were striving to find the winning issue; the Democrats, to maintain one.

Neither party ever lost sight of the relation of the League to the presidential election of 1920. The Republicans were confident that on domestic issues alone they could defeat any possible Democratic candidate: they had merely to capitalize on war-weariness and a desire to get back to "normalcy." But if Wilson should shove his grandiose scheme through the Senate, his increased prestige would be dangerous. So overshadowing a world figure might he become that he would perhaps dictate a Democratic successor—possibly his son-in-law, William G. McAdoo.

Even more disquieting was another possibility. Once the League was approved, would it not be logical that Wilson should stay in office at least another term to see that it got off to a proper start? The two-term tradition was still strong, but world reorganization was a grave responsibility. Wilson might consent to run by persuading himself that he was the "indispensable man." Worse than that, he might be able to persuade the voters that he was the "indispensable man." The nightmare of four more years of Wilsonism caused cold chills to run down Republican spines.

The hated professor might even aspire to head the League of Nations and become president of the world. Possibly this was his desire. Irwin H. ("Ike") Hoover, the White House usher, referring to the period shortly after Wilson's return from Europe, recalls that the President once turned to him and asked if he would like to go back to Geneva.

4

One of Wilson's gravest mistakes, it now seems, was his failure to announce early in the fight that under no circumstances would he attempt to shatter the two-term tradition. Partisanship would have remained; but a great deal of the personal spleen would have been removed, and the battle would have been fought out at ordinary partisan levels. As it turned out, a vast amount of Republican effort was devoted to thwarting and humiliating Wilson, largely because he was a potential candidate for a third term. He was in fact freely mentioned as such, down to the very week in 1920 when the Democrats nominated James M. Cox.

Wilson, as his private papers now reveal, was fully aware of this situation. On May 17, 1919, an editorial in the influential Springfield *Republican* called upon him to announce that he was not a candidate for a third term, and thus eliminate his personality from the debate. This editorial reached Wilson in Paris, and on June 2 he cabled his private secretary in Washington, Joseph P. Tumulty, asking for a consensus of opinion among his advisers as to what he should do.

Tumulty did not make it clear in his reply of the next day whether he had consulted anyone or not. But he vigorously advised against accepting a third nomination, even though the great majority of the Democratic leaders favored one. Another four years would not add to Wilson's dignity and honor. But in any case, Tumulty concluded, the time was not ripe for an announcement, because the Democrats were sorely depressed by their 1920 prospects.

Wilson did not reply to this urgent cablegram, but it is significant that he refrained to the very end from making a public pronouncement. We do not know whether he was impressed by Tumulty's advice, or whether he was moved by other reasons. Several possibilities offer themselves.

Before the two-term tradition was shattered in 1940, the President's power waned as his second term neared its end. Everyone knew that the king was dying. Perhaps Wilson wished to cultivate the third-term threat so as to hold his Democratic followers, many of whom were grumbling, securely in line. Perhaps he was actually keeping his mind open on the question of a third term, waiting to see whether it was necessary to arrange to have himself "drafted." Possibly he felt that a formal act of abdication would be not only unnecessary but slightly ridiculous: the two-term tradition had already become a part of the unwritten Constitution. And Wilson habitually recoiled from the unnecessary or the slightly ridiculous.

In politics one must often stoop to conquer. Wilson never fully learned that one must do irrelevant, repetitious, or even somewhat foolish things to attain the larger end. At least, he never learned to do these things willingly or gracefully.

5

The presidential election of 1920 was not the only one that cast a dark pall over the League issue.

In the campaign of 1912 the Republicans had broken into two snarling factions, and had defeated themselves. The penalty was Wilson and his works. At all costs the Republicans must not split again in 1920. Whatever position they took, it must be one which all of them, or the great majority of them, could support. If that position squared with world order and the cause of humanity, so much the better; but, if it did not, the nobler cause would have to go out the window. There must be unity at any price, for disunity might mean another 1912, with a triumphant Wilson or his heir apparent enthroned for four more years.

Much that is not otherwise understandable becomes transparently clear when we remember that the preliminary stages of the election of 1920 were fought on the floor of the Senate in 1919, with the League as the chief whipping boy. When the Republican leaders wavered under pressure of public opinion, and seriously considered accepting some kind of amended Wilson League, there were always bolters like Borah and Johnson to threaten that they would organize a third party in 1920 and repeat the horrors of 1912.

Our presidential form of government has many virtues, but in the field of foreign affairs it has serious drawbacks. Elections must come not by the crisis, as in England, but by the calendar; and the calendar is no respecter of events. The momentous debate of 1919–1920 was conducted with one eye on the political arena.

Both parties, it must be emphasized, were looking at the calendar. Democrats accused the Republicans of partisanship; Republicans accused the Democrats of partisanship. It was the age-old story of the pot calling the kettle partisan; purely political motives were absent on neither side. This is a fact that has often been overlooked by overzealous friends of the League, who have upbraided the political maneuvers of the Republicans while completely ignoring those of the Democrats. The innermost feelings of the Democrats were betrayed by one South Carolina newspaper which remarked, "The world has been made about as safe for democracy as this country for the Democratic party."

Democratic partisanship was quieter, less conspicuous, more subtle. The Republicans appeared to be flagrantly partisan, for they were attempting to pull down or at least reshape the Wilsonian League. They seemed to be attacking world peace. The Democrats on the other hand, while supporting Wilson's scheme for what were in some cases largely partisan motives, appeared to be fighting for peace on earth and good will among nations. They could make political capital out of Wilson's glowing successes, while professing to support the League for only the noblest motives. They sought partisan credit; the Republicans could not permit them to get unalloyed partisan credit.

The various newspaper polls show beyond a doubt that where the Democratic party was strong, sentiment for the League was strong. The Solid South was solidly behind the League. Where the Republicans were strong, opposition to an unamended Wilson League was strong. In the Senate, the Democrats lined up almost unanimously for an unamended League. If on the one hand there was blind Republican partisanship, on the other hand there was blind Democratic party loyalty. Both are partisanship.

6

Viewed in the large, the League of Nations was a national issue—a world issue—which should have been completely divorced from politics. There was nothing inherent in the League that should have enlisted the support of the cotton-

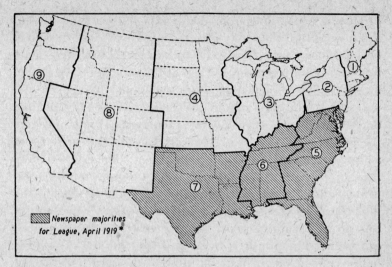

Newspaper majorities
for League, April 1919*

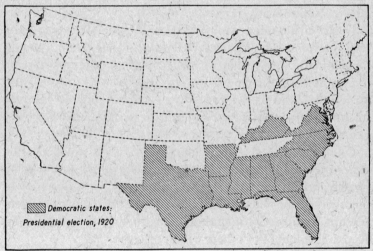

Democratic states:
Presidential election, 1920

* Based on *Literary Digest* poll (April 5, 1919, p. 15) of 1,377 daily U. S. newspapers on League of Nations. Responses by section: (1) 40 yes, 14 no, 41 conditional; (2) 122 yes, 37 no, 104 con.; (3) 166 yes, 48 no, 132 con.; (4) 85 yes, 29 no, 70 con.; (5) 75 yes, 13 no, 24 con.; (6) 45 yes, 4 no, 7 con.; (7) 88 yes, 8 no, 21 con.; (8) 33 yes, 8 no, 30 con.; (9) 64 yes, 20 no, 49 con. Total: 718 yes, 181 no, 478 con.

producing South and aroused the antagonism of the wheat-producing North. If party barriers could have been completely beaten down in the Senate, it is inconceivable that the same line-up would have been for and against the Wilson League. Men did not vote their consciences; they voted their party.

If the Republican candidate, Charles Evans Hughes, had defeated Wilson in 1916, and had presented a Hughes League, the Solid South almost surely would have been in favor of adding reservations to it or rejecting it. The Montgomery *Advertiser* was frank to admit that the League was supported in the South "largely because Southern Democrats regard the Treaty and its ratification as a Democratic issue." In a lighter but no less truthful vein, the Greenville (S.C.) *Piedmont* quipped: "The South is heart and soul for the Treaty. It hasn't read it, but it has read some of the speeches of them darned Republicans."

Isolationist enemies of the League liberally misquoted Washington's immortal Farewell Address. He did not say, as he was made to say, that we must avoid *all* alliances. But he did say to his countrymen—and this is a part of the unread and forgotten Farewell Address: "I . . . warn you in the most solemn manner against *the baneful effects of the spirit of party generally.*"

One other highly significant point must be stressed. The viciousness of the senatorial attacks on Wilson's League cannot be entirely disassociated from the fact that a dozen or so members of the Senate were active aspirants for the presidential nomination. Conspicuous among them were Johnson and Knox. The names of others will appear later.

The attacks which some of these men launched against the League, notably Johnson, were not currently popular, but, given time, the tide might turn against internationalism and in favor of rousing nationalism. It is always easier to implant doubts than to dig them up. Unquestionably much of the oratory and parliamentary jockeying in the Senate was related to the great national conventions of 1920. "Patience, Europe," counseled one Southern newspaper. "We can't bother with these little world-problems until we decide who is to get the office."

In political warfare as in military warfare the first casualty is the truth. The imminence of the battle of 1920 was all the more reason why Wilson, as noted elsewhere,* should have striven to keep a detailed League Covenant out of the treaty, so that it might be considered later in a less impassioned and less partisan atmosphere.

7

Partisanship and prejudice merged imperceptibly with pride of prerogative in the Senate fight over the League.

The Senate is the more important half of one of the three coordinate branches of the United States government. In normal times it is a coordinate body; in wartime it tends to become a subordinate body, because the Constitution confers upon the President dictatorial powers. When the war is over, the Senate naturally seeks to reestablish its former importance. This it did when the Civil War came to a close in 1865; this it did when the World War came to a nominal close in 1918. Lincoln died before the battle was fully joined, leaving Johnson to do unsuccessful battle; Wilson lived on, gave unsuccessful battle, and was crushed.

Wilson's position was in some respects even less favorable than Lincoln's would have been had he lived to face the music. From the very beginning of his administration in 1913, Wilson had "crowded" Congressmen in his attempts to drive through a sweeping program of reform. By 1919 there was a growing list of members who were not loath to pay off old scores.

The senators, by being left off the Peace Commission, had been ostentatiously denied an opportunity to help write the treaty in Paris; now was their opportunity to do a little re-

* See T. A. Bailey, *Woodrow Wilson and the Lost Peace*, pp. 190–192, 352–353.

writing on their own in the form of reservations. They owed it to their wounded pride to put some kind of senatorial stamp, major or minor, on Wilson's handiwork. They were in fact the first representative body in our democracy to have a chance at it. Wilson's group of experts ("The Inquiry") had been solely appointive; his Peace Commission of five had been solely

"Looks Black to Me"

(From New York *Evening World*; cartoonist Cassel; reprinted by permission)

appointive, and largely rubber stamps. If democracy had any validity, the people's elected representatives were entitled to a microscopic look at a treaty which had been negotiated behind guarded doors.

8

Wilson, it now appears, took an unduly narrow view of the constitutional powers of the Senate regarding treaties. To him advice and consent meant that the Senate would give its advice and consent *after* the completed pact had been laid before it, not while the pact was in the process of negotiation.

Such was the procedure that had ordinarily been followed in dealing with routine treaties, though previous Presidents had occasionally sought advice in advance of senatorial action. Wilson was legally justified in pursuing a policy of aloofness; but it was politically unwise. Ordinary methods would not suffice. This was more than an ordinary treaty: it was a charter for a new world order. The Senate would doubtless have been flattered, and probably to some extent mollified, if it had been invited to have some kind of share in the treaty's making.

The two-thirds rule interposed a formidable hurdle, but there it was, and Wilson had to play the game within the rules unless he was prepared to engineer a successful *coup d'état*. The Founding Fathers, with their distrust of George III, had piled up obstacles in the path of executive action, and had set the stage for deadlock. A prudent Wilson would have left no stone unturned in his efforts to avert the deadlock.

Wilson felt strong, because, as we have noted, public opinion was generally behind him. He knew that he was wiser than the Senate in that he could see the world aspects of the problem, whereas the mental ceiling of the senators from the sheep-and-corn country was relatively low. He believed that when the Senate was presented with an accomplished fact in peace-making it might grumble but could do no other than surrender.

This, as we shall see, was a woeful misjudgment of the temper of the prerogative-proud Senate. Public opinion might favor the League, but public opinion could be changed or confused. Besides, election day for individual senators was approximately two, four, or six years away; and the voters have an incredibly short memory. One wit has well said, "The President proposes, the Senate disposes, while the country dozes."

Two-thirds of the Senators would be in office after Wilson's two terms came to an end. The Senate in 1919 was composed of iron-willed, independent-minded men: the Brandegees, the

Reeds, the Borahs, the Johnsons, and the Shermans. They would not jump when the President cracked the whip; they would give more advice than consent. If Wilson made them angry enough, they would willingly commit political suicide provided, in so doing, they could but drag this vile League into the grave with them.

A certain amount of partisanship would of course have been present even if Wilson had treated the Senate with the deference of a Lord Chesterfield. But he would have lost nothing if at the very beginning he had tried to make partners of the senators rather than vicious partisans. By July, 1919, he had affronted them so seriously that it was difficult if not impossible to recover lost ground.

Wilson was now dimly aware of this situation, and under the proddings of his advisers undertook to make some conciliatory gestures in the direction of the Senate. But it was evident to all that he would extend no "nosegays" to the "pygmy-minded" members of that body.

CHAPTER FOUR

THE CAVE OF THE WINDS

"God made the world in seven days, but he didn't have a senate
to deal with." Greenville (S.C.) PIEDMONT, *September, 1919.*

1

THE FOCAL point of the fight over the treaty was the Senate
of the United States—what the presiding officer, Vice President
Thomas R. Marshall, remembering his classical mythology,
whimsically called "the cave of the winds." The opinions of
the senators ran the whole gamut from enthusiastic approval
of the treaty as it stood, to flat rejection of all it contained. An
analysis of these various groups is indispensable if one is to
understand precisely how the treaty met its doom.

The Democrats may be considered first. When the treaty
was submitted to the Senate there were 47 Democrats and 49
Republicans. The Democrats not only lacked a simple majority but fell far short of the necessary two-thirds. Not only
that, but four of the Democratic senators were outright opponents of an unreserved "Wilson treaty": the unbridled Gore
of Oklahoma, the independently minded Shields of Tennessee,
the Irish-sired Walsh of Massachusetts, and the leather-lar-
ynxed Reed of Missouri. By far the most important of these
four Democratic "irreconcilables" or near "irreconcilables"
was the silver-thatched Reed, an accomplished rabble-rouser
with a withering tongue and a buzz-saw voice. He seems to have
turned against the treaty primarily because of his isolationist
and anti-British prejudices.

The Democrats not only lacked numbers but lacked forensic
power. They had no one who could stand up against the oratorical blasts of Borah and Johnson, or match the sarcastic
sallies of Brandegee and Moses. Reed could, but he deserted
to the other side.

The Democrats also lacked parliamentary skill. Not even their ablest member could cross swords on equal terms with Lodge, one of the cleverest and most resourceful parliamentarians in the history of the Senate.

Altogether, the Democrats were conspicuously short of intellectual resources and general ability. In brilliance of mind, Senator Walsh of Montana, a bloodhound for facts who later made his mark in the Teapot Dome prosecutions, could, after careful preparation, stand up against Knox or Lodge, but he was lacking in personal force and adaptability. His older colleagues were in general average if not mediocre figures.

Most of the Democratic senators were from the Solid South, where party loyalty was a fetish closely associated with racial supremacy and the "Lost Cause" of 1861–1865. They were generally the products of a one-party system, and some of them had been elected and reelected for decades with little or no opposition. It was said with more than a grain of truth that if a Southern Democrat maintained his party allegiance, voted the straight ticket, and kept out of jail, he could be reasonably sure of being returned to Congress. This situation did not make for the ablest type of legislator.

2

The Democrats also lacked effective leadership. Their minority leader, the seventy-two-year-old Senator Martin of Virginia, had been seriously ill for more than six months, and was confined to his home. He died during the debate over the treaty. The acting minority leader was Gilbert M. Hitchcock of Nebraska, a newspaper editor with an honorable record and moderate ability, who was called upon to defend the breach against Lodge, the master parliamentarian. When we consider Hitchcock's mediocrity, his relatively little experience with the tricks of parliamentary jockeying, and his demoralizingly uncertain status as acting leader, it is surprising that he did as well as he did.

Hitchcock was further handicapped by not enjoying the complete confidence of Wilson, at least not at the outset. Having received two years of his education in Germany, the senator had developed a higher degree of sympathy for the German point of view than was common, and in a strongly worded letter to the President he had protested against going into the war. When he declared himself foursquare for the League, Wilson felt more kindly disposed toward him, but still there was lacking that close cordiality which was essential for effective cooperation.

After Wilson's physical collapse, an additional barrier was erected between the two men. Yet it must be confessed that before this time Wilson had not made the most of his opportunities. On the day he submitted the treaty to the Senate he incorrectly told his press conference that reservations could be added only by a two-thirds vote. This was extremely embarrassing to Hitchcock and other Democrats, for they had just been arguing on Capitol Hill that a simple majority would suffice.

The Democrats, for all their weaknesses, had three powerful advantages. One was party loyalty. Whatever their personal convictions, only four members of the entire group deserted the ranks, until it was clear that the battered ship was sinking. The great body of Democrats was blindly loyal to the ablest leader they had raised up since the days of Andrew Jackson. The dying Senator Martin wrote Wilson from Virginia, on July 27, 1919, that when the time came to vote he would get into the drawing room of a train, come to Washington, vote for the treaty, and return home.

The second Democratic advantage was a good cause—what at the outset seemed to be the superior moral cause. But in the mouths of skilled sophists the better position may be made to appear the worse, and the Republicans had a superfluity of skilled sophists.

The third great advantage of the Democrats was Wilson's
leadership. He was President of the United States, with all the
prestige and power of that exalted office. He was a gifted leader
who could sway opinion and turn the tide of events. But he
was the only real leader the Democrats had. This was all the
more reason why he should have worked closely with his following in the Senate, while carefully husbanding his energy
and safeguarding his health.

3

Complicated though the situation was in the Democratic
camp, it was simplicity itself when compared with that on the
Republican side.

No single Republican group unqualifiedly favored the treaty
as it stood. For the sake of the party, the Republicans could
not permit a Wilson pact to go through without some kind
of alteration—without "Americanizing" it or, to put it crudely,
"Republicanizing" it. If they did this, they could save face, and
in some measure share the glory, claiming that it was now a
Republican as well as a Democratic treaty.

Many of the Republicans (as well as some Democrats)
had honest doubts about the treaty. They were afraid that our
sovereignty might be jeopardized, that we could not control
our own tariff barriers or our immigration flood dikes. They
wanted reservations added to the treaty, of greater or less
force, to safeguard the interests of the United States, to clarify
our obligations, and to glorify the Republican party.

The reservationists among the Republicans divided into
two groups: those who favored mild reservations, and those
who favored strong reservations or amendments.

The "strong reservationists," cleverly led by Henry Cabot
Lodge, not only wanted to amend outright certain objectionable parts of the treaty, but insisted that the signatory powers
formally accept these changes. The "strong reservationists"
numbered about twenty, and included such dependable party

hacks as Harding of Ohio (later President) and Curtis of Kansas (later Vice President). It is probable that some of these men did not want the treaty in any form, but lacked the courage to attack it frontally.

Our Senatorial Hamlet
[To ratify or not to ratify]
(Courtesy of Spokane *Spokesman-Review*;
cartoonist Morris)

The "mild reservationists" (also called "middle grounders" or "moderates") included about twelve of the ablest and most liberal-minded senators, such as Kellogg (later Secretary of State) and McNary (Republican Vice Presidential nominee in 1940). They favored certain rather innocuous reservations which would protect our interests without undermining the basic structure of the treaty or requiring further action by the signatory powers.

The dozen or so "mild reservationists" played a crucial role in the unfolding of this great drama, and one that has not been properly appreciated. They were evidently sincere in wanting the treaty approved, and their reservations were relatively unobjectionable, differing hardly at all except in phraseology from the reservations which the Democrats themselves were belatedly willing to accept. If the 43 dependable Democrats had joined with the dozen "mild reservationist" Republicans, the Democrats would still have been short of a two-thirds majority, but *they would have had comfortably more than a simple majority.*

This is a fact of immense importance. The much-maligned Lodge reservations were all added by a simple majority vote. If the Democrats had opened their arms to the "mild reservationists," the resulting coalition *could have voted down every Lodge reservation;* more than that, *it could have voted through its own relatively innocuous reservations.* Even then the two-thirds vote might not have been obtainable; but the remaining Republicans would have been confronted with the painful alternative of defeating the treaty outright or getting onto the bandwagon. It is possible that under pressure of this kind enough "strong reservationists" would have swung over to insure victory.

One of Wilson's gravest strategical errors was his failure to hold out the olive branch to the "mild reservationists" in the summer of 1919, when they were in a mood to be bargained with. But Wilson, for understandable reasons, was cold to the whole idea of reservations. When he stingingly rebuffed the "mild reservationists," they had to respond to the tuggings of party loyalty and the growing popular demand for reservations. So they fell in behind Lodge; but they went unwillingly, with Kellogg freely damning Wilson and wishing "the treaty was in Hell."

4

As far as the public was concerned, the small phalanx of Republican "irreconcilables" overshadowed all other Senate groups. Numbering about fourteen, and irreconcilably opposed to the treaty in any form, they were also known as the "bitter-enders" and the "Battalion of Death."

The "irreconcilables" held the balance, or more than the balance, in oratorical ability and obstructive power. They dominated the Senate Foreign Relations Committee, and thus were able to pursue their strategy of delay. They had the loudest voices, the voices of Borah and Johnson, and they could shout down and silence their opponents. They could monopolize the Senate debate, and at times did, all the while dragging out the discussion, and further confusing the public mind with irrelevant or baseless arguments, against which their opponents were forced to dig up answers.

Nor were the "irreconcilables" merely noise. They had brains on their side as well, the brains of Knox and Brandegee. In parliamentary as well as in military warfare the advantage is usually with the side which is able to seize and hold the initiative. This advantage lay with the "Battalion of Death." Attacking the treaty with satire, ridicule, and invective, they could throw its proponents on the defensive. The League lent itself to ridicule; the "irreconcilables" did not lend themselves so well to ridicule, for they were proposing nothing. Their role was to tear down, and they did.

The compact little group of "irreconcilables" also held the balance of power in the voting. They joined with their Republican colleagues in saddling the treaty with as strong reservations as possible, and then joined with their Democratic opponents to vote the whole thing down.

This seemed like hypocrisy, and the "bitter-enders" were roundly condemned for it. But, to give the devil his due, they were playing the game within the rules. They believed—no doubt, some of them sincerely—that the Republic was faced with the most awful peril in all its history, and they were determined to forestall, by fair means or foul, this "unholy thing with a holy name." To them the end justified the means. If the rules permitted them to defeat the treaty by loading it down, they would be foolish not to take advantage of the rules. The Democrats, had they been in the shoes of the "irreconcilables," almost certainly would have done the same thing.

5

The "irreconcilables" had one other potent weapon: the threat to bolt. They constantly brandished it over the head of Lodge, loudly threatening to go over to the Democrats and vote down the Republican reservations, unless a substantial part of their wishes was granted.

Worse than that, these "bitter-enders" repeatedly declared that they would desert the party in 1920 if the Republicans surrendered to White House dictation. The bolters of 1912 had brought in Wilson; whatever the cost, there must be no bolters in 1920.

The stock in trade of the "irreconcilables" was obstruction, not construction. They were heatedly accused of not proposing anything constructive; of not coming forward with any practicable alternative. As the Syracuse *Post-Standard* remarked, "The League of Nations Covenant has flaws in plenty, but we should like to see the document that Senators Lodge, Borah, Johnson, Reed and Sherman could agree on." Yes, one would. But the "bitter-enders" felt no call to propose anything. They were quite content that the United States should stay out of any or all Leagues, and they made it their aim to bring this about.

The "irreconcilables" presented an almost perfect example of minority rule; theirs was the philosophy of the filibuster. They, and only they, saw the true light; theirs was the ultimate wisdom. They would prevent this treaty calamity even though some 80 per cent of their colleagues and an overwhelming majority of the American people favored the League in some form.

Almost fanatical in their desire to save the Republic, the "bitter-enders" did not scruple to use any weapon that came to hand. Senator Sherman openly appealed to religious prejudice when he asserted that Catholic peoples would predominate in the League, and that the new order would be ruled by the Pope. Senator Reed openly appealed to racial prejudice when he declared that colored peoples would outnumber whites in the new League of Nations.

It is impossible to determine with certainty the motives of each of the "irreconcilables." At best, emotions and motives tend to merge. Some of the senators, traditionalists and isolationists like Borah, appear to have really believed that the Republic had to be rescued from imminent peril. Others, like Johnson, probably saw the possibilities of using the senatorial sounding board for the advancement of their presidential candidacies—though it must be conceded that at the outset the fiery Californian took the unpopular side. Others were no doubt aware of the political profit to be derived from appealing to the Irish and German vote.

A detailed analysis of the motives or probable motives of the "irreconcilables" would doubtless reveal that their state of mind was compounded of varying amounts of traditionalism, ignorance, bigotry, fear of the untried, prejudice, personal pique, partisanship, political ambition, and a natural bent for destructiveness. But, whatever the motives, the result was the same. This group was one of the vitally important elements in keeping the United States out of the League of Nations.

6

The "irreconcilables" were such a colorful crew, and their names will appear so often in this narrative, that it would be well to make the acquaintance of some of them.

There was Medill McCormick of Illinois, relative of the inventor of the McCormick reaper, former publisher of the violently isolationist Chicago *Tribune*, husband of the daughter of Mark Hanna, and a senator who through his polish and connections was expected to go far.

There was George H. Moses, small-town newspaper editor from New Hampshire, filled with Yankee shrewdness and political craft, and noted for his gabbiness, flippancy of tongue, and cheap wit.

There was Albert B. Fall of New Mexico, with drooping mustaches, wide-brimmed western hat, and a wide-brimmed conscience, who, after having "saved" his country from European thieves, was to deliver his country's oil reserves to 100 per cent American thieves.

There was Philander C. Knox of Pennsylvania, "the brain" of the "bitter-enders." A distinguished lawyer whose mind had been whetted on the grindstone of corporation law, he had served as Secretary of State under President Taft. Short of stature, bald of head, rotund of paunch, he was dubbed by Theodore Roosevelt that "sawed-off cherub." Impeccably dressed, with striped trousers and wing collar, he looked like a statesman, and was still considered, despite his sixty-six years, presidential timber. He provided much of the legal acumen, the shysterlike shifts and dodges, which the "Battalion of Death" needed in waging what seemed at the outset to be a losing battle.

There was Frank B. Brandegee of Connecticut, the "tongue" of the "irreconcilables"—that is, the rapier tongue. A Connecticut Yankee, bitter to the point of vindictiveness, and so intense as later to commit suicide, he dressed like a fop and spoke in a peculiarly high, whining, nasal voice. Mrs. Alice Roosevelt Longworth, who was a constant visitor to the Senate galleries, especially enjoyed hearing him speak. He was usually brief, and though in deadly earnest he threw off sparks of sardonic humor. When Mrs. Longworth complimented him he replied, "Well, I get going and I can't stop, like a cat with a ball of catnip." He was one of the original "bitter-enders," and one of the few who never lost confidence that the League would be killed.

There was Hiram W. Johnson of California, the "noise" of the "irreconcilables." Thickset, ruddy-faced, silver-thatched, he was probably the most accomplished rabble-rouser of them all. If Brandegee wielded a rapier, Johnson wielded a meat-ax. Having made his reputation as a smasher of the corrupt Southern Pacific political machine in California, and having become governor and senator largely on the strength of that achievement, he continued to smash things. His noise-making ability came to be a standing joke: he did not attack, he "flayed." Yet no one could deny that the man had bulldog tenacity, a ripsaw voice, and the ability to move great crowds.

Friends of the League decried Johnson's cave-man mentality and his completely closed mind. They said if he was sincere then God deliver us from the sincere bigot. Probably he was sincere; but he was also sincere in desiring the presidency. He was also consistent. The fires of his presidential ambitions reduced to ashes, his stentorian voice reduced to a whisper, he was still holding the same antiquated castle twenty-five years later.

7

William E. Borah was the "soul" of the "irreconcilables." Tall of frame, massive of face and head, bushy of hair, and almost eccentric in appearance, the "Idaho lion" was generally regarded as the most eloquent and inspiring speaker of the Senate, if not of his generation. Admirers compared him with the "godlike" Daniel Webster. The murmured announcement that Borah had the floor was enough, during a critical debate, to depopulate the House floor and galleries. This was a compliment paid to few if any other orators of his generation.

Borah's eloquence was sincere, simple, lofty, moving. One did not have to agree with his isolationist convictions in order to admire his oratory. At one time during the Senate struggle, the bored presiding officer, Vice President Marshall, scribbled a note for Borah: "May a mummy say that you almost galvanized him to life?"

By instinct and training Borah was a conscientious objector. His daily horseback ride in Rock Creek Park was as unfailing as the Washington Monument; and one of the stock jokes of the capital was to express amazement that the senator would consent to go in the same direction as the horse. His mind naturally sought reasons why something should not be done, rather than why it should be done.

Borah's official biographer claims that he was "the original irreconcilable." As early as 1916 the senator was voicing vehement opposition to Wilson's proposed forsaking of the paths of isolationism. Early in 1919, when American public opinion overwhelmingly favored the League, and when the Republicans were timidly thinking that the best they could do would be to "Americanize" or "Republicanize" the Covenant, Borah demanded that the whole wicked contraption be hurled back across the Atlantic into the teeth of its authors.

After Borah's great speech of February 21, 1919, Lodge came to him with a word of congratulation, but added with a deprecatory wave of his hands: "What are you going to do? It's hopeless. All the newspapers in my state are for the League." Other admirers of Borah chimed in: "That was great; that was fine; we agree with you; but we have got to have some sort of League; everybody is for it." The fainthearted Senator Harding told Borah: "Bill, I'd like to get in the fight against this League of Nations, but the people of my state are all for it I'm afraid." (In 1937 Borah told the present writer that Harding was the "biggest moral coward" he ever knew in public life.)

It was Borah, probably more than any other man, who stirred up and crystallized public opposition to the League, at least in the early stages. He demonstrated that with the passage of time, and with the proper strategy, an anti-League program might prove to be politically profitable.

The leonine Idahoan was completely uncompromising. He declared that if he had his way the League would be "Twenty Thousand Leagues under the Sea." He wanted "this treacherous and treasonable scheme" "buried in hell," and he insisted that he would not change his course if Jesus Christ himself should come to earth and plead for the Covenant.

Newspapers might call Borah, as the Philadelphia *Public Ledger* did, a "political antiquarian and a pottering troglodyte"; but few doubted his sincerity. Borah had the rare ability to smash everybody's pet scheme and yet retain the friendship if not the admiration of those whose plans he had reduced to rubble. Completely free of a mean and petty spirit, he alone of the "bitter-enders" retained the respect of President Wilson.

To the very end the "irreconcilables" seem to have thought that they had done a noble thing: they had saved the Republic from dangers to which all others were blind. Borah's official biographer, writing with the Idahoan's sanction, says, "The Senator is proud of his part in keeping the United States out of the League . . ."

8

Closely associated with the "irreconcilables," at least in the public mind, was the leader of the "strong reservationists," Henry Cabot Lodge. He was so important in the treaty fight that one might almost say he was a group in himself.

Lodge was slender, narrow-shouldered, and aristocratically bewhiskered. Sprung from the stony soil of Massachusetts, and nurtured by the New England aristocracy, he fell heir to all the advantages of wealth, education, culture, travel, and social position. Educated at Harvard University, where he took the degree of Ph.D. in history, Dr. Lodge early undertook a literary career. From his pen poured a succession of books, chiefly on historical subjects, some of which had their brief day, but none of which has lived or has deserved to live. He also revealed a flair for politics, and by faithful party service he secured a strangle hold on his seat in the Senate, and became chairman of the Senate Committee on Foreign Relations. Cold, cautious, aloof, aristocratic as he was, one wonders at the secret of his appeal to the masses.

Three Little Elephants
(Courtesy of Brooklyn *Eagle*; cartoonist Harding)

For many years Dr. Lodge enjoyed the distinction of being "the scholar in politics." Then came Professor Wilson, whose political and scholarly attainments eclipsed those of Lodge, and the senator's flattering sobriquet dropped into disuse. This was no doubt displeasing to the learned solon.

All of Lodge's forbears had reached America before the Revolutionary War; all of Wilson's had come well after the establishment of the Republic. Lodge took naturally to nationalism; Wilson more naturally to internationalism—possibly as a result, in part, of his heredity.

Yet Lodge, before the arrival of Wilson on the scene, had shown signs of broadening horizons, as had other leaders of the traditionally expansionist and imperialistic Republican party. He had warmly supported his bosom friend, "dear Theodore" Roosevelt, in the various international adventures upon which the brandisher of the Big Stick embarked. He had made speeches in favor of some kind of international organization for peace, and in 1915 had even come out for *a* league of nations. But shortly thereafter Wilson began to advocate *the* League, and Lodge found himself in the other camp. The senator in his apologia strongly denies that this was anything but mental growth. Chronology and circumstance suggest that it was not disassociated from the feud with Wilson.

Contrary to a general misconception, Lodge was not an isolationist of the Borah or Johnson stripe. On the eve of the Peace Conference he was willing to go even further than Wilson in making the United States a part-guarantor of the European settlement. He said repeatedly that, League or no League, the world could count on us again to spring to the defense of Western civilization against ruthless aggression.

9

The whole bent of Lodge's thinking had naturally predisposed him to entertain kindly thoughts toward the Covenant that Wilson brought back from Paris. But it was a Democratic League, from which the Democrats could make political capital, and all the partisan instincts of the senator rose to the surface.

Above all things Lodge was a partisan, a narrow and bitter partisan, who believed that the Republican party was the embodiment of all the virtues. In 1914 he had made an eloquent speech about politics stopping "at the water's edge"; but this was pure rhetoric. He probably would have denied that he would basely subordinate the interests of his country to those of his party, but so ingrained was his Republicanism that he did not find it difficult to convince himself that the interests of both were identical. With him party regularity was a religion.

Lodge realized as clearly as anyone that it would be politically unwise for the Republicans to permit Wilson and his Democratic following to garner all the glory from the League. The Republicans must be allowed to add something to it, just enough to pose as co-authors of the pact.

With disarming candor, Lodge outlines in his posthumous book the strategy which he employed. He would load the treaty down with Republican reservations, and in this way "Americanize" or "Republicanize" the document, thus safeguarding both the country and the party. If Wilson accepted the Lodge reservations, then the Republicans would be sharers of the glory; if he did not, then the onus for rejecting the entire pact would be on the President's shoulders, not on those of the Republicans. Either way the Republican party could make political capital.

When the corpse of the treaty was finally dragged from the senatorial arena, the friends of international cooperation pointed the finger of accusation at Lodge, and since then have kept it unwaveringly there.

This is a gross oversimplification. The struggle was exceedingly complex; there were all shades of opinion; there were varying and conflicting motives; there were currents and cross-currents. To say that one senator alone killed Cock Robin is to betray obtuseness or mental inertia.

So poisonous were the hatreds stirred up by Lodge that his position has seldom been viewed in proper perspective. He was chairman of the Foreign Relations Committee. He was majority leader, not because of personal charm, but because men respected his skill as a party manager and parliamentarian.

His speeches were able, dignified, and usually on a high plane. His two-hour condemnation of the League, on August 12, 1919, was delivered at a time when the galleries were crowded with marines who had returned from Château-Thierry. The unprecedented roar that greeted his peroration lasted for three minutes, and sounded like the ovation accorded the home-town hero who knocks the ball into the right-field bleachers.

Lodge's responsibilities were heavy and conflicting. He was a foremost defender of senatorial prerogative. He was leader of the party in the Senate and the official spokesman for the various factions within the party. His immediate task was two-fold: first, to propose and carry through a specific program of reservations; second, to keep the party ranks intact, and pre-vent any such schism as had developed in 1912. His primary duty, as he conceived it, was not to unite the world but to unite the party.

The Massachusetts senator was in the plight of one attempt-ing to ride three horses trying to go in three different direc-tions. The body of the Republican senators—the "strong reser-vationists"—were not too difficult to manage; they were going down the middle of the track. But on one side the dozen "mild reservationists" were momentarily threatening to coalesce with the Democrats. On the other side the "bitter-enders" were threatening to bolt the party completely, or go over to the Democrats and vote through reservations objectionable to Lodge. At one time the Massachusetts senator complained that the "irreconcilables" were addressing him in language which "no man of my age should be obliged to hear."

While Lodge was trying to curb the three horses, he had to keep closely in touch with the party managers outside the Senate so that the strategy of the campaign of 1920 could be carefully mapped. Above all, he had to restrain his personal dislike of Wilson for fear that he would appear to be a "sore-head." It has been well said that Lodge had "a hard enough time keeping his temper without stopping to consult his con-science."

10

The bitterness of feeling between Lodge and Wilson was intense and was perhaps the most formidable single barrier in the way of compromise.

The two men simply rubbed each other the wrong way. Lodge insists that his distrust of Wilson was wholly on public grounds, and began with the administration's alleged misconduct of relations with Mexico. The feud broke out into the open in 1916, when Lodge accused Wilson of suppressing certain vital information regarding the *Lusitania* negotiations. Wilson, in a not altogether candid reply, delicately branded the senator a liar, and from then on the breach widened.

Colonel Bonsal talked with Lodge about the League Covenant in November, 1919. "As an English production it does not rank high," said Lodge, perhaps half jokingly. "It might get by at Princeton but certainly not at Harvard." Colonel House observed at Paris that President Wilson "bristled" whenever Lodge's name was mentioned. On the few occasions when the President and the senator had to meet, the interchanges were severely formal, and the atmosphere could seemingly be cut with a knife.

Both the senator and the President were bitter partisans, lasting haters. In life, Lodge outwardly restrained his innermost feelings, at least in public. But he forgot about the Old Testament patriarch who expressed the desire that his "adversary had written a book." The senator prepared an elaborate, posthumously published apology, in which his embittered spirit rose from the grave to reveal what he had previously been at pains to conceal.

"I never had the slightest personal hostility to Mr. Wilson," writes Lodge. He goes on to say that Wilson was not a true scholar at all, and as proof stresses the fact that, unlike Lodge, the Princeton professor did not stud his speeches with classical allusions—which any sterile wit may crib from compilations of quotations.

The senator finally convicts Wilson of not having been a scholar, and perhaps not even an educated man, when he gleefully reveals that on the one occasion when he found the Princetonian using a classical reference, it was used incorrectly. Wilson committed the terrible error of having Hercules, rather than Antaeus, renew his strength as he touched Mother Earth.

This does not prove that Wilson was unscholarly. All it proves is that Lodge had a jealous and petty spirit.

CHAPTER FIVE

THE STRATEGY OF STRANGULATION

"The mere fact that President Wilson wants something is not an argument against it." Philadelphia PUBLIC LEDGER, *quoted in the* LITERARY DIGEST, *December 6, 1919.*

1

ONCE THE Treaty of Versailles was formally before the Senate, it was referred as a matter of course to the powerful Foreign Relations Committee, a traditional graveyard of presidential hopes. The signs did not point to a hospitable reception.

When Congress had convened nearly two months earlier, the Republicans controlled the Senate by a narrow margin, and thus it was that Lodge became head of the Foreign Relations Committee. The "scholar in politics" went to great pains to see to it that the newly appointed members of his committee were not too kindly disposed toward the League.

Four new places were to be filled by Republicans. Kellogg of Minnesota was a logical choice for one of them, but the firmness of his opposition to the League was suspect. Lodge made it clear to him that he might have a place if he would promise in advance to support the chairman's decisions and carry out his policies. But Kellogg's self-respect would not permit him to be a Lodge rubber stamp, and he said as much. The vacancy was then filled by Moses of New Hampshire, a relative newcomer but an unflinching "irreconcilable."

The four new Republican members (Harding of Ohio, New of Indiana, Johnson of California, and Moses of New Hampshire) were all at least "strong reservationists." Two of them, Johnson and Moses, were among the most active "bitter-enders." Of the two new Democratic members (with whose appointment Lodge had nothing to do) one, Shields of Tennessee, was so independently minded on the League question as to be an "irreconcilable."

Altogether, there were ten Republicans and seven Democrats on the committee. Only one of the Republicans, McCumber of North Dakota, favored the treaty without alteration. Six of the ablest and most bellicose Republican "irreconcilables" (out of a total of fourteen) now had places on the committee. In addition to Moses and Johnson, there were Borah of Idaho, Brandegee of Connecticut, Knox of Pennsylvania, and Fall of New Mexico. *Thus the "bitterenders," though constituting about one-seventh of the Senate, were able to outvote the Republican majority representatives on the Foreign Relations Committee.*

Why did Lodge, who professed to want the treaty with adequate reservations, pack the committee with "irreconcilables" whose avowed purpose was to bring about the complete ruin of the treaty? The scholarly senator vouchsafes no answer in his apologia except to say, "It will be seen at once that this was a strong committee and such as the existing conditions demanded." Verily, it was.

Fair-minded persons naturally condemned this flagrant packing of the committee. Ex-President Taft openly voiced his dissatisfaction in public speeches. Even some of the Senate Republicans were quietly unhappy, while their Democratic colleagues protested stridently. When Senator Thomas of Colorado (Democrat) accused the Republicans of stacking the cards against Wilson by packing the committee, Senator McCormick of Illinois (Republican "irreconcilable") replied that Wilson had "stacked the Peace Conference with Democrats." This, unfortunately, was uncomfortably close to the truth.

2

We remember that when Wilson submitted the treaty to the Senate he announced that he was ready to confer with the

members and give them such information as he had. Nearly a
week went by, and there was no response to the invitation.
Wilson then decided to take matters into his own hands by
summoning individual senators to the White House for conferences. About twenty Republicans were invited and put in
an appearance.

This, on the face of it, seemed like a conciliatory gesture;
and in some ways it was. If it had been made before Wilson
went to Paris, it might have had far-reaching results; but it
now came much too late. The President, as a matter of fact,
undertook these conferences with great reluctance. Senator
Hitchcock later recalled that it was difficult to persuade him
to employ such tactics: he was temperamentally unable to
flatter and coax.

Hitchcock assisted in making up the list of Republican
senators who were to be invited. Some of the proposed names,
Wilson rejected out of hand. Finally, the list was complete,
and invitations were sent out by letter in three batches. The
Democrats were not included in these individual conferences,
although Wilson talked with eleven of them at one time late
in July. They could be counted upon to support the administration anyhow.

The great body of Republican invitees was drawn from the
"mild reservationists" and from those of the "strong reservationists" who seemed open to reason. The bitterest of the
"bitter-enders" were completely passed by; invitations were
sent to only two of the "irreconcilables," Fernald of Maine,
who came; and Norris of Nebraska, who in a courteous letter
declined to come. He gave as his reasons, first, that he would
be honor bound not to discuss afterward any of the matters
considered, some of which were public property anyhow; and
second, that it would take too much of Wilson's valuable
time to confer with each senator. It would be better, he said,
for the President to send over to the Senate, in the usual way,
such information as he wished to submit.

Wilson's omission of most of the "bitter-enders" seems to

have been fully justified. It would have been a complete waste of time to try sweet reasonableness with rigidly closed minds. Yet, because the Foreign Relations Committee was packed with "irreconcilables," only three of its ten Republican members were invited, and Lodge was not one of them.

3

The time-consuming private conferences with the Republican senators ran about an hour each. On one day Wilson was closeted individually for three hours with three; on another day he talked four hours with four during successive appointments. Most of the senators spoke freely to the reporters about their experience, and from these accounts we may piece together what went on behind White House doors.

The conferees were virtually unanimous in agreeing that Wilson did not try to browbeat them into accepting his views. He evidently conceived of his role as explicatory rather than hortatory. He explained what had happened at Paris; the reasons for certain decisions; and the nature of some of the secret data. He emphasized the necessity for haste, and especially the desirability of avoiding reservations. These, he said, would necessitate a reopening of the conference, cause further delay, and encourage Germany to make additional demands.

The senators were likewise unanimous in agreeing that Wilson's remarks had not altered their fundamental position, although Senators Capper and McNary admitted that he had somewhat softened their opposition to the so-called "surrender" of the Chinese province of Shantung to Japan. Many if not most of the senators made it clear to the President that the treaty simply could not be ratified without reservations of some kind.

Senator Watson of Indiana was the only one of the invitees who published his recollections of the event. He found Wilson very cordial, and asking, "Where am I in the Senate on this fight?" "Mr. President," replied Watson, "you are licked."

Wilson expressed amazement when Watson said that the administration could count on only twenty-four votes for the proposed mandate over Armenia. As the conference ended, Watson said to the President that there was only one way to take America into the League, and that was, "Accept it with the Lodge reservations."

"Accept the Treaty with the *Lodge* reservations?" Wilson replied scornfully. "Never! Never! I'll never consent to adopt any policy with which that impossible name is so prominently identified." Watson almost certainly did not remember Wilson's exact words, and possibly he misread their spirit; but the general import of his version squares with the President's known views.

It is doubtful whether these individual conferences helped the cause of the League in any appreciable way. But they did show that Wilson was prepared to make a fair and frank attempt, albeit belatedly, to meet the senators on their own ground. The conferences also indicate that the President recognized to some extent the necessity of wooing the "mild reservationists."

But the whole strategy of the conferences was poor. They involved an undue expenditure of time and energy. The same result, and possibly better results, could have been achieved if Wilson had invited the senators in small groups, with perhaps a few Democrats present.

Unfortunately also, the individual senators were forced into an awkward position. The news that they were going to the White House was heralded in advance on the front page of the newspapers. The question on the public lip was, "Will they bend the knee?" When they emerged from the White House the news hawks were there with pencil and notebook to record whether they had cravenly surrendered. The whole business savored of the naughty boy being called into the principal's office for a scolding. The natural disposition of the proud senators was to show their mettle by making up their minds in advance that they would not yield anything, and none of them apparently did. Much of this inevitable public pressure would have been removed if the senators had met with Wilson in quiet groups.

4

Informed observers generally agree that if the treaty could have been brought to a speedy vote it would have been approved with no worse than mild reservations. This is not only the judgment of present-day scholars; "bitter-ender" senators like Moses openly confessed as much when the fight was over.

The strategy of the foes of the treaty was, as we have seen, the strategy of delay. Time was on their side. The longer they kept the treaty tied up in the committee and before the Senate, the more they sent out speakers and distributed propaganda, the brighter their prospects of success. Public opinion would gradually become confused, less insistent on action, and finally somewhat indifferent to substantial changes or even outright rejection.

The "irreconcilables" were able to control time, because they were the controlling bloc on the Foreign Relations Committee. With the cooperation of Lodge, they could and did lock the treaty up indefinitely, while their orators and their propaganda were sowing doubts and winning converts. Early in the fight hundreds of thousands of copies of speeches by Lodge, Knox, Borah, and others were scattered throughout the country.

If the "irreconcilables" could control time, they had more trouble with money. A nation-wide campaign of "education" was costly, with such items as pamphlets, postage, clerical help, traveling expenses, the hiring of halls, and newspaper advertising. The game might be lost unless an adequate war chest could be scraped together.

One evening in May, 1919, a group of gloomy "bitter-enders" met at the home of Senator Brandegee. The campaign thus far had been progressing favorably, especially in the isolationist Middle West, where the powerful support of the Chicago *Tribune* and the Kansas City *Star* had been enlisted. But funds were melting away, and unless the campaign of starting backfires behind wavering senators was to be abandoned, new resources would have to be tapped.

Senator Knox suggested the name of a fellow Pennsylvanian, the multimillionaire "coke king" and art collector, Henry Clay Frick. One of the non-senatorial "irreconcilables," presumably George Harvey, who describes himself as the "delegated conspirator," journeyed to New York, where he laid the "stock" arguments before this hardheaded businessman.

When Frick heard that the United States, the richest of the nations, was going to join a League in which it could allegedly be outvoted by the other nations, chiefly its debtors, he exclaimed: "I am opposed to that. Of course I am. I don't see how any experienced businessman could fail to be. Why, it seems to me a crazy thing to do."

The aged philanthropist, who was bitterly anti-Democratic, liberally underwrote the "irreconcilable" campaign of "education," and followed it with keen interest. He died about six months later, and three days before the end, upon receiving encouraging report of progress, he smiled contentedly and pronounced it "good."

Senator Knox himself approached Andrew W. Mellon, another Pittsburgh multimillionaire and art collector, who for his services to the party was made Secretary of the Treasury and later Ambassador to the Court of St. James's. Mellon agreed to duplicate Frick's substantial contribution; and the "Battalion of Death," with two of the wealthiest "angels" in America behind it, could push on with renewed enthusiasm to ultimate victory.

The friends of the treaty, notably the League to Enforce Peace, also raised money for propaganda to support their views. But their efforts seem to have been far more open and aboveboard.

5

We must return to the meeting room of the Senate Foreign Relations Committee.

At the outset, and in pursuance of his strategy of delay, Senator Lodge read aloud the entire text of the 268-page treaty. This totally unnecessary and unedifying farce consumed a valuable two weeks, and can be explained on no other rational basis than a desire to play for time. It was unnecessary because the treaty had promptly been put into printed form, and it is fair to assume that the senators were sufficiently literate to read it themselves more rapidly than Lodge could read it to them. It was unedifying because the members could obviously study the treaty more effectively through the printed word than through the cultured intonations of their colleague.

Most of the oral reading was done before a sparse committee; some of the time only the clerk was present; and at one point on the last day the distinguished senior senator from Massachusetts was left alone to drone along before completely empty chairs. If haste had been a primary consideration, surely the learned Lodge could have completed 268 pages in less than two weeks.

Once the treaty had been read aloud, the committee arranged to protract the delay by holding public hearings, which began on July 31, 1919, and lasted to September 12, a total of six weeks. About sixty witnesses appeared, and a total of 1,297 pages of printed testimony was preserved for posterity. In a very real sense the League of Nations was drowned in a sea of words.

The hearings were ostensibly for the edification of the senators, and in some measure they undoubtedly served this purpose. But the unannounced objectives were to consume time, stir up prejudice, and further confuse the public mind. (The "confusionists" were in some ways more formidable than the isolationists.) The real purposes were betrayed at the outset when the committee decided to resort to the unusual expedient of public hearings.

Senator Lodge insisted that the Senate was not delaying the treaty unduly. It had taken Wilson nearly six months, with some thirteen hundred assistants, to draw up the pact, and the Senate, Lodge felt, ought to be pardoned for devoting a

"Stop Playing Politics"

(From New York *Evening World*; cartoonist Cassel;
reprinted by permission)

few weeks to a study of this exceedingly complicated instrument. The President had ignored the senators while drafting the treaty; now was their chance to find out what was in it. Lodge complained that neither he nor anyone whom he knew really understood it; yet Wilson was urging the Senate to rubber-stamp an instrument of immense importance—an instrument which would profoundly affect the foreign policy and perhaps the very structure of the United States government.

With such fears allegedly holding them to their task, the committee went ahead with the hearings. Some of the first witnesses who appeared had been at Paris, and they were in a position to contribute first-hand information of some value. Among those who took the stand were Bernard M. Baruch (who had worked on reparations); David Hunter Miller (an architect of the League Covenant who was badgered by his inquisitors); and Secretary of State Lansing, whose sensational testimony will be discussed later.

The committee had one inflexible rule. It would permit only American citizens to testify, and this eliminated a host of aliens who were eager to argue impassionedly and interminably for their native lands. Many of the witnesses were summoned; others came at their own request. Lodge says that it was impossible to deny these people a hearing.

This statement is open to serious doubt. The committee unquestionably was empowered to reject those whom it did not want to hear, even though there was great pressure from scores of groups to have their day in court. The circumstantial evidence indicates that the committee generally favored witnesses who were likely to embarrass Wilson and the friends of the League.

The closing stages of the hearings degenerated into flagrant and irrelevant appeals to partisanship and prejudice. Former friends who had broken with Wilson were allowed to unbosom themselves. A sop was thrown to the England-haters when the committee sought to establish the British origins of the League of Nations. Ireland, too, had her inning, with a Tammany-Irish orator, among others, evoking warm and frequent applause for the cause of Hibernian freedom.

Representatives of other national or racial groups were able to find some American citizen to plead their cause, while in at least one case they remained at his elbow with promptings. There were self-appointed spokesmen for the aspirations of the Negroes, Egypt, Persia, Ukraina, China, Greece, Albania, Czechoslovakia, Yugoslavia, Hungary, Esthonia, Latvia, Lithuania (moving pictures were shown of German atrocities in Lithuania), India, and Italy (represented by the future mayor of New York, F. H. La Guardia). Sweden's claims to the Åland Islands were argued by a man who admitted that he spoke no Swedish. The height of absurdity was reached when a woman with an Irish name urged the claim of Italy to Yugoslavia's Fiume.

Lodge insists that all this could not have been avoided, for the treaty was a world treaty. But he neglects to explain how the pact related to Ireland, or India, or Egypt, or Korea, or racial equality for Negroes in the United States. It looked as though the senators thought it their duty to prevent rather than complete the treaty; to hunt mare's nests for the discrediting of Wilson while Europe starved and the world slowly crumbled to pieces.

The sapient senators sat solemnly in their seats and listened to arguments for the independence of India, as though they understood the problem and could do something about it. Neither was a valid assumption. But silent listening to various grievance mongers seemed to indicate sympathy, and this might please the Irish, Italian, and Negro voters. It was good politics, if nothing else.

6

The Senate hearings were not usually front-page copy. When the testimony was relevant to the treaty, which much of it was not, the allegations were usually old information, minor information, or relatively minor shadings of something important. There were two exceptions. One was the bombshell of William C. Bullitt which, we shall later note, burst forth spectacularly while Wilson was on his western tour. The other was the testimony of Secretary of State Lansing.

Lansing presented a rather pathetic figure. He did not shed

much light on the treaty, because he had not had much to do with it; but he did shed a flood of light on himself and his relations with Wilson. For the first time it became painfully evident that the President had largely ignored his Secretary of State.

The most startling statements of Lansing were two. He expressed the opinion that Wilson could have secured justice for China without the alleged surrendering of Shantung to Japan. This, of course, was only the Secretary's personal opinion, but it was seized upon gleefully by those who were assailing the Far Eastern clauses of the treaty.

Lansing also said that until he arrived in Paris he knew nothing of the secret pact between Japan and Britain for the division of Germany's Pacific islands. Lansing's ignorance of the secret treaties in general, and of this treaty in particular, merely added strength to the isolationist argument that the other powers were dishonest tricksters who would trade us out of our eyeteeth if we ventured to sit down with them in any League of Nations.

The net result was that Wilson's position was weakened, and he was thrown further on the defensive.

7

The breach between the President and the committee had in the meanwhile been gradually widening. In particular, Lodge and his colleagues complained that Wilson was refusing to provide them with data necessary for an understanding of the pact.

We need do no more than sketch the outlines of this part of the story. The committee requested stenographic records of the secret conferences in Paris. Wilson refused on the ground that such confidences could not be revealed without breaking faith with the governments concerned. The committee likewise requested a copy of the protest against the Shantung decision which a group of his experts had sent to the President. Wilson refused on the ground that this document reflected unfavorably on friendly governments. The committee also requested copies of the draft treaties which were then being drawn up with Austria, Hungary, Bulgaria, and Turkey. Wilson refused on the ground that this would take the constitutional function of negotiating treaties out of the hands of the Executive.

In every case Wilson's decision seems to have been fully justified on the grounds of precedent and public interest. It is highly probable that these repeated senatorial requests were made with the expectation that they would be refused, and in the hope that they would be, for the President would then appear as obdurate, uncooperative, and dictatorial. Anything to discredit Wilson.

The committee now decided on a new tack. The parade of witnesses was not providing much information; Wilson would not send over secret data of a confidential nature. It finally dawned on the solons that the man who probably knew most about the making of the treaty lived in Washington, about a mile from the Capitol. If they were really seeking information, why not go to him?

It will be remembered that Wilson, when presenting the treaty to the Senate, had announced that he was at the disposal of that body. This, as it turned out, was poor strategy, for it placed the initiative squarely in the hands of his opponents on the Foreign Relations Committee. If, at the outset, he had invited the committee to meet with him, it could not very well have refused, and he might have been able to take the offensive and start the discussion off with greater momentum.

On August 14, 1919, more than a month after the submission of the pact, Senator Lodge, speaking for the members of his committee, requested the President to meet with them, provided the proceedings were completely public. Wilson promptly and graciously acceded, and in addition invited the committee to have lunch with him. He chose August 19 as the day, ten o'clock as the time, and the stately East Room of the White House as the place.

This was the first time that a President had ever consented to meet the Foreign Relations Committee at the White House and be publicly grilled by it. The newspapers and press associations were impressed with the importance of the occasion, and nearly a hundred correspondents gathered in the corridors, with desks, typewriters, and other equipment. Relays of expert stenographers were on hand to record a verbatim account of what was revealed, and put it on the wires while it was still "hot."

On the appointed morning, the big iron gates of the White House grounds were thrown open to the senatorial inquisitors, who arrived singly or in small groups. Senator Lodge drove up in a big automobile; Borah came on foot, carrying a bulky copy of the treaty under his arm, like a schoolboy about to attend class. Only Senator Shields, a Democrat not in sympathy with Wilson's views, failed to put in an appearance.

After greeting his guests with a smile, Wilson read a brief prepared statement in which he stressed our moral obligation to ratify speedily. Then he subjected himself to about three and one-half hours of interrogation. Though slightly nervous, he was seemingly candid, quick in his responses, and in good temper, as were his questioners. Only once did he reveal a trace of impatience, for the color mounted to his cheeks when it was recalled that Secretary Lansing had testified against the Shantung "surrender." At the end of the period, the President, plainly fatigued, accompanied the senators to the luncheon room, and when the meal was over the party broke up in evident good spirits.

8

We need concern ourselves here with only the most significant aspects of Wilson's testimony.

Much of the discussion centered about Article X, which

had been pictured by its foes as an agency to beget war rather than to promote peace. Wilson made it clear that he not only regarded Article X as the "backbone" of the covenant, but that he as much as anyone was the author of it. He pointed out that since the Article was permissive in its obligations, it was morally rather than legally binding. No superbody could order us about, he said, for *in any given case we would consult our consciences and act accordingly*.

When Senator Harding suggested that we would not have to honor a moral obligation, Wilson replied, "Why, Senator, it is surprising that that question should be asked." For his part, the President regarded a moral obligation as stronger than a legal one: a person might escape legal technicalities, but he could not escape his conscience.

Senator Johnson of California, no doubt mindful of his large anti-Japanese constituency, harped on the Shantung settlement, and drew from the President the candid admission that it was not completely satisfactory. The cause of Wilson and the League was not helped when it was made to appear that the Shantung decision was in the nature of blackmail to keep Japan in the League.

Wilson also made it clear that he was willing to accept reservations of a purely interpretive nature, as long as they were embodied in a *separate resolution,* and as long as they *did not require the assent of Germany and the Allied Powers*. This was rather surprising, because only four days earlier Senator Hitchcock had come away from the White House saying that Wilson opposed reservations.

The President made a curious slip when he said that any changes in the Covenant of the League would not require the consent of Germany. He was thinking of the Reich as a non-member of the League, rather than as a signatory of the treaty. Over in the Senate the Democratic leaders were further embarrassed, because they had been energetically taking the opposite point of view. Wilson's slip was excusable, but he further weakened and humiliated the Democratic leadership by betraying that he was not working in close harmony with it.

On the question of the secret treaties, Wilson was guilty of more than a slip. He insisted, under repeated questioning, that he had known nothing of them before going to Paris. This, as we now know, was untrue. Some have argued that he forgot, which seems improbable; that he was fatigued, as he no doubt was later in the session; or possibly that he was caught off guard. This seems hardly credible. Only two weeks before, Lansing had caused a sensation when the same question was asked him, and it is most improbable that Wilson could have failed to anticipate similar grilling.

The real explanation, which has been discussed elsewhere,* will probably remain buried in the crypt with Wilson. It seems likely that he did not want to weaken his position further by a candid admission. To have confessed that he knew all about the baleful pacts before going to Paris would no doubt have evoked embarrassing inquiry as to why he did not do more to bring about their abrogation.

Wilson had been the chief spokesman for American and Allied war aims. Yet here he was confessing that he had known nothing about the secret mortgages on the happiness of millions of peoples—mortgages, as George Harvey put it, "conceived in sin and born of the desire for empire grabbing." The *New Republic* brutally concluded that Wilson was either an "incompetent or a liar."

9

Opinions varied as to the skill with which the President had conducted himself at the senatorial inquest. His friends, like Senator Hitchcock, went away feeling that he had been "keen and careful," and that he had upheld the Covenant effectively. Wilson had seemed filled with the subject; he had handled the questions in a masterly manner. His worshipful private

* T. A. Bailey, *Woodrow Wilson and the Lost Peace*, pp. 147-148, 347-348.

secretary, Tumulty, felt that he had "parried every blow"; that he had never been "more tactful or more brilliant in repartee."

The President's enemies found fresh confirmation of their prejudices. Lodge was forced to admit that Wilson had taken the questions, which were "rather sharp at times," in "good

"We'll Never Sign It!"

(From New York *World*; cartoonist Kirby; reprinted by permission)

part." But the incorrigible Brandegee contemptuously remarked, "What is the use of probing into an intellectual apparatus like that?"

Wilson, on his part, found fresh confirmation of his low opinion of the senatorial intellect. A few days later, at a Cabinet meeting, he remarked that "Senator Harding had a disturbingly dull mind, and that it seemed impossible to get any explanation to lodge in it."

While it is probably true that the Democratic friends of

the League came away with heightened enthusiasm, there is no evidence that a single member of the committee changed either his mind or his vote. It is also probable that the "bitter-enders" were nettled by their inability to "show Wilson up."

As far as the committee itself was concerned, the affair was a failure. But other senators, not present, read the testimony, and newspaper readers all over the country were further instructed—or confused. The Chicago *Tribune* ran a headline above the report of the conference: "U.S. ARMS AT LEAGUE'S BECK, WILSON ADMITS." The printed testimony reveals no such admission.

But all is fair in love and war. And this was war—war on Wilson.

CHAPTER SIX

THE APPEAL TO THE PEOPLE

"I am ready to fight from now until all the fight has been taken out of me by death to redeem the faith and promises of the United States." WOODROW WILSON *at Spokane, Washington, September 12, 1919.*

1

WILSON'S DECISION to make a spectacular stumping tour across the country in behalf of the treaty was one of the most momentous decisions of his entire career, perhaps the most momentous. As it turned out, the tour was a disastrous blunder. It not only wrecked Wilson's health, but in a very real sense helped wreck the League of Nations, and with it the hopes of humanity.

The decision to make the trip is generally represented as a sudden impulse, an act of desperation, a supreme effort to build up a backfire of public opinion against the stubborn senators and thus save the treaty.

It was undoubtedly an act of desperation, but it was clearly not a sudden impulse. More than two months before returning from Paris the President stated that he expected to make a tour of the country, but he could not yet be certain that he would. There were even earlier intimations in the newspapers that he was going to barnstorm from the Potomac to the Pacific.

When Wilson reached home in July it was taken for granted that he would make his "swing around the circle." The question was not: Will he? It was: When will he? The anti-League senators were aware of his plan, and somewhat uneasy about it. Senator Moses proposed that the Foreign Relations Committee take advantage of the President's gracious offer to appear before it by requesting that he come every day at ten o'clock, and thus keep him from departing. This was a cheap trick, worthy of the "wisecracking" Moses, but it was so naked that not even the other "irreconcilables" dared push it.

2

While the general plan to swing West was no sudden inspiration, it is probable that Wilson would have spared himself such an ordeal if the fight for the treaty had been going well. Possibly he had let his intentions leak out in the first place so that he might hold the threat of a country-wide appeal over the Senate.

But the fight was not going well. The friends of the League were plainly losing ground. The results of the White House conference had been most discouraging, not only with regard to arousing public opinion, but also with regard to moving the senators. The Republican majority on the Foreign Relations Committee was now pressing forward with its plans to amend the treaty drastically.

Wilson was also distressed by growing signs of defection among his own followers in the Senate: some were betraying a friendliness for strong reservations, a few others were downright hostile to the League. The committee, moreover, had the treaty tied up, seemingly forever, and the protracted hearings were now degenerating into a Roman holiday of prejudice and passion. Some drastic and spectacular move must be made to pry the pact from the death grip of the "bitter-enders." "Seems easier to get into war than peace," gloomily remarked the *Wall Street Journal*.

The fever chart of Europe was reacting unfavorably to the exhibition of delay and impotence in the Senate. The final settlements with the other Central Powers were dragging because of the evident reluctance of Uncle Sam to jump into the international pond, certainly not without a superfluity of life-preservers. The prostrate Germans were taking heart, and there was still the alarming possibility that they might balk at going through with the final ratification of the Treaty of Versailles.

This was the discouraging predicament late in August, 1919, when friends of the treaty on Capitol Hill came to Wilson and urged him to make the contemplated tour. It was hardly necessary for them to use much persuasion; the President was already convinced that heroic measures were imperative.

Wilson, as we have seen, had indestructible faith in the power of public opinion—in democracy itself. The people

Going to Talk to the Boss

(Courtesy of Chicago *Daily News*; cartoonist Brown)

could be relied upon to judge correctly when the issues were placed clearly and truthfully before them. He had appealed over the head of Congress before, and with no little success, notably when he had built a fire under backward senators and had routed the insidious tariff lobby in 1913.

He would again appeal to the court of last resort—the court of public opinion. He would "go to the country" and arouse the people against their obstructive senators. He was tired of appealing to the better instincts of the politicians in Washington; he would go out and appeal to the source of their power, which was also the source of his power. He would keep his plea, as he wrote privately, on a strictly nonpartisan basis. Where the electorate was nation-wide, and the cause world-wide, there was no place for narrow partisanship. Yet Wilson apparently forgot that the President is the head of a great political party, and in a technical sense he can make no purely nonpolitical speeches.

Wilson was a fighter, and his Scotch-Irish blood quickened at the prospect of an open battle. It had been galling to his spirit to have to sit quietly in the White House and watch ignorant and designing men not only misrepresent but manhandle the League to which he had devoted so much of his intellect and energy. He was forced to be quiet, courteous, dignified, gentlemanly, while inwardly he was impatient, uncompromising, militant. He could now let himself go and fight for his great cause on a nation-wide stage. His imagination was fired, as Senator Hitchcock later testified, by the prospect of stirring up such a popular storm that the Senate would be forced to come to heel.

3

All these reasons for a western tour no doubt seemed plausible. But even without the wisdom of hindsight it should have been evident that, barring some kind of political miracle, the President had little to gain and everything to lose by this wild venture.

Wilson, it must be admitted, was not at his best on the stump. Thoroughly at home behind the lecturer's desk, he was an effective speaker of the academic type: cold rather than warm, intellectual rather than emotional, dispassionate rather than impassionate. Men might listen to his precise prose with respect and admiration, but he lacked Theodore Roosevelt's animal heat—the capacity for arousing mass affection. People did not "go insane in pairs" over him.

The pedagogue-President had no gift for dramatizing what he had done, for presenting his deeds in their heroic aspects. He was constitutionally incapable of brutally getting down to cases, and speaking in the most concrete of terms. His mind and his speech ran naturally to abstractions—to ideals, hopes, aspirations, responsibilities, and duties.

He had no desire to resort to cheap or undignified tricks, like Theodore Roosevelt, and was temperamentally unable to do so. Time and again his friends urged him to adopt the devices of the demagogue, and his answer was, "I can't make myself over." No man of his age could. On the trip it was suggested that he "warm up a bit," pull out all the stops, and give the audiences some "sob stuff." His answer was an indignant refusal to "capitalize on the dead." Wilson was too honest to make a convincing demagogue, even if he had tried to be one. Yet he deliberately chose to get down off his high pedestal in the White House and meet the rabble-rousers on their own ground and attempt to use their own weapons—weapons which they were more adept in using than he.

Many of Wilson's foes were joined by some of his friends in saying that the President was needed in Washington rather than in the West. The treaty was not the only issue before the country: at times it seemed like a minor one. Labor was uneasy; the high cost of living seemed much closer to home than the League. Two resolutions were actually introduced in Congress by Republicans who allegedly wanted the President to stay in the capital and deal with inescapable domestic problems. Even if he returned alive and well, he would still be gone for about a month, and that was a long time for the engineer to take his hand off the throttle.

A potent argument against Wilson's going was the necessity for his staying in Washington to direct the treaty fight. He needed to keep in close touch with the Democratic leaders, something he had thus far conspicuously failed to do. He needed also to entice the "mild reservationists" into the Democratic camp, something that there was still hope of doing. It was clear to every cool-headed observer that by this time the treaty could not be approved without at least mild reservations. Then let Wilson stay in the White House, work out a compromise, and get the pact out of the way. Certainly he had compromised enough in Paris; let him compromise a little in Washington.

This was logical reasoning, and Wilson, as the event proved, would have been well advised if he had followed it. But he was evidently not convinced of the necessity of doing these things, and he seems to have had an exaggerated conception of his influence over the people.

4

A final reason against Wilson's going was the unanswerable one that he probably could not succeed even if he did succeed. In less contradictory terms, he could hardly have forced the Senate into a speedy and unreserved approval of the pact even if the results of the tour had exceeded all reasonable expectations.

Wilson had written in 1908 that the Senate was much less responsive than the House to the pressure of public opinion. This was still true. The senators are elected for a six-year term, and only one-third of them come up for reelection every two years. The next election was to be in November, 1920, fifteen months ahead.

The average senator knew that he did not have to worry unduly about his stand on the League. His term was long; the memory of the voters is short. The League would presumably be a dead issue by 1920; certainly by 1922 and 1924. New problems would arise in the meantime, some of them vitally important to the people of the individual states; and, if the senator was "right" on local issues, why need he worry about the League?

There is no reason to believe that such "bitter-enders" as Borah of Idaho and Johnson of California faithfully reflected the views of their constituents. There is ample evidence to show that a great many of the California voters were dissatisfied with their senator's stand on the treaty, and on international affairs in general. But Johnson was reelected by tremendous majorities in 1922, 1928, 1934, and 1940. He might be all wrong on the League and the World Court, but he was "sound" on such local issues as the tariff on prunes, lemons, and nuts. Besides, old-timers could not forget that he had crushed the Southern Pacific machine, and why should young whipper-snappers try to displace their hero?

There is no reason to suppose that Idaho was as isolationist as Borah. But Borah was "sound" on the wool and potato issues, and besides he was the only man of really national stature whom the state had produced. In a political sense, he was Idaho's chief export, its principal claim to national fame. He was of presidential timber, and it would be a great honor to have an Idahoan in the White House. Borah would be re-elected, no matter how he stood on such seemingly unimportant things as European affairs.

Even if the senators had feared the results of Wilson's appeal many, if not most, of them were in no mood to bend the knee. If the "swing" had been started earlier, it might have been more effective; but by September the lines were drawn, and the senators had taken their stand. Tough-fibered men like Brandegee and Sherman would break before they would bend.

The supreme irony is that if Wilson had done the impossible and had defeated every Republican senator who was up for reelection in 1920, he would still have fallen short of a two-thirds vote. It is inconceivable that he overlooked this crucially important fact. Yet he may have thought that he could stir up a tremendous tidal wave of public sentiment which would roar up into the highlands of 1922 and 1924. In short, Wilson was staking everything on an upheaval which, though theoretically possible, was not at all probable.

The inescapable fact is that treaties, under our Constitution, are approved, not by public opinion, not by the President, not by the House of Representatives, not by a simple majority of the Senate, but by a two-thirds vote of the Senate. If the American people do not like this method, they are at liberty to change it. That was the system which existed in 1919, and Wilson would have done well to stay in Washington and try to effect an understanding with the only legislative agency under our Constitution empowered to approve treaties. Perhaps he would not have succeeded even then, but there was a better chance of success in the city of Washington than in the state of Washington.

This, of course, assumes a willingness on Wilson's part to accept reasonable compromise. If his mind was completely closed, then the only hope—and a slim one at that—lay in a personal appeal.

5

The best reason of all for not taking the desperate gamble of a nation-wide tour was that Wilson would almost certainly suffer a complete physical collapse. This was evident before he started; and the tragic result merely confirmed the worst fears of his close friends.

Wilson had never been physically strong. He had ruptured a blood vessel in one eye while president of Princeton University, and the doctors had recommended that he stop work. But he rose above that disability. When he came to the White House he was suffering from weak digestion and from neuritis in the arm and shoulder. His personal physician, Dr. Cary T. Grayson, prescribed a diet of raw eggs and orange juice, and had his arm and shoulder regularly baked and massaged. Wilson also followed a strict routine of recreation and exercise: he attended the theater regularly, and played golf dutifully— a conservative, down-the-middle game. Under this regimen his health markedly improved.

The events of the decade before the Peace Conference were enough to crush a more robust man. First, there were the bitter quarrels at Princeton; then the stormy two years as governor of New Jersey; the heated campaign of 1912 for the presidency; the early years of his administration when he had to drive his

reform program through Congress; the constant yawping of
the opposition; the perennial friction with Mexico; the tragic
death of his first wife; and the outbreak of the World War.
Then came the prolific vexations of neutrality; the losing
struggle to keep the nation out of war; and the final plunge
into the abyss.

During the war months Wilson conserved his strength carefully, choosing able assistants and delegating authority to
them. But at the Peace Conference the task seemed too important to delegate to others; he tried to do too much himself.
His recreation was limited to a few brisk walks and automobile rides; his diet was broken by banquets of strange and
indigestible food. He had to encounter formidable adversaries
like Clemenceau, to say nothing of showers of abuse from the
French press and backbiting within his own delegation. At
home he was nagged at by the Republican senators and the
Republican press. The volume of work at Paris was appalling.
It is no wonder that Wilson suffered a temporary breakdown
when, in April, 1919, he succumbed to a violent attack of influenza, an attack from which he may never have completely
recovered. The not-too-reliable "Ike" Hoover, the White
House usher who accompanied Wilson to France, says that he
was not the same after his illness: he began to do queer, fussy,
ungenerous little things.

Then came the trip home. Wilson expected that the Senate
would approve the treaty without undue delay, and that he
could quietly go back to the reform program interrupted by
the war. It was all a vain hope. Domestic problems allowed
him no rest; a railway strike had to be averted; a conference
between capital and labor had to be arranged. Royal visitors
were journeying to Washington. The heat was merciless.
There was no serenity in the goldfish bowl of the presidency.

The Senate, as we have noted, gave him no peace, what with
conferences and calls for data. The heat of prejudice and partisanship seemed to rise higher than that which shimmered
from the softening pavements outside the Capitol.

Wilson was a sick man before he started, and to the keen observer he looked sick. Late in July he had been forced into bed with an attack of dysentery; he was pursued by headaches, possibly premonitory warnings of a stroke. Sir William Wiseman lunched with him at the White House a few days before the ill-starred tour began, and he was shocked by the President's gray color, and by the twitching of his facial muscles.

What this haggard, tormented man needed was a vacation, not a transcontinental trip that would have taxed the strength of a "Bull Moose" like Theodore Roosevelt. He had in fact enjoyed no real vacation for several years, and in recent weeks he had been able to steal away for only a few hours during week ends on the presidential yacht.

6

Wilson's most intimate friends, including Dr. Grayson, repeatedly warned him that it would be plain suicide for a man approaching sixty-three, with hardening of the arteries and all his other disabilities, to undertake this ordeal—physical, nervous, and vocal. He was warned of the heat, the smoke, the cinders, the dust; of the interminable handshaking, the receptions, the dinners, the horrible food; of the "local committees," always demanding something for Podunk. He was warned of the dozens of speeches, and of the parades, during which he would have to stand in the back of a swaying automobile for hours at a time and wave his hat with robotlike smile at tens of thousands of curiosity seekers.

But the President had made up his mind, and to the end he was a stubborn man. He had the courage of determination and desperation. To him there was no other course; the treaty, so it seemed, was hopelessly bogged down in the Senate. To stay in Washington was to court certain defeat; to go to the country was the only chance of success. Of course there were dangers;

of course he might lose his life. But, as he told Grayson with a grim smile, "The boys who went overseas did not refuse to go because it was dangerous." To his wife he said that he could not break faith with the soldiers whom he had promised that this war was to end wars. "If I do not do all in my power to put the Treaty in effect," he said, "I will be a slacker and never able to look those boys in the eye. I must go."

In the face of his friends' opposition, Wilson developed something of a martyr complex. At one of the Cabinet meetings, when it was suggested that he might kill himself, he promptly replied that he would be willing to give up his life for the cause. He admitted to Tumulty that he was "at the end" of his "tether," but to save the world from the calamity that would flow from a rejection of the treaty, he was willing to make whatever personal sacrifice that was necessary. No man, he said, should count his own personal fortunes in such a crisis. "Even though, in my condition, it might mean the giving up of my life, I will gladly make the sacrifice to save the Treaty."

The stern Presbyterian was coming to the fore. Wilson felt, quite understandably, that he had a sacred mission. Like the early Christian martyrs he gloried in sacrificing himself for his principles.

It is well enough, when the occasion demands it, for men to die for their convictions. It is often better—as it would have been in this case—to live and work for them.

Wilson, as we have seen, was the only real leader his party had. The Democrats in the Senate were somewhat demoralized as it was; without him, they would be completely rudderless. The chief of staff does not seek the front-line trenches where he may die for his cause; he stays at the rear directing the general engagement.

The President was willing to give his life for his principles, and in a sense he did. He killed himself, and in killing himself killed the treaty in so far as the United States was concerned. It would have been better if he had been willing to give up some of the high ground he was defending, and compromise enough to save the pact. That was the only way it could have been saved.

7

The completed itinerary was not released until the eve of departure. It was evident at a glance that this was to be primarily a middle western and western trip; the West had re-elected Wilson in 1916 (see map on page 336), and this was the section to which he would again appeal. The Deep South was safely Democratic and could be passed by; the East was strongly Republican and could be ignored.

The speeches had been carefully scheduled with an eye to influencing wavering senators or "irreconcilables." There were to be addresses in Reed's Missouri, in Borah's Idaho, in Poindexter's Washington, in Johnson's California. The Golden State was to be honored with nine major speeches, evidently in an attempt to correct Johnson's misrepresentations regarding Shantung and other issues.

Illinois, with its metropolis of Chicago, was deliberately avoided. There was little point in going to a state notorious for the outspokenly isolationist Chicago *Tribune;* for the blathering Chicago Mayor ("Big Bill") Thompson; for the "irreconcilable" Senators Sherman and McCormick; and for a vociferous mass of German-Americans, Irish-Americans, and Italian-Americans. The name of Wilson had already been hissed in open meeting in Chicago.

All together, there were to be about forty formal speeches, in places ranging from tents and stadia to opera houses and tabernacles, to say nothing of various unscheduled appearances on the rear of the train. The first address would be given at Columbus, Ohio, on September 4; the last at Louisville, Kentucky, on September 29.

The preliminary schedules called for a week or so of rest at the Grand Canyon of the Colorado River. But Wilson vetoed

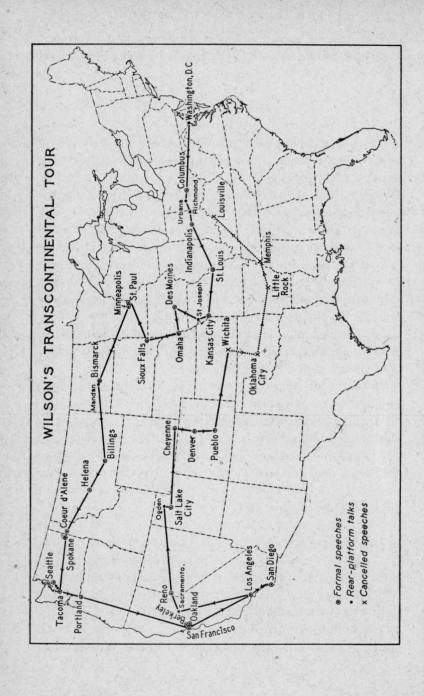

WILSON'S TRANSCONTINENTAL TOUR

⊙ Formal speeches
• Rear-platform talks
x Cancelled speeches

all such plans; he would not consent to even a day of vacation. As he sternly told Tumulty, he was going on a sacred crusade, and the people would never forgive him 'if he turned it into a sight-seeing junket.

The party was to be carried on a special train, which, for purposes of safety, was to be preceded by a pilot engine or a first section. The exact schedule was not announced until fulfilled city by city, presumably as a precaution against sabotage.

Only a few overnight stops were arranged, and the entire party was to live on whirling wheels. There were to be one baggage car, one dining car, one car for the correspondents (there were about twenty, plus the representatives of several moving picture concerns), one car for the stenographers and the Secret Service men, and one for the President. This was the last of the procession, and was called the "Mayflower," after the presidential yacht.

The wheeled White House contained sleeping accommodations for the President, Mrs. Wilson, Dr. Grayson (who kept an anxious eye on Wilson), Mrs. Wilson's maid, the President's Negro valet, and his Negro chef. A place was fitted up for a study, where the President deposited his portable typewriter. Here he consulted with his private secretary and others on matters of state.

8

The President and Mrs. Wilson arrived at the capital's Union Station at about seven P.M. on September 3, ready to board their private car. The crowd burst into hand clapping and cheers. The straw-hatted Wilson seemed to be in excellent humor, laughing and cracking jokes with the few personal friends who had come to see him off. Dr. Grayson had insisted that he rest up a few days for the ordeal, and spend a good deal of time in the open air.

But Wilson's mechanical smile was but the façade for a

troubled heart. He knew that he might crack under the strain. He knew that there would be no let-up in the cataract of current business. And when would he find time to outline those dozens of speeches, of which he had not prepared a single line?

One of the most fascinating might-have-beens of history is to speculate on what would have happened had there been then, as there was to be in a few years, a nation-wide radio hookup. Wilson had a fine voice and splendid diction. He probably would have been even more persuasive over the radio than in person. Sitting quietly in the White House, and needing only several half-hour speeches, he might in a series of "fireside chats" have informed and aroused the people, while at the same time preserving his health and strength. But this is all profitless speculation; there was no radio. Wilson had to do the job the hard way.

The train glided out of the yards to the accompaniment of no Godspeeds from the foes of the League. The "irreconcilables" had their heads together, laying plans to "trail" Wilson and wipe out whatever favorable results he might achieve. *Harvey's Weekly* railed against this "Covenanting Crusade," this "hippodroming excursion," this "tour of torment," this "cavorting and gallivanting" at the taxpayers' expense.

Wilson could expect no quarter from his foes, and he was in no mood to give any. The future lay in the lap of the gods.

CHAPTER SEVEN

THE SWING AROUND
THE CIRCLE

*"The only people I owe any report to are you and the other citi-
zens of the United States."* WOODROW WILSON, *at Columbus, Ohio,
September 4, 1919.*

1

THE WESTWARD-SPEEDING presidential party made its
first formal stop at Columbus, Ohio, on the morning of September 4, 1919. The visitors passed through streets that were
crowded three or four persons deep; but there was no evidence
of great interest, much less hysterical enthusiasm. The audience of some 4,000 at Memorial Hall was not so large as expected, possibly because of a morning rainfall and a local
streetcar strike.

This was Wilson's first popular defense of the treaty, and
he expressed pleasure at the opportunity of meeting directly
with the people, the only ones to whom he owed an accounting.
He drew warm applause when he praised the League as an
instrument for preventing wars. Alluding to the long lines of
men in khaki through which he had passed in coming to the
platform, he eloquently expressed the hope that they would
not have to be sent across again.

The address was well received, but as Wilson was leaving
the speaker's stand a Chinese youth in the gallery jumped to
his feet and shouted, "Mr. President, how about Shantung?"
In the general confusion, Wilson did not hear him, and consequently made no reply.

The next speech was scheduled for Indianapolis, Indiana,
later the same day, at the Coliseum on the state fair grounds.
Wilson was warmly cheered on the five-mile route from the
station, but the arrangements did not work out happily. There

was much disorder on the edge of the crowd, where curiosity seekers who had stared at the prize bulls tried to elbow their way in for a look at Wilson.

The President was loudly cheered; but he could not project his clear voice to the confused outer edges, and many of the spectators, their curiosity satisfied, wandered off to view the blue-ribboned boars. This exodus caused a ten-minute interruption, but when order was restored Wilson could be heard clearly, and he was listened to intently. Perhaps the greatest cheer greeted his statement that the peace was severe but just.

The next stopping point was St. Louis, the home of the renegade Senator Reed, and the center of a large German-American group. All during the day Wilson received an unexpectedly enthusiastic reception, quite in contrast with the coldness of Ohio and Indianapolis, and this welcome, the warmest since his return from Paris, must have renewed his faith in the people.

The high point in St. Louis was an address that night in the Coliseum, where Wilson had been renominated in 1916. The enthusiasm of the some 12,000 people who packed themselves into the hall resembled that of a great political convention. When Wilson reached the platform, he was applauded for three minutes, and when the presiding officer predicted that the President would soon be hailed as "Wilson, the Father of World Democracy," there was a wild roar of assent.

Wilson warmed to the occasion, and with fighting words painted the choice as one between partnership in peace or isolation in arms. The United States had by the force of events been thrust into the role of a world leader for peace, and he "for one" was not a quitter (great applause). Restressing his theme that the people were being misled because they could not or would not read the treaty, he offered to send a copy to anyone who had not done so. A lusty voice shouted "Reed," to the accompaniment of applause and loud cheers.

2

With Wilson hunched over his portable typewriter, laboring on his next speech, the presidential special sped toward Kansas City, where an eager crowd of some 15,000 packed Convention Hall to the rafters. When the distinguished guest appeared, the crowd surged to its feet and gave him a mass flag salute. Stirred by this reception, the President delivered himself of a vigorous address, in which he boasted that his "fighting spirit" had been aroused.

Des Moines (Iowa), Omaha (Nebraska), and Sioux Falls (South Dakota) were all taken in stride. The enthusiasm here was more restrained, for these places were strongly Republican, the wheat harvest was on, and there was an active German element, especially in Nebraska, where "irreconcilable" Senator Norris had a loyal following.

At Des Moines, as at St. Louis, Wilson evoked the greatest demonstration when he appealed for the establishment of a new world order. At Omaha he said that he would willingly die if he thought that he stood in the path of the realization of his aims.

Three major speeches were scheduled for St. Paul and Minneapolis, Minnesota, the home state of Senators Nelson and Kellogg, two of the most respected "mild reservationists." The reception was cordial, but not wildly exuberant. Wilson emphasized the familiar themes, and in addition declared that speedy ratification would reduce the cost of living and stabilize labor relations. The newspapermen accompanying the party received the impression that while the people of Minnesota favored the treaty, they were "mild reservationists" like their senators, and did not approve a whole-hog-or-none attitude.

Then came a speech at Bismarck, North Dakota, and a rear-platform appearance across the river at Mandan, where the President was cheered by the crowd, including a group of

Indians. One wonders if these original isolationists understood the issues involved.

The train was now puffing up toward the Rockies. Thus far Wilson and his advisers had little reason to feel unduly elated.

The New Peace Conference
(Courtesy of St. Louis *Post-Dispatch*; cartoonist Fitzpatrick)

Except for St. Louis, and possibly Kansas City, there had been nothing even approaching hysterical approval. Perhaps it was pro-Germanism; perhaps rock-ribbed middle western isolationism. Certainly there was a large degree of preoccupation. One prominent member of the Omaha Chamber of Commerce confessed, "We are so busy making money that we haven't had time to worry about the Peace Treaty." The Kansas City *Times* warned, "The nation is in a hardheaded mood just now."

3

The two stops in Montana, first at Billings, and then at the capital, Helena, were marked by reverent rather than warm-hearted crowds. Scores of persons in the first audience wore mourning. Their boys had fallen in the blistering Argonne, and they had come long distances to get what comfort they could from their President. As Wilson described in touching words the sacrifices of the lads who had gone abroad, tears streamed down the weather-beaten cheeks of his hearers.

The next state was Idaho, the stamping ground of the rampageous Borah. If the presidential party approached the "enemy's country" with misgivings, these were dispelled by the ovation at the one stop, Coeur d'Alene. The generous outpouring of good will indicated that the people in this part of the state did not agree with Borah's irreconcilable position.

The same was true of Spokane, Washington, the home city of the "bitter-ender" Senator Poindexter. The people turned out in droves to greet the first citizen of the land, and some seats in the packed armory were allegedly sold by scalpers for twenty-five dollars.

At Tacoma, and particularly at Seattle, the reception was so overwhelming and unrestrained as to recall Wilson's triumphal Italian tour. The welcome was warm, genuine, Western. The West had elected him in 1916; it was seemingly still with him.

At Tacoma, some 25,000 people had gathered in the Stadium, with thousands of children in posts of honor, waving a sea of red, white, and blue flags, and singing the national anthem. Wilson's voice shook as he prayed God that these boys would never have to carry that flag into battle. On the way to the armory for the second address, the crowds became so unmanageable that Secret Service men had to hurl people back from the presidential automobile.

In Seattle, where Wilson spoke twice, the exuberance of the outpouring approached fanaticism: it was the greatest ovation thus far. Multi-colored snowstorms of confetti descended upon the visitors, while Wilson waved his silk hat. The police, aided by sturdy Boy Scouts, could scarcely hold back the throngs. A part of the enthusiasm was no doubt due to the holiday spirit in the air. The great Pacific Fleet was there to be reviewed by the Commander-in-Chief, and Mrs. Wilson remembers how impressive it was at night, bedecked with fireflies of light.

There was only one sour note in Seattle. A good many alleged I.W.W.'s were sullenly displaying printed hatbands calling for the release of political prisoners, especially the Socialist leader, Eugene V. Debs.

4

As the barometer of enthusiasm arose, the barometer of Wilson's physical and nervous reserve sank correspondingly. Those terrible headaches dogged him; well-wishers and politicians would not leave him alone so that he might snatch a moment of rest or begin work on the next speech. Mrs. Wilson and Dr. Grayson watched him furtively, apprehensively. Yet he kept up a brave front, and no doubt impressed the audiences with his vigor. But shortly after Tacoma, says Tumulty, the fatigue of the trip began to write itself plainly on Wilson's face.

The show had to go on. Portland, Oregon, was no less enthusiastic than Seattle, though perhaps lacking the mob spirit. The main speech, that in the evening, was delivered to the fortunate 7,000 among the 30,000 who had applied for tickets. Earlier the same day the party took a fifty-mile outing on the soul-refreshing Columbia River highway. Along the road cars were parked, and constant cheering accompanied the procession. A tragic automobile crash took the life of one of the most popular of the news correspondents, and seriously injured another. This did not help to relax Wilson's taut nerves.

Southward through the Cascades wound the presidential special to California, the bailiwick of the envenomed Senator Johnson. The stay in the San Francisco Bay region was spread over September 17 and 18, and embraced San Francisco, Oakland, and Berkeley. The spectacle was much the same as that in Oregon and Washington, and the streets, windows, and roofs were packed with cheering masses of humanity.

The main San Francisco speech, that in the huge Civic Auditorium, was dampened by poor acoustics and by the disorders among alleged Irish agitators. On the other side of the bay, in Berkeley and Oakland, the program went off more smoothly. Some 12,000 people jammed into the Civic Auditorium in Oakland, with half as many stranded outside. When a voice in the gallery cried, "Are we with him?" a thousand throats hurled back the reply, "We are!"

In the California addresses Wilson tried with evident success to allay the peculiar apprehensions of the people of the Golden State. To the Irish he explained that the League aided rather than hindered the cause of Ireland's freedom; to the Chinese and their sympathizers he declared that the Shantung settlement would in the long run work out to the advantage of China; to the great body of anti-Japanese Californians he gave assurances that the United States would still have sovereign control over its immigration sluice gates.

The reception in Southern California was, in the judgment of the correspondents, the high point of the trip thus far. In San Diego the main address was delivered in the Stadium, where a glass cage with an electrical device had been prepared so that the 50,000 auditors might hear.

At Los Angeles, where he spoke twice, Wilson received the now-accustomed acclaim. Yet the intrepid Covenanter was beginning to falter. Those terrible headaches were taking their toll. At the urgent insistence of Dr. Grayson, the schedule was broken in Southern California, so that Wilson might spend a few hours at a quiet resort.

Returning to Central California, Wilson made a brief, unscheduled speech at Sacramento, Senator Johnson's home town. Then the train was pointed toward the undulating Sierras and home.

The visit to California was a great success. Expecting to find audiences hostile on the Irish, Japanese, and Chinese questions, Wilson had received unprecedented ovations. Veteran newspapermen estimated that he had the state two to one for a League without crippling reservations.

The tour was a triumph, except where the results counted: the vote of Hiram W. Johnson. If anything, he was more bitter than ever. The other senator, James D. Phelan (Democrat), had been a Wilson supporter all along.

5

They were now headed for home, with the worst of the ordeal behind. Wilson was still drawing too heavily on his pitifully small balance in the bank of nature. Yet his Scotch implacability was aroused; he was so enheartened by the rousing western reception that he was beginning to talk of carrying the fight into the "enemy's country"—Senator Lodge's Massachusetts.

Nothing noteworthy happened at thinly populated Reno (Nevada) or at Ogden (Utah), though the greetings were warm. But the Utah metropolis, Salt Lake City, recalled the ovations in California. The only address was scheduled for the famed Mormon Tabernacle, which was so tightly packed with humanity that the air became stifling. Mrs. Wilson, who herself almost fainted away, soaked a large handkerchief in lavender salts and sent it up to the wilting President.

Before Wilson began to speak, all doubts as to the attitude of the Mormon Church were dispelled when a high dignitary, Heber J. Grant, besought divine inspiration for the President, and evoked a deep-throated "Amen" from the audience. Wilson then spoke vigorously against wrecking the treaty with reservations; but the effort was an exhausting one, and at the close of the address his clothes were wet with perspiration.

On to Cheyenne, and then Denver. The end was fast approaching. Wilson was making feeble jokes, saying that his constitution was gone, but that his by-laws were left. He was running on his nerve. At Denver it was doubtful, when he rose, whether he could go on. Yet he seemed to be in fighting fettle, and he struck again at Senate reservations when he insisted, "We must either go in or stay out." From the crowd came cries, "Don't worry about the Senate."

Wilson was thinner, tired-looking: to Mrs. Wilson, a sick man. Before the Denver effort she suggested a few days of rest, but he refused, saying, "No, I have caught the imagination of the people." He cheered her, or tried to, by remarking that it would soon be over, and by promising that when they reached Washington he would take a holiday. The holiday never came.

6

The address at Pueblo, Colorado, was in some respects the high point of the entire trip. Wilson's fatigue was such that he planned to speak only a few minutes. But when he appeared the entire audience rose and cheered for several minutes, and he was moved to a supreme effort. Just before he began to speak, he remarked half-jocularly to the patient pressmen who had already heard about forty of his speeches, "Aren't you fellows getting pretty sick of this?"

This last address in Wilson's public career turned out to be one of the longest of the trip, and by common consent the most moving. It was as though he recharged the batteries of his energy from his sympathetic audience. Near the close he dramatically pictured the burial places of the American boys in France, and pleaded that it should not happen again. His eyes grew damp, as did those of some of the hardened newspapermen, while tears flowed freely down the cheeks of many in his audience.

At the end he received a tremendous ovation, the memory of which probably never left him. It was a fitting climax to an inspired speaking tour, and to a world-shaking speaking career—perhaps the most memorable in history.

Pueblo was journey's end. Contrary to the Hollywood version, Wilson spoke in a new auditorium, not from the rear platform, and he did not collapse while speaking. But that night on the train was a prolonged ordeal of insomnia and excruciating headache, accompanied by unmistakable symptoms of physical and nervous exhaustion. The rest of the speeches had to be canceled.

As a physical and vocal effort the three-week tour had been tremendous: some 8,000 miles of hurried travel (from sea level to high altitudes), innumerable conferences, a dozen or so wearying parades, and thirty-six set speeches (averaging an hour in length), to say nothing of several rear-platform addresses. The wonder is that Wilson did not crack sooner.

7

We must now analyze this noteworthy series of messages at some length.

The addresses were pitched, especially the early ones, on an extremely optimistic key. Wilson made it clear that he was not arguing or fighting with any one. He was traveling to find out what the people were thinking and saying; he wanted the pleasure of seeking fresh "inspiration" from them. He was merely explaining the treaty and making a report to the people. He never for one moment doubted that the treaty would be ratified; the only thing that concerned him, he said, was the delay.

He urged his audiences to read the treaty. It was a plain document couched in plain English; he could not find a

"single obscure sentence" in it. What he most feared was ignorance rather than prejudice; and he had found much ignorance.
Critics were concentrating their fire on the most liberal and
constructive parts of the pact. He had discovered that many
people thought the Covenant consisted of one article, Article
X; and all the rest of the treaty had but a few clauses, notably
that regarding Shantung. He was doing his best to correct this
false notion, and he was surprised by the number of people
who said to him, "Why, we never dreamed that those things
were in the treaty."

Wilson realized as well as any one that the pact was not
wholly satisfactory, but he also realized that it would be poor
strategy to confess this publicly. It seemed wise to put the best
possible face on things; so he did.

The treaty was, in his judgment, a great peace, a "just"
peace, and it had been the "crowning" privilege of his life
to sign it. It was a "thoroughly American document" and a
"people's treaty," the first of this kind. It liberated oppressed
minorities, abolished secret treaties, provided a Magna Charta
for labor and for women and children; and as such it was "the
great humane document of all time."

Above all, the pact contained the Covenant of the League
of Nations, which was designed for peace and not—according
to critics—for war. In this sense it was a "disentangling alliance." The League did not guarantee that there would be no
future wars. But it made war "violently improbable" by arranging for elaborate arbitral machinery and a cooling-off
period of nine months. Would not a scheme which provided a
10 per cent guarantee against war be worth while? Yet this
was a 90 per cent guarantee.

8

Much of Wilson's time was taken up with answering the
attacks of his Senate foes. He stressed the point that at Paris

he had brought about an amendment of the League Covenant in response to their demands, and now they were complaining that they did not like the wording of the changes.

He advanced the familiar arguments to meet the charges regarding six votes to one, the Monroe Doctrine, Shantung, and the control of immigration and other domestic problems. Article X was "the heart of the treaty"; and the real danger, he correctly felt, lay not in action but in inaction, in a failure of the League to function energetically when it should.

America would not, he said, be entrapped in the League. We could always get out after serving two years' notice. But he hoped that this mighty nation would not insist on sitting timorously near the door, on the edge of its chair, with one hand on the doorknob. This did not befit a great power.

Not content with parrying arguments, Wilson presented some of his own. All this delay was but aid and comfort to the Germans, whose propaganda and whose hyphenates were behind much of the obstruction. The world was still unsettled because of uncertainty as to the support of the United States.

Isolation, he insisted, had gone forever; the processes of history and modern mechanical miracles had turned the globe into a "single whispering gallery." We could not be peaceful or prosperous in an unpeaceful and unprosperous world; we could not "disentangle" ourselves from the rest of the earth. When the next war came the United States not only would be sucked into it but would have to bear the brunt of it.

The United States, Wilson concluded, had an inescapable moral obligation to bear its share of the responsibility for world peace. He believed that the overwhelming majority of the American people favored the League; and that America would have to join sooner or later. It was just a matter of time; this nation would enter either gracefully as a charter member or disgracefully as a laggard.

9

Wilson's speeches on this tour, when read today, impress one as having been a remarkable performance, especially in view of the physical and other disabilities under which he was laboring. In elevation of tone or beauty of diction his addresses do not measure up to his finest efforts; but the occasion called for a lower tone, and extemporaneous efforts can seldom approach the precision of carefully prepared essays.

Wilson probably gave ear to the proddings of friends that he come down off his pedestal and talk plain English, for he undertook at times to speak in the vernacular. But the vernacular did not become Wilson.

Such expressions as "It gravels me" or "It sticks in the craw" were acceptable colloquially but hardly Wilsonian. At Indianapolis, Wilson declared that the League was the only conceivable arrangement for preventing war, and that those who were criticizing it, or who thought they had a wiser scheme, had better "put up or shut up." He apologized a bit for using this "common" expression, but he employed it again at Kansas City and at Omaha. At St. Louis he won great applause when he said, "You hear politics until you wish that *both* parties might be smothered in their own gas." This was not a graceful expression, nor a tactful one, because he was the titular head of one of the two great parties, and he needed its support if he hoped to win.

Even more questionable were his attacks on the Senate, which he was trying to win over. At St. Louis he said that the senators ("some gentlemen") would be "absolute, contemptible quitters if they do not see the game through." He did not say that they *were* "contemptible quitters," but that they *would be* if they failed. He also declared that unless the senators did their duty they would be "gibbeted" in the annals of mankind.

These expressions were most ill advised. If Wilson was

merely expounding, why attack the senators in this fashion? They naturally struck back. Senator Harding said that nobody was a "quitter" and nobody would shut up. Wilson's statements also lent themselves to misrepresentation. *Harvey's Weekly* reported: "Yet he rushed about the country like a howling dervish, shrieking 'Put up or shut up, you contemptible quitters, before you are hanged on a gibbet!' "

To many unfriendly critics it looked as though the President were publicly airing a private quarrel.

10

At times Wilson used mistaken tactics, or made actual errors in tactics. To call upon great audiences to read the entire treaty was but to offer the counsel of perfection. To call upon them to read the French version with a French dictionary if they could not understand plain English was to offer the counsel of absurdity. To urge the senators, as he did at Indianapolis, to hold their own convention and draw up something better was foolish. The senators were of no mind to hold a convention, and they had no authority to do so. Treaty negotiation was the function of the President; treaty criticism was the function of the Senate.

A more serious tactical error was for Wilson to admit at Indianapolis that Article XI of the Covenant was his favorite article (see page 385 for text). At present, he said, we had to mind our own business; under Article XI, which permitted friendly intervention in the affairs of others, *"we can mind other people's business."* The logical inference was that if we could mind other people's business those people could start minding ours. This, of course, was gall and wormwood to the isolationists.

Fundamentally more serious was Wilson's generally uncompromising position on reservations. A reservation which merely quieted nerves, or which repeated in different words

what was already said, he would tolerate. But stronger reservations were too humiliating to accept. At Billings, he stated
bluntly, "It is this treaty or none." At Cheyenne, as well as at
Salt Lake, he declared that the Senate's proposed reservation
to Article X he would regard "as a rejection of the treaty,"
thus implying that he would not complete ratification on
these terms.

Whatever the reasons, Wilson made a number of statements
which were exaggerated or erroneous. His warm advocacy of
the treaty led him to say that it "has very, very few compromises
in it"; that it was not "a statesman's arrangement." His conscience must have twinged a bit when he said that "forward-
looking men" like Clemenceau and Orlando, who had helped
him frame the pact, "spoke the conscience of the world"; their
hearts "beat with the people of the world . . ."

His explanation of the six votes to one was occasionally
careless. It was misleading to say, as he did in Denver, that the
United States had a veto voice in the Council of the League
in all cases; our vote could not be counted in our behalf if
we were a party to the dispute. *Harper's Weekly* had a field
day at Wilson's expense, running numerous "fillers" which
read:

$$1 + 1 + 1 + 1 + 1 + 1 = 1$$

Inconsistencies or errors of fact appeared here and there, as
when Wilson repeatedly put Sarajevo in Serbia instead of
Austria-Hungary. But this sort of thing was relatively unimportant, except as a handle for his enemies.

Perhaps Wilson's greatest single failure was not to stress
more fully and clearly what America would gain. Although less
abstract than usual, he was still inclined to talk over the heads
of his hearers about problems they could not understand.
What they wanted to know was how the treaty affected them;
or, in the immortal words of the Tammany politician, "What's
in it for Mrs. Murphy and the children?"

Wilson characteristically stressed our obligations rather

than our gains. He undertook to appeal to America's unselfish self; to emphasize the duties of the strong; to demonstrate that the greatest nation must not be the master nation but the servant nation—the servant of mankind. We must not be afraid to dare new things; to take on new obligations; to measure up to our greatness.

America, as was soon to become apparent, wanted relaxation, not exertion; freedom, not responsibility; profits, not losses.

11

The apologists for Wilson insist that if he had not collapsed on the trip the Senate would have been forced to bow to the storm of public opinion. The President himself clearly shared this belief.

No one can deny that in the West, *the most thinly populated part of the country,* Wilson had succeeded in arousing lively demonstrations of enthusiasm. But there are important qualifications.

The size and exuberance of the crowds did not prove that the country was swinging to the treaty *without reservations.* Many of the people who turned out to cheer were merely curiosity seekers. Wilson had recently talked with kings; he had reordered the world. But more than that he was President; and the presidential office was entitled to respect if not reverential awe. Crowds will always turn out to see the President.

The audiences, as is almost always the case, were packed with Wilson sympathizers. Critics normally stay home and scoff; worshipers attend and approve. After Wilson's address to the St. Louis Chamber of Commerce, the New York *Times* correspondent interviewed forty or fifty of those present and found that they all favored unconditional ratification.

The length and volume of the ovations did not prove a great deal. Much of the noise was made by the "saved"; others doubtless cheered because one is always supposed to cheer the President. Others no doubt felt admiration for a "fighter" who would not submit to the Senate lying down. Also, the spirit of mob enthusiasm often takes hold of large crowds, and they cheer almost any ringing declaration. *Harvey's Weekly* was not far from the mark when it said that "some people would applaud a declamation of the binomial theorem or a proposal to repeal the Decalogue."

Using the Burning Glass on the Senate Opposition
(From New York *World*; cartoonist Kirby; reprinted by permission)

If we assume that all those who turned out and cheered for Wilson were cheering for the League, we still have not answered the question: What kind of League were they cheering for? Were they for the League as it stood; for a mildly reserved League; for a strongly reserved League; or for an amended League? This question is unanswerable, though there can be no doubt that many of the applauders favored a League with some kind of reservations.

But the question of applause is largely academic. Those who cheered could not vote on the treaty: that was to be done by the Senate. And how many senatorial votes were influenced?

It would be difficult to prove that a single vote was changed by Wilson's western appeal. It is true that a group of Democrats who had been toying with reservations lined up with the President while he was gone, but it is not apparent that the tour had any real bearing on their decision. At about the same time two other Democrats shifted over into the reservation camp.

Certainly not one of the "bitter-enders" abated his opposition. Probably Wilson's pressure tended to draw them together and further solidify their opposition. Two of the "mild reservationists," Kenyon of Iowa and Spencer of Missouri, issued unexpectedly unfriendly statements following the President's visit to their states. This further confirms the view that it would have been better to stay in Washington and attempt to win them over.

Finally, the appeal to the country gave Wilson's enemies additional ammunition to fire at him. Ex-President Taft, a friend of the League, was disgusted that Wilson should go barnstorming around the country, throwing "contemptuous phrases" at his opponents, and announcing undying opposition to effective reservations. Hostile newspapers cried, "Go back to Washington." *Harvey's Weekly* attacked Wilson for trying to be "President of the World," for setting out on his "terrifying tour," during which he unloosed the "boorish violence of his diatribes." And when the curtain fell tragically at Pueblo, the unsympathetic Harvey concluded that Wilson had "railed and raged and scolded himself into an alarming state of collapse . . ."

We have already observed that Wilson could not have succeeded if he had succeeded. The trip was not a success; it was a disastrous failure.

CHAPTER EIGHT

THE FALLEN WARRIOR

"I would rather lose in a cause that I know some day will triumph than triumph in a cause that I know some day will lose."
WOODROW WILSON, *September 12, 1912.*

1

IT WOULD be an error to conclude that Wilson's tragic breakdown was due solely to the physical strain imposed by the tour. There were numerous other harassments—some of the usual variety, some produced by postwar readjustment.

Domestic cares pursued the Chief Executive across the continent, and the presidential routine had to be carried on from the perambulatory White House. Time and energy had to be given to the approaching Industrial Conference in Washington, and to strikes, especially the steel strike.

Nor would foreign affairs stand still. The Mexican vexations continued unabated. The inflammatory Fiume problem again blazed its way into the headlines. While Wilson was in the Rocky Mountain area, the fanatical Italian poet, Gabriele d'Annunzio, seized this Adriatic port for his disappointed countrymen, and the fat was once more in the fire. Between speeches, Wilson had to concern himself with the Fiume affair, and even to prepare a cablegram to Paris expressing his amazement and distress that the Allied leaders should be acquiescing in Italy's grab.

Even the Democrats in the Senate were not standing too firm, and the Republicans were continuing their partisan maneuvers. Senator Penrose of Pennsylvania, whose own reputation was tainted, charged on the floor of the Senate that Wilson had improperly accepted gifts abroad valued at several million dollars. Such vicious misrepresentations must have been rasping to the spirit of the Princeton Puritan.

There were personal problems as well. In Los Angeles a proposed rest period was broken by a visit from Mrs. Mary H. Peck, "the butterfly of Bermuda," whom Wilson had known in happier days, and with whom he had exchanged innocuous but somewhat indiscreet letters. The tongue of scandal had smeared both. Wilson was shocked to find her a broken butterfly, completely wrapped up in her own penury and other troubles.

Only a few encouraging developments, aside from the customary ovations, interrupted the monotonous tale of toil and trouble. Not so many Democratic senators finally wobbled over into the reservationist camp as had been feared. The American Bar Association came out with an endorsement of ratification. And some 250 leaders in American life, including William H. Taft, Samuel Gompers, George W. Wickersham, and A. Lawrence Lowell, issued an appeal urging the Senate to reject the proposed Lodge amendments and ratify the treaty at once without crippling reservations.

2

While Wilson was in or near the bailiwick of Borah, doing battle for the League, William C. Bullitt (later Ambassador to France) took the stand before the Senate Committee, and did battle against the League.

The twenty-eight-year-old Bullitt was a personable man, deeply idealistic and markedly impulsive, who had been attached to the American Peace Commission in a minor capacity. He made a special trip to Russia for the purpose of clarifying relations with the Bolsheviks, but upon his return he was brushed aside by Wilson and Lloyd George. Angered by this reception, and disillusioned by the treaty, he wrote a scorching letter of criticism to Wilson, at the end of which he formally resigned. The work of peacemaking ther went forward without him.

The young man was subpoenaed by the Senate committee, though he was apparently eager to come. When on the stand he offered to read freely from notes he had taken on confidential conversations in Paris, and without restraint proceeded to reveal all he knew.

The Bullitt testimony was in the highest degree sensational. The witness testified that Secretary Lansing had told him at Paris that he considered "many parts of the Treaty thoroughly bad, particularly those dealing with Shantung and the League of Nations"; that the League as constituted was entirely "useless"; that the "powers had simply gone ahead and arranged the world to suit themselves"; and that the American people would "unquestionably" defeat the pact if they "ever understand what it lets them in for."

Lansing was now on the griddle. The witty Clemenceau, who had been wounded during the Conference by an assassin, remarked: "I got my bullet at the Conference, but Lansing got his afterward." The red-faced Secretary wired Wilson, admitting that he had criticized the treaty in Bullitt's presence, but explaining that he had not meant precisely what the witness had said. Lansing thereupon offered to make a public explanation along these lines.

Wilson was profoundly distressed. The bullet had glanced off Lansing only to hit him. "My God!" he cried out to Tumulty. "I did not think it was possible for Lansing to act in this way." As nothing but a flat denial would help correct the bad impression, and as Lansing had to admit that there was a considerable measure of truth in Bullitt's remarks, a labored public explanation would only make matters worse. So the President did not give Lansing the authorization to issue a statement; hence Lansing could issue none. Wilson did not even reply to the telegram or acknowledge it.

The Bullitt business stirred international reverberations. Abroad, the loquacious ex-diplomat was freely denounced, especially in England, where he was branded a Bolshevik and a cad. At home, the foes of the League were jubilant. Whatever ground Wilson may have laboriously won thus far on his tour was now partially lost, perhaps wholly lost.

Wilson had called upon the Senate obstructionists to put up or shut up; they had put up Bullitt. *Harvey's Weekly* gleefully reported that the witness had spoken out "in meeting"; and it printed a scathing editorial under the caption, "BULLITT BLABS." Harvey also called upon Lansing to resign: how could he in good conscience continue to serve when he had admitted that the treaty to which he had put his signature was in large part "thoroughly bad"?

Some critics were inclined to view the whole mess in a somewhat more jocose vein. One southern newspaper directed attention to Lansing's statement that the American people would reject the treaty if they understood it. If that was the case, concluded this paper, "they will never reject it."

3

The Bullitt sensation was from several points of view intrinsically unimportant. Nothing new had been revealed about the treaty; and it had long been common gossip that Lansing was not in complete sympathy with the President's idealistic aspirations.

But the shock probably contributed something to Wilson's collapse, undermined public confidence in the high officials of the government, and revealed how far disillusionment would cause otherwise honorable men to go.

Bullitt did what he did deliberately, after mature reflection, and no doubt with the conviction that the public weal demanded the defeat of the treaty. Where the public weal is involved no such thing as private confidences should stand in the way—at least some people can rationalize their conduct along these lines.

If Lansing was indiscreet in talking, and Bullitt was ungentlemanly in blabbing, what shall we say of Lodge and the other Republicans who summoned him before the committee and encouraged him to talk? This in some ways was the most reprehensible part of the whole affair.

Bullitt was sneaked in as a "surprise" witness before a rump meeting of the committee, from which all Democrats were absent. If they had known he was coming, they undoubtedly would have been present, and they would have attempted to shut him off. Lodge, who was privy to all this, wrote rather lamely to his friend Henry White that Bullitt's "breach of confidence" was "his affair"; he simply turned state's evidence and insisted on reading his report of the conversations. Lodge added that Bullitt would have gone ahead and revealed all his notes, but that he (Lodge) and Senator Knox stopped him. By this time they had accumulated enough evidence; they must not make the mistake of drawing the bow too far.

Henry White always blamed Lodge for this unsavory episode. "Really," he wrote to a friend, "it requires some patience at times not to become indignant with him."

The Bullitt testimony ended the six weeks of Senate hearings. It was a fittingly disgraceful ending for a thoroughly disgraceful episode.

4

The Bullitt affair was only one of Wilson's troubles. Before him on his tour went Irish agitators, who published in the local newspapers full-page advertisements attacking the League. When he left, another advertisement (also paid for by the Friends of Irish Freedom) assailed his arguments.

Behind him, like baying bloodhounds, came several of the Senate "irreconcilables," "trailing" him from city to city. It was enough to unnerve the faltering crusader.

Most of the "Battalion of Death" stayed behind and used the senatorial sounding board, but a few went out on the stump. Poindexter made several speeches in the East, while McCormick, Borah, and especially Johnson undertook to

speak in the Middle West. At some of the meetings enthusiastic listeners sprang to their feet, threw their hats into the
air, and shouted approval of a smashing argument.

Wilson had avoided Chicago; it was too full of isolationists
and hyphenates. The "irreconcilable" "trailers" went to the
Windy City, and there held what was perhaps their most ex-
citing meeting, with Borah, Johnson, and McCormick all
speaking from the same platform. Borah was in fine fettle.
He cried that Wilson had gone over to Paris preaching open
covenants, and had surrendered. "Who quit?" he shouted.
"Who was the quitter?"

From the crowd came the ringing response, "Wilson."

Borah referred to the hundred thousand (imaginary) men
whom England was going to ask Wilson to send to Constantinople.

"Impeach him! Impeach him!" screamed the audience,
many of whose members were not even American citizens.

Elsewhere Senator Johnson had a field day in exercising his
tub-thumping talents. At Kansas City he cried that the League
was an "infamous nostrum"; at Des Moines, "a gigantic war
trust." At Lincoln, Nebraska, he shouted, "Shall American
boys police the world?" At Sioux City he charged that Wilson
intended to adopt a new government for the United States.
Persistently and consistently he assailed Allied duplicity,
Article X, and the Shantung settlement.

Many Californians were not proud of their loud-mouthed
senator. In a telegram made public on September 27, over
thirty prominent citizens of the state, including President
Benjamin Ide Wheeler of the University of California and
President Ray Lyman Wilbur of Stanford University, protested to Johnson against the tactics he was using. But the
senator was not especially concerned about people at the university level; many more votes could be found among the
masses.

Johnson's campaign against the League—and for his presidential candidacy—was markedly successful. His friends de-

clared that he was running away with the nomination. Summoned back to Washington to vote for amendments to the treaty, he temporarily abandoned his trip with reluctance, insisting that if he could get "just sixty days" before the final vote the American people would make their wishes known in no uncertain fashion.

The Deadlocked Article X
(Courtesy of St. Louis *Post-Dispatch*; cartoonist Fitzpatrick)

The untamed Reed, after arousing the Senate galleries with a four-hour excoriation of the League, went out on the hustings. At Ardmore, Oklahoma, he was rotten-egged from the platform by a group of irate citizens, prominent among whom was a woman who had lost her sons in the war.

Proof is lacking, but it is reasonable to conclude that the efforts of the "irreconcilable" "trailers" to some extent canceled out the efforts of the President. Friends of Wilson complained that the conduct of the senators was unfair and un precedented. But the United States is a democracy, and the members of Congress have as much right to free speech—even though it be ignorant speech—as the President.

It certainly would have been more dignified and perhaps more useful, as the Boston *Herald* pointed out, if both the President and the senators had stayed in Washington, subordinating prejudice and passion, discussing the issues with moderation, and seeking to reach a compromise agreement.

5

When Wilson's body finally rebelled in Colorado, it was no easy matter to convince him that the remainder of the trip must be canceled. Dr. Grayson pleaded that any other course would mean complete disaster. But the stricken man replied, through tears of pain and disappointment, "No, no, no. I must keep on."

Wilson feared that Senator Lodge would say that he was a "quitter"—perhaps a "contemptible quitter"; that he was "quitting" because the western trip was a failure. If he stopped now, it seemed as though all the ground that he had so painfully gained would be thrown away.

Until the time the train slowed down at Wichita, Kansas, Wilson still had hopes of making a public appearance. But it was not to be; instead he issued a statement to the people of Kansas. He finally yielded completely, but only after it had been pointed out to him that the trip was a great success. He had presented his case fully, and he could add nothing new in the five or so remaining speeches scheduled for the area of Kansas, Oklahoma, Arkansas, Tennessee, and Kentucky.

The plan was suggested of having Wilson seek some near-by health resort before undertaking the rest of the trip back to Washington, but Dr. Grayson decided that the quiet and privacy of the White House would be better. Grayson issued a statement announcing that Wilson's condition was not alarming; he was suffering from a nervous collapse caused by overwork and dating back to his influenza attack of April. He needed rest and quiet.

The saddened presidential party, with curtains drawn, was spirited from the Rockies to the Potomac in forty-eight hours, hardly stopping long enough to change heated engines. A crowd of the curious and the worshipful gathered at the Union Station in Washington, and the wan Wilson raised his hat automatically in response to their cheers. Worn and shaken, he was able to walk to the White House car with some show of briskness, but to the careful observer he betrayed signs of exhaustion. Though his face was drawn and haggard, he did not seem desperately ill, and his critics were further confirmed in their suspicion that he was shamming illness because the trip had been a failure.

Little sympathy was wasted on the fallen Wilson by his enemies. *Harvey's Weekly* exulted: "He went away from Washington with the edifice of his ambition quaking and trembling about him. He returns to find it in utter ruins.

"He has had his say. He has shot his bolt. He has done his worst. He is no more to be considered. Now let the Senate act."

During the three days after his return Wilson slept fitfully, wandered about aimlessly, too shaken and pain-bedeviled to work, and went for a few short automobile rides. He did not feel able to see Sir William Wiseman, a representative of the British government, who appeared with an important message; and he put off several Democratic senators who called in the hope of consulting their leader on the all-important treaty fight.

On the evening of the third day Wilson felt so much better that before retiring he vigorously read a passage from the Bible to his wife, as he had habitually done during the war. He then wound his watch, and absent-mindedly left it on the table in Mrs. Wilson's bedroom. She took it to him, and he said, "That worries me—to have left that watch there. It is not like me."

Nature was warning Wilson of more tragic things to come.

6

At about eight o'clock the next morning (October 2), Mrs. Wilson found her husband sitting on the edge of his bed, complaining of numbness in his left hand. She helped him to the bathroom, and then hurried to telephone Dr. Grayson. While still at the telephone she heard a slight noise, and rushing back she found Wilson lying on the floor unconscious. He had suffered a stroke, which thickened his speech, paralyzed the left side of his face and body, and partially incapacitated his left arm and leg until his death.

Dr. Grayson soon arrived, and shortly thereafter appeared in the hall crying (according to "Ike" Hoover), "My God, the President is paralyzed!" Other doctors were summoned, nurses were engaged, medical apparatus was moved in, and the White House became a veritable hospital. When Wilson regained consciousness, says Josephus Daniels (then the Secretary of the Navy), he extracted a promise from both his wife and Dr. Grayson that his condition, if serious, should not be made known.

For several weeks Wilson spent practically every moment on his back. The initial stroke was complicated by indigestion and a painful swelling of the prostate gland, which failed to respond to local treatment and which, on October 17, produced an obstruction of the urethra. The doctors agreed that only an operation would save the President's life.

The dilemma was a frightening one to Mrs. Wilson. It seemed as though her husband in his weakness could not survive a major operation; if there was no operation, the body would be fatally poisoned. The doctors (there were six of them) patiently explained his plight by means of diagrams, and bluntly told Mrs. Wilson that the obstruction could not be allowed to continue beyond two hours. But on her own responsibility she decided that there should be no operation.

Near the end of three interminable hours the condition cleared up, and the crisis was passed.

During these early weeks the President was a desperately sick man. Mrs. Wilson later wrote, "For days life hung in the balance." But neither the Cabinet nor the public was made fully aware of his critical condition. There was no inkling in the White House announcement that Wilson had been laid low by a stroke; it was generally believed that he had suffered a nervous breakdown, complicated by digestive and prostatic trouble. All he apparently needed was seclusion and rest.

The reasons for this deliberate deception of the public are obvious. The domestic front was in a turbulent condition, and a frank admission would have further unsettled the country. Also, a truthful statement might have led people to conclude that Wilson had become incapacitated within the plain meaning of the Constitution, and a demand for his resignation might well have reached irresistible proportions. This may have been the main reason why the President wanted his real condition concealed.

Such a lack of candor, necessary though it may have seemed, had unfortunate by-products. When truth is crushed to earth, rumors multiply. There were wild reports that Wilson was paralyzed, dead, insane. Passers-by pointed to the bars on the White House windows (put there to protect them from the ball-playing children of Theodore Roosevelt), and whispered that a madman lay behind them. Senator Moses, one of the bitterest of the "irreconcilables," wrote a letter alleging that Wilson was suffering from a brain lesion. This was so uncomfortably near the truth as to bring a denial from one of the attending specialists.

The absence of truthful bulletins no doubt accounts in part for the lack of expressions of concern from public and private bodies. While it is true that certain individuals, like Senator Hiram W. Johnson, made gracious remarks, and prayers were offered in the churches, the absence of a formal resolution of sympathy from either the House or the Senate was painfully apparent. Even as big-hearted a man as Taft could write privately that Wilson had been so intent on "hogging" all the authority that he had broken himself down. An Irish mass meeting in New York City greeted a reference to Wilson's illness with raucous laughter.

The President had earlier told Tumulty, with perhaps a touch of clairvoyance, "People will endure their tyrants for years, but they tear their deliverers to pieces if a millennium is not created immediately."

CHAPTER NINE

THE LIVING MARTYRDOM

*"He fell, wounded unto death. He died . . . as much a victim
of the war as the Unknown Soldier who sleeps at Arlington."*
THOMAS W. GREGORY *(Wilson's Attorney General),*
January 23, 1925.

1

THE SUPREME tragedy would have been a clouding of
Wilson's splendid mind, but this seems not to have occurred.
He was apparently able to remember and reason as well as
before the stroke, that is, for relatively short periods, then
fatigue overtook him. But while the clarity of his brain could
pass muster, it was evident to those who observed him closely
that he was not the same Wilson. He was more irritable, more
sensitive to criticism, and apt to break down in tears under
unusual emotional strain.

Prolonged illness, accompanied by pain, depression, and
permanent physical impairment, frequently affects the patient's mental fiber. A man's brain may be clear, but he may
be unable, because of his affliction, to work more than a few
minutes a day. A man's brain may be clear, but he may lack
his old energy, his emotional balance, his ability to make
speedy and sound decisions, and above all to provide that type
of vigorous leadership demanded by high executive office.

As a leader, Wilson was never the same again. Something
went out of him; his mental resiliency fled. But his Scotch
stubbornness—the will not to yield—was apparently fortified.
An unkind stroke of Fate had withered one cheek, yet he
turned the good one more resolutely than ever toward his
adversaries.

With glacial slowness the sick man got better. He was permitted to grow a beard and mustache, about which he made

feeble jokes as his strength partially returned. No one was allowed to see him during these early weeks except the doctors and nurses and Mrs. Wilson, with Tumulty hovering about in the anteroom. As the patient improved, Mrs. Wilson read him fiction and light verses, and permitted him to listen to phonograph music.

Gradually, and near the end of the third week, Wilson improved so much that he could give a few minutes to the most urgent matters of state. On October 20, he sent for some public papers; on October 21, he overruled his doctors and prepared a letter to the chairman of the Industrial Conference; on October 22, he was propped up in bed to sign four bills; on October 25, he issued a statement regarding the coal strike; on October 27, he ineffectually vetoed the prohibition enforcement bill (Volstead Act).

An unusual departure from routine came on October 30, when Wilson was allowed for a few minutes to see the King and Queen of the Belgians. The President continued intermittently to transact public business for a short time, and on November 17—a red-letter date in his recovery—he was able to recline in a wheel chair on the White House lawn for the first time since his stroke. Two days later came the momentous vote in the Senate on the treaty.

When there were setbacks, as there were, Wilson could do little or nothing; when there were good days, as there were, he might work as much as an hour or two. But it is clear that from October 2, 1919, to March 4, 1921—a period of a year and a half—the American people had only a part-time President, a shell of the distinguished statesman who returned from Paris in July. He was a sick man with a tired brain.

2

The genius of a Sophocles or a Shakespeare never created a tragedy more poignant than that of Woodrow Wilson. Elevated to a pinnacle hitherto unattained by mortal man, glimpsing the promised land of perpetual peace, he suffered physical collapse, mental aimlessness, political defeat—and lived out the rest of his days in querulous impotence. The Greek concept of nemesis—of lightning striking the proudest tree in the forest—is nowhere better exemplified.

If the President had died that night on the platform in Pueblo, it seems almost certain that the results in the long run would have been happier for all concerned. Wilson himself was a fighter; he had lived a full life; and he could have hoped for no more glorious end than to go out fighting the good fight. Ex-Senator Beveridge, one of the President's most savage critics, later remarked that, had this happened, Wilson would have eclipsed Lincoln as a martyr.

No more dramatic exit from this vale of tears could have been imagined: Wilson actually giving up his life for the League. In all probability the Senate would have been jarred —perhaps shamed—into action. Much of the partisanship would have faded, because Wilson as a third-term threat would be gone, and Vice President Marshall, a small-bored Hoosier, was not to be feared.

Marshall of course would have been President for seventeen months. Having presided over the Senate for more than six years, and knowing the temper of that body, he probably would have recognized the need for compromise, and probably would have worked for some reconciliation of the Democratic and Republican points of view. In these circumstances it seems altogether reasonable to suppose that the Senate would have approved the treaty with a few relatively minor reservations.

If Wilson had been crushed less, he might still have had his old powers of leadership, and perhaps a willingness to compromise. If he had been crushed more, either he or those near him could have accepted the inevitability of resignation with good grace. As it turned out, he could still cling to his office, without the power to lead actively and sure-footedly, but with unimpaired power to obstruct. He experienced what few men ever experience: a living martyrdom. As a dynamic political force, as a doer of great deeds, as the voice of a nation—the old Wilson died in Colorado.

The Fates were unkind to Wilson. Having set the stage for a great martyrdom, they suddenly changed their minds. If he had died, the United States probably would have entered the League, and the League might have been more successful.

But this is all speculation. Wilson did not die until 1924. He lived to attend the funeral of his successor, President Harding.

3

One of the major mysteries of this stupendous tragedy is why Wilson did not resign, or why he was not permitted to resign.

It is evident to the layman, as it must have been to the physicians, that Wilson, if he did recover, would never be more than the ghost of a President. Cerebral thrombosis is a terrible affliction, and not uncommonly recurs. The patient requires complete rest and, above all, freedom from worry and responsibility.

The presidency of the United States is a killing office, especially so since the machinery of government has become infinitely complicated. Experts were beginning seriously to doubt if a man could actually live through more than two terms, when the already crippled Franklin D. Roosevelt came along with an iron constitution and an ability to laugh off cares that would have prostrated an ordinary man. From Grant in 1877, to Roosevelt in 1941, only one man actually served two consecutive full terms; and that was Wilson, who broke before the end.

What Wilson himself thought about resignation, we shall probably never know. His natural tendency was to cling to office; he did not want to be branded a "quitter." The doctors were probably not completely candid in explaining to him the nature of his disability; to have done so might have destroyed the will to live. Wilson was probably led to believe that within a few weeks he would be nearly as well as before, and able to direct the League fight to a successful conclusion.

What all six tight-lipped doctors thought, we shall probably never know. Possibly they disagreed, as doctors will. Mrs. Wilson says that the eminent Dr. Francis X. Dercum advised against resignation, *provided* she would undertake to shield her husband from all but the most pressing business. The doctor reasoned, according to Mrs. Wilson, that resignation would weaken the patient's determination to recover, and that the country needed his leadership.

George Sylvester Viereck, who later saw a good deal of some of the principals in the drama, has an entirely different story. He says that the doctors advised resignation, but that both Wilson and his wife disregarded their advice.

The general circumstances support the Viereck version. It is possible that Mrs. Wilson does not remember accurately what Dr. Dercum told her. To the layman it seems incredible that a distinguished physician could have prescribed anything other than absolute quiet, and a complete sloughing off of all official duties. Dr. Dercum must have been naïve indeed if he thought that the country could run itself indefinitely, or that Mrs. Wilson could keep brain-disturbing decisions away from her husband, or that the country needed the leadership of a broken man.

Mrs. Wilson has been accused of a thirst for power, of a reluctance to relinquish the honor of being First Lady of the Land. It is more probable that since she knew her husband's sensitiveness on the subject of being a "quitter," and realized that his whole life was wrapped up in the fight for the League, she concluded that the shock of resignation would kill him.

This was a decision so cruel and momentous that no interested person should ever be called upon to make it. Loyalty on the one hand to a loved and stricken husband; loyalty on the other to a vexed and leaderless nation—loyalty to one person or to one hundred million persons. "Woodrow Wilson," she writes, "was first my beloved husband whose life I was trying to save, fighting with my back to the wall—after that he was the President of the United States."

4

Mrs. Wilson had to make this decision because the Constitution, in one of its few glaring omissions, gave no one else the authority. Unless this defect is remedied, a similar situation will almost certainly develop again, and possibly under circumstances even more disastrous.

The Constitution clearly states that, upon the disability of the President, the duties of the office shall devolve upon the Vice-President. But who shall certify to the disability of the President? There is no answer.

Tumulty records that a few days after Wilson's collapse, Secretary Lansing called to suggest that Marshall be asked to "act in his stead"—presumably until recovery. With a great display of indignation, Tumulty replied (Dr. Grayson agreeing) that he would not be a party to any such act of disloyalty. Tumulty went further and threatened that, if anyone outside the White House attempted to certify to the President's disability, he and Dr. Grayson would repudiate such action.

To the devoted Irish secretary it seemed reprehensible that anyone should take advantage of the President's prostration, and even temporarily fill his place so that the government might function efficiently. Tumulty was willing to perjure himself for his stricken chief. Loyalty won at the expense of the public.

The position of Vice President Marshall was singularly difficult. He was being urged to declare Wilson disabled, and to force his way into the presidential office. His nerves were on edge, because he did not know at what moment he would be called upon to take over onerous new duties, and because the President's condition was carefully concealed from him. A current joke was that the Vice President had nothing to do but push the White House doorbell every morning and inquire ghoulishly after Wilson's health.

Among the President's critics there was some demand that he resign, or that Marshall seize the helm. This demand was strengthened by various rumors as to the extent of Wilson's illness. When the President recovered sufficiently to sign public documents, with a shaky hand which was steadied by his attendant, skeptics scrutinized the signature and wondered whether it was genuine. When the annual message to Congress was submitted in December, observers studied it carefully and concluded that it had not been written by Wilson at all.

Critics like the New York *Nation* remarked that Wilson treated the presidency as an hereditary monarch did his succession: it seemed like a personal possession of the Wilson family. The country was paying $75,000 for a President; it now had what amounted to a pensioned President, with someone else running the government, or the government running itself. To unfriendly observers it seemed like a dog-in-the-manger situation: Wilson could not discharge his duties, yet he would not get out (or Mrs. Wilson would not let him get out) and permit someone else to come in who could. He could not lead aggressively and effectively, but he would permit no one else to lead.

This distressing situation gave rise to various proposals for amending the Constitution so as to establish some kind of jury to determine the disability of the President, consisting perhaps of members of the Cabinet, of the Supreme Court, and of Congress. Several such proposals were actually introduced as resolutions into Congress, but nothing came of them. The American people were not properly impressed with the seriousness of the problem, even when they saw it before their faces. Perhaps some of them felt, as did the Knoxville *Sentinel,* that if Congress shall "pass upon the disability of the President . . . who shall pass upon the disability of Congress?"

5

The United States was virtually without a President for several troubled months, perhaps even longer. It was a period when of all times executive leadership of a high order was needed. Strikes convulsed the country; the treaty fight in the Senate neared its fateful conclusion; and the American peace commissioners in Paris, who were hard at work on the lesser settlements, needed presidential direction. While millions of people cried for bread and peace, the President lay inert, and the government functioned at slow motion or not at all. Events were controlling decisions, rather than decisions controlling events.

Wilson was undoubtedly incapacitated within the plain meaning of the Constitution. He was unable to discharge some of the simplest duties of his high office; or at least the guardians of the bedchamber did not feel that he was strong enough to be bothered with them. Senators could not see him about the crucial treaty struggle, but the King and Queen of the Belgians and the young Prince of Wales (who later yielded his throne for the woman he loved) were shown in for a few minutes. These conversations, of course, were but embarrassed chitchat.

While the White House remained a hospital, twenty-eight bills became law after the expiration of the ten-day period prescribed by the Constitution. Wilson presumably was too weak to sign them, or did not have the mental energy to study them and decide what action to take.

Secretary of the Interior Lane had been offered several positions paying $50,000 or more a year. He was eager to accept one of them so as to repair his shattered private fortunes. But he was unable to see the President and discuss his resignation; and he was unwilling to resign without prior consultation, lest he upset his chief emotionally, and create more wild rumors. This was as late as December 29, 1919—*nearly three full months after the complete collapse.*

An important presidential function is to receive ambassadors; in fact, they cannot officially take up their posts until they are so received. A dozen or so foreign envoys were forced to wait outside the White House gates, among them Viscount Grey of Great Britain, whose vitally important mission will be discussed later.

6

Who ran the government during the interregnum when Wilson was almost completely incapacitated? The answer seems to be that Mrs. Wilson acted as a kind of female regent and supersecretary. In a very real sense she was the first woman President of the United States; at least, she kept up the pretense of the presidency.

Though an amateur in statecraft, Mrs. Wilson undertook her difficult role with the medical advice of Dr. Grayson, and with the loyal Tumulty stationed outside the door. Her chief task was to go over the papers that came to the White House, decide which ones were so important that a decision on them could not be postponed, and reduce them to tabloid form. She would wait for an opportune time, when her husband was having one of his better days, and when Dr. Grayson would approve the intrusion of public business. Then she would present the problem to Wilson for his decision.

During these early weeks Mrs. Wilson scribbled down the President's reactions on small pieces of paper, many of which are preserved among the Wilson papers today. As the President grew stronger, he would scrawl his approval or disapproval on a document, and occasionally add a few remarks in a handwriting which became progressively less shaky.

Mrs. Wilson was undoubtedly a woman of great poise and personal charm, and she tiptoed through her role with commendable discretion. Her warm, womanly hand skillfully erected a Chinese Wall around the White House bedroom, and nursed the invalid back from the shadow of the grave.

But, much as we may admire her loyalty and devotion, we may be permitted to feel less admiration for her competence in political matters. Ill equipped and ill informed, she carried on as best she could.

Outsiders sneered about the "reigning monarch," and the "Woman who was President." She no doubt resented these implications, for in her memoirs she asserts with charming naïveté that she "never made a single decision regarding the disposition of public affairs." "The only decision that was mine," she qualifies, "was what was important and what was not, and the *very* important decision of when to present matters to my husband."

This is incredibly naïve. The proverb tells us that it matters not who writes the laws of a nation if one can only write its songs. It does not matter greatly who is President of the United States if one can decide whom he may see, when, and for how long. It does not matter greatly who is President if one can examine all executive papers, decide which are important, and present these to him in capsule memoranda, possibly not devoid of misinformation and personal bias.

The Cabinet during these fateful months was almost completely ignored, and it found out about Wilson's condition through grapevine channels. Left to its own devices, it met informally from time to time, and thus inspired some public confidence in the workings of the government.

The role of Mrs. Wilson must not be exaggerated. The government ran largely from its own momentum. When Lincoln was shot in 1865, James A. Garfield consoled an audience by saying that, even though the President was dead, "God reigns and the Government at Washington lives." In 1919 Wilson was all but dead, but the government lived. The various departments carried on their work; and that the government functioned as well as it did is a tribute to its toughness and resiliency.

7

Wilson's physical and mental condition had a profoundly important bearing on the final defeat of the treaty.

Protracted illnesses, particularly when accompanied by paralysis, tend to produce melancholy and bitterness. For many weeks Wilson had little to do but lie quietly and brood over the unkindness of Fate and over wrongs, real or fancied. It would have been strange indeed if his thoughts had not turned repeatedly to Lodge and the "bitter-enders," whose opposition had driven him forth to collapse. This may account for what seems to have been a stiffening of his already abnormal stubbornness and inflexibility.

William Allen White surmises, with much plausibility, that as Wilson lay in the White House his mind dwelt on his recent trip, and especially on the grand finale at Pueblo, where the people had seemed to want a League without reservations. But the world had kept moving; things were not as they had been at Pueblo. Wilson's dynamic leadership was gone, and public opinion and the Senate were turning more and more to a League with reservations. But this chilling fact had to be kept from the President. In his weakened condition he could not be told anything that would disturb him unduly; he might burst into tears and suffer a serious relapse. Tumulty was prompt to hasten to him with good news, as when some senator came strongly to his defense on Capitol Hill, and when the crippling amendment regarding Shantung was voted down. Wilson would smile a wan, pleased smile.

Tumulty remembers how he was warned by Dr. Grayson and Mrs. Wilson not to alarm the patient with pessimistic reports; hence he attempted to bring to Wilson "in the most delicate and tactful way" some hint of the atmosphere in the Senate. But the President, like many another man, wanted to believe what he wanted to believe, and such hints seem to have been largely lost on him.

The mail addressed to the prisoner in the White House was rigidly censored. Mrs. Wilson herself carefully sifted the correspondence so that nothing disheartening would shock the patient. H. H. Kohlsaat sent Wilson a letter late in October urging him to accept compromise reservations. Mrs. Wilson promptly returned it unopened, saying that, as she did not know the purport of his message, she assumed that it was not

As the World Sees Us!

(From New York *Evening World*; cartoonist Cassel; reprinted by permission)

important enough to bring to the attention of the President.

Colonel House addressed three important letters to Wilson, urging some kind of compromise. There was no answer, no acknowledgment. Mrs. Wilson disliked and distrusted the Colonel, and his advice did not square with what Wilson wanted to hear. It is altogether probable that these letters were never brought to the President's attention.

Henry White came to Mrs. Wilson and asked her to tell Wilson that it would be necessary to accept some reservations. She seemed disappointed, and accused White of "keeping bad company." It seems unlikely that the message ever reached the secluded President.

Wilson's collapse also deprived him of valuable consultations with the members of his Cabinet. These men were not sycophants, and they probably would have told him bluntly, if they had been permitted to do so, that the deadlock in the Senate demanded some kind of compromise. Their combined voices might have made an impression on Wilson; but they were never given a chance to speak. The first Cabinet meeting did not occur until the treaty had been rejected by the Senate for the second and last time.

Ironically enough, Wilson's personal isolation from his trained advisers and from public opinion accelerated the alarming drift toward national isolation.

8

The disability of the President left the Senate Democrats in a most awkward position.

They were without leadership. If Wilson had been completely incapacitated, they could have worked out a strategy of their own; but, since they did not know Wilson's mind, they could not. More than that, the President, before leaving on his trip, had laid down certain instructions. Until the Democratic senators heard from him again they were bound to follow those instructions, whether such orders fitted the existing situation or not.

Senator Hitchcock was in an intolerable position. Himself an acting minority leader who did not know when he might be displaced, he was trying to cooperate with a President whom he could not visit, the extent of whose disability was unknown, and who might momentarily be replaced by the Vice President. During the crucial month of October, Hitchcock did not see the President at all; during November he apparently consulted him only twice and for brief periods, just preceding the final vote.

Hitchcock, too, was forced to curse the unkindness of the Fates. He picked up what information he could about the President's true condition through the grapevine and through other private channels. That the leader of the minority, the bearer of Wilson's hopes, should have been forced into this position was not the only anomaly that the period presents.

Hitchcock despairingly told A. D. H. Smith: "Well, it looks as though the country would have to struggle along without a President, doesn't it?" And then, striking his hand on the desk, he exclaimed, "What a hopeless situation!"

CHAPTER TEN

THE BATTLE OF
RESERVATIONS

"He [Wilson] can not pass his treaty without some kind of reservations and he should have seen this a month ago." SECRETARY OF THE INTERIOR LANE, *September 11, 1919.*

1

As WILSON lay on his bed of pain, battling for his very life, the struggle in the Senate over the treaty moved into its final stages.

On September 10 the Senate committee finally relinquished the treaty from the strangle hold which it had been maintaining for the two months since July 14. The majority report, which was signed by Lodge and eight fellow Republicans, is a unique document.

Lodge denied at the outset that the committee had been unduly dilatory; surely it was entitled to a few weeks in which to consider this momentous pact. It was also handicapped by the unwillingness of the President to provide information, and by the necessity of having to ferret out data of its own. And as far as speed was concerned, how about the Allies? Great Britain had "very naturally" ratified at once (a suggestion of sinister British designs); but France, Italy, and Japan had not yet acted.

The popular clamor for haste, continued the report, was largely "artificial." It had been fomented by administration forces, by banking firms (the malign hand of Wall Street), and by the "unthinking outcry" of ignorant but well-meaning citizens who had not read the treaty beyond the words "League of Nations." Yet these were the people who were certain that the pact would bring about a beatific state of "eternal peace."

The cry that speed was necessary to restore our economic structure was just so much nonsense. Trade with Germany had already been reestablished, though on an informal basis.

The "unthinking" supporters of Wilson were crying that no amendments could be added to the treaty because such action would require a reconvening of the entire Paris Conference. This, said Lodge, was not true. The Peace Conference of Paris was still in session, working on the lesser settlements. It could be "at least as usefully employed" in considering amendments as in dividing up the booty of Southeastern Europe and Asia Minor, or handing over friendly Greeks to our enemy Bulgaria, or in seeking to shoulder off onto Uncle Sam burdensome mandates in Armenia, Anatolia, and Constantinople.

Not only was the conference in session, but the German representatives could be summoned once more to Paris. With another unseemly display of sarcasm, the report declared that "the journey is within the power of a moderate amount of human endurance . . ."

The committee then offered forty-five textual amendments, and four reservations, totaling forty-nine, the most important of which were later embodied in the well-known Lodge reservations. In general the committee amendments were designed to safeguard American sovereignty and freedom of action, and to veto a few objectionable parts of the treaty.

The Lodge group was certain that the unamended League was an alliance rather than a league, and that it was a fomenter of war rather than a preventer of war. "Unthinking" zealots were saying that the United States "must" join and "must" do this or that; they forgot that "must" was a word not to be found in the dictionary governing the intercourse of sovereign nations. No one could force us to accept this treaty as it stood, for we sought "no guarantees, no territory, no commercial benefits or advantages."

The majority report ringingly concluded: "The other nations will take us on our own terms, for without us their league is a wreck and all their gains from a victorious peace are imperiled."

2

The six Democrats on the committee filed a minority report which was less vigorous but no less interesting than that of the majority.

The minority strongly urged prompt ratification without either amendments or reservations. The long delay in committee had been totally unnecessary, it declared, because the Republican members had known how they were going to vote before the discussion began. Industry and commerce had suffered as a result of Senate obstructionism—an obstructionism which was clearly out of line with American majority opinion.

It was misleading to argue, the report continued, that commerce with Germany had been resumed. Admittedly there had been about $11,000,000 worth of trade since the Armistice —or two cents' worth with each German per month. This was not trade; it was a trickle.

The amendments proposed by Lodge, said the minority, were worse than useless: they would bring about a complete rejection of the treaty. It was true that a skeleton peace conference still lingered on in Paris; but Germany had signed, and we had lost the power to bring her back to sign something more. We should have to subject ourselves to the humiliation of going as suppliants to Berlin and of begging for such terms as our vanquished foes chose to give us.

It was both false and dishonest to say that we sought no material gain through the treaty. The minority report listed twelve important items, including valuable trade privileges, the retention of 500,000 tons of seized German shipping, the restoration of confiscated American property in Germany, and a validation of the seizure of $800,000,000 worth of German assets in the United States. All of these sweeping gains would be jeopardized by a renegotiation of the treaty.

The Republicans, concluded the minority, while seeking out "petty flaws" with a microscope, had nothing constructive to report. The League was the one hope of humanity, and the United States must not fail to throw its full weight behind this noble project.

Looking back on both these reports today, we cannot escape the impression that the Republican effusion was bitterly partisan, offensively sarcastic, somewhat frivolous, and largely specious. It was obviously not directed at the Senate, to which the majority was formally reporting, but at public opinion. Ex-President Taft could hardly believe that a man of Lodge's background could stoop to such "sneers" and "cheap sarcasm."

The Democratic report was also partisan, though less bitterly so, but it was badly out of line with reality in disclaiming the need for any reservations whatever. Yet on the whole it was a more honest and a more factual document.

Curiously enough, a second minority report was filed by Senator McCumber of North Dakota, the high-minded tenth Republican on the committee, who at first opposed all reservations, but who was now presenting six mild reservations. With conspicuous fairness he attacked the offensive partisanship and destructive criticism of his Republican colleagues, while censuring the Democrats for their subserviency to Wilson.

McCumber fortified the position of the Democrats when he pointed out that it would be both time-consuming and difficult to fill out again the skeleton of the conference at Paris. He opposed textual amendments on the ground that other powers would be encouraged to present additional ones of their own. On the other hand, he conceded that the purpose of some of the proposed Republican reservations was unobjectionable, though their tone was "defiant, discourteous," and "overbearing."

Altogether, the McCumber report came as a gust of fresh

air into an atmosphere fetid with partisanship, and remains a tribute to the fairness and balance of its author.

3

Before 1929, treaties were invariably debated in secret session of the Senate, unless by special vote the galleries were thrown open. The Republican majority cleverly arranged to have the Treaty of Versailles discussed in open session. The foes of Wilson realized that a public debate would give them yet another sounding board from which to hammer home their arguments and further confuse the people.

Public sentiment by this time was clearly drifting away from ratification without any reservations whatever. In July, the issue had been: ratification without reservations, or ratification with mild reservations. By September, the issue had become: ratification with reservations, or no ratification at all. As the great majority of the American people clearly favored the treaty in some form, the discussion centered on the kinds of amendments or reservations most acceptable.

The treaty as reported back to the Senate was now taken up section by section. The debate had been going on unofficially since about the previous December, and there was obviously nothing new to be said unless it was false, irrelevant, or unimportant. The senators on both sides had made up their minds how they were going to vote, and the final result could be calculated within just a few votes. Yet while Europe suffered, and the Allies marked time, and the other European settlements were delayed, and the Germans at home and abroad took heart, it seemed as though the Senate were engaged in splitting hairs and then trying to determine which pieces were the thickest.

Outright textual amendments had to be disposed of first. These were highly objectionable to the true friends of the treaty, because they would require a reopening of the negotiations not only with the Allies but also with Germany. Haggling of this kind would mean embarrassment, delay, and a further unsettling of world peace.

Scores of amendments were offered in the Senate, some of vital importance, others of no importance. Senator Sherman, an "irreconcilable," proposed an amendment that would invoke the "gracious favor of Almighty God." This was promptly objected to by Borah, who opposed anything that would seem to imply the blessing of the Almighty on "an infamous Covenant."

All the amendments were voted down by early November, principally because they would necessitate prolonged renegotiation. All were defeated by either comfortable or overwhelming majorities, except the Johnson amendment on six votes to one, which lost on October 27 by a narrow margin of 38 to 40.

The complete defeat of the amendments was a sweeping victory for the Democratic forces, and the news was doubtless enheartening to the sick Wilson. Possibly he took too much encouragement from this victory, and further developed false ideas about the needlessness of compromise.

Significantly, the victory was not won by Democrats alone. It was achieved by a solid block of Democrats (several deserted), with the assistance of about twelve "mild reservationists." The voting definitely proves that even at this late hour the "mild reservationists" were open to reason, and probably to compromise. *Nothing could better high-light the failure of the Democrats to win them over at an earlier date, or the necessity of gaining their votes if unobjectionable reservations were to be attached to the treaty.*

4

When the amendments were all rejected, Lodge presented from the Committee on Foreign Relations, on November 6, 1919, a series of fourteen reservations. In their final form these came to be known, somewhat inaccurately, as the "Lodge" reservations. (See pages 387-393 for the complete texts.)

Each one of the proposed restrictions was voted on separately, usually after debate, which in some cases was protracted. Dozens of amendments to the reservations or substitutes for them were presented by various senators, including the "irreconcilables" and the Democrats, led by Hitchcock. All such proposals lost. Only two of the fourteen reservations sponsored by the committee were defeated, but two others on different subjects were proposed from the floor and carried in their places. The Republicans, with the occasional defection of one member, voted as a compact unit for the reservations; while the Democrats, with the defection of from three to ten of their members (counting "irreconcilables" and "pairs"), voted as a group against them.

There can be no doubt whatever that a prompt and unqualified ratification by the United States would have started the treaty and the League more auspiciously, and would have caused us to appear to far better advantage in the international community. From this point of view Wilson was completely justified in opposing all qualifications. But since it was now clear that restrictions of some kind were inevitable, we may profitably examine the Lodge reservations to determine precisely how they affected the treaty.

The Lodge preamble stipulated that ratification by the United States would not become binding until three of the four principal Allied powers had accepted in writing the reservations adopted by the Senate.

As long as there were going to be reservations, much could be said in favor of this proviso. Vagueness and uncertainty are enemies of international accord. It is desirable that all parties to a compact, whether in civil or in international life, know as definitely as possible what they are undertaking to perform. Otherwise there will almost inevitably be false assumptions, friction, charges of bad faith, and perhaps an open rupture.

Yet Wilson, for quite understandable reasons, was strongly opposed to this preamble. He did not want strong reservations anyhow; but to be forced to go to the other powers, and to extort from them a solemn written statement, was humiliating in the extreme. It seemed like international bad manners, but more than that it was a confession that the President, after having drawn up the treaty, could not control the legislative body that was supposed to approve it.

So much for the preamble. The first reservation consisted of two parts, the first of which stipulated that in case of withdrawal from the League the United States would be the sole judge of whether it had fulfilled all its obligations.

This was designed to quiet the fears of nervous souls who suspected that other nations might try to hold us in the League on the pretext that we had not been faithful to our bond. Such an eventuality seemed most unlikely, for in actual practice a powerful sovereign nation is the ultimate judge of these matters. Besides, no weak League could possibly hold a great nation like the United States against its will. Since this was so, no real harm could be done by asserting the general proposition—a proposition which Wilson himself approved in the four mild reservations which he secretly prepared for Senator Hitchcock. (See pages 393-394 for text.)

The second part of the first reservation provided that notice of withdrawal from the League might be given by a concurrent resolution of Congress. A concurrent resolution, as contrasted with a joint resolution, does not require the signature of the President; nor is it subject to his veto.

Wilson was naturally much displeased by this move, for it was clearly another attempt to encroach upon the Executive in his conduct of foreign affairs. It was interpreted by the Democrats as unconstitutional, and also as a direct slap at Wilson. But, as Lodge pointed out, Wilson would not be President after March, 1921, and this limitation would be as binding upon a Republican as upon a Democratic Executive. Yet, whatever the political implications, it seems clear that the machinery set up by the United States for withdrawal would have no real bearing upon the actual functioning of the League.

5

The second reservation stabbed at Article X, and was beyond a doubt the most significant of the fourteen. If it had not been proposed, the senators and Wilson might have been able to compromise on other matters, in which case the treaty would have been ratified. The "heart" of the Covenant— Article X—was the "heart" of the difficulty.

The Lodge reservation to Article X declared that the United States "assumes no obligation" to preserve the independence or territorial integrity of any other country, or to employ the armed forces of the United States for such purpose, *unless* Congress should so provide.

We must note at the outset that the Lodge reservation did not wipe out Article X. This article could still function. The basic general obligation in the first sentence was left untouched. We *might* be willing to cooperate with other nations in employing our army and navy. But first Congress, which under our Constitution possesses the war-declaring power, would have to vote its approval. We could exercise our free choice, as the President himself had told the Senate committee, as to whether to get into the fight or not. But Wilson was unalterably opposed to the Lodge reservation because it specifically removed any *moral* obligation to exercise that free choice against the aggressor. It was, in his mind, a "knife thrust at the heart of the treaty."

It is difficult at this distance to understand why Wilson should have been determined to block all compromise, and with it the treaty, over the Lodge reservation to Article X. Actually, the more important articles which provided the machinery and the teeth of the League were left untouched or virtually untouched.

Pride of authorship, as Lodge suggests, was probably involved in Wilson's thinking. Like other successful authors, he did not care to have editors tamper with his style, and the seemingly clumsy efforts of the senators to change his literary creation were calculated to arouse great stubbornness. Lodge may in fact have had the ingenuity to concentrate his fire on Article X, rather than on the more formidable (boycott) Article XVI, because Article X was more likely to provoke the President into a politically disastrous course.

More important to Wilson, no doubt, was the idea of a *moral* obligation, which he felt was stronger than a *legal* obligation. When aggression occurred, the Council, in the words of Article X, "shall advise" as to what to do, which of course could mean much or nothing. But Wilson hoped that all the League members would be *morally* bound by the pledge "to respect and preserve" the territory and independence of all member states.

Theoretically, as was so often the case, Wilson was on sound ground. In private life a man may find a loophole in a contract; but if he is an honorable man he cannot escape a moral obligation. One of Wilson's great aspirations was to introduce into international affairs the same high standard of ethics that exists in private life among honest men.

This was a noble ideal, but like so many of Wilson's other ideals, it presupposed something for which the world was not yet ready—and may never be. The veriest amateur in diplomatic affairs knows, especially since the Munich surrender of 1938, that moral and even legal obligations may be of no real value unless they are strongly connected with self-interest.

One of the bitterest ironies of this great drama is that Wilson destroyed, or helped destroy, his dream for world peace, because he insisted upon his version of Article X—an article which meant no more than the good faith of the nations subscribing to it and the other articles.

6

The reservation to Article X, from many points of view, was unnecessary. Article X itself may have been unnecessary, as a number of distinguished international lawyers concluded, among them an American, Elihu Root, and a Frenchman, Léon Bourgeois, one of the framers of the League, the first president of its Council, and Wilson's successor as winner of the Nobel Peace Prize.

We have remarked that the unreserved Article X was vague and permissive, and that moral obligations provide a shaking foundation for world order. We should also note that no action could have been taken by the League Council to send American boys to the deserts of Arabia *unless* the vote of our representative was in the affirmative—as it almost certainly would not have been. In short, the reservation was unnecessary, except perhaps to forestall future disputes as to our good faith.

But things that are unnecessary for legal purposes are often necessary for political purposes. Ignorant and designing foes of the League had liberally sown the dragon's teeth of suspicion all over the country. There had to be a reservation to Article X as a sop to the Irish vote: American boys must never be used to crush Erin's coming revolt. There had to be a reservation to quiet nationalistic nerves: American boys must never be "hirelings" of some superstate. These fears were poorly founded, as the subsequent history of the League attests. But they were very real in 1919, and they were shared not only by Americans but by large numbers of Canadians, whose objections were later presented at Geneva.

The "strong reservationists" apparently wanted a reservation to Article X that would be sweeping enough to protect the peculiar interests of the United States, while leaving a substantial part of the article unaffected. On November 10 Senator Borah offered a reservation completely releasing the United States from any *legal* or *moral* obligation under Article

X. This attempt virtually to eliminate the disputed article was snowed under by a vote of 18 to 68, with mostly "irreconcilables" voting in the affirmative.

The Lodge adherents, whatever their motives, were evidently unwilling to kill the article completely, though that is what Wilson thought they were doing.

7

The third Lodge reservation stated that no mandate could be legally accepted by the United States except by action of Congress. This was obviously designed to prevent Wilson or some other President from taking on vexatious obligations in strange parts of the earth.

The mandate reservation, while not flattering to the President's discretion, cannot at this date be regarded as harmful. Mandates would cost money; only Congress under the Constitution may appropriate money; hence no American mandate could exist, regardless of the Executive, without the sanction of the Congress. The reservation was thus a warning to the President not to do what he probably would never have dared to do. As we shall later note, Wilson himself publicly admitted that there was no objection to a frank statement of this principle.

The fourth Lodge reservation declared that all questions pertaining to our domestic affairs were excluded from the jurisdiction, arbitral or otherwise, of any outside body. Also, the United States would be the sole judge of what were "domestic" questions.

This declaration reflected the ancient unwillingness of the Senate to submit "domestic" issues, such as those concerning tariffs and immigration, to the judgment of foreigners. In a sense the reservation was repetitious and unnecessary, for Article XV of the League Covenant (in response to Senate objections) specifically exempted questions of "domestic jurisdiction." But even though repetitious, the reservation could surely do no harm by apprising the outside world of our peculiar position on these matters. Wilson privately conceded this principle in his secret draft of the Hitchcock reservations.

The fifth Lodge reservation specifically exempted the Monroe Doctrine from the jurisdiction of the League.

This was another repetitious qualification, and in that sense unnecessary. At the behest of American and senatorial opinion, Wilson had forced an amendment into the final draft of Article XXI of the Covenant, providing that nothing in the Covenant should affect "international engagements" such as "regional understandings like the Monroe Doctrine . . ."

Lodge, Root, and others condemned these phrases as ambiguous, misleading, erroneous, and "ridiculous." The Monroe Doctrine was not then an "international engagement"; it was the *unilateral* policy of the United States. It was not then a "regional understanding"; it was *our* policy, not that of any region.

It must be conceded that Lodge and his cohorts were correct; but, inaccurate though such descriptive phrases were, the Monroe Doctrine was specifically named and specifically exempted. The famed Doctrine, like the elephant, is difficult to define but easy to recognize when seen—or rather when a situation involving it is seen.

The Lodge reservation was thoroughly unnecessary, except to give assurance to a host of Americans who set great store by the sacred shibboleth without knowing what it meant. In that sense it was thoroughly necessary. This Wilson privately conceded in his secret draft of the Hitchcock reservations.

8

The sixth Lodge reservation dealt with the "scandal of Shantung." It declared that the United States withheld its assent to the articles of the treaty countenancing this arrangement, and reserved full liberty of action in any controversy arising out of them.

This was an anticlimactic conclusion to the months of heated debate over the alleged "surrender" of Shantung province to Japan rather than to China. It was at best a futile gesture. We did not annul the arrangement; we simply refused to recognize it. The reservation would not move a single Japanese out of Shantung or a single Chinese in. Japanese policy in the Far East would run the course marked out for it, perhaps a bit more obdurately now that the senators had offended Japan by their ill informed fulminations against the "rape" of Shantung.

The reservation may have been futile, but it did salve senatorial consciences, and it did provide a sop to American opinion. With unctuous indignation we could declare that we would not be a party to this section of the settlement.

The senatorial reservation on Shantung was not without its ironical aspects. For more than twenty years the imperialistic Occidental powers—Russia, France, Great Britain, and Germany—had been carving out leaseholds and spheres of influence in China. Yet the Senate had not become unduly concerned, and silence is presumed to give consent. Now came the Japanese, who actually belonged in the Far East and who had dispossessed the Germans, and senatorial indignation boiled over.

The shade of Denis Kearney, king of San Francisco Chinese-baiters of yesteryear, must have stirred uneasily as Senator Johnson of California shed crocodile tears over the poor heathen Chinese. Certain cynics even concluded that the sapient senator was less concerned with helping China than he was with helping his presidential prospects. The New York *Evening Post* thought that he had "got all the famous hypocrites from Tartuffe to Pecksniff beaten hollow."

The blaring Borah was moving heaven and earth to stave off any world organization for peace that might get us into the broils of Europe. At the same time he was demanding that we rush headlong into the broils of the Far East in the interests of the underdog Chinese. "We have crawled and cringed long enough," he cried. "I do not anticipate war with Japan, but, if unavoidable, it might as well come now as at any other time."

Senator Johnson to the contrary, China had not lost her

The Discovery of China

(Courtesy of Brooklyn *Eagle*; cartoonist Harding)

sovereignty in Shantung to Japan, and no nation (including ourselves) could be forced under Article X to fight the Chinese in order to keep the Japanese there. German economic rights in Shantung, and not Chinese sovereignty over Shantung, had passed to Japan. The Japanese agreed to evacuate the province in due season, and did so in 1922. The best hope that China had of regaining complete control of Shantung, economic and otherwise, was to enter the League and negotiate on an amicable basis with Japan.

The loud and libelous outpourings of the senatorial "friends" of China angered the Japanese, stiffened Chinese obduracy, and made more difficult the negotiations between Japan and China leading to the final evacuation of Shantung. The Lodge reservation merely added to these difficulties. The Chinese could well pray for deliverance from their "friends" —friends who were more eager to discredit Wilson than Japan, more eager to help the party than to help China.

9

Reservations seven to thirteen inclusive (see pages 389-392 for texts) were all relatively minor, and did not interfere in any substantial way with the functioning of the League or the execution of the treaty. While somewhat ungracious in tone and suspicious in content, they were designed to reassert the primacy of the Constitution and safeguard the functions of Congress.

The fourteenth and last Lodge reservation asserted that the United States was not bound by any action of the League in which any member (with its political satellites) cast more than one vote. This was aimed at the six votes of the British Empire in the Assembly to the one for the United States.

The new six-to-one safeguard was the fruit of many proposed compromises. One bright senator had suggested that we demand forty-eight votes for ourselves—one for each state in the Union. Others urged that our vote be increased to six, while that of the British be reduced to one. (This led one commentator to propose that the vote of Idaho in the Senate be reduced in proportion to its population, and with it the vote of Borah.) Yet in the end it was decided that the British might keep their six votes, but we would not be bound by them.

Why were our fears of the British Empire so grossly exaggerated?

It was assumed that the six British votes would always be cast one way, which did not prove to be the case at all.

It was forgotten that while Great Britain had six votes in the Assembly she had only one vote in the all-important Council. This is what defenders of the League meant when they said that Britain had "six voices but only one vote." Or, as the Little Rock *Arkansas Gazette* put it, "Sort of a parallel to Hi Johnson's status in the Senate."

It was also forgotten that the United States controlled at least six votes in the Assembly through its influence over such "protectorate" nations as Cuba, Santo Domingo, Haiti, Panama, Nicaragua, and Liberia. It is probable that Washington could have "voted" these tiny countries with more consistency than London could have "voted" the component parts of the Empire.

It was also forgotten that on all decisions of substance the one vote of the United States in the Council or the Assembly could block any adverse vote by the British Empire.

There was one valid objection to the six-to-one arrangement. If we were a party to a dispute, our vote was not allowed to count in our favor, and it was conceivable, but extremely unlikely, that all six British votes would be cast against us. Yet the same was true of all other nations, and powers like Italy and France, which were more vulnerable than we, betrayed no undue suspicion.

Thus the Lodge reservation did not wipe out the six-to-one arrangement. It merely declared that in the eventuality that a decision should be rendered against us by British votes, we might refuse to be bound by it.

This of course reflected an unwholesome distrust of our associates in the world of nations. It was an affront to Canada and Australia, both of whom had sacrificed more of their sons on the field of battle than we had. We were clamoring that these highly advanced commonwealths should be denied votes

while gladly conceding them to black Liberia, revolutionary
Nicaragua, and (as one Canadian journal put it) "the half-caste
Greaser republics of the West Indies . . ."

10

It is hard to understand how Wilson could have insisted
that the fourteen Lodge reservations, ten of which concerned
the League only, completely nullified the whole treaty. Most
of the treaty, indeed most of the Covenant, was completely
unaffected. No attempt was made to touch the European settlement. While our obligations were somewhat limited under
the Covenant, the machinery of the League was left free to
function. By refusing to attach any reservation whatever to
some of the more important articles, including Wilson's favorite Article XI ("minding other people's business"), the
Senate merely underscored its acceptance of them.

It is true that some of the reservations were of no real consequence. One even gets the impression that a few were put
in to swell the number to fourteen, and thus offset Wilson's
Fourteen Points. But if they were of no real consequence, why
become unduly concerned about them?

It is also true that some of the reservations were completely
useless—except to pacify public opinion and save senatorial
face. But in this sense they were not useless.

It is also true that some of the reservations were repetitious
of the Covenant. But surely no real harm could be done by
saying in more words and more explicitly what the Covenant
said in fewer words and less explicitly.

It is also true that some of the reservations repeated what
was already in the Constitution of the United States. Colonel
Bonsal, talking with Lodge about these problems, remarked,
"It goes without saying." "If it goes without saying," replied
Lodge rather tartly, "there is no harm in saying it—and much
advantage."

It is true that Congress appropriates money and declares war. There is no harm in saying these things; in fact foreigners sometimes need to be reminded that Congress does not have to honor the commitments of the President.

It is also true that some of the reservations were tactless and offensively worded. Despite the fact that we were wealthy and powerful, they breathed an atmosphere of suspicion, as well as a determination not to be taken into camp by "slick" European diplomats. But foreign peoples had long since become used to our "shirtsleeve" tactics, and we were so rich and our support was so desperately needed that we could afford to indulge in bad manners. Nor was the reservation habit anything new: the Senate had already fallen into it in connection with other treaties.

It is also true that the reservations warned foreigners about our peculiar prejudices. Other nations no doubt had mental reservations which would have come out sooner or later; the American method at least had the merit of candor and of forestalling future misunderstanding as to our position.

Wilson thought that these few ill phrased and largely inconsequential reservations completely killed the 268-page treaty; the Republican majority professed to feel that these same reservations would save the United States from disaster. Nothing could better illustrate the distorting effect of pride, personal prejudice, prerogative, and partisanship.

A few ill chosen words, one way or another, were not going to make or break this great treaty. It was the spirit behind it that counted. If the people of the United States were unwilling to support it, the absence of reservations probably would have availed little; if the American people were willing to support it, the Lodge reservations did not prevent them from doing so.

CHAPTER ELEVEN

THE STRATEGY OF DEADLOCK

"The whole damn thing has gotten into the maelstrom of politics, of the nastiest partisanship, when it ought to have been lifted up into the clearer air of good sense and national dignity . . ." SECRETARY OF THE INTERIOR LANE, *October 2, 1919.*

1

AS THE day for the showdown vote in the Senate neared, the burning question was: Will Wilson accept the Lodge reservations? This problem is so vital that we shall have to retrace some ground in order to put it in its proper setting.

From the very outset, as we have seen, Wilson was hostile to reservations. They meant either something or nothing. If general and innocuous, they would mean nothing, and hence were ridiculous excess baggage. If they were specific and amendatory, they would involve the humiliation of further negotiation with the Allies, and possibly the even greater humiliation of treating with our once arrogant foe. This would mean further delay, at a time when all Europe was crying for peace; and it might mean, if Germany proved refractory, a complete loss of all our material advantages under the treaty.

Wilson was convinced that to ask for special treatment would cheapen us as a nation, and put us outside the concert of powers just as clearly and definitely as rejection. The brave new League could not start off with promising momentum if we joined half-heartedly, one eye furtively on our associates, the other longingly on the exits. We ought either to go in like a great power, "scorning privileges," or to preserve a dignified aloofness. And staying aloof would both injure our commercial prospects and forfeit our world leadership.

To Wilson the Lodge reservations were cowardly and unmanly. To load ourselves down with qualifications, when not even the tiniest nations were asking for them, would make us the laughingstock of the world. If changes were to be made in the League, we could work for them after we entered, just as our states had done after ratifying the federal Constitution in 1788, and as the League members actually did in amending the Covenant.

Above all, reservations seemed to Wilson like a base betrayal —a betrayal of our honored dead, a betrayal of our war aims, a betrayal of our associates at the peace table, and a breaking of the solid front that had crushed the Prussian threat to Western civilization.

Reservations not only cut Wilson's pride in the nation; they cut his own pride as well. Pride of authorship was hurt by the proposed changes in the Covenant. Pride of prerogative was hurt by the encroachments of Congress on the Executive. Pride of leadership was hurt by an inability to get the treaty approved as signed.

There can be no doubt that personal animus and partisanship in large measure lay behind the Senate reservations. Lodge plainly hated Wilson, and was out to discredit and humiliate him. If Wilson accepted these vexatious qualifications, he would merely be playing into the hands of his archenemy.

And why should he accept such a humiliation when he did not need to? Public opinion clearly favored the League (in some form), and the people ultimately would prevail over senatorial obstructionism.

There was in Wilson a strain of the Scotch Covenanter: having made up his mind that he was right, he saw evil in any other course. Personal pride and ingrained stubbornness partially blinded him to the public weal.

2

Two days after returning home from Paris, Wilson dictated this statement to the newsmen: "The President is open-minded as to every proposition of reasonable interpretation, but will not consent to any proposition that we scuttle." In short, Wilson would accept mildly interpretive resolutions which were not a part of the treaty, and which would not involve the hazards of renegotiation.

Under such encouragement both the Democrats and the "mild reservationists" in the Senate began working on interpretive reservations. By mid-August it seemed as though they might be able to get together.

But suddenly Wilson struck a more uncompromising attitude. No doubt he was irked by the dilatory tactics of the Senate committee, and by the agitation in the Senate for outright amendment. Whatever the reasons, he held a conference with Hitchcock on August 15, after which the senator issued a most unfortunate statement.

Hitchcock revealed that Wilson had not changed his position, but he now felt that even mild reservations "would prove tremendously embarrassing." They would betray half-heartedness on the part of America. All this talk about reservations, said Wilson, was premature: he was not even considering them; the Democratic senators were not even to think about them.

No less significant were Wilson's views about outright textual modifications. "Both the President and I agreed," reported Senator Hitchcock, "that the immediate task is to see to the defeat of the proposed amendments. We've got to remove absolutely any probability of the dotting of an 'i' or the crossing of a 't.'" Wilson also said (perhaps only half seriously) that, if the treaty was ruined by amendments, he would send Senators Lodge and Knox to Berlin to negotiate another.

Hitchcock was most indiscreet in repeating these statements,

even granted that he did so correctly. Wilson was attacking
amendments, not reservations; and that he was right is indicated by Republican support in the Senate. But the President's
remarks were wrenched from their context. George Harvey
and other partisans from then on quoted Wilson as being
opposed to *all reservations,* even to the "dotting of an 'i' or
the crossing of a 't.' "

The upshot was that, by mid-August, Wilson had stiffened
even on interpretive reservations, his followers had become
cold to the overtures of the "mild reservationists," the "mild
reservationists" were unwillingly being driven into the arms
of Lodge, and strong reservations were ultimately welded to
the treaty.

3

On August 19, as we have observed, Wilson met with the
Senate committee in their historic conference. Possibly in response to the unfavorable reaction to his interview with Hitchcock, he sounded a more conciliatory note, for he agreed to
accept purely interpretive reservations embodied in a *separate*
resolution.

Shortly thereafter Wilson left for his western tour, and in
his speeches he took essentially the same stand. But toward
the end he seemed to turn more sharply against reservations,
especially at Salt Lake City, when he branded the proposed
Lodge reservation to Article X as "a rejection of the Covenant." By this time he was certain that "any reservation" would
have to be carried back to all the treaty signatories, including
Germany.

Then catastrophe struck, and Wilson was borne back to
the White House. His closing speeches on the tour, combined
with his subsequent statements, gave rise to the legend that
he was unalterably opposed to *all* reservations.

It is not generally known that Wilson, just before leaving

on the western trip, drafted on his typewriter four interpretive reservations which, if necessary, he was willing to accept. (See pages 393-394.) These related to Article X, the Monroe Doctrine, domestic questions, and withdrawal from the League. Wilson gave the reservations to Hitchcock and instructed him to employ them as he saw fit, but not to reveal their source. The senator used them, essentially unchanged, as the basis for four of his five reservations, but the secret of their authorship was carefully guarded for a number of years.

The confidential Wilson reservations, which related to four of the most knotty issues in dispute, are of immense importance in revealing the President's mind. They were not substantially different from the corresponding Lodge reservations, though the latter were more sweeping and more offensively worded. No less significant, the secret Wilson reservations were in essentials so close to the similar reservations being backed by the "mild reservationists" in mid-August as to raise several searching questions. If Wilson could accept his own secret reservations without violating his principles, why could he not have accepted those of the "mild reservationists"? Instead of going West when he was so near this group, why did he not remain in Washington and work out a complete understanding with them?

Up to a point Wilson's strategy was sound. It would have been folly to announce publicly that he was quite willing to accept any kind of amendment. The obvious course was for him to seem unyielding, drive as hard a bargain as he could, and then at the last moment, when there was no danger of more reservations being added, make the grand gesture of accepting the Lodge reservations as of no fundamental importance.

Wilson had played this kind of game before in securing desirable legislation, but it is a dangerous game—a game that demands that one have one's wits about one, and that one observe the play closely at every stage. During the last weeks of the fight the President was a desperately ill man, and he could not watch the maneuvering carefully. He saw darkly through the windows of his sick chamber.

Throughout the entire struggle Wilson was consistent on several counts. He would not accept amendments, and amendments were defeated. He would accept only mild reservations that were not made a part of the resolution of ratification. The Lodge reservations were not mild, and they were definitely made a part of the resolution of ratification.

Some apologists for Wilson claim that if he had not collapsed he would have compromised with Lodge. Perhaps so, but there is nothing to support such a view in his public utterances, in his private papers, or in his character.

4

By the beginning of the third week of November, 1919, the resolution of ratification was moving sluggishly toward a final vote. The Lodge reservations were being voted up, the Democratic substitutes were being voted down.

It was as plain as a pikestaff, and had been for many weeks, that the Republicans, having attached the reservations by a majority vote, could not command the necessary two-thirds vote. The only way the treaty could be approved was for the Democrats to support the Lodge reservations, or for the Republicans to abandon their program and join the Democrats in supporting the treaty without reservations or with mild Democratic reservations.

This latter alternative was plainly out of the question. The country was now demanding reservations of some kind; and the Republicans, after all their talk about "Americanizing" the treaty, could not tamely hoist the white flag. Nor could the Democrats, after all their talk about the Lodge reservations emasculating the treaty, vote with the Republicans. It was bad politics for either side to give in to the other.

Everything depended on the invalid in the White House.

He was still the leader of the Democratic party. If he told the Democrats in the Senate to vote for the treaty with the Lodge reservations, most of them undoubtedly would do so, and the two-thirds majority would be won. If he told them to vote against the treaty with the Lodge reservations, the great body of them would do so, and the treaty would be lost.

Wilson was a sick man and in no condition to direct an

It "Shall Not Pass!"

(Courtesy of Chicago *Tribune*; cartoonist Orr)

intricate parliamentary battle. The Democrats knew this, and at one point it seemed as though their strategy was to delay until the President was well enough to familiarize himself with the situation. If they could get the word of command from him, they could push off onto his bent shoulders the responsibility for their final action.

Not only was Wilson enfeebled in body and weary in mind; not only was he embittered in spirit and unstable in emotion; not only did he have false notions about the public's views on reservations (that Pueblo applause would not stop); not only was he out of touch with the currents of public opinion and with the Democratic leaders in the Senate; not only were his few informants carefully instructed to withhold news that might shock him into a relapse; but the guardians of his bedside continued to censor his mail. This, though desirable from a medical point of view, was, as we shall note, perhaps disastrous from a political point of view.

5

One of the minor tragedies of the major tragedy is that Colonel House was not available to Wilson during these crucial hours.

For over six years House's peculiar talents as an adviser and compromiser had complemented and smoothed the Scotch-Irish traits of the somewhat stiff-necked Wilson. But at the Conference the two men had appreciably drifted apart, and busybodies had widened the gap. Colonel House continued his work in Europe, and did not return to America until October 12, 1919, ten days after Wilson's stroke. House himself was seriously ill, suffering from gallstones and other ailments, and was assisted from the ship to his home in New York.

Late in October, House sent Colonel Stephen Bonsal to Washington to talk with Senator Lodge about reservations. Bonsal, though out of sympathy with Lodge's position, nevertheless found the senator courteous, considerate, and in a mood for compromise. On a printed copy of the League Covenant the scholar-politician added a few words and inserted some others, all of which constituted the minimum he would accept in the way of reservations. These were complementary, relatively inconsequential, and far less binding than the official Lodge reservations which passed a week or two later. It is clear that Lodge, at least at this stage, was more conciliatory in private than in public, that is, if he was acting in good faith and not merely jockeying for further advantage.

Bonsal promptly sent this highly important document to Colonel House, who in turn mailed it to Wilson. The Colonel packed his bags, sick though he was, expecting a summons to come to Washington and work out a compromise with Lodge. The summons never came; the letter was never acknowledged; no action was apparently ever taken as the result of it.

Possibly Wilson rejected the new proposal out of hand on the ground that Lodge was merely up to another of his tricks. Possibly the very name of the senator caused the President to react so unfavorably that he put compromise completely out of his mind. At this date he apparently still thought that he could win the battle by placing Lodge "in a hole" and by forcing the Senate to "take its medicine."

It is also possible that Mrs. Wilson or Dr. Grayson preferred to keep this disturbing document from the President. Perhaps they thought that he was not well enough to consider it—this was about November 4 or 5. Yet the previous week he had chatted with the King and Queen of the Belgians, and a few days later he had conferred with Senator Hitchcock.

If the Lodge-Bonsal document was received at the White House, as it almost certainly was, Wilson's vice-regents shouldered a grave responsibility in keeping it from him—granted that they did. If such a decision was made on the ground of the President's ill health, then this is but further proof that he should have resigned. If the decision was made on the ground that Mrs. Wilson disliked Colonel House and distrusted his advice, as we know she did, then she should have resigned along with her husband.

If Wilson received the letter, and took no action on it, whether for reasons of health or personal pique, we could want no better proof that he should have relinquished the reins of authority.

Lodge was evidently offended by this episode, as well he might have been if he had acted with sincerity. He had so far unbent as to propose a compromise which was far less drastic than the official committee reservations. For his pains he got nothing but silence.

Four days after the interview with Bonsal, Lodge introduced the reservations that bear his name, and succeeded in carrying through twelve of them.

6

Senator Hitchcock's position was still singularly difficult. He privately confessed to Colonel Bonsal, the day before the November vote, that *he and most of the Senate Democrats favored getting the treaty ratified "in almost any form."* Yet for political reasons they had to oppose the Lodge reservations: Wilson was insisting that they do so.

Hitchcock's hands were tied until he could hear from the titular leader of the party, yet the titular head of the party lay prostrate behind a shroud of darkness. To communicate with him was like trying to communicate with the spirit world.

Finally, on November 7 and again on November 17, Hitchcock was permitted to see the ailing President. The first interview came the day after the Lodge reservations were introduced, and lasted a half-hour; the second came two days before the vote on the treaty, and lasted for about an hour. Each session was carefully supervised by Mrs. Wilson and Dr. Grayson, both of whom were there to shake an admonitory finger. Hitchcock promptly gave accounts of the interviews to the press, and while they were apparently candid, they were a good deal more cheerful than those which the senator later presented in public addresses and private conversations.

During the first visit Wilson was propped up in bed, with his paralyzed arm concealed beneath the covers. Hitchcock was shocked to find that within a few weeks the President had become a white-bearded old man, though his eye was clear and his resolve strong. While Wilson was willing to accept some of the minor Lodge reservations, he would not "budge an inch" on the preamble (acceptance by the powers) and on Article X. When the senator told him that the Democrats could not muster even a simple majority for ratification without reservations, the President fairly groaned, "Is it possible; is it possible!"

Hitchcock was loath to mention Lodge's name during the conferences: that was dangerously provocative. He could not present both sides of the question fully and fairly: that might shock the President unduly. He was not permitted to argue with the patient: that might kill him. He dreaded hearing Wilson speak, because that was final, and the door was slammed shut on compromise.

Several years later Hitchcock publicly told of one interchange:

"Mr. President," I said, "it might be wise to compromise with Lodge on this point."

"Let Lodge compromise," he replied.

"Well, of course," I added, "he must compromise also, but we might well hold out the olive branch."

"Let Lodge hold out the olive branch," he retorted, and that ended it for that day, for he was too sick a man to argue with in the presence of his anxious doctor and his more anxious wife.

In the two interviews Hitchcock outlined his strategy, and he reported to the press that Wilson had given it his full approval. The Democratic senators would unite to vote down the treaty with the attached Lodge reservations. Then through a favorable though questionable ruling by Vice President Marshall, they would carry a vote to reconsider, and move for the treaty without reservations or with the Hitchcock (Wilson) interpretive reservations, regarding which the President had given the Democratic leaders a free hand.

This scheme would work if enough "mild reservationists" and others came over to make a two-thirds vote. But if it did not work, then there would be deadlock, and the heat of public opinion (so Wilson hoped) would beat so heavily on both the "mild" and the "strong" reservationists that they would bolt to the Democrats and work out some kind of compromise. But first there had to be deadlock before there could be the kind of compromise that the Democrats would accept.

Wilson bluntly told Hitchcock on November 17 that the Lodge reservations were a "nullification" of the treaty, and that if they came to him he would pocket the whole thing. The President chose to have the treaty defeated outright in the Senate, with the Lodge reservations, rather than have to assume the responsibility for pigeonholing it himself. When Wilson was told that the Senate might adjourn while the treaty was still deadlocked, he thought that would be quite desirable. "I would like," Hitchcock quoted him as saying, "to have some of the Senators go home to their constituents while the treaty is still pending."

In short, Wilson wanted a deadlock (rather than the Lodge reservations); worked for a deadlock; and got a deadlock. He had unfaltering faith that public opinion would break the deadlock—in his favor.

7

Senator Hitchcock's strategy, as the event proved, was thoroughly bad. There is less excuse for him than for Wilson, because he was in the thick of the combat, knew the temper of the Senate, was familiar with the Senate rules, and presumably was aware of the shifting tide of public opinion.

Ominously, Lodge was saying, and in essence had long said, that if the Democrats would not take the treaty with his reservations, there would be no treaty. Its blood would be on their hands.

Lodge may have been bluffing, but he had the votes—more than a majority of them. And a majority of the Senate could block any motion to reconsider and to take up Democratic proposals. Of course the friends of the treaty still hoped that the "mild reservationists" would bolt, but these "moderates" had been treated so brusquely by Wilson that they were in no mood to help the Democrats out of the hole into which they had worked themselves. Even Hitchcock admitted that he was "taking a chance" in relying on the "mild reservationists."

Hitchcock was taking much more than a chance in counting on favorable rulings by Vice-President Marshall. The presiding officer, no matter how sympathetic, could be overruled by a simple majority vote—and the Republicans commanded such a vote.

It is true, as Hitchcock planned and Wilson hoped, that there would be a deadlock if the Democrats refused to support the Lodge reservations. But it is difficult to see what good a deadlock would do Wilson's cause. The country was now weary of talk and wanted action, one way or the other. It also seems reasonably clear that by this time public opinion favored either the Lodge reservations or something rather closely akin to them.

Lodge and his fellow Republicans could not afford to yield; they would lose face intolerably. They had first sought to separate the League from the treaty, and had failed. They had next talked of rejecting the treaty outright, but that was too dangerous. They had tried direct amendments, and had been defeated. They had then added the Lodge reservations, and that was the absolute minimum. They had set out to "Americanize," "Republicanize," and "Senatorialize" the treaty; and they would lose what political capital they had gained if they finally permitted their opponents to dictate a different program.

8

As the time for the fateful vote neared, the situation in the Senate and outside the Senate was complicated in the extreme. Much time was spent in parliamentary jockeying, with the clear intent of throwing the onus for rejection on the other party. Each side was trying to stare the other down. Neither wanted to go into the next political campaign with the dead albatross of a rejected pact tied around its neck.

Lodge was saying that this was the last chance for the Democrats, and he meant it. If they rejected the treaty with his res-

ervations, they would have no way of resurrecting it. "It may
lie in the Senate inert," he promised, "but the breath of life
will never be put into it again."

The "mild reservationists," angered by repeated rebuffs,
were insisting that they would not clasp hands with the Democrats, and they meant it. Though restive retainers of Lodge,
they were bound by pride and pledge to stand fast.

Senator Hitchcock was declaring that the Democrats would
kill the treaty rather than accept the "nullifying" Lodge reservations, and he meant it. He was still awaiting final instructions from the White House as to how to vote, and the
Republicans were taunting their opponents with being such
rubber stamps that they could not move until they heard
their master's voice. Yet on November 15, four days before
final action, Hitchcock wrote to Mrs. Wilson that in the absence of definite instructions he would undertake to have his
followers reject the treaty with the Lodge reservations.

The "irreconcilables" were saying that they would vote
against the treaty in any form, and no one doubted that they
meant it.

Of all four groups, the Democrats seemed the least dependable. The pressure was on them rather than on the Republicans. The Lodge men were proposing something concrete;
the initiative lay in their hands; and their reservations seemed
to a vast body of Americans like altogether sensible safeguards.
The Democrats, rather than the Republicans, were cast in the
role of obstructionists.

One of the nightmares of the "irreconcilables" was that the
Democrats, under the pressure of this tremendous responsibility, might throw themselves at the last minute into the arms
of Lodge, and the treaty would then be approved. This seemed
like a very real possibility up to the time of roll call.

To the very end it seemed as though there might be some
eleventh-hour compromise that would save face on both sides.
It was unthinkable that on an issue of this importance the
Senate should throw up its hands and confess that it was impo-

tent. To the very end both Lodge and Wilson seem to have entertained the dual delusion that the other would give way when the showdown came.

Strong pressure was being brought to bear on Wilson to yield ground, though we do not know how much of it reached him. He had reversed himself in the past, on issues like military preparedness and woman suffrage, and the hope was still cherished that he might do so again. The Senate Democrats no doubt would have been pleased with a Wilsonian capitulation, for they were none too comfortable in the role of obstructing the only ratifying resolution that had any chance of passing.

The "mild reservationists" were scurrying about to the very last moment, seeking to bridge the gap—a gap more psychological than actual, more rhetorical then real.

Yet Hitchcock, it seems clear, did not want compromise unless such compromise was a virtual surrender by the Republicans and an adoption of the Democratic program. The Republicans did not want to do this, and they did not have to do it; so they "sat tight."

9

As the zero hour approached, various last-minute attempts were made to induce Wilson to yield or to stand fast.

Herbert Hoover, who had won world-wide fame in Belgium and as United States Food Administrator, sent a long and penetrating telegram on November 19, urging compromise, pointing out that the Lodge reservations were on the whole unobjectionable, and declaring that all these rhetorical matters paled into insignificance beside Europe's need for haste.

Senator Hitchcock seems to have brought no real pressure, either through personal interview or by letter. The nearest he apparently came was on November 18, when he sent to the White House a letter of that date from Senator Walsh of Montana, one of the most intelligent and reasonable of the Democrats. Walsh argued that even though the Lodge reservation devitalized Article X, there was still enough left in Articles XII, XIII, and XVI to provide substance and teeth for the new world organization. Hitchcock significantly added in his covering letter that *many of the Democrats held the same views as those expressed by Walsh*. In brief, these good party men, unlike Wilson, did not think that the Lodge reservations nullified the treaty, but *for the sake of party regularity they would vote as the President directed*.

Why Senator Hitchcock was not more forthright in dealing with Wilson it is not easy to say. He was not a dominating personality, he had political ambitions, and he did not want to shock the President unduly with disagreeable truths. As between the danger of killing the President and killing the treaty, he apparently preferred to take a chance with the treaty.

Incredible though it may seem, even the "irreconcilables" tried to bring pressure on Wilson not to compromise. Senator Borah and his group were desperately afraid that at the last moment Wilson would consent to the Lodge reservations, or some modification of them. The "Idaho lion" sought out Senator Swanson of Virginia, a Democratic wheel horse, and induced him to do what he could at the White House to prevent compromise. This was deliciously ironical: two men teaming up for a common end, the one because he did not want the treaty at all, the other because he wanted the treaty exactly as it was.

Close friends of Wilson, like Bernard M. Baruch, urged compromise, arguing that "half a loaf is better than no bread." Mrs. Wilson also entered the lists, for she felt that with the treaty fight jeopardizing her husband's recovery, nothing mattered but to get it out of the way, even with the hated Lodge reservations.

At the critical moment she went to the President and pleaded, "For my sake, won't you accept these reservation; and get this awful thing settled?"

Wilson (according to his wife's account) stretched out his pallid hand and said, "Little girl, don't you desert me; that I cannot stand." He went on to explain that he had no moral right to accept those changes; the honor of the nation was at

"Where Do We Go from Here?"
(Courtesy of Brooklyn *Eagle*; cartoonist Harding)

stake. "Better a thousand times to go down fighting," he insisted, "than to dip your colors to dishonorable compromise."

Mrs. Wilson adds that for the first time she saw the issues clearly. Never thereafter did she plead with her husband to do what was manifestly so dishonorable.

Then, she relates, Wilson dictated his fateful message to the Senate Democrats.

10

Wilson's communication to Hitchcock, dated November 18, was without exaggeration one of the momentous documents of world history. It told the Democratic majority how they should vote, and it spelled the difference between ratification and nonratification of the Treaty of Versailles.

On the question of the Lodge reservations, Wilson minced no words: "On that I can not hesitate, for, in my opinion, the resolution in that form does not provide for ratification but, rather, for the *nullification* of the treaty. I sincerely hope that the friends and supporters of the treaty will vote against the Lodge resolution of ratification.

"I understand that the door will probably then be open for *a genuine resolution of ratification.*"

"I trust that all *true friends* of the treaty will refuse to support the Lodge resolution."

This letter was a direct slap at the "mild reservationists," whose support was not yet considered lost. They were classed as "nullifiers" and not as "true friends" of the treaty. Some of them were "true friends" of the treaty, and they were naturally angered by this tactless and unnecessary blow.

It is clear that Wilson wholeheartedly endorsed the Hitchcock strategy. First there would be deadlock, and out of the deadlock would come compromise, Wilson fondly believed, along lines that he was willing to accept. Then the way would be clear for a "genuine resolution of ratification," that is, a resolution with no more than interpretive Democratic reservations.

Wilson said nothing about pocketing the treaty if it should pass with the Lodge reservations, but the tone of the letter was so uncompromising as to reinforce his previous threats that he would.

Still strong in the faith, Wilson revealed his ingrained stubbornness, perhaps fortified by sickness and seclusion. Not fully aware of the receding tide of public opinion, he had supreme confidence in the righteousness of his cause and in his power ultimately to override the opposition, as he had done before in Congress. Angered by Lodge and his diabolically clever tactics, he permitted the pinpricks of the Republican reservations to blind him to the fact that the great structure of the treaty was virtually untouched.

Wilson was not asked to choose between a whole loaf and a half-loaf, as Baruch suggested. If those had been the alternatives, his choice would perhaps be less open to criticism. He was given three choices: a loaf with a Republican wrapper around it; a loaf with a Democratic wrapper around it (the chances were very slim); and no loaf at all.

Wilson thought he was choosing the Democratic wrapper, while apparently closing his eyes to the strong probability that he would get no loaf at all.

CHAPTER TWELVE

BREAKING THE HEART
OF THE WORLD

*"The League was defeated in the United States, not because it
was a League of Nations, but because it was a Woodrow Wilson
league, and because the great leader had fallen and there was no
one who could wield his mighty sword."* THOMAS W. GREGORY *(Wilson's Attorney General), January 23, 1925.*

1

THE SCENE was Washington, the hour was noon, the day
was November 19, 1919—one year and eight days after the
Armistice. The Senate of the United States, with galleries
packed and long lines standing out in the corridors, was convening to vote on the treaty.

The country was weary of debate; the Senate was even more
weary. Several days earlier Senator Ashurst of Arizona, a Democrat, had loudly objected to further palaver. They had all made
up their minds; further talk was just "making mud pies." "For
God's sake," he cried, "let us all keep our mouths shut and
vote, vote and only vote." (Applause in galleries.)

Last-minute maneuvers had already taken up a part of the
morning. The Democrats had just met together in secret
caucus, and Wilson's letter, now being published in the newspapers, was read to them. Their great President had asked
them to vote down the Lodge reservations, and they would
follow the leader. He had taken from their shoulders the grave
responsibility of having to make this decision themselves.

The Republican "irreconcilables" had their final hour in
court. Brandegee condemned the "pipe dream" of the League,
and declared that he would consider himself as a "candidate
for a madhouse" if he were to vote for it. Borah conceded that
sooner or later the pact would no doubt be approved with

reservations—"too soon" to suit him—but he wished it to be known that he still wanted no part of it. Sherman denounced the "boiling hell" of the treaty, and castigated the Covenant as the charter of an "international homicide club." He brought a ripple of laughter from the galleries when he said that he was pleased to follow the advice of Wilson and vote against the pact—the first time he had supported the administration since the Armistice.

Senator Hitchcock presented the final case for the Democrats. He went down the line to show that there was no wide gulf between his reservations and those of Lodge; in fact the Democrats could agree to most of the Lodge reservations in principle, though desiring a more tactful wording. The Republican majority, in his judgment, was using the caucus method of a political convention: presenting a group of reservations with a defiant, take-it-or-leave-it attitude. Let there be, he pleaded, the spirit of give and take; let those on the other side of the aisle who really wanted the treaty get together with the Democrats. (Applause in the galleries.)

Hitchcock's reference to the caucus method was not altogether fortunate. It was common knowledge that the Democrats had met that morning in caucus to follow the bidding of Wilson's letter. Senator Penrose (Republican) spoke up and said that "every Democrat" was "under orders from the White House." Senator Thomas (Democrat) snapped back, "I deny that." Penrose got in the last word by retorting that Thomas was the only one who could deny it.

2

The "mild reservationists" resented both Hitchcock's remarks and Wilson's tactless letter. With flushed face Senator Lenroot warmly rebutted the President's charge that the purely protective reservations were "nullification." He would resign his seat before he would consent to Article X without an adequate safeguard. Specifically, he challenged the Democrats to point out what harm there was in protecting the Monroe Doctrine and domestic autonomy.

Senator Kellogg, another "mild reservationist" friend of the treaty, was also irked by Hitchcock's last-minute appeal for compromise. This came "a little late and with bad grace." For about three months Hitchcock had been saying that there must be no substantial reservations at all; not until November 15—four days before—had he been willing to come out with any, and these did not differ essentially from those of Lodge. It was not true, declared Kellogg, that the Lodge reservations had been written by enemies of the treaty: the extreme amendments and reservations of the "irreconcilables" had all been voted down. The "mild reservationists" had long been trying to get a compromise, but the Democrats had refused to meet them halfway. "I am tired of this sort of talk," Kellogg burst out.

Senator McNary, another "mild reservationist," introduced a statement from the League to Enforce Peace, dated November 18. This highly important pressure group, with Taft at its head, had labored long and earnestly for the League of Nations. Now that the issue was clearly a League with the Lodge reservations or no League at all, it reluctantly declared itself for the Lodge reservations, except for the preamble, which it hoped could be modified so as to permit the silent acquiescence of three powers rather than to demand their written consent.

Senator McCumber, another "mild reservationist" and one of the truest friends of the treaty, had the final four minutes before the roll call. He insisted that as much compromise had gone into the reservations as was possible, while still leaving hope for a two-thirds vote. Turning to the Democrats, he pleaded with them not to retreat because they had suffered "some minor reverses." Will you bring your ship "into port," he argued, "though battered somewhat," or "will you scuttle your ship?"

3

It was now 5:30 in the afternoon, and five and one-half hours had been consumed in final debate. The Senate was impatient for action, and as McCumber took his seat cries of "Vote," "Vote," "Vote," arose from all over the chamber.

The question before the Senate was on approving the treaty with the Lodge reservations attached. The crowded galleries sat in tense silence as the roll was called, and as each senator responded to his name.

The result was then announced: 39 ayes, 55 nays. A murmur swept through the galleries. The treaty with its reservations had lost.

The Republicans (with four independently minded Democrats) had voted for the Lodge resolution of ratification. The Democrats, aided by thirteen Republican "irreconcilables," had voted as a body against it.

Then the parliamentary jockeying began. Hitchcock sprang to his feet and moved an adjournment. He evidently hoped to rally his forces before they could go over to the Republican fold and agree to some kind of compromise. His motion lost, 42 to 51. The "irreconcilables" were now back in their own camp.

Then Hitchcock sought to secure a vote on his own reservations. Vice President Marshall (evidently by prearrangement) thrice ruled favorably on his introducing them, but in each case the decision of the chair was overruled by a Republican vote.

Hitchcock's motion that the treaty be reconsidered with his reservations was next defeated 41 to 50, with the Republicans standing together.

Lodge, still in the driver's seat, then surprised the opposition by permitting another vote on the treaty with his reservations. This time he lost 41 to 51, as compared with 39 to 55 on the first vote. Three more Democrats, faced with the appalling prospect of a complete defeat of the treaty, joined the four who had already bolted.

Lodge then permitted Senator Underwood (a Democrat) to move approval of the treaty without any reservations. The motion was defeated 38 to 53, with all the Democrats (except seven) voting solidly in the affirmative, and with the "irrecon-

Nailed!

(From New York *Evening Telegram*; cartoonist Greene; courtesy of New York *World-Telegram*)

cilables" joining all their Republican brethren (except Mc-Cumber) in opposition. This was convincing proof of what had been evident all along—that the treaty could not be approved without some reservations.

Now that the Democrats had themselves defeated the treaty with the Republican reservations attached, Lodge made good on his threat that he would permit no further compromise. And he held the whip hand. Senator Swanson (a Democrat) walked over to him and, according to one press report, pleaded: "For God's sake, can't something be done to save the treaty?"

"Senator, the door is closed," replied Lodge. "You have done it yourselves."

After further vain maneuvering, the Republican majority carried a motion to adjourn sine die, with the Democratic regulars in opposition. The latter simply could not believe that Lodge had meant what he had repeatedly said: Either his reservations or nothing. Hitchcock and his following wanted to stay and work for further compromise, even though the hour for compromise had plainly passed.

Thus ended one of the most memorable legislative days in the history of the Senate of the United States. Thus ended the first session of the Sixty-sixth Congress. The Senate had labored for more than four months over the treaty, and finally had to confess that the narrow fissure which separated the two sides simply could not be closed.

4

At first blush it appears that Lodge, the master parliamentarian and the leader of the majority, was a failure. He had been successful in getting his reservations adopted, but on the final vote he fell far short of a two-thirds majority, and substantially short of a simple majority.

Contrary to a widespread misconception, *the treaty was not defeated in November by the two-thirds rule* (though it was to be in March). Neither side was able to command a simple majority for any constructive proposal.

If Lodge was a failure in mustering adequate support for his reservations, he was also a failure in holding the thirteen Republican "irreconcilables" in line. On the crucial votes, they turned against his reservations and went over to the Democrats.

Yet this was a successful failure. Lodge had so deferred to the "bitter-enders" that, even though they deserted him on the final vote, they were with him on other issues. This was the price he had paid to keep them from splitting the party wide open.

If Lodge had really wanted the treaty, he was a failure. But there is serious doubt as to whether he actually did, and it seems clear that he was lukewarm even about his own reservations.

If Lodge did not desire the pact at all, he was a complete success. He had kept the "mild reservationists" from deserting (thanks to the ineptitude of the Democrats); he had kept the "irreconcilables" in the fold on all important issues except the final vote; and he had forced the Democrats into a corner where they had to accept his terms or nothing. And if they accepted nothing, the blame for rejecting the treaty could be thrust onto them.

Lodge did not even permit the Democrats to present the Hitchcock reservations. If he had done so, and the Republicans had voted them down (as they certainly would have done), then the onus would have been shifted from the backs of the Democrats to those of the Republicans. Lodge no doubt thought that the Democrats, when faced with their horrible dilemma, would break and come over to him. But he seems not to have cared a great deal whether they broke or not: either way, the Republicans would make political capital.

Lodge was also a complete success in so far as general party harmony was concerned. Chairman Hays, of the Republican National Committee, was in Washington during the closing days of the fight, collaborating with Lodge at every step. He was apparently not unhappy over the result.

The "bitter-enders" were deliriously happy. Borah proclaimed the result "the second winning of the independence of America," and the "greatest victory since Appomattox." Fearing a momentary defeat through a Democratic bolt, the "irreconcilables" had won a resounding triumph for obstructionism. A group of them met for supper that night with some "strong reservationists" at the home of Mrs. Alice Roosevelt

Longworth. The treaty-scramblers ate scrambled eggs, cooked by Mrs. Harding.

The Republican regulars were not unhappy; they had jockeyed the Democrats into a politically disadvantageous position. Mrs. Longworth found that, now it was all over, they seemed as pleased as the "irreconcilables."

The "mild reservationists" were acutely unhappy, but their anger was directed at Wilson for his stubbornness and at the Democrats for their servile loyalty, rather than at Lodge.

So the Republicans were one big united family. That Lodge should have achieved this result, in the face of serious difficulties, is a tribute both to his skill and to the unwitting collaboration of Wilson and the Democratic minority.

5

Two of the Republican groups require more extended consideration.

The "bitter-enders" have been and still are savagely condemned for their alleged insincerity. They voted to attach the Lodge reservations; then they voted them down.

There is far more to the story than this. The "irreconcilables" did not want any part of the treaty. They did not believe that any reservations, however stringent, could make a silk purse out of a sow's ear. But since the great majority of the Senate favored the treaty in some form, it seemed highly probable that in the end the pact would be approved with some reservations. The aim of the "bitter-enders" was to tack on as drastic reservations as they could get, so that, if and when the treaty was adopted, American interests would have the maximum of protection. In this sense the "Battalion of Death" was sincere in supporting reservations.

The "irreconcilables" have also been blamed for the single-handed defeat of the treaty. Even today one reads how one-sixth of the membership of the Senate forced its will upon the other five-sixths.

This is a perversion of both figures and facts. The thirteen Republican "bitter-enders" alone could not have defeated the treaty. It takes 33 votes (one-third plus one of the full membership) to accomplish this result. The Democrats in many ways were more important. If they had voted for the treaty with the Lodge reservations, *instead of combining with the "irreconcilables,"* the Senate would have approved the pact (on the first vote) 81 to 13, or with 19 votes to spare.

Speaking broadly, there were more important "irreconcilables" than those in the "Battalion of Death." Lodge was an "irreconcilable" in that he insisted on his reservations or nothing. Hitchcock was an "irreconcilable" in that he and his following insisted on nothing rather than the Lodge reservations. Wilson was in some ways the most important of all the "irreconcilables." He insisted that the treaty be ratified on his terms, or not at all. There was too much irreconcilability all around.

When it came to the actual voting, the "mild reservationists" were in some respects more important than the "bitter-enders," and the fact that they have been largely overlooked testifies to the power of noise. We have repeatedly observed that these "middle-grounders," had they been won over by the Democrats, could have voted down the Lodge reservations, and then voted through the milder Democratic reservations. Perhaps the Republican regulars would have defeated the treaty so reserved, but if they had done so the blame for obstructing ratification would have been placed squarely on them rather than on the Democrats.

When the Senate adjourned, two of the "mild reservationists," Kellogg and Nelson, issued a joint statement declaring that they had done all they could to bring about ratification with adequate safeguards for the United States. "As a matter of fact," they concluded, "the Republicans Americanized the treaty and the Democrats killed it."

Privately, the "mild reservationists" expressed themselves more emphatically. Senator Colt exclaimed to A. D. H. Smith: "This is not good politics. It is not good Republican politics.

It is not good Democratic politics. It is not patriotic. It is un-American. We are losing sight of what we have been fighting for . . ."

With tears in his eyes Senator Kenyon of Iowa, another "mild reservationist," told A. D. H. Smith: "I am ashamed and disgusted. I cannot continue a member of a body which can be so small. If this is politics, I'm out of it. I'll get out as soon as I can."

In 1922, two years before the end of his term, Kenyon resigned his seat for the federal bench.

6

Senator Hitchcock and his colleagues prided themselves on having played a creditable role: they had gone down with their colors flying. They had put the odium for defeat, they felt, on the Republicans.

In point of fact their strategy was inexcusably bad. Hitchcock had counted on favorable rulings that were not sustained, on "mild-reservationist" support that was not forthcoming. He could not even muster a majority vote to get his own reservations before the Senate. All this, as we have noted, could have been confidently predicted.

Hitchcock afterward confessed that the one thing he did not foresee was that the Republicans would force an immediate adjournment. He was counting on a deadlock and continued discussion, with public opinion and the logic of the situation forcing his opponents to bend the knee. This strategy, as Hitchcock should have anticipated, also backfired.

The Democratic minority leader also failed to hold his ranks intact; four Democrats broke over on the first vote and seven on the second. Even so, his record was better than that of Lodge, who lost thirteen "irreconcilables." When it was all over, Hitchcock told a reporter, after pointing to the (temporary) division in the Republican ranks. "I think we made a pretty good showing."

It now seems reasonably certain that if it had not been for
the rigid bonds of party regularity, more than seven Democrats
would have bolted, probably enough to make a two-thirds
majority. But held together by partisan loyalty, and specifically directed by Wilson, the Democrats voted the treaty down,
in the confident hope that there would still be a chance to
"Democratize" it.

The Democrats, now the minority party, recognized the
absolute necessity of keeping their ranks solid, of standing
behind their great President, and of facing the campaign of
1920 with an unbroken front. The newspaper reporters noted
that Postmaster General Burleson, the political wheel horse of
the Cabinet, was conferring with Democrats on the floor of the
Senate during the day of the voting, presumably beating the
waverers into line.

The great majority of the Democrats no doubt wanted the
treaty; but for partisan reasons they could not accept the Republican reservations. So they voted the whole thing down.
The "bitter-enders" wanted neither the reservations nor the
treaty, so they voted the whole thing down. If the "irreconcilables" were insincere, what shall we say about the Democratic
regulars?

7

To criticize Wilson is ungracious but necessary. He was a
sick and secluded man, poorly advised by Hitchcock.

The President was still counting on an upsurge of public
opinion to break the deadlock and bring about ratification
with mild Democratic reservations. The upsurge did come, but
it had to be more than an upsurge: it had to be an earthquake.
Nothing less than that would have forced the Senate to act
against its will.

Wilson might have yielded to anyone but Lodge; but to
Lodge he could not yield. One evening before the final vote,
Senator Watson was at Lodge's home, and he expressed the

fear that Wilson might suddenly accept the Republican reservations, and then the United States would be in the League. Lodge replied with a confident smile that Wilson's hatred of him was such that the fear was utterly groundless. Watson demurred that this was a rather "slender thread on which to hang so great a cause."

"A slender thread!" Lodge scornfully replied. "Why, it is as strong as any cable with its strands wired and twisted together."

The longer the struggle continued, the more a refusal to yield became a sacred principle, both on the part of Wilson and on that of Lodge. Warm friends of the treaty, like ex-President Taft, cursed the stubbornness of the "mulish enigma" in the White House.

Wilson's Secretary of Agriculture, David F. Houston, concedes that the President was stubborn, but he asks, were not Borah and Johnson and Brandegee also stubborn?

What the apologists for Wilson often fail to see is that it was not Wilson's responsibility to be as stubborn as or more stubborn than the "bitter-enders." They might with good grace play a purely negative role. His task was to keep things moving, to get measures adopted. His executive leadership was at stake, and here, whatever the reasons, he failed. Deadlock was not to his credit; compromise and achievement would have been.

The champions of Wilson still argue that there was no point in his accepting the treaty with the Lodge reservations, because the three requisite Allied powers would not have approved them. We shall consider this whole problem later, but for the present we may note that these powers were never given an opportunity to accept or reject. This tremendous responsibility the President deliberately took upon himself.

If Wilson had advised his faithful followers to vote with the Republicans, then the problem of acceptance would have been placed squarely in the laps of the Allies. If these powers had rejected our terms, then the position of the Democrats would have been immeasurably strengthened, for they could have gloated that this was what they had predicted all along. If the

Allies had accepted our conditions, then we should have been in the League, with reservations which were of no real consequence, and which the Senate subsequently could have softened or eliminated.

The defenders of Wilson also insist that, if he had accepted the Lodge reservations, then Lodge would have screwed on more, until Wilson would have been forced to balk. This contention is no doubt sound for the early stages of the fight, but it falls to the ground when we consider the vote on the final day.

All Wilson had to do at the eleventh hour was quietly to instruct the Democrats to vote for the resolution of ratification with the Lodge reservations incorporated. Had he done so, the resolution would unquestionably have carried. Lodge might conceivably have moved a reconsideration so as to screw on more reservations; but such a gesture would have been so flagrantly obstructive that the Republicans probably would not have dared support it. Besides, the "mild reservationists" almost certainly would have joined with the Democrats to block any such transparent trick.

The fact that the "irreconcilables" were desperately afraid of a last-minute bolt by the Democrats to the Lodge reservations is final proof that the "screw-on" argument is flimsy.

8

We come now to a crucially important point which renders much of the preceding discussion purely academic.

Before his collapse and after his collapse—in private letter, White House interview, and public speech—Wilson made it clear, both explicitly and by indirection, that if the treaty came to him with the odious Lodge reservations attached, he would simply pocket it and not go through with ratification.

We cannot be certain that he would have carried out this threat, because he did not permit the treaty to get to this stage. But it seems likely that he would have done so. He was a stubborn man; he bitterly resented Lodge's tactics; his fighting spirit was aroused. And the events following his collapse strengthened his obduracy.

The outcome, at any rate, was a sad commentary on the functioning of the democratic process under our Constitution. More than 80 of the 95 or 96 members of the Senate professed to favor the treaty in some form, yet they could not muster even a simple majority vote for any constructive proposition. It was legislative impotence at its worst.

A. D. H. Smith relates that a Japanese correspondent for two important newspapers sat next to him in the Senate press gallery on the final day. He continued laughing to himself, quietly and politely. "It iss so fonny," he kept repeating. "It iss so fonny. Why do they do thiss so fonny? You excuss'? But I muss' laugh."

It is fruitless and to some extent childish to try to apportion blame, particularly in exact percentages. The situation was exceedingly complex, shot through with personal pride, prejudice, and partisanship. Much of the final debate was devoted to the possible effects of the Senate's action on the fortunes of both parties—to the battledore and shuttlecock of trying to leave the onus on the other side.

The "bitter-enders" were to blame for thinking that the unfledged League would destroy the United States; the "mild reservationists" were to blame for not overlooking the snubs of Wilson and the Democrats; Lodge and the "strong reservationists" were to blame for their stubbornness and blind partisanship; Hitchcock and the Democrats were to blame for their bad strategy and servile loyalty; Wilson was to blame for his insistence on the whole loaf or none.

If the senators could have foreseen that their vote would mean the eventual defeat of the treaty, and the probable ruin of man's noblest scheme for world peace, they might well have acted differently. But they—at least the Democrats—did not believe that this was the end. We can hardly blame them and Wilson for not having been soothsayers.

There comes to mind the remark of a Frenchman at the time of the French Revolution: "I do not blame anyone. I blame the situation."

9

The Senate had gone home, but the aftertaste lingered. The sorry exhibition of partisanship and impotence made a profound impression, not only at home but abroad.

Strangely enough, the newspapers and other media for expressing public opinion seem not to have been unduly concerned as the momentous vote approached. The debate had been too long dragged out; other diversions had come up, including John L. Lewis' coal strike. The wearied public found it difficult to appreciate the rhetorical difference between the reservations which in Democratic eyes would save the treaty and those which in Republican eyes would save face.

Another distraction was the approaching holiday season; a tremendous splurge of Christmas shopping struck the large cities in November. One enterprising merchant caught the spirit of the hour when he advertised in the Philadelphia *Public Ledger*:

> TREATY OR NO TREATY
> EVERYBODY MUST HAVE
> NEW WINTER CLOTHES

When the results of the voting were announced, the anti-League press naturally broke into extravaganzas of rejoicing. The editorial in the anti-League Boston *Transcript* (Republican) began, "Thanks be to God which giveth us the victory," and went on to rejoice over the defeat of "the evil thing with a holy name." Hearst's Boston *American* reached even dizzier heights:

> The treaty is dead!
> Thanks and congratulations and felicitations.

Thanks to God, who rules the affairs of peoples and directs the destinies of nations.
. . . .

These are great days for the republic—glorious, gallant, splendid, wonderful days!

They will live forever in the annals of the American people.
. . . .

Thank God, I am an American.

Sober anti-League journals, like the liberal New York *Nation,* were generally pleased over the result, though the *Nation* regretted that the treaty had not been rejected outright on the ground that it was a base betrayal of Wilson's ideals and an unjustifiable imposition on Germany.

A large group of Republican newspapers, many of them genuinely lamenting the result, were disposed to blame Wilson rather than Lodge. The New York *Sun* (Independent Republican) thought that the tragic farce was due to a surrender of American sovereignty in the unreserved treaty, and to Wilson's arrogance in trying to override the Senate.

Ex-President Taft, writing in the Philadelphia *Public Ledger,* blamed Wilson for a failure to effect an early compromise, and for his fatuous belief that by a frontal attack on the Republicans he could reduce a plain majority against the treaty to a two-thirds majority for it. Privately Taft boiled against both Lodge and Wilson, who continued "to exalt their personal prestige and the saving of their ugly faces above the welfare of the country and the world."

The Philadelphia *North American* (Progressive Republican) declared that Wilson had been consistent: his arrogance and unyielding nature had killed the treaty. The New York *Tribune* (Independent Republican), in an editorial entitled "Infanticide," concluded that Wilson was willing to sting his own to death rather than consent to coguardianship. The Boston *Transcript* felt that the responsibility should rest squarely on those Democratic senators who had docilely followed White House bidding.

10

Many sorrowful Democrats bemoaned "the greatest tragedy since the crucifixion of the Saviour of Mankind." Dyed-in-the-wool Democratic newspapers were especially bitter, and they heatedly denied that the fault was Wilson's. The New York *World,* an indefatigable champion of the League, blamed the result on Lodge's "rule-or-ruin" policy. He could not get his reservations through, so he would not let anyone else have the treaty. If partisanship and personal vanity had been subordinated to national needs, agreement would have been speedy.

The Peace Dove That Got Away

(Courtesy of Chicago *Daily News*; cartoonist Brown)

The St. Louis *Post-Dispatch* (Independent, with Democratic leanings) struck the same note under the heading, "THE SENATE'S DISGRACE." The treaty had not been considered on its merits: personal vanity, resentment, malice, and partisanship had brought disaster. Lodge had demonstrated that he could ruin but not rule. If he ran again for the Senate, his platform should be, "He kept us out of peace."

The Atlanta *Constitution* (Democratic) bitterly blamed "a little coterie" of Wilson-haters in the Senate, while the St. Louis *Star* (Independent) was especially savage with the "mild reservationists"—a name which was "a synonym for a plain coward." These men, of all the members of the Senate, merited the "greatest contempt," for "they went the farthest in violating the dictates of conscience."

To other newspapers the issue was not one of simple black and white. The Cleveland *Plain Dealer,* a prominent Independent Democratic paper, thought that both sides were to some extent at fault. The Lodge men were partisan, but the Democrats went to their fall with their eyes wide open. Compromise had been essential from the beginning, and much easier at the beginning than later. Wilson should have recognized at the outset that ratification on his terms, and only on his terms, was an impossibility. Or, as the Boston *Globe* (Democratic) put it, the great fault of the administration lay in not making a timely and genuine attempt at compromise.

The Philadelphia *Public Ledger,* an Independent journal with strong Republican sympathies, felt that the result was a blow at boasted American efficiency; we were discredited in the eyes of the world. Personal vanity and party prejudice were to be found on both sides. Wilson had snubbed the senators, including the "mild reservationists," and they had sunk a stiletto of hate into his sick body.

Other newspapers made much of the fact that only 64 votes were needed for ratification, and 81 Senators had voted for the treaty in one form or another. Surely the sweet reasonableness of compromise—the very basis of our democratic process—would ultimately triumph. The American people were disgusted with an exhibition of partisanship and wounded vanity which left the world in despair.

Many journals declared that the nation wanted peace and the treaty, not deadlock. Public opinion would not let the matter rest in suspense. The Senate sorely mistook the temper of the people if it thought that this was the end. Compromise was still possible, and compromise we must have. Let both Wilson and Lodge retreat from their high ground; let Wilson unbend; and let the Republicans soften the tone if not the substance of their reservations.

So argued the more reasonable editorial commentators.

11

Across the Atlantic, the British were disturbed, but on the whole they seem to have viewed the partisan impotence of the Senate with sorrow rather than with anger. They had been left in the lurch, but they would carry on and count upon the sober second thought of the United States to bring ratification.

The French were profoundly alarmed by the turn events had taken. Obsessed with a passion for security, and relying on the powerful military support of the United States, they condemned American politics, and felt keenly the bitterness of betrayal.

The attitude of the more important French journals toward the Lodge reservations is highly significant, particularly in view of the repeated statements by Wilsonians that the Allies would never accept them. The Paris *Liberté* favored a treaty with reservations rather than none at all. The influential *Journal des Débats* had held all along that, if slightly modified, they did not contradict the spirit of the treaty. The powerful *Temps,* which often spoke for the Foreign Office, took the same line; it believed that the Lodge reservations merely set forth restrictions which would in practice exist anyhow.

By December, and in the face of increasing German arrogance, the *Temps* thought the reservations wise, and to the best interests of France. The French would accept them as they were; the British would probably want to negotiate further over the preamble.

Italy was far less disturbed than France. She was acutely dissatisfied with her meager share of the spoils; she still had unrealized Adriatic aspirations. The withdrawal of America would weaken the concert of powers, and leave Italy in a position to push her demands with greater vigor, as she did.

The shocking decision of the Senate cooled very appreciably the enthusiasm of the recent European neutrals for the League of Nations. They felt that without the powerful participation of the United States the new world organization would be weak and fangless.

In China, every single one of the four hundred vernacular newspapers was reported as having commented favorably on the refusal of the Senate to "swallow" the "Shantung surrender."

In Japan, the press showed much less concern. It naturally could not applaud the Shantung reservation, but was inclined to dismiss it as of no real effect. On the whole, Japanese opinion seems to have regretted the blow to world order administered by the United States.

12

The German reaction to the tragic farce in Washington was confused and somewhat restrained. A great host of Teutonic treaty-haters regarded rejection by the Senate as a "tremendous moral victory"—a step toward final repudiation, as it no doubt was. Yet those who were hoping for the blessings of speedy and permanent peace were not sure that any good would come of America's defection.

The Germans now claimed that the desertion of the United States altered the fundamental character of the treaty which they had signed. They had approved it with the understanding that America would accept membership on the various commissions (including the all-important Reparations Commission); and they had counted on American fairness and disinterestedness to soften the execution of the pact. They therefore requested a modification of the treaty; but the Supreme Council in Paris turned a deaf ear to all such pleas. The fact is that the Germans would have had to sign anyhow, Senate or no Senate.

Certain German journals charged that the United States, by entering the war and blocking all possibility of a negotiated peace, had turned Europe into a scrap heap. The Americans had a moral obligation to help pick up the pieces; yet, now that they found they could not keep their tempers long enough to agree on terms of ratification, they were quitting the game and turning their backs on Europe as though it were a pesthouse.

The American desertion no doubt contributed substantially to the further deterioration of the European and Near Eastern situation. In early December, when the Allies attempted to assess damages for Germany's suicidal destruction of her fleet at Scapa Flow, a genuine crisis developed, the worst since June. The Berlin government refused for a time to sign the protocol necessary to make the Treaty of Versailles effective, and it was generally believed that this new flash of defiance was encouraged by the action of the Senate.

Thus the United States continued in the uncertain twilight zone between peace and war. Our material gains under the treaty were left in doubt and perhaps in jeopardy; we were not free to extend credits to Germany, or to resume trade relationships with her. We had impaired our prestige, abdicated our leadership, and had left the world in confusion and despair.

CHAPTER THIRTEEN

THE BIRTH OF A SOLEMN REFERENDUM

"Personally, I do not accept the action of the Senate of the United States as the decision of the Nation." WOODROW WILSON, *Jackson Day letter, January 8, 1920.*

1

THE SENATORS scattered to their homes for a brief vacation prior to the opening of the second session of the 66th Congress, on December 1, 1919. The treaty was left behind, suspended in mid-air. The mountain had labored for more than four months, and had not even brought forth a mouse.

Two days after the last futile vote, Lodge issued a statement to the press, throwing the blame on Wilson and declaring that the reservations were simple, direct, American. There was no more room for compromise. "I wish," Lodge asserted, "to carry those reservations into the campaign." In a word, let the people decide between simple Americanism and overweening Wilsonism.

This was an ominous note indeed. Senator Borah had long been urging that the question be thrust into national politics; Senator Johnson had already begun his bid for the presidency on the treaty issue. But the Republican leaders, not sure about the temper of the country, did not relish the prospect of having to defend themselves against the charge of being treaty-killers. So why not make one more attempt at compromise, and clear the explosive issue away?

Senator Hitchcock publicly rebuked Lodge for his latest maneuver, and declared that the Massachusetts senator was thinking more of politics than of patriotism. Reservations were inevitable, admitted Hitchcock, but they must be framed by the friends of the treaty for the purpose of securing its ratification, and not by the enemies of the treaty for the purpose of engineering its defeat.

Hitchcock appears not to have seen Wilson during the week or two immediately after the crucial vote. The press reported that the senator was invited to the White House, but that the appointment was canceled because of the President's ill health.

The senator nevertheless continued to keep Wilson informed—or at least he continued to address letters to the White House. On November 22 he wrote that the result was not defeat but deadlock: surely it would be possible to work out a compromise among the great majority who professed to favor the treaty. On November 24 he expressed the hope that something might be done with the "mild reservationists," a number of whom were most eager for a settlement. Hitchcock believed that the Democrats could still win, *provided they made concessions which were substantial* but which would leave the League in good working order.

This last assumption was no doubt correct. But it would have been better if the Democrats had made "substantial" concessions before the "mild reservationists" had been driven into the unwelcome embrace of Lodge. Above all, would Wilson ever consent to "substantial" concessions?

2

What were the shattered President's reactions to the Senate debacle?

Mrs. Wilson hesitated to bring him the disheartening news; she feared that the shock might cause a relapse. Finally she went to the bedside and gently explained the situation. Wilson lay there quietly for a few moments, and then said: "All the more reason I must get well and try again to bring this country to a sense of its great opportunity and greater responsibility."

While Wilson lay prostrate, physically unable to lead and temperamentally unable to retreat, Colonel House sent him two highly significant letters, dated November 24 and November 27, 1919. House advised that Wilson, having discharged his duty, leave the responsibility for further action at the door of the Senate. The Democratic senators could be instructed to secure as mild reservations as possible, but in the end to vote for ratification with reservations. Wilson could then dump the whole business on the doorstep of the Allies. If they accepted, Wilson's conscience would be clear; if they refused, his position would be vindicated. If they insisted on further negotiations, these could be undertaken. In any event, the treaty would be put into operation, and Wilson's great Covenant would live.

This scheme seems to have been the only practicable course that could have saved face all around. It was in fact supported by President Polk's way of handling the Oregon treaty of 1846.

Neither of House's two letters was answered or acknowledged. There is good reason to suppose that Mrs. Wilson did not permit her husband to see them. There is also good reason to suppose that Wilson, in his sick stubbornness, would have rejected this advice even if he had been permitted to see it.

3

As the dead line for the annual message to Congress approached, Wilson's feeling of helplessness was further borne in on him. He was physically unable to appear in person, as he had proudly done at the opening of every December session since 1913. He was also physically unable to prepare the lengthy document. The various heads of departments submitted memoranda, which Tumulty dovetailed together, and the whole thing was read to the President and slightly revised in the light of his criticism.

The message, as usual, was received sympathetically by the Democrats, critically by the Republicans. Much of it was obviously not of Wilson's composition. It was devoted almost exclusively to domestic affairs; there was only one vague allusion to the delay of the peace settlement. Many Republicans regarded this as a studied insult.

The ensuing debate over the authorship of the message revived rumors that the President was crazy. It seemed desirable that someone, aside from his intimates, look into the bedchamber and tell the country candidly what was going on.

An excuse was provided by the Mexican muddle, which had reached a crisis after the seizure for ransom of William Oscar Jenkins, United States consular agent at Puebla. Senator Fall of New Mexico pressed a resolution in the Foreign Relations Committee for the appointment of a subcommittee of two to wait on the President, ostensibly to discuss Mexican affairs with him, but actually to discover if his mind was clear. After a heated debate in the committee, the resolution passed by six Republican votes to five Democratic votes.

The two men appointed for this ungracious mission were Hitchcock and Fall. The latter was personally offensive to Wilson. He was a leading "irreconcilable," with a florid manner and with an affectation for the garb of a prosperous frontiersman—clothing which he ultimately exchanged for the more drab habiliments of the penitentiary. His reputation in Washington was unsavory, so much so that it was believed (without foundation) that he actually tore back Wilson's bedclothes to see how much of the invalid was left.

Wilson had been up that morning (December 5), but he was now propped up in bed, in a shaded corner of the room, and clad in a dark brown sweater. Fall brazenly entered with the embarrassed Hitchcock, and after washing his hands with invisible soap in invisible water, smirked, "Well, Mr. President, we have all been praying for you." "Which way, Senator?" shot back Wilson.

The interview lasted forty minutes, and the President bore up well. He seemed to be the brightest and most self-possessed person in the room. Mrs. Wilson hovered near by with a pencil and pad in her hand (this provided her with a good excuse for not shaking the oily palm of Fall), and scribbled down a summary of the discussion. In the midst of the session, by one of those dramatic coincidences which occasionally occur, the news was brought in that Consular Agent Jenkins had been released.

The whole affair was something of a triumph for Wilson: he had dispelled all doubts as to his sanity. Hitchcock emerged smiling; and even Fall admitted that the President was able to handle the Mexican situation. Wilson apparently enjoyed the episode, which, far from causing a relapse, had something of a tonic effect.

Nearly three months later, Wilson spoke to Secretary Houston about the "smelling committee" which had come over to find out whether "he was all there or not." He had been angered by Fall's unctuous reference to prayer. "If I could have got out of bed," he declared, "I would have hit the man. Why did he want to put me in bad with the Almighty?"

4

As the "smelling committee" prepared to leave the sickroom, Hitchcock inquired about the future of the treaty. Wilson's reply showed that he had not budged from his earlier position: the responsibility for the pact, he said, had been shifted to the shoulders of others (the Republicans), and he was content to let it rest there awhile.

In the week that followed, Wilson showed marked improvement, and by mid-December he was dressing himself and hobbling around with a cane. These encouraging symptoms of recovery may have increased his belligerency, for on December 14 a most uncompromising official statement came from the White House. Sharply rebutting the rumor that the President was preparing to make a conciliatory gesture toward the Republicans, the declaration continued: "He has *no compromise or concession of any kind in mind,* but intends, so far as he is concerned, that the Republican leaders of the Senate shall continue to bear the undivided responsibility for the fate of the treaty and the present condition of the world in consequence of that fate."

Wilson was evidently still hoping that the righteous wrath of an outraged public opinion would force the Republicans to accept his terms.

The country continued to be concerned over the inability of Wilson and his antagonists to unbend. "Let us take counsel together," the New York *Tribune* (Independent Republican) imagined Wilson saying; "and my idea of counsel is for you to sign here." The Philadelphia *Public Ledger* (Independent Republican), referring to both Wilson and Lodge, declared that each of these gentlemen "must come down from his high horse and get his feet on the ground and face the situation."

Even the Democratic senators were reported to be resentful at Wilson's unyielding statement. It put the party in an unreasonable light before the country, and branded the Democratic senators as traitors if they should turn against their great leader and even consider compromise.

The unfavorable reaction to this latest gesture of defiance made no impression on Wilson, assuming of course that he got some inkling of it. Writing to Senator Hitchcock (through his wife) on December 19, and responding to the overtures of Senator Glass at about the same time, he elaborated his unyielding views.

It would be a serious tactical mistake, Wilson insisted, for the Democrats *to propose* anything; any proposition must come from those senators who had defeated the treaty. Absolute inactivity on the part of the Democrats would be better than mistaken initiative. *No proposal or even intimation of compromise and concession should come from the Democratic side.* Surely there was enough parliamentary skill and ability among the Democrats to force the Republicans to vote on the treaty as it stood, or propose some new course regarding it.

The cloistered President was clearly in an unbending if not belligerent mood. He still failed to see that no amount of technical skill and maneuvering would overcome a hostile majority.

5

While Wilson lay secluded in his darkened bedroom, his brain concocted one of the wildest schemes imaginable. It finally took shape in the form of a document, clearly prepared late in January, 1920, which lies unsuspected among his private papers.

This striking statement was couched in the form of a public appeal, and was directed, as was his ill omened Congressional appeal of October, 1918, to "My Fellow Countrymen." It was unthinkable, Wilson said, that we should withdraw from the concert of enlightened nations. Germany was still technically at war with us; she was open to Bolshevist intrigue; she was raising her head in arrogance because of our desertion of the Allies. None of our war aims could be realized without the treaty and the Covenant.

All this, Wilson continued, was not what the American people desired. He knew that the overwhelming majority wanted the treaty, for he had found abundant confirmation of this view in his "recent" visit to seventeen states. (That "recent" visit had taken place about four months before, and Wilson was unwilling or unable to recognize the subsequent shifts in public opinion.) Yet he was not believed when he said that a majority of the people favored the treaty. It was assumed that he was no longer their spokesman, and that he no longer enjoyed the confidence which they had expressed when they reelected him in 1916.

There was, concluded Wilson, only one way to settle the dispute: direct reference to the voters of the country. Regrettably, the Constitution provided no machinery for such a referendum; but he had devised a method which was both legal and feasible, and he hoped that it would receive public support.

He thereupon boldly challenged all senators who had obstructed the Democratic program in the recent voting—a long list of them was specifically named—to resign their seats and seek immediate reelection on the issue of that record.

Wilson then solemnly promised that if all these senators, or a majority of them, were returned, he would resign the Presidency. Vice President Marshall had in this case agreed to follow suit. The office of President would then devolve upon the Secretary of State, and Wilson would invite one of the Republican leaders to accept that post. (Presumably Secretary Lansing would be induced to resign, or would be dismissed.)

This utterly fantastic scheme was finally pigeonholed, possibly at the insistence of Wilson's most intimate advisers. There was not the slightest prospect of its succeeding. The President completely misjudged the temper of men like Senators Shields and Borah, both of whom had more than four years left in their terms, if he thought that they would bow themselves out of the Senate at his behest. For that matter, would any of them resign? And even if they should, there could be no special elections under the constitutions of many of the states: the governors would have to appoint successors. Yet would the incumbents be reappointed?

The abortive January appeal is remarkably revealing of Wilson's mental processes. It spotlights his lifelong fondness for the parliamentary form of government, and his desire to engraft that form upon the American presidential system. It betrays his inability to shake off the appeal habit, which had backfired disastrously since October, 1918. It underscores his stubbornness, and particularly his quite understandable vindictiveness toward the senators. It shows that the applause of Pueblo was still ringing in his ears, and that he was interpreting that applause to mean no compromise when, as a matter of fact, the country clearly wanted compromise.

6

While Wilson was still toying with the idea of a public demand for the resignation of senators, he decided upon a step which, though less sensational, was more disastrous.

The occasion was the annual Jackson Day dinner in Washington, when the Democrats gathered ostensibly to honor one of their patron saints, the Hero of New Orleans, but actually to sing their own praises and promote their own political fortunes. These annual gatherings were not always love feasts; the fighting spirit of the indomitable Andrew Jackson seemingly brooded over the banquet hall.

Some little while before the memorable dinner, it was made known that the President, though unable to appear, would send over a statement to be read. No inkling was given as to its contents, and the tongues of political wiseacres wagged overtime. No doubt the document would be a ringing challenge to Wilson's senatorial enemies; possibly it would announce his determination to accept a third term and carry on the battle for four more years. The demand for tickets became so overwhelming that the original banquet hall had to be supplemented by another.

The Jackson Day letter—a fourteen-hundred-word document—was edited by some of Wilson's advisers, including Secretary Houston, who found so many errors in the original draft that he could not believe that the President had anything to do with its composition. Houston's corrections were generally accepted, but even the final product, while undeniably Wilsonian in ideas and spirit, was so unlike Wilson in style that it was generally believed to have been prepared for him by other hands.

The letter was addressed to Homer S. Cummings, chairman of the Democratic National Committee, and a spellbinder of considerable ability. On the night of the banquet he read it to a sympathetic audience, which interrupted him time and again with "the wildest enthusiasm."

Wilson declared that America had abdicated spiritual leadership, and that the world had come to dire straits as a result of our dallying. He simply could not believe that the country wished to remain outside the concert of powers which was organizing the League, and he refused to accept the action of the Senate "as the decision of the nation."

He had long asserted that the overwhelming majority of the American people desired ratification, and this impression had been "recently" confirmed by his western tour. He still had no objection to purely interpretive reservations accompanying the act of ratification, but he could not accept those that made it uncertain whether we had "ratified or rejected." We could not rewrite the treaty. We had to *"take it"* without changes which altered its meaning, or *"leave it"*; and if we left it we should have to face the "unthinkable task" of making a separate peace with Germany.

Wilson concluded by saying that his own assertions as to popular approval were not being credited. So, if there was any doubt as to the views of the people, the clear way out was to submit the treaty issue to the voters, and "to give the next election the form *of a great and solemn referendum . . .*"

This appeal was typically Wilsonian in that the President's statement unfortunately left the door wide open for misconstruction. Wilson did not appeal unqualifiedly, as many thought, for "a great and solemn referendum." This was merely implied; it was the only way out "if"—and this was a big "if"—there was any doubt as to what the people thought.

It is a striking fact that some of the ideas and actual phraseology of the Jackson Day letter were taken over from the unissued appeal for the resignation of senators.

7

William Jennings Bryan, the "Peerless One" and three-time nominee of the Democratic party, attended the Jackson Day jamboree. His relations with Wilson had been somewhat strained since his resignation from the Cabinet in 1915 over the *Lusitania* issue, and it was widely believed that he was piqued because Wilson had not taken him to Paris as a peace commissioner. (Wilson had in fact summarily dismissed this suggestion.) Bryan still had a large and worshipful popular following (more Democrats had voted for him in 1896, 1900, and 1908 than had supported the victorious Wilson in 1912), and despite his lack of success at the polls, he was no fool as a politician. He had learned a good deal the hard way.

Like Wilson, Bryan had at first opposed reservations, thinking quite logically that it was better to join the League and work for amendments later. But he was now convinced that the crippling effect of the Lodge reservations was much overestimated, and that without reservations there could be no ratification.

Bryan found himself strongly in disagreement with Wilson's Jackson Day letter, and after it was read he sprang to his feet to express objections in that once magnificent voice. All this talk of a "solemn referendum," he insisted, was complete folly. It was merely delaying the issue; and in the nature of things a presidential election could not be a referendum on a question of foreign policy. The thing to do was to work out a compromise, and get the vexatious issue out of the way before it completely wrecked the party. In a democracy the majority should rule, and the Democrats were merely placing themselves in the position of a filibustering minority.

Bryan's eloquent objections were not too favorably received. The audience was pro-Wilson, and it could not applaud the Commoner for putting ratification with reservations above party loyalty. When he asked if the Democrats could afford to "gamble" on getting control of the Senate and postponing the issue for fourteen months, cries arose of "Stand by the President!" "Stand by the President!" Others yelled, "Go on, Bryan." " 'Ray for Wilson." People jumped up all over the room, while Chairman Cummings impotently thumped his gavel.

There was sound if unpalatable advice in Bryan's unwelcome remarks. He had tried in the campaign of 1900 to get a solemn referendum on imperialism, but the issue had got tangled up with the trusts, free silver, Bryanism, and a host of

Who's Driving?

(Courtesy of Chicago *Daily News*; cartoonist Brown)

other domestic problems. Bryan's words were deserving of respectful attention; after all, he had acquired a good deal more experience than anyone else in losing presidential elections.

8

The Republican party chieftains, as earlier noted, were somewhat reluctant to take the treaty into the uncertainties of a presidential canvass. One exception was Lodge. He had urged that the issue be settled at the ballot box, and it is possible that his challenge had, in part, provoked Wilson into asking for a "solemn referendum."

The "irreconcilables" were overjoyed at the turn affairs had taken; Wilson was playing directly into their hands. Senators Borah and Johnson not only expressed delight—Johnson openly and defiantly accepted Wilson's challenge. The "bitter-enders," with their talents for confusing and distorting issues, could hope for nothing better than fourteen more months in which to plant doubts in the public mind. They could hope for nothing better than to pose as the champions of nationalism versus internationalism, as saviors of the Republic from the machinations of some horrendous superstate.

The Republican and liberal press was on the whole sharply critical of Wilson. Senator Capper's paper, the Topeka *Capital* (Republican), was sure that the President's letter had "spilled the beans" to such an extent that not even his own party leaders were behind him. Elsewhere Wilson was widely condemned for his obduracy. Already some promising compromise negotiations had started in the Senate, and it was feared that the President's obstinate attitude would put an end to them.

Other critics, like the New York *Nation,* pointed to an apparent inconsistency in Wilson's position. He had come home saying that there must be the utmost haste in ratification; speedy action would end labor troubles, revive business, and cure many of the world's ills. Six months had passed since the President returned demanding hot haste. Now he was proposing a scheme which meant postponing the issue until November, and then to the inauguration of the new government the following March—a total of at least fourteen months.

Republican journals rather generally felt that the spirit of Andrew Jackson had guided too closely the pen of Woodrow Wilson. Public opinion, they felt, was demanding a reasonable compromise, and acceptance of that compromise by the President.

9

The Democrats were sharply divided in their reaction to Wilson's appeal for a "solemn referendum." The pro-Wilson phalanx lined up squarely behind their chief, among them Senators Hitchcock and Underwood, both of whom desired Wilson's support for the Democratic senatorial leadership. In loyal Democratic circles Bryan was regarded as a "sorehead" who had forsaken principle for expediency, and who was making this "grandstand" gesture in the hope of capturing his fourth presidential nomination. "Mr. Bryan is indeed a hardy quadrennial," opined the Philadelphia *Public Ledger* (Independent Republican).

Elsewhere in Democratic ranks there was widespread but rather grudging support of Bryan. Senators Myers of Montana and King of Utah openly declared that it would be a great mistake to make the treaty a party issue: Wilson would have a desperate fight on his hands which would break the ranks of the Democrats.

An impressive number of Democratic newspapers, some of them hitherto foursquare in their support of Wilson, declared that Bryan had sensed more accurately the temper of both the party and the country. Among them were journals like the New York *Times*, the Brooklyn *Eagle*, the Hartford *Times*, the Dallas *News*, and the Montgomery *Advertiser*. The country was already sick of the much-debated issue, and the thing to do was to compromise and clear it out of the way. The Democratic party would cut its own throat if it went before the country opposing adequate reservations to preserve American sovereignty.

Some of the Democratic newspapers concluded that Wilson was much too bullheaded, and that there could be no true referendum in the fiery furnace of a national election. Compromise was the essence of democracy, and a majority of the people wanted a give-and-take adjustment. The Democratic Hartford *Times* went so far as to say that Wilson, through his Jacksonian opposition to conciliation, was putting himself in the same category as the Senate "irreconcilables," Brandegee and Borah.

All this was meat for the Republicans. Their editors and cartoonists had a field day, and again the hawklike features of the

Peerless One sprang into prominence. The Republicans had feared that Johnson and Borah would split the party wide open; instead it looked as though Bryan would split the Democrats wide open and, reversing the tables of 1912, enable the Republicans to win "in a walk."

Bryan in subsequent statements denied that he had broken with Wilson; he differed from him only in method and not in purpose. He could not allow the Democrats in the Senate to go to the country and stand on their record; delay was a "disgrace," and he would not permit his party "to commit this crime" of filibustering until November while the world slipped into the abyss of anarchy.

10

The Jackson Day letter was one of the most reverberating in a long series of Wilsonian blunders. In some ways it was Wilson's worst. It is true that he reaffirmed his willingness to accept mildly interpretive reservations; but many more people doubtless read comments on the letter than the letter itself, and these interpreters made Wilson appear more uncompromising than he actually was. Even so, his position was so unyielding as to cost him the support of many of his most loyal and influential followers.

The letter also had a depressing effect on several attempts at compromise in the Senate which had made promising headway since December. Inasmuch as Wilson preferred a popular referendum to a surrender, why should his faithful followers try to compromise? Push the issue off into the next election, and if things did not go well the reproach could rest on Wilson's frail shoulders. Or, as the Brooklyn *Eagle* put it, the "Congressional motto seems to be, 'Never put off until to-morrow what you can postpone until after election.' "

Clearheaded students of the American political scene shared Bryan's view that it would be impossible to get a referendum on the treaty in a national election. As in the 1918 Congressional elections, Wilson was asking for an electoral mandate when there could be none. The treaty issues were themselves confused; they would be further confused by local issues.

The Cincinnati *Enquirer* (Democrat) concluded that the people were not competent to decide such a complicated ques-

Why Wait Till 1920!

(From New York *Evening World*; cartoonist Cassel; reprinted by permission)

tion. The obvious lack of any machinery for recording a referendum on the treaty issue prompted Senator France of Maryland (Republican) to suggest a resolution providing for a poll on this single issue. Nothing of course came of it. The New York *Evening Post* (Independent) hit the nail squarely on the head when it declared: "To throw the Treaty into the campaign would bring about, not 'a great and solemn referendum,' but a great and solemn muddle."

The situation was further complicated by one inescapable fact which Wilson seems to have ignored all along. It was not mathematically possible for the Democrats to win enough Senate seats in 1920 to command the necessary two-thirds vote. By 1922 it might be possible; but by that time Wilson would presumably be gone, and the issue long since decided.

But would Wilson be gone by 1921? He had not yet declared himself out of the running, and his demand for a referendum in 1920 high-lighted himself as the logical standard-bearer in a cause for which he had already broken his body but not his spirit. This, of course, revived all the fears of the Republican Wilson-haters.

*　　*　　*

Meanwhile the Allied powers and Germany had come to final terms, and the formal ratifications of the Treaty of Versailles were exchanged in Paris, two days after the reading of the Jackson Day letter. America, the most powerful of them all and a co-author of the pact, was not represented. The bells of London pealed in honor of the peace, but they pealed dismally. The people were not unduly excited. The future did not look bright with America drifting further and further away from the entente which had won the war and which could have guaranteed the peace.

CHAPTER FOURTEEN

COMPROMISE WITHOUT CONCESSION

"The Anglo-Saxon idea of Government is founded on the principle of compromise. No public official can have his own way all the time." EX-PRESIDENT TAFT, *January 16, 1920.*

———

1

THE AMERICAN people have long preened themselves on their Anglo-Saxon genius for compromise, and their historical scroll bears the names of such immortal compromisers as Henry Clay and Daniel Webster. Yet both Wilson and the senators had been unable to tread in these illustrious footsteps. We had become the laughingstock of the world, and our vaunted Constitution was seemingly on trial before the bar of international opinion. American sentiment was plainly disgusted with the political dodges of both Democrats and Republicans.

A number of distinguished political and educational leaders urged compromise, among them Taft, Wickersham, Lowell, and Hoover. An appeal from the League of Free Nations Association urged the President to accept the necessary reservations and get the treaty into operation; he had done his duty, and any responsibility for reservations would rest with their authors, not with him. Among the signers of this appeal were Cardinal Gibbons, David Hunter Miller (Wilson's chief assistant in framing the Covenant at Paris), Dr. Isaiah Bowman (one of the leading American experts at Paris), and Ray Stannard Baker, director of the American Press Bureau in Paris, and destined to be Wilson's able and sympathetic biographer.

Various other groups and organizations, during December and January, petitioned for speedy ratification. The League to Enforce Peace continued its widespread propaganda; universities, church groups, and labor organizations added their voices to the swelling chorus. Business and banking leaders pressed for action, among them the mighty J. P. Morgan, whose advocacy evoked new blasts against Wall Street from Borah and others.

Mass meetings of aroused citizens insisted on some kind of agreement. Newspaper editorials, letters to the editor, and letters and telegrams to the senators added to the growing demand. If the rising tide of ink could float the treaty through the Senate, ratification seemed a certainty.

The high point of this pressure agitation came in mid-January and February. On January 13, 1920, the spokesmen for twenty-six organizations, representing twenty to thirty million people, waited on both Lodge and Hitchcock, urging ratification in such form as would not require renegotiation. On February 9, a committee representing twenty-six organizations, with a total membership of fifty million, memorialized both the President and the Senate to compromise their differences. This committee was unable to see any real distinction between the Lodge reservation on Article X and the Hitchcock reservation, the latter of which Wilson was prepared to accept.

This tremendous ground swell was an impressive tribute to the power of public opinion, and to its ability to secure action (if not results) when it makes up its mind that something must be done.

2

When the senators returned to Washington in December, 1919, after having taken a bath in local opinion, the atmosphere on Capitol Hill seemed highly favorable to compromise. There was general agreement that the corpse of the treaty should be brought in for a post-mortem examination, and that an effort should be made to breathe life into it. The Democrats were hopeful that some kind of adjustment could be worked out; the "mild reservationists" were receptive to compromise; and the rank and file of the Republicans seemed agreeable to changes in the Lodge reservations, provided there was enough of the original left to enable them to claim some credit for having "Americanized" the pact.

Outwardly, Lodge was as completely deaf to concession as Wilson. On the eve of the reassembling of Congress he declared that his reservations were the "irreducible minimum," and that any immaterial changes were "foolish and needless." If the President wanted ratification, he would have to accept the Lodge reservations as they stood. The senator was confident that his view reflected that of public opinion, and he was still quite ready to drag the issue into the election of 1920.

Privately, Lodge said that the treaty had been "killed by Wilson," who had been a "marplot from the beginning." The senator was tired of having Taft and others urge him to give ground. "Why," he asked, "do they not put their pressure on Wilson and make him yield?" Lodge thought that the next move was up to the President, but the senator did not think him capable of making a move; his condition was no doubt worse than the White House bulletins indicated.

Neither Wilson nor Lodge would give an inch, and each thought that the next move was up to the other. In such circumstances there can be only disagreement or complete surrender, with an intolerable loss of face to one of the antagonists.

Throughout the month of December various and complicated attempts at compromise were pressed in the Senate. Hitchcock, evidently nettled by all this shilly-shallying, accused Lodge of consulting with the "irreconcilables," who did not want the treaty at all, while declining to consult with the Democrats, who did want it. Lodge curtly replied that this was because the votes of the opposition party were not their own but (inferentially) Wilson's. When the Democrats sprang angrily to their feet to resent this insult, Lodge withdrew his remark. Yet there was enough truth in it to hurt.

The "mild reservationists," who wanted the issue cleared

away before the election, were much displeased with Lodge's obstinacy, and late in December they began to hold conferences among themselves. It was alleged that they were preparing to revolt against Lodge's leadership unless he would make some conciliatory moves. The "irreconcilables," who wanted the issue thrown into the election, were openly threatening to desert the Massachusetts senator and filibuster if he attempted to compromise. Senator Johnson was reported hurrying back to Washington to "stiffen Lodge's spine."

Lodge was evidently back with his tightrope act. If he yielded, the "irreconcilables" would push him off; if he did not, the "mild reservationists" might push him off. The way of both the transgressor and the party leader is hard.

3

If Lodge's position was difficult, that of Hitchcock was hardly less so. Various Democratic senators were bringing pressure to bear on him to yield, and by January 3, 1920, the press could report that four of them were giving signs of revolting from his leadership. Even such stalwart Wilsonian journals as the Cleveland *Plain Dealer* were saying, "Concession there must be, and the first move toward concession must come from the Democratic side."

Yet Hitchcock could not compromise unless Wilson would compromise; with Wilson refusing to make concessions, Hitchcock was not permitted to see him in order to persuade him of the necessity of making concessions. On December 31, six weeks after the rejection of the treaty, the senator was allowed to consult Tumulty for half an hour, after Tumulty had talked with Wilson. This kind of one-way negotiation was highly unsatisfactory, though Hitchcock bravely told the newsmen late in January that he had not seen the President and did not need to see him.

On January 5, 1920, the senator wrote Mrs. Wilson a candid

and somewhat pathetic letter. The thing to do, he said, was to win over the dozen or so moderate Republicans, with at least eight additional recruits. Once this was done, the treaty could be sent to Wilson, Lodge or no Lodge, with reservations that the President might accept. Yet to do this meant concessions, and thus far Hitchcock had "little encouragement" from the President to make them.

Wilson's answer to all such pleas (assuming that he saw them) came in his unflinching Jackson Day letter. He stood exactly where he had stood all along, only he was now suggesting that the issue be tossed into politics.

The Jackson Day letter, while no doubt providing some of the Democratic die-hards with justification for standing pat, spurred the movement for compromise among certain of their associates. These men felt the sting of public opinion, and recognized the folly of trying to solve the problem by pushing it off to the next election. The way things were drifting, neither side could claim political credit from postponement.

4

All this pulling and hauling in the direction of compromise resulted in only one development that seemingly had any real prospect of success. This was the bipartisan conference of senators, which met between January 15 and 30, 1920, apparently at the instance of Senator Owen of Oklahoma, a Democrat.

The group gathered in the committee room of the Foreign Relations Committee, and consisted of four Republicans and five Democrats. The Republicans were New of Indiana, Lenroot of Wisconsin, Kellogg of Minnesota, and Lodge of Massachusetts. None of the true "irreconcilables" was appointed, though Hitchcock regarded Kellogg as the only genuine compromiser of the lot.

The Democrats were Hitchcock, Walsh of Montana, Mc-

Kellar of Tennessee (later involved with the TVA), Simmons of North Carolina, and Owen of Oklahoma. It was unfortunate that such an interested party as Lodge was present, for it seems clear that his heart was not in compromise, and that he was just going through motions for the sake of party harmony and as a sop to public opinion. In any event, this was apparently the first time since the treaty rejection on November 19 that the leaders of the opposing groups were able to get their feet together under a table for full discussion.

The meetings were supposed to be held in secret, but this did not prevent the press from reporting developments in some detail. The "middle-ground" Republicans applied spurs when they threatened, unless the conferees moved rapidly, to call up the treaty and begin the debate all over—a repetitious performance which nobody really welcomed.

The high point of the bipartisan conferences came on January 23, 1920. On that day the "bitter-enders" learned that the conferees were nearing agreement on the points in dispute, and particularly that Lodge was about to break the log jam by working out a compromise with Senator Simmons on Article X.

Borah seized his telephone and summoned a group of "bitter-enders" to his office for a council of war. As the Idaho senator told the story to the present writer in 1937, they selected Moses, as the member of the group who had the most "nerve," to go over to Senator Simmons' office and haul Lodge out of his secret conclave.

Moses soon triumphantly returned with Lodge, who stood there pale and nervous. (Borah had never seen a man look so scared in his life.) Lodge protested, "Can't I discuss this matter with my friends?"

Borah spoke up, "No, Cabot, not without telling your other friends!"

Lodge leaned against the wall for support. "Well," he finally said, "I suppose I'll have to resign as majority leader."

"No, by God!" burst out Borah. "You won't have a chance

to resign! On Monday, I'll move for the election of a new majority leader and give the reasons for my action."

After a prolonged session, Lodge agreed to end his dickering with Senator Simmons on Article X, and the "irreconcilables" thereafter congratulated themselves on having by the narrowest of margins rescued the Republic from complete disaster. Senator McNary, a "mild reservationist," told the present

"Teacher, It Can't Be Done!"
(Courtesy of Dallas *News*; cartoonist Knott)

writer in 1937 that he had in his safe-deposit box a copy of the Simmons compromise resolution with interlineations in the handwriting of Lodge.

The details of Borah's dramatic story were no doubt improved by him with repeated telling. But this much is certain: the bipartisan meeting scheduled for the next day was postponed, and Lodge allegedly told his colleagues that he would never compromise on principle. On January 26, when the bi-partisan committee met again, Lodge was reported to have declared that there could be no concessions on the reservations regarding the Monroe Doctrine and Article X.

On January 30 the meetings broke down completely. Steps were thereupon taken to call up the treaty and to restart the verbiage mill on the floor of the Senate.

Hitchcock flatly announced that definite progress had been made when the conferences were broken up by the "irreconcilable" uprising. The committee had tentatively agreed upon a changed preamble and upon all the reservations except those relating to Article X, the Monroe Doctrine, and one or two minor matters. Agreement on Article X was in sight when the end abruptly came.

The assertions of Hitchcock were heatedly and categorically denied by Republican members of the committee, and the upshot is that only a few things emerge with clarity. There was a bipartisan conference; it did discuss certain concessions and tentatively agreed to set them down. Article X was the big stumbling block. The "irreconcilables" did threaten to go on the warpath, but it may be doubted whether agreement was as near as they feared or as near as Hitchcock wishfully thought.

It is also clear that Lodge would go so far as to make certain concessions, such as watering down the preamble and permitting withdrawal from the League by a joint rather than by a concurrent resolution of Congress. He was apparently willing to change the phraseology of his reservation on Article X, but he seems never to have been prepared to concede that there was a moral obligation, which was the kernel of the whole controversy.

5

On January 31, 1920, the day after the breakdown of the bipartisan conferences, the London *Times* published a document written by an eminent British statesman which had a vital bearing on the struggle for compromise. Behind this statement lies an extraordinarily interesting story.

Some weeks after Wilson had returned from Paris in an unbending mood, Colonel House and others in London urged Viscount Grey of Fallodon to undertake a special mission to the United States with the purpose of putting the President in a more reasonable frame of mind. Grey was the logical man for this delicate assignment, for he was by common consent one of the greatest living Englishmen, and one for whom Wilson had expressed deep admiration.

The ostensible purposes of the mission were to discuss the Irish question and the increasingly ominous naval race between Britain and America. But there can be little doubt that the real object was to bring about a breaking of the treaty deadlock. Britain already had a competent minister ad interim in Washington, and she was able to draw upon a large and well-trained diplomatic corps for men to handle routine problems.

Grey was nearing sixty, and in 1916 had retired from active service as Foreign Secretary, weary and in ill health. The world had grown morally dark for him in 1914, when war came despite his best efforts to avert it; the world was now growing physically dark, for he was losing his sight. It is perfectly clear that this man, broken in health and spirit, who delighted in the woodlands and bird calls of his home, would not come out of retirement and undertake a strange mission to a strange land unless he was convinced that this was an extraordinary task which only he could perform.

With a twilight world gathering around him, Grey reached New York the day after Wilson collapsed at Pueblo and began to enter a twilight world of his own. Grey's rank was that of ambassador on special mission, but he could not become an official envoy until he had presented his credentials to a President who was unable to see anyone. So the noble Briton had to content himself with marking time, pending Wilson's recovery, and during this period he undertook to inform himself by consulting with senators from both parties, and by trying to absorb all points of view.

Viscount Grey was an experienced diplomatist, and he seems to have moved with great caution. He was reported to have said that he remembered very well the fate of Lionel Sackville-West, the British minister who in 1888 was dismissed by President Cleveland for writing an indiscreet letter interfering with American politics.

6

Wilson did not receive or even see Grey. At first it was clear that he was unable to; but as the weeks wore on, and various visitors appeared at the White House, the suspicion developed that the President did not want to meet him. After about three months of heel-cooling the special ambassador went home, with little to show for his experience but the American point of view and an operation on his eyes which may have postponed the final curtain of darkness.

It seems certain that Wilson was physically able to receive Grey by early January, the time of his departure. A dozen or so visitors had been admitted to the White House, including the Fall "smelling committee." If Wilson could have seen the senatorial inquisitors for forty minutes on December 6, he surely could have seen Grey for a half-hour a month or so later.

Henry White, a Republican and a retired professional diplomat of much experience, privately defended Wilson. He wrote that there were a dozen or so traditionally jealous foreign envoys waiting to be officially received, and their noses would have been put out of joint if the President had singled out Grey for special consideration. This is no doubt true; but Britain was such a great power, and the issues involved were so world-shaking, that Wilson would have been justified in giving offense to a few protocol-bound diplomats.

The President did not even have to go through the bore-some routine of receiving Grey with great formality. All the customary flummery doubtless meant nothing to the distin-guished statesman. All he wanted was a chance to relay his message, and he could have done this just as well—perhaps better—in a half-hour of informal conversation.

The suspicion is not easily quieted that Wilson did not want to see Grey—or perhaps Mrs. Wilson did not want him to. The real purpose of the special envoy's mission was com-mon knowledge; and the President, who conceived of himself as fighting a holy crusade against the forces of evil, did not want to be talked into what he regarded as base surrender. Grey had moreover been giving a receptive ear to the senators on both sides. Secretary Houston relates that at a dinner in Washington he overheard Grey commenting sympathetically to Lodge on the senator's handling of the treaty. It is likely that such reports got back to Wilson. In his eyes even listening to Lodge was probably a serious offense, as it no doubt was to Houston, who may easily have exaggerated Grey's approval of the senator.

Dr. Grayson later remembered that an indiscreet attaché of the British embassy had been criticizing the President and spreading silly stories about Mrs. Wilson. Wilson attempted to have him removed, but there were objections and delays. Per-haps the President blamed Grey for this failure to secure prompt and satisfactory action.

There is one other disquieting explanation. It is possible that the President's bedside guardians did not like Grey, and that they did not permit Wilson to see him, or persuaded Wilson that Grey's mission was not really important. Mrs. Wilson confesses that she disliked Sir William Wiseman, of the British Embassy, and that it gave her pleasure when the President, just before his disastrous stroke, declined to see him.

If Wilson refused to receive Grey for reasons of health, this is but further proof that he should have resigned. If he refused to see him for reasons of personal pique, or because he was under the influence of advisers with petty spirits, the same conclusion seems warranted.

A final possibility—and the one most creditable to Wilson —is that he hesitated to stir up the anti-British elements in the country by appearing to fall under the influence of Grey. While there is admittedly some force in this argument, it is also true that the Irish and other England-haters were already arrayed against the League; and it is difficult to see how they could have become much more vocal.

7

Grey reached England on January 13, but refrained from public comment until January 31, when it became clear that the promising bipartisan negotiations in the Senate had collapsed. He doubtless had concluded that a premature statement would complicate the controversy by arousing resentment against outside meddling. His medium of expression was a lengthy letter in the London *Times* of January 31, 1920.

This able document is of the highest importance, and deserves much more emphasis than it has yet received. It is the report of a distinguished man, respected for his fairness and objectivity, who had come with the detached point of view of a foreigner, who had listened to the senatorial debates, and who had considered the problem from all angles.

Grey made it evident at the outset that he was speaking as a private individual in the hope of clarifying for the British people the much-misunderstood position of America. Outsiders must be patient and tolerant, he said, for the Senate was an independent body, and its refusal to approve the treaty was not evidence of repudiation or bad faith. While it was true that politics—the curse of all democratic legislative bodies —had entered into the struggle, partisanship was not the sole or even the main cause of deadlock over the League. More vital in Grey's judgment was the persistence of the isolationist tradition, with its fear of foreign entanglements. Also important was the conflict between the executive and the legislative—a conflict which was inevitable under our Constitution.

Without the United States, Grey continued prophetically, the League would lack moral force, and would become merely a league of victorious Allies. Without a real League the old order would return, and America would again be sucked into the European maelstrom. If the United States entered the League as a *willing* partner with *limited* obligations (reservations), this was much better than as an *unwilling* partner with *unlimited* obligations. The proposed reservations were admittedly material qualifications, but those persons who were experienced in statecraft knew that expected dangers often never arise. Hence these reservations might never have to be invoked, and they probably would not weaken the League nearly so seriously as was feared. It would therefore be a mistake to spurn the cooperation of the United States simply because strings were attached to it.

By implication Grey accepted the fourteen reservations, except one. The British dominions, he insisted, could not be deprived of their vote in the Assembly. They would in effect *all* be debarred from voting on an issue that arrayed *one* of them against the United States; and there was no objection to the United States' having more than one vote. But this whole problem could no doubt be solved by amicable negotiation between the two powers.

8

If the Grey letter created a profound impression in England, it was a front-page sensation in the United States. One of the strongest Wilsonian arguments had been that the other powers would reject the Lodge reservations. Now Grey, after presumably consulting the British Cabinet, was saying in effect that the mightiest of our former associates would accept them.

Some of the senators professed no great surprise. They reported that Grey when in Washington had secretly shown them
a cablegram from Prime Minister Lloyd George stating that
Great Britain would accept reservations. This, they alleged,
was the basis for Republican confidence that the Allies would
not balk at our terms.

Lodge and his following were jubilant: the props had been
completely knocked out from under Wilson and his "sub-
servient" senators. What, the "strong reservationists" insisted,
are we waiting for? Why not pass the Lodge reservations without further delay?

The "bitter-enders" like Johnson and Borah were much less
happy. Borah found in the Grey letter complete justification
for all his fears. Grey admitted that the League was a sharp
departure from American tradition—which was what the "bitter-enders" had been contending all along. Grey confessed that
once we were in the League the weakening effects of the "American reservations would not be felt in practice"— which merely
confirmed the "irreconcilable" suspicion that the Lodge reservations did not erect safeguards enough. Grey conceded that
the League could not work without the United States. Hence,
declared Borah, the Allies were admittedly bankrupt; they
were merely seeking a rich and gullible partner who would
carry all the burdens.

The Democrats were crestfallen, and their eyes instinctively
turned to the White House for guidance. The Grey letter was
clearly in the nature of an appeal to the American people over
the head of their ailing President, however much it might be
disguised as a simple report to the British public. Such appeals
are not regarded as good diplomatic form; ambassadors have
been bundled off home for less. But Grey could not be bundled off home; he was already home. He could not be dismissed; he had never been officially received. Yet it was felt
that he had been guilty of a breach of etiquette, for he was
still technically a special ambassador on leave of absence.

The Republican critics of Wilson remembered that during

the Paris Conference he had appealed over the heads of the Italian authorities to the Italian people. It was ironical indeed that the tables should now be turned. The unrelenting *Harvey's Weekly* poked another sharp jab at the President when it said that not even the League of Nations went so far as to prevent a freeborn Briton from writing to the London *Times* without the consent of Woodrow Wilson.

9

Wilson's inward reactions to the Grey letter were cloaked in official silence. It was reported in the press that he was very angry, and had drafted a rebuke to be secretly presented at Downing Street. The curious were partly satisfied when, on February 5, the White House issued a statement through Tumulty declaring that Grey had acted without consulting the President, and without even letting the President know his views.

The Wilson papers permit us to lift one corner of the veil of secrecy. Among them lies an undated note, written in Mrs. Wilson's hand and evidently dictated by Wilson or prepared at his direction as a White House release. It states that the President was as much surprised as the public by Grey's extraordinary attempt to influence both the Senate and the executive. If, the release concludes, Grey had undertaken to issue such a statement while still ambassador in Washington, his government would speedily have been asked to recall him.

Wiser counsels evidently prevailed, and this stinging reprimand was not published. It would have come with poor grace indeed from one who had less than a year before publicly appealed to the Italian people. It would have seemed a futile act of spite against a man who was not and never had been an official British agent in the United States, and who had not been permitted to convey his message to Wilson. Grey may in fact have been speaking not so much to the British and the American people as to the recluse in the White House.

Downing Street was put in an awkward position. Outsiders naturally took it for granted that Grey would not have made public so important a statement without consulting the British government and perhaps that of France. Prime Minister Lloyd George flatly told the American ambassador that there was no truth in the charge that Grey had shown a cablegram from him to the senators. Lloyd George wanted Wilson to know that he had no knowledge of the Grey letter until he read it in the London *Times*. (The Prime Minister may or may not have been telling the truth; his reputation for veracity was not good.)

In the same interview Lloyd George made one striking declaration regarding the Lodge reservations. As long as the other powers were not *expressly required to agree to American conditions,* it was up to the United States to determine what restrictions it desired to lay down. Unlike Grey, Lloyd George (if we may believe him) did not even object to the six-to-one reservation.

This statement casts a flood of light on the question of whether or not the Allies would have accepted our terms. Lloyd George's one objection was met when the preamble to the Lodge reservations was amended in March so as to provide for silent acquiescence rather than specific approval.

Even private official utterances like those of Lloyd George were probably rare. Governments have long since discovered that it is dangerous to try to influence pending legislation in foreign countries. But it is highly significant that Lloyd George's views were essentially those of the Grey letter, which probably reflected the general attitude of the British government, and which may well have been framed in informal collaboration with it.

10

The British press welcomed the reverberating letter as on the whole clarifying the situation. The editor of the London

Observer would go even further than Grey: Let the Americans bring over a whole shipload of reservations, with the understanding that they would apply to the other members of the League as well. The London *Morning Post* said that Grey was really proposing that America be allowed to enter the shallow end of the pool, and then gradually work toward the middle.

"Come on In, It Isn't Deep!"

(From St. Louis *Star*; cartoonist Tuthill; courtesy of St. Louis *Star-Times*)

The uproar on both sides of the ocean gave leading French journals like the *Temps* and the *Journal des Débats* another opportunity to repeat what they had been saying for many weeks. Better the United States with reservations than no United States at all. Inasmuch as these newspapers reflected official opinion, it was assumed that the French government would raise even fewer objections than the British.

Grey, it now seems clear, put his finger on one very fundamental truth. There are always more possibilities than actualities in this world. If one enters an organization with reservations designed to meet every possible contingency, those reservations tend to be forgotten with the passing of time.

The worst fears of those who shied away from the League were proved ridiculous by the event. If Uncle Sam had entered the pool at the shallow end, he no doubt would shortly have found himself moving toward the middle. And when he discovered that the water was not shark-infested, he probably would have ignored the reservations or repealed them. At all events the League would have got off to a far better start with Uncle Sam in the shallow end of the pool, even though loaded down with life preservers.

The upshot of the Grey letter was to strengthen Lodge, throw the Democrats further on the defensive, and portray Wilson as needlessly perverse. If the European nations, who were far more vulnerable than we, did not think that the Lodge reservations crippled the League, then why should Wilson continue to insist that they did?

CHAPTER FIFTEEN

THE NEW
WOODROW WILSON

"I shall always believe ratification would have been possible if Wilson's health had not given way; when that tragedy occurred, not even his best friends could exercise any considerable influence on him." SENATOR GILBERT M. HITCHCOCK, *December 7, 1922.*

1

AS THE Senate, under the lash of public opinion, prepared to call up the treaty on February 10, 1920, and renew the seemingly interminable debate, Wilson began to reveal increasing evidences of a marked improvement in health.

The terribly twisted, sunken expression on his face was smoothing out. Gradually more motion returned to his withered arm, and he was able to hobble around more vigorously on his blackthorn cane, which he whimsically called his "third leg." Much of the time he spent in the sun in a wheel chair near the south portico of the White House. The Washington correspondent of the Chicago *Tribune* found him there, hooking his cane to a post, swinging his chair around in a semicircle on the stone flagging, and exclaiming delightedly, "See how strong I am getting!"

By February 10 Wilson's recovery had progressed so far that Dr. Hugh Young of the Johns Hopkins Hospital, one of the attending physicians, could reveal through a reporter for the Baltimore *Sun* that Wilson had suffered an attack of cerebral thrombosis. This rather unusual departure from ordinary professional ethics may have been prompted by the White House, for the doctor's report (assuming that he was correctly quoted) was far more optimistic than the facts seem to have warranted.

By February 19 it could be announced that the President was

at his desk every day at 9:30 in the morning; but how much work he could do was problematical. And on March 3, Wilson went for an hour's motor ride—the first such outing in five months.

2

Politically minded Joseph P. Tumulty had repeatedly urged Wilson to prepare a statement that would expedite the compromise negotiations then being undertaken in the Senate. The President finally acquiesced when on January 26 he sent a letter to Hitchcock, and appended a note (in Mrs. Wilson's hand) saying that it might be published at the senator's discretion. Hitchcock held it back until the eve of the renewal of the debate, and then released it.

At the same time that Wilson sent the statement he returned a proposed compromise on Article X which had been debated by the bipartisan committee. He conceded in the letter to Hitchcock that he could not object to its substance, because he, like the senators, was under oath to observe the Constitution. But he found the form "very unfortunate." Any statement asserting that the United States declined to assume any obligations "unless or except" would "chill" our relationship with the other great powers in maintaining world peace.

Wilson went on to explain that his criticism was happily not all negative. He had gone over the five Hitchcock reservations again (he had drafted the first four), and he was glad to report that he could "accept them as they stand."

In concluding, Wilson affirmed that he had no reason to doubt the good faith of our recent associates; that he hoped the reservation regarding withdrawal from the League would provide for a joint Congressional resolution (which could be vetoed); and finally that he could see no objection to stating that the United States would not accept a mandate without the authorization of Congress.

This letter, though somewhat conciliatory in tone, was not

calculated to promote compromise in the Senate. While conceding the obvious point on the mandates, Wilson stood just where he had stood all along. He would tolerate interpretive reservations, such as those of Hitchcock, but he would go no further. This was where he had been back in November, and even in July. He apparently would not even accept a reservation to Article X that was unobjectionable in substance but "chilling" in tone.

If Wilson stood just where he had stood all along, the country and the Senate did not. Much water had flowed down the Potomac since the previous July. It takes two to make a compromise, just as it takes two to make a quarrel, and if neither Wilson nor Lodge would retreat an inch there could be no real hope of adjustment.

3

Wilson's new access of vigor, and the strengthening of his inflexible attitude, were sensationally high-lighted in mid-February by a public rupture of relations with Secretary of State Lansing.

On February 7, Wilson peremptorily wrote Lansing and asked if it was true that he had been calling Cabinet meetings. Lansing answered that he had frequently summoned the Cabinet in informal conferences during the past months. The members had regarded such gatherings as useful and necessary, and they had not believed that they were acting contrary to Wilson's wishes. Lansing thereupon volunteered to resign if by so doing he could relieve the President of embarrassment.

Wilson bluntly replied that he was much disappointed by the reasons which Lansing gave for usurping authority. The Cabinet could take no official action without the President; hence there was no point in having meetings. Wilson went on to say that these acts of insubordination merely deepened the distrust which he had begun to develop at Paris regarding the noncooperation of Lansing. He would therefore accept the

Secretary's resignation, and would endeavor to find a successor whose mind would run along more closely with his.

Lansing vigorously defended himself in his rejoinder of February 12. He denied that he had usurped authority; insisted that the Cabinet meetings had been necessary and proper; and contended that he would have been derelict in his duty if he had not called them. He had been planning to resign for a long time. He had wanted to at Paris, but had delayed doing so because he had thought it unwise to comfort the enemy and weaken the President's hand by advertising dissension within the ranks. He had wished to leave after the President's collapse, but that would have further shaken confidence in the government. Now that his services were no longer wanted, he could resign with a feeling of "profound relief." This no doubt was true; Lansing had too long been forced to choose between disloyalty and dishonesty.

The next day Wilson formally accepted Lansing's resignation, at the same time conveying best wishes for his future success and recalling most pleasantly "our delightful personal relations." But conspicuously absent was the customary appreciation of Lansing's long and laborious public services.

The President was evidently in an unforgiving mood. When Tumulty remonstrated that in the existing state of public opinion it was the wrong time to do the right thing, Wilson shot back from his invalid's chair, with a flash of his old fire: "Tumulty, it is never the wrong time to spike disloyalty. When Lansing sought to oust me, I was upon my back. I am on my feet now and I will not have disloyalty about me."

4

The publication at Wilson's instance of the correspondence between him and Lansing caused a reverberation throughout the country. The nation was left amazed and regretful at what seemed to be an unbecoming fit of temper.

Wilson remained serene throughout it all. To his secretary he remarked with a smile in his eye, "Well, Tumulty, have I any friends left?" "Very few, Governor," was the reply. Wilson then remarked that the whole thing would blow over in a few days, and that the country would turn against a Secretary who had put his signature to a treaty and then had come home to testify against it.

The country, though shocked, was hardly surprised. Rumors of friction between Wilson and Lansing had long been current, especially after the Bullitt testimony, and the Secretary had actually been forced to deny reports of resignation. It was Wilson's published explanation for his action, rather than the action itself, which deeply disturbed the public. The very fact that the President should have had the correspondence published, evidently thinking that it would vindicate him, is further proof that something had happened to his soundness of judgment.

Mrs. Wilson, with her woman's intuition, claims that she urged him not to send the letter as written, because it did not expose Lansing's more serious acts of disloyalty. To request his resignation because he had summoned the Cabinet would make the President "look small." But Wilson brushed aside her objections.

Most of the friends of Wilson were eloquently silent. Some of the newspapers that had defended him through thick and thin were openly critical. The loyal New York *World* (Democratic) remarked that the President is not obliged to give reasons for evicting a Cabinet officer, but when he does give them, they should be complete. It seems clear at this distance that Wilson would have appeared to better advantage if he had shown Lansing the door for alleged incompetence in handling Mexican affairs, rather than for usurping authority. As long as he was going to give reasons, they should have been good ones, whether the real ones or not.

Several other members of the Cabinet sprang to the defense of their colleague when they testified that they were equally guilty in arranging for meetings. In the public eye Lansing became something of a martyr, especially among those unfriendly to Wilson. His chief sin had apparently been to do his duty and serve the country in difficult circumstances. Lansing remained something of a martyr until he published his book about a year later, and then it became evident that he should have left much sooner than he did.

Discerning observers knew that Cabinet meetings in the absence of the President were not altogether without precedent, and that, Wilson to the contrary, such meetings could be useful in promoting an exchange of information and in making informal decisions. Besides, it was extremely desirable that public confidence in the government be bolstered. Lansing conferred a great favor on Wilson, for which he was ill repaid, by arranging for Cabinet sessions; otherwise public opinion might have risen up in its might and demanded the resignation of the incapacitated President and the installation of Vice President Marshall.

5

The unfortunate public quarrel with Lansing raised even more serious questions about the President's candor and his physical and mental health.

Wilson did not say in his letter that he had just heard of the unauthorized Cabinet meetings. He merely asked Lansing if the report was true, the implication being that he had but recently learned of them. This, as we now know, was false. At the very first meeting, that of October 6, Dr. Grayson appeared and (according to Secretary Houston) reported that Wilson was irked because of this evidence of independent action.

It was common knowledge that the Cabinet had met about twenty-five times. If, the public felt, Wilson had not until very recently had any hint of this, then an investigation had better be started to find out who was running the government.

Less defensible in some eyes was the arbitrary and even dictatorial tone of Wilson's letters. "That thrombosis," jocularly observed one southern newspaper, "evidently has not affected the President's kicking foot." The Secretary of State, whatever his shortcomings, occupies what is commonly regarded as the most distinguished appointive administrative post in the United States—a position second in importance only to the Presidency. Lansing had served long and diligently in

Dropping the First Mate

(Courtesy of St. Louis *Post-Dispatch*; cartoonist Fitzpatrick)

the Department of State, and his reward was to be dismissed as brutally as if he had been an insolent filing clerk.

If Wilson's friends were speechless or openly distressed, his enemies enjoyed a field day. Even more moderate critics regretted that he had not appeared to better advantage. *Harvey's Weekly* cried that the President had gone completely "mad."

It was widely felt that this latest exhibition of Wilsonism went far beyond mere petulance; perhaps it was the result of the thrombosis. The President's position seemed to be the dog-in-the-mangerish one that he would not tolerate having anyone share his authority. If he could not run the Cabinet, then the Cabinet should not run at all.

The real reason for Lansing's dismissal seems to have been an explosion of pent-up wrath against an associate who over many months had seemed insubordinate and downright disloyal. But the public reactions to the incident have been analyzed at length because they had an important bearing, hitherto unemphasized, on the final stages of the treaty fight in the Senate. The press teemed with such adjectives as "uncandid," "querulous," "petty," "pettish," "peevish," "petulant," "jealous," "ungenerous," "uncompromising," "egotistical," "overbearing," and "arrogant."

Enemies of Wilson were further embittered. Even some senators who were friendly to the treaty remarked privately that they would not yield a point and promote compromise, because compromise was impossible with a mentality which had become childishly unreasonable.

6

The headlines of February 26 announced that Lansing's successor would be Bainbridge Colby, a New York lawyer with considerable oratorical and literary talents. The resulting roar of criticism, from both Democrats and Republicans, approached in volume and vigor that which had greeted the dropping of Lansing.

Colby was rather generally known as a brilliant but erratic figure. He had been a Republican; he had bolted to the Progressives in 1912; but he had supported Wilson in 1916. There was some doubt as to whether he really was a Democrat; there was more as to his emotional balance. He was totally without experience in diplomatic matters, as most of our new Secretaries of State are; but the American people will excuse inexperience before they will instability.

The Democrats were quietly angry. Were there not enough of the faithful who had toiled in the vineyard for twenty or thirty years, without having to reach over into Republican ranks and come out with a turncoat Progressive? Frank L. Polk, who had served capably as Acting Secretary of State and who had headed the American Peace Commission in Paris after the return of Wilson, was widely regarded as the logical choice. Granted that his health would have permitted him to accept, he would have been an excellent appointment. But Wilson, who according to Dr. Grayson was worrying himself sick over the problem, did not react favorably to Polk's name.

Senator Lodge and his Foreign Relations Committee went over Colby's qualifications with a fine-toothed comb, and even haled the nominee before them. Lodge defended his conduct by saying that with the President broken in health, with the Vice President unwell, and with the Secretary of State next in line, it was necessary to be cautious. The Senate finally though belatedly confirmed the nomination.

The selection of Colby was so incredible that political experts racked their brains to guess its inner meaning. The New York *Nation* said that the appointment further demonstrated Wilson's unfitness to serve. The *New Republic* guessed that, since the treaty was to be thrown into the campaign, Wilson wanted an able speaker to take the stump in its behalf.

The reasons for the choice, otherwise inexplicable, seem to have been largely personal. Wilson wanted a man whose mind would "run along" with his; those of Lansing and Bryan had run in contrary directions. Wilson wanted a man who was loyal; Colby was worshipfully loyal. Colby was an idealist, like Wilson, and a gifted speaker who could represent Wilson in public. Finally, Colby could write beautiful prose. This was probably a large part of the answer. Wilson admitted to Dr. Grayson that as a result of his disability he would be unable to draft public papers with his former facility, and he needed someone to help him.

7

The scandal of Lansing's dismissal was still the talk of the nation when Wilson hurled another bombshell, which had international repercussions. On February 16 the press carried the summary of a note which the Department of State, clearly with the collaboration of Wilson, had recently sent to Rome, Paris, and London. In it the President objected in the strongest terms to a proposed settlement of the Fiume controversy with Italy in a manner contrary to the strong moral position already taken by the powers.

Wilson stingingly rebuked the Allies for going behind his back and drawing up an arrangement which flew in the face of every principle for which we had recently fought. The American people were fearful, Wilson declared with undeniable truth, of being inveigled into the unjust bargains of Europe, and this latest exhibition of chicanery provided the most "solid ground for such fears."

Then Wilson laid down his ultimatum. If the Allies would not carry through the just proposal already accepted by Britain, France, and the United States, the President "must take under serious consideration" the question of withdrawing the Treaty of Versailles from the Senate, and of leaving the Allies to carry out the settlement without our support.

To European peoples this sounded like dictatorial talk. The Liberal *Westminster Gazette* (London), while admitting that Wilson had justice on his side, felt that his tone recalled "a European monarch of the eighteenth century . . ." The French press was mightily aroused by the prospect of being left completely in the lurch, and denounced Wilson as an autocrat who outdid the Russian tsars. Back in America, the isolationist Washington *Post* chuckled, "Paris is puzzled about the stand of the United States in world affairs, and so is the United States."

Two more Wilsonian notes followed, somewhat more conciliatory in tone and context, but the controversy dragged on for many more months. We need concern ourselves here only with the effect of this Adriatic flare-up on the fortunes of the treaty.

Wilson's ultimatum undoubtedly injured the prospects of treaty ratification. The "irreconcilables" saw in the whole unsavory affair abundant confirmation of their worst fears. If such an exhibition of treachery was typical of our future associates in the League, then why not wash our hands of the whole wretched business? Perhaps the most common reaction of the press was that we should never have become involved in the first place.

The hyphenates, especially Italian-Americans, were again in full cry, with F. H. La Guardia of New York (the future "Little Flower") a leader of the pack. The Italians in distant San Remo did some renaming of streets: Corso Wilson became Corso Fiume.

The whole affair did not make for a sweet spirit of compromise in the Senate. This latest outburst of temper on the part of Wilson indicated that he was not in a state of mind to come anywhere near halfway. If the Adriatic snarl was a fair sample of European trickery, then there was all the more reason for attaching strong reservations to the treaty. And if the President was going to withdraw the whole thing, what was the point in trying to sew little patches of reservations on a useless garment?

In the Lansing affair Wilson was technically right; no President should be saddled with a Cabinet member whom he does not want. In the Adriatic affair Wilson was morally right, as he so often was. But in both cases his timing was poor. The main task was to conciliate the Senate and facilitate compromise, not to inject new distractions and antagonisms. Both the Lansing and the Adriatic showdowns could have been postponed a few weeks, until the treaty was approved. Then dismissals and ultimata, if necessary, would have been in order.

CHAPTER SIXTEEN

THE LAST CHANCE

"So far as the United States Senate is concerned, the dead of this war have died in vain." New York WORLD, *March 20, 1920.*

1

W HILE W ILSON was purging his Cabinet and laying down the law to the Allies, the senators were languidly moving toward a reconsideration of their previous action. Finally, on February 9, the Senate formally voted to reconsider the treaty, and the members entered upon a rehash of their old arguments with little evident relish. Vice President Marshall weariedly remarked to the news correspondents,. "Boys, why don't you just take your files on this treaty debate and print them over again?"

Yet an atmosphere of optimism pervaded the capital: this time the treaty must not be allowed to fail. Even the "irreconcilables" were privately conceding defeat. One of them remarked that, now they had "raised all the Cain possible," he would not be surprised to see most of them voting for ratification. Borah sneered that the only essential difference between the Lodge and Hitchcock reservations to Article X was the difference between "unless" and "until," and with all his oratorical talents he poured scorn upon the heads of the "unlessites" and the "untillites."

Senator Hitchcock was revealing an auspicious willingness to compromise. Lodge, on his part, agreed to accept the bipartisan conference changes on nine of the original fourteen reservations. But the stumbling block was a more satisfactory reservation regarding Article X. Hitchcock emphatically declared that the new proposal of both Lodge and the "mild reservationists" was worse than the original. By February 17

254

the Democratic leader was deeply discouraged; he feared that "we may come out at the same hole we went in."

Hitchcock openly blamed the Republicans. The Democrats, he complained, had agreed to accept two versions of a reservation on Article X which came so close to the original Lodge reservation that many senators could see no real difference between them. Whereupon the irrepressible Borah summed the situation up neatly: The Democrats had come nine-tenths of the way toward compromise; they were admitting that the remaining one-tenth amounted to little or nothing. Then why not, after having gone this far, go the whole way?

2

The Senate at first moved with gratifying speed. Between February 21 and March 7 it adopted or revised eight of the fourteen so-called Lodge reservations.

The withdrawal reservation was approved as it stood (45 to 20), with Lodge vainly trying to secure a joint resolution of Congress, *as Wilson desired,* rather than a concurrent resolution.

The reservation declining to accept a League mandate without the consent of Congress carried by the overwhelming vote of 68 to 4. Wilson had conceded that there was no real objection to this.

The reservation on Shantung was changed (48 to 21), as the Democrats had urged in the bipartisan conferences, to a more tactful version, with the words "China" and "Japan" omitted.

These three reservations all received a two-thirds vote, quite in contrast with the narrow margins of November. Strong Democratic support was mustered for all of them, which indicated that Hitchcock would be unable to hold his followers completely in line on the final vote. Nevertheless a feeling of hopelessness overtook the Senate by the end of February. The "irreconcilables" were voting the reservations on, as before, but they would vote against the whole thing at the end, and barring a surrender by Wilson they would be joined by enough Democrats to defeat the treaty.

The blast that chilled the Democrats, and indirectly the Republicans, came from the White House. About the last week in February, Senator Glass of Virginia (Democrat) was

Can't Even Remove the Victim

(Courtesy of Brooklyn *Eagle*; cartoonist Harding)

delegated to visit the convalescing President and ascertain whether he would pocket the treaty if it should be approved with the Lodge reservations. Wilson emphatically told Glass that he would, according to a newspaper account which is confirmed by their private correspondence. This being the case, why waste more time?

Late in February, Hitchcock told the reporters that he expected the present attempt at ratification to fail, but he was "quite confident" that there would be another one which would succeed. This was incredibly purblind. Only by the grace of a tidal wave of public opinion were the Democrats having their second chance; such tidal waves would not roll up indefinitely. Henry White talked with Hitchcock and was vexed by his "light and airy way" of referring to the treaty, and of expecting that another deadlock would force the Republicans to yield.

Hitchcock's confidence may have been bolstered by Borah, who was declaring that he intended to present a strong anti-League plank at the coming Republican convention, and bolt the party if it was rejected. The prospect of another Republican schism was highly tempting to the Democrats. Why should either Hitchcock or Wilson yield too much in the way of compromise and get the League issue out of the way, when there was this high political premium on continued deadlock?

3

During the first week in March the debate over reservations was alternately listless and heated. The "bitter-enders" were again cheerful. Everywhere there was a feeling that the treaty white elephant should be dragged from the Senate floor and pushed into the coming campaign. There seemed to be no other way to get rid of it.

Yet the debate ground on, to the amusement of well-filled galleries. Having made up their minds to kill the treaty, the senators could not decide on a prompt and decent burial. Borah baited the Democrats by charging that they would all finally surrender and be in there voting for the Lodge reservations at the end. This naturally hardened Democratic resistance, as did the rumor that the President, if his followers surrendered, would head a third party in the approaching campaign and ruin their chances of reelection.

Lodge was at his wit's end. He had endorsed most of the changes which the Democrats had pushed in the bipartisan conferences, and had succeeded in getting some of them adopted. But the "irreconcilables" were threatening to bolt if he gave ground on Article X; the "mild reservationists" were threatening to bolt if he did not; and the Democrats were under orders from the White House to vote down whatever was agreed upon. On March 4 Lodge flared up and said that since the Democrats seemed unwilling to support some of the amendments which they had presented in the bipartisan conferences, he would offer no more. He solemnly admitted for the first time that the treaty had "fallen by the wayside."

Yet to the very end a few of the faithful never gave up hope that some compromise might be worked out on the reservation to Article X. Senator Simmons of North Carolina (a Democrat) was one of these, and he enlisted the support of Senator Watson (a Republican), who in turn secured the assent of Lodge to a part of the plan.

Simmons was anxious to talk with the President about his proposal. On or about March 5 (the letter is undated), Hitchcock wrote directly to Wilson urging that Simmons be called to the White House, and giving reasons why. At the bottom of this letter is a brief notation in the writing of Mrs. Wilson, presumably dictated by the President and sent on to Hitchcock. The note curtly said that it would be folly to undertake individual interviews. (Wilson was probably thinking of the fruitless conferences with individual senators back in July.)

The upshot was that Senator Simmons and his fellow compromisers were not permitted to see Wilson, and Senator Watson records that Simmons was much vexed. The President was probably vexed, too: why should people be constantly bothering him about compromising on Article X, especially since he had already made it clear that he would not compromise?

Wilson's Olympian seclusion from the Senate during these critical days is puzzling. Senator Glass, a warm friend, seems to have been the only one whom he did consult, though others were reported as anxious to see him. There can be no doubt that he was physically able to talk with individual senators, and might have done so if his mind had been open and if he had realized the importance of keeping in touch with developments in the Senate. Evidently Wilson had reconciled himself to the rejection of the treaty, and looked forward to a triumphant vindication at the polls.

4

The President fired another verbal bombshell, on March 8, 1920, when he addressed a communication to Senator Hitchcock setting forth his objections to the Lodge reservations. The letter was in the nature of a reply to Hitchcock's request that Wilson see Senator Simmons and one or two of his colleagues.

No devitalizing reservation to Article X, Wilson insisted, would be acceptable, for Article X was a moral obligation—a sacred pledge to our gallant boys. Without this article we should get nothing out of the war but regrets for having gone in. Either we should enter the League fearlessly, accepting responsibility for world leadership, or we should retire "as gracefully as possible" from the concert of powers.

Wilson went on to say that at Paris he had run afoul of "militaristic" forces, particularly those of France, and they had fought Article X. The Lodge reservation would be a victory for them.

The President further explained that "practically every so-called reservation" was a "rather sweeping nullification" of the actual terms of the treaty. He had heard of "reservationists" and "mild reservationists," but he could not understand the difference between "a nullifier" and a "mild nullifier." In concluding, Wilson expressed the wish that Hitchcock would communicate these views to his fellow Democrats in the Senate for their guidance. In brief, reject the Lodge reservations because they nullified the treaty.

This letter is one of the most striking that Wilson ever wrote. In his discussion of Article X he soared again into the empyrean idealism of his Fourteen Points and other war addresses. But he was clearly out of touch with reality. Some of the things he said were no doubt true but they would not get the treaty approved. It was, for example, a gross exaggeration to assert that practically every one of the proposed reservations was in effect a sweeping nullification of the treaty.

The letter disclosed not only a stubborn mind, but a closed mind. By the day that Wilson wrote these instructions, *about half of the Lodge reservations had not yet been voted upon* (including that to Article X), and in general they were the less important ones. The others were still taking shape, and were subject to amendment. The reservation to Article X was still being hammered out, and at the time Wilson sent the letter there was still a lively hope of some kind of compromise along the lines of the Simmons-Watson proposal. Yet Wilson *vetoed all the rest of the reservations without even waiting to see what they were going to be.*

5

The reverberations from this March letter were both national and international.

The wavering Democrats were beaten back into line by the crack of the Wilsonian whip. Most of them, especially those up for reelection, did not care to go before the voters and admit that they had defied the sickbed wishes of their great President.

Some of the more reasonable Democrats, like Owen of Oklahoma, were forced to choose between Wilson and Lodge, and they sadly chose Lodge. Owen openly announced that he would fall in behind any leadership that would take us into the League, with or without reservations.

The "mild reservationists," who had not completely abandoned hope of a compromise on Article X, were again slapped in the face. They were branded as "nullifiers," when in their judgment they were trying to save the treaty from a stubborn zealot who would destroy it.

The "irreconcilables" were delighted. Senator Brandegee, "overjoyed and exultant," hastened with a copy of the letter to Mrs. Alice Roosevelt Longworth. It meant that the angered "mild reservationists" would stand with the "bitter-enders" in voting reservations onto the treaty. Senator Moses sacrilegiously rejoiced that he, an "irreconcilable," had been united in the holy bonds of "political wedlock" with Senator Kellogg, a "mild reservationist," by the Reverend Woodrow Wilson.

The "Lodge reservationists" were now more determined than ever to carry through their program with dispatch, and dump the dead treaty on Wilson's doorstep. Lodge snorted that the President's letter contained some "delightful" passages, especially on French militarism and imperialism. He rose in the Senate several days later to explain that he had meant this sarcastically.

The French were stunned by the attack upon their militarism. Wilson had promised them security through the League and the Security Treaty. The League was dying; the Security Treaty was dead. Could France be blamed, after this betrayal, for building up a strong system of alliances and trying to safeguard herself against future aggression?

The French Ambassador in Washington, Jules Jusserand, promptly sent a note of remonstrance to Acting Secretary of State Polk, who forwarded it to Wilson. The President replied on March 15 that he resented Jusserand's rushing in, and expected Polk to have a frank and firm talk with him. Wilson evidently was piqued because Jusserand was piqued. The same trace of asperity that had crept into the Lansing and Adriatic notes again had come to the surface.

Across the Atlantic, the French press flared forth in anger. It was shocking to learn that Article X had been devised to hold France in check. It was hypocritical for America (who had not reduced her armaments) to blame France (after betraying her) for maintaining large armies. Some of the less moderate French journals referred to the maunderings of a sick man. The Paris *Midi* said bluntly, "The American nation is directed by an idiot." The Paris *Matin* quoted *Harvey's Weekly* as saying, "No, Mr. Wilson has not become insane; *he* is just as he always was."

The London *Globe,* the first English paper to break silence, wondered if Wilson was now physically or temperamentally capable of dealing with a complicated international situation which demanded give-and-take. His illness had aroused the sympathy of the whole world; his recent petulant outbursts elicited "a certain degree of sympathy for the United States."

6

On March 8, the day that Wilson wrote his disturbing letter, the weary senators, convinced of the futility of what they were doing, unanimously adopted a motion to limit debate. Most of the remaining reservations were rapidly carried through, all of them by lopsided if not overwhelming votes, all of them with some Democratic support, and one of them without debate. The six-to-one reservation, in revised form, was approved 57 to 20, *with 17 Democrats supporting it.*

By March 10 the crisis was approaching on Article X. There were rumors that the Simmons-Watson proposal might yet win enough votes. Even Lodge alarmed the "irreconcilables" by presenting a watered-down version of his own reservation, though he admitted he had changed the phraseology and not the basic principle. Senator Reed then told the story of the boy who was fishing for suckers: when they would not bite, he merely reversed the same worm on the hook, saying, "Oh, these are just fish I'm after; they don't know much."

Senator Hitchcock took the trouble to send the new Lodge reservation to the White House about March 12 with a note (undated) saying he assumed it would be unacceptable. Wilson curtly noted on the bottom of the page that the senator was

quite right, and returned it. The "irreconcilables," by threatening dire things, were finally able to force Lodge to accept
an amendment to his revised reservation on Article X which,
if anything, made it more sweeping. In this form it was adopted
on March 15 by a vote of 56 to 26, *with 14 Democrats voting
for it*.

The irate Senator Simmons taxed Lodge with twice having
surrendered on Article X when agreement was in sight, and
with twice having entered into an alliance with the "irreconcilables." Lodge replied that the Republican senators had
been "endeavoring to act together." Then, with an acid thrust
at Wilson, he added: "We cannot conduct matters on this side
of the aisle as they are conducted on that side. *We have no one
to write us letters.*"

Simmons snapped back that no one had to write Lodge letters. All that was necessary was for Borah, the leader of the
"irreconcilables," to "tell" the Massachusetts senator what
to do.

Borah then spoke up for the "irreconcilables" to say that
they were standing foursquare with Wilson in seeking "to
defeat the treaty." "There is just as much of an understanding
between the President of the United States and myself as there
is between the Senator from Massachusetts and myself."

7

On March 18, appropriately enough the day after St. Pat-
rick's Day, an astonishing development occurred. Senator
Gerry of Rhode Island, a stalwart Democrat, proposed a
fifteenth reservation putting the Senate on record as favoring
self-determination and independence for Ireland.

This was the acme of legislative absurdity. Ireland was completely irrelevant to the subject matter of the treaty. The
fourth Lodge reservation warned other powers to keep out of
our domestic concerns, and now we were rushing headlong

into those of Britain. Such an indefensible irrelevancy would give Wilson complete justification for pocketing the entire treaty, even assuming that he would not have done so anyhow. Finally, the British would be strongly impelled to object to the Irish reservation and perhaps defeat or delay final ratification.

It was crystal-clear by this time that the only chance of securing ratification lay in the Lodge reservations. The last-minute Ireland dodge was but a transparent trick by the Democrats to make the preceding fourteen reservations so offensive that not even the Republicans would vote for them. The regular Democratic senators apparently did not want agreement, and they preferred to take their chances in the coming campaign, unless they were allowed to put the stamp of their own interpretation on the treaty. From now on the Democrats were hardly in a position to accuse the "irreconcilables" of bad faith in voting for reservations with the plain intent of later voting them down.

Lodge frantically sought to wriggle out of this diabolically clever trap. He finally proposed a recess so that he might rally his demoralized ranks. But the outspoken Ashurst of Arizona (Democrat) cried out in piercing tones against further delay. The Senate, he shouted, should either take this treaty in a pair of tongs and drop it into the Potomac, or ratify it without more palaver or delay, for the people were heartily tired of it. This sally brought such a tremendous outburst of applause from the packed galleries that not even the stern hammerings of the presiding officer could check it.

The Irish reservation carried by the close vote of 38 to 36, with the "bitter-enders" and *over half the Democrats present voting for it,* among them men like Hitchcock who had consistently opposed the Lodge reservations. Such are the mutations of politics.

Just before the final vote, on March 19, the Senate adopted without record vote a Lodge amendment to the preamble of the original reservations. This provided for silent acquiescence

by all the Allied powers, rather than explicit written acceptance by three of the major four. (It will be remembered that
Wilson had strongly objected to the original reservation because it required written consent.)

By this time it was hardly accurate to speak of the "Lodge"
reservations. That regarding Ireland was vehemently opposed
by the Massachusetts senator. Others had been revised to meet
Democratic objections and had received strong Democratic
support, notably the preamble, the Shantung reservation, and
the League-expense reservation. Lodge seemingly was willing
to yield more than this but was repeatedly beaten back by the
"bitter-enders." Generally speaking, the revised Lodge reservations (except for that on Ireland) were more tactful, less likely
to wound foreign sensibilities, and more carefully worded.

Throughout the debate Hitchcock consistently presented
substitute reservations, and was as consistently voted down. A
careful analysis of his proposals shows that in principle, if not
in phraseology, they differed little if any from the corresponding ones of Lodge. The difference was not so much between
tweedledum and tweedledee as between Democratic political
face and Republican political face. Throughout the debate,
repeated and unabashed references to the impending campaign again demonstrated that the curse of party politics was
ever present.

8

As the hour again approached for the crucial vote, it was
apparent that the tide of public opinion, even within Democratic ranks, had begun to turn strongly against the uncompromising President. This was quite in contrast with November, when Wilson had radiated something of the aura of a
martyr. But the Lansing and Adriatic affairs, combined with
the peremptory letter to Hitchcock, had caused the President
to appear in a less lovely light.

When it became clear that the choice was either a reserved

treaty or nothing, all but the most partisan and stubborn shrank from the terrifying responsibility of giving the country and the world nothing. Men like Herbert Hoover, William Jennings Bryan, and ex-President Taft begged Wilson not to throw away nine-tenths of a loaf because he could not get the whole loaf. Personal friends of the President added their voices to the swelling chorus.

Highly significant was the defection in March of a number of the most influential Democratic newspapers. The Cleveland *Plain Dealer* turned a somersault and reluctantly declared for the Lodge reservations. The Brooklyn *Eagle* was sadly urging the senators to ignore the President and vote their own convictions. The powerful New York *World,* an unflagging defender of the League, now belittled the Lodge reservations, and while insisting that Wilson was right in principle, admitted that on occasion every statesman must yield to expediency. The President's position, from this point of view, was "weak and untenable."

The Louisville *Courier-Journal,* which carried on the violently outspoken tradition of "Marse Henry" Watterson, had long been, like the other Democratic newspapers, a foe of reservations. It now reversed itself and urged ratification on "the best terms possible." The St. Louis *Post-Dispatch* (nominally Independent, though strongly Democratic in its leanings), had supported the treaty all along with great vigor. It now parted company with Wilson because he was "endangering the cause"—and the cause was greater than any man or any party.

9

It was in this changing atmosphere that, on March 19, 1920, the Senate prepared for the final vote. The galleries were jammed; the air was electric; but the excitement was less tense than in November. Barring some kind of miracle or last-minute shift, the treaty would be rejected.

Several of the senators took the floor to make their final

arguments. Among them was Senator Walsh of Montana, who contributed one of the few really impressive speeches of the entire debate. He would reluctantly vote for reservations, partly because the influence of Article X had been exaggerated, but primarily because there was no alternative.

The zero hour had now arrived. The question was on agreeing to the resolution of ratification with the Lodge reservations incorporated. With stentorian tones the clerk began to call the roll. Three of the first four Democrats turned against Wilson and voted for the treaty. Then came the name of Senator Culberson of Texas, a Democrat who had grown gray in the service and who was high in the esteem of his colleagues. If he too voted "Yea" he might touch off a Democratic stampede. His face was perplexed, but after a moment's hesitation he voted "Nay." (Later in the street he turned to a friend, and after speaking in the highest terms of Walsh's speech, remarked, "You know, for a minute in there I didn't know how to vote.")

The roll call continued. Some of the Democratic stalwarts stood fast; others deserted. Then came the name of Hitchcock. If he voted with Lodge, he might yet start a stampede among the remaining Democrats. But he remained true to Wilson's leadership and voted "Nay." (Some years afterward he told Dr. Nicholas Murray Butler that he was the man who had really defeated the treaty, at "virtually the command" of Wilson. "It was," Butler reports him as saying, "the mistake of my life.")

When the votes were all tallied, the count stood 49 to 35, which meant that the treaty, *though commanding a simple majority this time,* lacked seven votes of the necessary two-thirds. Twenty-one Democrats went over to the Lodge camp, but twenty-three remained loyal. If seven of the twenty-three had followed the others, the treaty would have carried. Thus twenty-three old-line Democrats, acting at the behest of the uncompromising Wilson, joined with the "bitter-ender" Republicans to bring about the second and final defeat of the treaty.

The "irreconcilable" Brandegee turned to Lodge and said, "We can always depend on Mr. Wilson. He never has failed us."

10

Once the treaty was rejected, the Senate passed the customary motion (47 to 37) to return it to the President. No effort was made, as in November, to approve the treaty without reservations, or with the Hitchcock reservations. All this was regarded as completely hopeless.

Yet a feeble attempt was made to reconsider the vote of rejection. It was generally felt that such a motion would be acceptable, once the wheel-horse Democrats had stuck by their guns and Wilson long enough to salve their consciences and stay in the good graces of their constituents. The loyal Democrats could then support a motion to reconsider, and leave the final decision up to the President.

The press reported that the administration Democrats had worked out a "deal" with the "mild reservationists" to carry a vote to reconsider. Senator Robinson (Democrat) actually made such a motion. Senator Watson moved to table it, but this maneuver lost 43 to 34, with the "mild reservationists" joining the Democrats.

The president of the Senate pro tempore (Senator Cummins of Iowa, Republican) thereupon declared the Robinson motion to reconsider out of order. He expressed misgivings as to the soundness of his ruling, and plainly invited an appeal from the decision of the chair. If such an appeal had been made, the loyal Democrats doubtless would have combined again with the "mild reservationists" to declare the Robinson motion in order, and there would have been a final chance to save the treaty. Incredible though it may seem, *not a single one of those who professed to favor the treaty with reservations,* either Republicans or Democrats, *rose to challenge the chairman's questionable ruling.*

Then Lodge came forward. He said that since some of the senators obviously wanted another chance to vote, he would propose unanimous consent for a motion to reconsider, and in this way give the Democrats one more opportunity to approve the treaty with his reservations. But Hitchcock flatly

Entirely Unadoptable

(Courtesy of San Francisco *Chronicle*; cartoonist Bronstrup)

objected to unanimous consent, and Lodge's last attempt to revive the pact had to be dropped. The Treaty of Versailles was never again formally considered in the Senate of the United States.

It is clear that, if those Democrats who voted against the treaty had really wanted a second chance, they could have had it. The conclusion must be that they did not want it. The twenty-three loyal Democrats were standing so steadfast that another roll call would obviously have been a waste of time. Wilson was insisting that he would rather have the treaty thrown into the tumult of politics than have it approved with the Lodge reservations; so the administration Democrats, for whatever reasons, gave their crippled leader what he wanted.

As before, the "irreconcilables" met at the home of Mrs. Longworth for a victory supper. But the affair was not a great success; they were all tired and suffering from the feeling of an anticlimax. "For weeks," says Mrs. Longworth, "it was really comic how we missed having the League to fight about."

Bright and early the next morning after the final vote, the secretary of the Senate appeared at the White House Executive Offices with the big bound volume of the official treaty, wrapped securely in brown paper and tied generously with red tape. The President had personally presented it to the Senate for approval; the senators could not agree on a resolution of ratification, so they were sending it back.

The next move, as Lodge explained, was up to the President. If he wanted to resubmit the treaty, the Senate would treat it as new business. If he wanted to toss it into the campaign, then the Republicans would gladly meet him on the hustings.

CHAPTER SEVENTEEN

THE SUPREME
INFANTICIDE

"As a friend of the President, as one who has loyally followed him, I solemnly declare to him this morning: If you want to kill your own child because the Senate straightens out its crooked limbs, you must take the responsibility and accept the verdict of history." SENATOR ASHURST *of Arizona (Democrat),* March 11, 1920.

1

THE TREATY was now dead, as far as America was concerned. Who had killed it?

The vital role of the loyal Democrats must be reemphasized. If all of them who professed to want the treaty had voted "Yea," it would have passed with more than a dozen votes to spare. If the strait-jacket of party loyalty had not been involved, the necessary two-thirds could easily have been mustered.

In the previous November, the Democrats might have voted against the treaty (as they did) even without White House pressure. But this time pressure had to be applied to force them into line, and even in the face of Wilsonian wrath almost half of them bolted. On the day of the final balloting the newsmen observed that two Cabinet members (Burleson and Daniels), possibly acting at the President's direction, were on the floor of the Senate, buttonholing waverers. The day after the fateful voting Hitchcock wrote Wilson that it had required the "most energetic efforts" on his part *to prevent a majority of the Democrats from surrendering to Lodge.*

Desertion of the President, as we have seen, is no light offense in the political world, especially when he has declared himself emphatically. Senators do not ordinarily court political suicide. Wilson still had the patronage bludgeon in his hands,

271

and having more than a trace of vindictiveness, he could oppose renegade senators when they ran again, and in fact did so.

Many of the loyal Democrats were up for reelection in 1920. They certainly were aware of the effects of party treachery on their political fortunes. They knew—or many of them knew —that they were killing the treaty; they made no real effort to revive it; they must have wanted it killed—at least until after the November election.

One striking fact stands out like a lighthouse. With the exception of Hitchcock of Nebraska, Johnson of South Dakota, and Thomas of Colorado, *every single one of the twenty-three senators who stood loyally with Wilson in March came from south of the Mason and Dixon line*. Only four of the "disloyal" twenty-one represented states that had seceded in 1860–1861. At the polls, as well as on the floor of the Senate, decent southern Democrats voted "the way their fathers shot." As between bothersome world responsibility on the one hand, and loyalty to President, party, section, and race on the other, there was but one choice. Perhaps world leadership would come eventually anyhow.

Democratic senators like Walsh of Montana and Ashurst of Arizona were not from the South. When the issue was clearly drawn between loyalty to party and loyalty to country, their consciences bade them choose the greater good. Ashurst had gone down the line in supporting Wilson; but several days before the final vote he declared, "I am just as much opposed to a White House irreconcilable as I am to a Lodge irreconcilable."

2

A word now about public opinion.

In March, as in November, more than 80 per cent of the senators professed to favor the treaty with some kind of reservations. All the polls and other studies indicate that this was roughly the sentiment of the country. Yet the senators were unable to scrape together a two-thirds vote for any one set of reservations.

The reaction of many newspaper editors, as before, was to cry out against the shame of it all—this indictment of the "capacity of our democracy to do business." We had astonished the world by our ability to make war; we now astonished the world with our "imbecility" in trying to make peace. How could we blame other countries for thinking us "a nation of boobs and bigots"? The Louisville *Courier-Journal* (Democrat), referring to our broken promises to the Allies, cried that we stood betrayed as "cravens and crooks," "hypocrites and liars."

Partisan Republican newspapers loudly blamed the stiff-backed Wilson and his "me-too" senators. Two wings of "irreconcilables"—the Wilsonites and the "bitter-enders"—had closed in to execute a successful pincers movement against the treaty. The New York *Tribune* (Independent Republican) condemned the "inefficiency, all-sufficiency and self-sufficiency of our self-named only negotiator," Woodrow Wilson. If the treaty died, said the *Tribune,* the handle of the dagger that pierced its heart would bear the "initials 'W. W.' "

If Republicans scolded Democrats, Democrats scolded Republicans. Lodge and his cheap political tricks were roundly condemned, and the general conclusion was that "the blood of the Treaty stains the floor of the Republican wigwam." A few of the less partisan Democratic journals openly conceded that Wilson's obstinacy had something to do with the final result. William Jennings Bryan asserted from the platform that this "most colossal crime against our nation and the civilized world in all history" made his "blood boil." He began a vigorous campaign against the two-thirds rule in the Senate. "A majority of Congress can declare war," he cried; "it ought to be as easy to end a war as to begin it."

The leading liberal journals, as before, were sadly happy. They rejoiced that the result would clear the way for a renovation of the treaty, but they regretted that the pact had been defeated as a result of partisanship rather than as a result of the betrayal of Wilson's promises.

An impressive number of the more discerning editors deplored the fact that the issue was now in the dirty hands of

"He Did It!"

(Courtesy of Los Angeles *Times*; cartoonist Gale)

politicians. An electoral referendum, it was felt, would merely confuse the issue; such a canvass could not possibly reveal anything more than was already known, namely, that *an overwhelming majority of the people wanted the treaty with some kind of reservations.*

3

Is it true that the invalid in the White House really strangled the treaty to death with his own enfeebled hands?

It is seldom that statesmen have a second chance—a second guess. They decide on a course of action, and the swift current of events bears them downstream from the starting point. Only rarely does the stream reverse itself and carry them back.

In November, Wilson had decided that he wanted deadlock, because he reasoned that deadlock would arouse public opinion and force the Senate to do his bidding. The tidal wave of public opinion did surge in, and Wilson got his second chance. But he threw it away, first by spurning compromise (except on his terms), and then by spurning the Lodge reservations.

There had been much more justification for Wilson's course in November than in March. In November he was sick, secluded, was fed censored news, and was convinced by Hitchcock that the strategy of deadlock was sound. In March, he was much improved in health, far less secluded, more in touch with the press and with the currents of opinion, though probably still not enough. He consulted even less with the Senate, presumably because he had made up his mind in advance to oppose the Lodge reservations. In November, there was a fair possibility of reconsideration; in March, it was clear that the only possibility lay in making the League an issue in the coming campaign. Wilson, with his broad knowledge of government and politics, should have seen that this hope was largely if not completely illusory. Perhaps he would have seen it had he not been blinded by his feeling for Lodge.

The evidence is convincing that Wilson wanted the issue cast into the hurly-burly of politics. He could not accept Lodge's terms; Lodge would not accept his terms. The only possible chance of beating the senator—and this was slim indeed—was to win a resounding mandate in 1920.

Yet this strategy, as already noted, meant further delay. At

Paris, the feeling at times had been, "Better a bad treaty today than a good treaty four months hence." Europe was still in chaos, and increasingly in need of America's helping hand. Well might the Europeans cry, "Better a treaty with the Lodge reservations today than a probable treaty without reservations after the election." Or as Dr. Frank Crane wrote in *Current Opinion,* "It is vastly more needful that some sort of League be formed, *any sort,* than that it be formed *perfectly.*" (Italics Crane's.)

Yet Wilson, for the reasons indicated, could not see all this clearly. Four days after the fatal vote he wrote Hitchcock, praising him for having done all in his power to protect the honor of the nation and the peace of the world against the Republican majority.

Mrs. Wilson, no doubt reflecting her husband's views, later wrote, "My conviction is that Mr. Lodge put the world back fifty years, and that at his door lies the wreckage of human hopes and the peril to human lives that afflict mankind today."

4

To the very end Wilson was a fighter. When the Scotch-Irish in him became aroused, he would nail his colors to the mast. He said in 1916 that he was "playing for the verdict of mankind." His conception of duty as he saw it was overpowering. He once remarked that if he were a judge, and it became his duty to sentence his own brother to the gallows, he would do so—and afterwards die of a broken heart.

It is well to have principles; it is well to have a noble conception of duty. But Wilson, as he became warmed up in a fight, tended to get things out of focus and to lose a proper sense of values.

The basic issue in 1920 was the Hitchcock reservations or the Lodge reservations. Wilson accepted those of Hitchcock while rejecting those of Lodge, which, he said, completely nullified the treaty and betrayed his promises to the Allies and to the American dead.

This, as we have seen, was a gross exaggeration. Minds no less acute than Wilson's, and less clouded with sickness and pride, denied that the Lodge reservations completely nullified the treaty. To the man in the street—in so far as he gave the dispute thought—there was little discernible difference between the two sets of reservations. How could one decry statements which merely reaffirmed the basic principles of the Constitution and of our foreign policy? To a vast number of Americans the Lodge reservations, far from nullifying the treaty, actually improved it. This was so apparent to even the most loyal Democrats in the Senate that Wilson could barely keep them in line.

In the final analysis the treaty was slain in the house of its friends rather than in the house of its enemies. In the final analysis it was not the two-thirds rule, or the "irreconcilables," or Lodge, or the "strong" and "mild reservationists," but Wilson and his docile following who delivered the fatal stab. If the President had been permitted to vote he would have sided with Borah, Brandegee, Johnson, and the other "bitter-enders"—though for entirely different reasons.

Wilson had said that the reservation to Article X was a knife thrust at the heart of the Covenant. Ironically, he parried this knife thrust, and stuck his own dagger, not into the heart of the Covenant, but into the entire treaty.

This was the supreme act of infanticide. With his own sickly hands Wilson slew his own brain child—or the one to which he had contributed so much.

This was the supreme paradox. He who had forced the Allies to write the League into the treaty, unwrote it; he who had done more than any other man to make the Covenant, unmade it—at least so far as America was concerned. And by his action, he contributed powerfully to the ultimate undoing of the League, and with it the high hopes of himself and mankind for an organization to prevent World War II.

5

The preceding dogmatic observations are of course qualified by the phrase, "in the last analysis."

Many elements enter into a log jam. Among them are the width of the stream, the depth of the stream, the swiftness of the current, the presence of boulders, the size of the logs, and the absence of enough lumberjacks. No one of these factors can be solely responsible for the pile-up.

Many elements entered into the legislative log jam of March, 1920. Among them were isolationism, partisanship, senatorial prerogative, confusion, apathy, personal pride, and private feuds. No one of them was solely responsible for the pile-up. *But as the pile-up finally developed, there was only one lumberjack who could break it, and that was Woodrow Wilson.* If at any time before the final vote he had told the Senate Democrats to support the treaty with the Lodge reservations, or even if he had merely told them that they were on their own, the pact would almost certainly have been approved. So "in the last analysis" the primary responsibility for the failure in March rested with Wilson.

What about Lodge? If the treaty would have passed by Wilson's surrendering, is it not equally true that it would have passed by Lodge's surrendering?

The answer is probably "Yes," but the important point is that Lodge had far less responsibility for getting the treaty through than Wilson. If Lodge had yielded, he probably would have created a schism within his ranks. His ultimate responsibility was to keep the party from breaking to pieces, and in this he succeeded. Wilson's ultimate responsibility was to get the treaty ratified, and in this he failed. With Lodge, as with any truly partisan leader, the party comes before country; with the President the country should come before party, though unhappily it often does not.

It is possible that Wilson saw all this—but not clearly

enough. He might have been willing to compromise if his adversary had been any other than Lodge. But so bitter was the feeling between the two men that Wilson, rather than give way, grasped at the straw of the election of 1920.

Lodge did not like Wilson either, but he made more of a show of compromising than the President. He actually supported and drove through amendments to his original reservations which were in line with Wilson's wishes, and he probably would have gone further had the "irreconcilables" not been on his back. He fought the crippling Irish reservation, as well as others supported by the "bitter-enders." Finally, he gave the Democrats a fair chance to reconsider their vote and get on the bandwagon, but they spurned it.

If Lodge's words mean anything, and if his actions were not those of a monstrous hypocrite, he actually tried to get the treaty through with his reservations. When he found that he could not, he washed his hands of the whole business in disgust.

The charge is frequently made that, if Wilson had yielded to his adversary, Lodge would have gleefully piled on more reservations until Wilson, further humiliated, would have had to throw out the whole thing.

The strongest evidence for this view is a circumstantial story which Secretary Houston relates. During a Cabinet meeting Wilson was called to the telephone, and agreed to make certain concessions agreeable to Lodge. Before adjournment the telephone rang again, and word came that Lodge would not adhere to his original proposal.

This story is highly improbable, because Wilson attended no Cabinet meetings between September 2, 1919, and April 13, 1920. By the latter date, all serious attempts at compromise had been dropped; by the earlier date the treaty was still before the Senate committee, and the Lodge reservations, though in an embryonic stage, were yet unborn. But, even if the story is true, it merely proves that Lodge veered about, as he frequently did under "irreconcilable" pressure.

In March, as in November, all Wilson had to do was to send

over Postmaster General Burleson to the Senate a few minutes
before the final vote with the quiet word that the Democrats
were to vote "Yea." The treaty would then have passed with
the Lodge reservations, and Lodge could hardly have dared
incur for himself or his party the odium of moving to reconsider for the purpose of screwing on more reservations. Had
he tried to do so, the "mild reservationists" almost certainly
would have blocked him.

6

A few days after the disastrous final vote, Wilson's only comment to Tumulty was, "They have shamed us in the eyes of
the world." If his previous words said what he really meant,
he was hardly more shamed by the defeat of the treaty than by
the addition of the Lodge reservations. In his eyes it all
amounted to the same thing.

If the treaty had passed, would the President have been willing to go through with the exchange of ratifications? Would
he not have pocketed it, as he threatened to do prior to the
November vote?

Again, if Wilson's words may be taken at their face value,
this is what he would have done. He had not backed down
from his pre-November position. His Jackson Day message
and his letter to Hitchcock made it unmistakably clear that
he preferred the uncertainties of a political campaign to the
certainties of ratification with the Lodge reservations. The
addition of the indefensible Irish reservation provided even
stronger justification for pocketing the entire pact.

It is probable that some of the loyal Democrats voted as they
did partly because they were convinced that Wilson was going
to pigeonhole the treaty anyhow. From their point of view it
was better that the odium for defeat should seemingly rest on
Lodge rather than on their President. It also seems clear that
Wilson preferred, as in November, to have the blood of the
treaty on the Senate doorstep rather than on his. As he wrote

to Secretary Colby, on April 2, 1920, the slain pact lay heavily
on the consciences of those who had stabbed it, and he was
quite willing to have it lie there until those consciences were
either awakened or crushed.

Yet it is one thing to say, just before Senate action, "I will
pocket the treaty." It is another, after the pact is approved and
sent to the White House, to assume this tremendous responsibility. The eyes of the world are upon the President; he is the
only man keeping the nation out of the peace which it so
urgently needs; he is the one man standing in the way of the
rehabilitation which the world so desperately demands. Public
pressure to ratify in such a case would be enormous—probably
irresistible.

Some years later Senator Hitchcock said that in the event
of senatorial approval Wilson would possibly have waited for
the November election. If he had won, he would have worked
for the removal of the Lodge reservations; if he had lost, then
the compulsion to go through with ratification would have
become overpowering. By November more than six months
would have passed, and by that time Wilson might have developed a saner perspective.

But this is all speculation. Wilson gave orders that the treaty
was to be killed in the Senate chamber. And there it died.

7

One other line of inquiry must be briefly pursued. Is it true,
as some writers allege, that the thirty-odd Allied signatories
of the original treaty would have rejected the Lodge reservations when officially presented? We recall that under the terms
of the preamble these nations were privileged to acquiesce
silently or file objections.

One will never know the answer to this question, because
Wilson denied the other signatories a chance to act. But it
seems proper to point to certain probabilities.

One or more of the Latin American nations might have objected to the reservation regarding the then hated Monroe Doctrine. Yet the Monroe Doctrine would have continued to exist anyhow; it was already in the Covenant; and these neighboring republics might well have swallowed their pride in the interest of world peace.

Italy probably would have acquiesced, and the evidence is strong that France would have done likewise. The Japanese could not completely overlook the Shantung reservation, but it was generally recognized in their press as meaningless, and for this reason it might have been tolerated, though not without some loss of face. It is noteworthy that the most important Japanese newspapers regretted the Senate stalemate as an encouragement to world instability, particularly in China.

Great Britain probably would have been the chief objector. The reservation on Ireland was highly offensive but completely innocuous, for the British lion had long endured Irish-American tail-twistings in pained but dignified silence. The reservation on six-to-one was a slap at the loyal and sacrificing Dominions, but it did not mean that their vote was to be taken away. Moreover, the contingency envisaged by this proviso was unlikely to arise very often, and in the long run would doubtless have proved inconsequential.

In sum, there were only two or three reservations to which the outside powers could seriously object. If they had objected, it is probable that a satisfactory adjustment could have been threshed out through diplomatic channels. For when it became clear that only a few phrases stood between the United States and peace, the dictates of common sense and the pressure of public opinion probably would have led to an acceptable compromise. If the Senate had refused to give ground in such a case, then the onus would have been clearly on it and not on Wilson.

The World Court is a case in point. In 1926 the Senate voted to join, but attached five reservations, four of which were accepted by the other powers. By 1935 a compromise was worked out on the fifth, but an isolationist uprising led by William

Randolph Hearst and Father Coughlin turned what seemed to be a favorable vote in the Senate into a narrow defeat for the World Court. The one-third minority again triumphed, with the aging Borah and Johnson and Norris and Gore still voting their fears and prejudices.

But the World Court analogy must not be pressed too far. In 1920 Europe was in a desperate condition; the only real

The Accuser

(From New York *World*; cartoonist Kirby; reprinted by permission)

hope for a successful League lay in American cooperation. Unless the United States would shoulder its obligations the whole treaty system was in danger of collapse. In 1926 the powers could afford to haggle over the World Court; in 1920 there was far less temptation to haggle while Europe burned. The European nations were under strong compulsion to swallow their pride, or at the very worst not to drive too hard a bargain in seeking adjustment.

But this again is pure speculation. Wilson never gave the

other powers a chance to act on the reservations, though Colonel House and others urged him to. He assumed this terrific responsibility all by himself. While thinking that he was throwing the onus on the consciences of the senators, he was in fact throwing a large share of the onus upon his own bent shoulders.

8

What were the reactions of our recent brothers in arms on the other side of the Atlantic?

The British viewed the Senate debacle with mixed emotions. The result had been a foregone conclusion, and there was some relief in having an end to senatorial uncertainty—at least this stage of it. Some journals were inclined to blame the two-thirds rule; others, the unbending doctrinaire in the White House. The London *Times* sorrowfully concluded that all the processes of peace would have to be suspended pending the outcome of the November election.

The French were shocked, though hardly surprised. The Paris *Liberté* aptly referred to the state of anarchy existing between the executive and the legislative in America. Other journals, smarting under Wilson's recent blast against French militarism, blamed the autocrat in the White House. "At the most troubled moment in history," gibed the Paris *Matin*, "America has a sick President, an amateur Secretary of State, and no Treaty of Peace. A President in the clouds, a Secretary of State in the bushes, and a treaty in the cabbage patch. What a situation!"

But the French did not completely abandon hope that America might yet honor her commitments. Meanwhile they would keep their powder dry and pursue the militaristic course which widened the growing rift between Britain and France, and which proved so fatal to the peace of Europe in the 1930's. The French finally became disgusted with German excuses (which were probably encouraged by America's defection), and in April, 1920, the month after the Senate rejected the treaty, their tanks rumbled into the Ruhr and occupied several German cities as hostages for reparations payments. Bullets were fired, and some blood was shed. This was but a dress rehearsal for the catastrophic invasion of the Ruhr in 1923.

The action—or rather inaction—of the United States had other tragic consequences. It encouraged German radicals in their determination to tear up the treaty: they were finding unwitting collaborators in Senator Borah and President Wilson. It delayed by many months, as British Foreign Secretary Curzon openly charged, the treaty with Turkey, thus giving the "Sick Man of Europe" (Turkey) a chance to prove that he was the "Slick Man of Europe." It held up the economic and moral rehabilitation of the Continent, and even hampered the work of relief then going forward. It further disillusioned the liberals of Europe and others who had clung to Wilson as the major prophet of a new order. It gave new comfort to the forces of disorder everywhere. It left the United States discredited, isolated, shorn of its prestige, and branded as a hypocrite and renegade. It marked the first unbridgeable rift in the ranks of the victorious Allies, a coalition that might have kept the peace. Instead they now went their separate ways, perhaps not as enemies, but certainly no longer as close friends. The United States was the first to break completely away.

America—and the world—paid a high price for the collapse of the treaty-making process in Washington. We are still paying it.

9

One final question. Who won after all these months of parliamentary jockeying?

Lodge the master parliamentarian had not won—that is, if he really wanted the treaty with his reservations. As in November, he was unable to keep the "irreconcilables" in line on the crucial vote, and he was unable to muster a two-thirds majority. He finally had to confess failure of leadership, except in so far as he prevented a schism.

The Republican party had not won. Lodge had avoided a serious split with the "bitter-enders" by knuckling under when they laid down the law. But the Republican leaders did not

Strange Bedfellows

(From St. Louis *Star*; cartoonist Chapin; courtesy of St. Louis *Star-Times*)

really want the issue in the campaign, and they had made strong efforts to keep it out. Now it was on their hands to cause them no end of embarrassment.

Wilson had not won. He has been praised for having kept the party ranks intact, and for having retained undisputed leadership of his following. But the Democrats in the Senate split 21 for the treaty to 23 against it, and that is hardly holding one's followers in line. Wilson lost irreparably because he did not get his treaty, even with reservations, and because he was doomed to lose again by insisting on a referendum where there could be no referendum.

The Democrats had not won. The treaty issue had caused a serious rift in the Senate, and Bryan, who was still a great leader, was on the rampage. Except for Wilson and some of his "yes men," there were few Democratic leaders who wanted this troublesome issue catapulted into the campaign. Yet there it was.

The United States had not won. It had won the war, to be sure; but it was now kicking the fruits of the victory back under the peace table. We had helped turn Europe into a scrap heap, and now we were scrapping the treaty. We were going to stand by the Allies—with our arms folded. We were throwing away the only hope of averting World War II.

The real victor was international anarchy.

CHAPTER EIGHTEEN

ADVANTAGES
WITHOUT OBLIGATIONS

*"A separate peace with the Central Empires could accomplish
nothing but our eternal disgrace . . ."* WOODROW WILSON, *at San
Francisco, September 17, 1919.*

—————

1

THE POPPIES were now growing for the second spring on
the graves of American boys in France. Other American boys
were helping keep the watch on the Rhine. Millions of men
all over the world were under arms, and brother was still killing brother. The fine ideals of ending war and establishing a
lasting peace seemed now but hollow mockery. As the Los
Angeles *Times* cynically observed, "It is quite impossible to
tell what the war made the world safe for."

The first meeting of the Council of the League of Nations
had convened at Paris on January 16, 1920, in response to an
invitation issued by President Wilson. The American delegate
was conspicuously absent, and the presiding officer, Léon
Bourgeois, regretted the absence of the United States. Without the active participation of the freshest and most powerful
of the nations, the League was getting off to a wobbly start.
Men had no real confidence in what they were doing.

In America, the "irreconcilables" pointed to the tramping
hordes of men in Europe, and said: "Aha, we told you so.
Wilson's League is powerless to prevent war!" The friends of
international cooperation rejoined that some of these clashes
antedated the birth of the League, and that one should not expect a babe in swaddling clothes to go forth and do battle with
Mars. To internationally minded persons the weakness of the
League was a challenge to make it stronger; to nationally
minded persons the weakness of the League and the disorders

in Europe were unanswerable arguments for staying out of
the whole mess.

It seems never to have dawned upon the isolationists, then
or later, that their obstruction had prolonged and worsened
the chaos in Europe, that a strong League might have been
able to deal with some of the current disorders, and that the

On the Outside Looking In
(Courtesy of Los Angeles *Times*; cartoonist Gale)

chief handicap of the League at this stage was the refusal of
the United States to join it. We had dealt the League a crippling blow; yet we stood on the sidelines and loudly blamed it
for being a cripple.

Interest in the League began to fade rapidly in America
during the spring of 1920; there were actually expressions of

relief when the treaty was unloaded at the White House door. A few of the faithful still nourished the hope that the President might return the pact to the Senate. But it was evident to everyone with postadolescent acumen that such a move would be useless unless Wilson was willing to give ground, and plainly he was not. He had unalterably decided to appeal from the Senate to the sovereign people.

The secluded invalid in the White House could contemplate with serenity the eight-month wait until November, and the twelve-month wait until the following March. But others were more impatient. When the leaders of both parties stopped accusing each other of having blocked the treaty, they realized that no matter where the blame lay, the country was still technically at war, and would continue to be until some legal action was taken to end it.

The United States was still suffering economically from its uncertain status. The complaints of American bankers and exporters were increasing in volume and vigor; we could not even station consular officials in Germany. Several score of wartime measures were still on the statute books, and some of these were hobbling American industry. Plainly something drastic had to be done to cut the Gordian knot.

2

The only alternative to further costly delay seemed to be for Congress to declare peace by a simple majority vote, just as it had declared war by a simple majority. This, of course, would anger Wilson, but he had in large measure brought it on himself.

The separate-peace resolution, which had been seriously considered since the November rejection of the treaty, was a curious admixture of practicality and politics. It was practical because it would merely declare a state of peace which everyone knew existed, while freeing the hands of business enterprise. It was excellent politics, because everyone knew that Wilson would veto it. This would put him and his henchmen further "in the hole." He had "kept us out of peace," it could be charged, by blocking treaty ratification; he would now keep us out of peace by blocking the only other way out—a Congressional resolution. Some of the Republican members of Congress were reported to be saying quite openly that partisanship was the primary purpose of the maneuver. The proposed resolution was obviously designed to make politics rather than peace.

The first separate-peace resolution was introduced in the House by Representative Porter, a fellow townsman of the "irreconcilable" Senator Knox. It was reported from the Foreign Affairs Committee by a strictly party vote. The floor of the House then became a verbal bullfighting arena, for the Democrats showed much heat during the fifty or so speeches on the proposal. Representative Pou of North Carolina cried that it was a "bastard resolution" designed to embarrass the President, a "damnable plot" to discredit Wilson. Representative Kitchin of North Carolina attacked the scheme with such vehemence that he collapsed and suffered a stroke of paralysis.

Nothing daunted, the Republican steamroller in the House pushed the resolution through on April 9, by a vote of 242 to 150. Virtually all of the Republicans, joined by a scattering of Democrats, voted in the affirmative.

The Senate produced a somewhat different resolution, framed by Senator Knox, working hand in glove with Lodge. It provided (1) for a repeal of the war declarations against Germany and Austria-Hungary and for a declaration of peace; (2) for a retention by the United States of *all the advantages accruing to it under the Treaty of Versailles*. This resolution was also reported from committee by a purely partisan vote.

The aging Senator Knox supported his proposal with vigorous words, and he was listened to intently, for his speech was regarded as one of the opening guns in his presidential boom. He declared that although we were actually at peace

the President, "with stubborn irresponsibility," kept us in a
state of technical war so that he might coerce the Senate into
accepting his terms. The only war then existing was the war
which Wilson was waging "against American citizens and
American industry."

After acrimonious debate, and after the usual charges and
countercharges about keeping the nation out of peace, the
Knox resolution passed on May 15 by a count of 43 to 38. Only
one Republican voted against it; all the others, aided by three
Democrats, voted for it. Among them was Reed of Missouri,
who cried with his usual intemperance but with unusual accuracy, "Nobody outside of a lunatic asylum believes unqualified ratification possible."

3

The Knox resolution differed in some particulars from that
already passed by the House. The usual procedure would
have been for the two measures to go to a conference committee; but this would have taken so much time that the completed draft could not have been laid on the President's desk
before the Congress disbanded for the Republican convention
in Chicago. To avoid such delay the House hastily took over
the Knox resolution and adopted it verbatim.

This was politics of the crassest kind. The Republicans not
only wanted to put Wilson "in the hole," but they wanted to
do it on the eve of the convention. The Democrats of course
might have obstructed the Knox resolution by filibustering
tactics, but they failed to do so. The press reported—and this
seems plausible—that Wilson sent word to the Democratic
minority not to delay the resolution. Homer S. Cummings,
who was in close touch with the White House, declared that
the President was just as willing to make the separate peace
resolution an issue as he was the League and the treaty.

Wilson did the expected. His veto message of May 27 was
a ringing document, reminiscent of the old Wilson and his

burning idealism. Ignoring the fact that he had himself threatened a separate peace in his Adriatic note, he decried such a
course as dishonorable and ignoble. It "would place inef-
faceable stain upon the gallantry and honor of the United
States."

The Democrats applauded Wilson's stirring message; when
it was read in the House the prolonged cheer from the Democratic side was led by ex-Speaker Champ Clark. The Republicans, on the other hand, defended their position by saying that
Wilson had left them no alternative.

Liberals throughout America were scandalized not so much
by the declaration of peace as by what they regarded as the
cool effrontery, indecency, and moral degeneracy of claiming
all the advantages of the treaty without assuming a single
obligation. The Europeans, it was felt, were completely justified in all the unpleasant things they were saying about us;
henceforth, said the New York *Nation,* no honorable American
could hold up his head in a foreign land.

Everyone knew that Wilson would veto the Knox resolution. He did. Everyone knew that the Republicans could not
scrape together enough strength in either house to override
his veto by a two-thirds vote. They did not. The vote in the
House (May 28) was 220 to 152, or substantially short of the
requisite number.

The Republicans were happy. They could further pillory
Wilson as the only real obstacle in the road to peace. The
blame, they said, was now on the Democrats; the Republicans
had made every possible effort to bring hostilities to a formal
end. Significantly, Republican leaders like Will H. Hays, who
had tried to keep the peace issue out of politics, were now
welcoming it. They sensed that the drift of public opinion
was to their side.

Wilson and the Democrats on the other hand were not displeased. They felt that, far from being forced "into a hole,"
they had allowed the Republicans to fall into a pit of their own
digging. During the war the very suggestion of deserting the

Allies and making a separate peace had been enough to bring expressions of anguish even from Senator Lodge. If the Republicans could go into the campaign shouting, "He kept us out of peace," the Democrats could cry back, "The Republicans will bring us disgrace, ignominy, and dishonor."

It seems reasonably clear that Wilson welcomed a chance

Peace by Resolution!

(From New York *Evening World*; cartoonist Cassel;
reprinted by permission)

to veto the Knox resolution. He wanted the election of 1920 to be a "solemn referendum" on the treaty. If he signed the separate peace proposal, he would dampen the burning issue. If he vetoed it, he would bring into even sharper relief the clash of views between himself and his foes.

4

By the late spring and early summer of 1920 Wilson was much improved in health. He was able to hold a Cabinet meeting on April 13, the first since he departed for his tragic tour in September.

Secretary Houston's diary etches a vivid picture of the occasion. The President looked "old, worn, and haggard"; one of his arms hung useless. His jaw tended to drop to one side as he spoke, and his voice was weak and strained. He attempted to keep up a brave front for a few minutes, feebly cracking jokes. Then there was painful silence: he would not or could not take the initiative. One member brought up the railroad situation, and Wilson seemed to have difficulty in keeping his mind fixed on it. Dr. Grayson peered in anxiously through the door several times, as if to suggest that the President should not be worn out with prolonged discussion. Finally, after about an hour, Mrs. Wilson appeared, looking rather disturbed, and suggested that they had all better go. They went.

The next meeting was held two weeks later. Houston was pleased to note that Wilson looked much better, and took a more vigorous part in the discussion.

Symptomatic of Wilson's improvement was his more active interest in Armenia. On May 22 he accepted an invitation from the powers to arbitrate its boundaries, though there were many who questioned his fitness for such a task. Two days later he submitted a special message to Congress urging it to grant him authorization to assume the mandate over Armenia.

Sentiment throughout the country seems to have been strongly if not overwhelmingly opposed to shouldering this strange burden. It is true that the Armenians wanted us; that we had missionary interests in Armenia; that it was to our advantage to stabilize the Near Eastern situation and prevent another world war; and that we had a moral obligation to help others less favored than ourselves. But on the other hand the mandate would cost hundreds of millions of dollars (at a time when taxes were high), involve tens of thousands of boys (at a time when they were homesick), and drag us into the quarrels of the powers (at a time when we were in a mood to stay out).

The suspicion was not easily quieted that Uncle Sam was being "played for a sucker." Britain had made off with Palestine and Iraq, and France with Syria. This left Armenia, poor in natural resources but rich in the possibilities of trouble and expense. It was a persimmon rather than a plum, for if it had been a plum the Allies, it was believed, would have kept it themselves. One Chicago paper was sure that Armenia would not find a desirable foster parent "until she discovers oil or something."

We wished the Armenians well, but we wished them well at a distance. We hoped the resilient Sick Man of Europe would stop butchering them; we sympathized deeply with them in their troubles; we would send missionaries; we would dole out some bread; but that was all. We were not our brother's keeper—especially on other continents.

A final argument against the Armenian mandate—at least in Republican ranks—was that Wilson wanted it. On June 1 the Senate soundly rebuffed him when it rejected his request, 52 to 23. The close-knit Republican phalanx, joined by 13 Democrats, constituted the majority, while the opposition came from a solid block of undying Democrats. The vote seems roughly to have reflected public sentiment.

Why Wilson invited this species of humiliation on the eve of the nominating conventions is not easy to explain. (The Republican platform condemned him roundly for his action.) He could easily have ascertained by a few discreet inquiries what the outcome would be. Possibly he felt that the Republicans, by spurning the Armenian proposal, would appear to even poorer advantage in the coming campaign. Certain it is that by this time he had set his heart on the mandate, and perhaps he was hoping for some kind of miracle.

5

Before either the Knox resolution or the Armenian mandate was killed, Wilson showed his fighting spirit in another statement.

Senator Chamberlain of Oregon, a prominent Democrat, was running for renomination in the primaries of his state. Wilson, it is safe to assume, had no great love for him. The senator had in 1918 undertaken a most embarrassing investigation of the alleged ineptitudes of the War Department, and he had been one of the Democrats who had forsaken the President in the March voting.

Chamberlain's chief rival for the Democratic nomination, H. G. Starkweather, was running on a platform which endorsed the Treaty of Versailles without any reservations whatever. One of Starkweather's leading backers, G. E. Hamaker, conceived the idea of asking Wilson if it was important to nominate candidates pledged to no reservations.

Wilson's telegraphed reply, which was promptly published, left no doubt in anyone's mind. It condemned the Lodge reservations as dragging us into the depths of dishonor, and it inferred that no reservations whatever would be the ideal arrangement. It reechoed the unquenchable idealism and uncompromising tone of the speech in Pueblo.

The telegram caused much fluttering in the political dovecotes. Senator Chamberlain could hardly fail to conclude that it was a vindictive outburst aimed at him, though Tumulty denied that it was directed at any local situation. Other Democratic senators who had bolted in March were up for reelection, and they could derive no comfort from Wilson's stern message.

It seems obvious that Wilson was shooting at larger game than the Oregon primaries. There was already some talk among the Democrats of pledging the party to compromise on reservations in the approaching nominating convention. The Oregon bombshell would rout such traitors. There was also a growing tendency to praise the bolting Democrats as sensible people. The Oregon ultimatum would brand them with dishonor and make personal allegiance to Wilson the supreme test. In short, the telegram would clear away the mists gathering about the League issue, and bring it back into the clear light of day.

Various Democratic groups registered varying reactions. Senator Thomas of Colorado resented the tarbrush of dishonor. Senator Reed condemned the no-reservation policy as political suicide. Every member of the Senate, except six, he declared, had voted for at least one of the Lodge reservations. Bryan, then in Florida, blamed Wilson for blocking majority rule, and opined that the secluded President was denied information "essential to sound judgment and safe leadership." But the faithful Senator Hitchcock concluded that a majority of the Democrats would applaud the Oregon telegram.

The Republicans were more nearly unanimous. Some of their newspapers praised the Democratic bolters for their good sense and statesmanship. These senators, they said, were unwilling that "the test of faith in democracy shall be faith in Wilson." Ex-President Taft called Wilson "the greatest obstructionist in Washington. He desires to destroy all if he cannot get all."

The "irreconcilables" likewise applauded. Senator Johnson remarked that at least Wilson was consistent in opposing reservations. Senator Moses declared that "once more the President has shown that he is our best friend."

There could be no doubt whatsoever about Wilson's stand as the date for the two great conventions approached. He wanted a "solemn referendum" on the paramount issue of the League. He would scuttle his own ship before he would surrender. It was neck or nothing.

CHAPTER NINETEEN

A TALE OF TWO
CONVENTIONS

*"What a hell of a condition the land is in politically. Cowardice
and hypocrisy are slated to win, and makeshift and the cheapest
politics are to take possession of national affairs."* EX-SECRETARY
OF THE INTERIOR LANE, *October 28, 1920.*

1

EARLY IN June, 1920, like long lines of ants hastening to
a giant anthill, the delegates to the Republican convention
began to converge on the windy city of Chicago.

The Old Guard senatorial oligarchy was everywhere in evidence, and firmly in the saddle. Lodge, partly as a reward for
his services in blocking a "Wilson treaty," was made both
keynoter and permanent chairman. (In the latter capacity he
made two highly arbitrary rulings to help the cause of the
oligarchy.) Senator Watson was named chairman of the subcommittee which framed the platform; and associated with
him were Borah and two other senators. Nine senators were
active candidates for the Presidency. Senator ("Boss") Penrose
was seriously ill in his Pennsylvania home, but he kept in touch
with the proceedings by private wire. The New York *Times*
pointedly referred to the convention as "government of the
Senate, by the Senate, and for the Senate."

The "irreconcilables" were there to make the most of their
"nuisance value." Borah loudly announced that he would bolt
the party if the convention declared for the League in any
form. Senator Johnson, the darling of the hyphenates and a
leading candidate, took the polyglot city by storm. He was
going to see that there was no "pussyfooting" or "sulking" on
the League issue. He appeared with Borah before a giant crowd
in the Auditorium Theater, and after the strongly pro-German

299

and pro-Irish ovation had died down, he declared for no straddling.

The Old Guard was mortally afraid of Borah and particularly of Johnson, who was an experienced bolter. He had left the party to run with Roosevelt on the ill-fated "Bull Moose" ticket in 1912, thus insuring victory for Wilson. It had all happened in this same city of Chicago, and it must not be allowed to happen again.

On June 8, 1920, the convention opened tamely, dutifully, mechanically. The slender and bewhiskered Senator Lodge appeared to deliver the keynote address, clad in black cutaway, white vest, and black tie. With crisp and cultured accents he read for over an hour from a manuscript, employing a minimum of gestures, but now and then smiling smugly at one of his phrases.

The speech was a prolonged "hymn of hate" against Wilson and Wilsonism. The President had twice kept us out of peace, declared the orator, by spurning first the Lodge reservations, and then the Knox resolution. "Mr. Wilson and his dynasty, his heirs and assigns, or anybody that is his, anybody who with bent knee has served his purposes, must be driven from control," cried Lodge, to the accompaniment of approving handclaps.

The address was not regarded as a great success. It was the uninspired and uninspiring utterance of a weary and cynical politician. Only a few passages evoked enough applause to stir the hot air of the convention oven. A few Republican apologists blamed the lack of enthusiasm on the advent of prohibition and the consequent increase in the price of hard liquor from six to nine dollars a pint.

Yet the keynote speech struck the keynote: anti-Wilsonism. This was both the dominant theme and the cohesive force in the convention as well as in the Republican campaign. "Make an end of this Wilson" were the words everywhere heard on delegates' lips.

2

The platform was the most ticklish business of all. The problem was to prepare a League plank so vague that the "irreconcilables" would not be driven out of the party, and so ambiguous that even the League advocates and "mild res- ervationists" could stand on it. Every man could be his own interpreter. "Harmony at any price" was the actual if un- proclaimed slogan of the convention.

The subcommittee that drafted the platform not only con- tained four senators (two of them "irreconcilables"), but it worked closely with Senator Lodge, Senator Brandegee (an "irreconcilable"), George W. Pepper (the successor to the dying Senator Penrose), and ex-Senator W. Murray Crane of Massachusetts, a sick man who died four months later. Crane wielded considerable influence, and he insisted that the con- vention declare for the treaty with reservations. This seems to have been, as Lodge privately conceded, the wish of the great majority of the delegates and of the people.

But a declaration for reservations would drive the "irrecon- cilables" berserk. It would also cause the Republicans to ap- pear as the tail to Wilson's kite. They would be conceding that the President was 95 per cent right, and that all they wanted to do was to renovate the remaining 5 per cent. In politics one must never admit that one's opponent is even 2 per cent right.

Lodge flared up against ex-Senator Crane's proposal. He threatened to lay down his gavel, take the floor, and fight against his own reservations if the committee took any such action. Wilson must be beaten and the party kept united, even at the cost of consistency.

After the committee had wrangled for three days and two nights, the deadlock was finally broken when one of ex-Senator Elihu Root's associates produced a compromise formula which the elder statesman had earlier prepared. (Root was then on his way to Europe for the purpose of organizing the World Court.) After a bitter fight in the committee, this compromise was adopted.

It was a masterpiece of ambiguity. It excoriated the treaty which Wilson had signed at Paris; it commended the senators for doing their duty and refusing to be his rubber stamps. Nothing was said specifically about the League; nothing about reservations to the League, though the Senate, inferentially, was praised for having voted through the Lodge reservations. Instead there was a mumbo jumbo about "international justice," "international association," and "general international conference." The first two paragraphs of the plank seemed to promise international cooperation, the next four paragraphs seemed to take it away, like the small print in a fraudulent contract. All one had to do was pick one's favorite paragraphs and be happy.

The platform was read to the perspiring delegates by Senator Watson, but he raced through the manuscript with such haste and inaudibility that it was impossible to hear all he was saying. Yet the delegates cheered happily. They knew that a rift had been avoided, and that all they had to do was to pick their paragraph.

The "irreconcilables" were delighted; they applauded the platform as meaning that there would be no League whatever. At all events they were determined to fasten their interpretation upon it. Again they had won a signal victory for minority rule; again they had blackjacked the majority into submission.

The Republican friends of a League with qualifications were less happy, but there was nothing in the platform which forbade reservations, and the reservationists were more determined than ever to work for them. Besides, the rest of the platform denounced Wilsonism, and this was eminently satisfactory.

Professional Democratic politicians like Senator Hitchcock were reported as highly pleased; the Republicans had played squarely into their hands by straddling on the "great issue."

Even William Allen White, a member of the drafting committee, frankly described the League plank as a "Pandora's box of seemingly contradictory propositions," worthy of Machiavelli at his best. It was indeed a superb example of a collection of words which made sense but not meaning.

3

The Senate oligarchy had by a narrow margin scraped over the platform reef. The next task was to pick a safe and manageable candidate.

General Leonard Wood and Governor Frank O. Lowden of Illinois were the two leading candidates, but their chances (whatever they may have been) were killed when it was learned that money had been spent too plentifully or too indiscreetly in their behalf. Senator Johnson had the third largest number of delegates, and he had enjoyed considerable success in the primaries. His rabble-rousing tactics had proved effective among isolationists and hyphenates, and his opponents had managed to split the pro-League vote. But he was too independent, too headstrong, too much of the bull-in-the-canebrake. The Senate oligarchy wanted no part of him: they could never forget his apostasy in 1912.

Senator Knox, another "irreconcilable," had a brief hour of notoriety; but he was too old and too sick. (His weak heart sputtered out the next year.) President Nicholas Murray Butler of Columbia University commanded a modest amount of support, but the country was weary of internationalists and professor-presidents.

The candidacy of Senator Warren G. Harding was hardly taken seriously by the public, and scarcely more so by the senator himself. He had run unimpressively in the primaries (even in his own state), and only the prodding of his wife and designing "friends" kept him from closing his forlorn headquarters in Chicago.

But the bosses were eyeing the statuesque senator far more

seriously than the senator was eyeing himself. He came from Ohio, which commanded many electoral votes. He was a regular politician with his hand on the rail of the escalator. He was not one to kick over the apple cart; weak of will and befuddled of mind, he would take orders from his cronies in the Senate oligarchy. He was "sound" on the League issue, having voted for strong reservations. While it is true that he had few if any original ideas, and no real force of character, these were not necessary; the oligarchy would provide the ideas and the momentum. He was admittedly a colorless party hack with low mental visibility, and without executive experience; but the times, as Senator Brandegee remarked, did not demand "first-raters."

Harding looked like a statesman; he was the perfect "stuffed shirt." He had made few enemies. He could make meaningless speeches of the bowwow variety with a great deal of noise and even more unction. He had been preaching the gospel of "normalcy," and although this word was not then in general currency, it was what the people wanted. They were tired of "moral overstrain" under Wilson; they would warm to a good, red-blooded, "average" American from the Middle West who would let them till their cornfields in peace without trying to take on all the burdens of the world.

The people were tired of the cold academic aloofness—the "highbrowism"—of Woodrow Wilson. No one ever accused Harding, the small-town newspaperman, of "highbrowism." He could set type in his newspaper plant; pitch horseshoes behind the house; and play poker of an evening with "the gang." He was a "regular fellow" who could be counted on to "go along" and be "one of the boys." Big, handsome, affable, plausible, he was "just folks"—"folksy," as one admirer put it. He loved dogs (he brought "Laddie Boy" to the White House); he loved people and liked to clasp their hands in his warm palm; he was a great backslapper and "first-namer." He liked to please every one, and he was unusually successful as a conciliator of differences.

4

As the Senate cabal expected and planned, General Wood and Governor Lowden cut each other's political throats, and the convention became deadlocked. The temperature was mounting; the hotel bills were mounting; the impatience of the delegates was mounting.

Then the Senate clique took hold, with George Harvey one of the mainsprings, though he was not a senator, not even a delegate, and nominally still a Democrat. After dinner on that humid Friday night (June 11) they met with him in the "smoke-filled" Room 404 of the Hotel Blackstone. It was an informal gathering, and lasted for a number of hours, with various persons wandering in and out—among them at least eight senators. They canvassed all the possibilities, and finally came to the unofficial conclusion that Harding was the most "available" of the possible candidates.

There was one hitch. Rumors had begun to go the rounds that the handsome but flabby Harding had become involved in some scandal which might prove damaging to the ticket. The dazed senator was called in and asked, man to man and before God, if there was anything in his "past life" which would endanger his candidacy. Harding was silent for a moment, and then he asked to be alone. After having stepped into an adjoining bedroom for about fifteen minutes, and after having presumably wrestled with his conscience and communed with his Maker, he came back and said firmly: "Gentlemen, there is no such reason."

(Seven years later Miss Nan Britton published her sensational book, *The President's Daughter,* alleging that a child had been born to her of which Harding [then Senator] was the father.)

The "smoke-filled room" took Harding at his face value, the whispered word was passed along, and the convention sweatily stampeded to the enemyless Harding on the tenth ballot.

The senatorial soviet had planned to nominate Senator Lenroot of Wisconsin for the vice presidency. Senator Hiram W. Johnson had indignantly announced that he would take no second-fiddle consolation prizes; he would have no single

On the Same Platform

(Courtesy of Dallas *News*; cartoonist Knott)

heartbeat between him and the presidency. (If he had been willing to stoop so low he would have satisfied in 1923 his consuming ambition to be President.) The senatorial cabal was pushing the Lenroot nomination through when the boss-ridden delegates suddenly took the bit in their teeth and stampeded to "Silent Cal" Coolidge, governor of Massachusetts. "Silent Cal" had recently talked himself into national prominence by issuing a smashing denunciation of the Boston police strike, albeit somewhat belatedly.

The delegates wearily pulled on coats over their wilted shirts, and entrained for home with a prolonged sigh of relief rather than a whoop of enthusiasm. They had avoided a split on the platform and a split on the candidate. Victory was in the bag.

The selection of the rubber-stamp Harding was something of a shock to the country. As George Harvey later testified, "He was nominated because there was nothing against him, and because the delegates wanted to go home." He was a respectable mediocrity—or at least a mediocrity. And that mediocrity was what nominated him; ability in Chicago was suicidal. The Republicans must have been confident of victory to reach so far down into the sack for their standard-bearer. People were saying that the country was so "fed up" on Wilsonism that all the opposition had to do was to nominate a "rag baby" or a "yellow dog." They nominated Harding.

Editorial reactions were varied. The Chicago *Tribune* (Independent Republican) regarded Harding as a "four-square American" who had worked his way up from the "humblest beginnings." The liberal Springfield (Massachusetts) *Republican* thought the nominee the "feeblest" Republican candidate since 1876, when the bewildered Grant bowed himself out. The New York *Times* (Democratic), usually more restrained, branded Harding as "the fine and perfect flower of the cowardice and imbecility of the Senatorial cabal." The liberal New York *Nation* dismissed him as "a colorless and platitudinous, uninspired and uninspiring nobody," who was but an errand boy of the Old Guard, put forward "like a cigar-store Indian to attract trade."

5

The nomination of a wooden-Indian candidate on a patchwork platform presented the Democrats with an enviable opportunity. But it was doubtful whether they would capitalize on it, for they were torn with doubt and dissension, and completely without aggressive leadership.

A strong majority of the Democratic conventions in rock-ribbed Democratic states endorsed either President Wilson or his administration or his stand on the League of Nations. But in other states the situation was badly confused by local politics, prohibition, Anglophobia, and resentment against Wilson's leadership. The Tammany-mottled New York state convention adjourned without endorsing the administration; the Democrats in the Rhode Island convention (many of them with Irish names) unanimously adopted a plank opposing Article X of the League Covenant.

The Georgia Democratic convention flatly refused to endorse the administration, and the primaries were, superficially at least, a rebuke to Wilson. Attorney General Palmer, who supported the President on the treaty, ran third; Thomas E. Watson, who condemned both Wilson and the League, polled the largest vote. One of his reported slogans was that "Woodrow Wilson should be in prison and Eugene V. Debs in the White House." Yet the situation in Georgia was so complicated by local feuds that one must not try to read too much into these primary election results.

The confusion in the state primaries was closely connected with another and more important puzzle. One of the chief embarrassments of the Democrats during these preconvention months was speculation regarding a possible third-term for Wilson. Did he really want it? Was he angling for it? Would he take it if offered? Was he physically able to serve? Would the country permit a violation of the sacred two-term tradition?

It is incredible that Wilson—the pathetic shadow of a once great leader—should have been eyeing a third term. But the circumstantial and direct evidence points so strongly in this direction that the riddle must be given some attention.

Several months before his collapse, Wilson seems definitely to have made up his mind to retire. He assumed, of course, that the treaty would be ratified, and the League started off under the most favorable auspices. There would be no reason or excuse for his arranging to have himself "drafted."

Then why did he not publicly renounce any designs on a third term? As we have seen, the Republicans were suspicious of him, and this was one of the basic reasons why they could not permit a "Wilsonized" League to go through. We have earlier noted that in May, 1919, so influential a newspaper as the Springfield *Republican* urged him to declare himself out of the picture. But Wilson, for reasons that may never be known, turned aside this suggestion.

After his tragic collapse and the first defeat of the treaty, there was more excuse for a third term, but the flesh was obviously too weak. Here and there one could find some support for Wilson, but conspicuously not in the South. On March 25, 1920, Representative Humphreys of Mississippi delivered a speech against the third term which elicited tremendous applause from both Democrats and Republicans.

Still Wilson did not declare or even hint that he was out of the running. His Jackson Day letter and his other public utterances completely ignored the question, and by ignoring it emphasized it. Indeed, if the League was going to be the burning issue in the election of 1920, was not Wilson the logical candidate?

Wilson's supporters intended to run him in the Georgia primary, but under the law the candidate had formally to file. A request that the President comply with the law met with stony silence from the White House, and his candidacy had to be dropped.

In the spring of 1920 the *Literary Digest* undertook an extensive poll of the voters in an attempt to ascertain their preferences for the presidency. It is significant that Wilson, despite his known physical disabilities, was highly regarded by the Democratic rank and file. He placed behind his son-in-law, ex-Secretary McAdoo, but well ahead of the other three leading Democratic aspirants.

6

On June 15, 1920, three days after the adjournment of the Republican convention, a striking development occurred. Possibly encouraged by the nomination of a "bungalow-minded" Harding on a shilly-shally platform, Wilson decided to take more decisive steps. He arranged for a three-hour interview with Mr. Louis Seibold, Washington correspondent of the New York *World*, one of the most powerful Democratic newspapers in the country.

Wilson was confident that the Republicans were cooperating in making the coming campaign a "solemn referendum" which would result in a Democratic victory. He dictated letters with his old-time decisiveness, observed Seibold, made decisions unwaveringly, and signed papers "with the same copper-plate signature." The reporter found that Wilson had gained twenty pounds, and that his face was not much changed, except for lines of suffering. He was still a bit lame, but—and this was a revealing touch—his leg did not drag so badly as that of General Wood, who had led on the early balloting in Chicago.

After Seibold had talked for about two hours to Wilson, and had loitered about to see him sign papers decisively and make decisions unwaveringly, the two men and Mrs. Wilson attended a White House showing of a "Bill" Hart western "thriller." (During these tedious days Wilson looked forward with juvenile delight to the frequent exhibition of films by what he called his "movie doctor.")

The Seibold interview, which was published on the morning of June 18, was a front-page sensation, and subsequently won for its author a coveted Pulitzer prize. That same afternoon the news "broke" that McAdoo, the leading Democratic contender for the nomination, had withdrawn from the race. He denied that he had done this with the prior knowledge of Wilson, but if he did bow himself out to clear the way for his father-in-law, he could not very well have revealed his hand so early in the game.

On the next day, George W. Harris, a leading Washington photographer, spent an hour with Wilson taking a series of photographs of the revitalized President. Harris later told reporters that Wilson looked fine, "better than I had expected. But the pictures speak for themselves."

The photographs were released on June 21, a week before the Democratic convention in San Francisco, and in time for the Pacific Coast newspapers to print them. It was reported that they would show a new and dynamic Wilson. The picture that was published in the San Francisco *Chronicle* on June 27 (the day before the convention opened) was taken from the unparalyzed right side, and shows Wilson decisively signing a document.

7

It is difficult to believe that all these developments were unrelated to the approaching Democratic convention. Newspaper correspondents do not ordinarily interview the President alone; they do not ordinarily interview a sick President for three hours; and after the interview is over they do not ordinarily hover about, gazing at the President while he signs documents and transacts other business.

All this does not prove—though some newspapers concluded as much—that Wilson was pulling wires for a third nomination. But it seems to indicate that on the eve of the Democratic convention he was eager to appear before the country as substantially recovered and able to discharge with old-time energy the duties of his high office.

Not only did Wilson refuse to declare himself out of the race, but he steadfastly declined to throw his support to any of the candidates. A sense of delicacy forbade any statement as long as his son-in-law, McAdoo, was in the race. To have come out for him would have savored of nepotism; to have come out for someone else would have savored of disloyalty.

But McAdoo had now withdrawn. If Wilson wanted a candidate who would faithfully carry out his ideals, why did he not back the most promising of the lot? He had not scrupled to support the program of Senator Chamberlain's opponent in Oregon. Why should he decline to do so when the issue was fundamentally the same but the scale of action much larger? Is it possible that Wilson did not issue a statement favoring someone else because he really favored himself?

On June 10 Postmaster General Burleson told Senator Glass (according to the latter's diary notes) that in his judgment the President wanted another nomination. Earlier the same day Dr. Grayson confided to Glass that Wilson "seriously" contemplated a third term, but that such an ordeal "would kill him." Six days later Grayson again expressed to the senator the "greatest anxiety about [the] President's third term thoughts," for the exactions of the campaign alone would "probably kill him." Yet the faithful doctor believed that Wilson's sole concern was for the League; if reelected, he would resign after the adoption of the Covenant. Tumulty, records Glass, shared Grayson's concern about a third nomination.

As the zero hour for the convention approached, Wilson closeted himself with some of the Democratic leaders. Homer S. Cummings, the keynote speaker, conferred with the President for about two hours, and then told reporters that Wilson approved his address. (Cummings remembered in 1929 that the President had expressed no preference for a candidate.)

Senator Glass, author of the Wilson-approved Virginia Democratic platform and Wilson's preference for chairman of the platform-drafting committee, was at the White House for about an hour, and this visit multiplied third-term rumors. But subsequent events, taken in connection with the senator's diary notes, indicate that Glass was there primarily to discuss the League of Nations plank. Wilson handed him a copy of a proposed plank on Armenia, and hoped that it would be included in the platform.

Later that day (June 19) both Dr. Grayson and Tumulty saw Glass off on the convention-bound train, and were anxious to know whether Wilson had said anything about a third term.

"Are You in the Race, Woodrow?"

(Courtesy of Brooklyn *Citizen*; cartoonist Norris)

The senator replied in the negative. Grayson again begged Glass to save the "life" and the "fame" of the President from "the juggling of false friends."

Even more mysterious were the comings and goings of Secretary of State Colby. He was an accomplished orator, and an inspiring convention speaker. We know that at Wilson's insistence, and apparently as a last-minute arrangement, he consented to go out to San Francisco as a delegate from the

District of Columbia—something that Secretaries of State do not ordinarily do. We also know that the President wanted him to be chosen permanent chairman of the convention.

It is possible that Wilson planned to have, or hoped to have, Secretary Colby seize the opportune moment, present the President's name to the convention in a stirring speech, and engineer a stampede for a third nomination.

The third-term movement was not sentimental but serious. Wilson, as already noted, ran well in the *Literary Digest* poll. Moreover, the hardheaded Wall Street operators reported on June 30, two days after the San Francisco convention opened, that *Wilson had taken the place of the favorite in the betting*.

Perhaps Wilson was merely seeking to control the convention. Perhaps he wanted no more than a courtesy nomination, which would have been flattering to anyone in his position, and which could easily have been declined. But it seems as though he were more than receptive to a nomination of some kind. He did not say one word in public to discourage a move in this direction. He probably was not thinking in terms of personal glory: he had had enough of that. But he may have concluded that he was the only man who had the prestige and vision to consummate his great dream.

8

Late in June, bands of train-weary Democrats were disgorged from ferryboats leading to the hill-crested city of St. Francis by the Golden Gate. This was the first and last great national nominating convention west of the Rockies.

It was a motley group, and the delegates in their persons emphasized the fact that during these years the most important elements in the Democratic party were the Solid South and the political machines of the northern industrial centers. There were three factions fighting for control: the Wilsonites, the Bryanites, and the bosses of the northern cities—Murphy of

Tammany Hall, Taggart of Indiana, and Brennan of Illinois. If the Chicago convention had its Senate bosses, the San Francisco convention had its Irish bosses.

The Republicans had fought their fights in Chicago, but they had concealed them pretty well behind the walls of smoke-filled rooms. The Democrats fought violently in public. The Irish bosses made no bones about what they were after. They wanted no more of Wilson and his ideals; they wanted a Democratic edition of Harding (a man who would "take orders"); and they wanted "booze." They and their crimson-nosed henchmen, liberally besprinkled with hoarse-throated Irishmen, detested prohibition, and they demanded as "wet" a plank and as "wet" a candidate as would float. They also wanted a declaration in favor of Irish independence.

The Wilsonites won only a partial victory in organizing the convention. Cummings, the keynote speaker, was there to present a Wilson-endorsed address. Senator Glass, likewise fresh from the White House, was made chairman of the platform drafting committee. But the convention choked on Colby as permanent chairman. The Senate bloc was finally able to shake off White House domination and select Senator Robinson of Arkansas.

Just as the formal sessions were opening, a beflagged and illuminated portrait of Wilson was dramatically unveiled, and it touched off an eighteen-minute demonstration. The New York delegation, possibly fearing a stampede for the President, sat in sullen silence among the 10,000 cheerers. Whereupon young Franklin Delano Roosevelt and a colleague seized the state standard from protesting Tammany hands, and after a fist fight and a football rush, carried it into the aisle with the other demonstrators.

When order was restored, Cummings, the keynoter, presented with great vigor and militancy the Wilson-endorsed speech. The President, he shouted, had been "physically wounded" by his enemies, just as Lincoln, Garfield, and McKinley had been. Wilson was not opposed to reservation but to "nullification." The League was the paramount issue; and "the only trouble with the treaty is that it was negotiated by a Democratic President [applause]."

The Republican platform, Cummings shouted, was a "masterpiece of evasion." [Cries: "Go to it. Hit 'em again. That's the stuff."] He called the roll of the nations who had joined the League, and asked if his audience wanted to hear the list of those who had not joined. "Yes, yes, tell us," came from all parts of the floor. "Revolutionary Mexico, Bolshevist Russia, unspeakable Turkey, and—the United States of America." [Tremendous roar.]

9

The first big fight was in the committee that framed the platform. The three most knotty problems were "booze," Ireland, and the League. Prohibition was neatly sidestepped, and an innocuous plank was adopted on Ireland. But the League was a different matter.

After an exhausting all-night session, the committee finally agreed upon a compromise. Senator Glass had presented the rather general formula which Wilson had approved: "We advocate the immediate ratification of the treaty without reservations which would impair its essential integrity." But Senator Walsh of Massachusetts, one of the Democratic near "irreconcilables," was able to add a qualification, *"but we do not oppose the acceptance of any reservations making clearer or more specific the obligations of the United States to the League associates."* (Senate reservations even pursued Wilson to San Francisco!)

After this reservation carried, Senator Glass and Secretary Colby, making a virtue of necessity, declared that the whole statement was in accord with Wilson's position. This may well be doubted. The platform now endorsed reservations that would define our "obligations"—which was essentially all that the Lodge reservations did, or all that their authors claimed they did. "Reservation" or "nullification" depended somewhat on who was doing the reserving or nullifying. In short, the Democratic plank opened the door to the Lodge reservations, or something akin to them.

This augured poorly for a clean-cut "solemn referendum." Strong reservations were permissible under the Chicago platform, by indirection; they were permissible under the San Francisco platform, by interpretation. The two pronouncements were not so very far apart after all.

The bleary-eyed Senator Glass, his voice husky from the all-night debate in committee, undertook to read the 8,000-word platform to the assembled convention. The League was given the place of honor, and those of the delegates who could hear waved flags and cheered lustily. The others cheered also. As Glass droned on for two hours, many cried "Louder." Someone shouted, "Let somebody read it who knows how." "Let Bryan read it." The plank for woman suffrage evoked a ten-minute cheer, and the band struck up, "Oh, You Beautiful Doll."

The crowd was eagerly waiting to hear the silver-tongued Bryan, who was there to seize demon rum by the throat in what was probably his last great convention speech. As he began, a foghorn voice in the audience shouted, "Grape-juice." The Commoner pleaded eloquently for the abolition of the two-thirds rule in the Senate, and for the ratification of the treaty with necessary reservations. This part of his address was well received. But when he argued for a dry plank he was booed by the thirsty Tammanyites.

After an eight-and-one-half-hour debate on the floor, all proposed amendments to the platform were defeated. Bryan, as usual, got many cheers, but not enough votes.

10

The nominations and the balloting were the next major tasks. Wilson continued to keep his hands off the candidates; his chief concern was apparently for the League. After the favorite sons had been eliminated, the contest settled down to a three-cornered struggle among McAdoo, the unfavored son-in-law, Attorney General Palmer, who had recently treated the country to an obscene orgy of red-baiting, and the "wet" Governor Cox of Ohio, who was from a politically important state and who was not closely identified with Wilsonism.

The Cox men were indefatigable. They had brought along a glee club which made the galleries ring with:

> Ohio! Ohio!
> The hills send back the cry,
> We're here to do or die!
> Ohio! Ohio!
> We'll win with Cox or know the reason why.

The parched Irish bosses killed off the "dry" McAdoo. He was too close to the White House (he was sneeringly dubbed the "Crown Prince" at a time when the German Crown Prince was most unpopular), and he had been too niggardly in doling out patronage plums while Secretary of the Treasury. Cox won on the forty-fourth ballot.

The vice-presidential nomination went by acclamation to the thirty-eight-year-old Assistant Secretary of the Navy, Franklin Delano Roosevelt. He was handsome, personable, intelligent, and was an able speaker. He was also a member of the administration (a sop to Wilsonians), an Easterner (to offset Cox), from New York (with its great block of electoral votes), anti-Tammany, and progressive. It was felt that his liberal views might seduce Progressive Republicans from the reactionary Chicago ticket. *Harvey's Weekly,* which was sparing of compliments to anyone associated with Wilson, remarked: "Mr. Roosevelt deserves to go far in public life, and will, even though he does have to suffer defeat next fall."

The exhausted delegates packed their bags without any general feeling of satisfaction. Even the League plank had turned out to be something of a straddle, though far clearer than its Republican counterpart. Cox was a boss-dictated nominee, the first one in many years. The convention had completely evaded the issue which was to it personally the most burning: "booze." Bryan shook the wicked dust of San Francisco off his feet, sadly remarking, "My heart is in the grave."

11

Wilson could hardly have been overjoyed. His plans had partially miscarried. Colby had not become permanent chairman; his personally drafted Armenian declaration was watered down; even the League plank was "weasel-worded." How could there be a "solemn referendum"?

It was an open secret that Cox was the most objectionable of the leading candidates to Wilson. McAdoo and Palmer had both been a part of the administration and outspokenly enthusiastic about the League. Cox had been neither. When Senator Glass had mentioned his name at the White House on June 19, Wilson had broken in, "Oh! you know Cox's nomination would be a joke."

Yet Wilson could hardly blame anyone but himself. During the balloting repeated messages had come to the White House, pleading for support for one candidate or another. But Wilson turned a deaf ear. He would lean over backward to the very end.

When the Cabinet members who had been at the convention returned to Washington, Wilson was reported to be cool toward them. Something had gone wrong. There had been much cheering for the President's portrait, but not even a complimentary nomination. He had received only two votes, and those on the twenty-second ballot.

Wilson's private papers reveal that on July 2, the crisis of the convention, Secretary Colby wired the White House in *secret code*. He had been conferring constantly with Wilson's friends; it was definitely a Wilson convention. None of the other candidates could break the deadlock. Colby thereupon proposed, unless otherwise definitely instructed, to take advantage of the first opportune moment, move a suspension of the rules, and place Wilson's name in nomination.

A telephoned reply which has not been preserved came from the White House, and on the strength of it Colby, as reported in his code telegram of July 4, summoned the Democratic leaders into a council of war. All those present, except Colby, regarded the move for a third nomination as most unwise. Wilson, for various reasons, could not command the necessary support in the convention, and his failure to do so would promptly though unfairly be seized upon as proof of anti-League sentiment among the Democrats.

The evidence is convincing that Wilson seriously considered accepting a third term. But it was obvious to the hard-headed Democratic leaders that the two-term tradition, if broken at all, could not be broken by an invalid.

CHAPTER TWENTY

THE GREAT AND SOLEMN MUDDLEMENT

"Cox will be defeated not by those who dislike him but by those who dislike Wilson and his group." EX-SECRETARY LANE, *September, 1920.*

1

FOR THE first two weeks or so after his nomination, Governor Cox seems to have had no strong desire to make the League the paramount issue. The people were tired of hearing about it; it was "old stuff." But on July 18 he and Roosevelt made a pilgrimage to the White House, and they came away fired with new zeal. Publicly, Cox announced that he was in complete accord with Wilson; privately, he told Tumulty that no one could talk with the crippled idealist about the League without becoming "a crusader in its behalf."

Cox and Roosevelt have been blamed for going to the White House and permitting themselves to fall under the Wilsonian spell and the Wilsonian liability. If they had stayed away and soft-pedaled the League, could they not have won on domestic issues alone?

The answer is that the Democrats, after nearly eight years in office, were on the defensive. Negation was not enough. They had to have some positive issue. The only important one available was the League, and it seemed to offer a real prospect of victory.

Such was the general atmosphere when Cox, on August 7, appeared before some 50,000 persons at the Dayton Fair grounds to deliver his speech of acceptance. With his collar rapidly wilting, he stood squarely for the League with such clarifying (not devitalizing) reservations as were necessary. "I am ready to go in," he cried, to the accompaniment of such shouts as "That's the way to talk, Jimmy!"

Cox then took the stump in one of the most ambitious barn-storming tours on record, one which carried him 22,000 miles and brought him before an estimated 2,000,000 people. He gestured vigorously, stamped his foot emphatically, and called spades spades, crooks crooks, and liars liars. He declared that this was "no pink tea campaign," "no pillow fight." When accused by Republicans of "getting rough," he cried that they had hit Wilson "below the belt"—"a sick man in his sick-room." Now they were squealing because someone was punching back.

Cox, in spite of the injection of idealism at the White House, did not really make the League the paramount issue until the last few weeks of the campaign. During much of the canvass he emphasized the alleged "slush" fund. The Republicans, he charged, were raising $30,000,000 by high-pressure methods to "buy" the election. He called Republican Chairman Hays a liar, and branded the two chief Republican money-raisers as the "Gold Dust twins." The Republicans were distinctly annoyed by such "barroom talk"; they were convinced that Cox was no gentleman. The subsequent Senate investigation did not arouse the voters from their apathy, especially when it was revealed that the money-getters were using the techniques of the Y.M.C.A. and the Red Cross.

Cox was constantly "assailing" other things besides "slush," among them the *Saturday Evening Post*, the Senate oligarchy, and the "wobbles" of Harding. He assailed the Republicans for charging that he was "wet." He would enforce the law; besides, as he truthfully pointed out, Harding owned stock in a brewery. The noble referendum—the great spiritual cru-sade—was clearly degenerating into something ignoble and un-spiritual.

2

During the last three or so weeks of the campaign Cox struck a more lofty note when he strongly emphasized the League. He had some little difficulty in explaining Article X to Irish and German audiences, and the wind was almost completely taken out of his sails when, on October 25, the distinguished Frenchman, Léon Bourgeois, one of the framers of the League, announced that Article X did not amount to much anyway. Why were the Americans making all this fuss? The really vital articles could be found elsewhere.

In the face of the drift away from Article X, Cox himself "wobbled." He announced in his Madison Square Garden speech that he now favored a reservation stating that the United States assumed no obligation to defend other members of the League *"unless approved and authorized by Congress in each case."*

Here we find Cox cheerfully cutting out the moral obligation from Article X—the moral obligation on which Wilson had insisted all along, and on which all compromise had been wrecked. Cox's position was now essentially that of Lodge on Article X. Charles Evans Hughes caustically remarked that before the week was out the Democratic candidate would be running on the Republican platform.

Franklin Delano Roosevelt was only slightly less energetic than Cox. He barnstormed from coast to coast for 18,000 miles, making many vigorous speeches and gaining some fruitful political experience. He betrayed no little naïveté when he promised that if Cox were elected the treaty would be ratified in sixty days. He blundered badly at Butte, Montana, when he said (or was quoted as saying) that the United States would really control about twelve votes in the League Assembly; that while Assistant Secretary of the Navy he had himself controlled two Caribbean republics (Haiti and Santo Domingo); and that he had written the new constitution of Haiti himself. When

Harding made an issue of this statement, Roosevelt heatedly denied having said the part about the votes. But all this was relatively minor; to the very end the Democratic nominee fought vigorously for the League and against "League Liars."

Theodore Roosevelt, Jr., son of the famed Rough Rider, was sent out by the Republican high command to "trail" his Democratic cousin. "Little Teddy" did some "assailing" on his own. In Wyoming he spoke to a thinning band of Rough Riders, and sneered at the Democratic degeneracy of Cousin Franklin: "He is a maverick—he does not have the brand of our family."

There can be no doubt that the Democrats, especially Cox, put on a fighting campaign which in its closing stages suggested a crusade. But all this did not appeal to the temper of the people. They were tired of crusades; they wanted repose. They did not want to arouse themselves again to noble deeds; they had done so once, and the results had been most disillusioning.

There was more than a grain of truth in the observation that in this campaign more enthusiasm was generated on the speakers' platform than was aroused in the audiences.

3

The Republicans adopted a completely different strategy. They did not need to embark upon a holy crusade; they did not have to prod a nation that wanted only repose. All they had to do was to stand on their ambiguous platform, be all things to all men, and wait for the tidal wave of reaction against Wilsonism to wash them into the White House.

Harding was a seasoned campaigner, whose statesmanlike profile appeared well on the stump. He had a magnificent voice and a superb string of meaningless and mangled words. He exuded amiability and love for his fellow man. He liked nothing better than to go out to the people, spread his muscular arms, and—as he put it—"bloviate," which he could do with considerable success.

But Harding's managers—"masters," Cox called them—did not want their "stuffed shirt" to go out on the stump. They wanted to keep him at home in Marion, Ohio, where he could run a small-town front-porch campaign, in the McKinley tradition. There his talents for glad-handing could be exercised to their full. There he could read carefully prepared little "straddles," censored if not written by his "masters."

Out on the stump Harding might betray himself. He might reveal that his "bungalow" mind did not measure up to his statesmanlike shoulders. His great gush of "bloviating" words might, through some horrible mischance, mean something definite. It was much too dangerous.

There were two opposing factions in the Republican party, and Harding was in the middle. "Irreconcilables" like Senator Johnson tried to interpret his words to mean that he would wash his hands completely of the nefarious League; pro-Leaguers like Taft tried to interpret his words to mean that he would take us into some kind of pasteurized League. The harassed Harding was shoved back and forth between the two factions like a giant pushball.

If the Republicans took liberties with the truth in misrepresenting the views (such as they were) of their confused candidate, the Democrats took liberties with the truth in attacking a Republican straw man. Their strategy was to say that the Republicans were unalterably opposed *to any kind of League.*

The Republicans, for their part, had a different straw man. They insisted that the Democrats were for the "Paris League," or the League "just as Wilson brought it back from Paris." (Few persons with any political discernment were now expecting that there could ever be senatorial approval of an unreserved League.)

So while the Democrats belabored the straw man of No League Whatsoever, and the Republicans belabored the straw man of Unreserved League, the two Republican factions propped up their straw-man candidate and promised that he would lead them in opposite directions at the same time.

For most of the campaign Harding sat benignly on his front porch at the Mecca of Marion, being "folksy" to the numerous bands of front-porch pilgrims. He clasped the hands of representatives of various walks of life, and when the Chicago "Cubs" appeared, he donned a glove and dexterously caught a half-dozen pitches from the great Grover Cleveland Alexander, appropriately remarking that our "one-man team" had "muffed domestic affairs badly," and had then "struck out at Paris."

4

July 22, 1920, was a gala day in Marion, Ohio; Warren G. Harding was to deliver his speech of acceptance. The crowds poured in, among them a Columbus glee club which sang lustily:

> We'll throw out Woodrow and his crew,
> They really don't know what to do.

Marion's favorite son stood before 30,000 of the curious and admiring, clad in cutaway coat, purple tie, and striped trousers, and spoke for an hour and a half, while his collar and cuffs grew limp, and his voice grew husky. For an hour and a half he wobbled all over the spacious Republican platform. He rejected the League of Nations (though not completely); hinted vaguely at a substitute Association of Nations; and asserted that we would help in international affairs (but in our own way).

Harding's most important front-porch speech was that of August 28, in which he vaguely sketched his ideas for the Association of Nations. He did not outline clearly what he had in mind, probably because (as he admitted one month later) he was "without specific program about an Association of Nations."

The Democrats promptly attacked "Harding's False Teeth Proposal." There was only one association of nations, and that was the League. It was actually functioning, and had a roster of some thirty members. These countries were all bound by Article XX of the Covenant to make no other compacts. It was ridiculous to suppose that all the other nations would abandon a going concern and stampede to an Association of Nations which did not even exist in the sterile mind of Harding.

Harding's Way Out of the War
(Courtesy of St. Louis *Post-Dispatch*; cartoonist Fitzpatrick)

Late in September, the Republican high command decided to run the risk of permitting their candidate to go out and "bloviate." Cox was putting on too dynamic a campaign; Harding had better venture forth and show his statuesque profile. At Des Moines, Iowa (October 7), the confused senator made the mistake of coming out flatfootedly about the League. He was quoted as saying: "I do not want to clarify these obligations; I want to turn my back on them. *It is not interpretation, but rejection that I am seeking.*"

Senators Borah and Johnson let out a whoop of delight. Up

to this time, they had been pouting or campaigning half-heartedly; now they were in the fight with both fists. Johnson went out on the stump to shout that Harding had never been ambiguous, that he had never wavered, and that he had been foursquare against the League all the time.

Cox was delighted also, remarking, "Now he's against the League, I'm for the League." "Evidently," sneered Cox, "Harding has been pulled over into the 'irreconcilable camp' by 'Brother Borah.' "

The angry protest among pro-League Republicans against the Des Moines blunder apparently frightened Harding into appearing more friendly toward the League. Cox seized gleefully upon this unexpected advantage, and counted up his opponent's alleged fourteen wobbles on the issue, both as senator and as candidate. Actually, in most of his speeches Harding condemned the "Paris" or "Wilson" League, while conceding that an amended League was within the range of possibilities. His most consistent theme in the closing weeks of the campaign was that when elected he would summon to Washington the "best minds" of the country, male and female, Republican and Democrat. (There would be no more "one-mannism.") His task would be to harmonize divergent views and, with these "best minds," work out some kind of association of nations or even a reconstructed League.

Wobble though he did, Harding could hardly be accused of having uttered one friendly sentiment about the League *as then constituted*. On the contrary, he said some very bitter things about it ("a stupendous fraud"), while not slamming the door on salvage operations. He seems to have felt that his chief task was to sit on the fence, keep the "irreconcilables" reasonably quiet until after election, and then work out something in line with majority wishes. This led the Grand Rapids *Press* to observe: "There are two sides to every question, and even if there were three we believe that each of our splendid Ohio candidates for President could be on all of them at once."

Harding walked down a tortuous path, with Hiram W.

Johnson holding one hand and William H. Taft the other. Both men claimed that they held the controlling hand. That Harding could do this, and keep a semblance of peace within the family, while at the same time commending himself to the electorate, was no mean political achievement.

One of the Republican campaign slogans was, "Let's have done with wiggle and wobble." It could better have been applied to the Republicans themselves.

5

On October 14, one of the most striking documents in American political history was given to the press. It was an appeal to the public, signed by thirty-one eminent people (mostly Republicans), later joined by twenty-five more. The list was an impressive one, containing the names of Root (who drafted it), Hughes, Hoover, and a distinguished group of educators and other public men. Here were the brains and conscience of the Republican party.

The gist of this curious document was that the alternatives in the campaign were the (straw-man) *unreserved* Wilson League or a *modified* Harding League. No matter what Harding said, the United States under his leadership would enter a reserved League of Nations. This assertion was unique in that it virtually proclaimed, under the most respectable auspices, that Harding was a liar, or he did not know what he was saying, or he could be controlled by the elder statesmen after election.

Root's biographer reveals that the real purpose of the declaration was to bolster Harding's backbone, particularly after his Des Moines wobble, by trying to force him out of the camp of the "irreconcilables." The statement was probably also designed to stop the alarming desertion of prominent pro-League Republicans to the Cox banner, and to prevent the inevitable Harding victory from being interpreted as a decisive mandate against the League.

Some of the arguments set forth in the appeal were thoroughly dishonest, and worthy of a shyster rather than Elihu Root. But the logic of the situation was such as to give the statement much plausibility. A case could be made out as follows.

The Republican party, which probably had a majority of the "best minds," had long stood for international cooperation; the Republican Senate had tried to get us into the League with the Lodge reservations, but had been blocked by Wilson. Cox, even if he won, could not get the treaty through. The Republican platform did not preclude a League, and while Harding had admittedly been blowing both hot and cold, he had twice voted for the League, and he conceded the possibilities of an amended League. Regardless of what he was now saying, when he came to high office the force of circumstances would compel him to accept a reserved League. He would then see that the League was operating hopefully, and that the other nations would not accept his vague association.

Harding was known to be a weak character. He would fall under the spell of the "best minds," and they would lead him and the country into a revised League. After the election, Dr. Frank Crane concluded in *Current Opinion:* "There have been Presidents elected on the strength of what they promised before election; *this one was elected in the belief that he will not keep his promise.*"

The appeal of the Illustrious Thirty-one undoubtedly had a great though undeterminable influence. It was primarily useful in enabling a large number of pro-League Republicans to salve their consciences and justify their natural desire not to leave the party.

The Democrats and some pro-League Republicans vigorously condemned this specious appeal. Harding was too amiable a character; he would say "Yes" to those who got to him last. If he could be counted on to consort with Hughes and Taft and Root and Hoover, all might be well. But the Senate oligarchy had nominated Harding, and he knew it. These men were his associates; they spoke his language; and he would be grateful to those who had befriended him. The Senate oligarchy would get to him last, *and they were not friends of international cooperation.*

One pro-Leaguer pointedly remarked that to support Harding on the ground that he would take us into the League was like "supporting the Devil in order to get to Heaven."

"Let Not Thy Left Hand Know What Thy Right Doeth"

(Courtesy of New York *Times*; cartoonist Marcus

6

President Wilson naturally could not make an active contribution to the campaign, though he evidently watched it with much interest. About September 17 he sent a check for $500 to the Democratic campaign chest, announcing that he wanted to make this contribution as a private in the ranks. This touched off a Match-the-President Fund, which met with considerable success.

In the closing weeks of the campaign, Wilson, in his feeble

way, became more active. Evidently displeased with the emphasis on "slush" and with the misrepresentations of Article X as a war pledge, he issued an appeal on October 3, beginning with the familiar, "My Fellow Countrymen." He pleaded for a vindication of the nation's honor, and for a repudiation of the "gross ignorance" and "impudent audacity" of those who were urging a policy of "defiant segregation." We had to keep faith with those nations which were anxiously awaiting our verdict, and with the boys who were sleeping "beneath the sod of France." He rejoiced that the election was to be "a genuine national referendum," in which the people would deliver a "solemn mandate" to the politicians.

But the President's most dramatic personal effort came on October 27, when he received and addressed a delegation of fifteen prominent pro-League Republicans. Seated in a wheel chair, and reading from a manuscript in a voice so thick and a tone so low as to be almost inaudible, he pleaded that we go through with our moral obligation to finish the job. His voice betrayed deep emotion as he referred to our fallen heroes. Possibly as an offset to Cox's last-minute wobbling and to Léon Bourgeois' startling disclaimer, Wilson stressed Article X as the redemption of our pledge that Germany should not be allowed to break loose again. He feared that the real issue in the campaign had become obscured by partisanship (which was no doubt true), but he was sure that the nation had never been called upon to return a more solemn referendum.

The delegation went away saddened and shocked. This was Wilson's first public appearance since Pueblo. He had occasionally met with his Cabinet, and now and then outsiders had seen a muffled figure speed by in an automobile. It was evident either that Wilson had suffered a severe setback or that his condition had been reported by Seibold and others in too optimistic a vein. The latter explanation is probably the correct one.

On the eve of the balloting, Wilson sent his congratulations to Cox, expressing admiration for his courageous efforts. He could hardly have been pleased with the candidate's emphasis on "slush," or with his fatal wobble on Article X. Probably Wilson was trying to keep up a brave front in the interest of the greater good.

7

The closing days of the campaign were marked by two scandalous developments.

The venomously anti-Wilson *Harvey's Weekly* published a sacrilegious burlesque of a famous painting by Raphael which satirized both Cox and the League. The Republican leaders immediately made what shamefaced amends they could, but this unseemly sneer at the Catholic faith undoubtedly dampened the enthusiasm of thousands of Democratic Irishmen who were flocking over to Harding's banner because of Article X.

For some little while the rumor had been spread by word of mouth and by pamphlet that Negro blood coursed through the veins of the handsome Harding. Several days before the election a professor in an Ohio college was dismissed because of his alleged connection with the preparation of pseudo-genealogical tables, and the whole affair, though discussed by the press in veiled terms, was a sensation.

Either one of these developments might have been enough to ruin Harding in a close election. Wilson, of course, had nothing to do with either; in fact he rebuked Tumulty, who was overjoyed at the appearance of the Negro-blood scandal, by saying that the campaign would be fought out on principle, not on backstairs gossip. But it is a sardonic commentary on Wilson's appeal for a "solemn referendum" that the whole sorry mess should have degenerated in the last days to a crass appeal to religious and racial antagonisms.

As the American people prepared for their quadrennial tramp to the polls, the result seemed a foregone conclusion to all but purblind partisans and professional Pollyannas. The straw votes all pointed one way; and despite the "Coxsureness" of the Democrats, the Wall Street betting odds were ten to one for Harding. It was not a question of who was going to win; it was just a question of how big the Republican plurality would be.

Election Day dawned for some 26,000,000 voters. Wearied of Wilson and Wilsonism, sated with idealism, disillusioned and morally dulled, bewildered by the various "wobbles" of the candidates, bored by the protracted debate and deadlock over the League, preoccupied with domestic problems, and fondly hoping for a return of "the good old days," the electorate rose up in its sovereign might and cast 16,152,000 votes for the apostle of "normalcy"—an unprecedented plurality of more than 7,000,000 votes. This was a popular vote of 60.35 per cent, a figure not equaled since Washington's day, not even by the extraordinary vote-getting ability of President Franklin D. Roosevelt. Cox failed to carry even his own state and his own district. Harding won Tennessee, the first state of the Secession since Reconstruction days to bolt over to the Republican column. It was not a landslide, remarked Tumulty, it was an "earthquake."

Long-term Democratic governors, congressmen, and senators were smothered beneath a blizzard of ballots. The Republicans increased their majority in the Senate, and the "irreconcilable" Brandegee and Moses (though running behind Harding) were triumphantly returned. The "Battalion of Death" was now stronger than ever.

It was not a "solemn referendum"; it was an awe-inspiring cataclysm.

8

The kind of crusade that Wilson hoped for never came. Enthusiasm was conspicuously lacking. An unusually large percentage of the eligible voters (among them newly enfranchised women) did not even bother to go to the polls. Many people openly said that it made no real difference who won. Cox was for the League with reservations; Harding (so the Illustrious Thirty-one promised) would get us in with reservations.

There was also a vast amount of dissatisfaction with each of the standard-bearers. Both candidates straddled, obscured the issues, stirred up offensive irrelevancies, or raked over dead ashes. There was little that was clear-cut. *Current Opinion* felt that the result was a victory for "General Grouch," while the New York *Nation* concluded that Harding was elected "by disgust."

Further evidence of disgust and protest is to be found in the remarkable showing of the Socialist candidate, Eugene V. Debs. As an involuntary guest of the federal government in the Atlanta penitentiary, Convict No. 2253 polled over 900,000 votes, the best showing quantitatively that the Socialists have ever made. Part of the Debs vote was certainly a protest against keeping men in prison for merely talking, but some of it was undoubtedly a protest against the "devil's choice" presented by Cox and Harding.

While the stunned Democrats shoveled the last clods on their dead hopes, the Republicans were hardly less stunned by their prodigious plurality. In the face of such a tremendous social phenomenon, it was impious to gloat. Warren G. Harding, who had made a poor showing in the three spring primaries which he had entered, was chastened rather than boastful.

But within a short time the spell wore off, and Republicans began to sense what they might do with their victory. Wilson had asked for a "solemn referendum." Cox had come out for the League; Harding had criticized the League (though the Illustrious Thirty-one said he did not really mean it). The Republicans had won by a stupendous plurality. Did they not have a solemn "mandate" to inter the League?

It is the time-honored privilege of the winner to place whatever interpretation he cares to on the result. His opponents

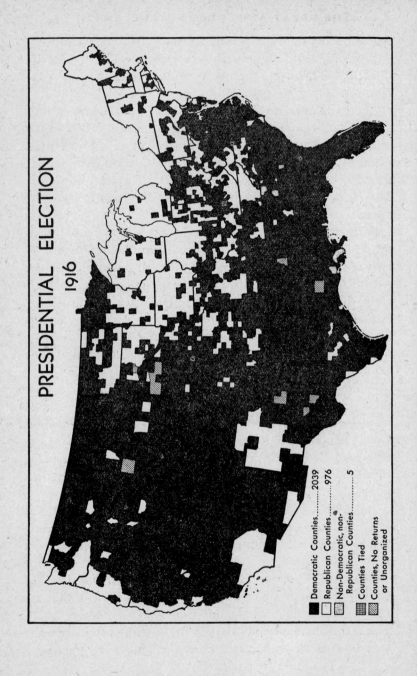

PRESIDENTIAL ELECTION
1916

Democratic Counties.........2039
Republican Counties..........976
Non-Democratic, non-
    Republican Counties...........5
Counties Tied
Counties, No Returns
    or Unorganized

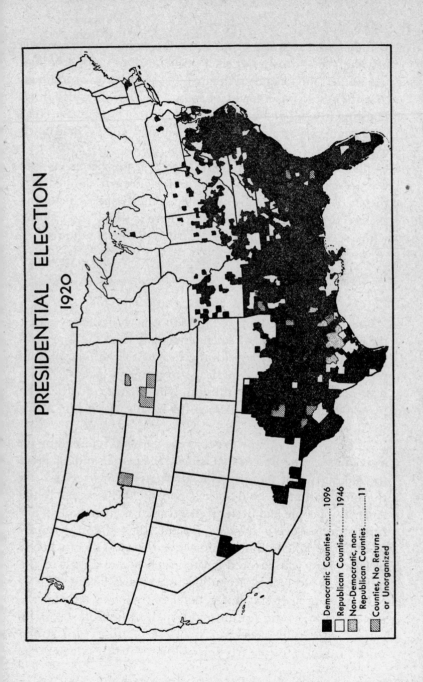

PRESIDENTIAL ELECTION

1920

Democratic Counties........1096
Republican Counties........1946
Non-Democratic, non-
    Republican Counties.........11
Counties, No Returns
    or Unorganized

will deny the accuracy of his interpretation, but the cymbals of victory will drown out such protestations. Those who had not wanted the League in the first place stridently proclaimed that the result was a mandate against foreign intermeddling. Harding himself announced, two days after the election, that the League was "now deceased." It was now safe to come down off the fence.

The Republicans not only claimed that the victorious vote was a solemn mandate to scrap the League, but claimed that they had a mandate to do anything else they wanted, including the erection of a high tariff wall. There is simply no arguing with a seven-million plurality. It strikes politicians dumb.

9

One of the most enduring myths in American history is that the election of 1920 was a solemn mandate from the American people to have no traffic with the League of Nations. Wilson, the great authority on American government, had asked that it be made a referendum, thus implying that it could be. The people could hardly be blamed for having taken him at his word.

The only possible way to get a true national referendum on a given issue is to present that issue to the people and ask them to vote on two or more specific alternatives. Switzerland was the only nation to hold such a poll on the League. If the American people had been given a similar nonpartisan opportunity to approve a *reserved* League, they almost certainly would have done so by a comfortable margin. The great body of Democrats who favored it would have been joined by the millions of pro-League Republicans who also favored it.

In 1920 there were four general positions to take on the treaty: (1) rejection; (2) unconditional ratification; (3) ratification with mild reservations; (4) ratification with strong reservations. It was clearly impossible to register one's views on four questions by voting for one of two major candidates, one of whom "wobbled" at the end, and the other of whom publicly admitted that he did not know what he had in mind, while the best brains of his party announced that, regardless of what he had in mind, he did not mean what he said.

Even if the candidates had taken clear-cut positions on the League, there still would not have been a referendum, because the League was by no means the only issue, though it was clearly the most talked-about issue. Aside from purely local problems, there were about a hundred issues or subjects for discussion, ranging from the Armenian mandate to the tariff on California lemons.

The Republicans concentrated their fire on Wilsonism ("one-mannism," autocracy, extravagance, meddling with business, dreamy internationalism), and the sins of the war government (heavy taxes, the railroad muddle, civil liberties, the price ceiling on wheat). The Democrats emphasized the treaty, but also progressivism versus reaction, with special attention to the Senate oligarchy and the "smoke-filled" room. To say that the final vote was a clear mandate on any one of the scores of issues involved is plainly absurd.

There is even some doubt as to whether the League was the leading or "paramount" issue. Various leaders on both sides said contradictory things at different times. To Taft, "Wilsonism" was paramount; to Bryan, prohibition was paramount. Cox at one time made "slush" the leading issue; Roosevelt at one time said progressivism was the "big" issue, though both men shifted back to the League. Harding wobbled over the many issues, though perhaps talking most about Wilsonism and world organization. A few prominent newspapers like the Portland *Oregonian* (Independent Republican) said that the League was not an issue at all: it was (or should be) completely nonpartisan. The Newark *Ledger* (Independent) insisted that no red herring of foreign policy should blind us to more pressing domestic problems. The Socialist New York *Call* scoffed that, as an issue, the League was as "vital as a dead cat in a gutter."

One of the issues in the campaign was, "What is the paramount issue?"

10

The elementary facts are these. Several million congenital Republicans and several million congenital Democrats (especially from the Solid South) were going to vote the straight party ticket, no matter who the candidates were or what the alleged issues might be. These voters were partisans by birth, race, heredity, habit, environment, conviction, and even by marriage. There is little reason to suppose that the Democrats would have won if Cox had declared flatly against the League and Harding had declared flatly for it.

Senator Reed of Missouri, a violent Democratic opponent of the League who had been snubbed and booed by the delegates in San Francisco, voted for Cox, and displayed his marked ballot to prove it. Did this mean that he was voting for the League which Cox was advocating? Not at all. His vote was a victory not for the League but for party regularity.

William Jennings Bryan, who had been hooted and jeered at by the convention, more or less sulked in his tent. Yet he announced that he had voted for the personally "wet" Cox against the personally "wet" but politically "dry" brewer, Harding. What was this a mandate on?

Pro-League Republicans were presented with a horrible dilemma, especially if they were "big business" Republicans as well, and desirous of fattening under a protective tariff. Should they bolt the party and vote their consciences against their pocketbooks? An impressive number did bolt, and no doubt tens of thousands of others would have done likewise if they had not been able to ease their consciences by the ambiguities of the platform, of the candidate, and of the Illustrious Thirty-one. George W. Wickersham, favoring the League but distrusting the motley crew of Democrats, said that there was nothing to do but "to retire to private life and cultivate roses."

When the tidal wave of votes poured in, the Hearst press and other isolationist newspapers raucously proclaimed that Wilson had asked for his solemn referendum and he had got it in no uncertain terms. The League was dead.

Washed In by the Waves
(From New York *World*; cartoonist Kirby; reprinted by permission)

But other newspapers, among them the most discerning and well balanced journals in the country, soberly denied that there had been a mandate on the League. The great majority of informed observers interpreted the vote as evidence of a revolt against Wilsonism, and of a desire for some kind of change.

This was undoubtedly true. The results were a victory that

could not be explained in purely political terms. The magnitude of the pluralities even in normally Democratic areas was evidence of something hardly less than a social or psychological upheaval. Cox *lost* New York City by about 440,000 votes; Governor "Al" Smith, running for reelection on the same ticket, *carried* the city (though narrowly losing the state) by some 320,000 votes. This was partly evidence of Smith's personal popularity, and perhaps of an Irish bolt from the national ticket, but it is unmistakable proof of a protest against Wilsonism and all that it implied.

The crippled Wilson, not the dynamic Cox, was running in 1920. The result was not a vote for Harding, but a vote against the minority party and Wilson—a Wilson who was made the whipping boy for all that had gone wrong during the previous eight years, both at home and abroad. In addition to the rank and file, countless thousands of disappointed and embittered Irish-Americans, German-Americans, and Italian-Americans vented their spleen at the polls. One English observer summed it up when he said that the crucial question had been, "Are you tired of this Administration?" And the answer was, "By God, we are!"

If there was any mandate it was in the mighty shout from the people to throw the minority party out of power.

11

Many of the pro-League journals denied that the outcome was a solemn referendum; they simply could not accept the results as final, for if they did the League would be lost. Some of these protestations were no doubt of the "sour grapes" variety. If Cox had won, the friends of the League would have claimed a mandate. But the fact remains that *long before the election*, scores of men in both parties had urged that the issue be kept out of the campaign because it was impossible to secure a true referendum.

Wilson's final blunder—and in some ways the most costly of all—was to insist that there be a referendum when there could be none. Deep in his heart he must have known this; but so great was his devotion to the League, and so unshakable was his faith in the people, that he was prepared to take this chance. Taft was right when he insisted that it was grossly unfair to condemn the League to death in a test which might well prove fatal and which was certain to be misleading.

Wilson's hopes and cause were buried beneath some 16,000,-000 votes. If he had kept the issue out of the campaign by judicious compromise, the United States almost certainly would have entered the League. Yet he insisted on the impossible. Catastrophe struck, and the champions of the League were never able to disentangle the remains of Wilson's brain child from the wreckage.

CHAPTER TWENTY-ONE

THE FINAL CURTAIN

*"The carrying out of that promise [an association for peace] is
the test of the entire sincerity, integrity and statesmanship of the
Republican party."* HERBERT HOOVER, *October 9, 1920.*

1

THE TREMENDOUS tidal wave that washed in Harding
should have come as no surprise to Wilson. The signs all
pointed so clearly in one direction that his friends tried to
cushion the inevitable blow. On the very day of the election
the Cabinet members met, but in response to their warnings
Wilson insisted: "The American people will not turn Cox
down and elect Harding. A great moral issue is involved." As
ex-Secretary Lane later noted, "Such faith, even in oneself,
is almost genius!"

When the election returns poured in, Wilson took the
shock unflinchingly. To Tumulty he remarked simply, "They
have disgraced us in the eyes of the world." At the next Cabinet
meeting Wilson looked worried; but he expressed concern, not
for himself, but for the distraught world.

A host of admirers addressed letters to the White House,
urging Wilson not to be downhearted; he had fought the good
fight, and the people were proud of him. To his daughter
Eleanor he wrote that no harm had been done to him or to
anything essential; but he was distressed because the country
now had to face a period of great trial. Symptomatic of a heavy
heart was his request that Secretary Colby draft the annual
Thanksgiving proclamation; while Wilson bore no resentment, he found it difficult to frame a proper statement.

The outspoken Bryan publicly called upon Wilson to appoint Harding his Secretary of State, and then resign along
with Vice President Marshall. But Wilson ignored such ap-

peals. Strong as was his admiration for the parliamentary system, he was unwilling to carry his convictions through to their logical conclusion. He had asked for a vote of confidence, and he certainly had not got one, whatever it was. But he stayed on to the bitter end.

The sands of the final weeks inexorably drained out. Tumulty submitted a draft of the last annual message to Congress, which Wilson edited in his own hand; Secretary Baker was called upon to write a veto message. Occasionally, Wilson would meet visitors, but he could not shake hands with them because his left arm was useless and his good arm had to support him on his cane. Senator Carter Glass, who was seeking an interview, wrote to Wilson in jest about a newspaper report to the effect that the President had refused to shake hands with Lodge because of his "third leg." Wilson replied rather sharply that it made him very cross that so good a friend as Glass should associate himself, even in fun, with Senator Lodge.

The last days were brightened somewhat by the news that Wilson had been voted the Nobel Peace Prize (about $40,000) in recognition of his heroic efforts to establish a new international order. This coveted honor brought a flood of congratulatory letters and telegrams.

Harvey's Weekly awaited the demise of the Wilson administration with satirical impatience. Week after week, with devilish iteration, it ran fillers: "Only 237 Days More"; "Only 230 Days More"; and so on. In the issue of February 26, 1921, it could gleefully announce, "Only 144 Hours More!"

The last Cabinet meeting was a painful experience for all present. When asked what he was planning to do in retirement, Wilson replied (no doubt thinking of the troublesome Theodore Roosevelt) that he was "going to try to teach ex-Presidents how to behave." But, he added, one difficult thing for him to have to endure was "Mr. Harding's English." At the very end, following a touching tribute from his associates, his lips trembled, tears rolled down his cheeks, and he choked out, "God bless you all."

On inauguration day, Wilson rode bravely to the Capitol with the incoming President. The contrast was striking: Wilson stooped, trembling, pallid; Harding square, strong, and bronzed. At the Capitol the President was waited upon by a Congressional committee which, through the voice of Senator Lodge, asked if there were any final communications. As if pulling himself together for a final effort, Wilson turned to his bitter foeman and in icy tones said: "I have no further communication. I would be glad if you would inform both Houses and thank them for their courtesy—good morning, sir."

The ceremony ended on this chilling note. A few minutes later the reign of normalcy began.

2

Upon retirement Wilson went to live in a recently purchased house on S Street. He had chosen Washington for his home largely because he was planning to write a book, and he wanted to be near the rich resources of the Library of Congress. He actually completed only the dedicatory page—a touching tribute to his wife. His total literary output consisted of a two-page article which appeared in the *Atlantic Monthly,* and for which he received three hundred dollars.

Needing additional income, Wilson proposed to ex-Secretary Colby that they form a law partnership. Colby acquiesced; offices were opened in both New York and Washington; but Wilson went to his desk only once. The partnership was in fact more hampered by Wilson's moral strength than by his physical weakness: he flatly refused to accept cases growing out of his connection with the government. His honor and his prestige were not for sale, even though one fee of $500,000 had to be rejected. From an ethical standpoint such standards are in the highest degree admirable; but Colby had to eat, and the partnership was dissolved. This was the final irony. Disliking the law and lawyers, and having failed early in life as a lawyer, Wilson ended his career as an unsuccessful lawyer.

The routine at S Street was quiet and secluded. Wilson spent much of his time resting, reading and being read to, and dictating answers to a heavy correspondence. A few of these letters betrayed the crotchets of a sickly and elderly man, and they were suppressed by those who were caring for him. He enjoyed automobile rides and attendance at the theater, where his appearance was invariably greeted by gratifying applause. He received an ovation when he appeared briefly in a procession preliminary to the dedication of the tomb of the unknown soldier at Arlington, in November, 1921, and rode to the White House on the day of Harding's funeral, in August, 1923. On his last birthday, his sixty-seventh, a group of admirers touched him deeply when they presented him with a handsome Rolls Royce limousine, painted in Princeton colors.

Wilson more than kept his promise to show how ex-Presidents should behave. He refrained from criticizing publicly either the bad English or the bad government of Harding, though there was much to condemn in both. But he did thrust his hands into state politics, and among other things wrote letters designed to defeat for reelection both Senator Reed and Senator Shields, two of the Democratic "irreconcilables" who had not supported him on the League. Privately, he criticized Senator Underwood of Alabama for cooperating with the Republicans in carrying through their separate peace and their Washington Conference program. "If Underwood is a Democrat," he remarked to a friend, "then I am a Republican."

Weakened though he was, and failing rapidly, Wilson still regarded himself as a leader not only of the Democrats but of liberals everywhere. He met with the Democratic chieftains, and laid plans for making the election of 1924 a true referendum on the League. He did not want the defeated Cox to carry the banner again; and when Tumulty conveyed a message purporting to come from Wilson which was construed to be an endorsement of Cox, the devoted ex-secretary was dropped from the throne of grace.

Late in 1923, just a few months before his death, Wilson

seriously considered serving as United States senator from New Jersey. Evidently he thought himself stronger than he was, and his chances for complete recovery far better than they were. But considerations of health, combined with the trial of having to associate with senatorial minds, caused him to abandon the whole idea. As he told James Kerney, they "haven't had a thought down there in fifty years." He added that he had a temper, and if he were to go to the Senate, he "would get into a row with that old Lodge, who no longer counts for anything."

3

A procession of visitors, distinguished and otherwise, journeyed to the S Street shrine. The grizzled Georges Clemenceau, associate and antagonist of peace conference days, paid his respects, and was so distressed by what he saw that he canceled a dinner invitation for that evening.

Lloyd George, both an adversary and a supporter at the peace table, also came and tried to get Wilson to repeat some of the limericks which had amused them at Paris. One impression that the distinguished Briton carried away was the ex-President's enduring bitterness against the then French Premier, Raymond Poincaré. "He is a cheat and a liar!" burst out Wilson.

Viscount Cecil, faithful collaborator on the League of Nations Commission in Paris, also put in an appearance. To him Wilson exclaimed: "We are winning! Don't make any concessions." In other words, the League should not offer to accept such reservations as the United States might care to propose. This was as late as April 20, 1923.

Wilson's steadfastness in the faith seems to have been unshakable. It was perhaps his strongest trait, while at the same time his greatest weakness, for it led to self-deception. He believed that the people would soon see the light; they had merely been misled by false Republican prophets. He wrote to

Rabbi Wise (July 11, 1923) opposing any cooperation with the League of Nations *except on the basis of full membership*. A partial cooperation might damage the prospects of complete participation. To the very end Wilson was a whole-loaf man.

Shortly before the curtain fell, Wilson surprised his friends when he told them (according to Josephus Daniels), "I am not

Afraid of His Own Shadow!

(From New York *Evening World*; cartoonist Cassel;
reprinted by permission)

sorry I broke down." He went on to explain that as it turned out the American people were thinking their way through to their own decision, "and that is the better way for it to come." This may be the key to his unwillingness to compromise on the Lodge reservations, and to his demand for a "solemn referendum."

The day before Armistice Day, 1923, Wilson undertook the ordeal of giving a brief address over the radio—his first and last experience with the microphone. He was in an enfeebled condition, and the unperfected radio of those days did not produce the best results. Yet he managed to stir up another hornets' nest abroad when he condemned both Italy and France for having made "waste paper" of the Treaty of Versailles. (Privately he told James Kerney that he "would like to see Germany clean up France . . .") But with even-handed justice, Wilson condemned the "great wrong to civilization" resulting from our "cowardly and dishonorable" withdrawal into a policy of "sullen and selfish isolation."

The next day—Armistice Day—a worshipful crowd came to S Street for the purpose of honoring Wilson. He hobbled out onto the porch for his last public appearance, and made a few appropriate remarks. The band then struck up "How Firm a Foundation," and the aging Covenanter, as though moved by the grand old hymn, interrupted to add:

I am not one of those that have the least anxiety about the triumph of the principles I have stood for. I have seen fools resist Providence before, and I have seen their destruction . . . That we shall prevail is as sure as that God reigns. Thank you. [Great and long-continued applause.]

Early in February, 1924, it became known that the intrepid spirit of the great idealist was about to take flight. Scores of the faithful gathered outside the house, and kneeling in the snow they kept their chilly vigil day and night. Amazing as were the demonstrations of esteem accorded Wilson in France and Italy, they seem hollow when compared with this last meed of devotion. It was an unprecedented tribute to courage, sincerity, vision, and a stern sense of duty.

Wilson died on February 3, 1924—on God's Holy Day. The last whispered words that Dr. Grayson heard were, "I am ready."

4

Turning from the sublime to the scandalous, we must consider briefly some of the high lights of the Harding administration.

The photogenic new President partially redeemed his promise to gather about him the "best minds." His Cabinet contained some of the "best minds" in the country, notably those of Charles Evans Hughes and Herbert Hoover, both of whom had signed the appeal of the Illustrious Thirty-one. It also contained some of the worst minds, including ex-Senator Albert B. Fall (who later served a term in the penitentiary), Harry M. Daugherty (who was brought to trial but was saved by two hung juries), and Edwin Denby (who was so incredibly stupid that responsible people did not seriously think he was implicated in the Teapot Dome "steal"). The goings-on of some of the Harding appointees gave much point to a current quip: The difference between George Washington and Warren Harding was that while Washington could not tell a lie, Harding could not tell a liar.

The hope was still cherished, not only in America but in Europe, that Harding would redeem the assurances of the Illustrious Thirty-one and take definite steps toward international cooperation. But, as the Scripture tells us, no man can serve two masters. During the campaign Harding had clasped both devils and angels to his broad bosom. Now he had to make a choice, and it seems clear that he was swayed by his "masters" and by the awesomeness of the 7,000,000 plurality. Harding seems to have become convinced, after hearing the Republican politicians repeat the refrain endlessly, that the election was truly a mandate against the League, and that it would be politically disastrous to touch the issue even with a ten-foot pole.

In his inaugural address, Harding did not even mention the

League by name, though it had been the leading issue in the recent election. In his first message to Congress he stated bluntly that America would have nothing to do with the League; in one of his last speeches he said that the issue was as "dead as slavery." The Association of Nations died a quiet death—granted that it had ever fuzzily existed in the brain of Harding.

The isolationist newspapers and the partisan Republican press did not even wish the League well. These journals sneered at its successes and jeered at its failures, as if to prove that they had been right in opposing it. Letter after letter from the League Secretariat lay unanswered in the files of the Department of State. It seemed unwise politically even to acknowledge communications from a League which had seemingly been rejected by a 7,000,000 plurality. But public opinion became aroused when it found out what was happening, and in September, 1921, the State Department daringly acknowledged the receipt of these communications, without, of course, committing the country to anything. Some of our early notes for the League were timorously routed through the Swiss and Dutch governments. Beware of 7,000,000 votes!

5

Frightened though it was by the League, the Harding administration did pull itself together long enough to make a separate peace with our technical enemies. In July, 1921, Congress declared peace; and late in August, *nearly three years after the Armistice,* the United States negotiated treaties of peace with Germany, Austria, and Hungary. In these pacts it was stipulated that this country, while not ratifying the treaties originally negotiated with those nations, "shall fully enjoy" *all of the advantages and privileges flowing therefrom.* All three pacts were promptly approved by the Senate.

Thus the Harding administration kept faith with the boys who had thought they were giving their lives in a holy crusade.

The regime of normalcy retreated into a policy of "sullen and selfish" isolation. Immigration barriers were erected against the destitute of Europe; tariff barriers were erected against the products of an industrially shattered Europe which could not pay its debts to us except in goods.

But the conscience of the Republicans was not greatly troubled. Only one of the Illustrious Thirty-one made any real public protest against the betrayal of the electorate, and he was President Lowell of Harvard University. The two signers in the Cabinet did not resign in protest: both held their posts well into the Coolidge administration, and the available record does not show that they took energetic steps to prod Harding into a redemption of the promises they had made for him.

With the League spurned, and the Association forgotten, Harding was under some moral obligation to show that he meant well toward the outside world. The result was the Washington Disarmament Conference of 1921-1922, which was acclaimed by Republicans as a safe substitute for the League. Not only was the Conference almost completely illusory in its long-run disarmament results, but it also interfered seriously with the disarmament program of the League of Nations.

Harding died with scandals beginning to break all about his befuddled head; death was a merciful refuge. We had exchanged a President who was physically sick for one who was morally sick, and one result was to prove that there could be worse things than a cripple in the White House.

Charity begs us to drop the curtain here; Truth insists that we record certain brutal conclusions.

The Senate oligarchs betrayed the country when they nominated Harding, knowing that he was weak and suspecting that he was immoral.

The Illustrious Thirty-one betrayed the country when they

vouched for Harding, and then did nothing effective to force him to redeem their promises.

The Republican chieftains betrayed their party not only by backing Harding, but by wishfully interpreting the results of the election as a mandate against the League, and by acquiescing in Harding's timorous policy of do-nothingism. This gross

"A Banner with a Strange Device"
(Courtesy of Brooklyn *Eagle*; cartoonist Harding)

betrayal of the party and of the country was not soon to be forgotten; in the campaign of 1944 it was repeatedly brought up in an attempt to prove that a Republican administration under Thomas E. Dewey could not be entrusted with the high responsibilities of peacemaking.

The voters betrayed their obligation to their country and its obligations to the world when they elected a spineless and double-talking candidate.

Harding betrayed his party, his country, and the world, when he permitted his administration to fall into the hands of thieves, and when he turned his back upon that international cooperation which he had ringingly—and perhaps sincerely—promised.

CHAPTER TWENTY-TWO

THE GREAT BETRAYAL

"If ye break faith with us who die,
We shall not sleep, though poppies grow
In Flanders fields."

JOHN MCCRAE

1

WILSON HAS been savagely denounced for having made commitments at Paris which the American people were ultimately unwilling to honor.

The truth is that only the President was in a position to make such pledges for the nation, and that the assurances which Wilson gave were in line with his war addresses, which the people either had warmly applauded or had seemingly accepted. Wilson erred not so much in making commitments—for commitments of some sort had to be made—as in assuming that the same high degree of wartime idealism would continue indefinitely after the signing of the peace.

But whoever was at fault, the unwillingness or inability of the United States to carry through the promises made in its behalf was catastrophic.

(1) One result was a betrayal of the League of Nations. The newly formed organization was crippled at birth when this nation, the most powerful of its sponsors, left it an orphaned waif on the international doorstep. With the United States in a position to hamstring the boycotts of the League—the League's most potent economic weapon—the other countries had little faith in what they were doing. While preaching peace they prepared for war. They could not hope to carry through a successful disarmament program as long as the United States would have no traffic with them. Under the League ideal there were to be no neutrals: either one was for

the League, or one was against it. By not being for it, the United
States was against it.

It is possible of course that the League would have proved
a failure even with our participation. But that is speculation.
It is a demonstrable fact that the League was weakened and
demoralized at the outset by the defection of the mightiest
of the nations.

(2) Another result was a betrayal of the Treaty of Versailles
—or better, the Truce of Versailles. This pact became a different treaty as a result of our desertion, and a much harsher
one. Wilson had counted on the Covenant—the "heart" of
the treaty—to soften its punitive features and provide a forum
for wronged peoples. But the treaty could not work unless
the "heart" worked, and the League could not work unless
we worked with it.

The two chief instruments for giving flexibility to the
Treaty of Versailles were the League of Nations and the
Reparations Commission. We spurned the one, while declining
representation on the other. The all-important commission
then fell under the domination of France, although at Paris
it had been assumed that the United States would use its great
influence in the direction of moderation. The result of our
withdrawal was that Germany was saddled with an impossible
reparations burden, which unsettled Europe (and America)
economically for more than a decade, contributed to the coming of the Great Depression, and helped prepare the path for
Adolf Hitler.

The same sad story must be told elsewhere. The commission
for the administration of the Saar was to have been headed by
a high-minded American historian, but it fell under the influence of a nationalistic Frenchman, who was made no less
nationalistic by fears growing out of the retirement of the
United States. This was the sort of thing that Lloyd George
had in mind when he said that the great failure lay not in the
Treaty of Versailles but in the failure of the powers to carry
out its provisions in the manner intended. To this tragic result

the United States, by mere abstention, contributed powerfully.

(3) Another result was a betrayal of the Allies. The United States, by seceding from the victorious Allied coalition, made the first major breach in an alliance which might have kept the peace. In so doing, we indirectly joined with our former enemy, Germany, against the Treaty of Versailles. If the original entente had been kept intact, Hitler today might be ranting in the beer halls of an unbombed Munich.

Our sins were sins of omission; the sins of Britain and France were sins of commission. But our failure to stand by our associates gave them justification in their own minds for blaming us for many of their ills, and provided a plausible excuse for not acting together resolutely in the face of their common dangers.

(4) Another result was a betrayal of France. Suffering from a security psychosis, the French were stunned by our renunciation of the League, of the Treaty of Versailles, and of the Security Treaty. The resulting state of "jitters" was largely responsible for harsh measures against Germany, particularly the disastrous invasion of the Ruhr in 1923, all of which further aroused German nationalism and provided combustibles for demagogues like Adolf Hitler.

(5) Another result was a betrayal of Germany. The Treaty of Versailles, as noted, became a different treaty from the one which the Germans had thought they were signing. One of the Fourteen Points was a League of Nations—presumably a potent, *world* League of Nations. It was partly on the strength of such a promise that the Germans laid down their arms in 1918. But through our defection the League was condemned to anemia, and at the outset it became essentially a European league, in large part aimed at Germany, rather than a world league with the United States as a moderating member.

(6) Another result was a betrayal of liberal opinion the world over, not only in England, France, and America, but also in Germany. The black eye given German liberalism helped

undermine faith in the Weimar Republic and smoothed the way for Adolf Hitler and other apostles of oppression.

(7) Another result was a betrayal of American boys who had died, and of American boys yet unborn. Those who had died had been assured that their lives were being expended in a war to end wars; those yet unborn had to go over and do the job—a bloodier job—all over again.

(8) Another result was a betrayal of the masses everywhere, particularly the unredeemed minorities who through Wilson had been promised a better world.

(9) Another result was a betrayal of our humanitarian, missionary, and educational interests not only in Europe, but particularly in the Near East. Our retirement from the scene delayed the Near Eastern settlement, and infused new life into the Turks, with resulting disaster to the Armenians and other peoples for whom we had something of a moral responsibility.

(10) Another result was a betrayal of the legitimate interests of American merchants, manufacturers, bankers, and investors. We adopted a policy of ostrichism: trying to play the role of a debtor nation when we were now a creditor nation; seeking to eat our cake and have it too; raising high tariff and other barriers. In so doing we contributed heavily to the economic ills of Europe in the 1920's and 1930's, which in turn prepared the foundations of the Great Depression, which in turn brought in Adolf Hitler.

(11) Another result was a betrayal of America's responsibility to assume that world leadership which had been thrust upon her. First of all, there was a kind of *noblesse oblige*—an obligation to help the less fortunate. Secondly, there were the dictates of both selfishness and common sense—of playing an active role so as to safeguard our interests and prevent our being dragged into World War II. Instead, we cravenly retreated, while our prestige sank to a new low in Europe, the Far East, and Latin America. Instead of trying to control events, we left ourselves at the mercy of events which inexorably drew us again into their vortex.

(12) Another result was a betrayal of the nation's plighted word and of good faith in international dealings. The world will be long in recovering completely from the shock of our desertion in 1919–1920. The cooperation of the United States had been indispensable for victory; it was no less indispensable for a victorious peace. We achieved the one gloriously; we botched the other ingloriously. Henceforth other nations, in laying their plans for a world order, must choose not what they think is desirable but what they think the political situation in America will permit the Senate to accept. All this makes for world instability, and militates against that maximum of international cooperation which might otherwise be possible.

The moral is that the ill effects of broken pledges are worse than those resulting from no pledges at all. If our government is so unworkable that we cannot carry through commitments which the President makes and a majority of the people want to honor, then we had better warn other nations in advance, so that they can count on only limited American cooperation —or no cooperation at all.

(13) Another result was a betrayal of our clear moral obligation to finish the job. If we had stayed out of the war in 1917, Europe would have worked out something different if not better—perhaps a negotiated peace. By throwing our power into the balance, we brought victory to one side and prostration to the other, all the while creating problems which we were morally bound to help solve. Vice President Marshall pointedly remarked that we were like the man who rushed into his neighbor's house to beat off a burglar, and then rushed back home, leaving the victim bleeding to death on the floor.

It ill became the United States to sit self-righteously on the side lines during the 1920's and 1930's and blame the Europeans for not solving their problems, when some of those problems would never have been created if we had stayed out altogether, or had not turned away from the plow when the furrow was only half completed.

(14) Another result was a betrayal of the American people. An overwhelming majority of our citizens clearly wanted the League—at least with some reservations. Wilson's instincts were sound when he vainly sought to find some way by which the people might express their will through their government. But our method of approving treaties is so antiquated, illogical, undemocratic, and unworkable that the American people had no mechanism through which to implement their desires. And Wilson's own inflexibility, as we have noted, tightened the deadlock.

The Gap in the Bridge

(Reproduced by permission of the Proprietors of *Punch*)

In 1919 and in 1920, the American people were willing to forsake the ancient path of isolation, at least with reservations. By the 1930's they were in a different mood, because by that time they saw that the League (which they had helped condemn to impotence) was a failure in preventing aggression by a major power.

This long and disconcerting list of "betrayals" does not necessarily mean that our withdrawal was solely, or even primarily, responsible for all the ills that befell Europe from 1919 to 1939. But it does mean that the United States cannot escape a very considerable share of the blame for what happened.

2

At the conclusion of the volume *Woodrow Wilson and the Lost Peace,* certain general principles were set forth regarding peacemaking. It now seems proper to list a few maxims relating to peace-ratifying and peace-executing.

(1) Politics, in so far as possible, should be kept out of foreign affairs. Nothing should be more nonpartisan than international relations, because what is good for one party is presumably good for both parties and the entire country. This, of course, suggests the counsel of perfection: politics is a bacillus which laughs at three-mile lines. Yet we should never wantonly throw a delicate issue on foreign affairs into the turbulence of a political campaign. The result is certain to be misleading and possibly disastrous. We must seek senators to match our mountains—men who will put the good of the country above the good of the party; who will put the advancement of humanity above the advancement of self. We should select senators and members of the House as much (if not more) for their position on foreign affairs as for their position on domestic affairs: the two, as we shall note, are inextricably intertwined.

(2) The two-thirds rule in the Senate should be eliminated. It is the refuge of the filibusterer, the obstructionist, and the devotee of minority rule, all of whom are foreign to a true democracy. This antique restriction adds immeasurably to clumsiness and deadlock in the treaty-ratifying process. In March, 1920 (though not in November, 1919), it was directly responsible for the defeat of the treaty.

(3) A postwar slump in idealism is inescapable in the cold, gray dawn that follows victory. The urge to return to a normalcy that can never be again is age-old; the growth of distrust in one's allies, once the common cause is won, is inevitable. The peacemakers should never lose sight of these things when

they come to design the temple of the future, and not try to attain the unattainable.

(4) Perfectionism is impossible in this workaday world. Our statesmen and our people, whether fashioning treaties of peace or fashioning new world organizations, should seek what will work—not what seems ideally desirable. The League was not perfect. It was, said one critic, only half a League—but it was half a League onward. Even today, after more than a century and a half of experience—our Constitution is far from perfect; yet we have changed it and are changing it.

(5) Compromise may be as essential in peace-ratifying as in peacemaking. Certainly this was true in Washington during 1919–1920. A stubborn refusal to compromise when the people demand compromise not only is undemocratic but may, as it did in 1920, lead to the defeat of the entire treaty.

(6) Sovereignty is a sacred cow tied across the path of international cooperation. It conjures up all kinds of unwarranted fears. But an impairment of sovereignty—of national freedom of action—is a characteristic of treaties entered into on a free and friendly basis. Broadly speaking, a treaty is a promise to give up, in return for something else, that which we would ordinarily do. The United States has entered into hundreds of international agreements, but our sovereignty is essentially unimpaired.

(7) Effective international cooperation demands a price. That price is the yielding of some small part of our freedom of action—our sovereignty—so that we may, through preventing international disorders, enjoy greater freedom of action. The good things of life may be free, but peace is not one of them. One of the supreme follies of the American people in the post-Versailles years was to demand rights, while shunning responsibilities. We found ourselves in the immoral and disastrous position of seeking all the immunities, privileges, and advantages of riding in the international boat, while refusing to pull the laboring oar of liabilities, responsibilities, and costs.

(8) An excess of suspicion—a Yankee horse-trading trait—

is a barrier to international cooperation. Peace can be preserved only among men of good will, for it is a blessing which rests not so much on paper pacts as on attitudes of mind. Peace can no more be maintained by parchment than sobriety can be maintained by constitutional amendments.

In 1919 we were the most powerful and secluded of the great nations, yet we acted as though we were the weakest and most vulnerable. Rich though we were, we feared that we might be asked to contribute one cent more than our proper share; powerful though we were, we feared that a few thousand of our soldiers might be sent abroad to prevent ten million from following them. We confessed by our conduct that our representatives were not intelligent enough to sit down at the same table with those of other nations, even though we had the highest stack of chips and most of the high cards.

If we enter a world organization for peace, eyeing our colleagues distrustfully and momentarily expecting them to try to "put something over on us," then failure is inevitable. There is usually more to be gained through an excess of confidence than through an excess of suspicion.

(9) Domestic affairs are but the obverse side of the shield of foreign affairs. In the 1920's the American people fatuously sought to crawl into a hole and pull the hole in after them. But they discovered to their sorrow—or at least some of them did—that immigration barriers, tariff walls, reparations payments, and foreign debts all stir up international reverberations. World depressions leap lightly across international boundaries; bumper wheat crops in the Argentine and Australia bring impoverishment to American farmers. The wars of Europe and Asia have an ugly and inexorable habit of becoming our wars.

(10) It is better to desert one's associates before the peace is drawn up than after. In 1919 we forced the Europeans to adopt a kind of treaty they would not have adopted if we had stayed out. Then we left them in the lurch and loudly condemned them because they could not make our kind of peace

work. If we are unwilling or unable to ratify and help execute a world peace, then we owe it to our associates to say so, in order that they may draw their plans accordingly.

(11) Isolationism as a physical fact is dead (granted that it ever existed), even though the isolationists are not. The desire to draw apart and mind one's own business is entirely natural and often commendable. But on this shriveling planet such an ideal is impracticable. With new inventions annihilating both time and distance, the Atlantic Ocean today is far smaller than the Aegean Sea was in the day of Pericles. It is now "One World," and we cannot secede from it. This whirling ball has now become so small that an international quarrel anywhere becomes our business. Wilson recognized all this, and it explains why he fought to the death for his ideal.

Since 1689, there have been nine world wars, and the American people have been drawn into *every single one of them.* This disconcerting fact lends much force to the truism that the only sure way for us to keep out of a great world conflict is to prevent its outbreak. If we are unwilling to recognize that we are a part of this planet, and if we are not utter fools, *we had better start preparing for the next world war right now.*

(12) Power creates responsibilities. The United States has become so wealthy and so powerful that, whether we do nothing or something in regard to an international organization, our influence will be felt for good or ill, positively or negatively. Aloofness merely accelerates the chaos which will inevitably engulf us. As long as this power exists, and as long as it will be felt one way or the other, elemental common sense commands us to direct it actively into channels which will be most helpful to the rest of the world and indirectly to ourselves.

(13) The United States, as the richest of the powers, has as vital an interest in world peace as any other nation. Another world war may bankrupt us. In 1919 we prided ourselves on not asking for anything at the peace table—in spurning reparations which we did not need and mandates which we did not

want. But we did have an enormous material stake, *and that was in making the peace last.* Because it did not last we were forced to incur a debt of over $200,000,000,000 and mobilize a force of over 11,000,000 men. Compared with this colossal outlay, the cost of making a world order operate would be nothing.

False Security

(Courtesy of Denver *Rocky Mountain News*; cartoonist Cory)

(14) American opinion must be educated to its responsibilities in international affairs. If a new world organization is to work, we as a people must have a better appreciation of our long-run interests and our long-range responsibilities. One of the most formidable barriers to international cooperation is the pursuit of the immediate, short-run advantage to the exclusion of the less immediate but more profitable longer-run advantage. Unless man is willing to labor for the interests of

all (which are his long-run interests); unless he is prepared to avoid the selfish short-run gain which hurts his neighbor and indirectly himself; unless he can assume that most people are decent human beings striving toward a common end—then we might just as well start preparing to go back into the jungle and up into the trees. *There can be no long-range peace without a long-range view.*

3

A few final observations.

Should the United States have ratified the treaty and joined the League? In the face of the evidence herein presented, there can be only one answer. We had very little if anything to lose— perhaps the trivial expenses of the League; and everything to gain—possibly a preventing of so-called World War II. No nation was ever trapped in the League, as our isolationists feared: Japan got out, Germany got out, Russia was thrown out. Where the possible losses were so negligible, and the probable gains so tremendous, the United States, as Wilson repeatedly pointed out, was more than justified in taking the chance.

Would the results have been essentially different if we had joined the League?

The conclusions here must of course be more speculative. But it seems clear that some kind of "slump in idealism" would have come sooner or later, and it may legitimately be doubted whether, when the pinch came, the United States would have provided adequate support for the League of Nations. The events of the 1930's would seem to support such a view, but we must remember that the set of circumstances then encountered might not have come into being if we had joined the League in the first instance.

General Jan C. Smuts said that not Wilson but "humanity" failed at Paris. This is a striking statement that has little meaning, in part because the real failure came after Paris. If a horseman spurs his mount at a twelve-foot brick wall, who is responsible for the ensuing accident: the horse that fails to make the jump, or the rider who has attempted an impossible feat?

A horseman must know his horse and its limitations; a statesman must know his people and their limitations, as well as the limitations of foreign peoples. Otherwise he is not a statesman. He must not set for his people impossible goals, however desirable they may be in the abstract. He must train public opinion by gradations for the new tasks—not try to shoot Niagara all at once. He must educate the people in advance for the responsibility which he is asking them to shoulder. Otherwise, even though they may temporarily take on the burden, they are likely to find it too wearisome and cast it aside.

Wilson engineered a revolution in our foreign policy when he undertook to lead the American people out of the path of isolationism into that of effective world cooperation. Yet the isolationists, aided by the circumstances set forth in this book, were able to effect a counterrevolution, and take us back into the old paths. But it is possible that this counterrevolution would have come within a few years anyhow; the people were not yet fully ready for a major departure.

The great Covenanter was eternally right in recognizing that isolationism was but a mirage, and that the next war would surely drag us in, and that the new organization for peace had to be based upon justice for all. The stakes were enormous; they were worth giving one's life for. He failed in part because he seems not to have realized that his was a dual task: making a peace and changing a national—perhaps a world—psychology.

Wilson was the greatest of the neutral statesmen, the greatest mediator, the greatest war leader, the greatest peacemaker, the greatest tragedy, and the greatest disappointment. Reaching for the stars, he crashed to earth.

But his was a magnificent failure, and in some ways a successful failure. Wilson once said, "Ideas live; men die." His ideas have lived. The Wilsonian tradition has been kept alive, and countless thousands of men and women have vowed that we shall not make the same mistakes again. We shall know better how to do it next time. We know better our limitations and those of other peoples, for we have before us the successes and failures of the League. We know better what machinery will work, and what will not. We know that a League without teeth is little better than a debating society.

We must never forget that there are two phases to a war: the fighting duration, and the peace duration. Partly because men did not recognize this, the Treaty of Versailles became an armistice, and the postwar era a prewar era. Only a handful of statesmen can actually draw up a treaty of peace. *But in a democracy every citizen can actively participate in its ratification and in its execution.* Upon him rests a sacred obligation not only to do so but to do so intelligently. The record is there for him to read, and he should read it—*with due regard for changed conditions.*

We do not want to have to do the ghastly job a third time.

BIBLIOGRAPHICAL NOTES

INTRODUCTION

THIS BOOK, like its predecessor, *Woodrow Wilson and the Lost Peace,* is to some extent a synthesis and largely an interpretation or reinterpretation of certain basic facts. It contains more significant new data than the earlier volume; hence the Bibliographical Notes are somewhat more fully documented. Footnotes are not included in the text, primarily because it should be reasonably clear to the specialist after examining these Notes where the material in question may be found.

Public opinion was even more vitally important in peace-ratifying than in peace-making, and for this reason more emphasis is placed upon it than in the preceding volume. The New York *Times* was followed throughout, and for specific periods use was made of the various other newspapers herein listed. The periodical press was most helpful, including the *Independent,* the *Outlook,* the *New Republic,* the New York *Nation,* the *Review of Reviews,* and particularly *Harvey's Weekly, Current Opinion,* and the *Literary Digest.*

Although the already-exploited House Papers at Yale University were of some value, the significant manuscript discoveries were made in the Ray Stannard Baker Collection, the Lansing Papers, the Hitchcock Papers, and particularly the Wilson Papers—all in the Library of Congress.

In the bibliographies and notes that follow, the full citation is given the first time only; thereafter the shortened form. Where quoted material appears in italics, both in the notes and in the text, these have been inserted by the present writer, unless otherwise indicated.

CHAPTER ONE

THE RETURN OF THE MESSIAH

FOR THE events connected with Wilson's return, see the relevant issues of the New York *Times;* also Alice R. Longworth, *Crowded Hours* (New York, 1938), pp. 285–286; David F. Houston, *Eight Years with Wilson's Cabinet* (Garden City, N.Y., 1926), II, 4–6. Joseph P. Tumulty, *Woodrow Wilson As I Know Him* (Garden City, 1921), is useful, but the historian must use with caution all reports of conversations with Wilson reproduced verbatim from memory. The texts of Wilson's two speeches appear in Woodrow Wilson, *War and Peace: Presidential Messages, Addresses, and Public Papers* (1917–1924), eds. Ray Stannard Baker and William E. Dodd (2 vols., New York, 1927), I, 532–535, 537–552.

PUBLICATION OF THE TREATY. Wilson's views on the publication problem were expressed to the Council of Four on May 17 and June 12, 1919 (Minutes of the Council of Four, Wilson Papers, IX–C). See also R. S. Baker, *Woodrow Wilson and World Settlement* (Garden City, 1922), I, 158; Allan Nevins, *Henry White* (New York, 1930), pp. 449, 452–453; Claudius O. Johnson, *Borah of Idaho* (New York, 1936), pp. 236–237; Philip C. Jessup, *Elihu Root* (New York, 1938), II, 396–399. Root's role during the treaty fight was a devious one. Though an outstanding friend of international collaboration, he worked closely with the Senate Republicans in planning a program of reservations, and either wittingly or unwittingly played into the hands of the obstructionists.

WILSON'S GENERAL ATTITUDE. On Wilson's state of mind, particularly regarding the Senate, both before and after his return, see Wilson to Lansing, May 24, 1919; Wilson to Tumulty, June 14, June 16, 1919 (Wilson Papers, IX–A). Also Tumulty to Wilson, May 26, 1919 (in *ibid.*); Stephen Bonsal, *Unfinished Business* (Garden City, 1944), pp. 48, 58–60, 153; Charles Seymour, *The Intimate Papers of Colonel House* (Boston, 1928), IV, 487; Herbert Hoover, *America's First Crusade* (New York, 1942), p. 63; Henry Cabot Lodge, *The Senate and the League of Nations* (New York, 1925), chaps. VII, IX; David Lawrence, *The True Story of Woodrow Wilson* (New York, 1924), p. 269; C. T. Thompson, *The Peace*

Conference Day by Day (New York, 1920), p. 415; W. Stull Holt, *Treaties Defeated by the Senate* (Baltimore, 1933), pp. 272–276. The incident recorded by Butler appears in N. M. Butler, *Across the Busy Years* (New York, 1940), II, 197–201. The time element in this situation is not altogether clear. Especially useful is John McCook Roots, "The Treaty of Versailles in the United States Senate," a manuscript Senior Honors Thesis (1925) deposited in the Widener Library, Harvard University. The author interviewed a number of the surviving participants (including Hitchcock, Taft, Glass, and Borah), and was given access by Senator Borah to the confidential minutes of the Senate Foreign Relations Committee.

THE SECURITY TREATY WITH FRANCE. For the text of the treaty and Wilson's message of presentation, see *Cong. Record,* 66 Cong., 1 sess., pp. 3310–3311. For general backgrounds and bibliography, consult T. A. Bailey, *Woodrow Wilson and the Lost Peace* (New York, 1944), pp. 230–237, 357–358. Also Robert Lansing, *The Peace Negotiations* (Boston, 1921), chap. XV; Wilson's press interview, July 10, 1919 (Wilson Papers, II–C); and Lodge, *op. cit.,* pp. 152–156. For the sympathy of certain anti-League leaders with the idea of the treaty, if divorced from the League and limited in time, see Allan Nevins, *op. cit.,* p. 450; Claude G. Bowers, *Beveridge and the Progressive Era* (Boston, 1932), p. 507; Jessup, *op. cit.,* p. 401; and particularly the leading article in *Harvey's Weekly,* Aug. 9, 1919, pp. 1–2.

CHAPTER TWO

THE PARADE OF PREJUDICE

MUCH OF the material used in this chapter has been drawn from the contemporary press, both newspaper and periodical. The general background for the period may be best found in F. L. Allen, *Only Yesterday* (New York, 1931), and Mark Sullivan, *Our Times,* vols. V, VI (New York, 1933, 1937). There is also some sketchy general material in Roger Burlingame and Alden Stevens, *Victory*

Without Peace (New York, 1944); in David Loth, *Woodrow Wilson: The Fifteenth Point* (Philadelphia, 1941); and particularly in W. E. Dodd, *Woodrow Wilson and His Work* (Garden City, N.Y., 1922). The viewpoint of the isolationists is set forth in C. O. Johnson, *Borah;* in C. G. Bowers, *Beveridge;* and in W. F. Johnson, *George Harvey* (Boston, 1929).

THE LIBERALS AND THE TREATY. Probably the best source consists of the files of the *New Republic* and the New York *Nation.* See Oswald G. Villard, *Fighting Years* (New York, 1939), and the same author's sketch of Herbert D. Croly (the *New Republic*'s editor) in the *Dictionary of American Biography*, XXI, Supplement One. The influence of J. M. Keynes' book, *The Economic Consequences of the Peace* (New York, 1920), can hardly be overestimated. The *New Republic* not only published parts serially, but sold a cheap edition to its subscribers. On May 15, 1919, five minor members of the Peace Commission wrote to Joseph C. Grew, severely criticizing the treaty and in some cases threatening to resign. They were Adolf A. Berle, Jr., Joseph V. Fuller, Samuel E. Morison, George B. Noble and John Storck (Lansing Papers, vol. 43). William C. Bullitt's sensational letter of resignation, dated May 17, 1919, is in this file. On the question of resignations, see Robert Lansing, *Peace Negotiations,* pp. 274–275; the New York *Nation,* Feb. 21, 1920, p. 224.

CHAPTER THREE

THE PALL OF PARTISANSHIP

THE GENERAL backgrounds of partisanship are well set forth in D. F. Fleming, *The United States and the League of Nations, 1918–1920* (New York, 1932); in W. S. Holt, *Treaties Defeated by the Senate,* chap. X; and in J. M. Roots, "The Treaty of Versailles." See also W. E. Dodd, *Woodrow Wilson;* P. C. Jessup, *Elihu Root;* C. G. Bowers, *Beveridge;* H. F. Pringle, *The Life and Times of*

William Howard Taft (New York, 1939), vol. II; David Lawrence, *Woodrow Wilson;* and Alice R. Longworth, *Crowded Hours.* On the rebuffing of Wood and Roosevelt, see Hermann Hagedorn, *Leonard Wood* (New York, 1931), vol. II; and H. F. Pringle, *Theodore Roosevelt* (New York, 1931).

THE THIRD-TERM ISSUE. For the documentation of this episode, and the further elaboration of it, see pp. 409–411. David Lawrence, early in 1919, wrote for the London *Times* that the League cause in the United States would be strengthened if divorced from a third term. Wilson, Lawrence says, cabled to Tumulty from Paris, asking whether he should renounce a third term; Tumulty replied that this was unnecessary. About a year later, when Lawrence published a story setting forth these developments, he noted evidence of White House displeasure. (Lawrence, *Woodrow Wilson,* pp. 299-300.)

SENATORIAL ASPIRANTS FOR THE PRESIDENCY. Republican senators who were mentioned more or less prominently, or actually nominated, were: Johnson, Knox, Poindexter, Lenroot, Harding, Sutherland, France, Capper, and Borah. The Democratic senators were Underwood, Hoke Smith, Pomerene, Sheppard, Simmons, and Hitchcock. Senators Calder and Lenroot were well regarded for the Republican vice presidential nomination.

CHAPTER FOUR

THE CAVE OF THE WINDS

USEFUL BACKGROUND accounts appear in D. F. Fleming, *The United States and the League of Nations;* in W. S. Holt, *Treaties Defeated by the Senate;* in C. A. Berdahl, *The Policy of the United States with Respect to the League of Nations* (Geneva, 1932); in H. B. Learned, "The Attitude of the United States Senate Towards the Versailles Treaty: 1918–1920," in H. W. V. Temperley, ed., *A History of the Peace Conference of Paris* (London, 1924), vol. VI, chap. V; in J. M. Roots, "The Treaty of Versailles";

and in G. A. Finch, "The Treaty of Peace with Germany in the United States Senate," *American Journal of International Law,* XIV (1920), 155–206. See also J. E. Watson, *As I Knew Them* (Indianapolis, 1936), by a "strong reservationist" Republican senator from Indiana; Allan Nevins, *Henry White;* P. C. Jessup, *Elihu Root,* vol. II; H. F. Pringle, *William H. Taft,* vol. II; Alice R. Longworth, *Crowded Hours.* Considerable ephemeral material exists on the "irreconcilables," but two books must be particularly mentioned: C. G. Bowers, *Beveridge* (ex-Senator Beveridge was closely associated with the "irreconcilables"); and C. O. Johnson, *Borah,* a high-grade campaign biography, written in close collaboration with the senator. On Lodge the most revealing work is the senator's apology, H. C. Lodge, *The Senate and the League.* See also, Stephen Bonsal, *Unfinished Business;* Allan Nevins, *op. cit.;* William Lawrence, *Henry Cabot Lodge* (Boston, 1925), a most sympathetic account; and the most recent biography, Karl Schrift-giesser, *The Gentleman from Massachusetts: Henry Cabot Lodge* (Boston, 1944), which presents the conventional interpretation of Lodge's wickedness in the treaty fight. See also the revealing account in Fleming, *op. cit.,* chap. XIX.

THE SENATE GROUPS. It is difficult, if not impossible, to make accurate statements regarding the exact composition of the various Senate groups throughout the entire fight. Their personnel changed from time to time; and in each classification there were marginal senators who fluctuated back and forth. This was notably true of the "mild reservationists" and the "strong reservationists." The Democratic regulars were on the whole constant, as was the "Battalion of Death," but even here there was a marked contrast between these two groups in the November and the March voting. See particularly W. S. Holt, *Treaties Defeated by the Senate,* p. 296.

CHAPTER FIVE

THE STRATEGY
OF STRANGULATION

ON PACKING the committee see H. C. Lodge, *The Senate and the League;* J. M. Roots, "The Treaty of Versailles"; David Bryn-Jones, *Frank B. Kellogg* (New York, 1937); D. F. Fleming, *The United States and the League of Nations.* On the conferences with individual senators, consult Lodge, *op. cit.;* J. E. Watson, *As I Knew Them;* and Hitchcock's speech of Jan. 13, 1925 (Nebraska Historical Society). On the Senate Committee hearings, the best source is *Sen. Docs.,* 66 Cong., 1 sess., no. 106. See also Fleming, *op. cit.;* Lodge, *op. cit.;* Allan Nevins, *Henry White;* W. S. Holt, *Treaties Defeated by the Senate.* The official record of the White House conference appears in *Sen. Docs.,* 66 Cong., 1 sess., no. 76; the correspondence between Lodge and Wilson leading up to it is published in the New York *Times,* Aug. 16, 1919. See also Lodge, *op. cit.;* J. P. Tumulty, *Woodrow Wilson As I Know Him;* and David Lawrence, *Woodrow Wilson* (Lawrence apparently was there).

SENATORIAL INVITEES TO INDIVIDUAL CONFERENCES. As the Wilson papers show, the President, on July 16, invited Jones of Washington, Colt of Rhode Island, Nelson and Kellogg of Minnesota, Kenyon of Iowa, Capper of Kansas, and McNary of Oregon. On July 19, he invited McLean of Connecticut, Cummins of Iowa, Calder of New York, Edge of New Jersey, Newberry of Michigan, Page of Vermont, and Norris of Nebraska. On July 29, he invited Watson and New of Indiana, Keyes of New Hampshire, Lenroot of Wisconsin, Fernald of Maine, Harding of Ohio, and Dillingham of Vermont. The New York *Times* reported that in addition to these, McCumber of North Dakota, Sterling of South Dakota, and Spencer of Missouri were invited, though carbon copies of the invitations were not found in the Wilson Papers. Lodge's list, *op. cit.,* p. 157, is somewhat inaccurate. Twenty-four in all seem to have been invited.

THE UNSUMMONED WITNESSES. On August 13, 1919, Borah and Johnson sent a letter to Lodge saying that it was "absolutely essential" to have the testimony of Bliss, White, House, Williams, Hornbeck, Young, Bullitt, Ferguson and Millard—all experts at Paris. Bullitt was subpoenaed by a strict party vote of 9 to 7, and all the others, except Bliss, House, and White, without roll call. The last-named three were still at work with the Paris Conference, and to have brought them home would have involved a serious interruption of their labors. When Borah moved that the committee subpoena these three, the vote was 8 to 9, with Harding and McCumber defeating the motion by shifting to the Democrats. (Roots, *op. cit.*, pp. 56–57, from committee minutes.) For plans to summon House, who arrived home in ill health after the hearings ended, see Stephen Bonsal, *Unfinished Business*, pp. 272–274; Charles Seymour, *House Papers*, IV, 505–506.

WILSON'S REFUSAL TO PROVIDE DATA. Two letters of Wilson to Lodge on this subject are printed in *Sen. Docs.*, 66 Cong., 1 sess., no. 106, pp. 252–253. The letters regarding secret data and the draft treaties were sent by Wilson to Lodge on Aug. 8 and Aug. 28, 1919, respectively (Wilson Papers, II–C). Lodge later complained that Wilson provided only two of the many documents requested by the committee (*op. cit.*, p. 167). He further complained that the treaties with Poland and France, as well as the Rhine protocol, which were all parts of the treaty with Germany, were first secured from documents laid before the British and French legislative bodies.

CHAPTER SIX

THE APPEAL TO THE PEOPLE

ON THE origins of the trip and Wilson's health, see D. F. Fleming, *The United States and the League of Nations;* J. P. Tumulty, *Woodrow Wilson As I Know Him;* Edith Bolling Wilson (Mrs. Woodrow Wilson), *My Memoir* (Indianapolis, 1939); and G. S.

Viereck, *The Strangest Friendship in History* (that is, of Wilson and House—New York, 1932); and Irwin Hood Hoover, *Forty-two Years in the White House* (Boston, 1934). Although Hoover had unusual opportunities for observation, he is unreliable; he apparently knew nothing of Wilson's pre-Conference ill health. On this general subject, see the record of Dr. Grayson's interview with Ray Stannard Baker (Feb., 1926), Baker Collection. See also the Hitchcock speech of Jan. 13, 1925 (Nebraska Historical Society). Secretary of the Navy Josephus Daniels, who was a first-hand witness, says that Wilson did not regard the trip as a strain; it would be a pleasure and a relief to meet the people and speak from a heart so full of the subject (*The Life of Woodrow Wilson* [Philadelphia, 1924], p. 327). Perhaps Wilson was whistling in the dark —granted that Daniels remembers correctly. In any event, this evidence differs from that found elsewhere. For Wilson's evident expectation that the White House Conference with the senators would prove more fruitful, see Lansing to House, Aug. 21, 1919, Lansing Papers, vol. 45. On Wilson's determination to keep politics out of the tour, see Wilson to E. F. Goltra, Sept. 3, 1919, Wilson Papers, II–C.

THE SENATE AND THE ELECTION OF 1920. The number of seats to be filled was 32: 17 Democratic and 15 Republican. If the Democrats had retained all 17 (which they did not) and had captured all 15 (which they did not), they would still have been 2 short of a two-thirds majority. In addition, certain of their members, such as Reed, Gore, Shields, Smith of Georgia, and Walsh of Massachusetts, could not be counted on to support Wilson's position.

ORIGINS OF THE SWING AROUND THE CIRCLE. Mrs. Wilson in *My Memoir*, p. 273, and Tumulty in *op. cit.*, pp. 434, 438, both indicate that the trip was the result of a sudden impulse; also D. F. Houston, *Eight Years with Wilson's Cabinet*, II, 20. Yet as early as February, 1919, when Wilson was in the United States on his return trip, the press announced that he was going to swing around the circle on his final return. (New York *Times*, Feb. 25, 1919. See also earlier rumors from Paris in *ibid.*, Jan. 15, 1919.) Wilson's cablegram to Tumulty of May 2, 1919, announcing his intention of going, is printed in Tumulty, *op. cit.*, p. 546. On June 13, 1919, Thomas W. Lamont wrote to Wilson from Paris that the plans for the trip should then be announced, so that the people would get into a fever of expectation (Wilson Papers, IX–A). On June 17, 1919, the New York *Times* stated that the plans were in full swing; Wilson hoped to go to Washington, Idaho, and California, the states of the "irreconcilable" Poindexter, Borah, and Johnson. The next day the *Times* reported a White House spokesman as announcing that Wilson planned a three-week swing in July, shortly after addressing Congress. The same journal also divulged the news that the senators would make plans to "trail" him as soon as they got the itinerary. On June 24, 1919, the *Times* confirmed the same general announcement. At his press conference on July 10, 1919, two days after returning to Washington, Wilson said that he could not make any announcement about the projected trip: he had been home only long enough to see the terrible table in his study piled high with documents (Wilson Papers, II–C). For the proposal of the Foreign Relations Committee to prevent the trip by demanding a daily conference, see New York *Times*, July 12, 1919. For further talk of the trip, consult *ibid.*, July 26, 28, 30, 1919.

CHAPTER SEVEN

THE SWING AROUND THE CIRCLE

THE ADDRESSES on the tour are published in Woodrow Wilson, *War and Peace*, vols. I and II. For the incidents on the trip, consult the New York *Times*. A good running account appears in D. F. Fleming, *The United States and the League of Nations;* a superficial narrative, in R. Burlingame and A. Stevens, *Victory Without Peace*. See also Robert E. Annin, *Woodrow Wilson* (New York, 1924). Valuable intimate glimpses may be found in Edith B. Wilson, *My Memoir;* in J. P. Tumulty, *Woodrow Wilson As I Know Him*; and in David Lawrence, *Woodrow Wilson*.

THE SITUATION IN WASHINGTON. Rudolph Forster (White House Executive Clerk) wired to Tumulty (Sept. 8, 1919) Senator Pittman's enthusiastic comment on the success of the tour. Yet on Sept. 22 Guy Mason telegraphed from Washington to Tumulty at Reno that the "mild reservationists" and Lodge had come to terms, and had been joined by some Democrats. However, on Sept. 24 Hitchcock informed Tumulty by wire that the situation had not materially changed in the Senate. He advised postponing a discussion of reservations until Wilson returned, because Johnson and Borah would oppose any compromise. They wanted, Hitchcock thought, to throw the issue into the presidential campaign. (Telegrams in Wilson Papers, II–C.) For the announcement of Ashurst and several other wavering Democrats that they would support Wilson foursquare, see New York *Times,* Sept. 26, 1919. See also Thomas W. Lamont to Wilson, June 13, 1919, for advice as to how to conduct the trip (Wilson Papers, IX–A).

WILSON'S SPEECHMAKING ERRORS. For a hypercritical analysis of the speeches, see William Bayard Hale, *The Story of a Style* (New York, 1920), chap. IX. The author, an estranged Wilsonian, stresses the President's infelicities of style; his geographical errors in relation to Serbia, Poland, Rumania, and Persia; and his various contradictions as to the causes of the war. On this point, see also O. G. Villard, *Fighting Years,* p. 469. It is clear from these speeches that Wilson's thinking on the situation in 1917 changed under the impact of his exalted objectives. See T. A. Bailey, *Woodrow Wilson and the Lost Peace,* pp. 330–331. Wilson also made careless statements as to the American origins of the League, as to the ease with which the Covenant was inserted in the treaty, and as to the incorporation of American ideas into the pact (Woodrow Wilson, *War and Peace,* II, 95, 121, 122, 398). Near the start of the tour he said that German rights in Shantung were promised Japan in order to induce her to enter the war. The secret agreement in question actually was negotiated in 1917, some three years later. After Senator Norris had directed his attention to this misstatement, Wilson acknowledged his mistake. (Fleming, *op. cit.,* p. 347.) There were many other errors, contradictions, or arguable statements of more or less minor importance, some of which were inevitable under the circumstances.

CHAPTER EIGHT

THE FALLEN WARRIOR

ON WILSON's collapse, three published accounts have been left by occupants of the White House: Edith B. Wilson, *My Memoir;* J. P. Tumulty, *Woodrow Wilson As I Know Him;* and I. H. Hoover, *Forty-two Years in the White House.* Of these accounts, Mrs. Wilson's is the most trustworthy; Tumulty's, the least trustworthy, at least on this general subject. Tumulty says that Wilson was stricken with paralysis on the trip, which is not true, and which is the basis for many of the erroneous accounts on the subject. See also the daily White House bulletins as printed in the New York *Times,* and the account of an interview with Dr. Hugh H. Young (an attending physician from Johns Hopkins) which appeared in the Baltimore *Sun,* Feb. 10, 1920, and was reprinted in the New York *Times,* Feb. 11. The present writer also had access to the data, oral and written, which Dr. Grayson later gave Ray Stannard Baker (Baker Collection).

For backgrounds, see the general works previously cited, including the biographies of Wilson. Some material on German-Irish propaganda appears in G. S. Viereck, *Spreading Germs of Hate* (New York, 1930).

THE BULLITT AFFAIR. The testimony is published in *Sen. Docs.,* 66 Cong., 1 sess., no. 106, pp. 1161–1297. The facts regarding Bullitt's subpoena appear in J. M. Roots, "The Treaty of Versailles." For Lodge's connection with the affair, see Allan Nevins, *Henry White,* pp. 462–467. Lansing's published apology is in his *Peace Negotiations,* chap. XIX. Lansing's telegram to Wilson of Sept. 16, 1919, reproduced in part by Lansing (pp. 270–271), appears in full in the Wilson Papers, II–C. Lansing seems to have been vacationing at Henderson Harbor, New York, and the Acting Secretary of State wired him on Sept. 13, saying that everyone in Washington, including the press men, felt that Bullitt's conduct was reprehensible; the Acting Secretary himself felt that some kind of denunciation was necessary. A notation at the bottom of this telegram, dated Sept. 15, records that on this day the Acting Secretary telephoned from Washington to say that Senator Hitchcock believed that silence was best unless Lansing wished to issue an absolute denial. But Hitchcock thought that Lansing could give him a statement on behalf of the treaty which could be used in case the opposition began to exploit the Bullitt testimony improperly. Lansing did send a personal and confidential telegram to the Acting Secretary (undated). All these Bullitt materials appear in the Lansing Papers, vol. 46. The clippings which Lansing preserved show that the British and the French were greatly disturbed, and that there was much speculation as to Lansing's imminent resignation and his succession by Undersecretary of State Frank L. Polk.

CHAPTER NINE

THE LIVING MARTYRDOM

THE MOST revealing book is Edith B. Wilson, *My Memoir*. See also J. P. Tumulty, *Woodrow Wilson As I Know Him*, and I. H. Hoover, *Forty-two Years in the White House*, for personal glimpses. T. R. Marshall, *Recollections of Thomas R. Marshall* (Indianapolis, 1925), is not very helpful. For accounts by those who made direct or indirect contacts with the White House, see G. S. Viereck, *The Strangest Friendship in History*; Stephen Bonsal, *Unfinished Business*; David Lawrence, *Woodrow Wilson*; and A. D. H. Smith, *Mr. House of Texas* (New York, 1940). Bits of information appear in H. H. Kohlsaat, *From McKinley to Harding* (New York, 1923), pp. 220, 223; Allan Nevins, *Henry White*, p. 481; A. W. Lane and L. H. Wall, eds., *The Letters of Franklin K. Lane* (Boston, 1922), pp. 325, 330; and James Kerney, *The Political Education of Woodrow Wilson* (New York, 1926), pp. 429, 434.

PRESIDENTIAL DISABILITY. For an able discussion of this problem, consult Edward S. Corwin, *The President: Office and Powers* (2nd ed., New York, 1941), pp. 51–56, 333–339. There is much material here relevant to Wilson's collapse. Corwin thinks, as others thought, that he was plainly disabled within the meaning of the Constitution. The current view was that the initiative lay with Marshall in taking over. For proposals to correct this defect in the Constitution, see D. F. Houston, *Eight Years with Wilson's Cabinet*, II, 39–40; New York *Times*, Feb. 19, 20, 21, 27, 1920.

CHAPTER TEN

THE BATTLE OF RESERVATIONS

THE THREE reports from the Senate committee appear in *Sen. Reports*, 66 Cong., 1 sess., no. 176. The debates and voting on the various reservations may best be followed in the *Congressional Record*, although G. A. Finch, in the *American Journal of International Law*, XIV (1920), 155–206, has a convenient digest. See also W. S. Holt, *Treaties Defeated by the Senate* (note the useful tabulations of votes); H. C. Lodge, *The Senate and the League;* D. F. Fleming, *The United States and the League of Nations;* and Dexter Perkins, *Hands Off: A History of the Monroe Doctrine* (Boston, 1941).

THE HARMFUL EFFECT OF RESERVATIONS. The tendency has been to accept Wilson's conclusion that the reservations "nullified" the entire treaty. This uncritical view has recently been elaborated by Ruhl J. Bartlett, in *The League to Enforce Peace* (Chapel Hill, N.C., 1944), pp. 162–166, although the League to Enforce Peace itself conceded (*ibid.*, p. 154) that its purposes could be accomplished by the Covenant with the Lodge reservations. For an elaborate and masterly analysis demonstrating for the State Department (Mar., 1920) that the effect of the reservations had been much exaggerated, see David Hunter Miller, *My Diary at the Conference of Paris* (21 vols., New York, 1924–1926), XX, 569–593. Miller, who had been at Paris, and who probably knew as much about the League as any other man, later testified, "for as far as the Lodge reservations made changes in the League, they were of a wholly minor character, they left its structure intact, and they would have interfered with its workings not at all." (E. M. House and Charles Seymour, eds., *What Really Happened at Paris* [New York, 1921], p. 424). Fleming, *op. cit.*, chap. XVII, follows the lengthy Miller memorandum rather closely in his analysis. Gen. Tasker H. Bliss (one of the American commissioners in Paris) prepared a penetrating memorandum along the same lines for Secretary Lansing, dated Jan. 21, 1920 (Lansing Papers, vol. 50). Another able statement, anonymous but apparently written by an American diplomat, appears in the New York *Times*, Dec. 16, 1919; see also the analysis of the League of Free Nations Association, in *ibid.*, Dec. 7, 1919. Taft and Hoover both recognized that the effect of the Lodge reservations had been much overplayed (Taft to Hitchcock, Nov. 15, 1919, Hitchcock Papers; Hoover to Wilson, Nov. 19, 1919, Wilson Papers, File VIII, vol. 6). Similar views were expressed by Henry White, one of the American Commissioners at Paris (Allan Nevins, *Henry White*, p. 480), and by President A. Lawrence Lowell of Harvard University (Stephen Bonsal, *Unfinished Business*, p. 280). See also the remarks of Senators Lenroot and McCumber, on Nov. 19, 1919, and Senators Lenroot, Pomerene, and especially Walsh of Montana, on Mar. 19, 1920 (*Cong. Record*, 66 Cong., 1 sess., pp. 8771–8773, 8786; *ibid.*, 2 sess., pp. 4574–4577, 4578–4585.

Covenant of the League of Nations

(THE PORTIONS BEARING MOST DIRECTLY ON THE RESERVATIONS FIGHT)

Article I

. . . .

Sec. 3. Any Member of the League may, after two years' notice of its intention so to do, withdraw from the League, provided that all its international obligations and all its obligations under this Covenant shall have been fulfilled at the time of its withdrawal.

Article V

Sec. 1. Except where otherwise expressly provided in this Covenant or by the terms of the present Treaty, decisions at any meeting of the Assembly or of the Council shall require the agreement of all the Members of the League represented at the meeting.

. . . .

Article VI

. . . .

Sec. 5. The expenses of the Secretariat shall be borne by the Members of the League in accordance with the apportionment of the expenses of the International Bureau of the Universal Postal Union.

Article VIII

Sec. 1. The Members of the League recognize that the maintenance of peace requires the reduction of national armaments to the lowest point consistent with national safety and the enforcement by common action of international obligations.

Sec. 2. The Council, taking account of the geographical situation and circumstances of each State, shall formulate plans for such reduction for the consideration and action of the several Governments.

Sec. 3. Such plans shall be subject to reconsideration and revision at least every ten years.

Sec. 4. After these plans shall have been adopted by the several Governments, the limits of armaments therein fixed shall not be exceeded without the concurrence of the Council.

. . . .

Article X

Sec. 1. The Members of the League undertake to respect and preserve as against external aggression the territorial integrity and existing political independence of all Members of the League. In case of any such aggression or in case of any threat or danger of such aggression the Council shall advise upon the means by which this obligation shall be fulfilled.

Article XI

Sec. 1. Any war or threat of war, whether immediately affecting any of the Members of the League or not, is hereby declared a matter of concern to the whole League, and the League shall take any action that may be deemed wise and effectual to safeguard the peace of nations. In case any such emergency should arise the Secretary-General shall on the request of any Member of the League forthwith summon a meeting of the Council.

Sec. 2. It is also declared to be the friendly right of each Member of the League to bring to the attention of the Assembly or of the

Council any circumstance whatever affecting international relations which threatens to disturb international peace or the good understanding between nations upon which peace depends.

Article XII

Sec. 1. The Members of the League agree that if there should arise between them any dispute likely to lead to a rupture, they will submit the matter either to arbitration or to inquiry by the Council, and they agree in no case to resort to war until three months after the award by the arbitrators or the report by the Council.

Sec. 2. In any case under this Article the award of the arbitrators shall be made within a reasonable time, and the report of the Council shall be made within six months after the submission of the dispute.

Article XV

. . . .

Sec. 8. If the dispute between the parties is claimed by one of them, and is found by the Council, to arise out of a matter which by international law is *solely within the domestic jurisdiction* of that party, the Council shall so report, and shall make no recommendation as to its settlement.

. . . .

Article XVI

Sec. 1. Should any Member of the League resort to war in disregard of its covenants under Articles 12, 13, or 15, it shall *ipso facto* be deemed to have committed an act of war against all other Members of the League, which hereby undertake immediately to subject it to the severance of all trade or financial relations, the prohibition of all intercourse between their nationals and the nationals of the covenant-breaking State, and the prevention of all financial, commercial or personal intercourse between the nationals of the covenant-breaking State and the nationals of any other State, whether a Member of the League or not.

Sec. 2. It shall be the duty of the Council in such case to recommend to the several Governments concerned what effective military, naval or air force the Members of the League shall severally contribute to the armed forces to be used to protect the covenants of the League.

Sec. 3. The Members of the League agree, further, that they will mutually support one another in the financial and economic measures which are taken under this Article, in order to minimize the loss and inconvenience resulting from the above measures, and that they will mutually support one another in resisting any special measures aimed at one of their number by the covenant-breaking State, and that they will take the necessary steps to afford passage through their territory to the forces of any of the Members of the League which are co-operating to protect the covenants of the League.

Sec. 4. Any Member of the League which has violated any covenant of the League may be declared to be no longer a Member of the League by a vote of the Council concurred in by the Representatives of all the other Members of the League represented thereon.

Article XXI

Sec. 1. Nothing in this Covenant shall be deemed to affect the validity of international engagements, such as treaties of arbitration or regional understandings *like the Monroe Doctrine,* for securing the maintenance of peace.

Article XXII

Sec. 1. To those colonies and territories which as a consequence of the late war have ceased to be under the sovereignty of the States which formerly governed them and which are inhabited by peoples not yet able to stand by themselves under the strenuous conditions of the modern world, there should be applied the principle that the well-being and development of such peoples form a sacred trust of civilization and that securities for the performance of this trust should be embodied in this Covenant.

Sec. 2. The best method of giving practical effect to this principle is that the tutelage of such peoples should be entrusted to advanced nations who by reason of their resources, their experience or their geographical position, can best undertake this responsibility, and *who are willing to accept it,* and that this tutelage should be exercised by them as Mandatories on behalf of the League.

. . . .

The Lodge Reservations

(Those of November, 1919, appear unindented; those of March, 1920, were exactly the same, except that the italicized and bracketed passages were deleted, and the indented passages were added. Such comments as appear in footnotes are in addition to those in the text of this book. For originals, see *Cong. Record,* 66 Cong., 1 sess., p. 8773; *ibid.,* 2 sess., p. 4599.)

Resolved (two-thirds of the Senators present concurring therein), That the Senate advise and consent to the ratification of the treaty of peace with Germany concluded at Versailles on the 28th day of June, 1919, subject to the following reservations and understandings, which are hereby made a part and condition of this resolution of ratification, which ratification is not to take effect or bind the United States until the said reservations and understandings adopted by the Senate have been accepted [*by an exchange of notes as a part and a condition of this resolution of ratification by at least three of the four principal allied and associated powers, to wit, Great Britain, France, Italy, and Japan:*]

> as a part and a condition of this resolution of ratification by the allied and associated powers and a failure on the part of the allied and associated powers to make objection to said reservations and understandings prior to the deposit of ratification by the United States shall be taken as a full and final acceptance of such reservations and understandings by said powers:

1. The United States so understands and construes article 1 that in case of notice of withdrawal from the league of nations, as provided in said article, the United States shall be the sole judge as to whether all its international obligations and all its obligations under the said covenant have been fulfilled, and notice of withdrawal by the United States may be given by a concurrent resolution of the Congress of the United States.

2. The United States assumes no obligation to preserve the territorial integrity or political independence of any other country [*or to interfere in controversies between nations—whether members of the league or not—under the provisions of article 10, or to employ the military or naval forces of the United States under any article of the treaty for any purpose, unless in any particular case the Congress, which, under the Constitution, has the sole power to declare war or authorize the employment of the military or naval forces of the United States, shall by act or joint resolution so provide.*]

> by the employment of its military or naval forces, its resources, or any form of economic discrimination, or to interfere in any way in controversies between nations, including all controversies relating to territorial integrity or political independence, whether members of the league or not, under the provisions of article 10, or to employ the military or naval forces of the United States, under any article of the treaty for any purpose, unless in any particular case the Congress, which, under the Constitution, has the sole power to declare war or authorize the employment of the military or naval forces of the United States, shall, in

the exercise of full liberty of action, by act or joint resolution so provide.

3. No mandate shall be accepted by the United States under article 22, Part 1, or any other provision of the treaty of peace with Germany, except by action of the Congress of the United States.

4. The United States reserves to itself exclusively the right to decide what questions are within its domestic jurisdiction and declares that all domestic and political questions relating wholly or in part to its internal affairs, including immigration, labor, coastwise traffic, the tariff, commerce, the suppression of traffic in women and children and in opium and other dangerous drugs, and all other domestic questions, are solely within the jurisdiction of the United States and are not under this treaty to be submitted in any way either to arbitration or to the consideration of the council or of the assembly of the league of nations, or any agency thereof, or to the decision or recommendation of any other power.

5. The United States will not submit to arbitration or to inquiry by the assembly or by the council of the league of nations, provided for in said treaty of peace, any questions which in the judgment of the United States depend upon or relate to its long-established policy, commonly known as the Monroe doctrine; said doctrine is to be interpreted by the United States alone and is hereby declared to be wholly outside the jurisdiction of said league of nations and entirely unaffected by any provision contained in the said treaty of peace with Germany.

6. The United States withholds its assent to articles 156, 157, and 158 [regarding Shantung], and reserves full liberty of action with respect to any controversy which may arise under said articles [*between the Republic of China and the Empire of Japan*].

7. [*The Congress of the United States will provide by law for the appointment of the representatives of the United States in the assembly and the council of the league of nations, and may in its discretion provide for the participation of the United States in any commission, committee, tribunal, court, council, or conference, or in the selection of any members thereof and for the appointment of members of said commissions, committees, tribunals, courts, councils, or conferences, or any other representatives under the treaty of peace, or in carrying out its provisions, and until such participation and appointment have been so provided for and the powers and duties of such representatives have been defined by law, no person shall represent the United States under either said league of nations or the treaty of peace with Germany or be authorized to perform any act for or on behalf of the United States thereunder, and no citizen of the United States shall be selected or appointed as a member of said commissions, committees, tribu-*]

*nals, courts, councils, or conferences except with the approval of
the Senate of the United States.*] [1]

No person is or shall be authorized to represent the United
States, nor shall any citizen of the United States be eligible,
as a member of any body or agency established or authorized
by said treaty of peace with Germany, except pursuant to
an act of the Congress of the United States providing for
his appointment and defining his powers and duties.

8. The United States understands that the reparation commission will regulate or interfere with exports from the United States
to Germany, or from Germany to the United States, only when
the United States by act or joint resolution of Congress approves
such regulation or interference.[2]

9. The United States shall not be obligated to contribute to
any expenses of the league of nations, or of the secretariat, or of
any commission, or committee, or conference, or other agency,
organized under the league of nations or under the treaty or for
the purpose of carrying out the treaty provisions, unless and until
an appropriation of funds available for such expenses shall have
been made by the Congress of the United States.[3]

Provided, That the foregoing limitation shall not apply to
the United States proportionate share of the expense of the
office force and salary of the secretary general.

10. [*If the United States shall at any time adopt any plan for
the limitation of armaments proposed by the council of the league*

1 This reservation was minor as far as the functioning of the League was concerned. It further betrayed postwar senatorial suspicion of the Executive. It
was primarily a matter of internal administration; such details were left to
the jurisdiction of the individual member states.

2 This was relatively minor. The situation referred to was most unlikely to
arise, and if it did the American representative in the Council could cast his
veto vote. But the reservation would clear us of charges of noncooperation
should such a contingency occur. As a matter of fact the problem never arose;
the powers handled the reparations question themselves.

3 This also was minor, and almost completely unnecessary. No appropriations
can be lawfully made under our Constitution without Congressional approval.
The reservation was a sop to certain imaginative senators who feared that our
annual share of the League expenses might run into hundreds of millions of
dollars, and who feared that the League would accuse us of bad faith if the
President did not immediately provide the money. As a sedative to such nervous
senators, and as a possible preventive of foreign criticism, the reservation was
not wholly pointless. But it was ungracious, for it implied that unscrupulous
foreigners might in some way commit the United States, the wealthiest of
nations, to pay more than its just share of the League expenses.

*of nations under the provisions of article 8, it reserves the right to
increase such armaments without the consent of the council whenever the United States is threatened with invasion or engaged in
war.*] [4]

No plan for the limitation of armaments proposed by the
council of the League of Nations under the provisions of
article 8 shall be held as binding the United States until
the same shall have been accepted by Congress, and the
United States reserves the right to increase its armament
without the consent of the council whenever the United
States is threatened with invasion or engaged in war.

11. The United States reserves the right to permit, in its discretion, the nationals of a covenant-breaking State, as defined in article
16 of the covenant of the league of nations, residing within the
United States or in countries other than [*that violating said article
16, to continue their commercial, financial, and personal relations
with the nationals of the United States.*] [5]

such covenant-breaking State, to continue their commercial,
financial, and personal relations with the nationals of the
United States.

12. Nothing in articles 296, 297, or in any of the annexes thereto
or in any other article, section, or annex of the treaty of peace with
Germany shall, as against citizens of the United States, be taken to
mean any confirmation, ratification, or approval of any act otherwise illegal or in contravention of the rights of citizens of the United
States.[6]

[4] This, theoretically, was of major importance. But actually any disarmament
plan adopted by the League probably would have contained such escape clauses,
as was true of the naval disarmament treaties of the 1930's. Article 8 of the
Covenant clearly provided for a reconsideration of all disarmament plans "at
least every ten years." Even if such safeguards had not been provided, there
can be little doubt that the United States, or any other nation similarly situated,
would have taken matters into its own hands anyhow. The reservation was
useful in that it would have cleared us of charges of bad faith had we been
forced to increase our armaments in the face of aggression.

[5] This, actually, was not of great importance. A League boycott against, say,
Japan would not have been critically weakened if the United States had continued trade with Japanese outside Japan. But, theoretically, the reservation
was unfortunate, because it weakened in principle the concept of international
sanctions.

[6] This was designed to permit American citizens to seek redress in American
courts for injury sustained by seizures under the Alien Property Custodian. It
was relatively unimportant, and probably unnecessary. No real harm was done
by inserting it.

13. The United States withholds its assent to Part XIII (articles 387 to 427, inclusive) [International Labor Organization] unless Congress by act or joint resolution shall hereafter make provision for representation in the organization established by said Part XIII, and in such event the participation of the United States will be governed and conditioned by the provisions of such act or joint resolution.[7]

14. [*The United States assumes no obligation to be bound by any election, decision, report, or finding of the council or assembly in which any member of the league and its self-governing dominions, colonies, or parts of empire, in the aggregate have cast more than one vote, and assumes no obligation to be bound by any decision, report, or finding of the council or assembly arising out of any dispute between the United States and any member of the league if such a member, or any self-governing dominion, colony, empire, or part of empire united with it politically has voted.*]

Until Part I, being the covenant of the League of Nations, shall be so amended as to provide that the United States shall be entitled to cast a number of votes equal to that which any member of the league and its self-governing dominions, colonies, or parts of empire, in the aggregate shall be entitled to cast, the United States assumes no obligation to be bound, except in cases where Congress has previously given its consent, by any election, decision, report, or finding of the council or assembly in which any member of the league and its self-governing dominions, colonies, or parts of empire in the aggregate have cast more than one vote.

The United States assumes no obligation to be bound by any decision, report, or finding of the council or assembly arising out of any dispute between the United States and any member of the league if such member, or any self-governing dominion, colony, empire, or part of empire united with it politically has voted.

15. In consenting to the ratification of the treaty with Germany the United States adheres to the principle of self-determination and to the resolution of sympathy with the aspirations of the Irish people for a government of their own choice adopted by the Senate June 6, 1919, and declares that when such government is attained by Ireland, a con-

---

[7] This revealed undue suspicion of the Executive and of foreigners, but it was not of fundamental importance. It seems evident that full participation would not have been possible without the approval of Congress anyhow, and that such approval would have been speedily forthcoming if we had joined the League. Even without League membership, Congress voted to join the International Labor Organization in 1934.

summation it is hoped is at hand, it should promptly be admitted as a member of the League of Nations.

Democratic Reservations

Secret Wilson Reservations [1]
(September, 1919)

[1] Inasmuch as Article ONE of the Covenant of the League of Nations provides no tribunal to pass judgment upon the right of a member State to withdraw from the League, the Government of the U.S. understands the provision of Article ONE with regard to withdrawal as putting no limitation upon the right of a member State to withdraw except such as may lie in the conscience of the Power proposing to withdraw with regard to its having fulfilled "all its international obligations and all its obligations under the Covenant" in the sense intended by the instrument.

[2] It understands that the advice of the Council of the League with regard to the employment of armed force contemplated in Article TEN of the Covenant of the League is to be regarded only as advice and leaves each member State free to exercise its own judgment as to whether it is wise or practicable to act upon that advice or not.

Hitchcock Reservations [2]
(November, 1919)

[1] That any member nation proposing to withdraw from the league on two years' notice is the sole judge as to whether its obligations referred to in article 1 of the league of nations have been performed as required in said article.

[2] That the advice mentioned in article 10 of the covenant of the league which the council may give to the member nations as to the employment of their naval and military forces is merely advice which each member nation is free to accept or reject according to the conscience and judgment of its then existing Government, and in the United States this advice can only be accepted by action of the

1 Text in D. F. Fleming, *The United States and the League of Nations*, p. 493; also *Canadian Historical Review*, X (1929), 197–198; both from copies provided by Senator Hitchcock; original now in Wilson Papers.
2 *Cong. Record*, 66 Cong., 1 sess., p. 8800. The order has been changed to parallel the Wilson reservations.

Congress at the time in being, Congress alone under the Constitution of the United States having the power to declare war.

[3] It understands that under Article FIFTEEN of the Covenant of the League no question can be raised either in the Assembly or in the Council of the League which will give that body the right to report or to make any recommendations upon the policy of any member state with regard to such matters as immigration, naturalization, or tariffs.

[3] That no member nation is required to submit to the league, its council, or its assembly, for decision, report, or recommendation, any matter which it considers to be in international law a domestic question such as immigration, labor, tariff, or other matter relating to its internal or coastwise affairs.

[4] It understands, also, that the reference to the Monroe Doctrine in Article TWENTY-ONE of the Covenant of the League means that nothing contained in the Covenant shall be interpreted as in any way impairing or interfering with the application of the Monroe Doctrine in the American Hemisphere.

[4] That the national policy of the United States known as the Monroe doctrine, as announced and interpreted by the United States, is not in any way impaired or affected by the covenant of the league of nations and is not subject to any decision, report, or inquiry by the council or assembly.

[5] That in case of a dispute between members of the league if one of them have self-governing colonies, dominions, or parts which have representation in the assembly, each and all are to be considered parties to the dispute, and the same shall be the rule if one of the parties to the dispute is a self-governing colony, dominion, or part, in which case all other self-governing colonies, dominions, or parts, as well as the nation as a whole, shall be considered parties to the dispute, and each and all shall be disqualified from having their votes counted in case of any inquiry on said dispute made by the assembly.

CHAPTER ELEVEN

THE STRATEGY
OF DEADLOCK

THE CHIEF sources for this chapter are the Wilson Papers, the Hitchcock Papers, the *Congressional Record,* and the New York *Times.* The Wilson letter to Hitchcock of Nov. 18, 1919, is published in the *Cong. Record,* 66 Cong., 1 sess., p. 8768. The Hitchcock-Wilson colloquy on compromise is related in Hitchcock's speech of Jan. 13, 1925 (Nebraska Historical Society). The Borah-Swanson negotiations are discussed in J. M. Roots, "The Treaty of Versailles," pp. 82–83. Roots got the story direct from Borah, who thought that his pressure had some effect. The Lodge-Bonsal incident is set forth in Stephen Bonsal, *Unfinished Business,* pp. 272–280. Bonsal quotes House as suggesting (*ibid.,* p. 279) that Wilson's letter to Hitchcock of Nov. 18 was drawn up in September when the outlook was more favorable, but the context proves that it was written a day or so before sent. Also useful are Edith B. Wilson, *My Memoir;* H. C. Lodge, *The Senate and the League;* J. P. Tumulty, *Woodrow Wilson As I Know Him;* and the more general works previously cited.

WILSON AND RESERVATIONS. Wilson's antipathy to asking Germany to accept our reservations was set forth in his speeches, and also in a letter to John C. Shaffer, Aug. 27, 1919 (Wilson Papers, II–C). On Sept. 18, Vance C. McCormick wired Wilson (then on his tour) that three of the "mild reservationists" had prepared a reservation to Article X which Lodge was said to favor but which Taft opposed; Wilson replied the next day that he would regard such a reservation as a practical rejection of the Covenant (Hitchcock Papers). On Nov. 13 Hitchcock wrote Mrs. Wilson outlining his proposed strategy and saying that the Democrats would like Wilson's guidance; on Nov. 15 he added that it was their plan to vote down the Lodge reservations unless the President advised otherwise. On the back of this letter (which had been brought by a special messenger) appears a notation in the handwriting of Mrs. Wilson to the effect that the program outlined by Hitchcock had Wilson's approval, for the President could not in any case accept ratification with the Lodge reservations. (Wilson Papers, File VIII, vol. 6.) On Dec. 17, after the treaty rejection, Hitchcock told Tumulty that Wilson's instructions (presumably obtained during one of the November interviews) had been to go ahead and do the best he could, which apparently meant that Hitchcock was to secure such mildly interpretive reservations as were possible. (Tumulty to Mrs. Wilson, Dec. 18, 1919 [reporting a conversation with Hitchcock], Wilson Papers, File VIII, vol. 7.) See also New York *Times,* Nov. 8, 1919. When Hitchcock was unable to block the Lodge reservations with his own, the President sent the letter of Nov. 18, 1919.

CHAPTER TWELVE

BREAKING THE HEART
OF THE WORLD

THE BEST source for the Senate voting is the *Congressional Record,* which may be supplemented by the New York *Times.* A long and moving letter from Taft to Hitchcock (Nov. 15, 1919), urging compromise and setting forth the reasons therefor, may be found in the Hitchcock Papers. Analyses of the final votes appear in the works by Learned, Holt, Roots, Lodge, and Fleming previously cited. Allan Nevins, *Henry White,* has useful material on French reactions. For the attitude of the League to Enforce Peace, see R. J. Bartlett, *The League to Enforce Peace* (especially pp. 154–155). See also Alice R. Longworth, *Crowded Hours;* A. D. H. Smith, *Mr. House of Texas* (especially p. 343); and J. E. Watson, *As I Knew Them* (especially p. 200).

WILSON'S PRESSURE TO DEFEAT THE TREATY. As late as Jan. 4, 1930, the New York *World* wired Hitchcock, seeking confirmation of certain charges that had recently been made in a public address by Henry Morgenthau. A draft reply appears in Hitchcock's handwriting among his papers. The ex-senator said that both he and the President were convinced that, if they relaxed their opposition, the treaty with the Lodge reservations would be adopted; also, that until the last moment Lodge labored under the delusion that Wilson would give in.

WOULD WILSON HAVE POCKETED THE TREATY? On June 23, 1919, Wilson cabled Tumulty from Paris that since reservations infringed on the President's power of negotiation, ". . . I would be at liberty to withdraw the Treaty if I did not approve of the ratifications." Wilson authorized the publication of the entire telegram, with this sentence omitted. (J. P. Tumulty, *Woodrow Wilson As I Know Him*, pp. 531–532.) In the speech at Pueblo, Wilson virtually declared that he would decline to go through with ratification if objectionable reservations were attached (Woodrow Wilson, *War and Peace*, II, 412). As the treaty approached a vote, it was believed in Washington that Wilson would pocket it (New York *Times*, Nov. 15, 1919); and on Nov. 17 he told Hitchcock that he would do so (*ibid.*, Nov. 18, 1919). The letter of Wilson to Hitchcock of Nov. 18 is so uncompromising as to support the belief that the treaty would be pocketed (*Cong. Record*, 66 Cong., 1 sess., p. 8768). See the President's correspondence with Glass on this subject, in R. Smith and N. Beasley, *Carter Glass* (New York, 1939), pp. 201–204. Wilson's subsequent vetoing of the Knox separate peace resolution (May 27, 1920) lends further support to the belief that he would have dropped the entire treaty had it been approved with the Lodge reservations.

PUBLIC OPINION AND THE TREATY REJECTION. Useful symposia appear in *Current Opinion* and in the *Literary Digest*, especially Nov. 29 (pp. 11–13) and Dec. 6, 1919 (pp. 14–15). Views unfriendly to the treaty are expressed in the New York *Nation* (see Nov. 22, p. 652; Dec. 6, pp. 711–712) and in the *New Republic. Harvey's Weekly* was an "irreconcilable" mouthpiece (see particularly issue of Nov. 22, p. 1). Fairer and more conservative in judgment were the *Review of Reviews* and the *Outlook*, especially *ibid.*, Dec. 3, 1919, pp. 407–408. For this period the New York *Times,* the *Christian Science Monitor,* and the Springfield *Republican* have been rather closely followed. The New York *Times* is gratifyingly full on Hitchcock's relations with Wilson.

A partial list of newspaper editorials which proved useful follows: Hearst's Boston *American,* Nov. 21 (quoted herein); the Boston *Transcript,* Nov. 19, 20 (quoted herein); the New York *World,* Nov. 20; the Boston *Herald,* Nov. 18, 20, 21; the Philadelphia *Public Ledger,* Nov. 22 (the quoted advertisement is from the issue of Nov. 20); the Cleveland *Plain Dealer,* Nov. 21; the Boston *Post,* Nov. 20; the Boston *Traveler,* Nov. 21; the St. Louis *Post-Dispatch,* Nov. 20; the Philadelphia *North American,* Nov. 21; the Boston *Globe,* Nov. 21; the New York *Tribune,* Nov. 18; the San Francisco *Bulletin,* Nov. 21; the San Francisco *Chronicle,* Nov. 20. The quotations from the St. Louis *Star* and the Atlanta *Constitution* appear in *Current Opinion* (Dec., 1919, p. 274) and in the *Literary Digest* (Dec. 20, p. 15). The conclusions expressed in this study regarding public opinion square generally with those in W. S. Holt, *Treaties Defeated by the Senate,* p. 288.

CHAPTER THIRTEEN

THE BIRTH OF A SOLEMN REFERENDUM

MOST OF the unpublished materials used for this chapter appear in the Wilson and Hitchcock papers, which were supplemented by the press. The texts of the annual message and the Jackson Day letter may be found in Woodrow Wilson, *War and Peace,* II, 428–442, 453–456. See also Edith B. Wilson, *My Memoir;* David Lawrence, *Woodrow Wilson;* D. F. Houston, *Eight Years with Wilson's Cabinet,* vol. II; G. S. Viereck, *The Strangest Friendship in History.* Symposia of press reactions to the Jackson Day letter are published in the *Literary Digest,* Jan. 17 and 24, 1920, pp. 11–13 and 15–16. The typescript House letters to Wilson of Nov. 24 and 27 (published in Charles Seymour, *House Papers,* IV, 509–511) were accompanied by brief, longhand notes to Mrs. Wilson, in which the Colonel spoke of his solicitude for Wilson's place in history, of the necessity of having the great work at Paris live, and of the possibility of later securing modification of objectionable reservations (Wilson Papers, File VIII, vol. 6).

WILSON'S UNISSUED APPEAL. On Dec. 22, 1919, Attorney General Palmer wrote to Wilson setting forth the laws of the various states regarding vacancies created by the resignation of United States senators. A draft of the note requesting this information for the President appears in the handwriting of Mrs. Wilson (Wilson Papers, File VIII, vol. 8). The senators who were called upon to resign (it is not indicated who made up the list) were all the Republicans, except McCumber, Nelson and Norris, plus nine Democrats: Bankhead, Gore, Kendrick, Kirby, Reed, Smith of Georgia, Thomas, Trammell, and Walsh of Massachusetts. Postmaster General Burleson was asked to criticize this list, which he did in collaboration with Senator Hitchcock. The two men believed that it was not fair to include the Democrats Kirby, Trammell, and Thomas; and that the "irreconcilable" Norris and the "mild reservationists" Nelson, McNary, Kellogg, and McCumber should be added. Some of the "Lodge reservationists" favored the treaty but, said Burleson, were more anxious to promote the welfare of the party than to secure ratification. The "mild reservationists," by voting for the Lodge resolution, had done as much to hinder the treaty as the other Republicans. This group was listed as consisting of Colt, Hale, Jones of Washington, Kellogg, Kenyon, Keyes, McCumber, McNary, Nelson, Spencer, Sterling, and Townsend—a different list from that conventionally accepted. (Burleson to Mrs. Wilson, Jan. 28, 1920, *ibid.*) In writing to Wilson on Nov. 24, 1919, Hitchcock had included, among others, Lenroot, Edge, and Cummins (*ibid.*, vol. 6). The copy of the unissued appeal (tentatively dated Jan. 26 by a custodian of the papers) appears in *ibid.*, vol. 8. Wilson had earlier considered resignation, particularly during the Canal Tolls repeal fight and the campaign of 1916.

WILSON AND HITCHCOCK. In response to rumors that Wilson was dissatisfied with Hitchcock's handling of the fight, Tumulty issued a statement to the press, on Nov. 22, denying all reports of a breach, and declaring that the President was very appreciative of the senator's efforts; he added that Wilson was not taking sides in the fight for minority leadership between Hitchcock and Underwood (New York *Times,* Nov. 23, 1919). On Jan. 13, 1920, Hitchcock wrote to Mrs. Wilson, suggesting that something be done to influence the vote of Senator Harris in the close contest for minority leadership between himself and Underwood. Hitchcock pointed out that he had alienated the support of the Democratic "irreconcilables" by his stand during the treaty fight. A note in Mrs. Wilson's handwriting, attached to this letter, states that the President could not accede to this request, because he did not want to give grounds for the accusation that he had exceeded the proper bounds of executive authority. Nevertheless, he was profoundly grateful for Hitchcock's leadership in the struggle for the treaty. (Wilson Papers, File VIII, vol. 7.) This rough draft was put into final form and appears in the Hitchcock Papers under date of Jan. 13, 1920. Wilson was probably wise, in view of the troubled situation, in keeping out of the fight, though it may be observed that he did not scruple to interfere in Democratic primaries to bring about the defeat of candidates whom he did not like. The note is interesting also as proving that at this late date Mrs. Wilson was still scribbling down the thoughts of her invalid husband.

WILSON AND POSSIBLE COMPROMISE. The letter to Hitchcock, dated Dec. 19, and referred to on p. 213, appears in the Wilson Papers, File VIII, vol. 7. It was drafted in Mrs. Wilson's hand, with Wilson's shorthand notes attached. The finished letter is in the Hitchcock Papers under the same date. The response to Senator Glass's suggestion for a compromise on Article X is drafted in Mrs. Wilson's blue pencil on an undated chit (Wilson Papers, File VIII, vol. 7); the similarity in wording suggests that it was prepared about the time of the Hitchcock letter referred to above. (See also R. Smith and N. Beasley, *Carter Glass,* pp. 201–204.) Another undated chit in Mrs. Wilson's hand, presumably written about Dec. 22, 1919, shows that Wilson was disposed to stress the fact that the attitude of the Senate was encouraging Germany to make a scrap of paper of the treaty (Wilson Papers, II–C).

CHAPTER FOURTEEN

COMPROMISE WITHOUT CONCESSION

FOR DATA relating to the general subject matter of this chapter, see the works by Roots, Fleming, and Bartlett previously cited. Much material on public opinion appears in the daily and periodical press, and in the memorials and petitions listed in the *Congressional Record*.

POLLS ON THE LEAGUE. Newspapers ranging from the (Portland) *Oregon Journal* to the Omaha *Bee* and the Baltimore *Sun* took polls of reader sentiment, which uniformly favored speedy ratification in some form. The most significant poll was conducted by the Intercollegiate Treaty Referendum, which addressed a questionnaire to colleges in every section of the country. The totals from 48 institutions as given by Hitchcock on Jan. 19, 1920 (*Cong. Record*, 66 Cong., 2 sess., p. 1695), follow:

Unreserved ratification	48,232
Complete rejection	13,933
Ratification with Lodge reservations	27,970
Compromise between Lodge and Democratic reservations	61,494

This poll is significant, for it seems to have been the closest thing to a "solemn referendum" on the issue that the country had. Even though the colleges were strongly pro-League, there was much sentiment for the Lodge reservations and for compromise. It seems probable that such sentiment was even stronger among the masses. See also the New York *Times*, Jan. 17, 1920; and particularly the letter of Hamilton Holt to the New York *World* (Jan. 19), published in the *World* on Jan. 20, 1920. It is an impressive recapitulation of various League polls and other expressions of public opinion.

LODGE AND THE BIPARTISAN CONFERENCES. Lodge apparently did not originate the conference, as he suggests (H. C. Lodge, *The Senate and the League*, p. 193), but it was brought about through the initiative of Senator Owen (Hitchcock to Tumulty, Jan. 16, 1920, Wilson Papers, File VIII, vol. 7). The Lodge account contains other errors. The dramatic session described by Borah is taken from notes of a personal interview which the present writer had with the senator on Apr. 21, 1937. A less lurid account appears in C. O. Johnson, *Borah*, pp. 246–247. The press and Lodge both put the meeting in Johnson's office, and Lodge's account says that Senator New was with him. Naturally, Lodge gives no inkling that he was bulldozed by Borah (Lodge, *op. cit.*, p. 194). Lodge also published the tentative changes that were proposed in the bipartisan conferences (*ibid.*, pp. 195–203). His secretary, Charles F. Redmond, later testified that the senator never thought agreement could be reached: he merely went through motions in response to public pressure (J. M. Roots, "The Treaty of Versailles," p. 100). See Hitchcock's speech of Jan. 13, 1925 (Nebraska Historical Society), in which he says that the "irreconcilables" "kidnapped" Lodge; also Senator Johnson's version in the *Cong. Record*, 69 Cong., 1 sess., p. 2351 (Jan. 19, 1926). H. Maurice Darling, "Who Kept the United States Out of the League of Nations?" *Canadian Historical Review*, X (1929), 196–211, throws some light on this whole episode. He reveals that Senators Colt and Kenyon, both "mild reservationists" active in the bipartisan preliminaries, were left off the final committee by Lodge, apparently because they were inclined to be conciliatory (p. 200). The Democrats were willing to accept a Taft reservation to Article X, but Lodge declined to do so. Darling blames Lodge for the final result, unaware of the fact that Wilson (in an undated chit among his papers) also rejected the Taft version. (See also R. Smith and N. Beasley, *Carter Glass*, p. 202.) Senator McKellar, who was one of Darling's informants, testified that Lodge was called to the telephone by Viscount Grey at a crucial moment in the negotiations (p. 209). As a matter of fact, Grey was then in England, or en route to England.

THE GREY MISSION. For general backgrounds see Charles Seymour, *House Papers*, IV, 494–496, 499–500, 508; and A. D. H. Smith, *Mr. House of Texas*, pp. 340–341, 350–354. Smith had a close connection with the British Embassy. See also D. F. Houston, *Eight Years with Wilson's Cabinet*, II, 49; Allan Nevins, *Henry White*, pp. 485–486; and E. S. Corwin, *The President*, pp. 215–216. There is also some

material in W. E. Dodd, *Woodrow Wilson*. The undated and unissued White House statement reprimanding Grey appears in the
Wilson Papers, File VIII, vol. 7. It is interesting to note that at this
late date, about Feb. 2, 1920, Mrs. Wilson was still serving as her
husband's private secretary. Lloyd George's views were relayed
from London by Ambassador Davis to Lansing, Feb. 6, 1920
(Lansing Papers, vol. 51). For senatorial recollections of the Lloyd
George cablegram to Grey, see New York *Times*, Feb. 3, 1920. The
Democrats found comfort in a statement by a distinguished British
statesman, Arthur J. Balfour, to the effect that American reservations would weaken the efficiency of the League (*Christian Science
Monitor*, Feb. 16, 1920).

CHAPTER FIFTEEN

THE NEW
WOODROW WILSON

THE LETTER from Wilson to Hitchcock of Jan. 26, 1920, is
published in Woodrow Wilson, *War and Peace*, II, 460–461; the
Adriatic notes appear in *ibid.*, pp. 462–479. The Wilson-Lansing
interchanges may be found in the *Cong. Record*, 66 Cong., 2 sess.,
pp. 2882–2883. Further material on the Lansing resignation appears in Robert Lansing, *Peace Negotiations;* D. F. Houston, *Eight
Years with Wilson's Cabinet*, vol. II; Edith B. Wilson, *My Memoir;*
J. P. Tumulty, *Woodrow Wilson As I Know Him;* David Lawrence,
Woodrow Wilson; Samuel F. Bemis, ed., *The American Secretaries
of State and Their Diplomacy* (New York, 1929), vol. X. On Colby
see *ibid.;* also Houston, *op. cit.*, II, 68–69. There exists an interesting memorandum of an interview which R. S. Baker had with
Colby on June 19, 1930 (Baker Collection).

HITCHCOCK'S RELATIONS WITH WILSON AND TUMULTY. Hitchcock
seems not to have seen Wilson at all during the period between
the November and March votes, except when he came with the
Fall "smelling committee" (Dec. 5, 1919). He saw Tumulty at least

once, and addressed letters to him, and to Mrs. Wilson, and finally
to Wilson. Tumulty acted as a go-between, and urged Wilson in
two notes to send Hitchcock a statement encouraging compromise
(Tumulty to Mrs. Wilson, Jan. 15, 17, 1920, Wilson Papers, File
VIII, vol. 7). On Jan. 16 and 17 Hitchcock sent two letters to
Tumulty advising him of progress in the bipartisan conferences
(*ibid.*). On Jan. 22 Hitchcock addressed a letter to Wilson directly,
enclosing a draft of the Article X reservation then being considered
(*ibid.;* also printed in New York *Times,* Feb. 8, 1920). On
Jan. 26 Wilson, probably responding to Tumulty's prompting,
sent his memorable letter to Hitchcock, which was in part a boiling
down of a draft submitted by Tumulty with his letter of Jan. 15.
Mrs. Wilson added a chit in her own hand saying that in Wilson's judgment the letter should not be published then, but permitting Hitchcock to make what use of it he saw fit (Hitchcock
Papers). What is presumably an earlier draft of this letter, in Mrs.
Wilson's hand, suggests that she was urging her husband to throw
responsibility on the Senate for making the peace (undated memorandum, Wilson Papers, File VIII, vol. 8).

THE WILSON-LANSING BREAK. Wilson had appointed Lansing with
misgivings, and had regarded him as an administrative assistant
(Houston, *op. cit.,* II, 67). At Paris their views had been sharply
divergent on the League (Lansing, *op. cit.*). Lansing's testimony
before the Senate committee, though perhaps unavoidable, had
displeased Wilson (Tumulty, *op. cit.,* p. 445). The Bullitt affair
had also put Lansing in a bad light. Wilson was irritated by the
first meeting of the Cabinet (Houston, *op. cit.,* II, 39, 69). His explosion in February may have been touched off by first learning of
Lansing's inquiries as to whether Marshall should take over, following the stroke. (See Tumulty, *op. cit.,* p. 444.) It was further
rumored that Wilson was angry because Lansing had allegedly
influenced the published views of Viscount Grey. The President
seems also to have been displeased with Lansing's handling of the
Mexican crisis. (*Ibid.;* W. E. Dodd, *Woodrow Wilson,* pp. 406–
407.) Dr. Grayson later remembered that Wilson wanted an
offensive member of the British Embassy dismissed, and that
Lansing had failed to secure satisfactory action (memorandum of
Baker interview with Grayson, Feb., 1926, Baker Collection). David

Lawrence, who was rather close to the White House, suggests that Wilson had thought that the Cabinet meetings were purely informal, and that he blew up when he learned otherwise (Lawrence, *op. cit.*, p. 287). Pent-up exasperation, illness, and a new access of energy, combined with some or all of the other factors mentioned above, probably provide the explanation of the President's summary action.

CHAPTER SIXTEEN

THE LAST CHANCE

THE CONTEMPORARY press and the *Congressional Record* are the best general sources. Analyses of the votes on the reservations appear in the works by Fleming, Finch, and Holt previously cited. The tables in Holt are especially useful. For the reservations and the final vote, see H. C. Lodge, *The Senate and the League;* and J. M. Roots, "The Treaty of Versailles." Incidental items appear in Alice R. Longworth, *Crowded Hours,* pp. 299–304; Allan Nevins, *Henry White,* p. 482; J. E. Watson, *As I Knew Them,* pp. 195–196; and N. M. Butler, *Across the Busy Years,* II, 201. The Wilson letter to Hitchcock of Mar. 8 is printed in the New York *Times* of Mar. 9, 1920. Hitchcock gives some personal glimpses in his speech of Jan. 13, 1925 (Nebraska Historical Society).

THE FINAL TREATY VOTE. All Republicans voted affirmatively on Mar. 19, 1920, except the following fifteen "irreconcilables," who voted negatively or were paired against the treaty: Borah, Brandegee, Fall, Fernald, France, Gronna, Johnson, Knox, La Follette, McCormick, Moses, Norris, Penrose, Poindexter, and Sherman. In the previous November all these, except Penrose, had voted against or had been paired against the Lodge resolution of ratification. The following twenty-one Democrats bolted and voted for the treaty: Ashurst, Beckham, Chamberlain, Fletcher, Gore, Henderson, Kendrick, King, Myers, Nugent, Owen, Phelan, Pittman, Pomerene, Ransdell, Smith of Georgia, Smith of Maryland,

Trammell, Walsh of Massachusetts, Walsh of Montana, and Wolcott. The seven who had bolted on the second vote on the Lodge resolution in November were: Gore, Myers, Owen, Pomerene, Shields, Smith of Georgia, and Walsh of Massachusetts. See *Cong. Record,* 66 Cong., 1 sess., p. 8802; 66 Cong., 2 sess., p. 4599.

CHAPTER SEVENTEEN

THE SUPREME
INFANTICIDE

ON THE general subject matter of this chapter see the previously cited works of Holt, Fleming, Roots, and Lodge. The incident of Wilson's telephonic negotiations with Lodge is taken from D. F. Houston, *Eight Years with Wilson's Cabinet,* II, 56–57. R. J. Bartlett, in *The League to Enforce Peace,* holds that the Allied powers would have rejected the Lodge reservations (pp. 164–166). This does not follow from the evidence herein presented, and particularly from the testimony of Grey, Lloyd George, and the French press given in a previous chapter. For further evidence see N. M. Butler, *Across the Busy Years,* II, 200–201.

PUBLIC OPINION AND THE SENATE VOTE. Material was taken from the editorial comments of all the journals listed on pp. 397–398; in addition, the Washington *Post,* the Chicago *Tribune,* and the Portland *Oregonian.*

WAS LODGE SINCERE IN SUPPORTING HIS RESERVATIONS? Much of the evidence about Lodge is contradictory. His daughter believed that his heart was with the "irreconcilables"; his grandson (later senator) denied this. (Fleming, *op. cit.,* p. 476.) A sister of Theodore Roosevelt, who was Lodge's house guest at the time, thought Lodge sincere (*ibid.,* p. 475); Roosevelt's daughter regarded the senator as basically an "irreconcilable" (Alice R. Longworth, *Crowded Hours,* p. 295). Lodge stirred up so much bitterness by his course that we must view with suspicion the numerous reports about him based on hearsay, supposition, and wishful thinking. The often quoted story of ("my dear James") Senator Watson (*As I Knew Them*, pp. 190–191), to the effect that Lodge diabolically sought to defeat the treaty by indirect means, does not have the ring of verisimilitude, as is true of other Watsonian tales. The present writer has preferred to judge Lodge more by his actions than by the guesses of others as to his motives. For what it is worth, it may be noted that Senator Borah told the present writer in 1937 that Lodge at heart was a "League man." (Further favorable evidence appears in P. C. Jessup, *Elihu Root*, II, 402–403.) Charles F. Redmond, then Lodge's private secretary, stated later in an interview that the senator had no strong convictions about the League one way or another, but as the fight developed he put party unity foremost in his thinking (J. M. Roots, "The Treaty of Versailles," p. 88). There is an excellent summary statement in Fleming, *op. cit.*, chap. XIX. Lodge's refusal to respond to White's invitation to submit amendments to the League when he might have done so may be plausibly explained on political grounds (Allan Nevins, *Henry White*, pp. 397–401). Positive judgments regarding Lodge's motives should be tempered pending an opening of his private papers.

JAPAN AND THE TREATY REJECTION. The Japanese press was much concerned about the proposed Shantung amendment, and rejoiced when it was defeated. But the purely negative Shantung reservation aroused no such opposition, largely because it was regarded as having no international weight. (See symposia of editorial opinion in the *Japan Times and Mail* [Weekly Edition], Nov. 22, 1919, p. 1477; Nov. 29, 1919, p. 1505.) This was also the conclusion of Viscount Ishii, former ambassador to the United States (*ibid.*, Nov. 22, 1919, p. 1483). The Japanese newspapers somewhat resented the violent senatorial attacks on Japan, but it was recognized that much of this was pure partisanship (see *ibid.*, Sept. 6, 1919, p. 1171). Of the six prominent Japanese newspapers referred to, none expressed satisfaction over the treaty rejection, either in November or March, and most of them regretted the action of the United States as bolstering Chinese obduracy and further unsettling world peace. The conclusion seems warranted that Japanese opinion preferred treaty ratification (even with the Shantung reservation) to treaty rejection. (*Ibid.*, Nov. 29, 1919, p. 1505; March 27, 1920, p. 405.) For a summation of Senate arguments on the

Shantung question, see Robert E. Hosack, "The Shantung Question and the Senate," *South Atlantic Quarterly*, XLIII (1944), 181–193.

CHAPTER EIGHTEEN

ADVANTAGES
WITHOUT OBLIGATIONS

ON THE separate-peace movement, see the *Congressional Record* and the New York *Times*. For public opinion on this issue and the others herein treated see the journals previously mentioned. The text of the Knox Resolution appears in the *Cong. Record*, 66 Cong., 2 sess., p. 7102, as does the final vote. Nelson was the only Republican voting against it; Reed, Shields, and Walsh of Massachusetts were the Democrats who voted for it. The account of the Cabinet meeting of Apr. 13 appears in D. F. Houston, *Eight Years with Wilson's Cabinet*, II, 69–70. For the Hamaker Oregon letter, the message to Congress on Armenia, and the veto message regarding the Knox Resolution, see Woodrow Wilson, *War and Peace*, II, pp. 483 ff. Some of the same ideas which appear in the Oregon letter also appear in a letter which Wilson wrote to Jouett Shouse, to be read to the Kansas Democratic State Convention. (See New York *Times*, Apr. 23, 1920.)

CHAPTER NINETEEN

A TALE OF TWO
CONVENTIONS

THE TWO most helpful accounts of the nomination of Harding are in Samuel H. Adams, *Incredible Era* (Boston, 1939), and Mark Sullivan, *Our Times*, vol. VI. Useful material appears in Hermann

Hagedorn, *Leonard Wood,* vol. II; Claude M. Fuess, *Calvin Coolidge* (Boston, 1940); William A. White, *A Puritan in Babylon: The Story of Calvin Coolidge* (New York, 1938); Harry M. Daugherty, *The Inside Story of the Harding Tragedy* (New York, 1932); W. F. Johnson, *George Harvey;* N. M. Butler, *Across the Busy Years,* vol. I; C. G. Bowers, *Beveridge;* P. C. Jessup, *Elihu Root,* vol. II; C. O. Johnson, *Borah.* More general accounts may be found in D. F. Fleming, *The United States and the League of Nations,* and in Charles P. Howland, ed., *Survey of American Foreign Relations, 1928* (New Haven, 1928). The smoke-filled room has become something of a legend, for the meeting was more informal, more protracted, and less definitive than is commonly supposed. See Henry L. Stoddard, *It Costs to Be President* (New York, 1938), pp. 73–75.

The materials on the backgrounds and course of the Democratic convention are less full. Consult the previously cited works by Dodd and Tumulty; and James Kerney, *The Political Education of Woodrow Wilson.* The pre-convention photograph of Wilson which was published in the newspapers appears in Gerald W. Johnson, *Woodrow Wilson* (New York, 1944), p. 108, but is four years out of context.

WILSON AND THE THIRD-TERM ISSUE. Wilson had earlier put himself on record as against a third term, and on Feb. 28, 1919, he rather definitely announced his retirement to a private gathering of Democrats (Tumulty, *op. cit.,* p. 378). On Aug. 27, 1919, shortly before leaving on his Western tour, Wilson wrote Cyrus T. Brady that when his *term came to an end* he hoped he would have enough vigor to propose some much-needed university reforms (Wilson Papers, II–C). While on the trip he laughed aside a suggestion of a third term (New York *Times,* Sept. 20, 1919). Mrs. Wilson told Henry White (prior to July 2, 1919) that under no circumstances would Wilson run again (Allan Nevins, *Henry White,* p. 456).

The editorial in the Springfield *Republican* urging Wilson to declare himself out of the running, was published on May 17, 1919. Wilson cabled Tumulty, on June 2, 1919, asking his opinion of it and that of Secretary Glass, Secretary Baker, Secretary Wilson, and Homer S. Cummings. Nothing, Wilson said, should be allowed to stand in the way of the League. On June 3 Tumulty advised against both a third nomination and a public renunciation at that time (Wilson Papers, IX–A). No further action seems to have been taken on this matter. See also pp. 44, 374 of the present book.

The last figures of the *Literary Digest* poll (*ibid.*, June 12, 1920, p. 20) showed the five leading Democratic contenders to have the following votes: McAdoo, 102,719; Wilson, 67,588; Edwards, 61,393; Bryan, 46,448; Cox, 32,343.

In an undated rough draft of some kind of proclamation or statement, tentatively dated by the custodians of the Wilson Papers Oct. 3, 1920, Wilson asked the rhetorical question whether the people wanted to make use of his services as President for another four years. There was no point in raising such a question after the nomination of Cox, and the internal evidence suggests that the statement may have been drafted before the Democratic convention with the thought of promoting a third-term candidacy. (Wilson Papers, File VIII, vol. 7.)

First-hand evidence from Dr. Grayson regarding Wilson's desires was recorded by Glass in his diary (R. Smith and N. Beasley, *Carter Glass,* pp. 205–209).

On June 30, 1920, Cummings wired Wilson that the platform committee was in the hands of friends, and that everything thus far had moved beautifully according to plan (Wilson Papers, II–C). See Colby's press interview (New York *Times,* July 1, 1920). For Colby's statement that he went to the convention as a result of Wilson's personal desire that he should go and also serve as permanent chairman, see Colby to Wilson, June 18, 1920, Wilson Papers, II–C. Stoddard thinks that Colby was sent out to put his chief's name in nomination, but that the "right moment" never came (Henry L. Stoddard, *As I Knew Them* [New York, 1927], pp. 515–518). Colby told R. S. Baker in 1930 that he had been on the point of nominating Wilson, and possibly of stampeding the convention. He promised to develop the story more completely, but evidently failed to do so. (Interview of June 19, 1930, Baker Collection.) A memorandum of Homer S. Cummings, dated Jan., 1929 (in *ibid.*), reveals that Mrs. Wilson told Colby (according to Colby) that the President was receptive to a third nomination, though the Democratic leaders at San Francisco (except Colby) thought such a nomination impossible. This memorandum is paraphrased in Charles W. Stein, *The Third-Term Tradition* (New York, 1943), pp. 248–249.

The code telegram from Colby at San Francisco to Wilson (July 2, 1920) is in the Wilson Papers, File VIII, vol. 7; his follow-up telegram to Wilson (July 4) is in the Baker Collection, A, Box 3 (Cummings).

For Wilson's alleged anger with the Cabinet members after the convention, see I. H. Hoover, *Forty-two Years in the White House*, p. 107, and G. S. Viereck, *The Strangest Friendship in History*, p. 336. Neither is particularly reliable. James Kerney, who is more trustworthy, states in his *Political Education of Woodrow Wilson*, p. 456, that Wilson summarily asked Burleson to resign because he had supported McAdoo. All this does not prove that Wilson had expected a third nomination; he doubtless was displeased over the whittling down of the League plank and the nomination of Cox. For the White House policy of hands-off, see Tumulty, *op. cit.*, pp. 493–496, 498.

Wilson's relation to the third-term issue is most fully developed in Stein, *The Third-Term Tradition*, chap. IX. Although this account is gratifyingly full, the author comes to the incredible conclusion (which he himself admits is flimsy) that, beginning with mid-1918, Wilson decided to exploit the League issue in such a way as to make necessary a third term. Here, says Stein, is the explanation of a long series of deliberate attempts to antagonize the Senate (pp. 263–264). The author not only misreads Wilson's character, but overlooks the fact that there were other and more plausible reasons for each of his acts.

CHAPTER TWENTY

THE GREAT AND SOLEMN MUDDLEMENT

GENERAL ACCOUNTS of the campaign of 1920 appear in the works by Fleming, Howland, Sullivan, Adams, and Berdahl, all previously cited. P. C. Jessup, *Elihu Root,* II, 413–414, throws some new light on the appeal of the Illustrious Thirty-one. On the essential dishonesty of this statement, see R. J. Bartlett, *The League to Enforce Peace,* and the commentary of ex-President Charles W. Eliot of Harvard University in the New York *Times,* Oct. 21, 1920. Samuel Colcord, in *The Great Deception* (New York, 1921), develops fully the thesis that the effort of the "irreconcilables" to misrepresent the result of the election as a clear-cut mandate against the League was "the great deception." A detailed analysis of the 1920 vote appears in Edgar E. Robinson, *The Presidential Vote, 1896–1932* (Stanford University, 1934).

COULD THE ELECTION HAVE BEEN A REFERENDUM? Following the Jackson Day appeal it was widely felt that there could be no clear-cut referendum. See the statements of Taft, Bryan, and Lowell, the comments of Democratic newspapers, and the observations of political experts in the New York *Times,* Jan. 10, 19, 1920. After the March rejection of the treaty such doubts multiplied. The New York *Nation* (Mar. 13, p. 322) recommended a true referendum in the Swiss style, as did the San Francisco *Bulletin* (Mar. 22). The Baltimore *Sun* (Mar. 20) said it was foolish to hope for a mandate; the New York *Evening Post* (Mar. 20) declared the result would be a "solemn muddle"; the Boston *Globe* (Mar. 20) observed that the issues, already muddy, would be further muddied by months of mud-slinging; and the Brooklyn *Eagle* (Mar. 20) remarked that the people would know no more after the election than before about public sentiment on the League. For similar expressions by other journals, domestic and foreign, see *Literary Digest,* Apr. 3, pp. 17–19, July 24, pp. 9–10; *Current Opinion,* Aug., 1920, p. 156. Curiously enough, foreigners, especially the French, seem to have been more realistic about the problem than some Americans. Among the many individuals who declared that domestic preoccupations would preclude a mandate were Senator McCumber (*Cong. Record,* 66 Cong., 2 sess., p. 6853), and Senator Walsh of Montana (*ibid.,* p. 4582).

WAS THE ELECTION A MANDATE? A majority of the newspapers sampled regarded the result as a repudiation of Wilsonism. See Philadelphia *North American,* Nov. 4; New York *Evening Post,* Nov. 3; New York *Sun,* Nov. 4; New York *Call,* Nov. 3; Brooklyn

Eagle, Nov. 3; New York *Herald,* Nov. 3; Springfield *Republican,* Nov. 3; Boston *Herald,* Nov. 3; Detroit *Free Press,* Nov. 4; Kansas City *Star,* Nov. 3; San Francisco *Chronicle,* Nov. 3; San Francisco *Examiner,* Nov. 3. There is a useful symposium in the *Literary Digest,* Nov. 13, 1920, pp. 11–14. Other papers stressed the desire for a change ("normalcy"), among them *Current Opinion* (Dec., 1920, p. 759), which said that the result was a victory for "General Grouch." See also the New York *Times,* Nov. 4; the Portland *Oregonian,* Nov. 3; the Boston *Post,* Nov. 3; the New York *World,* Nov. 4; the Columbus *Dispatch,* Nov. 3; the Boston *Globe,* Nov. 3; the Louisville *Courier-Journal,* Nov. 4; the Chicago *Tribune,* Nov. 3. Those which declared that there could be no mandate, or that the results were confused, were the New York *Times,* Nov. 3, 4; the Boston *Globe,* Nov. 3; the St. Louis *Post-Dispatch,* Nov. 3; the New York *Tribune,* Nov. 2; the Cleveland *Plain Dealer,* Nov. 3; the Philadelphia *Public Ledger,* Nov. 3 (it was "dishonest" to say that a "downright or unmistakable mandate had been written"); the Atlanta *Constitution,* Nov. 4; the Sacramento (Calif.) *Union,* Nov. 3; the San Francisco *Bulletin,* Nov. 1 (the difference on the League issue was that between "Tweedledum and Tweedledee"). See also *Literary Digest,* July 24, pp. 9–11, Aug. 21, p. 14; *Current Opinion,* Dec., 1920, pp. 778–779. Those which stressed the reaction against idealism were the Kansas City *Star,* Nov. 3; *Current Opinion,* Dec., 1920, p. 778. Those which pointed out that it was not a partisan victory but a national upheaval were the Washington *Evening Star,* Nov. 3, and *Current Opinion,* Dec., 1920, p. 761.

Only a few newspapers came out flatfootedly and said that the result was clearly and unmistakably a mandate against the League; among them, the Hearst chain. (See Boston *American,* Nov. 3.) Other isolationist journals, like the Boston *Transcript* (Nov. 2) and the Washington *Post* (Nov. 3), coupled the League with something else, as did the San Francisco *Chronicle* (Nov. 3). Some newspapers accepted the proposition that the election doomed the League, among them the New Yorker *Staats-Zeitung* (Nov. 3); the *Wall Street Journal,* Nov. 4 (the country needed "an audit" rather than a referendum); and the San Jose (Calif.) *Mercury-Herald,* Nov. 3 (the same general result would have been obtained if the League had never been heard of).

Borah and Johnson and other foes of the League of course hailed the result as a clear-cut mandate (New York *Times,* Nov. 4). Lodge later said essentially the same thing (*The Senate and the League,* p. 210). Others, then and later, were of a contrary view. See Samuel Gompers, *Seventy Years of Life and Labor* (New York, 1925), II, 502; D. F. Houston, *Eight Years with Wilson's Cabinet,* II, 58; Walter Lippmann, *Public Opinion* (New York, 1922), pp. 195–196. Calvin Coolidge remarked that the outcome was not a verdict on the League (New York *Times,* Nov. 24). On Nov. 23, Senator Pittman wrote to Wilson that the result was not a mandate but a remarkably successful campaign of "deception" (Wilson Papers, II–C). See also David Lawrence, *Woodrow Wilson,* p. 300; and Colcord, *op. cit.,* who estimates that more than one hundred and fifty pro-League Republican newspapers supported Harding. Consult also *Official Report of the Proceedings of the Democratic National Convention* (Indianapolis, 1924), pp. 250–276, for the debate in 1924 on the plank for a national referendum on the League.

CAMPAIGN ISSUES. In the field of foreign affairs the Republicans talked mostly about the League, which also embraced the Association of Nations, Article X, the Monroe Doctrine, six votes to one, and Shantung. Wilsonism was clearly the most discussed domestic issue. It embraced such items as "one-mannism" and personal rule; autocracy; dictatorship; overcentralization; interference with business; attempting to make over the government; catering to labor; inefficiency; maladministration; extravagance, incompetence, and waste; "socialism"; impractical idealism; and government by deadlock. Reaction to the war government was tied up with Wilsonism, and involved such items as heavy taxation, restrictions on freedom of speech and other civil liberties (Debs), postal censorship and inefficiency (Postmaster General Burleson), Red-baiting (Attorney General Palmer), the railroad muddle (Secretary McAdoo), the price ceiling on wheat, profiteering, and the absence of curbs on the high cost of living.

The Republicans also stressed peace, prosperity (with a high tariff), and "normalcy," which no doubt was the winning slogan. Other themes were the Armenian mandate; farm relief; soldiers' bonus; justice for the Indians, Jews, and Irish; immigration bars;

Japanese in California; relief for labor; prohibition; a ship sub-sidy; partisan credit for woman suffrage; Panama Canal tolls repeal; the World Court; Democratic unpreparedness in 1917; the Mexican muddle; failure of the League in Poland; the who-won-the-war issue (the Republicans?); Democratic patriotism, 1917–1918; and the injustices of the treaty.

The Democrats stressed the League, so the Republicans charged, to obscure their failures at home. The Democrats also emphasized progressivism; the straddles of the Republicans; their keeping the nation out of peace; their isolationism; their Senate cabal; their class rule; their appeal to the hyphenates. On other issues the Democrats generally took opposite sides from the Republicans, or promised to do the same thing better.

THE WOMAN VOTE. It is difficult to make sound observations as to how the women responded. Many mothers no doubt voted for Cox because they hoped the League would keep their boys at home. Other mothers no doubt voted for Harding because they feared that Article X would take their boys abroad; the Association of Nations looked somewhat safer. The Woman's Christian Temperance Union was unfriendly to the "wet" Cox. It was generally believed that the women, who had felt the pinch of high prices and war-time restrictions more keenly than the men, joined disproportion-ately in the anti-Wilson protest vote.

CHAPTER TWENTY-ONE

THE FINAL CURTAIN

FOR WILSON'S final days, Mrs. Wilson's *My Memoir* is the most revealing of the published works. The private Wilson Papers contain much material, and the present writer is deeply indebted to Miss Katharine E. Brand for her invaluable *précis* of the S Street files. The works previously cited, by James Kerney, Tumulty, Josephus Daniels, Houston, and Bonsal all contain some material. Bainbridge Colby, *The Close of Woodrow Wilson's Administration and the Final Years* (New York, 1930), p. 12, indicates that Wilson at times despaired of ultimate success, for he feared that the enemies of the League had poisoned the wells of public thinking for at least thirty years. See also J. P. Tumulty, *Woodrow Wilson As I Know Him*, p. 455. For Wilson's post-presidential third-term aspirations, see C. W. Stein, *The Third-Term Tradition*, pp. 252–253.

On the Harding administration in general, consult the works by Adams, Sullivan, and Daugherty previously cited. See also M. R. Werner, *Privileged Characters* (New York, 1935). Bartlett, *op. cit.*, has some important new material on the plight of the Illustrious Thirty-one. On the relations of Harding with the League, consult the works by Berdahl and Howland previously cited, and D. F. Fleming, *The United States and World Organization, 1920–1933* (New York, 1938).

CHAPTER TWENTY-TWO

THE GREAT BETRAYAL

THIS CHAPTER consists of general conclusions drawn from the materials that were used in preparing this volume and the preceding one on Wilson. A sketchy bibliography would not do justice to the subject or to those who have written about it; a full bibliography would be unmanageably voluminous and not in consonance with the author's purposes.

INDEX

Adriatic notes, 252–253. *See* Fiume
Alien Property Custodian, 391
alliances, 7, 48
Allies: and treaty publication, 3; duplicity of, 128; delay ratification, 149; must accept reservations, 155–156, 198–199, 240, 264–265, 281–284; severe with Germany, 206, 207; ratify treaty, 224; U.S. betrays, 358. *See* Adriatic notes; public opinion; *and countries by name*
amendments to treaty: proposed, 150; McCumber on, 152; debated, 153–154; Wilson against, 173. *See* reservations
America. *See* United States
American Bar Association, 124
Anglophobia, 25, 28–29, 236. *See* Great Britain; Ireland; Irish
Armenian mandate, 76, 150, 295–296, 313, 339, 359. *See* mandates
Article X: early attacked, 13–14; Irish hate, 27; Wilson explains, 85–86, 116, 119, 259; misrepresented, 115; Johnson attacks, 128; reservation to passed, 157–160; necessity of, 159–160; and Shantung, 163–164; Wilson opposes reservation on, 171, 177, 244, 395–396; reservations on, 182–183, 226, 254–255; final compromise attempts on, 230–232, 258, 260, 402, 404; aimed at France, 261–262; final reservation on, adopted, 262–263; importance of, exaggerated, 267; Rhode Island Democrats oppose, 308; in 1920 campaign, 323; text of, 385; text of reservations on, 388–389, 393. *See* Bipartisan conferences; League of Nations
Article XI, 116, 118, 385. *See* League of Nations
Article XII, 183, 386
Article XV, 160–161, 386
Article XVI, 158, 183, 386–387
Article XX, 327
Article XXI, 161, 387

Ashurst, Senator H. F., 187, 264, 271, 272, 380, 405
Assembly (of League) : voting in, 164–165. *See* League of Nations
Association of Nations: in Republican platform, 302; Harding on, 326–327; in campaign, 328; dies, 352
Australia: distrusts U.S., 165–166
Austria: peace with, 352
Austria-Hungary: and separate peace, 290–294. *See* Austria; Hungary

Baker, R. S., 225
Balfour, A. J., 403
Baruch, B. M., 81, 183
"Battalion of Death," 59. *See* "irreconcilables"
Belgium: rulers of, in U.S., 136, 142, 176
Beveridge, ex-Senator A. J., 22, 32, 137
bipartisan conferences, 229–232, 244, 254, 258, 401–402. *See* compromise
"bitter-enders," 59. *See* "irreconcilables"
Bliss, Gen. T. H., 377, 384
Bolsheviks, 19, 20
Bonsal, Col. Stephen, 166, 175–176
Borah, Senator W. E.: publishes treaty, 4; a Progressive, 22; irresponsibility of, 31, 33; characteristics of, 61, 63–65; on Foreign Relations Committee, 73; at White House, 85; misrepresents constituency, 96; "trails" Wilson, 127–128; objects to an amendment, 154; fights Article X, 159; on Shantung, 162–163; pressures Wilson, 183; condemns treaty, 187–188; rejoices, 193; urges referendum, 208, 220; wrecks compromise, 230–232, 402; and Grey letter, 238; on reservations, 254; on compromise, 255, 380; threatens bolt, 237; baits Democrats, 257; defends self, 263; against World Court, 282–283; at 1920 convention, 299–300; in campaign, 327–328; presidential aspirant, 374; and

417